MW01632430

# Antahkarana: Celestial Fullness
## Esoteric Acupuncture
## Volume VI

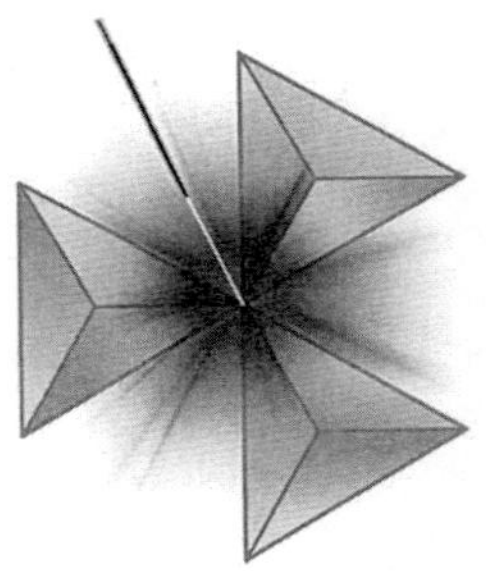

To Jeff -
Enjoy the Journey.

Much Love -
Mikio
07/19/17

*Mikio Sankey, Ph.D., L.Ac.*

Published by
Mountain Castle Publishing
208 West 64th Street
Inglewood, CA 90302



Front Cover Kanji by:
Master Calligrapher Eri Takase
Characters on front cover say: *Tian Man* "Celestial Fullness"

Permission given by the Academy for Future Science to reprint quotes from ***The Book of Knowledge: Keys of Enoch*** by J.J. Hurtak

Permission granted by Jason Aronson Publishers, Inc. to reprint the Pathways of the Tree of Life from the book ***Ten and Twenty-Two*** by Michael Jacobs

***Antahkarana: Celestial Fullness, Esoteric Acupuncture, Volume VI***
Mikio Sankey, Ph.D., L.Ac.

Includes bibliographical references.

ISBN 978-0-9670637-5-1
Printed in the United States of America

First Printing, 2014
Second Printing, 2015

# Antahkarana: Celestial Fullness
# Esoteric Acupuncture
# Volume VI

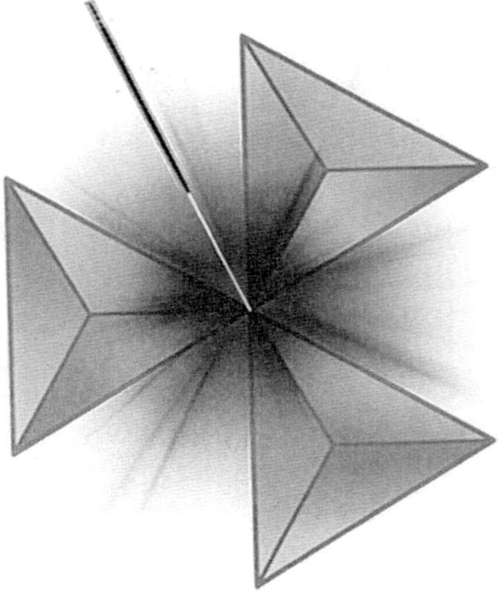

*Mikio Sankey, Ph.D., L.Ac.*

This book is dedicated to:

**Jikun Kathy Sankey, OMD, L.Ac.**
**and**
**Nataraj Muni Baba Swami.**

**And to all the**
**Masters of Wisdom**
**and the**
**Lords of Compassion**

## Acknowledgements

I would like to give a special thank you to the following individuals who have recently helped to spread the word and work of Esoteric Acupuncture: Dr. Kevin Soltani (Dean) and Monica Soltani of American Liberty University in Orange County, California; Alison Clarke of Into Freedom in Boronia, Victoria, Australia; Trevor of China Books in Melbourne, Victoria, Australia; Dr. Jacques MoraMarco, OMD, L.Ac., Dean of Emperor's College and Gretchen Badami, DAOM, L.Ac. Associate Dean of Emperor's College in Santa Monica, California; Wendy Nelson of Energy Wisdom in Boulder, Colorado; Christina Souza Ma and Segovia Smith of Yoga Hub in Silver Lake, California; Glenn Wollman, M.D. of Santa Barbara, California; Alexander Joannou, M.D. of New South Wales, Australia; Francesca Habermehl of Niwot, Colorado; Dr. John Stan of Eastern Currents in Vancouver, British Columbia, Canada; Tony Tavares and Douglas Doolittle of Toronto, Ontario, Canada; Dr. Yury Kronn and Constance Kronn of Energy Tools International in Eagle Point, Oregon; Anna Kelly, L.Ac., Jack Pessin, M.S., L.Ac., Jacquelin Payne, M.S., L.Ac., Nancy Parks, L.Ac., Therese Sibon, L.Ac., and Dr. Carlene DeVito, L.Ac. of New York, New York; Priya Advani, L.Ac. of Wilmington, California; Dr. David Weinthal, L.Ac. of Georgetown, Texas; Sara Sas, L.Ac., Kimberly Hoover, L.Ac. and Karen Lamont, L.Ac. of San Diego, California; Daphne Fung, Toowoomba, Queensland, Australia; and Barbara Hughes, EAMP, L.Ac. of Stanwood, Washington. I would like to give an extra special thank you to Dr. Will Morris, Dean of the Austin Graduate School of Integrative Medicine in Austin, Texas who was the first to invite me to speak on Esoteric Acupuncture (in 1998) when he was the Dean of Emperor's College in Santa Monica, California.

I would like to thank Priscilla Liekkio, June Kim and Diane Viera who have assisted me with my seminars in the Los Angeles and Orange County areas. Thank you to Aurica Berger for your input in this book. A very special thank you to Rick Reynoso for the graphics and assistance in putting the book together and to Revital Wachtel of Royal Printing.

A very special thank you to Howard Carlip for your keen eyes and the many hours you spent editing this book. I also want to thank you for your humorous comments you left throughout the book.

And, a big thank you to my brother Edwing who has always been there for me throughout my challenges.

# Preface

Esoteric Acupuncture is a work in progress that had its genesis in California in 1995. There have been bits and pieces of the puzzle that I remember as a young child growing up, but it was not until 1995 that the name Esoteric Acupuncture had its genesis. As I have evolved my inner awareness and expanded my overall consciousness, I have become better equipped to receive and to share the information that I have downloaded during meditation and quiet times. I do not channel this information from the Astral Planes. Information is received instantaneously and telepathically from the higher Causal Planes during waking hours, sleep and also while meditating or during "dreamtime" states of consciousness. In this regard, my job in bringing forth Esoteric Acupuncture may be somewhat likened to that of an amanuenses, but with much traditional and academically accepted information intertwined throughout the work.

Since Esoteric Acupuncture is constantly growing and evolving as I personally evolve, there have been a few changes from earlier works to my later books. Several times I have suggested certain angles to insert the acupuncture needles in a few New Encoding Patterns. In my demonstrations at lectures today, I may insert the acupuncture needles in a slightly different manner. If there are any discrepancies from an earlier work versus a later version of how I am currently presenting any materials from Esoteric Acupuncture, follow the later version. Any slight discrepancies will not discredit or negate the information of the earlier version. As I have gathered more light, the information I receive may also change due to the fact that I am gathering the information with a clearer heart and lighter mind. As I said earlier, Esoteric Acupuncture is a work in progress.

There is some overlapping of information with other volumes in the Esoteric Acupuncture Series. There are two reasons for this. The first is that I wanted to have each volume in this series stand on its own without a person having to read the books in sequence. Some of the information that is discussed is needed to be in more than one book. Secondly, in my own search for the esoteric truths, I have found that as I read difficult concepts or theories more than once, but in slightly different contexts, it was often easier to comprehend what the author was trying to convey.

As with the earlier Esoteric Acupuncture books, most of the Chinese names will be in italics. The exceptions will be the commonly used words such as: yin, yang, qi and the two primary vertical midline meridians known as Ren and Du. Some acupuncture texts used in the acupuncture schools in the United States will denote the anterior Ren channel as conception vessel and the posterior Du channel as the governing vessel. In the instances where qi is used with another word, such as *Wei Qi* or *Yuan Qi*, then both of the Chinese words will be italicized. When qi is used by itself, it will not be italicized. If you run across unfamiliar words that are not italicized, they will not be from the Chinese language.

There may be some grammatical confusion with the Chinese terms *Po*, *Hun* and *Shen* which can be both singular or plural. Just be aware that sometimes you may see one or more of these words used in a sentence in a singular format, while in another paragraph that same word will be used as a plural.

When discussing the acupuncture points for those who have been taught the American/English terminology for the points, certain abbreviations will be used such as: Lu for lungs; LI for large intestines; Sp for spleen; St for stomach; Ht for heart; SI for small intestines; Per for pericardium; SJ for san jiao;; Ki for kidneys; UB for urinary bladder; Liv for liver; and GB for gallbladder. I prefer using the Chinese names of the points. Both the Chinese and American/English names will be given for the acupuncture points, unless the acupuncture point or group of points do not have an American/English name. *Sishencong* is an example of four points grouped together as one set that does not have an American/English name.

Some of you who are more interested in the accepted traditional academic works from the past may question the information in the Esoteric Acupuncture series. I have no interest or desire to convince anyone of the credibility, validity or usefulness of any of the information presented in Esoteric Acupuncture. The scientific research protocol of reproducibility is almost impossible when working with consciousness. If you are interested in the Ageless Wisdom Teachings and find the information presented in the Esoteric Acupuncture Series has validity and may be useful to you, please use the information presented in this book and in the other books of the Esoteric Acupuncture series. See for yourself if the New Encoding Patterns work. If you require more proof of the validity of the Esoteric Acupuncture, please stick to the modalities that resonate with your own belief system.

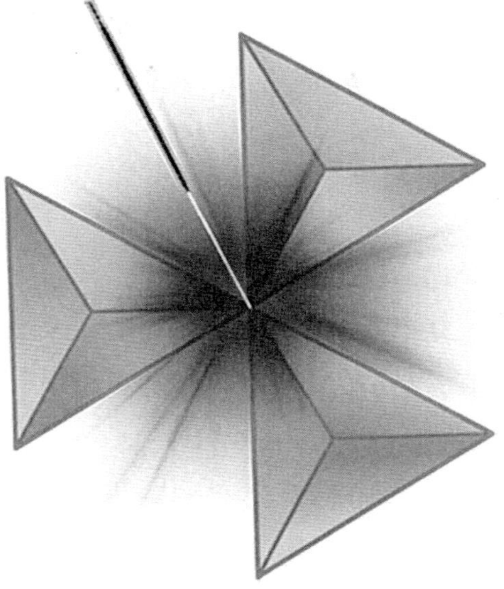

# Table of Contents
## Antahkarana: Celestial Fullness, Esoteric Acupuncture, Volume VI

### Chapter I: The Spiritual Side of Esoteric Acupuncture
### The Awakening of Humanity

## Chapter II: Master Window Groups of Esoteric Acupuncture

## Chapter III: Fabrics of Consciousness and Chinese Medicine

## Chapter IV: What is the Antahkarana?

## Chapter V: Tiers of Density and New Encoding Patterns

## Chapter VI: Final Thoughts



## Addendum

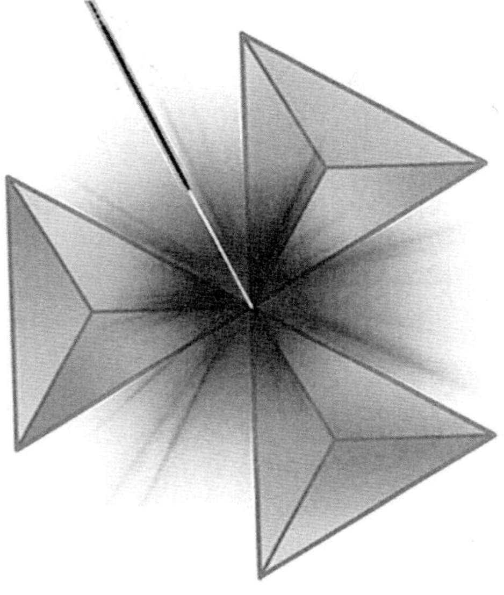

# Chapter I: The Spiritual Side of Esoteric Acupuncture
# The Awakening of Humanity

*"Nature, in order to force us forward, always confronts us with problems that we can answer only by growing wiser. This does not mean that we must become all-wise—only a little wiser.... It may be that we must temporarily turn to others for help, but only in order that they can direct us so that we can solve our own problems. In spite of all the advice we get, we must do the work ourselves, or it will never be done."* [1]

Manly Palmer Hall

*"Know that the knower is greater than knowledge, and the One who seeks is greater than the sought."* [2]

Djwhal Khul

## What is Esoteric Acupuncture?

How can information, knowledge and concepts developed in centuries past, or even millennia past, be the final authority or final criteria that defines the scope of how a present society decides to extend the use of that information and incorporate those teachings into a modern society? Should a current society be exclusively tied to those ancient theories and systems from past generations? How important is tradition in today's society?

In the clothing fashion industry, although current styles may reflect some ideas and designs from the past, the current fashion industry uses materials and fabrics that are of a much finer and more exquisite quality than was available earlier. In sports today, athletes are bigger, faster and better than the athletes in bygone generations. The professional training methods, the dietary regiment and thinking process of current athletes are way beyond that of only a few decades ago.

In the mathematics/physics world of unification, did academic thinking stop with the concepts of Einstein? The various theories associated with superstring physics go way beyond what Einstein or his peers could have even imagined back then. In the world of astrophysics, did the thinking stop with those concepts put forth by Copernicus or Galileo?

The various other Asian schools of thought concerning acupuncture, such as those from Korea or Japan, may say their ideas and theories have been expanded beyond those theories brought forth by the scholars in China. Are those newer Asian theories that much different from what was presented to the world by the ancient Chinese scholars? The dance steps may be newer and different, but the dance is the same. The ideas from Korea and Japan on how to treat a patient may be different from that of the Chinese system, but the systems are the same as the Chinese role model. You learn how to treat disease, not address wellness without the disease stage being addressed first.

In the western world of acupuncture in the 21st Century, are we to believe that the purest academic thinking and final authority concerning acupuncture theories should remain with the ideas and concepts brought forth in an ancient time? Is it in the best interest of acupuncturists today to remain strictly in the field and scope of the Traditional Chinese Acupuncture system?

One of the first steps that I feel is necessary to bring acupuncture more into alignment with the needs and thinking of society today, especially here in the West, is to expand the language of acupuncture. Secondly, it is definitely not necessary to get rid of the old dance (the Chinese system), but add a newer dance (system) that is more encompassing and more in alignment with the needs of the 21st Century. This means not merely learning new dance steps to dance to the old tune.

Those who hear about Esoteric Acupuncture for the first time think that this system is merely a different type of acupuncture style to treat physical or emotional challenges. Since acupuncture needles are inserted at traditional acupuncture sites, Esoteric Acupuncture treatments can be used to address those types of ailments. But, Esoteric Acupuncture is a system designed to bring the healthcare professionals, especially acupuncturists and their clients, into the mindset of treating wellness and expanding consciousness. Focusing on wellness will automatically start the process of prevention of disease.

There are several basic principles underlying Esoteric Acupuncture. The first basic principle is to pierce your temple (your physical vehicle) with acupuncture needles (or other positively energized tools) at specific acupuncture sites using a very specific sequencing order with any number of New Encoding Patterns to unlock the gateways to the finer frequency levels of consciousness that are stored in the planes above the dense mental planes of consciousness.

A second basic principle is to balance and strengthen the opposing energy fields of the heart and love versus the kidneys and fear (*Esoteric Shaoyin*) for the most optimum usage of those fields for the recipient of an Esoteric Acupuncture treatment.

A third basic principle is to assist the client to be able to access the Ageless Wisdom teachings in order to find or discover his or her puzzle piece in life. Who are you and what is your purpose in this incarnation? Finding your puzzle piece in life requires you to become very still and enter a certain level of consciousness that allows you to reach your Inner, Higher, Spiritual Heart Center. It is possible to reach this level of consciousness if you have done a certain amount of inner plane work plus receive a treatment with the proper New Encoding Pattern.

The fourth principle of Esoteric Acupuncture is to expand

both the vocabulary and the field of acupuncture to bring this grand traditional system more into alignment with the needs of the people in the western countries in the 21st century. Once you have completed your academic schooling at an accredited acupuncture institute, some of you may wish to begin incorporating into your thinking the idea that acupuncture is also art, not merely a left-brained modality to treat an old paradigm of thought. In reality, Esoteric Acupuncture is a way of life, or at least a way of looking at life, that involves trying to find and constantly refine your Inner, Spiritual Heart Center.

Very often other people, including your spouse or family members, require you to fulfill monetary and other social obligations. There may be other factors involved that dictate who you are and how you should pursue your short-term goals in life. Why are you here in your specific physical vehicle at this particular time frame in history? Often your short-term goals become so demanding that they encompass your life's journey and you do not fulfill your Soul Journey or your Inner Spiritual Journey.

Esoteric Acupuncture is designed to assist you with discernment, so you are able to make wiser choices in life that will be the most beneficial, or at least guide you on a path of least resistance, on your journey of trying to remain on your own individual Inner, Spiritual Heart Path. When in doubt, ask yourself this question: "Will this choice or this decision help me to further my Inner, Spiritual Heart Journey, or will this choice take me away, or lead me astray, from my Inner, Spiritual Heart Path?"

As a way of life, Esoteric Acupuncture emphasizes that each of you make wise choices in the foods and drinks you ingest. Everything that goes into your physical body "shapes" all the various fields surrounding you and influences who you are. If you are interested in foods for consciousness, read ***Support the Mountain: Esoteric Acupuncture, Volume V***. Everything you eat and drink, as well as the people you associate with, the things that occupy your time and mind, as well as the electromagnetic radiation you are exposed to (cell phones, computers, television, battery operated vehicles and other devices) all contribute to the energy that surrounds you and the energy that is within all of your fields. All of these different factors contribute to the frequency of the energy you carry and possess and make up what is known as energy consciousness. Energy is a transporter of information. This means that an advanced soul will be aware and conscious of the all the types of fields surrounding that person, as well as knowing what benefits or acts as a hindrance to that person's inner, spiritual growth.

Some of the esoteric teachings within Esoteric Acupuncture are adapted from the teachings of the Ageless Wisdom schools. Viewing acupuncture as art requires that we must become more inwardly directed, rather than merely following the outward influences imposed upon the acupuncture community by academia and the controlling constrictions of the somewhat outdated, traditional acupuncture world. Anyone with some academic skills at a college level is able to learn the traditional ways of utilizing acupuncture. One way of moving past the restrictions of Traditional Acupuncture requires an artistic perspective with connections to the inner worlds of the heart. The finer frequency levels of the heart will allow the inner spiritual essence of acupuncture to unlock the inner key codes for the maximum benefit of the client being treated.

The scope of Esoteric Acupuncture encompasses much more than treating the dense physical body for pain, or for merely relaxing the astral and mental stressors. For example, anyone can be taught how to paint a picture by using one's left-brain and with rote memorization of the very base principles of painting. It requires the Inner Spiritual Heart and an artistic right brain to be able to create an original artistic painting using colors and new ideas of your own. Likewise, anyone can learn to be an acupuncture technician by going to an acupuncture school. It requires much more to be able to reach into the consciousness realms of the Causal, Buddhic, Atmic, Monadic, Logoic and even higher consciousness planes for the purpose of using acupuncture in a different way than the model taught by the traditional acupuncture schools today.

This is where the "art" in acupuncture is applied. I am encouraging acupuncturists to break from the constrictions of the old thinking and move into the fields of energy that are opening up for humanity in the Age of Aquarius. We, as licensed acupuncturists, must not forget that merely passing exams in an accredited academic setting is not enough. We must also remember that besides the academic requirements for achieving some level of competency in acupuncture, that essence of "true" acupuncture is art. Acupuncture is energy. Energy is life. Life is energy. Art is energy. Life is art. Acupuncture is art.

The inner essence of the Ageless Wisdom teachings are still left intact within Esoteric Acupuncture, but the wording or phrasing may have been changed slightly to make the teachings more understandable for the thinking of today. The esoteric teachings of the Ageless Wisdom are not designed to draw you into being a follower of one specific teacher or of one specific type of philosophy. There is an inner plane connection of spiritual intention and love among all the disciples, initiates and teachers of the Ageless Wisdom schools of thought. The esoteric Ageless Wisdom teachings, for those who are ready to receive the knowledge and wisdom emanated by the vibrations of the words, will spark an inner push to seek and find the one true Master—the Master within your Higher, Inner, Spiritual Heart. Esoteric Acupuncture is designed to help you to move you in your Higher, Inner, Spiritual Heart Center so you will always be able to follow the wisdom of your own heart. You do not need an external guru when you already have an inner guru in the form of the Guru Chakra situated directly below the Sahasrara (Crown Chakra). You must first be aware of your inner guru and then learn how to access this inner guru.

When I say the frequencies that emanate from certain words or phrases, I am not talking about specific words or a dictionary meaning of those words. For those who have done the inner plane work, the vibrations from certain words or phrases may trigger "something" that makes you feel there is a truth to the teachings. Although you may not completely understand what the words or phrases are conveying to you, you know in your heart that there is something that is drawing you to seek further, to delve deeper into the untold mysteries within those words or phrases. You know in your heart that there might be something else to unravel that will benefit you.

To understand Esoteric Acupuncture, one must understand fields. We are not merely talking about systems, but are now working with fields. As we quickly move into the Age of Aquarius, some of you may realize that the acupuncture meridian system, as understood and taught by the acupuncture academia today, is very limiting in terminology, especially for the western mind. The meaning and characteristics of the various planes of consciousness such as: the Dense Physical Plane, Etheric Body, Astral and Mental Planes are not taught in acupuncture schools in the United States today. Those four levels are the planes most affected by the insertion of acupuncture needles at acupuncture sites using the principles of Traditional Acupuncture theory.

From the Traditional Acupuncture viewpoint, qi moves within the channels, collaterals and the connecting pathways throughout the physical body. The acupuncture channels are within the etheric levels. With this type of thinking, whether the acupuncture instructors understand systems or not, they are confining the qi flow in the body to only the etheric levels within the closed meridian network system. With Esoteric Acupuncture, the triangular visualization connections bring the system into the realm of fields and not merely etheric channels.

The Etheric Plane is the intermediary between the dense physical vehicle and the Astral Plane of our emotional body. The Astral Plane is in turn the level directly below the Mental Plane. This makes the Astral Plane the intermediary between the Etheric Planes of consciousness and the four lower Mental Planes of the concrete mind. Although the Traditional Acupuncture professors do not use the terminology being presented in the Esoteric Acupuncture series, the realm of all the Traditional

Acupuncture systems consists of the Lower Quaternary of the Dense Physical Plane, the Etheric Sub Planes, the Astral Plane and the Mental Plane.

No matter how quickly qi travels through the acupuncture meridians and channels, those movements are still linear. There is another type of connection that is not linear. This non-linear connection between two or more distant locations is an instantaneous consciousness connection called a morphic resonant connection. By understanding the properties of morphic resonance and incorporating this understanding into your acupuncture practice, you will break out of the closed system of thinking that qi only flows within the meridians, connecting channels, muscular channels, cutaneous and sub cutaneous pathways and any of the other linear pathway connections. If you understand morphic resonant connections, then something "else" and something "new" is now possible.

Fields extend much further outward from the dense physical vehicle than the Etheric Plane of the acupuncture meridians. With the activation of any of the New Encoding Patterns, you are initiating spin point activity at each acupuncture site that is needled. The collective energy of the spin point activities created by the correct activation of any New Encoding Pattern will, in turn, create a Spin Field around the client. A Spin Field is not confined to the Astral Plane or Mental Plane of the client. Spin Fields extends into the Causal Sub Planes, the Buddhic, atmic, Monadic, Logoic Planes and even beyond into the cosmic levels of consciousness. With a different understanding of how the acupuncture sites create spin field activity, one is now able to at least have a basic understanding that the acupuncture system is not a closed system. Our acupuncture community, as a whole, must move forward and expand our understanding of energy and consciousness and accept that consciousness is connected to everything. This will move us from the traditional, limited closed system into an expanded open system.

Consciousness is contained within all fields. A Spin Field has a much greater intensity with a higher, lighter frequency than the frequencies created by more traditional acupuncture treatments. A Spin Field inherently has various tetrahedral geometrically formed fields that create an overall frequency that allows the individual, who is in alignment with this frequency, an opportunity to quickly accelerate into a higher plane of conscious. This possibility may occur when two criteria are met while the client is receiving an Esoteric Acupuncture treatment. Firstly the recipient of the Esoteric Acupuncture treatment must be able to quiet his or her chattering mind and become very Still. Being Still is not synonymous with silent thinking. Secondly the frequency of the practitioner inserting the acupuncture needles must be resonating at a high level of light quotient. The key for moving into the higher consciousness planes requires that both the practitioner and the recipient of the treatment are actively engaging in some level of inner plane work such as: meditation, pranayama (breathing exercises), *QI Gong* or other inner, calming, centering work.

The practitioner must understand the vastness of the concept of Six Surrounding One, or more precisely Six Surrounding "The One." Since "the six" are six points placed along the circumference of a circle, Six Surrounding The One is also Three Hundred Sixty surrounding The One. This numbering is related to 3-6-1. Remember there are 361 acupuncture points in the twelve major vertical meridians plus the vertical Du and Ren channels. Of course there are hundreds of additional acupuncture points when you add the various hand, facial, auricular and other micro systems of acupuncture. Just know that 361 is a very important esoteric puzzle to assist you to unravel the mysteries of who you are. The concept of 3-6-1 is discussed in more detail later in this chapter.

You should also understand that Six Surrounding The One cloaks another frequency of Twelve Surrounding The One. The Twelve Surrounding The One is also the clue to unlock the frequency of the "hidden gate" located at the acupuncture site of *Tian Man*, the esoteric Du-20 that is the pathway to the Jewel in the Lotus of the Anahata (Heart Chakra). "The One" in this instance refers to the Jewel that is surrounded by the twelve petals of the Anahata (Heart Chakra).

There are also twelve petals surrounding the Jewel within the Guru Chakra. The "Jewel" within the Anahata (Heart Chakra) plus the "Jewel" within the Guru Chakra are known in Esoteric Acupuncture as the Higher Twin Flames Within. The merging and communication between your Higher Twin Flames Within is an initiation into the deeper and more advanced realms of the Ageless Wisdom teachings. It was mentioned in an earlier work, in the Esoteric Acupuncture series, that in the Age of Aquarius we do not need an outside personal guru. We only need to know that we have our own teacher or guru within in the form of the Guru Chakra. We merely need to access and activate our own guru within.

When the practitioner is intimately familiar with the complexities of the concept of Twelve Surrounding The One, that esoteric information is passed through the practitioner to the recipient of the New Encoding Pattern. Energy is a transporter of information, which is consciousness. The key is to first acknowledge and understand that we all have higher levels of the heart. Then we should access and activate the higher, finer frequency levels of our Anahata (Heart Chakra).

Do not merely strive to be a technician. I have had many acupuncturists tell me how they have memorized a certain number of Chakra Balancing Patterns or New Encoding Patterns. When I look directly into their eyes and into their energy fields, I know they do not really understand the esoteric teachings that are infused within the Esoteric Acupuncture Patterns. The true seeker of the Esoteric, Ageless Wisdom is dedicated, disciplined and becomes the true seer. The term seer is not being used to describe those who can make futuristic predictions. Seer is used here to mean those who have clear insight into "the now" and are on their way to becoming clairsentient/clairvoyant or are already at some level of clairsentience/clairvoyance.

The true seeker is always hungry for "The Truth." This is the path to unraveling your true puzzle piece in life. There may seem to be variations of The Truth depending on your light quotient. But, variations of The Truth are not The Truth. "The Truth" is singular. Knowing The Truth requires that you seek and obtain the highest, inner light within. This is the goal of Esoteric Acupuncture, which is to reach the highest possible light quotient (light frequency) obtainable in this particular incarnation. "The Truth" is not something explainable. You will Know when you reach that level of Light Quotient.

### Triangles

One of the fundamental principles involved in Esoteric Acupuncture is the use of triangulation when inserting acupuncture needles at various acupuncture sites. Triangles are the signature for tetrahedrons. Triangles with the apex pointing upward represent fire, the heart frequencies and love. Triangles with the apex pointing downward represent water, the kidneys and fear. When the two opposing triangles are layered one on top of the other, a two-dimensional six-pointed star is formed. When this geometric form is expanded and viewed from a three-dimensional perspective, a double tetrahedral structure is formed. Some people may feel that working with triangles, tetrahedrons and six-pointed stars represent the old system.

One thing to keep in mind is that triangles in a two dimensional plane are actually open systems and not closed systems. A closed system represents the thinking of the old ideas and a finite number of possibilities within a closed field. An open system represents the idea of an infinite number of possibilities and an infinite number of fields. If you draw a triangle of any shape or size starting at point A then forming the three vertices by moving from point A to point B to point C and back to point A, the two vertices that intersect at point A are not actually touching each other. This means that the triangle is not closed. One line lies on top of the other line at point A. On a two-dimensional plane, two points cannot occupy the same space at the same time. This means that no matter how tiny the opening that is created by the overlapping vertices at point A, there is nonetheless a gap. This makes triangles an open system on a two dimensional plane. (See figure 1.1 below.)

Fig. 1.1

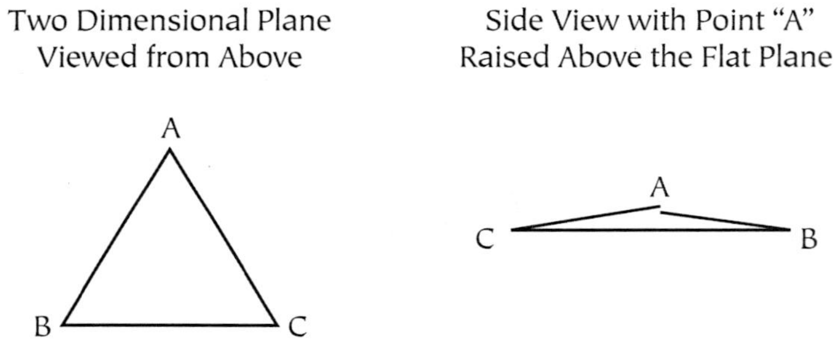

If the triangle is opened at one end, then the triangle is also a spiral. When people think of a spiral, they usually think of a spring or other type of revolving energy field. How many links or sections of a spring does it require to make it a spiral? A triangle represents one link or one section in a larger spiral. (Remember that the triangle is an open triangle, not a closed triangle.)

In the submicroscopic world and sub worlds, spirals are always moving and spinning. The constant spiraling movement of the triangles creates an open system. I want to make it perfectly clear that in Esoteric Acupuncture with the New Encoding Patterns and the Chakra Balancing Patterns, we are working with open systems and not closed systems. When you align your frequencies with the new frequencies of our evolving Earth, evolving solar system and with the evolving cosmic changes, then what may seem like old geometric shapes, patterns and thought forms automatically take on a higher, more refined vibrational frequency. It is not the same frequencies of an older age.

You will notice that the New Encoding Patterns and the Chakra Balancing Patterns are made up of various interconnecting triangles and intersecting triangles. Triangles are the signature of tetrahedrons and tetrahedral geometry. After you have correctly needled any of the acupuncture patterns on the posterior side with the proper sequencing, it is best to have your client make mental visual triangular connections of these acupuncture sites. The practitioner must guide the client with the visual triangular connections. The triangular connections will consist of both fire and water triangles. Fire triangles have the apex pointing upward toward the head. Water triangles have the apex pointing downward toward the feet. These mental visualization connections are exercises for the abstract mind and allow the client an opportunity to more readily move into his or her Inner, Higher, Spiritual Heart Center. This process may then allow the client to transition into a tetrahedral geometrical spin field while the acupuncture needles are still inserted and also allow the client an opportunity to access information encoded in his or her Inner Key Codes.

The New Encoding Patterns are designed to shift the client into a tetrahedral spin field. It is while in a tetrahedral geometric spin field consciousness that the client will be given the opportunity to work with a more expanded form of energy and an expanded form of consciousness. If the client has done the proper amount of inner plane work, he or she may eventually access the Akashic Records. The visual triangular connections within the New Encoding Patterns create a stronger, more centered energetic field than the field obtainable by more traditional acupuncture protocols.

It was mentioned in ***Support the Mountain: Esoteric Acupuncture, Volume V*** that qi (prana), as well as other forms of energies are transporters of information. Constructing triangular formations through mental visualization connections of the needles inserted at specific acupuncture sites create more energy and a more complex field than just placing the needles at those same acupuncture sites in a random fashion with no clue of the power of utilizing triangulation in your treatments.

I feel that with any complex system, the intricacies and the nuances of these complexities must be broken down to a level that can be explained in a simpler format. If a person cannot explain a complex system or complex theories in an easier to understand manner, than that person does not really know that system or theory very intimately. Now the system or theories may still remain difficult to comprehend by some, but the presenter must be able to at least simplify the explanations of the system. I have tried to present Esoteric Acupuncture in the manner that I hope will be the most understandable to those who are truly seeking "The Truth" (not merely a truth) and are interested in uncovering their individual puzzle piece in life. The one difficulty with Esoteric Acupuncture may be the languaging of certain concepts and the use of certain terms. In cases where there might be ambiguity with the concept, I have tried to use the phrasing that I felt was the least difficult to understand and tried to approach that idea from the angle of most accessibility for the reader. Often the same esoteric terms may have different meanings depending upon different authors or different systems. To eliminate ambiguity with certain terms, whenever possible, I have tried to explain how those specific esoteric terms are used within the context of Esoteric Acupuncture.

## Qi As a Transporter of Information

A big part of the lifestyle of Esoteric Acupuncture involves the choices of foods and drinks you decide to ingest. Esoteric Acupuncture encourages you to only ingest the foods and drinks with the highest vibrational frequencies possible. That means ingest only organic, pesticide-free and no genetically modified foods of any kind. This also means that one must eat at home as much as possible. Elisabeth Rochat De La Vallee states in her book ***A Study of Qi***:

> *The tastes activate and guide the qi. There is a very strong primitive link between food and qi. It is a vitally important to eat carefully because it is not only a question of good health but a question of good qi and its regulation. The qi is able to make the will solid, and the will is able to direct and form the inner disposition. It is your inner disposition that determines what you say.* [3]

All of the particles and qi in the foods and drinks are transformed into energy that directly affects consciousness. What types of energies do you want to create and maintain? Energy (qi) is a transporter of information. What types of information do you want to store and share with others?

A human being, with body, mind and spirit, has an amazing, inherent, inner drive to move in a positive, progressive, expansive manner. The mind has a limitless field with no borders. That is why children are always curious about new things. We all want to grow and expand our awareness. We all want to see and explore new places and things.

As we age, we begin to place restrictions on ourselves. We want to follow proper etiquette and try to be politically and socially correct. Many want to be part of a group, so we do not say or do things that are outside of the group mentality. But those who start to wake up eventually come in touch with that inner place that feels the need to explore and discover new things. For some people, this need to learn and explore new ideas becomes more like an urgent passion. In reality they want to remember information that is stored deep in their subconscious. Much of this information may be from past life experiences. The inner heart is expansive, not constrictive.

The physical body has the inherent ability to heal itself naturally. If you bruise or cut your body, you do not have to mentally direct your body to heal. The body will heal by itself over a certain sequential period of time. Likewise, our spirit has the inherent quality of wanting to know more and to experience all that is possible in one human lifetime. If our spirit is bruised or even crushed, there is an inherent force field within that wants the spirit to mend and be whole again. This requires the heart.

What happens is that many times we are programed to not believe in the beauty and miraculous ability of our body, mind and spirit to guide us on the most marvelous adventure possible, known as our own individual journey of life. We do not trust ourselves to make decisions and usually follow someone else's advice or try to follow someone else's dreams. Parents often attempt to pursue their dreams through their children by shaping their children's lives based on what the parent may want. Even grandparents sometimes may try to pursue their own unfulfilled dreams through a grandchild. Esoteric Acupuncture is designed so that we may uncover our own true puzzle piece of life. It is important that we pursue our own dreams and our own goals. We must learn to trust our Inner, Spiritual Higher Heart again. I am not merely talking about the emotional heart, but our Higher, Inner, Spiritual Heart.

## Transformations

We have moved past the Year of the White Rabbit (2011) {How far down the rabbit hole did you go to find your own truth?}, the Year of the Black Dragon (2012) {wash away the old to allow rapid, new realities to unfold} and the Year of the Black Snake (2013) {Did you allow the serpent energy to ascend in your inner transformational journey?} to enter into a new and exciting phase for humanity. It has become increasing clearer that the emphasis for Esoteric Acupuncture has shifted from merely the "healing phases" to a greater emphasis on assisting in the alignment and awakening of higher consciousness of the New Humanity for the purpose of full awakening. The various fields of healing are contained within the larger field of awakening. Awakening is healing and much more.

In reality, there may not be such a thing as an individual "total all-encompassing," complete full awakening. As we continue to grow and awaken on our own individual inner journey, there are always expanded levels of consciousness to unfold beyond the cosmic and multiverse consciousness planes. The full awakening I am referring to is the awakening of our present collective global consciousness to embody the heart frequencies, rather than the kidney frequencies of fear, scarcity and control. Of course, some souls have already opened to an accelerated and expanded level of awakening. This awakening I am referring to is merely a state of consciousness. We all possess this vibrational state of consciousness, but most of humanity has chosen to remain in a denser state of consciousness.

Light workers must learn to hold their ground and to maintain a high level and high intensity of light. This means keeping a fairly constant high light quotient. The old guard and the old school of fear, scarcity and control do not want changes. This old school model has been in control for many millennia. Because the old school creates and thrives on confrontation, fear and control, we should try to not be confrontational with the old thinking. They have the power in that arena and will usually win in that arena. But, the old school of darkness cannot handle the amount of light being showered on the planet at this time with so many light workers holding the higher frequencies of light. There are also additional light workers awakening every day. The planet, as a whole, is also moving toward a lighter frequency vibration, which is also transforming darkness into more light. Total transformation from darkness to lightness will not happen overnight. We need to be diligent and patient.

In Chinese medical thought, the kidneys are said to rule the water element and are associated with fear. The Chinese also say that the heart controls the fire element that is associated with joy and happiness. The heart system and fire element oppose the kidney system and the water element. Those two systems are the black and white colors seen in the Chinese yin and yang symbol. The black represents the kidneys and water, while the white represents the heart and fire. In an earlier work of the Esoteric Acupuncture Series, it was stated that the concepts of joy and happiness that are associated with the heart were not strong enough to overcome the various levels of fear. Joy and happiness are not the direct neutralizing frequencies of extreme fear. Joy and happiness are not strong enough frequencies to overcome fear at the extreme end of the spectrum of fear. It is love that is powerful enough to oppose extreme fear. Joy and happiness are tentacles of love. Love does not come from joy or happiness, which are both denser frequencies. We must expand the field of the fire element of the heart in Chinese medicine (Five Element Theory) and understand that it is love that is the most fundamental starting frequency of the heart and not joy and happiness.

Esoterically the number associated with the heart and love is the number 1. Esoterically the number associated with the kidneys and fear is the number 2. A divine, inner spiritual force resides within each of us. This divine, inner spiritual frequency resonates with the number 1. But, we are socialized to embrace the frequencies of two. We are taught at an early age about division. We are told that we have to go outside of ourselves to pray to a source for spiritual guidance, even thought this same fundamental frequency is within each and everyone of us. We have learned to disconnect from this inner, spiritual source. We are taught about our family, racial differences, cultural differences. Various social organizations, political, religious, ethnic and national groups perpetuate this belief in division. We are taught about "us and them." Within your own group you are the insiders. Anyone who is not an insider is automatically an outsider. We are taught that our group is better, or our group has something special that the outsiders do not have or possess. This is especially true with the different religions. This mind program often does not allow people to move past their old thinking, old ways of doing things or to move out of their neighborhoods even if they are not happy with their current situation. We are programmed to feel safe within our group. We must stay connected to the hood (neighborhood). This is the group mentality and one of the energies encoded within the Swadthisthana (second chakra).

Traditional thinking, such as Traditional Chinese Medicine as taught in the United States, does not incorporate spirituality within the practice. Although we are taught some level of *qi gong, tai qi* or very basic meditation, the acupuncture schools in the United States do not stress the spiritual aspects of Traditional Chinese medicine outside of mental or emotional centering.

## Use of the Name Esoteric Acupuncture Not Allowed in California

In late 2012, I learned that the California Acupuncture Committee would not allow CEU's (continuing education units) for Esoteric Acupuncture classes or workshops presented in California. (Acupuncturists need a certain amount of continuing education units to be able to renew their license to practice acupuncture.) Up until that time, I had been teaching Esoteric Acupuncture for approximately fourteen years. My lectures and workshops had always been approved for CEU's, in California as well as other states. I called the California Acupuncture Committee in early 2013 and was told that the committee would not approve any acupuncture courses that had any reference of a spiritual nature. One individual within the acupuncture committee did not like the name esoteric. I was told that using the moniker Esoteric Acupuncture implied that I was teaching astrology or something spiritual. They were perfectly fine with the course description and the material that was being taught, but did not like the name Esoteric Acupuncture. One lawyer told me they could not make me change the name of Esoteric Acupuncture without a legal explanation and even said he would take the case for no charge. As in Sun Tzu's ***The Art of War***, I felt it was best to avoid a conflict at this particular time. So for any of my courses to be given CEU status in California, I had to change the name of Esoteric Acupuncture.

If the California Acupuncture Committee's treatment protocol for licensed acupuncturists in California is to strictly follow and adhere to the Traditional Chinese Medical role model, the California Acupuncture Committee is definitely unfamiliar with ***The Yellow Emperor's Classic of Internal Medicine***. The version translated by Ilza Veith states: "*How can a disease be cured when there is no spiritual energy left in the body.*"[4] The statement does not say "no energy left." The translation by Ilza Veith says: "*no spiritual energy left.*"

How could a supposedly rationally thinking, academic governing board in the 21st Century be afraid of a word such as esoteric? According to ***Webster's Third New International Unabridged Dictionary*** esoteric means: 1) "designed for or understand by the specially initiated alone;" 2) "difficult to understand;" 3) "confined or limited to a small circle."[5] If you believe that ***Webster's Third New International Unabridged Dictionary*** is a legitimate, authoritative, academic reference source, then the definitions in ***Webster's*** can apply to any traditional acupuncture curriculum in the United States today. 1) Acupuncture is "designed for or understood by the specially initiated alone" can also be read as acupuncture can only be understood and used by those who have gone to an accredited acupuncture institution and are licensed by the state or country. 2) The idea that something is "difficult to understand" can also mean that a person will not understand acupuncture unless he or she studied in an accredited acupuncture institution. 3) The idea that something is "confined or limited to a small circle" can mean that only those who are licensed acupuncturists (limited to a small circle) are allowed to practice acupuncture.

After some time contemplating on different titles for

Esoteric Acupuncture, I decided to go with Dr. Mikio Sankey Acupuncture. I was not comfortable with this name because in the yogic world, they do not like the lower ego to influence the work. Names like Pasteurization and many healing modalities with the creator's name are not looked upon favorably in the yogic world. Renaming Esoteric Acupuncture to be called Dr. Mikio Sankey Acupuncture might seem like I was trying to push my name above the work. I called Swami Nataraj Muni Baba for advice. I wanted to talk to a realized yogi master at the swami level and not just any yogi guru. After a lengthy discussion, he gave me blessings and an approval from the yogic world to use the name Dr. Mikio Sankey Acupuncture. When I lecture internationally or in other states outside of California, I still use the name Esoteric Acupuncture. I teach the same material in California, but I use Dr. Mikio Sankey Acupuncture. How interesting that in a state that may appear to be liberal, open-minded and trend setting in the health field, California is the one place that has a problem with the moniker Esoteric Acupuncture.

## The Super Human Within Us

I have heard many times how a practitioner cannot really understand Traditional Chinese Medicine unless the person speaks and reads Chinese. Ancient systems were built and evolved around the energetics and needs of the people of those ancient times. Even the generations that followed and used the traditional model had to incorporate newer ideas because of the differences in the thinking and needs of each new generation. Those sticking to the dogma of the superiority of "knowing" the intricacies of the traditional ways because of being able to speak or read a certain language better than those who cannot read or speak that particular language have created division. Creating division resonates with the number "Two" associated with the state of fear and its many tentacles. Esoteric Acupuncture emphasizes staying within our Higher Heart Center, our Divine Spiritual Center that resonates with the frequency of the heart and the number "One." Esoteric Acupuncture was not developed to pit traditional methods and theories versus a newer way of thinking. Esoteric Acupuncture has merely expanded the field that includes the traditional, as well as the newer thinking.

In this time phase of rapid change on Planet Earth, it seems that relying strictly on the old paradigm is much too slow. In acupuncture we are taught to treat the signs and symptoms of an imbalance, to treat a particular organ system or to focus on certain areas of challenge such as: lower back pain, stiff neck, achy knees, digestion, hormones, coughing, palpitations and other physical health challenges of this nature.

I am suggesting that treating a small portion of the whole (signs and symptoms or an organ system) is too slow for this time of accelerated consciousness awakening. It is very beneficial to take herbal supplements and rely on a healthy dietary regime, but those modalities alone are not enough for the complexities of today. Radiation from nuclear fallout, the spraying of massive amounts of chemicals in the air (called chemtrails) and all of the electromagnetic frequencies radiating from television, cell phone towers, satellites, electric cars and radiation from all of the myriad of electromagnetic devices are all contributing to our inability to stay centered in our hearts.

I feel it is of utmost importance to learn how to quickly align our inner frequency heart center that is the center of all our systems. This Inner, Spiritual Higher Heart Path is our own ever-evolving Tree of Life. Esoteric Acupuncture treatments are designed to align the whole body on all levels, not merely the Dense Physical, Etheric, Astral and Mental Planes. The mind controls the lower, denser planes. This is healing in its most basic sense. I am using healing to mean moving from one plane of consciousness to a more desirable plane of consciousness. That is what we expect when we take herbs, go to a western medical doctor who may prescribe pharmaceutical medicines, have massage or have an acupuncture treatment. We are attempting to move from one level of consciousness to a more desirable state of consciousness. This thinking only makes sense if the person is aware of consciousness and is conscious of the awakening that is happening today. An individual stuck in a denser plane of consciousness might not wish to move from where he or she is at to an expanded level of awareness and consciousness. For those types of people, my definition of healing would not make sense. If you are happy or at least content with where you are at presently, why would you want to move into another plane of consciousness? But, a great portion of humanity feels there is "something" happening right now.

There is definitely "something" happening now that reflects humanity's desire for some level of consciousness shift to a more awakened state. The masses may not be sure of what that consciousness shift entails. Nonetheless, there seems to be an urgent search for something new, something different.

Have you noticed in these past recent years (as least since the early 2000's) how many movies made in Hollywood, California are based on super action heroes from comic books? These action heroes all have super powers with an emphasis on indestructibility, immortality and staying the same (staying young) forever. Do Hollywood films program our consciousness, or is the group consciousness of the masses influencing what types of movies are produced? The overall effect is that people want to believe in the possibility of some level of "super" human existence.

We hear about stem cell research in the scientific field through the various news outlets. There is so much interest in discovering new herbs, supplements and elixirs to help us stay young and retain all our youthful attributes, especially among the boomer generation (those born approximately from 1945 through 1965) of today. Men want the latest testosterone "magic pill" or ointment to keep physically and sexually fit. Men are taking steroids to keep their muscles toned to look younger. Women want the latest anti-aging treatments and anti-aging herbs, hormones and drugs available to keep their youthful appearance forever. Botox to remove wrinkles and sagging skin and less invasive cosmetic laser surgeries or facial surgeries are very important to those who can afford those types of treatments. These are all geared toward trying to retain some level of a youthful appearance. Athletes all over the globe are shattering athletic records and achievements from past generations of athletes, some without concern over what artificial steroids will do to the body.

There seems to be a global desire for something "super human." This consciousness is in reality about some level of genetic mutation for positive shifts in humanity. There will definitely be new discoveries to assist us to retain some of our physical youthful attributes. The genetic mutation I am referring to revolves around the awakening of the dormant portions of the brain, as well as the awakening of that larger portion of our DNA now called junk DNA to bring humanity into a golden age of enlightenment. If we merely focus on the dense physical portions of our reality, it may be more challenging to awaken the higher frequency realities above the Lower Quaternary plane of existence. If we emphasize awakening the higher levels of our hearts, we will be able to bring about both a dense physical and lighter, higher consciousness shift. The New Encoding Patterns within Esoteric Acupuncture were and are developed to assist one in uncovering those "hidden" key codes of wisdom locked away within the cellular, intracellular and spaces between the cells. Unlocking these hidden key codes of wisdom will help to align and accelerate the awakening of our divine Inner, Spiritual Heart Center.

In reality, each and every one of us has everything we need and will ever need. Everything is contained within our consciousness. We are all already "enlightened" beings. The reality of the situation is that the majority of humanity have forgotten how to access the fields of consciousness directly triggering these areas known to realize and accept "enlightenment." We have been programmed to think, feel and react in particular ways depending upon the program and the situation we find ourselves. Consciousness is a very vast and all-encompassing field. Part of our spiritual journey is to discover how to deprogram those portions of our reality that no longer vibrate with the frequencies we wish to embrace today. It is important that we learn to accept our new consciousness and new way of life. The old thinking of the old society does not like change, especially rapid change. Change is expansion and is related to the heart and the many branches of love. Tradition is rigidity, constriction, stagnation and is related to the kidneys and its many tentacles of fear and contraction.

Esoteric Acupuncture is one method to help an individual find his or her true quiet center, which is the heart field. There are many layers of the heart field. We are first attempting to enter into the center alignment of the Field of Silence. Then our focus shifts to refining this center alignment to a more refined vibration that leads to the Field of Stillness. It is within this particular field of consciousness that all is available to us. There are many methods to obtain this vibrational frequency. Some of the older traditional methods are very constricting following rigid guidelines and strict rules. Those methods may indeed work, but often those older teachings are more about rigid forms and less about formlessness, which is the Field of Stillness. Often being excessively nitpicking about the rules of the form may obstruct, or at least impede the pathway to the formless. The form is the kidney field. The formless is the heart field.

Being Still is not synonymous with stagnation. There is expansion and subtle movement within Stillness that is not a part of the reality of the chattering, cluttered three-dimensional mind of the masses. Stillness does not impede change. Stillness creates change.

By striving to stay within our Inner, Spiritual Heart Center, we will be the super human that we idolize on the movie screen or in comic books. We may not have the physical powers and be able to perform amazing physical feats, but awakening Kundalini, expanding consciousness and remaining in our Inner, Spiritual Heart Center will reveal a whole new world, both inner and outer, that will indeed make us "super" humans. The key is being able to find that quiet Stillness within your body, mind and spirit.

## Development of A New Humanity

One desired goal of Esoteric Acupuncture treatments is to align and harmonize the major chakra centers of the body. Another goal is to build the Antahkarana for the recipient of the Esoteric Acupuncture treatment. The Antahkarana is the energetic spiritual bridge, or a main connection from the dense concrete mind to the higher head centers and beyond. This bridge is formed by wave frequencies of consciousness. With an Esoteric Acupuncture treatment, we are attempting to reach some level of the field of formlessness. Eventually, it will be possible to tap into the field of spacelessness and formlessness whenever we are able to Still the Mind. This requires diligence, perseverance and devoted inner plane work. Unlocking the inherent Esoteric Ageless Wisdom encoded within the geometric patterns of the various New Encoding Patterns is one method to reach a certain level of Stillness.

Although there are specific numbers of acupuncture sites and a certain sequencing of those acupuncture sites within each of the New Encoding Patterns required to activate the overall field of that pattern, the form is not as important as the intention of the treatment. In other words, do not get too hung up on memorizing all the New Encoding Patterns and trying to understand why certain patterns use a certain number of acupuncture points. Do not try to memorize which specific pattern to use for any particular individual. Do not get too caught up in the form and trying to be the perfect technician while forgetting the formless. Utilizing the formless aspect of Esoteric Acupuncture by working with qi and consciousness is the intention of the treatment. We should also utilize the frequencies of the compassionate, inner heart.

I have included in Chapter Five of this book a guideline of which New Encoding Patterns to use by the practitioner depending on the Tier of Density of the client. These treatment protocols are only recommendations. It would be more beneficial to you as the practitioner to integrate your higher, intuitive powers and the selective, discerning reasoning power of your Higher Heart into your daily life regime. Involve your Higher Heart in the selection of any New Encoding Pattern for a particular client.

I am not suggesting any particular method over another to reach this level of Stillness. Some of your family members, close friends or acquaintances may not wish to follow this doctrine of discovering one's Inner, True Spiritual Heart. But, you would not be reading this book if you did not already have the inner desire to unravel the concealed, esoteric consciousness within you. You have the desire to light the inner violet flame of spiritual transformation to open the gates of your Antahkarana for higher spiritual awakening. You may choose to follow one or more of the older traditional methods, or choose to merely follow your heart. No matter what method or pathway you desire and eventually choose to follow to obtain this Field of Stillness, know that each of us already has this Field of Stillness inherent within. The "pathways" to this Field of Stillness are merely blocked by excessive mental chatter and excessive worldly, emotional desires. Fear and the many tentacles connected to this dense realm will impede the process of moving into and staying in your Refined, Inner, Spiritual Heart Center.

Have you ever experienced a massage session from a particular massage therapist where you felt very relaxed, "light" and very centered. This feeling was more than merely having a few kinks and blockages removed from your physical body. The feeling from the session lasted weeks and maybe even longer than your normal sessions where you usually felt relief for only a few days. Something else happened during that particular session. There was a special electromagnetic connection. That massage therapist, at that particular date was able to tap into the vibratory rate of your magnetic field and was able to align your own electromagnetic center with the qi flow within the acupuncture meridians and the finer frequency nadi system.

This same electromagnetic connection often happens during an Esoteric Acupuncture session. I have been saying throughout my lectures how important it is for the practitioner to only ingest healthy foods and drinks. Everything we ingest becomes a part of the physical cells of the body, as well as shaping and creating a certain vibrational frequency for our etheric, astral and mental planes. The foods and drinks we ingest are transformed into energy that we use. Energy is a transporter of information. When we do healing work on other people, we are transferring information to that person. This information transference may occur by way of verbal communication, when we massage or touch the client or by the insertion of an acupuncture needle into the client. Even those who do some type of energy healing where the practitioner does not physically touch the client, but rather sends energy to the client, is still transferring information to the client by way of the energy transference. If both the practitioner and recipient of an Esoteric Acupuncture treatment are vibrating on an equally high frequency plane, than the chances for a special magnetic, electromagnetic and consciousness shift will be greatly enhanced. The shift will occur simultaneously on the Physical, Etheric, Astral, Mental and Higher Planes of consciousness. Once again, I will mention the importance of being very selective of what you put into your body.

The question is: How do we tap into the electromagnetic field of the client? With Chinese pulse diagnosis or tongue diagnosis, we are taught how to differentiate the subtleties of the physical and emotional levels. In Esoteric Acupuncture, we are not so interested in the denser energy fields. Although the seven primary chakras are associated with the astral levels and the astral plane is often thought of as a lower, denser plane, we are using a specific chakra balancing protocol as a means to align with the higher head chakras. The desired goal is to open and connect to the expanded consciousness planes from the causal level and above. It is important to harmonize and align the levels of the Anahata (Heart Chakra) so we are able to connect and align with the higher head chakras. When we involve our higher intuitive powers to assist us in selecting the most appropriate New Encoding Pattern for that client on that particular day with its specific astrological alignments, we will be able to offer the most beneficial treatment. We do not have to know astrology to be able to intuit the most beneficial treatment protocol to use on any particular day. We must learn to discern the True Whisper of our own heart and trust that our higher heart will always offer us the highest truth each and every time.

I mentioned in other volumes of Esoteric Acupuncture that we are not interested in manipulating the needles to tonify, sedate or to influence qi flow in a specific manner, such as taught in the traditional schools of acupuncture. We are only interested in a gentle and shallow insertion of the acupuncture needle at the "correct" gateways. By correct gateways, I am referring to the acupuncture sites that have qi. By trying to locate an acupuncture site following the guidelines set down by the traditional acupuncture books, you may find that you have needled a point that has very little qi. I am encouraging all licensed acupuncturists to now utilize your sensitivity and higher intuitive abilities to try and see or feel where the qi is located. You will often see that your point location is slightly different from the location you learned in acupuncture school. Any type of rough insertion, very deep needle insertion, turning, thrusting or other types of aggressive needling will only negate what we are trying to achieve. The traditional aggressive methods of needling will only reach the denser levels of *shen*. We are trying to awaken the most subtle, inner *shen*, attempting to unlock the hidden, Inner Key Codes.

It is very important to think of qi as information. The qi (information) stored at the specific acupuncture site, along with the qi of the needle, the qi of both the practitioner and the client, the qi and electromagnetic stress of the treatment room, the particular astrological forces at the time of the treatment, plus the total synergistic alignment of information from all the acupuncture points within a specific New Encoding Pattern will collectively influence and form the vibrational frequency for the client during that treatment. If you, as the practitioner, have your higher intuitive, discernment powers aligned with the frequencies of your client and are able to select the most appropriate New Encoding Pattern for that specific treatment, then the client will receive a harmonious, healing treatment that will simultaneously allow your client the opportunity to tap into his or her fields of higher consciousness.

Seeking out and understanding esoteric teachings are very inspiring and rewarding endeavors, especially for the intellectual seekers of the Ageless Wisdom. Many people are driven to explore new and exciting information. Exploring new ideas and philosophies in the vast world of academia and the esoteric realms can be very seductive. But, information for information's sake, even the esoteric Ageless Wisdom, is merely collecting something else to "clutter the mind." Unless you integrate the esoteric Ageless Wisdom teachings into your daily life, you are missing the true reason to seek out and learn this wisdom. The esoteric teachings will eventually become an integral part of the daily life of a "true" esoteric seeker. When esoteric knowledge becomes a part of the fabric of who you are, then the knowledge you have gathered transforms into wisdom.

Merely repeating esoteric teachings and esoteric knowledge that you have read or heard about is meaningless, unless you are walking that talk. Many lecturers merely store esoteric knowledge as information to be retrieved at certain favorable moments to allow their lower concrete minds an opportunity to exhibit the ability to recite tidbits of interesting facts to others. If you are one of the many esoteric teachers and/or lecturers that recite spiritual teachings but have a gap between your real life actions and your talk, then your words have little or no power. No matter how interesting your topic may be, you are merely expounding words. People today are becoming so consciously aware that many in the audience can automatically tell when a teacher or lecturer is not walking his or her talk. If you are a known lecturer or teacher, it is important to move as close to the high vibrational frequencies of those teachings and the knowledge and wisdom you are sharing with others. It is important to walk your talk from your Heart Space.

The esoteric teachings are to assist and guide you in finding your Puzzle Piece in Life. Your Puzzle Piece is not about finding your "perfect" job, or finding what makes you happy in life. This inner Puzzle Piece contains the clues to your pathway to discover and understand who you are, or rather to assist you to remember who you truly are. You are a magnificent spirit who chose a particular three-dimensional physical vehicle to allow you the opportunity to experience the human journey on Earth with the objective of reaching the highest levels of consciousness possible for you at this particular time. Finding your Puzzle Piece in Life means you will know your true Inner, Spiritual Heart.

Things, ideas and perceptions are constantly changing. As the world evolves, things just naturally change. It would be great to have a strong, stable heart center. During times of chaos, turmoil and challenges, we are then able to access this quiet, compassionate space to help us remain centered and grounded. If your true Inner,, Spiritual Heart Center has been developed solidly with devotion and discipline, it will remain a constant throughout time. A solid heart center will assist us in each new incarnation. That is why sometimes you may meet someone who is very grounded, centered, compassionate and wise without having meditated or without having done any inner plane work in this lifetime. His or her karmic development carried over into this present incarnation. On the other hand, a person may have done much inner plane work in a previous incarnation, but that individual needs other experiences to fulfill his or her karmic destination and may not seem spiritual, centered or wise in this incarnation.

The true heart center has a high vibratory rate that resonates with truth, integrity, gratitude, tenderness, friendliness, compassion and spiritual love/wisdom. Our heart center has the quietude and balance that will help us to evolve and grow through rapidly changing, chaotic and challenging times and to better deal with difficult situations and difficult people.

We must first choose to activate this center. Why do you think that heart related problems are the #1 cause of deaths in the United States today? People of North America have not connected with their hearts. The inner *shen* of the heart is not perceivable for those who cannot turn off the mental chatter of the mind. (In Chinese medicine, excessive mental chatter is an imbalance of the heart.) Our heart center is the calm within the storm of our daily lives in the complex, hectic world of the 21st Century. Meditation is one of the very best methods to strengthen our Inner Spiritual Heart Center.

There is also a lower center that revolves around the energies of survival, sex, greed, accumulation, lower ego gratification and power that many people desire and even cling to. This lower center is a very powerful and controlling center. The constant center, which I feel is the more desirable center to activate and build, is the heart center, not the sexual and lower power center.

The heart center has a particular fabric of vibrational, inner spiritual awareness that is always within each individual, but for many, these vibrations have been deeply concealed. Gratitude is a frequency that seems to be lacking in many people born in the Generation Y group (1980 to 2000) and in the Generation Z group (2000 & 2001 to the present). There seems to be an overall attitude of entitlement among many people born in those two generations. Gratitude is not a vibration these two groups seem to embrace. Overall I have not noticed much gratitude within these groups

Everything is moving so quickly and with information being so readily accessible through the internet and wireless phone systems, these younger generations do to not seem to grasp the idea of patience. Patience is a frequency of the heart. No matter how much the times are changing and how the consciousness of people today are rapidly expanding, patience is still a virtue that is very important to cultivate and utilize.

Through the teachings of Esoteric Acupuncture, it has been stated that the real healing is achieved through finding your own true Higher, Inner, Spiritual Heart Center that will assist in your own spiritual awakening and healing. There are infinite states of awakening that make life so exciting and rewarding. Esoteric Acupuncture provides one method to assist the seekers to move toward their heart path and to fine tune their own Inner, Spiritual Heart Center. This can be accomplished by inserting acupuncture needles in the body in various specific geometric patterns using very specific sequencing for each of the New Encoding Patterns. The New Encoding Patterns are designed to create a spin field that allows the recipient of the treatment to align with a very high consciousness frequency with the goal of expanding higher consciousness. The level of expanded consciousness obtainable is dependent upon both the level of consciousness of the practitioner and the amount of inner plane work done by the recipient of the treatment. The lighter and finer the frequency levels that the practitioner possesses will allow the recipient of the treatment to receive higher vibrational information. Remember that energy is a transporter of information. What vibrational frequency of information is the practitioner transmitting to the client? If you, as the practitioner, are only interested in being a skilled technician, then your Esoteric Acupuncture treatment will most likely focus only on the physical, etheric, astral and mental levels of consciousness.

Why did you originally choose to become involved in the healing fields? Maybe you decided to go to a more traditional, accredited institution and pursue a career as a licensed acupuncturist, medical doctor, chiropractor, osteopathic physician or massage therapist. Perhaps you decided to go another route and investigate other types of healing modalities such as color therapy, Pranic Healing, Reiki, toning, Mahikari or other healing practices, Was there an inner voice or inner spark that guided you to pursue this journey? Some of you may have entered the healing field to help a loved one who was suffering from some physical or emotional problems. Many may have chosen the healing profession to help the general public to begin the healing process.

Once you dedicate yourself to learning any of the various healing modalities and become knowledgeable and proficient in that particular form, you automatically become a teacher. A teacher does not mean that you have to lecture to large groups of people or stand in front of a class and teach students. All of your patients/clients are your students. They are coming to you to learn something, or gather information about a certain condition that is a challenge to them. The information, inspiration or relief from a physical challenge they are seeking requires that you teach your clientele how to maintain a healthy state of daily existence, as well as maintain a certain higher level of vibrational radiance. A healthy condition radiates at a higher frequency than the stages of emotional, mental or physical problems. Once you view your problems as merely challenges in your life, you have already changed your vibratory rate to that of a higher frequency. Even though your emotional or physical challenges are still with you, changing your mental view to a higher state of consciousness means that you have already initiated the healing process.

You, as an advanced energy healer, must guide your clients in that positive direction and show them how to become proactive in their own healing. The true teacher does not do the work for the student. The true teacher gives instructions or guidance and then leaves it up to that individual to see if he or she decides to follow the teacher's advice.

Your guidance and wisdom must come from the heart. This means that you must walk your talk from the heart. This means you propose or suggest certain guidelines, not from the denser realms of the lower ego and superiority, but from a place of compassion, understanding and love. You, as the healer and teacher, already have more responsibilities than those who are coming to you for help or advice. That is why it is so important to walk your talk from your heart. You cannot be a true healer who follows the heart path by giving advice that you do not follow yourself. Do not be a hypocrite. An example might be giving advice about the negative aspects of ingesting certain types of processed sugars to a patient/client who has a condition of excessive dampness that may have manifested as candida (overgrowth of yeast) or diabetes. Yet, you eat those same processed sugar in foods such as: pastries, ice cream, pies, cookies and drink alcohol yourself. How can you tell your patient/client about the undesirable attributes of certain types of foods and to not consume those foods, if you, yourself, eat or drink those same types of foods?

There is a higher calling and a higher purpose to why you became involved in the healing arts. There is a series of books by Alice Bailey published by Lucis Trust. Although Alice Bailey is given credit by Lucis Trust as being the author of those series of books, most of the books are the teachings of Djwhal Khul. Djwhal Khul was a Tibetan monk/scholar/teacher living in Tibet who telepathically transmitted information to Alice Bailey who lived in England. Alice Bailey was merely the vehicle on the receiving end of Djwhal Khul's messages. Alice Bailey manually wrote down and edited the messages, but the source of the information came from Djwhal Khul. Alice Bailey was able to use her gift of automatic writing to be able to telepathically and automatically write down the information by means of thought transference. Although Alice Bailey wrote several of the books in the Alice Bailey series, she was mainly a telepathic amanuensis for Djwhal Khul's teachings.

One of the books in the Alice Bailey collection is entitled ***Externalization of the Hierarchy***. When I first saw the title of the book in a bookstore many years ago, the vibration of the title was so powerful and magnetic to me that I literally yanked the book off the shelf. I did not know what ***Externalization of the Hierarchy*** meant, but I knew I had to read and investigate its contents.

That book was copyrighted and first published in 1957. The actual message in that book was written and presented for the consciousness of that time frame. We are in a much higher frequency now than that of the 1950's and the plan for elevating the consciousness of humanity has changed dramatically. Djwhal Khul's information revealed the Inner Plane Hierarchy's plan for the manifestation of other very high conscious beings to incarnate into the three-dimensional plane of Earth to assist humanity in our awakening and ascension into a higher spiritual consciousness.

That message is not in alignment with what is happening on this planet in this particular time frame. Earth of the 21st century has risen to a much higher vibrational frequency than the Earth of fifty plus years ago. The Piscean message was that an inner plane "savior" would appear in a physical three-dimensional body to assist humanity. We are now moving more and more into the frequency of the Age of Aquarius and we do not need to be saved by an external source. That view is no longer in alignment with the frequencies and consciousness of today.

There will be no one external savior from any one religious group who will uplift planet Earth. Today with the polarization of the major religions and even the separation between various factions within each religion, each with their own agenda and with disdain toward other religious philosophies, make it almost impossible to come to a universal agreement on how to deal with the problems of the Earth and humanity from a religious viewpoint. There is no love between the various religious factions. The political views and dogma within the major religious factions and the wide separation between the groups will not allow a savior that is outside of their one's own religious beliefs.

The Externalization of the Hierarchy has a different meaning today than in the 1950's. Externalization of the Hierarchy means that the consciousness of the multitude of individuals who have heard and responded to their own inner spiritual calling and have raised their level of Light Quotient to a very high frequency will emerge as a group body and blend this collective higher consciousness with the consciousness of the inner plane masters who are showering the planet with light. In other word, the higher consciousness of this group of spiritual light workers on Earth will keep ascending and merge with the consciousness held by the Inner Plane Hierarchy to create a new level of consciousness for the whole planet. If you are currently doing the proper inner plane work, this means that you are a part of the Externalization of the Hierarchy. The new Hierarchy will be a large group body, not one or several beings who have densified their physical vehicle to guide humanity as our saviors. Our individual awakening will automatically pull us, as a group body, up to a higher plane to merge with the downward pouring of the esoteric Ageless Wisdom that is being showered upon us today.

The Externalization of the Hierarchy will be a group event encompassing many individuals from around the globe from many different countries and many different religions and every race and ethnic group. Those of you reading this book are a part of the new Externalization of the Hierarchy. You would not be reading this book if you did not resonate with a very high frequency of light.

We are in the phase that I call the genesis of the New Humanity. The newborn souls of today are much different than those of previous generations. Many are incarnating with a very high Light Quotient, which means they are already vibrating at a very high level of consciousness. Remember all those special children chose their parents. It is up to the parents to encourage and help develop and maintain that higher level of consciousness of those special souls incarnating today.

In this time of great transition for humanity and the planet as a whole, each of you already knew in the deepest regions of your higher, Inner, Spiritual Heart that you were put on this planet at this particular time to hold and build the center light of your heart. You would not be reading this book if you did

amounts of information today. The expansion of consciousness does not merely mean gathering new tidbits of information. But, being open to ideas and thoughts that are not generally discussed by the mainstream media is a portion of this expanded consciousness. Some of this information has been purposely hidden until now. Some of this hidden information has newly been uncovered, while other information has been known by a select group of individuals who are the advanced seekers of The Truth. Do not be afraid of information that you have not heard or read about before. Being afraid is a mechanism that constricts your mind from expansion. Just gathering information does not mean that the message in that information is The Truth or that it is useful for your spiritual awakening and evolution. One way to differentiate useless information from useful information is to go inward to your own Inner Heart field.

The portion of expanding consciousness that is related to the Externalization of the Hierarchy is the unfolding of the Inner, Spiritual Higher Heart. Wisdom vibrates at a much higher frequency than mere knowledge. It is beneficial to learn to Be Still. Stillness will allow us to be better equipped to tune into the frequencies of wisdom rather than merely downloading information from the ethers. Being able to Still the Mind will allow us to infuse discernment into our daily lives for all planes of consciousness.

As we evolve into this next phase for humanity and a New Humanity is coming into fruition, the acupuncture community must realize that the majority of information being taught in the traditional academic setting is rapidly being outdated by the growth in our spiritual and technological advancements, our heightened awareness and our interconnectedness with the global community. We are no longer confined to a small local community. We are moving from a local consciousness to a global consciousness and beyond. Esoteric Acupuncture is an evolving system developed to make us aware of our interconnectedness to the global community, as well as to the cosmic community.

We are taught in acupuncture school about the balance of yin and yang within a harmonious system. We must have a certain amount of balance between the masculine (yang) aspects and feminine (yin) aspects of energy. This does not necessarily mean that there must be a balance of 50% male with 50% female. To be harmonious means there must be balance. Yet, we have been dominated by the male yang frequencies on Earth for millennia. We are a part of the Milky Way galaxy, which resonates with a feminine frequency. That is a main reason why during this transition period in Earth's history, humanity as a group, is starting to awaken to the right brain, creative, feminine aspects of existence. We are becoming more bicameral, rather than strictly relying on the rational, intellectual left-brain. Why do you think our galaxy is called Milky Way? It is the feminine aspect symbolized by our mother's milk (Milky Way Galaxy) that gave us this name. We are now becoming more aware of the Andromeda Galaxy next door to us. Andromeda resonates with a higher masculine, higher yang frequency. This higher frequency includes the "knowing" aspect of the heart. As we expand our consciousness to a greater cosmic awareness, we will eventually incorporate more of the higher masculine frequencies from the Andromeda Galaxy to balance the higher feminine frequencies of our own Milky Way Galaxy. The higher masculine frequencies do not need to utilize the lower energies of fear, scarcity, conquering, dominance and control of the lower masculine mindset. Understanding how the frequencies from two different galaxy systems fit into a greater whole is a beginning stage of moving into an expanded level of cosmic consciousness, or at least cosmic awareness.

Something new and exciting is taking place right now. One suggestion that I would like to present is that acupuncturists, as a group, start recognizing the concept of fields and levels of consciousness, rather than merely comparing and contrasting traditional acupuncture systems and theories. There are various mainland Chinese systems that differ from the systems used in Taiwan or Hong Kong that in turn are very different from the Korean and Japanese styles. A system is already a limiting concept. Although fields may also be somewhat limiting, some fields are very expansive and much more encompassing than the fields within the Lower Quaternary closed system of the present acupuncture community today.

The fields referred to in this book are the various fields of consciousness on the seven planes of consciousness. We are expanding into even greater heights of awareness and higher levels of consciousness than we thought possible only a few decades ago. It is consciousness (waves) that affects the particles (physical tissues of the physical body). The way we think affects our emotions, which in turn affects our dense physical vehicle.

As we move further into the 21st century, I feel that the scope of the acupuncture profession and acupuncture community needs a more encompassing and much broader field to work with in order to include the multiple levels of consciousness that are opening up for humanity at this time. This expanded field also includes new languaging and new terms that are not within the limiting scope of traditional acupuncture and traditional thinking teachers of the various Asian medical modalities. We need new expressions and an expanded vocabulary to explain and integrate the new concepts being brought forth today so these newer ideas can be woven into the fabric of acupuncture. If you are able to understand the language of Esoteric Acupuncture, these concepts become clearer and easier to grasp.

In my search for what I consider the fundamental starting point for consciousness, the place that controls everything in our 3-D world and beyond, my conclusion is that everything revolves around the various levels of our heart and heart systems. The fundamental starting point for expanding inner consciousness is to first find that space of inner Stillness. Then work with the Inner, Spiritual Higher Heart, that is an extension from our Original *Shen*. We must tap into the thinking aspect of the heart, not merely the emotional aspect then later work with the knowing aspect of the heart.

In our present understanding of the fundamentals of the Universe, we only know of particles/waves and space-time continuum, or space-time curvature. Even our understanding of space-time has expanded to now recognizing simultaneous multiple space-time lines. Also, our understanding of space-time curvature has evolved from only few decades ago with the knowledge now that curvature in space can be manipulated. This leaves us with particles and waves as the fundamental starting point for humanity. Waves as consciousness came first. Consciousness is the most fundamental starting place for humanity. Original Consciousness includes Original *Shen* (heart). To make lasting positive changes in our lives, we must go to the heart.

When there is reference to the Inner, Spiritual Higher Heart Center, this is not about the condition of your physical or emotional heart. Of course you must take care of your physical heart in order for all of the other systems to be harmoniously aligned. The Inner, Spiritual Higher Heart Center refers to the wave aspect of the heart (consciousness aspect) and not the particle aspect (physical heart).

All the various New Encoding Patterns are designed to align the recipient of an Esoteric Acupuncture treatment with his or her Inner, Spiritual Higher Heart Center. This alignment is the key for a spiritual awakening to occur. We must first align, balance and tonify our own heart center. If we want to change the world into a better place to live, then we must first change our own world. The Higher, Inner, Spiritual Heart Center is the fundamental starting point for each individual to uplift himself or herself to become a part of the awakening of the whole of mankind into the realms of the New Humanity. The Higher, Inner, Spiritual Heart Center contains our Original *Shen* and our Original *Hun*. These are Chinese terms for frequencies of consciousness connected to the heart (*shen*) and the ethereal soul (*hun*) of the liver. (The *shen* and *hun* will be discussed in detail in Chapter Three.)

## Choices of Foods

It was mentioned earlier that Esoteric Acupuncture is a way of life. Our Muladhara/Root Chakra involves our day-to-day activities. One of our daily rituals is eating. Unless you have no food, or are purposely fasting, then most people eat on a daily basis. The Muladhara influences our choices of the foods and drinks that we decide to consume each day. The Muladhara is our base chakra and is the building block for the physical to be able to harmoniously house all the others levels of consciousness.

People have asked me if eating healthily meant having to become a vegan or a vegetarian. I said no. The basic difference between a vegan and a vegetarian is that vegans do not eat any animal products including butter, cheese, milk or eggs. Also a vegan diet is usually raw or very close to being raw with the enzymes left intact within the live foods. Vegetarians eat both cooked and raw foods. Followers of a macrobiotic diet are mostly vegetarians, but eat cooked and fermented foods with little or no raw foods.

My suggestion is to eat the highest vibrating foods of your choice. Of course, highest vibrating depends upon your level of consciousness. As you move up the ladder of consciousness, your selection of foods will also evolve. If you are working toward being in your true Inner, Spiritual Higher Heart Center and pay close attention and are honest with yourself, then your physical body will start dictating to you what types of foods and drinks to select. You will automatically start refining your diet. You will eliminate the foods that are too dense for the frequency you are vibrating at in that particular time frame. If your heart does not control your thoughts and actions, then the earth element of the spleen system will dictate what types of foods and drinks to select. Food choices controlled by the spleen system are usually are not those with the highest vibratory rate and may be denser in frequency. You can tell if the heart (fire system) or the spleen (earth system) controls your diet. The heart system of the fire element burns up the undesirable things (thoughts, emotions, fat) as well as the unproductive things in your life. This allows you a chance for new growth, and new productive things to come into your life. The fire system moves upward and outward and has two main frequencies. One is a very rapid frequency that allows rapid change. On the complete opposite end, the fire element allows one to become very Still. Fire can be very rapid, or very Still.

The natural movement of qi of the spleen system of the earth moves downward and spreads outward to the extremities. The spleen system is a heavier system than that of the fire element. The earth-type body is often solid with a firm grasp to earth and heavy grounding energy. Remember, the earth element goes downward. So if you are ruled by the earth element, you may eventually end up with an earth-type body, which is a larger midriff, larger buttocks, larger thighs and a big gut. Look at the typical American body of today and you will see an earth body with the expanded rib cage, huge gut and big buttocks and thighs. This type of physical condition is a contributing factor to the high incidents of diabetes and heart-related problems in the United States today. Unless you were born with a mother who was emotionally challenged while you were in the womb or you inherited some congenital heart conditions, any present physical heart problems you might have were caused by the lack of listening to your higher heart.

There are no accidents that have no reason for their occurrence. There is always a reason why something happens. You may not want to know the real reason, so you justify it as an accident. If you are able to view the larger picture, then you will understand the reason for an "accident." You may not like the reason, but nonetheless there is always a reason for an action occurring.

There are no hard-set rules in Esoteric Acupuncture about your diet. You will be the one making those decisions. The beauty of this philosophy is that your choices of your actions, not just the foods and drinks you decide to consume, but of everything within your daily life and the life style you choose are influenced and dictated by the frequency of your current level of consciousness. The intention of your choices should be based upon moving you closer to your heart center.

One phrase that presents an obstacle for moving into a more heart-based, truth-seeking frequency is the phrase, "It's too scary or that's too scary." People say: "I don't want to hear or talk about that. It's too scary." The phrase "it's too scary" carries a vibrational field that is programmed to prevent people from experiencing an expanded level of thought. People who use that phrase do not want to hear or learn something outside of a certain comfort zone they have built around themselves to cope with their closed system of belief. They have built certain limiting parameters around themselves and are not willing to move outside of those parameters.

Today most people are programmed to merely repeat information that is from an outside source and not of their own. It is much more difficult to be programmed if you are truly in your heart center. The biggest programmers today are not only the internet and television, but also your parents, school and religion have all programmed us to a certain extent. People have asked me how do I know what is going on around the world if I do not watch television? Do you really think you know what is happening around the nation and around the world by watching television? Certain controlling groups only show you or tell you the news that they want you to see or hear about.

## Anti-Asian Acupuncturist

I have been lecturing on the subject of Esoteric Acupuncture for a number of years in Orange County California. I live in the Los Angeles area, and Orange County is just to the south of Los Angeles County. As a whole, Orange County is much more conservative than Los Angeles county. I find it amusing that I have been given the name "the anti-Asian acupuncturist" by a certain portion of the Asian acupuncture community (not the American born Asians) in Orange County.

First of all, I love and respect the theories and systems that were presented by the Ancients who wished to preserve and further the work of acupuncture in Asia in the early genesis stages. Secondly, I bow to the past Asian giants in the acupuncture world who laid the foundation for what is evolving in the western acupuncture world today. If Esoteric Acupuncture has the truth and wisdom to withstand the scrutiny and critical analysis by the professional acupuncture community and society as a whole and is able to stand the test of time, it is only because the work being presented in the Esoteric Acupuncture series is standing on the shoulders of the Asian acupuncture giants that came before me. If not for the wisdom and the documentation of the various Asian acupuncture theories that came at an earlier time, Esoteric Acupuncture would not have the foundation to spring forth the newer thinking that is needed as we move into the Age of Aquarius.

There is no need for me to rehash someone else's work from the past. The traditional acupuncture teachings stand as a complete body of work. This body of traditional work is a starting point to understand the basics of acupuncture and does not require additional tidbits as an addendum to make the traditional works more complete. The traditional works are finished and complete for what was needed for the consciousness of that time period. The originator of any work is able to give the most honest and truthful presentation of his or her work. If you merely rehash in your own words and style what was already presented to the Universe, then you have not added anything new for advancing and expanding the scope and the world of acupuncture for the requirements of society today. Just because I do not present workshops or seminars on past theories from Asia that have been presented in various forms again and again by hundreds and even thousands of lecturers around the world should not imply that I anti-Asian. I just have to smile at that moniker.

If the acupuncture community only wishes to embrace an imbalanced condition after its formation, we cannot move forward into a more desirable paradigm for the 21st Century. The amount of money and time being squandered on our so-called heath system is staggering. If we only followed the path of the western medical role model, acupuncturists will always be in second place next to the western doctors. It might be time to embrace and develop a healing system that focuses on health and not disease. Esoteric Acupuncture is an attempt to introduce a healing system that focuses on prevention, wellness and the expansion of consciousness.

## Planes of Consciousness

Any system in itself is contained within a constricting field, or at least a field with certain defined parameters. Being confined to the boundaries of a system, no matter how large or complex the system is, means you will still be encapsulated within a limited field. Even if you combine several systems, the nature of a system is self-containing and thus is self-limiting.

That being said, systems definitely have a place in society. The difference between Esoteric Acupuncture from the other more traditional based acupuncture systems is that the frequencies created by the sequential activation of acupuncture sites during a treatment with any of the New Encoding Patterns of Esoteric Acupuncture are designed to work with consciousness planes above the dense mental planes and to assist one to break out of constricting habits that keep us tied into an older, sometimes outdated way of viewing and living life. Consciousness is only restricting if your concrete mind is not flexible or expansive enough to allow qi to flow into your abstract mind. Esoteric Acupuncture is designed to awaken, develop and expand your abstract mind. One's diet is an inseparable focus in Esoteric Acupuncture.

The Traditional Chinese model for acupuncture treatments

is not interested in giving a specific name to the diseased process or to the imbalanced state of the patient. The Traditional Chinese model involves identifying the signs and symptoms of the diseased state, then correcting those imbalances. One Korean model for acupuncture treatments deals with identifying the specific organ or organs, then treating that organ or organs. Both the Chinese model and the Korean model are treating a small portion of the whole. An Esoteric Acupuncture treatment involves working on the whole. Esoteric Acupuncture is interested in aligning and refining the frequencies within our Inner, Spiritual Heart Center so we may be able to balance and allow for growth on all levels of consciousness available to us at this particular time in the evolution of Earth. We are attempting to open consciousness and move out of our restrictive, programmed minds to be able to access the unlimited Universal conscious that has no limits.

Think of the New Encoding Patterns of Esoteric Acupuncture as grids. Whenever a person has a New Encoding Pattern needled on him or her, following the correct needle sequencing, that person will have an energetic field imprinted on his or her energy bodies that are not created with traditional acupuncture treatments. The sensitive individual will intuit and know that something is happening that is in addition to merely feeling relaxed or feeling very peaceful. A spin field has been created with an Esoteric Acupuncture treatment. The action of inserting an acupuncture needle at the correct acupuncture site following the correct needling sequence for that particular New Encoding Pattern sets in motion an event known as spin point activity. Each of the acupuncture sites will have spin point activity. The qi, as information, from each of the acupuncture sites communicates with one another. Because of the geometric interconnectedness between the acupuncture sites that are linked together by the mental visualizations done by the recipient and practitioner of the Esoteric Acupuncture treatment, a unique type of communication network is formed. The qi from the collective spin point activity creates the field known in Esoteric Acupuncture as a spin field. A spin field is merely a term that states that the field is vibrating at a certain high frequency level that creates an accelerated spin. A spin field creates a different type of qi activity than the qi activity created by traditional models of acupuncture treatments. This special type of spin movement formed within a spin field raises the vibration of the field and allows the recipient of the treatment an opportunity to experience levels of consciousness not often experienced with more traditional types of acupuncture.

When that individual can tap into that spin field mentally (not the astral plane, which is the emotional field of an individual) and then later release the mental body attachment, then another reality is being shaped. Mentally giving energy to the spin field then releasing the attachment means that the person is given the opportunity to shift from the denser mental levels into the causal levels and possibly above. We have moved from the constricting concrete mind into the expansive abstract mind. If we can move from the empty mind to the clear mind to the No Mind, then we are given the opportunity to experience a whole new vibrational field of consciousness. Although merely having a treatment with a New Encoding Pattern will not automatically, consciously transport you to this higher realm, the New Encoding Pattern treatments are designed to activate the "hidden" frequencies at the cellular level called our Key Codes" to assist you in your own individual awakening and ascension. Unlocking one's Key Codes should be a desired accomplishment for the true seeker of the Esoteric Ageless Wisdom.

With the correct sequencing of the acupuncture sites and the geometric patterns being formed during an Esoteric Acupuncture treatment, a spin field is being created. If the client is able to Still his or her mind and the practitioner also has done the adequate amount of inner plane work, then the correct frequencies will form allowing the client to move into the causal sub plane levels of the mental plane and beyond. For this to happen, the practitioner must guide the client with the correct visual triangular formations on the posterior pattern.

The planes of consciousness are numbered with one being the lowest plane and seven being the highest. (See the chart below.) Also within each plane, there are seven sub planes. The causal sub planes occupy sub planes five, six and seven of the mental plane.

**Planes of Conciousness**

|  |  |
|---|---|
| Adi/Logoic Plane | 7 |
| Anupadaka/Monadic Plane | 6 |
| Spiritual/Atmic Plane | 5 |
| Intuitive/Buddhic Plane | 4 |
| Manas/Causal Plane (Sub Planes 5, 6 & 7)<br>Mental Plane | 3 |
| Kama/Astral Plane | 2 |
| Etheric Plane (Sub Planes 6 & 7)<br>Sthula/Physical Plane | 1 |

The geometric patterns created by the needling sequences within the various New Encoding Patterns will move qi (energy) very quickly. It is advisable to have your client visually connect the acupuncture sites in a predetermined triangular connection at least during the very first treatment with a particular posterior pattern. This means that the practitioner must be familiar with the order of the visual sequences of the posterior patterns.

Visually having your clients making triangular connections means that the geometric patterns are on the mental plane, instead of merely having meridian connections on the etheric plane. (The acupuncture meridians are in the etheric plane directly above the dense physical vehicle.)

The goal of these treatments is to raise consciousness and not merely manipulate qi to balance activities on the physical, astral (emotional), or mental levels. The raising of awareness will lead to a certain level of awakening. Esoteric Acupuncture is designed to balance, awaken and unlock the locks that prevent us from moving into higher levels of consciousness. We are more interested in waves versus working on particles. Traditional Asian acupuncture is more interested in treating particles by manipulating qi within the acupuncture meridians on the etheric level. Since the practitioner is inserting an acupuncture needle in his or her client utilizing the principles of Esoteric Acupuncture, the client is also receiving treatments on the same planes as those of a traditional acupuncture treatment. Working with qi within the acupuncture meridians means that we will be confined to the four densest planes of consciousness (Lower Quaternary) from the four lower sub planes of the mental plane down to the astral planes, etheric sub planes and the dense physical realms. Esoteric Acupuncture is especially designed to connect to the planes above the four lower sub planes of the mental plane. Esoteric Acupuncture is Energy Consciousness. Consciousness is not bound within a field. Consciousness in its purest form is merely energy, which is synonymous with waves. Energy has no boundaries. Consciousness has no limits. Energy Consciousness has no boundaries or limits.

As we work on ourselves and become very conscious of our actions, our thoughts, our words and especially what we choose to eat and drink, we will automatically shift our consciousness to a higher level. Esoteric Acupuncture, as a way of thinking and a way of life, encourages the individual to expand consciousness and awareness by refining his or her Higher, Inner, Spiritual Heart Center at all times and not just when you have an audience.

Basically, the difference between the traditional Asian theories of acupuncture taught in the schools in the United States and that of Esoteric Acupuncture is that the traditional Asian theories deal with the physical, etheric, astral and mental planes of consciousness. (The acupuncture meridians are on the etheric plane.) The etheric is actually part of the physical plane, so the traditional Asian system of acupuncture involves three planes with four distinct levels. The traditional Asian system is a closed field of four levels known as the Lower Quaternary. Esoteric Acupuncture involves those Lower Quaternary levels of consciousness plus the Causal, Buddhic, Atmic, Monadic, Logoic planes and expanded planes above the Logoic level of consciousness. Esoteric Acupuncture is an open system and is still in the infancy; its developmental stages. Esoteric Acupuncture is still a work in progress. How will Esoteric Acupuncture grow in the future?

For Esoteric Acupuncture, there is included a simplified division of consciousness known as the Three Tiered Levels of Consciousness. With the Three Tiered Levels of Consciousness, it is a little simpler to explain some of the concepts later on, especially the Monadic Ray Chart in Chapter III.

When the seven planes of consciousness are placed within the Three Tiered Model of Consciousness, the Lower Quaternary of the dense physical, etheric, astral and the four lower sub planes of the mental are placed within the Personality Consciousness Plane.

The upper three sub planes of the Mental Plane are collectively called the Causal Body or the Causal Plane. The Causal Plane has three sub planes. The lowest sub plane of the three sub planes of the Causal Plane is an intermediary step from the Personality Plane to the Soul Plane. The upper two sub planes of the Causal Plane, plus the Buddhic and the Atmic Planes are part of the Soul Plane level. The very top plane within the Three Tiered Levels consists of the Monadic and Logoic Planes. (See the chart on the next page.)

## Three Tiered Levels of Consciousnes

|  |  |
|---|---|
| Monadic Plane | Logoic |
| | Monadic |
| Soul Plane | Atmic |
| | Buddhic |
| | Higher Causal |
| Personality Plane | Lower Causal |
| Lower Quaternary | Mental |
| | Astral |
| | Etheric |
| | Dense Physical |

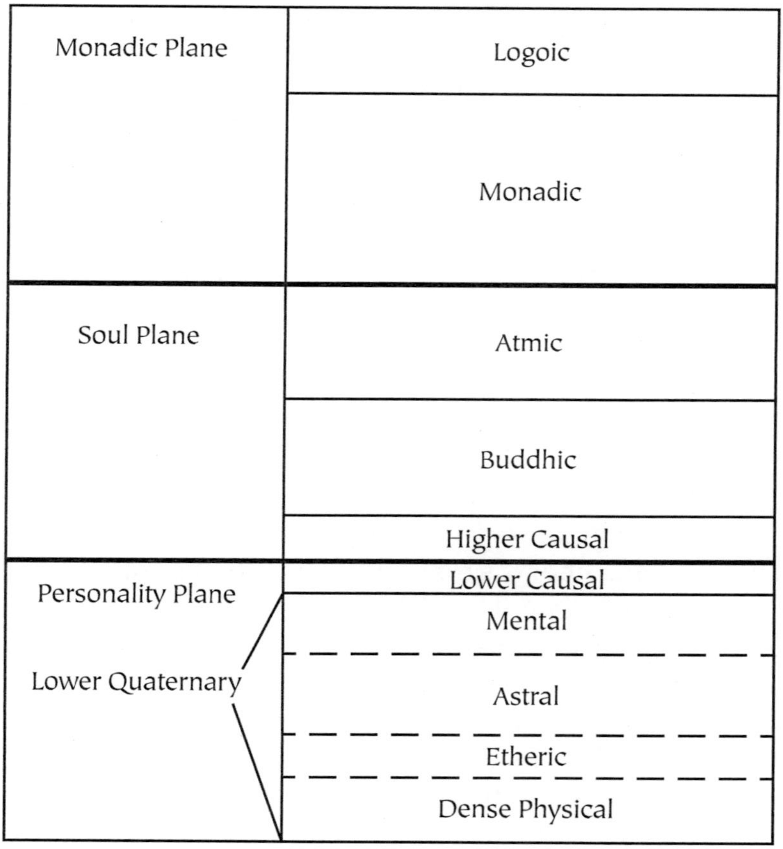

Although the chart may seem like a closed system, the Monadic Plane in the Three Tiered Levels of Consciousness is a gateway from our planetary levels of consciousness to an expanded, unlimited field of consciousness that moves into the solar, galactic, cosmic and universal realms of consciousness. Consciousness in the Esoteric Acupuncture model is an open-ended field, not a closed field like Traditional Asian Acupuncture styles or modalities following Traditional Acupuncture Theories based upon qi movement in the etheric planes of the acupuncture meridian pathways.

The esoteric teachings say that most of the physical diseases for humanity begin on the various astral levels. These are the emotional levels. The chakras are also connected to the Chitrini Nadi Pathway within the Sushumna in the Astral Plane. (See figure 1.2-bb on page 114.) Working with and balancing the chakras will also address imbalances that arise in the emotional bodies of people that often densifies in these astral realms to later manifest as a physical challenge.

We are now moving into hyper dimensional realities that are beyond Kundalini awakening experiences and beyond balancing the Chakra Systems of the Hindus. The earlier books on Esoteric Acupuncture placed an emphasis on first balancing the seven major chakras, then activating and balancing the higher chakras. Remember the chakras are located in the astral plane of consciousness and are part of the Lower Quaternary. Balancing the chakras is only one part of an Esoteric Acupuncture treatment and is not the main goal. The focus of Esoteric Acupuncture is to assist your client to shift into a heightened state of awareness and become conscious of the various planes of consciousness above the dense mental sub-planes. Eventually this expanded of state of awareness becomes the platform for even finer frequency states of consciousness to awaken. The shift into finer frequency states of awareness occurs as we move to refine our true center, our Higher, Inner, Spiritual Heart Center. Continued Esoteric Acupuncture treatments with the various New Encoding Patterns will assist in moving the recipient of the treatments into a more refined, spiritual center.

One thing to keep in mind when viewing the planes of consciousness charts is that the various levels of consciousness are not strictly confined within each plane the way they are depicted in the charts. There is always some overlapping between the levels. In reality, consciousness is not stacked linearly as depicted in the charts shown in this book.

One confusing point with the chakras may concern the higher head centers and their connection or influence in moving one into the state of heightened consciousness and expanded awareness and awakening. If the chakras are connected to the Astral Plane and the Astral Plane is part of the Lower Quaternary, how can awakening the higher head chakras move us into the higher levels of consciousness above the Lower Quaternary?

Think of the chakras as both areas that hold and store information, as well as being consciousness doorways. We are interested in finding pathways or the connections from the lower ranks of the higher chakra to the other higher chakra above. We would like to align the higher head centers with the correct vibrational frequencies so these head centers are locked in and can communicate freely. When the higher head centers are in alignment with the correct frequencies and communicating with each other, this is when the opportunity arises to move into higher, awakened states of consciousness. The challenge is that the conscious awareness that something happened in the higher planes may be fleeting. We may only get a glimpse, but not quite remember what we received—somewhat like in a dream. The key is to continue to ingest clean, high frequency foods and drinks and to surround yourself as much as possible, with high vibrational people. Try to maintain clean, clear thoughts and try to be in an environment that is the healthiest to all your denser planes and to the spiritual field you are creating around you.

Our Inner Spiritual Higher Heart Center has a wide frequency band that allows an individual to benefit on many tiers of density. (Tiers of Density are discussed in Chapter 5.) If your focus is on improving the physical vehicle, then being in your heart center will afford you the most advantageous paths to heal and tune the physical vehicle. If you have emotional or mental challenges, then being in your heart center will allow you the most beneficial opportunity to heal those challenges. Sometimes a person may have a physical challenge but the mental overrides the physical so that individual has decided to work on his or her spiritual growth. For that person, the New Encoding Patterns will greatly benefit his or her inner plane work to assist that individual in achieving those higher spiritual aspirations.

Although one goal in Esoteric Acupuncture is to focus on refining the frequency of our Higher, Inner, Spiritual Heart Center to be able to move into finer frequency fields of consciousness, every Esoteric Acupuncture treatment will also strengthen and balance our physical vehicle and our immune system. Every time we receive an acupuncture treatment, we are also tonifying our *ying qi,* which is a level of our kidney qi, while simultaneously strengthening and balancing our *wei qi* known in English as our protective qi. The *ying qi* addresses a deeper level of the physical body. The *wei qi* strengthens the our lung qi and the outer, protective layers of our physical body. Thus, we are simultaneously harmonizing and strengthening the yin and yang levels of the physical vehicle.

What do we mean by the term spiritual? Spirit is life force, something within us and is incorporeal. Spiritual in Esoteric Acupuncture is used to mean the life force within each individual that resonates with a higher frequency that is often thought of as God. This "God Force" flows through everyone and is a part of everyone. Not everyone is aware of this "God Force." This same life force resonates with the heart frequency and contains the vibrations that are associated with honesty, honor, trust, integrity, compassion and all of the other attributes we think of as goodness and kindness in humans. I want to make it perfectly clear that spiritual is not synonymous with religious. In many instances religious practices may be included within what I term "the spiritual aspects of humanity." Many religious people are indeed very spiritual. There are also many people who go to church, to a temple or synagogue on a regular basis who are not what I would call spiritual. Although everyone has the God Force within, most people only believe in an external God Force. I do not include the dogmatic side of the extreme religious zealots as necessarily being equated to what is called spiritual. On the other hand, there are many people who are not religious but are very spiritual. I am using the term spiritual to mean those individuals who are following their inner heart path regardless of their connection to, or lack of, affiliation to a recognized religious organization. This is how the term spiritual is used in Esoteric Acupuncture. Spirituality must have very similar vibrations to The Truth, love and goodness.

When I say spiritual side of Esoteric Acupuncture, you must understand the full meaning of Esoteric Acupuncture. Most people who hear of Esoteric Acupuncture think that it is merely a new type of acupuncture. I have mentioned in earlier works of the Esoteric Acupuncture series that the deeper explanation of Esoteric Acupuncture means "a commitment to a certain way of life." This way of life includes selecting the foods and drinks you ingest which must be of the highest vibrational frequencies as possible all the time. You will always continue to move toward your heart center and to refine the frequencies of your heart center.

When you decide what foods to eat, in what events to participate and with whom you are going to align or be associated, the unasked question should always be: "Is this going to move me closer to my heart center, or is it going to pull me from my center heart path?" Sometimes we may need certain karmic experiences that deviate from this center path. These types of events may often be necessary in order to gain and experience a fuller understanding of our karmic path or to resolve past karmic connections. Sometimes the events that seem to pull us from our center heart path give us the opportunity to understand a deeper level of our karmic commitments and to assist us in a deeper understanding of our puzzle piece on Earth in this particular incarnation.

Many New Agers have magnificent and expansive aspirations and goals but want to obtain things and have quick results with the least amount of effort. They may seek out the latest guru or teacher with the latest techniques and newly discovered shortcuts. With the internet and the information highway in full gear, there are plenty of sources to receive information. Check the vibratory rate of the information you are receiving. Also, closely discern the vibratory rate of the person disseminating the information. Just remember that information is merely information and not necessarily truthful.

The inward journey of our inner spiritual growth and development is an objective for those studying Esoteric Acupuncture. The journey itself is the reward, not necessarily some result at the end of the journey. Getting to the "top of the mountain" by helicopter is not the same as making that journey on your own with all of the challenges, lessons and rewards you will experience. The experience of the journey itself should be the major part of your inner thrust to begin your search for your own truth and to discover your puzzle piece in life.

## What Is Healing?

*You can never be awaken using the same system that put you to sleep in the first place.*

Gurdgieff

What comes to mind when you hear the word "healing"? Healing is defined in ***Webster's Third New Unabridged International Dictionary*** as: "the act or process of curing or of restoring to health; the process of getting well."[6]

Most people use the term healing to describe changing from some level of physical pain, or physical, emotional and mental stressors to what they consider is a more "normal" way of existence. For Esoteric Acupuncture, healing is defined as moving or shifting from one state of existence to a more desirable state. (We might say that healing is moving from one state of consciousness to a healthier and expanded state of consciousness.) For those who resonate with this philosophy, real health on all the various planes of consciousness can be our daily goal.

If the acupuncture community wants to be a true positive force with greater influence in the healthcare industry for the betterment of the future of this country and the planet, we must shift our attention from merely the treatment of diseases and medical problems to now stress the prevention of disease, the maintenance of wellness and the growth and enhancement of the spiritual aspects of individuals and our society as a whole. Prevention and wellness of our physical, emotional, mental and spiritual health requires a lifestyle change and a rethinking of how we choose to define health. The prevention and maintenance of at least a certain level of wellness requires re-educating the public about choices of foods and certain lifestyle changes that will help the masses to reduce future healthcare costs (treatment of disease) tremendously.

The real beauty and power of acupuncture, herbs and Oriental (Asian) Medicine is in the prevention and wellness portion of healthcare and not the treatment of disease stage. Wellness requires that we are in tune to consciousness and understand how this consciousness is connected to the various planes of our existence. Expansion of consciousness is an inherent quality within the field of wellness. Consciousness is energy. The human body is a residing place for this energy. This energy renews itself when we have depleted it, eliminates waste products that have accumulated within the human body, even if we do not consciously try to remove the excess toxins, and also repairs the physical body when it is injured or broken. There is a magnificent healing quality within this energy. This inner working of this inherent inner, very fine frequency of qi strives to keep all aspects of our consciousness in a harmonious vibrating mode. This requires that we stay in touch with our Inner Heart Center. It is when we deviate from the path of our Inner, Spiritual Higher Heart Center that we start to manifest challenges that may eventually turn into disease or other obstacles. View these challenges as steps for our forward progress and growth.

The information highway through computers and other electronic gadgets has allowed us a gateway to endless amounts of information. It is much more difficult to hide information today, and there are more whistle blowers exposing injustices, lies, deception, corruption and other types of hidden, manipulating activities. We are bombarded daily with all sorts of topics. We are awakening to the outer world outside of ourselves through the internet, satellite television and cell phones. But, there is another gateway available to everyone on this planet and it does not include the 3-D information available "out there." This gateway has been called the Gateway of Liberation that leads to discovering your own true identity and finding your puzzle piece on Earth. Your "true identity" does not mean to uncover your personality or to identify with your job or your career. This other gateway leads to the inner plane realities. You only have one lifetime on this planet with your current physical vehicle. Building and utilizing your Antahkarana is one path leading to your inner gateway to expanded consciousness.

We have been programmed to not have the aspirations to actualize our true nature and to not reach for our highest goals. We have been told that only special people are able to achieve certain levels of awakening and certain spiritual heights because they were either the "ordained ones," or they were special because of their birthright. When you have the belief system that you cannot obtain certain spiritual awakenings or that these aspirations are not important, then you will not put forth the required qi necessary to reach those levels.

If there is a possibility of the reality of ending suffering, then we must at least consider a possibility that certain systems within our society keep us "locked" into a mentality that states that suffering is a part or our reality. Here in the West, we are programmed to not seek medical advice or seek medical attention until something negative happens to our physical vehicle. We are then flooded with all sorts of magic bullet products including: aspirin and other painkillers or anti-inflammatory drugs, anti-depressant drugs, digestive aids, blood pressure medications, diabetic medications, insomnia medications and a host of other drugs. In the alternative medical field, we have many of the equivalent pharmaceutical products but these herbs and supplements are marketed as alternative products to the drug world. But, the alternative medical field still uses the same system as the western role model. That system is based on the premise that once you get sick or have a problem, we have the solution or we will find a solution for you. So whether you take pharmaceutical drugs, herbal medications, or homeopathic remedies, receive acupuncture or massage treatments or any of the many other modalities, most people still wait until there is a problem before making changes.

Today in the United States, it seems like a major goal for the acupuncture profession is to be included in the mainstream, western healthcare system. A few states, such as California, have already included acupuncturists as primary healthcare practitioners. It seems that this inclusion as primary healthcare professionals justifies to the powers that are shaping the direction of acupuncture and Oriental Medicine that our entire profession must bow to the western medical role model. Today in some of the acupuncture colleges in California, there are almost as many classes based on western medicine as classes dealing with acupuncture and Chinese Medicine. The acupuncture system in California is being pushed towards including more western medical terminology, western medical treatment protocols and overall having the acupuncture students learn more about the western medical way of thinking and dealing with disease.

On the one hand it is very beneficial as legitimate primary healthcare professionals to be able to understand western medical terminology and the western medical thinking so we are better equipped to answer questions and to communicate with patients who only have a western medical viewpoint.

On the other hand, why should we, as a group, be swallowed into a system that is not efficiently meeting the needs of all the medical problems of today? The western medical model is not curing people or helping to prevent disease, but rather temporarily fixing the signs and symptoms of disease. This old system has put the public to sleep and finds no reason to change. Why not build a bigger, more efficient system that not only includes the disease treatment mentality, but includes the prevention of disease as a focal point with wellness and optimal health as the logical next step. This requires that we become familiar with the consciousness realms above the Lower Quaternary and begin to focus on these higher consciousness planes.

## A Brief Treatise on The Law of 3-6-1

### The "Hidden" Keys Within 3-6-1

All the keys that you will need to assist you in finding your personal puzzle piece in life are contained within the encoded field of 3-6-1. Although there are certainly other paths or other esoteric concepts or methods to help you unravel the mysteries of why you are here, if you unlock the secrets within 3-6-1, the process will help you discover your puzzle piece in life. The concept of 3-6-1 includes geometry plus sacred geometry, sacred numbers, Qabbalah (Kabbala, Cabala), Hindu Chakra System, acupuncture and other systems that have been discussed in other volumes of Esoteric Acupuncture.

Geometry is the study of lines, angles, points, surfaces and solids. Sacred geometry is much more interesting, intriguing and may hold the answers to questions concerning your inner journey of life. Sacred Geometry contains esoteric knowledge and wisdom within the shapes, angles and structures. You will need to understand what the geometric structures are concealing. Sacred Geometry is one pathway that may offer you clues to assist you on your journey to discover your puzzle piece in life.

The concept of 3-6-1 includes the Hermetic axioms of: "As Above, So Below" and "As Within, so Without" that were discussed in ***Climbing Jacob's Ladder: Esoteric Acupuncture,***

*Volume III*. The field of 3-6-1 also includes Rupert Sheldrake's concept of morphogenetic fields and the belief that everything is connected to everything else in a systematic fashion. The field of 3-6-1 also includes Bell's Theorem of chaos stating that even chaos has order, if the field is large enough. The encoded messages contained within 3-6-1 will show you one way to expand your field of consciousness.

The question was asked in an earlier volume of the Esoteric Acupuncture Series: "Why do you think there are 361 major acupuncture points in the major acupuncture meridians (channels)? What is the significance of the number 361? Do you think it is a mere coincidence that there are exactly 361 major acupuncture points within the fourteen major Chinese acupuncture meridians? Of course, there are many hundreds of additional points within the various microsystems including: auricular (ear acupuncture), facial acupuncture, Korean Koryo hand acupuncture, scalp acupuncture and various other microsystems. But, there are exactly 361 acupuncture points in the fourteen main meridians of Chinese acupuncture theory. Why was the number of acupuncture points on the major meridians not equal to 360 points or 365 points? Those two numbers might seem more logical. There are three hundred sixty degrees in a circle. There are three hundred sixty-five days in most years. So, why the number 361?

The significance of the number 361 has two major esoteric meanings. One esoteric meaning is that 361 is the number that is created by multiplying 19 by 19. The plane created by multiplying 19 by 19 creates a unique grid. The number 19 is a very highly vibrating number that represents the frequency of the consciousness state known as "All That Is." The 361 acupuncture points in the major meridians form the grid within our etheric template or our etheric plane. The acupuncture meridians are located within our etheric plane, not the dense physical plane. The field represented by the 19 X 19 grid reminds us that there are connections to the planes of our solar, galactic, cosmic and even higher fields by way of our Axiatonal Grid. An Axiatonal Grid is a network that allows a person to connect to planes and fields not usually accessible with our normal 3-D consciousness. The grid of our etheric body joined together by the 361 major acupuncture points in the fourteen major acupuncture channels represents our Axiatonal Grid System. But, there is more to being able to connect with the planetary, solar and universal life fields than merely studying traditional acupuncture that deals with the dense physical, emotional or mental planes of treatment. Just because you are receiving regular acupuncture treatments by a traditional-based acupuncturist from any of the many systems does not mean that the acupuncture practitioner even knows of the concept of Axiatonal Grids, let alone knowing how to activate your Axiatonal Grid system. Besides understanding the intricacies within Esoteric Acupuncture and knowing how to activate your Axiatonal Grid through the correct needling of a New Encoding Pattern, your consciousness connection to higher planes occurs by being very Still and centered within your Higher, Inner, Spiritual Heart Center.

The number 19 is also seen within the Hindu Flower of Life Theory and within the Flower of Life pictograph or diagram that is contained with the New Encoding Patterns of Esoteric Acupuncture. The Flower of Life can also be expanded into a Yantra that is an antennae that receives energy waves from outside. There are nineteen circles in the Flower of Life. These interlacing circles are intimately connected to the concept of Six Surrounding One. The field of Six Surrounding One connects Platonic solids to various Pythagorean theories, to the Hebrew Qabbalistic Tree of Life, to both the Hindu Nadi system, and Hindu Laya Yoga Chakra System, as well as to the Chinese acupuncture system. When needling certain acupuncture sites in a very specific order, the qi and information stored at those acupuncture sites will communicate in such a way as to create an Axiatonal Grid. The Axiatonal Grids are not limited to the acupuncture meridians that are part of the etheric body. That is why we have the client receiving an Esoteric Acupuncture treatment make triangular connections on the mental plane as well. In fact, if your acupuncture treatment is limited to moving qi on the etheric levels, then you most likely will never create an Axiatonal Grid with that type of acupuncture treatment. When needling both the posterior and the anterior of the body in one acupuncture session, the practitioner will start the process of building the clientele's Axiatonal Grid system. (For additional information on the 3-6-1 and other Six Surrounding One connections, see ***Climbing Jacob's Ladder: Esoteric Acupuncture, Volume III***.)

The second esoteric puzzle hidden within the number 361 involves the idea of a circle with 360 degrees surrounding a dot in the center. The 360 degrees of the circle plus one equals the 361. See how the circle with a center dot is connected to the Field of 3-6-1 and how it is related to the ancient Hebrew doctrines.

It has been said that everything is connected to everything else. How is this possible? Some things seem so far away that from a linear perspective, there is no way everything could possibly be connected to each other. Is there some sort of thread or glue that connects everything?

If you are able to understand the field of 3-6-1, then you will begin to understand how everything is interconnected and interrelated. There are linear grid systems, as well as non-linear, morphic resonant connections that are not known by the majority of the human population on Earth today. To even begin to comprehend the concept of the interconnectedness of everything, we must first think in terms of fields. Then we must understand the importance of grids and the massive Axiatonal Grid systems in our Universe.

Everything including sand, dirt, clay, rocks, water, plants, insects, cells, animals, humans, space, stars and star systems, planets and solar systems, galaxies and Universes all contain an energetic, geometric grid within them and outside of them. These geometric grids are contained within a field. What connects us within a field? We are connected because of grids.

Albert Einstein became famous with his equation E = MC

squared basically proving that energy equals matter. Einstein even stated that what people think of as matter is merely energy densified or compactified so as to be visible to the human eye. His conclusion basically answered the question of what came first, particles or waves? If we believe that Einstein's thinking was correct, then waves came before particles. Consciousness came first before the physical form manifested. Waves are energy without solid form. Energy, prana, and qi are synonymous with consciousness. Consciousness is made of frequencies. Waves are frequencies. The geometric structures within the 3-6-1 Encoding also contain waves and are representations of Creation and the universe.

There is a defined system of pathways known as Axiatonal Grids that are not material or made up of matter. The Axiatonal Grid Systems are made up of waves, which in turn are transporters of consciousness and information. Axiatonal Grids are not limited to the structure or system that contains the grid. This is not the case with either the Traditional Acupuncture System contained within the etheric planes, or the Hindu Nadi System contained within the astral levels. In those two examples, the pathways define the structure, as well as give life to the structure. Both the pathways of the Chinese and Hindu systems are contained within the Lower Quaternary of the human body consisting of the Dense Physical, Etheric, Astral and Mental Planes. In the teachings of Esoteric Acupuncture, Axiatonal Grids will be used to describe a non-physical pathway system made up of both linear and non-linear, non-physical pathways that collectively, as a grid, has the capability to be able to connect to systems outside of the actual defined pathways within the system.

In Esoteric Acupuncture, the grid system created within the various New Encoding Patterns by the mental visual connections of specific acupuncture sites create multi-plane grids that are not confined to the acupuncture meridians. The grids within the New Encoding Patterns are Axiatonal Grids. Axiatonal Grids are the connections to everything and everywhere. The Axiatonal Grid created by an Esoteric Acupuncture treatment will allow you the possibility to travel to unlimited planes of consciousness.

There are many other Axiatonal Grid Systems throughout Earth and throughout our solar system, galaxy and our universe that connect us to every other universe known and unknown. We are trying to best utilize our internal Axiatonal Grid by understanding the spin field created by unraveling the mysteries of 3-6-1.

Pythagoras is well known for several of his theories including the theory that the square of the hypotenuse of any right triangle is equal to the sum of the square of the other two sides. Although this theory may not seem to have any relationship to acupuncture, decoding the mathematical relationships contained within triangles will assist one to understand other esoteric Laws of Life. Within the Pythagorean Theorem of this particular right triangle are contained the numbers 3, 4 and 5. The number 5 is the length of the hypotenuse AB. The numbers 3 and 4 are the lengths of the other two sides AC and BC. (See figure 1.2-a below.)

## Pythagorean Theorem

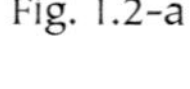


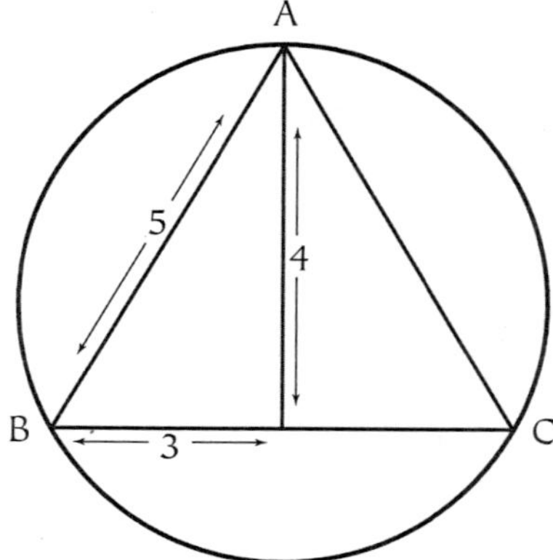

One of the basic building blocks of Esoteric Acupuncture is to utilize the energetic powers inherent in triangles by needling the acupuncture sites within any New Encoding Pattern in a triangular formation. Triangles are also said to hold the secrets of our universe. Those of you who have utilized any of the New Encoding Patterns of Esoteric Acupuncture will know how the needling sequence follows a triangulation format creating triangles that have the apex pointing upward, as well as forming triangles with the apex pointing downward. The upward pointing fire triangles oppose the downward pointing water triangles. This is Esoteric *Shaoyin,* the heart and love opposing the kidneys and fear.

No matter what acupuncture channels or systems we are needling, if you work with creating opposing Esoteric *Shaoyin* triangles and overlay both the heart and kidney systems over the channels or systems that you have selected to needle, you will create multiple layers of energy fields. By merely understanding and needling in a triangular format, you have increased the power and field of your treatment from that created by merely following the traditional protocols of inserting needles in the etheric level of your client/patient. Needling the acupuncture in a triangular formation creates a Spin Field that moves qi with more force than merely needling those same acupuncture points without consciously triangulating the needling sequence. If you grasp this thinking, you will know how important triangles are in Esoteric Acupuncture.

Draw or imagine an equilateral triangle of any size. Place a dot or imagine a dot at each of the three angles of the triangle. Next divide each of the sides into three equal sections by placing dots on the three lines of the triangle that divide each line into three equal length portions. When you to do this, you will see the sides now have an additional two points between each of the three angles of the triangle. Adding all the dots on the three sides plus the three dots at the three angles gives you a total of nine dots. Next divide the section between each of the two inside dots on each of the sides of the triangle, into two smaller, equal linear parts. Make a mark at the division points between the larger dots that are on each of the three sides of the triangle. You will notice that each side is now divided into nine equal linear parts. Now connect all of the dots and smaller marks that you have made in the manner shown in figure 1.2-b below. You will notice that the larger triangle has been subdivided into a series of smaller, but proportionately same shaped triangles as the original triangle. The fact that each smaller triangle is the exact shape as the original larger triangle references the idea of holograms or holography. The similar triangles can go on ad infinitum and are not merely confined to the boundary of the larger triangle.

### Holographic Representation

Fig. 1.2-b

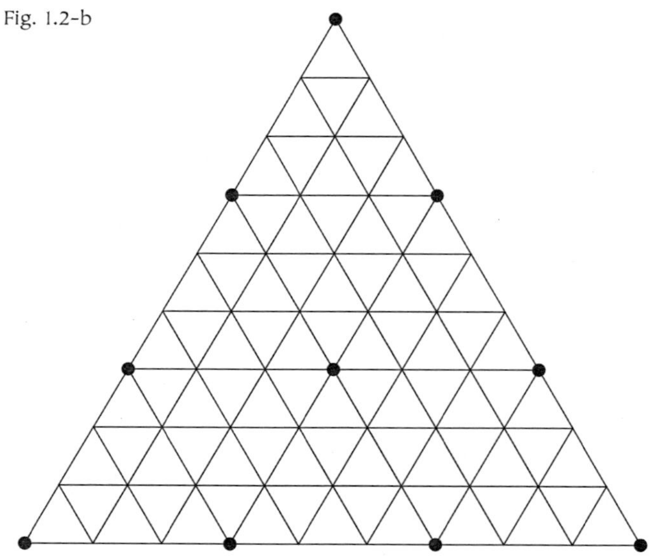

This idea states that the whole is contained within a small part of the whole. It has been stated that our universe is holographic in nature. This exercise with the smaller but identical shaped triangles is a representation of the holographic nature of our reality.

Pythagoras is also known for his presentation of the Tetractys. (See figure 1.2-c below.) The Tetractys reveals another view on the field of 3-6-1. There is the triangle with it's own encoding plus ten dots concealing certain information. Some scholars have said that the Tetractys hold the keys to unlocking the "secrets" of the universe. Viewing figure 1.2-d shows that the Tetractys is merely another sequencing of 3-6-1. The larger dots in figure 1.2-e show six surrounding the center dot with three dots on the three angles of the triangle.

## Pythagorean Tetractys

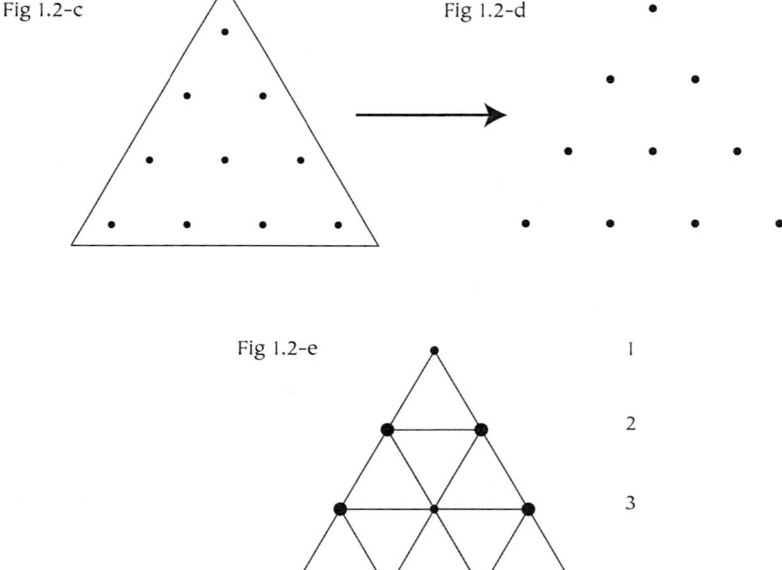

In the Pythagorean Tetractys, there are four horizontal rows of dots. The number four also refers to the four natural elements: fire, air, water and earth. Each of the horizontal rows contain a specific number of dots. The first row has one dot that is representative of no dimensions. The second row has two horizontal dots representing one dimension. The third row has horizontal three dots representing two dimensions on a flat surface or flat plane. And the bottom row has four horizontal dots representing an esoteric encoding that means moving into a reality of being conscious of a three-dimension spatial world. The four rows with the four numbers represent the esoteric numbering for form meaning one is moving upward from a two-dimensional reality without form to the three-dimensional reality that contains form. (See figure 1.2-f below.)

**Tetractys = 1 + 2 + 3 + 4 = 10**

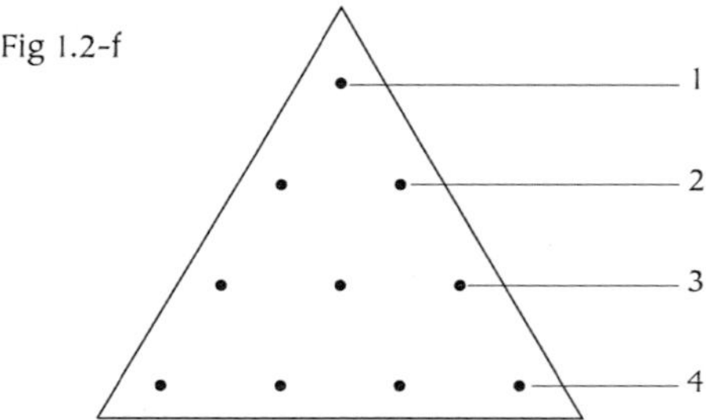

Fig 1.2-f

When discussing the esoteric numberings that are related to form, we start with the power of the number 1 that is represented by the Dot, The Absolute or the Monad. The dot and the Absolute are also other names for what some people call God. Monads are the sparks of the Supreme Fire or can be thought of as a fragment of Divine Life that resides in the Monadic Plane of consciousness. In the Theosophical teachings, a monad is not merely pure consciousness, but consciousness combined with an extremely refined form of matter. Although the roots of the manifestation of monads begin in the Logoic Plane (Adi Plane), monads dwell on the Anupadaka Plane (Monadic Plane).

The power of the number 2 refers to The Manifest and refers to a Line. We have moved from the Dot representing the unmanifested into The Manifested. The One is not easily explained or understood, but we can begin to make sense and gather some information and understanding with the number 2. The power of the number 3 refers to evolution, self-regenesis and a Plane which, on a two dimensional surface, is the triangle. A triangle is a self-regenerating polygon containing much hidden powers and properties.

The power of the number 4 refers to form, stability and solids and is the esoteric number that represents a tetrahedron. The four conceals the six. The tetrahedron with its four sides and six vectors is the simplest structure in a three-dimensional reality that contains insidedness and outsidedness.

## Beginning of Tetrahedral Consciousness

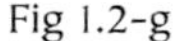
Fig 1.2-g

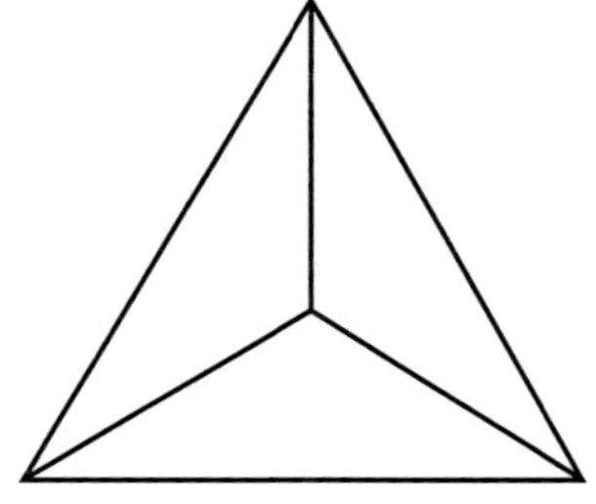

The number 1 is also the esoteric number for the heart and the field of love. The number 2 is the esoteric number of fear and the kidneys. The number 3 is the number that represents the Divine Trinity. (More on this later in this section.) The three also hides the four. The number 4 refers to the tetrahedron that is the simplest structure in our known Universe and to completeness and wholesomeness, such as having a square meal.

When the four numbers are added up (1 + 2 + 3 + 4) you will have the number 10. The single digit 1 stands for the male frequencies and yang. The 0 stands for the female frequencies and yin. The numbers 1 and 0 combine to form 10. As one unit, 10 stands for the blending and the balancing of the polar opposites of the male and female and the yang and the yin.

See how the Hebrew Tetragrammaton is a similar in form to the Pythagorean Tetractys. The Tetragrammaton represents the Hebrew name of God transliterated in four letters as Yod-He-Waw-He. The four letters are read as either YHWH that means Yahweh or JHVH that reads as Jehovah. (See figure 1.2-h below.)

**Tetragrammaton**

Fig 1.2-h

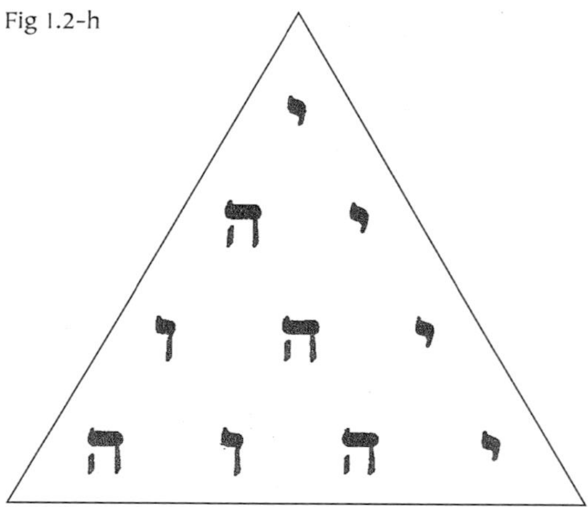

The field of 3-6-1 also encompasses the hidden esoteric Inner Seed of Life that is also known as our Inner Key Code. Our Inner Key Code houses our Original Consciousness, our Original *Shen* and our Original *Hun*. A representation of the Inner Seed of Life is seen in the figure as the center dot with the six petals emanating from the central dot. This Inner Seed of Life transforms, or evolves, into both the Hindu Flower of Life with all of the outward petals and the Qabbalistic/Kaballistic Tree of Life as shown by the three central vertical columns of dots. The number ten, that refers to the ten Sephiroth (excluding Da'ath), corresponds to the ten dots of the Pythagorean Tetractys. (See figure 1.2-i below.)

**Flower of Life / Tree of Life**

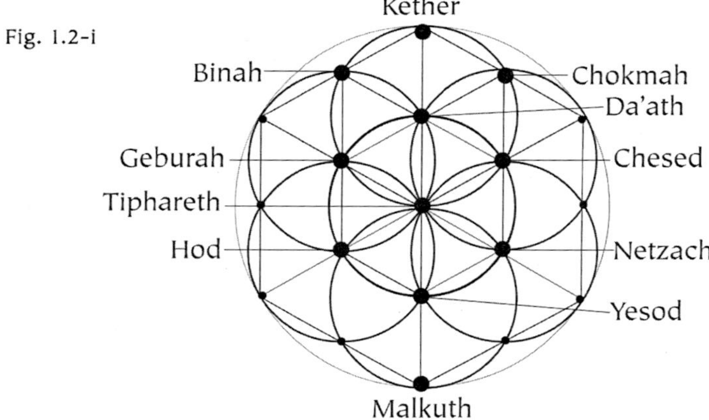


Fig. 1.2-i

The field of 3-6-1 also includes the extremely intricate and vast Hindu Nadi system with its tens of thousands of pathways. According to Swami Muktananda, there are seventy-two thousand pathways in the Hindu Nadi system.[7] (Swami Muktananda is talking about the many pathways and not acupuncture points.)

Within the seventy-two thousand pathways, three are the

supreme pathways or channels. The three main channels of the Nadi system are the Sushumna pathway (the main pathway) in the center, the Pingala pathway (masculine energies) to the right of the Sushumna pathway and the Ida pathway (feminine energies) on the left hand side. These three pathways are seen in the three central vertical columns of dots that also include the ten Sephiroth of the Qabbalistic Tree of Life, plus the eleventh dot representing Da'ath. (See figure 1.2-j below.)

**Three Main Nadis / Seven Chakras**

Fig. 1.2-j

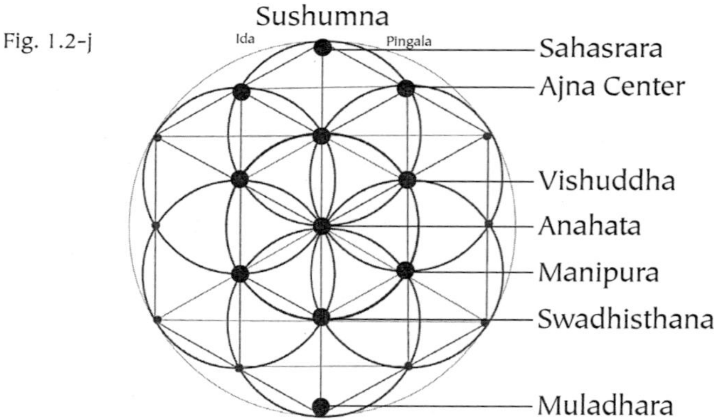


You can also readily see from the above figure that the field of 3-6-1 also includes the Hindu chakra system. You can also see how the Hebrew Tree of Life is directly connected to the Hindu chakra system within the field of 3-6-1.

One of the challenges of esoteric works is to be able to unearth connections and other underlying information that is not readily visible or obvious by the first glimpse of the work. I call this being able to jump the "esoteric synapses" in your mind.

We now go back to the significance of the number 361 that is the number of major acupuncture points/sites on the fourteen major acupuncture meridians. Through these multiple connections that have been presented, one is able to more clearly understand how the number 361 contains an Esoteric Encoding within the field of the number itself, plus esoteric connections within the field of Sacred Geometry and beyond.

The principles of Sacred Geometry shape and guide the theories underlying Esoteric Acupuncture. Due to the fact that there are 361 acupuncture points in the fourteen major meridians of Traditional Acupuncture, the field of 3-6-1 is also a basic starting point for Traditional Acupuncture. However, since Traditional Acupuncture does not recognize the importance of the 361 encoding, they are not able to take advantage of this window of advancement that will allow Traditional Acupuncture the opportunity to expand from a finite system, developed in the Age of Aries and the Age of Pisces, to move into the newer consciousness of today. As we transition into the Age of Aquarius, with many more complexities and the consciousness of humanity expanding at a very rapid pace, it seems to be necessary to adopt a more complex and infinite system of acupuncture. Esoteric Acupuncture is an open system with no limitations except that of your own consciousness. And Universal Consciousness has no limitations. It is infinite.

Some acupuncture practitioners and scholars may feel that since there are additional acupuncture points, often known as extra points or extraordinary points being added to the scope of Traditional Acupuncture, these newly discovered acupuncture points show that Traditional Acupuncture should not be viewed as a closed, static, finite field. What those same thinkers may not realize is that the newly discovered acupuncture points are not actually new points at all, but are acupuncture points that have recently been given “official” recognition. The functions of these newly named acupuncture points are mainly to address imbalances on the Physical, Etheric, Astral and Mental Planes of consciousness. The emphasis of the treatment plan is to address physical diseases or emotional and mental imbalances. As long as traditional acupuncturists only use the old paradigm of treating diseases once they have developed, this makes Traditional Acupuncture a finite, closed system.

Esoteric Acupuncture is specifically designed to enhance wellness and expand consciousness. Esoteric acupuncture was not developed with the intent to address physical imbalances or disease. The visual linear connections used in Esoteric Acupuncture are on the mental plane and are used to activate the right brain of the abstract mind. Of course, since acupuncture needles are used in Esoteric Acupuncture to pierce the physical vehicle, we are also addressing issues on the dense physical, etheric, astral and mental planes of consciousness. But, that is not the main goal for Esoteric Acupuncture treatments.

The main fundamental New Pattern that is the basic foundational pattern for many of the major posterior New Encoding Patterns is the Crown Infinity Pattern. When lecturing to licensed acupuncturists, doctors and other healthcare professionals on the fundamental and the foundations needed to understand Esoteric Acupuncture, I always stress the importance of the Crown Infinity Pattern. If you are a licensed acupuncturist using Traditional Acupuncture protocols but are curious about incorporating Esoteric Acupuncture into your practice, this is the one New Encoding Pattern I recommend you start with. The geometric layout, the significance of the number of acupuncture sites activated and the multi-layered energetics surrounding the Crown Infinity Pattern are all based on the principles of six surrounding the one that are inseparably fused into the concept of 3-6-1. The Crown Infinity Pattern is a 3-6-1 encoding. Traditional Chinese Acupuncture with its 361 acupuncture points in the fourteen major acupuncture meridians is also a 3-6-1 encoding. The 3-6-1 encoding is one pathway to The All Field or to Universe.

If you wish to move into the planes above the Etheric Plane level, the one thing to keep in mind is that you must be able to visualize geometric patterns as sometimes being twisted, compacted, expanded or having a flop transition. View the depiction of Six Surrounding One as it is used in Esoteric

Acupuncture. In figure 1.2-l, notice the asymmetrical figure eight produce by needling the seven acupuncture sites. (See figures 1.2-k and 1.2-l below.)

## Six Surrounding One (Posterior)

Fig. 1.2-k

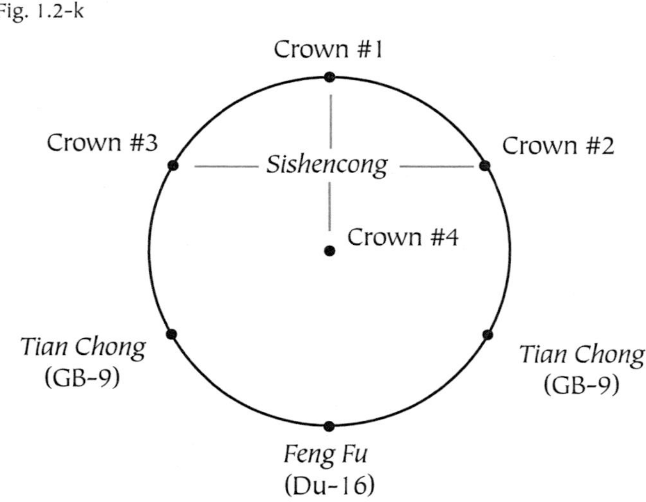


Fig. 1.2-l

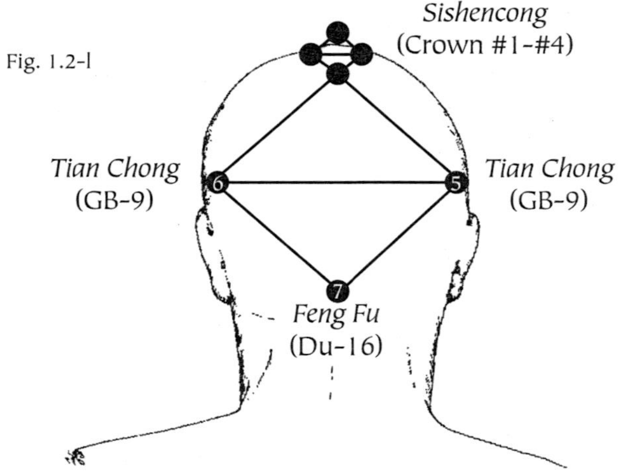

The major, basic anterior New Encoding Pattern is the Extended indigo Triangle Pattern. This is the "sister" pattern to The Crown Infinity Pattern on the posterior of the body. The Extended Indigo Triangle Pattern is another example of the energetics of Six Surrounding One and the field of 3-6-1 being used in a practical format. (See figures 1.2-m and 1.2-n below.)

### Six Surrounding One (Anterior)

Fig. 1.2-m

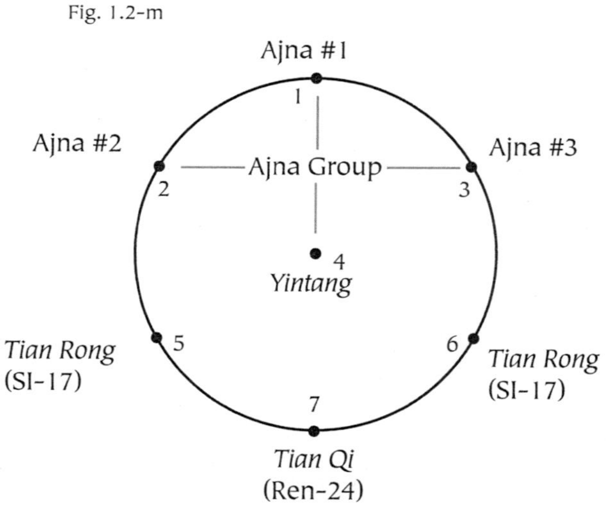


Fig. 1.2-n

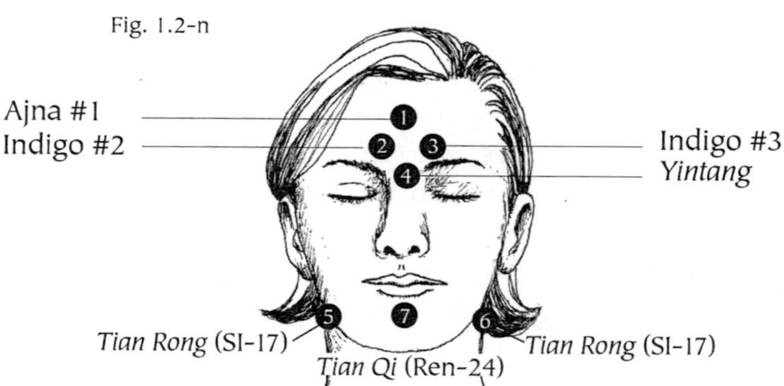

The Extended Indigo Triangle Pattern is used within the Cube On Cube Window Pattern, The Crystalline Grid Pattern, The Crystalline Heart Grid Pattern and The Extended Crystalline Grid Pattern.

I feel there is a need to repeat once again the importance of these two New Encoding Patterns, the Crown Infinity Pattern and the Extended Indigo Triangle Pattern. A practitioner who wishes to use Esoteric Acupuncture in his or her practice, or the individual who merely wishes to understand the intricacies and the concealed encoded information within the Esoteric Acupuncture works should become very intimate with these two New Encoding Patterns. These two New Encoding Patterns are the very basic foundational structures in the practical part of Esoteric Acupuncture that utilize the inherent powers in the concept of Six Surrounding One, which is itself a part of the larger theory of 3-6-1.

The very first lecture on the very first day of class at the acupuncture school I was attending was, to me, a very boring and very slow moving lecture. Partly because of boredom on my part, for some reason during the lecture I decided to add up the number of acupuncture points contained within the fourteen major acupuncture meridians. Very often, there are other forces or consciousness fields that we tap into that guide us on a path, or perhaps nudge us, toward a path that we might not ordinarily take. Yet that path, at that specific time, may have something to reveal to us that will help us or is beneficial to us in the larger picture of our Soul Journey. (There are no coincidences or unexplainable events.)

The total number of acupuncture points added up to 361. My very first thought was 361 equals 19 multiplied by 19. The 361 corresponded to the number of intersections on a "Go" board used by those who play the Japanese game of "Go." There are two colors of stones that opposing players use. The weaker of the two players makes the first move and uses the black stones that symbolize the yin aspect of water and the kidney system of fear. The stronger of the two players uses the white stones representing the yang aspects of fire, the heart system and love.

At that time in my Soul Journey, I did not know how the 19 multiplied by 19 fit into the overall picture of Sacred Geometry and what the significance of this information had to do with my eventually writing the Esoteric Acupuncture series of books. But, I knew there had to be some connection to acupuncture because there are no mere coincidences. Although at a quick initial glance at a Japanese Go board the intersecting lines may seem to form squares, I knew that the intersecting lines actually form very slight rectangular polygons. (See figure 1.2-o below.)

**"Go" Board**

Fig. 1.2-o

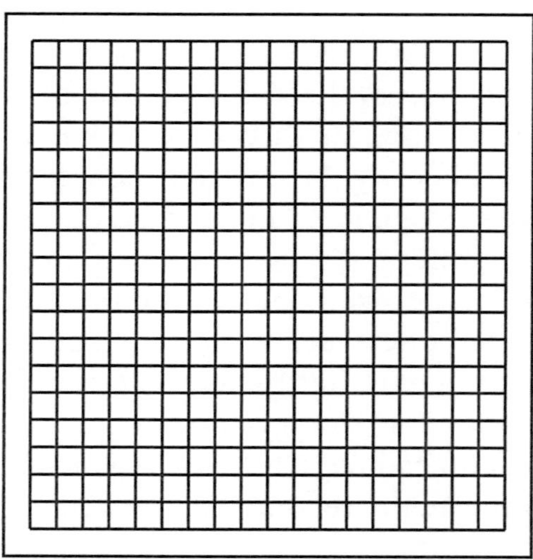

Being so engrossed in my acupuncture studies, I did not further investigate the significance of the esoteric energetics behind 19 multiplied by 19 until a couple of years later. At that time I remembered that the electromagnetic Hartmann lines that intersect the total surface of Earth also formed a rectangular grid. The Hartmann lines (discovered and named after Dr. Ernest Hartmann of Germany) are approximately six feet to seven feet apart and are intersected by lines that are approximately eight feet to eight and a half feet apart creating rectangular grids. (For more on the Hartmann Grid, please go to the glossary.) Although the rectangular formations of the Hartmann Grid are not as symmetrical as the rectangles on a "Go" board, the crossing of the Earth pathways still formed a pattern that had some esoteric connection to the 361 intersecting points of the "Go" board. The 361 intersecting points on the "Go" board corresponded to the exact number of acupuncture points on the fourteen major acupuncture meridians. Was there some sort of interconnection possible or a communication bridge that could be built by the action of inserting acupuncture needles at various acupuncture sites on the human body that would allow the creation of a specific sympathetic resonant frequency to be able to communicate with Mother Earth? Was that possible? When I realized the connection of the rectangles on a "Go" Board to the rectangles of the Hartmann Grid lines, I knew the connection between 19 multiplied by 19 and its meaning concerning the Earth grid. It was possible to build an axiatonal grid network that had the capabilities to extend communication outside the field of one's body and even beyond the field of Mother Earth.

Just because one receives an Esoteric Acupuncture treatment does not mean that the correct sympathetic resonant frequencies for planetary or extra planetary communications will automatically take place. The very slim possibility of forming the correct sympathetic resonance between the recipient of the Esoteric Acupuncture treatment and that of Mother Earth and extra planetary bodies requires that the recipient of the treatment has been doing some sort of inner plane work to quiet the chaotic mental chatter of the concrete mind. It also requires that the practitioner inserting the acupuncture needles or using other energy activating tools at the acupuncture sites must carry a certain level of light quotient and also have knowledge of the esoteric teachings infused within Esoteric Acupuncture.

Another factor involves how the planetary, solar and cosmic frequencies would influence the information being activated by the recipient of the Esoteric Acupuncture treatment on that particular day and time frame. Nonetheless, the possibility of this sympathetic resonant connection between a person, Mother Earth and extra planetary bodies can be set in motion with an Esoteric Acupuncture treatment when all the other correct alignments are in place.

***The Book of Knowledge: The Keys of Enoch***

*"There is at work within all biological systems a path of interchangeability to standardize unique vibratory levels. Our galactic body of creation controls its renewing functions through meridian axiatonal lines which are the equivalent of acupuncture lines that can connect with resonating star systems.*

*These axiatonal lines are not limited to a physical body or a biological creation, but are open-ended and can connect the body vehicle with axiatonal lines that emanate from the various star populations.*

*For the human body is a microcosmos or a small space-time field within a larger field. If we can maintain this view, we can recognize that acupuncture is one of the first empirical demonstrations of biological scaling within the universe."*

*If we are to approach acupuncture from the standpoint of biophysics and also understand the higher force fields which go through the human system as a small open-ended universe, then we can understand how this thinking organism known as the human being can be attached to other thinking organisms within the local universe.* [8]

J.J Hurtak

The number 361 can also be divided into 360 plus 1. The 360 is the number of degrees that form the circumference of a circle. The "plus one" is a dot placed in the center of the circle forming a geometric figure of 360 surrounding one dot. The concept of Six Surrounding One is an esoteric symbol of the 360 Surrounding One. Remember that in Sacred Geometry, the "six" are placed on the circumference of a circle equally spaced from one another. Six Surrounding One is similar in vibrations to 360 Surrounding One.

In the Hebrew tradition, the dot in the center symbolizes The One or what many people refer to as God. (More is discussed later on in this section.) But in reality, "The One" is you. Everyone has this inner "God Force" surrounded by an inner "God Matrix" (symbolized by the circle) within us. But, we have been programmed to feel that we need something outside of ourselves to guide and give us directions in life. Most of humanity has lost its connection to this inner God Force. The 360 Surrounding "The One" symbolizes the fact that if you are resonating within your Higher, Inner, Spiritual Heart Center, then you will be in control of your life and not be controlled by your surroundings. The compelling factor of everything that directs and controls your life should be you, not an external source.

For those who have done the necessary inner plane work and are interested, the secrets of 3-6-1 begin by knowing that those numbers are an encoding to unlock and build your inner antenna known as the Antahkarana. This is an inner consciousness antenna made of very fine mental frequencies. The Antahkarana is your energetic Rainbow Bridge to All-Things, No-Thing, everything seen or unseen, knowable or unknowable, in all Dimensions or No-Dimensions and into the All Field. One expansion of the original Six Surrounding One includes the Antahkarana Yantra. Yantra merely means an antenna depicted in a geometric design.

Water is a conductor of electricity. The human body contains at least 70% water. What is a better antenna for electromagnetic energy than the human body? The building of one's Antahkarana by receiving Esoteric Acupuncture treatments is one way to allow you to engage your inherent consciousness antenna within. (See The 3-6-1 Antakarana Yantra in figure 1.2-p below.)

## Antahkarana Yantra

### Within a Field, Without a Field

Fig 1.2-p

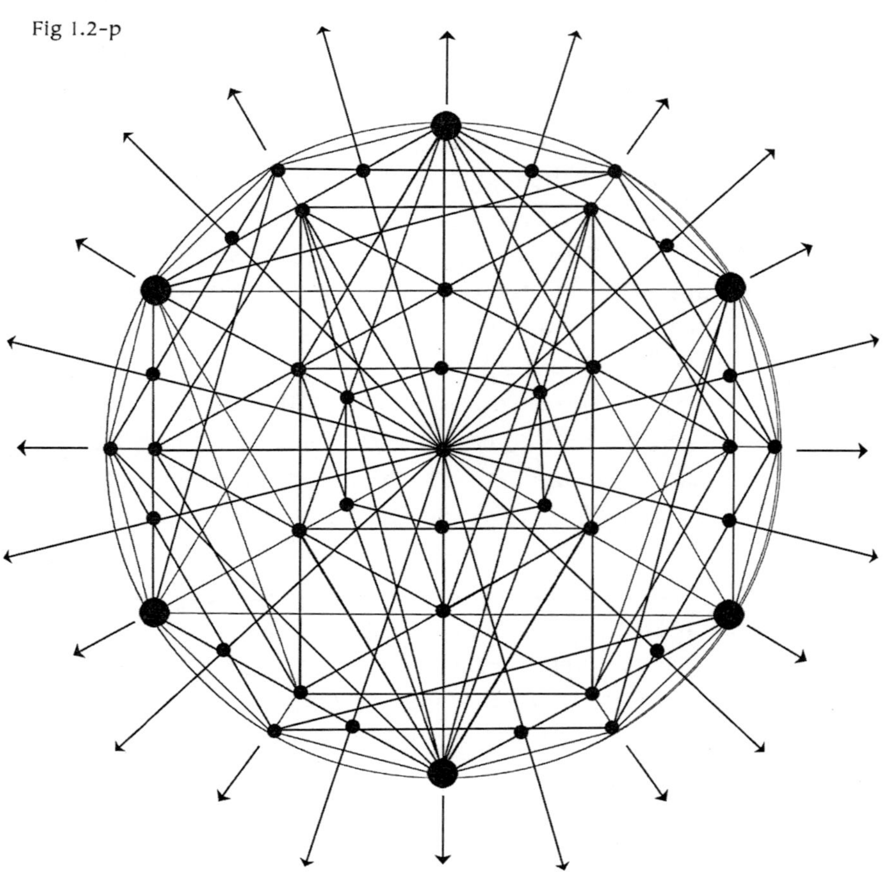

## The Law of Three

The Law of Three is a very important subdivision within the Law of 3-6-1. The Law of Three states that everything in our manifested universe in our three-dimensional world has a three-fold nature. The number "3" has an esoteric perspective known to disciples and initiates of the Ageless Wisdom who emphasize the inner planes over merely working on the outer planes. One particular aspect of the number 3 refers to the three principles of life of: 1) the aspirants; 2) the initiates; and 3) the more evolved masters/teachers on their esoteric spiritual journey. The three principles are: Truth, Simplicity and Love.

Those three principles will not have much meaning or make sense to those who abide by the phrase that "time is money." Those who believe in that phrase are also very tied into the concept of reproducibility and tied to the concrete mind. This is the world of scientific endeavors. Everything must fit into a well delineated, rigid belief system. "We must utilize our time wisely, because time is money." According to Jose Arguelles, Ph.D. in his book ***Time & The Technosphere*** he states:

> *We must keep in mind that the calendar systems are the chief instruments for establishing and maintaining the human mind and social order within very specific programs of behavior. These programs, at least in the Old World, were characterized by the introduction of artificial systems of exchange called money, and accompanying programs of taxation.... In this we find the root of the slogan, 'time is money,' where money is the artificial medium to negotiate artificial time.*[9]

Time is not money. Jose Arguelles, Ph.D. also says that "Time is Art." Art is defined in the Apple Internet Dictionary as: "the expression or application of human creative skill and imagination, typically in a visual form such as painting or sculptures, producing work to be appreciated for their beauty or emotional power." But, the concept of art is not limited to what people think as objects or physical creations that are recognized by a select group of critics who have the power to proclaim something as being a work of art. The concept that "time is art" brings forth the idea of having time, or utilizing time, to create something of beauty that will be appreciated by others. This can include cooking nutritious food and presenting the foods in a very beautiful, creative, artistic setting. Time is art refers to playing beautiful music, creating beautiful poetry, writing heart-felt stories, planting a garden, creating and sewing beautiful clothing, expressing yourself through vocal or instrumental music or any number of other "artistic" endeavors that bring forth beauty and joy to others. When you have discovered your own true puzzle piece in life, your Spiritual Journey will be following the three principles of Truth, Simplicity and Love.

Most of humanity has been driven downward to the level of focusing only on their own survival needs, their need for more money or wanting the things that go along with having more money. As you move toward your inner spiritual path of your puzzle piece in this life, your day-to day work will eventually morph or evolve into something that produces beauty or emotional power for others and not merely working to provide for the basic necessities of survival.

The number 3 also has a history of standing for the Holy Trinity in different cultures or the three bodies in Buddhism. A very simplistic overview of a few of the concepts of trinity and religions are listed below.

Christianity: Father, Son, Holy Ghost (Holy Spirit)
Egyptian: Osiris, Isis, Horus
Hindu: Brahman, Vishnu, Shiva Creator,
Sustainer, Destroyer
Zoroastrian: Ahura Mazda, Asha Vahista, Vohu Mana,
Father, Son, Holy Spirit

Sumeria: Anu = Domain of the Sky
Enlil = Domain of Earth
Ea = Ruler of the Waters
Greece: Zeus, Poseidon, Adonis
Buddhism: Trikaya Doctrine, the Three Bodies of Buddha:
1) Dharmakaya: The Truth Body; Emptiness, and the "groundless ground"
2) Sambhogakaya: Body of Bliss; Body of Clear Manifestation; Death of the Old, Birth of the New
3) Nimanakaya: Body of Time and Space; Physical Body; and the "ground of existence"

The Law of Three also refers to the esoteric teachings of the three permanent atoms of both the Upper Spiritual Triad and the Lower Physical Triad. These two triads also represent the kidney and heart fields of Esoteric *Shaoyin*. The Lower Physical Triad refers to the three permanent atoms that are at the atomic sub planes of the Physical, Astral and Mental Planes. This lower field is the kidney field and refers to form. The Upper Spiritual Triad refers to the permanent atoms that correspond to the spiritual heart field.

Upper Spiritual Triad:
Atmic Permanent Atom
Buddhic Permanent Atom
Manasic Permanent Atom

Lower Physical Triad:
Permanent Mental Unit
Astral Permanent Atom
Physical Permanent Atom

The Three Esoteric Flames
Electric Fire
Solar Fire
Fire by Friction

The three esoteric flames and the Lower Physical Triad of permanent atoms are parts of a "puzzle" that for the dedicated seekers may eventually lead to another piece of the puzzle in the Upper Spiritual Triad. (For more on the permanent atoms, see ***Esoteric Acupuncture: Gateway to Expanded Healing, Volume I*** and ***Sea of Fire-Cosmic Fire: Esoteric Acupuncture, Volume IV***. For more detail on the three esoteric flames, see ***Sea of Fire-Cosmic Fire: Esoteric Acupuncture, Volume IV.***)

The bridge that connects the Lower Physical Triad to the Upper Spiritual Triad is a portion of the esoteric Antahkarana. The permanent atoms of the Lower Physical Triad are connected to the Sutratma (energetic cord) of the heart and are also contained within the lotus of our Anahata (Heart Chakra). The Soul Lotus (sometimes called the Egoic Lotus) of our Anahata (Heart Chakra) consists of three sets of three petals. (In the Theosophical teaching, ego and egoic refer to the soul level and is not the same as the ego talked about in western psychology or psychiatry.) When the nine outer petals of the Soul Lotus are vibrating at a certain frequency, an additional "hidden," inner group of three petals reveals itself and surrounds the Inner Key Code known as The Jewel In the Lotus. So there are three sets of outer petals (each set has three petals) that encompass an inner set of three petals. When discussing The Jewel In the Lotus, the lotus refers to the outer three sets of three petals plus the inner three petals giving the Lotus a total of twelve petals that envelope the inner Jewel. This inner jewel is the Jewel In the Lotus.

On the cover of the first four books of the Esoteric Acupuncture Series are two geometric figures both depicting a similar, but different 3-6-1 Energy Grid that is within the Field of Six Surrounding One. The figure I am referring to shows three tetrahedrons with one star of each tetrahedron merging into the center with a needle being inserted into the center where the three tetrahedrons meet. This picture does not have the hand inserting the acupuncture needle. The acupuncture needle piercing the center is actually activating the closed qi at the "hidden" Thirteenth Gate. In order to activate the "Hidden" Gate, the needle must be inserted at the acupuncture site of the esoteric Du-20 called *Tian Man* and not the traditional Chinese location of Du-20 known as *Bai Hui*. The three tetrahedrons represent the three innermost petals encapsulating the Jewel in the Lotus. The three merging tetrahedrons (lotuses) meet at the center and are communicating with the central force of our Key Code. When the correct spin and frequency are achieved, the Jewel Within the Lotus will reveal itself. Our Key Codes are usually in a dormant stage until some activity such as: Kundalini rising; trauma to the head; extreme fright, or an event such as meditation or a dreamtime activation opens the doorway to access the Key Codes. (See figure 1.2-q below.)

**Activating the Hidden Thirteenth Gate**

Fig. 1.2-q

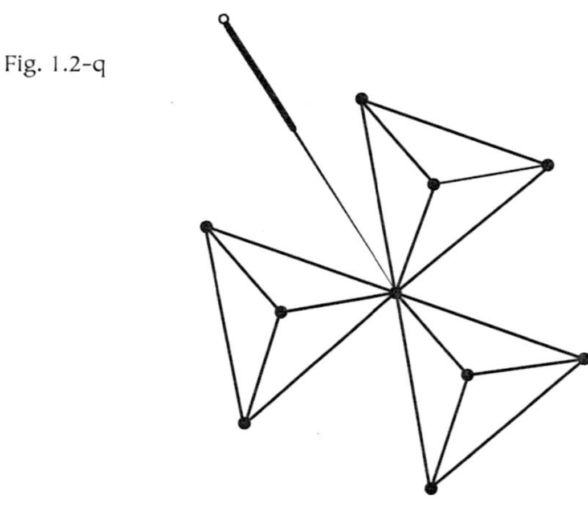

Three is the smallest number that can define a plane on a two dimensional surface. Remember the third horizontal row of dots in the Pythagorean Tetractys. That horizontal row contains three dots. The number three represents a plane. The plane is represented by a triangle.

The number three also stands for the three ordinary states of human consciousness:

1. Waking
2. Dreaming
3. Sleeping

There are also three higher states of human consciousness.

1. Cosmic Consciousness
2. Planetary/Global Awareness
3. Self Realization

The Three-fold nature is found in the Qabbalistic and Theosophical Teachings concerning creation and the beginning. This will be discussed later.

1. Ain
2. Ain Soph
3. Ain Soph Aur

One way to explain our three-fold nature is by understanding the fact that everything contains three states of existence:

1. Active
2. Passive
3. Neutralizing

According to R. Buckminster Fuller's works in geometries and mathematics, the three-fold nature consists of:

1. Action
2. Reaction
3. Resultant

R. Buckminster Fuller discusses the three-fold nature in terms of triangles and the attraction that is created by the polar opposite triangles. See how the two open triangles come together to form a tetrahedron. In the microscopic world of waves, opposites attract one another. When the opposites unite, something greater is created. (See figure 1.2-r below.)

### Synergy: One Plus One is Greater than Two

Fig 1.2-r

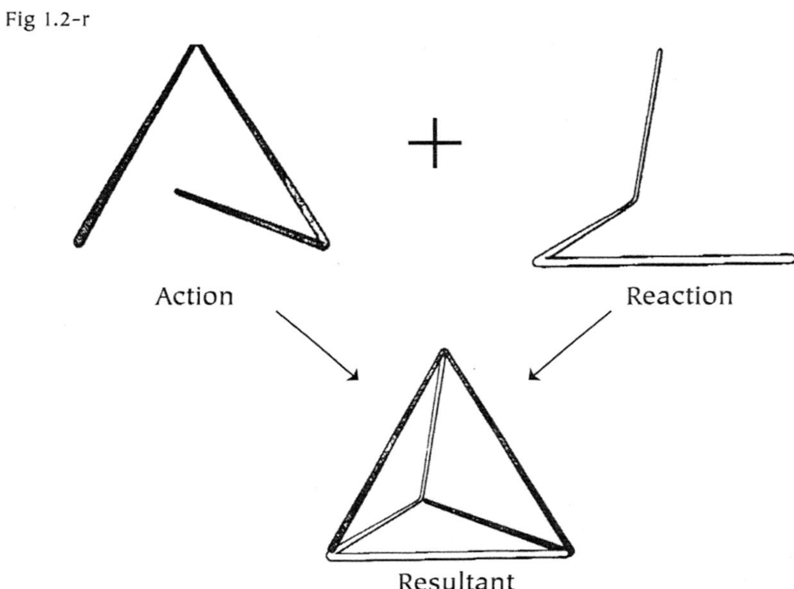


The resultant shows a three-dimensional figure with four triangles, not merely two triangles. There are also four stars or four points of the tetrahedron. This is an example of the concept of the number "Three hides the Four. Although in this case, the four is very obvious. To be able to grasp the basic principles of how Sacred geometry is related to both consciousness and to Esoteric Acupuncture, this esoteric truth is important to know and to understand. You must know that the three hides the four, or the three inherently contains four. You must remember the inherent powers contained within a triangular structure and why triangular formations are used so often in the New Encoding Patterns of Esoteric Acupuncture. A flat two-dimensional triangle "moves" into something greater in a three-dimensional reality.

When viewing a triangle on a two-dimensional plane, the most noticeable feature is that there are three sides (vectors) that form the triangle, Also know that when viewing a geometric figure that looks like it is on a flat two-dimensional plane, may really mean that you are viewing a three-dimensional figure from only one side or one face. (See figure 1.2-s below.)

**Three Vectors**

Fig 1.2-s

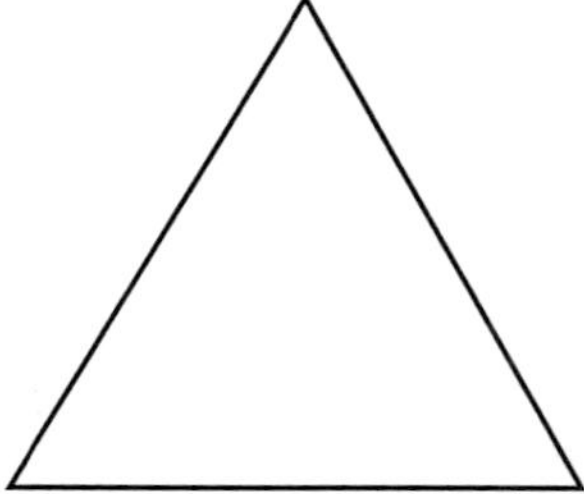

Esoterically, the triangle is the "signature" of a tetrahedron. In order to realize the triangle as a tetrahedron, we must first be able to visualize how a triangle on a two-dimensional plane will expand within a three-dimensional plane. This means a dot (star) will be revealed in the center of the triangle. But, the dot may be on the side that is not seen in a two dimensional plane. When you view the triangle from the opposite side, then you will see a polygon such as that in figure 1.2-t shown below. This is the esoteric meaning of three "hides" the four.

**Three "Hides" the Four**

Fig 1.2-t

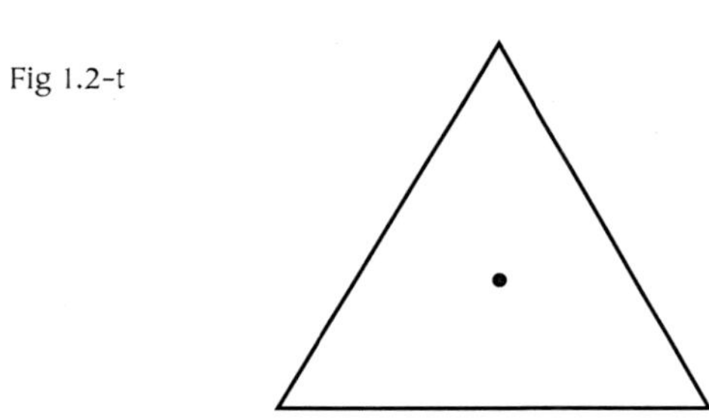

After the meaning behind the "three hides the four" is understood and the three-dimensional figure is completed in your mind, the next phase is to understand the statement "four moves into the six." This is also the concept that there is an inherent sixness contained within fourness. The central dot (star) within the triangle is the fourth point and represents the formation of a tetrahedron in a three-dimensional plane. When we connect the three outer stars (three points of the triangle) to the central star (dot in the center), three additional vectors are revealed now "creating six." From the four stars, six vectors are created. There are four sides, also known as faces, plus six vectors which form a tetrahedron. Each of the sides of a tetrahedron is a triangle. Each of the triangles has three angles and three edges adding up to six.

Knowing that the tetrahedron has four triangular sides with six vectors and an additional energy "Field of Six" stored within each of the four triangular faces, we are then able to understand the esoteric meaning of the "four moves into the six" and the tremendous amount of power inherent in this geometric figure. The specific numbers associated with the tetrahedron and the inherent powers associated with those numbers reveal the energy and power contained within a tetrahedral structure. (See figure 1.2-u below.)

**Fourness Has An Inherent Sixness (#1)**

Fig 1.2-u

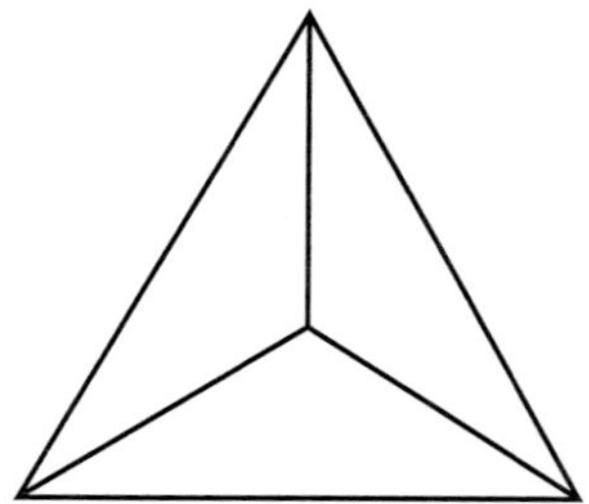

The tetrahedron, with six vectors, reveals to us that the number six is the smallest number that is required to create a structure in our known three-dimensional reality. There can be no structure in three dimensions with the number five, four or smaller numbers. The number six refers to interrelatedness and connectedness. The six vectors constitute all the possible relationships between the four stars and to the tetrahedral structure as a whole. One has to understand the esoteric links to appreciate this statement of six and its interrelatedness and its connectedness. "*The four stars have an inherent sixness of interrelationship.*"[10]

In a three-dimensional reality as we know it, a structure must have height, width and depth. A structure, as defined by R. Buckminster Fuller is:

> "*a self-stabilizing energy-event complex and a system of dynamically stabilized self-interfering and thus self-localizing and recentering, inherently regenerative constellar association of a minimum set of four energy events.... Constellar means an aggregation of enduring, cosmically isolated, locally co-occurring events dynamically maintaining their inter-positioning.*"[11]

Again according to R. Buckminster Fuller: "*Four stars are the minimum we can have for a thought. If I can at first discover only three stars in a thought challenge, there must be at least a fourth lurking somewhere in the critical neighborhood....The tetrahedron turns out to be the fundamental increment out of which all thoughts are constructed.*"[12]

The tetrahedron is the simplest structure known to man that has structural integrity. The number 4 is inherently tied to the tetrahedron. The number six is inherently connected to the tetrahedron. The number 4 is the minimum number that has the inherent arrangements of: 1) insidedness and outsidedness; 2) withinness and withoutness; and 3) inwardness and outwardness. The esoteric meaning of having both insidedness and outsidedness at the same time reveals the grasping of a concept of something called consciousness. The tetrahedron is the signature for consciousness. The triangle is the signature for the tetrahedron. When we visually connect the acupuncture sites in a triangular formation in an Esoteric Acupuncture treatment, we a setting in motion the possibility of a profound inner awakening of consciousness for the recipient of the treatment.

### Fourness Has An Inherent Sixness (#2)

Fig 1.2-v

Figure 1.2-v above shows a two-dimensional square with four boundaries and four angles. The square is viewed from a certain perspective, or a certain side.

When we view the square from a slightly different angle, the figure now reveals a cube. A cube has six sides. From one angle, we see fourness. Viewing this same fourness from a different angle shows us another perspective on how fourness has an inherent sixness when the dimensions are expanded. (See figure 1.2-w below.)

### Fourness Has An Inherent Sixness (#3)

Fig 1.2-w

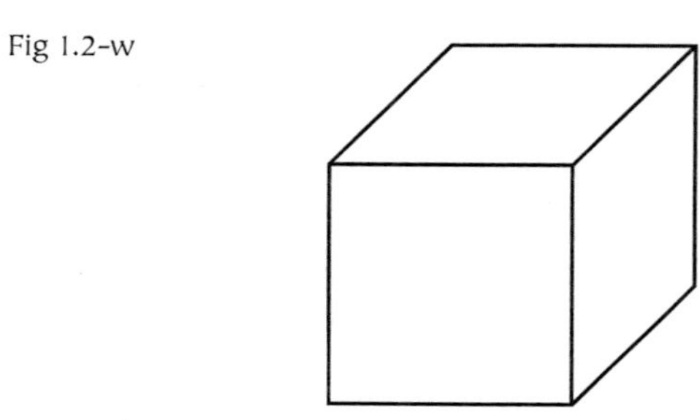

When Sacred Geometry is introduced into the concept of a cube, we are able to see a tetrahedron within the space of the cube. The tetrahedron is the symbol for the concept of sixness. (See figure 1.2-x below.)

## Fourness Has An Inherent Sixness (#4)

Fig 1.2-x

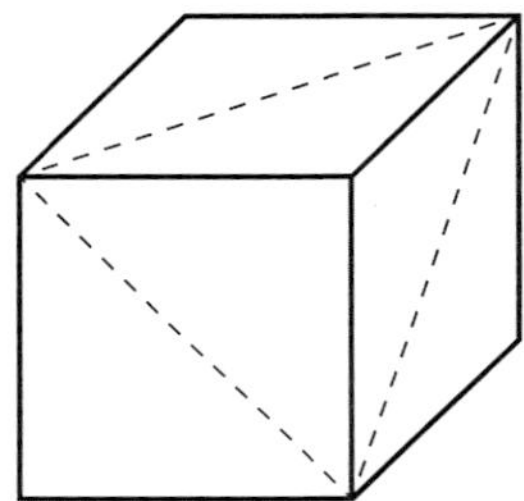

One stable concept today is the idea that everything can be further subdivided into particles and waves. Superstrings are waves and are much more fundamental than particles. Waves (as energy) have always existed, even prior to the formation of particles. Waves are synonymous with consciousness. Since consciousness has always existed, and tetrahedrons are the symbol for consciousness, does this mean that the tetrahedron has existed from the very beginning of time even before humans were able to grasp the concept of consciousness?

## In Beginning, Created Six

In Hebrew, Bara Shith, Bara Sheth or Bara Shesh can be translated to mean "created six." Bereshith can be translated to mean "In Beginning, Created Six." One esoteric idea contained within the number six means that six is connected to something that was created "in the beginning." Perhaps consciousness never had a beginning and has always existed. But, six still refers to something in the genesis stage at the beginning of something or some event. Think of the number six as symbol for creation, expansiveness and consciousness.

Six is a very powerful and important number that contains other hidden Key Codes within its frequency field. You must be able to go to a place of Stillness in order to uncover other esoteric encryptions within the concept of six.

Perhaps the consciousness that has always existed had no beginning and has no end is a level of consciousness so above the comprehensive capabilities of even the minds of people today with post college education, that it is impossible for the masses within humanity with less formal education to try and describe, or even begin to grasp a basic understanding of what this level of consciousness encompasses. In Esoteric Acupuncture, this level of consciousness is synonymous with what is known as "pure consciousness," something that is primordial. If we accept the definition of primordial according to ***Webster's Third New International Unabridged Dictionary*** that states: *"existing at or from the beginning or constituting a basic or starting point,"*[13] then the level and type of consciousness referred to as "In Beginning, Created Six" may be something different from primordial consciousness.

There was no beginning or starting point for the level of what is being called pure consciousness. The level of pure consciousness always existed. This same consciousness existed before the introduction of humanoid life and before the introduction of Homo Sapiens on planet Earth. This level of pure consciousness still exists but is not recognizable for most of modern humanity today who are known as Homo Sapiens Sapiens versus the Homo Sapiens of the Cro-Magnon era. The high adepts of yoga and most likely those who work in the field of superstrings physics, plasma physics and the cutting-edge geometers and mathematicians understand the concept of pure consciousness.

Not always, but often when a person studies traditional

philosophies such as Traditional Chinese Medicine and acupuncture or the Hebrew Qabbalisitc/Kabbalistic Doctrines taught by scholars very well versed in those traditional views, the student may be compelled to strictly adhere to the old views and guidelines set by scholars in those particular schools of thought. To control the students into only studying the old, traditional viewpoints, the scholars may say that outsiders cannot grasp the true meaning of the traditional teachings. This may create a situation where the student is so influenced by the old thinking and the old guidelines that he or she is not able to, or willing to, envision a different "slant" on the traditional views of thought.

Perhaps the meaning behind the esoteric connection of the numbers four and six to the tetrahedron and the Hebrew word Bereshith meaning "In Beginning, Created Six," had it's genesis at the very beginning of the creation, the birthing of the very earliest Homo Sapiens on Earth. Within the scope of the Esoteric Acupuncture teachings, the activation and formation of this specific type of consciousness created the birthing of Tetrahedral Consciousness.

Tetrahedral Consciousness did not exist before some event occurred that created a need for this type of consciousness. Tetrahedral Consciousness was not needed or usable for the small brains of the species known as homanids or the group that followed called humanoids. Tetrahedral Consciousness is a denser frequency within the frequency realm called pure consciousness, but of a finer frequency than the consciousness usable by either homonids or humanoids. Tetrahedral Consciousness was not required by the species known as Australopethicus Afarensis, Australopethicus Africans, Homo Habilis, Homo Erectus/Homo Ergaster, Homo Heidelbergensis or Neanderthal Man.

Perhaps the event that was required for the birthing of Tetrahedral Consciousness was the transitioning on Earth of the humanoids to early Homo Sapiens with much larger brains. This did not happen through a "normal" evolutionary timeline. Something happened that created this larger brain and the sudden appearance of the group known as Cro-Magnon. The

Cro-Magnon group is now generally classified as Homo Sapiens.

The larger capacity of thought and the greater thinking potential of the larger brains of the very early Homo Sapiens, necessitated the creation of an expanded capacity consciousness. This was the genesis of Tetrahedral Consciousness. "In Beginning Created Six" can refer to the need for a higher level of consciousness for a more advanced, larger brained species called Homo Sapiens. The number six and the tetrahedron refer to consciousness. The transition of Homo Sapiens to Homo Sapiens Sapiens now allows the larger brains and the expanded levels and expanded fields of consciousness of Homo Sapiens Sapiens, or modern man/woman, to make sense of both the concept of "In Beginning Created Six" and the connection between six and the tetrahedron to consciousness.

Tetrahedrons also contain the number three. Helena P. Blavatsky and her Theosophical teachings state that the number 3 stands for force. Force can also be thought of as energy, qi, prana or waves. The number 4 stands for matter or particles. (Remember from the three emerges the four.) Energy came before matter. According to the Theosophical teachings of Madame Blavatsky, the number 3 represents the invisible and the male essence. The number 4 represents the visible and the female essence. The number 6 also represents the invisible and the male principles. The number 6 is hidden within the 4. From the invisible came the visible. From waves came particles. From light emerged physicality.

We will very briefly discuss three states of consciousness or existence from a Hebrew Qabbalistic viewpoint, but also add a more modern outlook.

1. Ain = Unmanifested consciousness, Negative Existence or the No-Thing
2. Ain Soph = Limitedless and Boundless
3. Ain Soph Aur = Boundless Universal Light

The first stage of reality in this model is known as Ain.

*"The Ain itself, or Negative Existence, is what might be referred to as infinite energy. It is not in the created world but in its own state of consciousness."*[14] Ain is also sometimes known as Unmanifested Consciousness and is represented by a circle. Both Unmanifested Consciousness and Negative Existence are merely different phrases for the same reality. Both are the consciousness that "had no beginning and has no end." The level called Unmanifested Consciousness existed before the creation of anything known as photons or light. Unmanifested consciousness existed before the need for a denser Tetrahedral Consciousness to come into existence.

At the level of Ain, there is no form, only pure consciousness. In Esoteric Acupuncture, unmanifested consciousness is a synonymous term for pure consciousness. Negative Existence is also synonymous with pure consciousness. The realm of unmanifested consciousness is an extremely fine, high frequency level of consciousness that is unreachable, ungraspable and unobtainable by the masses within humanity today. Only those fully awakened, very advanced seekers today will be able to grasp and make sense of what is meant by unmanifested consciousness and negative existence. Unmanifested consciousness refers to consciousness that existed before the manifestation or the creation of homo sapiens and before the creation of galaxies.

Toward the end of this period when there was only Ain, a slightly denser reality started to take shape. As this slightly denser reality had not reached a level where it could move past pure consciousness, there was still no form. Although the circle depicting the consciousness of Ain may seem to represent the beginning of form, the plain circle is merely a representation of consciousness at the level of Ain and does not mean there is form. In the context being discussed, form refers to something besides pure energy. But the awareness of the creation of the circle meant that pure energy was beginning to transmute from pure Formlessness into something else. The Formlessness was beginning to transmute into Form at a very fine, high vibrating frequency.

Could there be a connection to what the ancients called Ain

or Negative Existence and what is known today as Black Holes? Negative Existence does not mean there was no existence of anything. It implies that there was yet no form and no light. Those knowledgeable with superstring physics may say that gravity contains gravitons that are thought to be the smallest particles within the field of gravity. What we will be referring to as form or Negative Existence is the opposite of the blackness of black holes. What we know as photons today had not gathered in a manner necessary to form light within the black holes. There was no light yet. The creation of light meant the creation of Positive Existence. Positive and Negative in this sense merely refers to polarities.

In ***The Qabbalah and the Zohar*** by Isaac Myer it states:

> *"Above Kether is Ayin or Ens, Ain, the No-Thing. It is so named because we do not know, and it is impossible to know, that which there is in Principle, because it never descends as far as our ignorance and because it is above Wisdom itself."*[15]

Black holes contain such massive amounts of energy called gravity that no light can exist within black holes. Even photons are pulled into the Black Holes. Anything that comes close enough to a Black Hole cannot escape the pulling force of that Black Hole. A Black Hole draws everything into its field. This corresponds to the ancient Hebrews saying that nothing could penetrate the circle of Ain or escape outward from the circle. Nothing could leave the circle.

According to ***The Secret Teachings of All Ages*** by Manly P. Hall, he states:

> *"It should be borne in mind that in the beginning the Supreme Substance, AIN, alone permeated the area of the circle; the inner rings had not yet come into manifestation."*[16]

According to a ***Scientific American*** article January 7, 2009 by George Musser, he quotes Christopher Carilli and his colleagues at the National Radio Astronomy Observatory New Mexico as saying: *The holes came first....Black holes came first and somehow—we don't know how—grew galaxies around them.*"[17] Carilli and his team used the very large array radio telescope in New Mexico and the Plateau de Bure Interferometer in France to peer back into the history of the universe. They believe that the very beginning of our known universe started around 13.7 billion years ago and believe that is when galaxies started forming. In an internet article by Andrea Thompson titled ***Black Holes Preceded Galaxies,*** Chris Carilli is quoted as saying: *"It looks like black holes came first. The evidence is piling Up."*[18]

The very ancient, massive Black Holes are not the same as the smaller more recently formed Black Holes that are thought to form within the galaxies. Fabian Walter of the Max Planck Institute for Radioastronomy in Germany says:

> *"We finally have been able to measure black holes and bulge masses in several galaxies seen as they were in the first billion years after the Big Bang and the evidence suggests that the constant ratio seen nearby may not hold in the early universe. The black holes in these young galaxies are much more massive compared to the bulges than those seen in the nearby universe. The implication is that the black holes started growing first."*[19]

According to Marianne Vestergaard, Ph.d., who did her astrophysics and postdoctoral research at both Ohio State University and the University of Arizona states: *"A study at Ohio State University has uncovered more evidence that black holes form before the galaxies that contain them."*[20] Even if the hypothesis about Black Holes forming before the creation of the galaxies is not universally accepted today, there is such a gathering of information concerning this thinking that this idea should not merely be dismissed. Although the name, Black Holes, was not known to the ancient scholars. I feel that a vague knowledge of the existence of the very early massive Black Holes created the concept of Ain and its description as Negative Existence and the No-Thing. The No-Thing of Ain did not mean there was no consciousness. All energy has consciousness. Also, Black Holes contain gravitons. (Gravitons were not known to the ancient scholars.) Possibly the No-Thing in those earlier writings meant that there was a form of energy or consciousness that was not understood by the scholars of those ancient times. (See figure 1.2-y below for the representation of Ain.)

**Negative Existence / Unmanifested Consciouness**

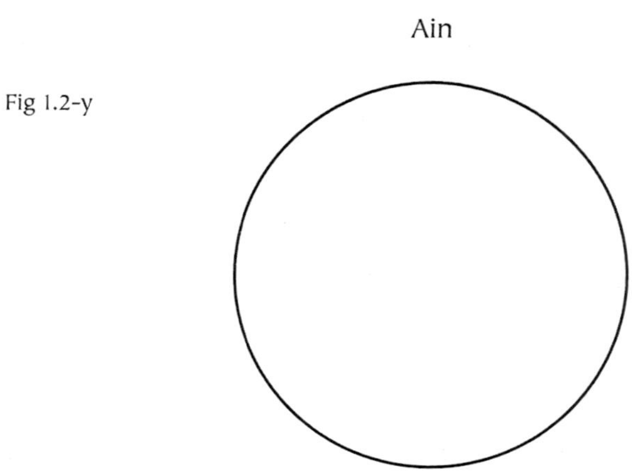

Fig 1.2-y

If the Negative Existence of Ain referred to a reality of complete blackness with absolutely no light, then what followed must have been the creation of another type of reality. This other reality may be referred to as Positive Existence. Only darkness existed in Negative Existence. The advent of the creation of light birthed a reality now called Positive Existence. With only Black Holes and the world of Negative Existence, the Ancients were not able to view that reality as having opposing, yet complimentary forces such as the concept of yin and yang. There was no push-pull, no male-female, no differentiation of good-bad or any other opposing-complimentary forces. The existence of Black Holes and No-Thing, or nothing else, meant that it was the time before the consciousness of the ancient scholars were able to conceptualize the universe splitting into yin and yang. The Chinese philosophers called this era the period of *Wuji, t*he time before the universe split into yin and yang. *"Ji means beginning and wu is negation, so  means before the beginning, i.e., the big void or nothingness."*[21]

The next stage of existence following the level of Ain is known as Ain Soph. From the writings of the ancient Qabbalistic (Kabbalistic) texts, the transition of reality moving from Ain into Ain Soph marked the genesis of light. With the creation of galaxies, we had the creation of photons and light. It was stated earlier that some astrophysicists believe that the massive Black Holes formed before the creation of the galaxies that contain the Black Holes. With the creation of light, we now had a reality that was split into yin and yang, having both complete darkness (Black Holes) and light (galaxies). There were both photons of light, as well as gravitons comprising gravity of the Black Holes. We had moved out of the phase of *Wuji* into the dualistic properties inherent in our known three-dimensional realities of life and everything that surrounds us.

*"AIN SOPH is a limitation of AIN, and AIN SOPH AUR, or Light, is a still greater limitation...."AIN SOPH was referred to by the Qabbalists as 'The Most Ancient of all the Ancients'."*[22] Referring to Ain Soph as "The Most Ancient of Ancients" or the "Concealed of the Concealed" may lead you to believing that the ancient Qabbalists were talking about a Divine Entity or a personal God. If you think of Ain or Ain Soph as entities or some level of a super, divine, personal god, then difficulties may arise when attempting to understand these Qabbalistic concepts from an

Esoteric Acupuncture viewpoint. It may be more desirable to view the Ain, Ain Soph and Ain Soph Aur as three states of existence or three different, but interconnected states of reality.

With reality now split into yin and yang, this newer phenomenon signaled a different consciousness plane now called Ain Soph. This consciousness plane followed the consciousness plane of Ain. Eventually over a period of time, Ain Soph reflected back into itself resulting in the creation of more light. The 360 degrees of the circle representing the consciousness of Ain also represented the 360 degrees of blackness, or "that without light."

> *"The nature of AIN SOPH is symbolized by a circle, itself emblematic of eternity. In the process of creation the diffused light of AIN SOPH retires from the circumference to the center of the circle and establishes a point, which is the first manifesting One—the primitive limitation of the all pervading O. When the Divine Essence retires from the circular boundary to the center, It leaves behind the Abyss, or, as the Qabbalists term it, the Great Privation. Thus, in AIN SOPH is established a Twofold condition where previously had existed but one."*[23]

The new consciousness and the new field with the dot in the center of the circle now symbolized the very beginning formation of light and a new reality. Moving from Negative Existence to the new reality of Positive Existence meant consciousness had moved out of the formless into form. This referred to the phrase "let there be light." The Negative Existence of the many massive black holes eventually led to the formation of galaxies and Positive Existence within our universe. The beginning of this level of new consciousness signaled the formation of light?. Now the formlessness of a prior time called Ain had begun its transformation into a very different reality. The process of transitioning from formlessness into form, or blackness into lightness is represented by the circle with a dot in the center, the realm of Ain Soph. (See figure 1.2-z below.)

### Genesis of Light

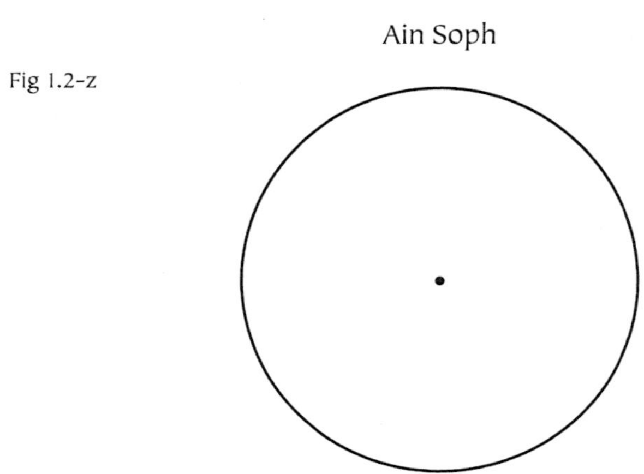

Fig 1.2-z

The circle with the dot in the center, or 360 Surrounding One, represents the results of the transformation of an extremely high vibrational consciousness into a newer, denser reality. The 360 degrees of the circumference of the circle with a central dot is also 361. The field of 361 also encompasses the fields of 3-6-1, Six Surrounding One and the 361 acupuncture points within the fourteen major meridians of Traditional Chinese Acupuncture system. We have connected the basic fundamental principles of ***Qabbalah*** to Sacred Geometry, astrophysics and to the basic principles behind the energetics of acupuncture, the Hindu Chakra System and the numbering of 361. The ancient theorem that everything is connected to everything else in our universe is now starting to make a little more sense. Can we reveal other esoteric encodings within 361?

The Ain had now birthed the new consciousness of Ain Soph. The dot in the center of the circle of Ain Soph also represents the supreme individualization of what is known as the Universal Essence. Some religions call this Universal Essence God or Allah. The dot or the Universal Essence is also known by other names in various other systems. The I Am Schools created by Godfre Ray King (Guy Ballard) and often referred to as the St. Germain teachings call this central dot the "I Am That I Am," which is above the consciousness of "I Am" or "I Am That."

Although the energy consciousness at the Ain Soph level still contained some of the vibrations of pure consciousness, the pure consciousness contained within Ain Soph was not as refined as the pure consciousness at the level of Ain. The creation of light meant that pure consciousness now had another factor that was denser than the pure consciousness at the level of Ain.

At the level of Ain Soph, Tetrahedral Consciousness did not yet exist. The energy consciousness at the level of Ain Soph was also referred to as the No-Thing or the Unknown of All the Unknowns. The reason this level of consciousness was also named the No-Thing by ancient scholars and teachers of Qabbalah was because the ancient scholars felt ancient humanity could not know this level of consciousness. Remember, that in the period of the creation of light and the genesis of the creation of galaxies, there were no Homo Sapiens or Homo Sapiens Sapiens. The consciousness at the level of Ain Soph was so refined and pure that it not yet descended down to a level comprehensible by the human consciousness, a species that would appear in a later time frame. That is one reason why the ancients said: "we could never know." But the consciousness of humanity is elevating and expanding at such a rapid pace today, compared to what was happening only a few decades earlier, that it is possible today for some advanced souls to reach the level of consciousness referred to by the ancients as that level "We Could Never Know."

As the dot in the center of the circle at the level of Ain Soph eventually started to gather more energy, tremendous amounts of heat were being generated. This heating action created even more energy and a stronger form of energy. The dot eventually generated enough energy and began to densify. This compactified and concentrated energy began to turn into such a tremendous force that this newly concentrated energy created two additional concentric circles within the larger circle. In Esoteric Acupuncture, the figure of the three concentric circles with a dot in the center is the representation for the level of consciousness now called Ain Soph Aur. (See figure 1.2-aa below.)

Ain Soph Aur

Fig 1.2-aa

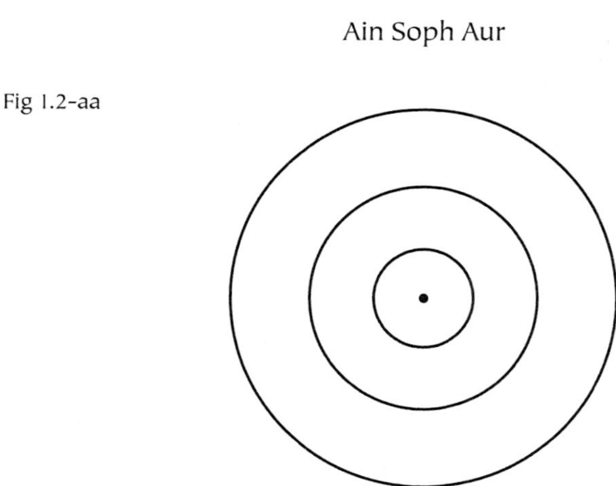

The figure with the two concentric circles within a third outer circle represents manifested universe and its subdivisions. From the circle with no dot representing Ain, through the circle with a central dot representing Ain Soph, came forth the manifested universe called Ain Soph Aur.

The Ain Soph Aur is also called "The Boundless Universal Light." This name refers to the boundless, universal consciousness. From the very beginning of the creation of the galaxies and light, we now had tremendous amounts of light and energy as a newer form of life called Homo Sapiens was created. At the level of Ain Soph Aur, there is both pure consciousness and now the need for a denser consciousness called Tetrahedral Consciousness.

The dot in the center of the three concentric circles of Ain Soph Aur represents one Sephira known in the Hebrew teachings, as Kether. Kether is the top Sephira in the Hebrew Tree of Life teachings. In any of the New Encoding Patterns of Esoteric Acupuncture that starts with the *Sishencong* Window Group of four acupuncture points, the first point within this group that is the closest to the anterior hairline represents Kether of the Qabbalistic Tree of Life. In the Tree of Life Astral Pattern discussed in Chapter V, *Tian Man* (Du-20) is the site of Sephira Kether.

A big part of my work in presenting the Ageless Wisdom Teachings within the context of Esoteric Acupuncture is to show how various esoteric teachings are interconnected and how these wisdom teachings can be used for the betterment of humanity in this time period we are experiencing. Are the Ageless Wisdom teachings still valid and important today in the 21st Century? These teachings are called "Ageless Teaching" for a reason. Ageless Wisdom Teachings are not synonymous with merely gathering information to clutter one's concrete mind. The basic, inner truths contained within the Ageless Wisdom Teachings will always stand the test of time for each group of humanity, no matter how evolved we become. Esoteric teachings always contain "hidden" meanings that change as one's consciousness evolves and as a person is able to understand a more advanced level of teaching. We just need to jump the "esoteric synapses" of our abstract minds and "see" the interconnectedness of all things to understand the importance of keeping alive these Ancient, Ageless Wisdom Teachings.

Do not be afraid to go beyond the safety net of your concrete mind. Unless one is able to expand his or her inner, spiritual consciousness, a person may not see how things fit together or understand the interrelationship between seemingly very different and separate concepts and theories. We will need to tap into the space that holds our inner knowingness frequencies (our Higher Spiritual Heart) to assist with seeing and understanding various abstract connections. These types of inner, spiritual fields or these consciousness vibrational frequencies can be activated and set in motion by having an acupuncture treatment with any New Encoding Patterns that have the 3-6-1 configuration within the pattern. This means any of the posterior New Encoding Patterns that contain the Crown Infinity Pattern or an anterior New Encoding Pattern that contains the Extended Indigo Pattern within the larger pattern. These New Encoding Patterns are discussed later in this book in Chapter V.

Besides the figure representing Ain Soph Aur, where else in the Esoteric Ageless Wisdom Teachings do we again see three circles surrounding an inner dot? There exists a very ancient and extremely complex system outlining energy flow throughout the human body known as the Nadi System. In the Hindu Nadi System, that predates the Chinese acupuncture meridian system, energy is referred to as prana. Prana travels throughout the entire physical vehicle through astral energy pathways known as Nadi pathways. In the Hindu Nadi system are three major central pathways that flow in a upward manner along and around the spine. The major astral pathway in the Nadi System is called the Sushumna pathway. The Pingala flows upward to the right of the Sushumna. The Ida flows upward and is to the left of the Sushumna.

Kundalini is a very subtle force that is not discussed in the western scientific worlds. In the world of superstrings where the superstring physicists have claimed to have found the key to unite all the known force field into one united theory known as The Theory of Everything (TOE), they did not include the force fields of Kundalini or the subtlest frequencies of qi within the tiniest luo (connecting) channels in the acupuncture system.

The main function of the Sushumna pathway is to allow Kundalini to ascend from the base of the spine in the perineum region upward to the Brahmarandra Chakra. Remember that the Brahmarandra Chakra is located within the cranium and directly inferior to the esoteric location of the **Sishencong** Window Group on the top of the head.

The Hindu Sushumna pathway is not the same pathway as the Du meridian pathway of the Chinese acupuncture system. The Sushumna pathway is made up of astral substance and is located in the astral planes. The Du meridian is constructed of etheric matter and is located in the etheric levels. The astral planes are made up of much finer frequencies than the waves of the etheric plane. This means that the Hindu Sushumna pathway is of a much finer frequency than the Du pathway of the acupuncture system.

There are additionally three smaller astral pathways located within the Sushumna pathway and flowing along the same length as the Sushumna pathway. If you examine the figure of the three concentric circles and enhance the circles to reveal pathways, you will notice that figure 1.2-bb below is another esoteric form of three concentric circles with a dot in the center. The central dot is the pathway of the extremely fine Brahma Nadi tube.

**Hindu Nadis / Astral Tubes**

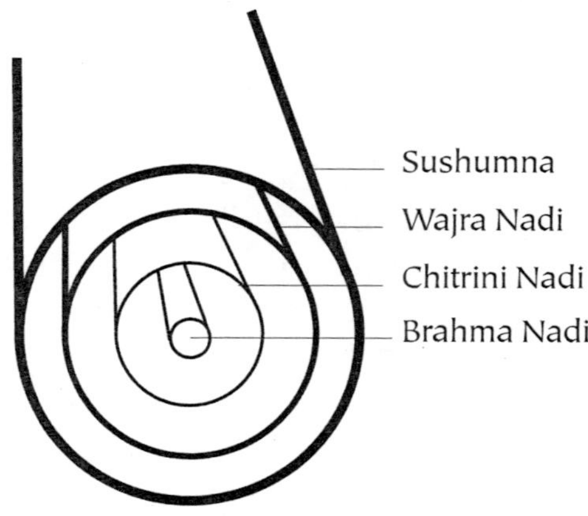

In the Hindu Nadi pathway theory, the chakras are connected to the Chitrini Nadi. Remember that the chakras are located within the astral planes and not within the dense physical planes.

The primary function of these four astral pathways is to have accessible pathways for the ascension of Kundalini. (Kundalini also ascends through the Pingala Nadi pathway to the right of the Sushumna and the Ida Nadi pathway to the left of the Sushumna, but these two nadi pathways are not a part of the three concentric circles with a central dot.) Kundalini usually stays dormant in the Muladhara (Root Chakra) unless there is an event that allows Kundalini to rise. The event may be the practice of pranayama (breathing techniques), the dedicated repetition of a particular mantra, the intake of certain drugs or herbs, receiving an Esoteric Acupuncture treatment or perhaps some trauma to the physical body or to the head. In most cases, Kundalini will only ascend as far as the Brahmarandra Chakra located within the cranium and below the esoteric location of the *Sishencong* Group and the esoteric location of the Du-20 known as *Tian Man*. There is a bridge that has to be built in order to harmoniously allow Kundalini to ascend to the Sahasrara (Crown Chakra) located above the cranium.

The chakras are located within the astral plane and are specifically connected to the Chitrini Nadi. You will notice that the Chitrini Nadi is located within the Wajra Nadi that is, in turn, located within the Sushumna Nadi. Since the Sushumna pathway of the Hindu Nadi system is made of a much finer frequency than the Du meridian of the Chinese acupuncture system, do not consider those two pathways to be identical pathways. The Sushumna Nadi is within the astral levels. The Du meridian is within the denser etheric levels. Most of the pathways of the Chinese acupuncture system are located in the etheric levels. (Some of the extremely tiny channels known as either minute luo channels or tiny connecting channels are part of the pathways located in the astral levels. But, the major acupuncture channels are in the etheric levels.)

At this high frequency stage in the development of consciousness in humanity, there will be some level of Kundalini awakening, even for those who are not aware of the concept of Kundalini. The goal for those who consciously work with awakening and trying to make Kundalini ascend is to have the finest essence Kundalini travel through the central, extremely fine pathway called the Brahma Nadi. If you are aware of Kundalini and are consciously working to refine and allow for the smooth and harmonious ascension of Kundalini, then the possibility arises to allow Kundalini to ascend through the Brahma Nadi. If this event occurs, you will have an opportunity to enter into a very elevated and advanced state of consciousness sometimes called Samadhi, Nirvana, Bliss, Cosmic Consciousness or various other names. This is a process that requires dedication, perseverance and discipline. Kundalini may arise in many individuals, but the ascension of the finest frequency Kundalini takes inner plane work and much dedication.

The dot within the circle in the Hebrew teachings represents what some people call the God Force. In the Hindu teachings, this same inner circle has a similar connotation in that the Brahma Nadi is one pathway to connect with your inner God Force, your God Within. The dot within the concentric circles that represents the Brahma Nadi is telling us how fine and narrow is the pathway of the Brahma Nadi. Only those with the most discipline and dedication to inner plane work and development will access this finest frequency of Kundalini.

Going back to the Hebrew Qabbalistic teachings of Ain Soph Aur with the three concentric circles and a dot in the center of the three concentric circles, one will eventually see that the two inner concentric circles within the larger circle representing the consciousness of Ain Soph Aur are replaced by two opposing inner triangles. The two inner circles actually transform into the opposing triangles within a larger circle with the three apexes of each triangle touching the circumference of the outer circle. The Fire Triangle with its apex pointing upward interlocks with the Water Triangle with its apex pointing downward. This action of the formation of the interlocking triangles within a larger circle signaled the subdivision of the universe into yin and yang, female and male, top and bottom and within and without. With the separation into opposing forces of energies, the Wuji era came to an end. The opposing forces of fire versus water and heart versus kidneys are known in the Esoteric Acupuncture teachings as Esoteric Shaoyin. (See figure 1.2-cc below.)

Moving from Black Holes to the creation of light was the genesis of the formation of the concept of yin and yang. During the time when there were only Black Holes and galaxies had not been created yet, there was no division of yin and yang. The figure below represents the completion and solidarity of the universe dividing into yin and yang.

**Ain Soph Aur**

Completion and Solidarity of Yin and Yang

Fig 1.2-cc

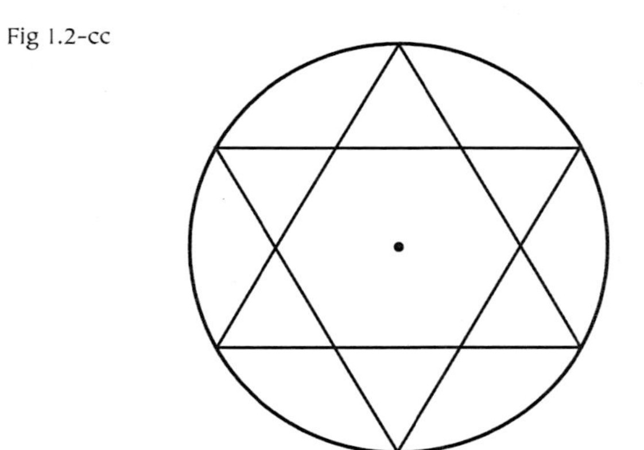

It was discussed earlier that three "hides" the four or that four is contained within the three. Each of the two triangles in the figure above is moving into the Energy Field of Four. The Energy Field of Four is the field of the tetrahedron. The three moving into the four symbolizes a lower dimensional reality expanding into a higher dimensional reality. The two-dimensional reality of the number three moves into the three-dimensional reality of the number four. This also represents a consciousness expansion.

The dot within a circle represents Universe being divided into two parts. The dot symbolized just the very beginning of photons and light, moving from the Negative Existence of Darkness and gravitons into the Positive Existence of Light and photons. The small dot within the large circle meant that although Universe was dividing into two parts, the parts were not of equal value. There was still more blackness than lightness. The figure with the opposing triangles within a circle was the first to divide Universe into two equal parts. The figure with the opposing double tetrahedron represented the expansion of Universe into more dimensions and an expanded consciousness. The double opposing tetrahedrons represents the idea of all within the system and all outside of the system. This particular frequency of consciousness is called Tetrahedral Consciousness. Tetrahedral Consciousness began at the level of Ain Soph Aur.

The original figure representing Ain Soph Aur transforming from the three concentric circles with a dot in the center to the opposing triangles within a circle and a dot in the center represents our reality moving into yin and yang. When reality was contained within Ain (Black Hole), there was no opposing yin and yang. With the transformation into darkness and lightness, reality had moved into opposing polarities. The transformation into the opposing triangles within an enclosed circle symbolized a more complete and equal representation of yin opposing yang. This is shown by the two opposing triangles, the Fire Triangle of love opposing the Water Triangle of fear.

The two dimensional triangles opposing each other within a circle, as shown in figure 1.2-cc, eventually transformed into opposing interlocking tetrahedrons within a circle. This new figure now represents an expanded consciousness with the accompanying expanded reality. The figure of the circle with the opposing, interlocked double tetrahedrons contained within the boundaries of the circle represents the union of female and male, yin and yang and up and down, withinness and withoutness all within a three-dimensional reality. (See figure 1.2-dd below.)

Withinness / Withoutness
Insidedness / Outsidedness
Inwardness / Outwardness

Fig 1.2-dd

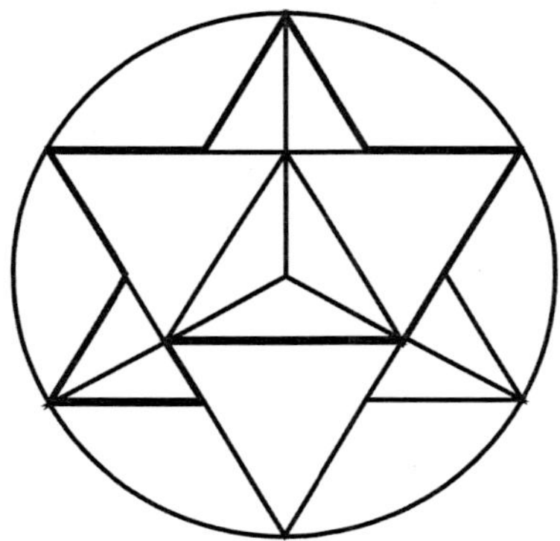

The major, basic posterior New Encoding Pattern within the Esoteric Acupuncture Teachings is the Crown Infinity Pattern. Those of you who are the most dedicated, the most curious and the most interested in learning and understanding Esoteric Acupuncture and the hidden Key Codes inherently encoded within 3-6-1 and Six Surrounding One will be shown how to unlock the locks to those inner secrets tightly guarded behind the closed inner doors of your mind. A treatment with a New Encoding Pattern of Esoteric Acupuncture will not necessarily catapult you through those previously closed locked doors. An Esoteric Acupuncture treatment will only unlock some of the inner locks on the doors to consciousness. You must take the locks off the doors, open the doors, then go through the doors to discover and unravel your own mysteries of life and existence. Below is the Six Surrounding One/3-6-1 encoding in the Crown Infinity Pattern.

**In Begining, Created Six**
**Six Surrounding One**

Fig. 1.2-ee

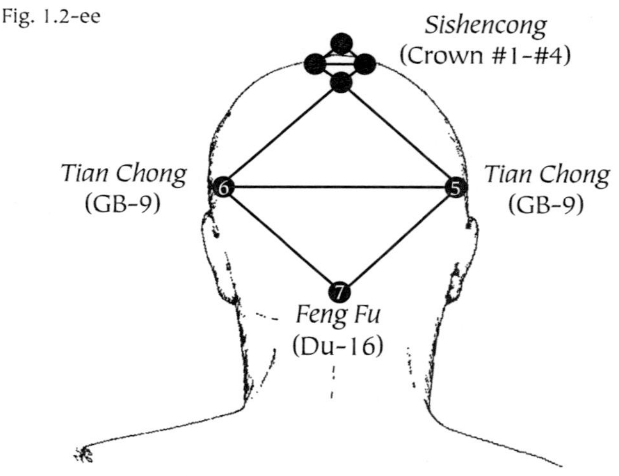


Remember the Hebrew concept of Bereshith, "In Beginning Created Six." We have been discussing the concept of "In Beginning, Created Six" as the event that was needed to reveal a new, expanded consciousness for the expanded brain of Homo Sapiens. I have always recommended that the practitioner begin an Esoteric Acupuncture Pattern by needling a posterior New Encoding Pattern on his or her client. You will notice that various posterior New Encoding Patterns begin with the Crown Infinity Pattern that has six acupuncture points surrounding one acupuncture point. Just remember that the Six Surrounding One is also three hundred sixty surrounding one and is equal to 361.

This means that with each Esoteric Acupuncture treatment that contains the Crown Infinity Pattern, we are needling six points surrounding one. Since at the very beginning of certain Esoteric Acupuncture treatments we are starting with six acupuncture points surrounding one point, we are following the Qabbalistic saying of: "In Beginning, Created Six."

At this stage, the concealed will be revealed. Some of you may feel that at a certain level, there will be no more searching and no need to seek. But for the true disciplined seeker, there will always be more levels to unfold. You merely need to be Still and go inward. Do your inner plane work. There is no end to the depths and heights of consciousness. But eventually, the seeking will be smoother. The "true" esoteric seeker will always adhere to the Buddhist saying of: "Chop wood. Carry water."

## Having Fun

As we move further into the 21st century, more people are awakening to the fact that our true nature is not scarcity, jealousy, greed and fear but is in reality happiness, joy, love, bliss and abundance. Yet, if you look closely around you, you will still see that many people are sad, angry, depressed or defeated. Many people have given up on ever having a joyful, loving life. They are merely existing in a haze carrying little or no light. Look at people's eyes. They may have a forced smile on their face and say everything is fine, yet their eyes reveal a deep underlying level of sadness and regrets in their lives. In others, regardless of how they want to present themselves to the outside public world, their eyes reveal the deep levels of despair and hopelessness in their lives. Many people today in the United States are living at the survival level, living from one paycheck to the next with only a step away from being unemployed and being homeless. Many people are merely existing and not enjoying life. Many of those same people do not have much hope for a better life. It is challenging and often very difficult to "live in the now" and be content with the present when there is little or no hope or no foreseeable positive changes or positive options available in the near future for a better lifestyle change.

Many people are looking for fun and things to do or see that will give them a temporary moment of laughter, amusement and some level of entertainment to take them out of their daily, mundane predicament. For many people, finding something fun to do is a temporary reprieve in those people's daily lives.

How many times have you said to yourself or to others: "I just want to have fun, " or "I want to do something fun?" What do you consider fun or having fun? Having fun is a nice place to be, but that should not be the goal of an acupuncturist, healthcare professional or anyone who has found his or her puzzle piece in life. Have you ever done something for the "fun of it" while knowing in your heart that the action was not the wisest of choices? Fun or having fun is merely one extension in the spectrum of love. In the overall realm of the vibrations of love, fun is among the lower frequencies of that realm.

The higher tentacles in the field of the love frequencies refer to the energy fields of a finer frequency and lighter vibration. The finer frequencies within the field of love last longer than the denser frequencies. Love will last forever, even into your next life or carry over from past lives. Joy can also last a long time. Fun has a very short time span. You can have fun one minute and something can upset you the next minute and completely cancel the energies created by having fun. Happiness is a finer vibration than fun and lasts longer than the energies of fun. Love lasts forever. You can have a situation happen to you that greatly stresses your life. But your love for someone, your love for life or your deep love of the inner, spiritual world will not be canceled out by a negative or very challenging incident in your life.

When you have found your puzzle piece in life and are resonating harmoniously in that space, you will not have to look outside for fun. The frequencies emanating from you after you have found your true puzzle piece in life will resonate, at the very least, at the frequency levels of "fun." Finding and staying on the path of your true puzzle piece in life will automatically assist your movement into the higher frequencies of happiness, joy, contentment and love. If you have found your puzzle piece in life, then your lowest frequency level of your day-to-day existence should be fun. If you are resonating with the frequencies of your true puzzle piece in life, then your life should never become boring or mundane. There are no limits to the expansiveness of consciousness of your true puzzle piece. As you expand in consciousness, your field also expands. Esoteric Acupuncture is designed to assist you to first find your puzzle piece in life, then to assist you in refining your constantly expanding consciousness along your own individual Soul Journey. Later your soul Journey will evolve to your Inner Spiritual Journey.

If you need a break from work or feel that you need a vacation, then your work is not your true puzzle piece. Sometimes your puzzle piece in life might not be able to support you on the day-to-day three-dimensional reality of paying bills. You may be forced to take a job to be able to "pay the bills." Not everybody is fortunate enough to discover one's true puzzle piece in life and have that puzzle piece be directly connected with the work you have chosen. If your true puzzle piece in life is not the same as your day-to-day work, then at least try to find work that will not take you too far off the path of your puzzle piece. Try to find work that will not drain your energy so much that you will not have time or energy to develop your True, Inner Spiritual Pathway.

What we are attempting to achieve with each treatment with a New Encoding Pattern of Esoteric Acupuncture is to build, strengthen and later to refine a person's Antahkarana so he or she may have a less obstructive pathway to higher levels of consciousness.

Think of building the Antahkarana as building one's own personal spiritual antenna to connect with your own higher consciousness planes. First we must have a desire to obtain an antenna. Later we must adjust the antenna to be able to pick up certain frequencies. Your body is similar to a radio that is able to pick up various frequencies. Sometimes we need to adjust the dial on the radio to pick up a particular frequency. Sometimes the signal is very faint and we must play with the dial within a very tiny range to try and hear, with clarity, that particular signal. What happens if you are trying to pick up a very faint signal and once you pick up the signal, the message is in a language foreign to you? Will you be able to interpret what is being sent through the radio waves?

Remember that energy is a transporter of information. The frequencies coming to you are vibrational energy pathways within various fields of consciousness that also carry information. In the beginning stages after you have started the process of building your own Antahkarana, you will most often not be able to clearly interpret the vibrational frequencies you are receiving. That is because you do not understand the language that is being transmitted and because you are using a denser system to try and interpret the information coming through a finer frequency channel.

If the acupuncture community wants to be a true positive force in the healthcare industry for the betterment of the future of this country and the planet, we must shift our focus from merely administering treatments for disease to the prevention and wellness of individuals. It may be beneficial for the acupuncture community to rethink our strategy for the future. We need to find solutions to the multitude of medical problems. Prevention and wellness means a lifestyle change that will reduce healthcare costs (treatment of disease) tremendously. Merely lobbying to be included in the disease treatment system by working in the western hospital system gives power to the disease system. We need to create a new category and lobby to have this new category included within the existing healthcare system. This new category will reward licensed acupuncturists and other licensed healthcare practitioners (payment from insurance companies) for the prevention of medical problems and for the maintenance of wellness. The real beauty and power of acupuncture, herbs and Oriental Medicine is in the prevention and wellness portion of healthcare. Wellness means expanding one's consciousness to understand oneself. Understanding what works and does not work for you will automatically reduce the occasions you may need to treat yourself for a disease process. It is time for the acupuncture community to forge a new and different pathway for true healthcare and not follow our present disease treatment system.

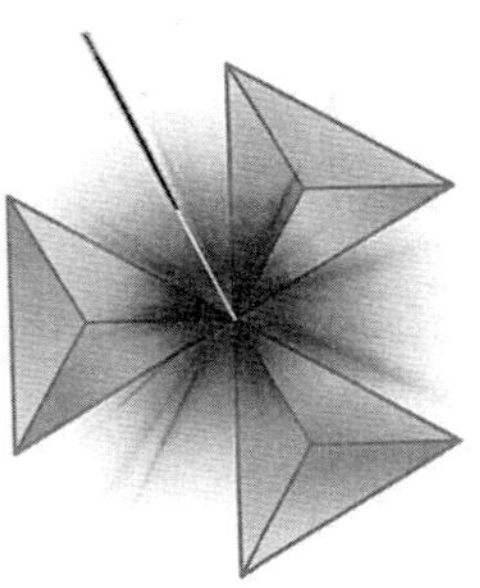

# Chapter II: Master Window Groups of Esoteric Acupuncture

*Be, in all time, in a grateful frame of mind, and let gratitude be evident in your speech. Gratitude will help you to own and control your own field of thought.*[1]

Wallace Wattles

*Whoever thinks deeply on things, even though he may carefully consider the future, will usually think about the basis of his own welfare. When your thinking rises above concern for your own welfare, wisdom, which is independent of thought, appears.*[2]

Miyamoto Musashi
(Samurai Warrior)

## Master Window Groups

Although all the various acupuncture points used in Esoteric Acupuncture are important, some of the points, or certain groupings of points, seem to have a little more "power" or more ability to activate the hidden Key Codes within us. This chapter discusses two Master Points, one on top of the head and one posterior point on the spine, plus the Master Window Groups. Each of the Window Groups consists of three to five acupuncture points. The basis for using certain acupuncture points and specific point combinations is always done with the goal of awakening, aligning and strengthening one's Higher, Inner, Spiritual Heart Center for the purpose of expanding consciousness. Although many people are constantly trying to stay in their physical, emotional and mental centers, it is important for those individuals who are on an Inner Spiritual Journey and have awakened to some degree to constantly refine the vibrational frequencies of their Higher, Inner Spiritual *Shen*, an aspect of a truly expanded heart system. (*Shen* is discussed in Chapter III.) The constant refinement of the Inner, Spiritual *Shen* is initially an important component of one's individual Soul Journey. The persistent and disciplined refinement of one's Inner, Spiritual *Shen* will eventually lead to the full awakening of one's very fine frequency *Shen*. This event will point one in the direction of his or her Inner Spiritual Journey.

You will notice that the Window Groups of points are all joined in some from of a triangular connection. Those of you who have followed the Esoteric Acupuncture series of books will know how much I have emphasized the importance of triangles.

Some of the acupuncture points used in Esoteric Acupuncture may have an alternate Chinese name that is different from the name of that particular point as taught to the Chinese speaking acupuncture students in the United States. (English speaking acupuncture students are taught the names of the meridians with a number assigned to the points such as: Liver-1, Liver-2, Liver-3 and so on).

I sometimes felt that an older, less known alternative name was more appropriate to be able to convey certain types of esoteric energetics inherent to that acupuncture point. You will notice that the alternative name has an esoteric, hidden meaning within the translation of the name that is closer to what is being presented in the Esoteric Acupuncture series of works. The name of an acupuncture point carries a certain vibrational frequency that may be able to reveal more information to the overall energetics of that point. (Remember qi is a transporter of information.) Such is the case with the first Master Acupuncture Point *Tian Man* (Du-20).

## *Tian Man* (Du-20): "Celestial Fullness"

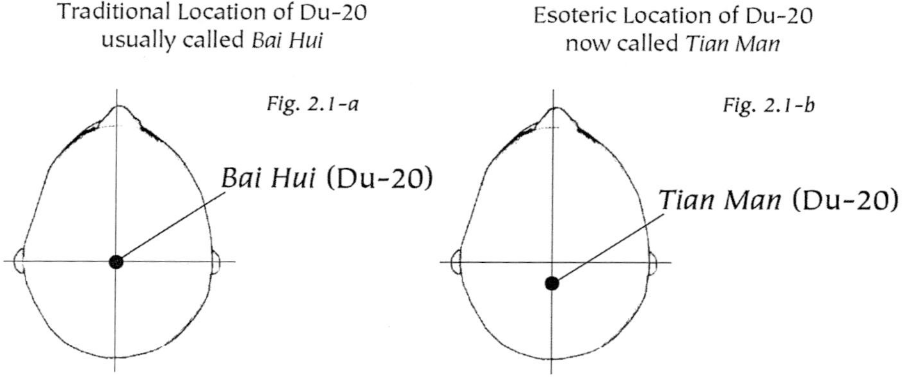


### Point location of *Tian Man* (Du-20)

One very important point to remember is that the location of *Tian Man* (Du-20) in Esoteric Acupuncture is different from the location of *Bai Hui* (Du-20) taught in the acupuncture books used in the United States. The traditional location for *Bai Hui* (Du-20) is found by drawing an imaginary horizontal line across the top of the head connecting the apex of one ear to the apex of the other ear. Next draw an imaginary vertical midline across the top of the head intersecting the imaginary horizontal line. Where the two imaginary lines intersect is the traditional location of *Bai Hui* (Du-20). (See figure 2.1-a above.) The esoteric location for *Tian Man* (Du-20) is approximately and inch or slightly more than an inch posterior to the location of *Bai Hui* (Du-20). Feel for a soft spot on the head posterior to the traditional location of *Bai Hui* (Du-20). To understand and most effectively utilize Esoteric Acupuncture, you must needle this esoteric site of *Tian Man*. (See figure 2.1-b above.) You will later learn why it is so important to needle the esoteric location of Du-20/*Tian Man* and its connection to the "Big Hammer" point known in Chinese as *Dazhui,* or to the English speaking practitioners as Du-14.

Both *Tian Man* (Du-20) and *Dazhui* (Du-14) are included in the Window Group Section because these two points are also "Window" points. The esoteric location of *Tian Man* (Du-20) is the gateway or window for allowing Kundalini to rise from within the cranium to the Sahasrara (Crown Chakra) above the cranium.

As I have mentioned in my previous books, I prefer an older Chinese name *Tian Man* for this acupuncture site instead of the more commonly used Chinese name of *Bai Hui* taught in the acupuncture schools in the United States today. *Bai Hui* is often translated as "100 Meeting." You gather at a location or meet at a certain place to discuss something or to make something happen. The traditional location of Du-20 (*Bai Hui*) is where much energy gathers. *Tian Man* can be translated as "Celestial Fullness" implying that the gathering has already taken place and a celestial occurrence has already been set in motion. *Tian Man* (Du-20), or rather the Chinese translation of "Celestial Fullness," is part of the title of this book. Also using a different Chinese name for the acupuncture point Du-20 allows one to differentiate the traditional acupuncture site at *Bai Hui* from the esoteric site at *Tian Man*.

Names have a vibrational field attached to them. I have heard from certain acupuncture professors that the names of acupuncture points do not matter and have no significance whatsoever in learning acupuncture theory. Just ask any woman who is married and has changed her last name to that of her husband and ask if the new married name has changed her personality and outlook on life. Of course names matter! In my opinion, *Tian Man* carries a much higher vibrational frequency than *Bai Hui*. *Tian Man* translated as Celestial Fullness tells us there is a possibility of a celestial event occurring. I again emphasize the importance of needling the energy at the esoteric *Tian Man* site and not the traditional location for *Bai Hui* (Du-20) when treating your client with any Esoteric Acupuncture pattern that has the Du-20 point as part of the pattern.

### *Tian Man* (Du-20): The Thirteenth Gate

In the sacred geometry section of the book ***Climbing Jacob's Ladder: Esoteric Acupuncture, Volume III,*** the concept of Six-Surrounding-One was discussed. There was a step-by-step progression of diagrams showing how the concept of Six-Surrounding-One evolved through various stages of evolutions. One of the steps along the Six-Surrounding-One Journey showed the Twelve Directions with an Inner Thirteenth Gate. (See figure 2.2 below.)

**The Twelve Directions Reveal The Thirteenth Gate**
***Tian Man* (Du-20)**

Fig. 2.2

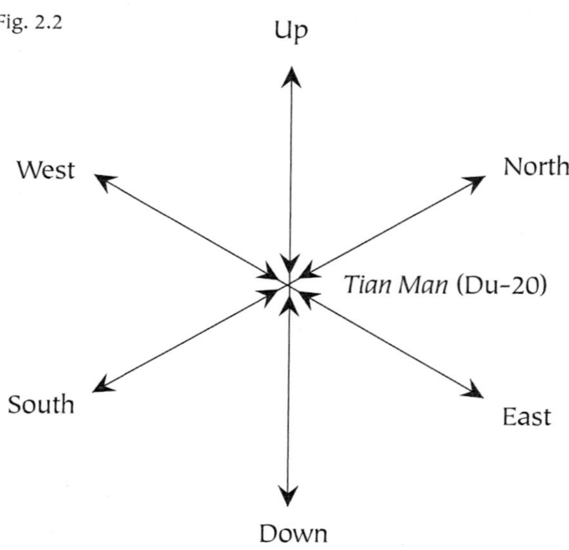


Eventually the Six-Surrounding-One Journey leads to the Tree of Life Yantra. Think of any yantra as merely a spiritual antenna moving through the various higher earthly planes of consciousness to reach and connect to the Cosmic Spiritual Planes of Consciousness. But, Du-20 is only the Thirteenth Gate and a passageway to the higher planes of consciousness if you needle the esoteric location that is surrounded by the esoteric *Sishencong* Window group. The Thirteenth Gate leads to the connection to the Sahasrara (Crown Chakra) and to the building of your Antahkarana.

When you needle the New Encoding Patterns such as: the Discern the Whisper Pattern, the Esoteric *Shaoyin* Heart Pattern, the Esoteric *Shaoyin* Kidney Pattern, the Esoteric *Shaoyin* Heart Window Pattern, the *Hun* Follow the *Shen* Pattern or the *Wei Qi* Grid Strengthening Pattern, you needle the esoteric location of the four *Sishencong* points first. This action sets up the field for the Thirteenth Gate to be accessed and activated. The site of *Tian Man* (Du-20) is needled after the *Sishencong* sites are needled and after other specific acupuncture sites are needled in a very specific sequencing order. Just know that the energy to activate the Thirteenth Gate is initiated by needling the esoteric location of the *Sishencong* Group as it is taught in Esoteric Acupuncture.

The Thirteenth Gate refers to an esoteric opening that allows movement of refined qi and Kundalini to ascend from the intracranial Brahmarandra Chakra (also known as the Nirwana or Nirvana Chakra) to begin the construction of a power bridge known as the wisarga. There are actually several wisargas. (See ***Sea of Fire, Cosmic Fire, Esoteric Acupuncture, Volume IV.***) This particular wisarga (power bridge) we are now working with connects the intracranial Brahmarandra Chakra to the Sahasrara (Crown Chakra) that is located superiorly to the cranium. Stimulating the Thirteenth Gate is one method of building our subtle spiritual antennae called the Antahkarana.

Pay attention to the larger dots in the diagram of the Thirteenth Gate Yantra. The larger dots in the diagram form the Crown Infinity Pattern. If you turn the yantra in a clockwise or counterclockwise manner, you will notice various angles of the Crown Infinity Pattern within the yantra. The central white dot represents *Tian Man* (Du-20), that is the symbolic activation site of the Thirteenth Gate. The Thirteenth Gate is only revealed when *Tian Man* (Du-20) is needled in the correct location on top of one's head. No matter what angle you view the two-dimensional yantra as you turn the diagram of the Thirteenth Gate Yantra, you will still have the 3-6-1 Encoding within. (See figure 2.3 below.)

**Thirteenth Gate Yantra**

Fig 2.3

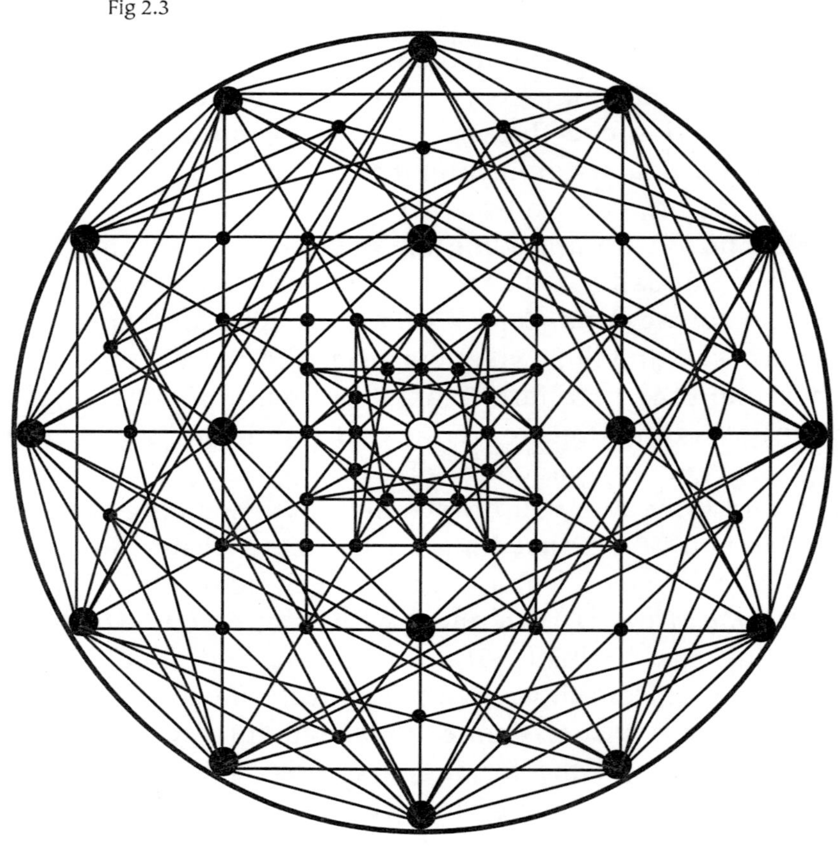

In advanced Chinese Acupuncture Theory, when the acupuncture site at *Feng Fu* (Du-16) is needled, part of the qi follows the etheric pathway of the Du meridian on the outside of the skin to connect with Du-20 (*Bai Hui*) on the top of the head. An internal branch of the Du meridian traverses inward to the brain from the site of *Feng Fu* (Du-16). The qi from the internal branch of the acupuncture Du channel then exits through Du-20 (*Bai Hui*). Just because qi exits the Du channel through the traditional Du-20 location does not mean that the qi will connect with the Sahasrara (Crown Chakra) located above the cranium. When the internal qi flow from the internal branch of the Du meridian exists through the site of *Bai Hui* (Du-20), the qi will flow along the etheric acupuncture pathway of the Du meridian. There is still a gap from the cranium to the Sahasrara (Crown Chakra that is situated on top of the cranium. No matter how tiny the gap may seem to appear, there is nonetheless some physical space that needs to be gapped or bridged to make this particular connection from the Brahmarandra Chakra to the Sahasrara (Crown Chakra).

For those who are doing the necessary inner plane work, eventually Kundalini will ascend through the Sushumna (central pathway) to the Ajna Center (*Yintang*). With additional inner plane work, Kundalini will flow from the Ajna Center to the intracranial Brahmarandra Chakra, but will not usually go any further unless additional criteria are met. The additional criteria using Esoteric Acupuncture are: 1) activating the esoteric *Sishencong* Window Group first, then later needling the site of *Tian Man* (Du-20); 2) needling *Dazhu*i (Du-14) for the purpose of activating *Yintang* (Ajna Center); 3) bringing the qi upward from *Dazhui* (Du-14) to connect with *Feng Fu* (Du-16); and 4) connecting *Feng Fu* (Du-16) with *Yintang* and simultaneously bringing the qi from those two points to connect with *Tian Man* (Du-20). These visual connections will initiate the building of the wisarga and the formation of your spiritual antennae. (Diagrams of these connections are shown in Chapter V.)

For the dedicated and disciplined individuals, Kundalini

will eventually become refined and may eventually transcend to a very subtle, refined frequency known in Hinduism as Wayu. This refined level of Kundalini will ascend through the most refined pathway within the Sushumna. This refined pathway is called the Brahma Nadi. The denser forms of Kundalini will ascend through the Sushumna and the other astral pathways contained within the Sushumna: the Wajra Nadi and the Chitrini Nadi.

It was mentioned in another book on Esoteric Acupuncture that the energy field created by the needling of the *Sishencong* Window Group formed a Radial Singularity field in that region of the head. In order to break through the Radial Singularity, other factors have to be in place. If you are interested in connecting the lower chakras with the Sahasrara (Crown Chakra), then it may be beneficial to understand and know the correct location of the esoteric Du-20 (*Tian Man*). If you are going to place the acupuncture needles in the correct location at the four acupuncture sites of the esoteric *Sishencong* Window Group, then it is best to first find the esoteric location of *Tian Man* (Du-20) as the guide post. It is at this esoteric site ("The Thirteenth Gate") that the wisarga (power bridge) will be built and extended from the cranium to connect with the Sahasrara (Crown Chakra) situated superiorly to the skull. The wisarga is built from extremely fine mental matter and assists the person to "jump" the gap that exists between the intracranial Brahmarandra Chakra and the outer cranial Sahasrara (Crown Chakra). Since the wisarga (power bridge) will not just automatically form, it has to be built in some manner for those who choose to work with one's Antahkarana.

When the esoteric Du-20 (*Tian Man*) is activated within certain posterior New Encoding Patterns such as: the Esoteric *Shaoyin* Heart Pattern, the Esoteric *Shaoyin* Kidney Pattern, the Esoteric *Shaoyin* Heart Window Pattern or the *Hun* Follow the *Shen* Pattern, plus the proper triangular visualization connections are made after the acupuncture needles have been inserted, these two actions initiate the building of this particular wisarga.

Think of this wisarga as the pathway that bridges the gap that exists from the Brahmarandra Chakra to the Sahasrara (Crown Chakra). Remember that it is the needling of the esoteric site of the Du-20 (*Tian Man*) and not the qi leaving the traditional location of *Bai Hui* (Du-20) or the energetics associated with the traditional site that activates and opens "The Thirteenth Gate." This particular wisarga has to be built from the site or opening at *Tian Man* .

*Tian Man* (Du-20) is also the capstone acupuncture site on the physical body for many of the New Encoding Patterns discussed in Chapter V of this book. When your client is standing up and you ask him or her to visually connect *Tian Man* (Du-20) to the esoteric location of the bilateral Ki-1 points on the soles of each foot, known in Esoteric Acupuncture as *Dichong*, you are creating the longest visual triangular connection on the human body using acupuncture sites. (For a description on how to locate *Dichong* versus the location of the traditional Ki-1 point called *Yongquan*, go to the Esoteric *Shaoyin* Kidney Pattern in Chapter V of this book.)

Activating and opening the pathway of the Thirteenth Gate does not automatically create a fully completed and functioning wisarga (power bridge) from the intracranial Brahmarandra Chakra to the Sahasrara (Crown Chakra) located above the skull. It is the action of first needling *Dazhui* (Du-14) to allow a morphic resonant connection to *Yintang*, the Third Eye at the Ajna Center that triggers the unfolding of one's spiritual antenna when using acupuncture to accomplish this process. When the qi has ascended from the acupuncture site of *Dazhui* (Du-14) to the acupuncture site of *Feng Fu* (Du-16), guide your client to visually make a triangular connection from both *Feng Fu* (Du-16) and *Yintang* upward to communicate with *Tian Man* (Du-20). It is all of these processes that initiates the building of the wisarga (power bridge). The very key is knowledge that *Dazhui* (Du-14) connects to *Yintang* via an instantaneous consciousness connection.

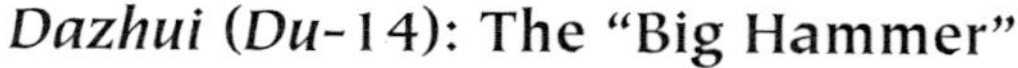

## *Dazhui* (*Du*-14): The "Big Hammer"

Fig. 2.4

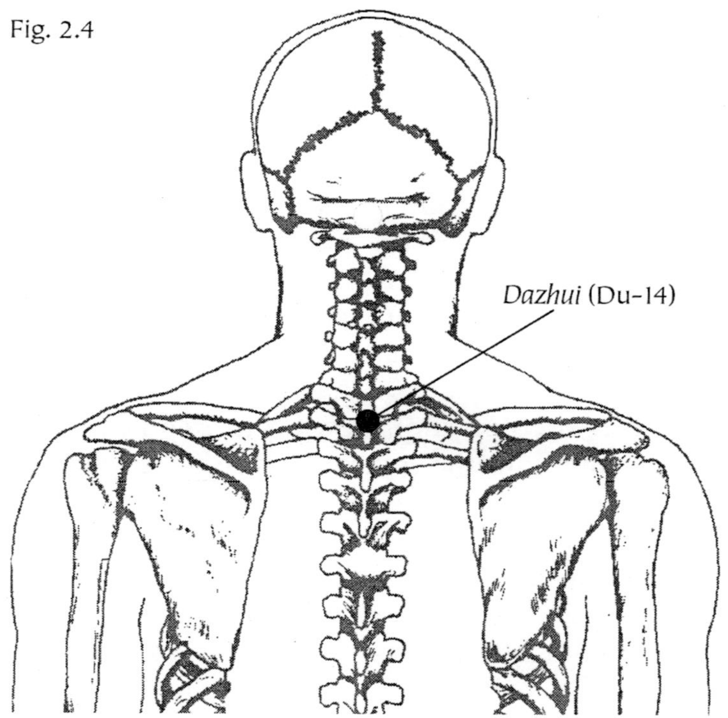


### Point location of *Dazhui* (Du-14)

*Dazhui* (Du-14) is located directly on the posterior spine below the spinous process of the seventh cervical vertebra. This vertebra is often, but not always, the largest protruding vertebra on the lower part of the neck where the neck joins the upper body. If you are not sure of the location of *Dazhui* (Du-14), while your client is lying face down on your treatment table, place one of your fingers on the vertebra that you think is the seventh cervical vertebra (C-7). Place another finger on the vertebra above C-7 (closer to the head) that you think is C-6. Have your client slowly lift his or her head and tilt it backward slowly. The sixth cervical vertebra will go inward, while the seventh cervical vertebra will not move, or at least not move much.

### *Dazhui* (Du-14)

This acupuncture point is also known as "the Big Hammer" and is located directly on the posterior spine. This is the key acupuncture site that introduced the concept of morphic resonance or morphic resonant connections into the vocabulary of Esoteric Acupuncture. A morphic resonant connection is an instantaneous consciousness connection that is not a linear connections or a connection flowing through the acupuncture meridian system on the etheric levels. Morphic resonance is a phrase introduced by Rupert Sheldrake referring to a consciousness connection that is not dependent on distance, time or dimensions.

Activating *Dazhu*i (Du-14) within any of the New Encoding Patterns automatically allows *Dazhu*i (Du-14) to communicate with *Yintang,* the acupuncture point on the vertical midline of the forehead between the eyebrows and superior to the bridge of the nose. *Yintang* is the site for the Ajna Center, which is also known as one's "Third Eye."

*Dazhu*i (Du-14) can also activate the Vishuddha (Throat Chakra), while simultaneously stimulating the dormant frequencies of the Ajna Center. *Dazhui* (Du-14) is one of the major acupuncture points in Esoteric Acupuncture because of its unique ability to instantaneously communicate with *Yintang*.

In Esoteric Acupuncture, we are attempting to align, harmonize and strengthen our Higher, Inner, Spiritual Heart Center while simultaneously building and refining our Antahkarana. In certain posterior New Encoding Patterns such as: the Discern the Whisper Pattern, the various Esoteric *Shaoyin*

Patterns and the *Hun* Follow the *Shen* Pattern, you will notice that the acupuncture points *Dazhui* (Du-14), *Feng Fu* (Du-16) and *Tian Man* (Du-20) are all needled. Since these three acupuncture sites are all on the Du channel, of course they communicate with each other through the etheric Du meridian pathway. But, it is the process of *Dazhui* (Du-14) first communicating with *Yintang* through an instantaneous consciousness connection, then asking the client to mentally move the qi from *Dazhui* (Du-14) up to *Feng Fu* (Du-16) and next mentally connecting *Feng Fu* (Du-16) to *Yintang* that is important. These mental connections are the foundations for building the Antahkarana at a more accelerated pace.

A very astute and extremely aware, highly sensitive student in Australia named Alex Nigol asked me during one of my workshops in Melbourne, Australia why I had not chosen an alternative Chinese name for *Dazhui* (Du-14). *Dazhui* is translated as "the Big Hammer." A hammer is thought of as a tool that is used to strike another object, usually a nail. By gently inserting an acupuncture needle at the site of *Dazhui* (Du-14), the acupuncture needle is esoterically "striking" and releasing the stored energy at that site, or more correctly activating the consciousness at the site to instantaneously communicate with the consciousness stored at *Yintang*, the site of the Third Eye. That is the hidden meaning in Esoteric Acupuncture of the acupuncture point known as the Big Hammer. During one of my meditations, the information that I received about the morphic resonant property of *Dazhui* (Du-14) hit me like a "Big Hammer."

If we understand the energetics of morphic resonance, then we will understand that the action of gently "tapping" the point at *Dazhui* (Du-14) allows an opportunity for dormant information (as energy) to instantaneously awaken creating a big reaction. Moving information from the back of the spine to your Third Eye area is this opportunity. It is this very action of inserting a needle at the site of *Dazhui* (Du-14) that activates the possibility for an Esoteric Acupuncture treatment to assist the recipient of the treatment an opportunity to awaken dormant frequencies within the higher head centers for the purpose of strengthening one's Inner Spiritual Higher Heart Center. The ability for qi stored at the acupuncture site of *Dazhui* (Du-14) to create a mini wormhole places *Dazhui* (Du-14) in the section with the Window Groups. The mini wormhole offers an individual a window for something exciting and important to take place, a spiritual awakening.

### Window Groups with Four Sites

The Window Groups in Esoteric Acupuncture are mostly groups of three or four acupuncture sites with one group having five acupuncture sites. All the window groups are triangular or polygon configurations that connect very specific acupuncture points that create special energetic fields. These types of energetic fields are not created by the needling action of the various traditional acupuncture modalities.

The idea of a window can refer an opening that leads somewhere or an opening that reveals something behind the window. Sometimes a window may be clear so you may peer through the opening and see what is on the other side. Other times a window may be clouded, foggy and closed so you are not able to clearly see through the window.

Another type of window might refer to a short duration of time when an advantage may open up for an individual, such as a window of opportunity. These window groups in Esoteric Acupuncture allow the recipient of the treatment a window of opportunity to tap into his or her higher, inner plane consciousness fields. If the person can quiet the mind and relax into his or her higher heart frequencies, these "windows" may open up one's inner pathways to expanded levels of consciousness. You may experience a special "ah ha" moment.

All the Window Groups are found within various New Encoding Patterns discussed in Chapter V of this book. Although the various Window Groups can be used within a more traditional style of acupuncture treatment, the Window Groups of points are utilized as part of various New Encoding Patterns that are presented in Chapter V of this book. If you decide to needle any of the Window Groups without a specific New encoding Pattern, you must needle the Window Group in the exact sequence given in this Chapter.

## *Sishencong* Window Group

Traditional Location of Du-20
usually called *Bai Hui*

Fig. 2.5-a

*Bai Hui*
(Du-20)

1 2 3 4

Esoteric Location of Du-20
now called *Tian Man*

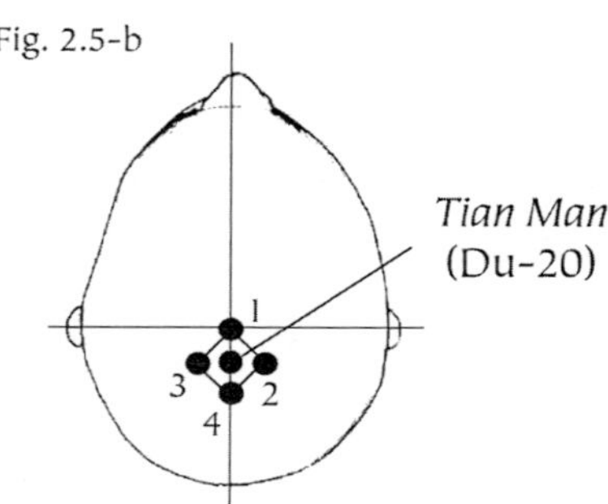


## *Sishencong* Window Group

Of all the Window Groups in Esoteric Acupuncture, the *Sishencong* Window Group activated in the correct esoteric location is the most important and allows a person the best opportunity to align and strengthen his or her gateway to the Sahasrara (Crown Chakra) and even beyond to the higher planes of consciousness. When the acupuncture sites of the four *Sishencong* Window Group points are needled in the correct order within a New Encoding Pattern of Esoteric Acupuncture, an energy field is created that allows the initial formation of the wisarga (power bridge) to form. The wisarga (power bridge) is the pathway that connects the intracranial head chakras to the Sahasrara (Crown Chakra) located above the cranium.

This window group surrounds the esoteric opening known as "Celestial Fullness," or the point known in Esoteric Acupuncture as *Tian Man* (Du-20). The four *Sishencong* points surrounding *Tian Man* (Du-20) create an energetic field that is known as a radial singularity. Singularity has various meanings depending upon the field of science for which it is used. In Esoteric Acupuncture, radial singularity means an energetic field that usually cannot be penetrated unless other factors are in place, or certain other factors are being set up. Radial singularity is different from an events horizon. In an events horizon, once the energy has passed a certain barrier, the crossing energy cannot return through the events horizon. In a radial singularity, the energy cannot initially penetrate the barrier.

The factors that create a Radial Singularity field with the *Sishencong* Window Group that will impede or prevent qi from ascending through the Brahmarandra Chakra within the cranium to the Sahasrara (Crown Chakra) include: 1) not knowing about Kundalini; 2) not knowing about the wisarga (power bridge) that usually requires building through mental matter; 3) needling the traditional *Sishencong* location; 4) not first activating the energetics at the acupuncture site of *Dazhui* (Du-14) to allow a morphic resonant communication with *Yintang* (Ajna Center); 5) not visually connecting *Feng Fu* (Du-16) to *Yintang* (Ajna Center); 6) not first activating the energies at the acupuncture site of *Tian Chong* (GB-9) before activating *Tian Man* (Du-20); and 7) not inserting an acupuncture needle or otherwise activating the correct esoteric location of the Du-20 point called *Tian Man* in Esoteric Acupuncture. If these impediments are rectified by the practitioner, then the process of removing the radial singularity from that area and the building of the wisarga (power bridge) can begin. The beauty of using Esoteric Acupuncture is that we are going to initiate the building of the Antahkarana (Rainbow Bridge) and the initial building of the wisarga (power bridge) without the older method of having to concentrate using mental matter through hours of meditation to first create the wisarga (power bridge)

The energetics at *Tian Man* (Du-20), when needled within a New Encoding Pattern of Esoteric Acupuncture, will create a field with a harmonious vibratory rate for allowing some level of awakening. Unless the client receiving an Esoteric Acupuncture treatment has recently taken an herbal hallucinogen, presently on psychotropic drugs or is extremely fear-based, the treatment will not create an unwanted potential challenge to the person such as an abrupt, unexpected Kundalini awakening.

The wisarga (power bridge) is an energetic pathway that has to be mentally created, or can be created by the posterior New Encoding Patterns where the practitioner activates certain acupuncture sites. These specific acupuncture sites include: *Shendao* (*Du*-11), *Dazhui* (Du-14), *Feng Fu* (Du-16), the bilateral *Tian Chong* (GB-9) points, *Yintang,* the *Sishencong* Window Group and *Tian Man* (*Du*-20). The *Sishencong* Window points and *Tian Man* (Du-20) must be needled in the location describe in Esoteric Acupuncture and not the traditional point locations. The New Encoding Patterns that contain those specific points are: the Discern the Whisper Pattern, the Esoteric *Shaoyin* Kidney Pattern, the Esoteric *Shaoyin* Heart Pattern, the Esoteric *Shaoyin* Heart Window Pattern, the *Hun* Follow the *Shen* Pattern and the 3-6-1 Antahkarana Meditation Pattern in ***Sea of Fire-Cosmic Fire: Esoteric Acupuncture, Volume IV***. The *Wei Qi* Grid Strengthening Pattern also contains those same acupuncture points.

You must also needle the four *Sishencong* points in the order that is given. This means that the first *Sishencong* site needled is the point closest to the front of the head. The next site needled is the *Sishencong* point that is approximately one *cun* lateral to *Tian Man* (Du-20) on the client's right side. The third site needled in the *Sishencong* Window Group is the point that is approximately one *cun* lateral to *Tian Man* (Du-20) on the client's left side. The fourth acupuncture site needled in this grouping is the point located approximately one *cun* posteriorly to *Tian Man* (Du-20) and directly on the Du channel. The four points of the *Sishencong* group has three functions when needled within the New Encoding Patters: 1) reinforce the power of *Tian Man* (Du-20): 2) assist in the unlocking of the stored consciousness at *Tian Man* (Du-20) that connects to one's "Keycodes"; 3) assist in the building of the wisarga (power bridge) that will build the Antahkarana, our antennae of consciousness to awaken our Higher, Inner *Shen*.

## Wing Maker Frequency Window

Fig. 2.6

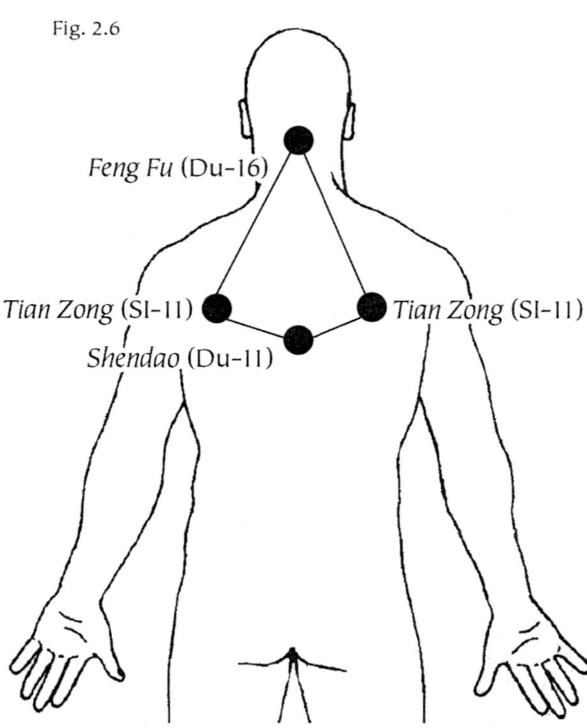

## Wing Maker Frequency Window

This next window group is known in Esoteric Acupuncture as the Wing Maker Frequency Window. The two scapulae of the body symbolically make up the "Wings of your Heart." When you are needling the posterior side of your client, it is beneficial to have him or her place the arms along the sides with the palms facing upward as shown in figure 2.6. The palms are directly connected to the heart field. With the arms extended in this manner, the client is able to open the wings of the heart.

In Esoteric Acupuncture, you will notice that the bilateral *Tian Zong* (SI-11) points are used in several of the posterior New Encoding Patterns. *Tian Zong* (SI-11) can be translated to mean "Celestial Gathering" and are important gathering points for spiritual energies to connect to the heart grid. In Chinese Medicine, the small intestine system is often paired with the heart system to form a yin and yang relationship. The heart system is considered the yin aspect, while the small intestine system is the yang aspect.

The four acupuncture sites should be accessed in this particular sequence. The acupuncture site of *Feng Fu* (Du-16), found in the depression inferiorly to the posterior occipital protuberance of the head, is the first site activated. Next insert an acupuncture needle in the client's right scapula at the site of *Tian Zong* (SI-11), followed by needling *Tian Zong* (SI-11) on the client's left scapula. The fourth acupuncture site activated is *Shendao* (Du-11) located below the lower border of the spinous process of the fifth thoracic vertebra. (For more description of the point locations, see the Discern the Whisper Pattern in Chapter V.) To visualize the Wing Maker Window, see figure 2.6 on the proceeding page. Once you have this particular window needled, you do not have to make a visual connection. Just say: "Bring me into Wing Maker Frequency." If the energy surrounding your field is very dense or heavy, you may wish to visually connect the points. In those instances, start at *Feng Fu* (Du-16) on the posterior of the head, go to *Tian Zong* (SI-11) on the client's right scapula, move downward to connect the *Shendao* (Du-11) point, move upward to connect to the *Tian Zong* (SI-11) point on the left scapula, then return to *Feng Fu* (Du-16).

The Wing Maker Frequency is a heart frequency intended to assist the person to a rapidly center himself or herself to their individual heart center. When I go into a lecture hall or classroom that has dense energy, I will step out into the hallway and say: "Bring me into Wing Maker Frequency." When I re-enter the hall or classroom, my lighter, clearer heart frequency will allow me to not take on the denseness of that particular room. There is additional discussion of the Wing Maker Frequency Window in the visualization section of the Discern the Whisper Pattern in Chapter V of this book.

## Wind Mansion Window

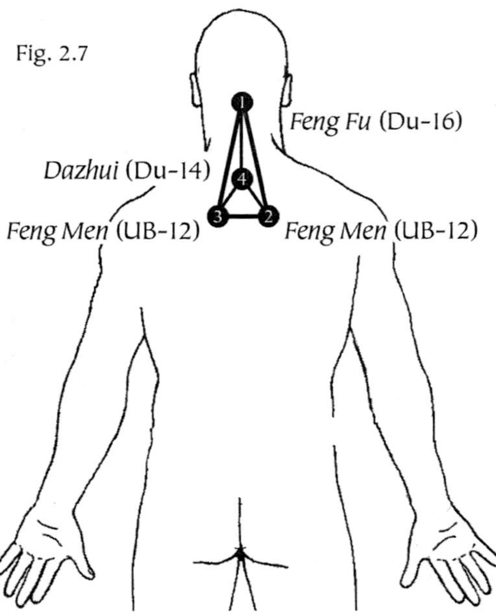

## Wind Mansion Window
## The Three Winds

In Chinese medicine, the concept of wind is usually associated with the liver system. Remember it was mentioned that the Chinese name of *Feng Fu* is often translated as Wind Mansion. The idea of wind is not just the idea that westerners think of when we talk about wind and how wind is a part of nature and a natural movement of nature. Wind can also be thought of something more nebulous, such as energy or spirit.

In Esoteric Acupuncture, the idea of wind is further subdivided into three different, but interconnected energy fields. The Three Winds consist of: 1) the Winds of Earth; 2) the Winds of the *Hun* of the liver system; and 3) the Winds of Spirit and the Celestial Spirits. This higher aspect of wind is further subdivided into three interconnected, but distinct vapors.

1) Think of the Winds of Earth as the denser frequency that also includes what are known as the winds of Nature. From a Traditional Chinese Medicine viewpoint, the concept of wind can be from an external source such as the wind from a storm, hurricane or tornado that may create physical challenges coming in contact with an individual. Have you ever been outdoors when the weather changed and a cool or cold wind developed, hitting your body? If your defensive qi, also known as either the protective qi or the *Wei Qi*, is weak, you may later develop sniffles and tightness around your shoulders and neck. These symptoms may later express themselves as a runny nose and overall aches and pains. Cold winds in the winter can cause stiffness and pain in the neck and shoulders, cause headaches, may lead to symptoms of a cold or flu and even frostbite. You may initially be very cold, then a fever sets in and you become very hot. Damp wind may sometimes lead to an irritable disposition and itchy skin (candida). Very dry, hot wind may lead to cracked, parched and scaly, dry and wrinkled skin. But, the Winds of the Earth will cool and energize your environment and clear and clean the air of unwanted or undesired energies

and man-made pollutants. The physical symptoms caused by the Winds of the Earth can often be changed and ameliorated by needling *Feng Fu*/Du-16 ("The Wind Mansion") and the bilateral *Feng Men*/UB-12 ("The Wind Gates"), while holding the intention of clearing the wind and the symptoms caused by the external wind.

2) When the Winds of the lower *Hun* of the liver system are triggered by internal or external pathogenic factors, sometimes discomforting and challenging physical symptoms may manifest in the acupuncture channels and other parts of the body. This event is known in Traditional Chinese Medicine as internal wind that circulates within the meridians of the body creating physical or emotional challenges. Some of these symptoms include: tics, jerky movements, spasms, Parkinson's Disease, twitching, facial paralysis such as in Bell's Palsy, hemiplegia from strokes or other causes, blurred vision, mental disorientation, anger, shouting and outward, aggressive behavior and other mental disorders. To change those unwanted symptoms into a more harmonious state, we must work on the liver system of the body. This level of the Winds of *Hun* refers to the denser frequencies of our lower *Hun* on the Etheric and Astral Planes.

The winds of the lower *Hun* also includes one's emotional and physical aspects that are guided and shaped by the strength or weakness of our *Hun*. This level of *Hun* controls our physical eyesight, our emotions, gives us directions in life and gives us guidance in how to best plan things in life for optimum manifestation. This level of wind within the lower *Hun* allows qi within our etheric acupuncture meridians to flow smoothly throughout the body.

3) The Winds of Spirit or the Celestial Spirits are those energies and energetic events connected to the realms above the everyday three-dimensional realities of one's day-to-day existence. These realms involve the energies of our Higher *Hun*. This level of wind is divided into three additional sections that influence and controls our Ethereal Soul, our Insight and shield one's field of "Sound without Sound."

Certain higher planes above the three-dimensional realms contain what people call spirits, our spirit guides, entities, ghosts, discarnate souls, lower fourth dimensional extraterrestrial beings and other beings not of our three-dimensional reality. Sometimes these spirits are here to assist us. Other times they can bring us great distress and unwanted challenges. Using the more advanced New Encoding Patterns will bring your frequency to a higher Light Quotient so you will not attract the lower, heavier, darker frequencies. Also, the *Wei Qi* Grid Strengthening Pattern in the Addendum section of this book will help to install a psychic protection grid around the body to ward off unwanted entities and negative energies.

The Winds of Spirit is further subdivided into what is called the Three Vapors. The energy stored at the acupuncture site of *Feng Fu* (Du-16) will be activated when receiving an Esoteric Acupuncture treatment that utilizes that point. The degree to which level of winds are activated depends upon your own internal work and other factors such as the cosmologic alignment of that day and the consciousness level of the practitioner inserting the acupuncture needle or using other means to activate the qi stored at *Feng Fu* (Du-16).

### The Three Vapors and *Feng Fu* (Du-16)

1) Sound without Sound
2) Light without Light
3) The Lost Chord of AUM

*Feng Fu,* also known as Du-16 by the English-speaking acupuncturists is also one of the most important acupuncture sites in Esoteric Acupuncture and is sometimes known as the "Wind Mansion." The acupuncture site of *Feng Fu* (Du-16) always has at least two or three entrances that are stacked very closely together one on top of another. *Feng Fu* (Du-16) is located directly on the vertical midline on the posterior of the head and in the depression below the occipital protuberance. On a treatment day when both the practitioner and client are vibrating at a high frequency level, and the practitioner is able to locate and needle the acupuncture site at *Feng Fu* (Du-16) that has the most qi, then the recipient of the treatment has an opportunity to experience some level of an inner awakening.

When talking about vapors or something vaporous, one usually thinks about a substance that is suspended or is diffused in the air and can be seen by the naked eye. This type of vaporous substance was initially a liquid or a solid. Vapors are not synonymous with gases. Gas cannot be liquefied by pressure alone. But, the Three Vapors being discussed in Esoteric Acupuncture is of a much finer frequency than what is thought of as gas.

It was mentioned earlier that the field of "Sound without Sound" is hidden within the chakra found at the acupuncture site of *Feng Fu* (Du-16), the Wind Mansion. Sound without Sound is not something that a person with extra sensitive hearing can distinguish or hear on the three-dimensional reality. Sometimes a person on cocaine, methamphetamines or other drugs has such sensitive, acute hearing that the level of perception is way beyond the range of normal hearing. This type of acute hearing is still controlled by the kidney system of the physical body. Dogs can pick up the sound of certain whistles, known as dog whistles, that emits a sound beyond the range of human hearing. This range is not what is meant by Sound without Sound. Physical hearing is controlled by the kidney system. Celestial Hearing, that encompasses the field of Sound without Sound, is dependent upon the awakening of one's Inner Heart Center and one's Inner *Shen*. Celestial sound is under the domain of the Higher Heart System. To reach this level of experience usually requires that the person has also done a certain amount of inner plane work. The possibility exists to activate the hidden gateway to reach the field of the esoteric "Inner Sound without Sound" by receiving an Esoteric Acupuncture treatment or by meditating during or after receiving an Esoteric Acupuncture treatment. Sound without Sound is an extremely fine frequency state of consciousness that only the most awakened souls can have the awareness. If you wish to have any sort of opportunity to enter this extremely fine frequency of reality, you must quiet the chaotic chatter of your concrete mind first. Quieting a chattering mind is not easy.

*Feng Fu* (Du-16) is one of the ten "Window of Heaven" points that are also known as the "Window to the Sky" points. Eight of the ten acupuncture sites of the Window of Heaven points are located on or around the neck.

> *"The points and orifices of the head and face are like the great windows of a high pavilion by virtue of which qi moves."*[3]

Often when Kundalini ascends from the Muladhara (Root Chakra) through the central Sushumna pathway, it will intersect a granthi (astral knot) or granthis at various locations. The granthis are astral blockages that do not allow Kundalini to rise smoothly through the astral pathways. A common region for a granthi to form is at the Vishuddha (Throat Chakra) and at the location of *Feng Fu* (Du-16). This blockage of Kundalini at the Vishuddha (Throat Chakra) may lead to mental confusion and other mental challenges. Remember the Vishuddha (Throat Chakra) is the storage center and location of the mental body.

There is a head chakra at the acupuncture site of *Feng Fu* (Du-16) with various names depending on the chakra system. In the Djwhal Khul Tibetan system, this chakra is called the Alta Major Center. In various Hindu systems, this chakra is called Taluka, Talu or the Lalana Chakra. If there is an astral knot in this region, then rising Kundalini may descend back downward to the Throat Chakra and may cause mental challenges.

The Window to the Sky Points will open energies in the neck region to allow Kundalini to smoothly ascend to the higher head centers. If you study Esoteric Acupuncture diligently, you will notice the use of many of the Window to the Sky Points.

*Feng Fu* (Du-16) is the gateway to pierce the medulla oblongata of the brain. The medulla oblongata is that portion of the brain that controls the Muladhara (Root Chakra). Most people only know of the lower functions of the Muladhara (Root Chakra). The Muladhara (Root Chakra) also has higher consciousness levels. The lower realms of the Muladhara (Root Chakra) involve: our day-to-day, routine activities, our survival instincts, as well as focusing on me, myself and I. At this level of existence, you always place yourself in first place without consideration for others.

The bilateral *Feng Men* (UB-12) points, that are a part of the Wind Mansion Window, are often translated to mean "Wind Gate." With the three acupuncture sites of the Wind Mansion Window, we are activating and opening the bilateral "Wind Gates" and visually bringing the qi upward in a triangular formation to connect with the energetics of the Wind Mansion at the site of *Feng Fu* (Du-16). We are not so interested in the functioning of these three acupuncture points on the etheric plane of the traditional acupuncture meridian pathways. The mental visualization of the triangular geometric form places the energetics of this window grouping in the higher realms extending from the Causal Planes and above.

The bilateral *Feng Men* (UB-12) points are part of the inner urinary bladder channel. The *Feng Men* (UB-12) points are located on either side of the spine approximately one and a half *cun* from the center of the spine and bilaterally to the lower border of the spinous process of the second thoracic vertebra.

The central acupuncture site in The Wind Mansion Group is *Dazhui* (Du-14), the "Big Hammer," discussed earlier in this section. The main reason why *Dazhui* (Du-14) was placed in this chapter with the window groups is because *Dazhui* (Du-14) is a window site or window point by itself. *Dazhui* (Du-14) has the power and function to communicate with *Yintang*/Ajna Center instantaneously through a morphic resonant connection. In Esoteric Acupuncture Theory, this type of consciousness connection at this particular site is known as a special type of cosmic mini-wormhole connection.

The extremely fine frequency field of Light without Light is stored in the Ajna Center, the site of the acupuncture point *Yintang*. Light without Light is not visible with the most sensitive, finely tuned three-dimensional eyesight of a human. Light without Light is a vibrational field of extremely fine "vapor" that only reveals itself to someone who understands and works with the refinement and ascension of Kundalini, and most importantly has done the necessary inner plane work.

When acupuncture needles are inserted at the four acupuncture sites of the Wind Mansion Window Group, you will notice the formation of a tetrahedron. A tetrahedron has inherent fourness that also includes a "hidden" sixness. Both the number 4 and the number 6 symbolize consciousness. (The concept of "four hides the six" was explained in Chapter 1). The six vectors of the tetrahedron stands for the creation of a certain level of consciousness that can be accessed because of the energetics of the four points and their connection to the various layers of wind and vapors. Activating the qi at both the acupuncture sites of *Feng Fu* (Du-16) and *Dazhui* (Du-14) in this window group has the potential to trigger a very special, inner spiritual expansion.

The third vapor field of The Three Vapors of Esoteric Acupuncture is the field of the Inner AUM. A-U-M is not synonymous with OM or O-M. AUM is an inner field that some dedicated and devoted inner plane devotees may strive to reach. This inner field is not the field or the state of consciousness that can be obtained by the repetitive physical sounding of OM out loud, such as one would do with a mantra. This is the third portion of the Vapor Field that is simultaneously connected to and contained within the field of Sound without Sound and the field of Light without Light. Although the Three Vapors are three distinctly different realms of consciousness, they are closely connected within an indivisible state of consciousness that is locked together in the highest inner spaces of one's consciousness.

For additional information on the Wind Mansion Window

Group, please refer to The Wind Mansion Pattern in the Addendum at the back of this book.

## Ajna Window Group

Fig. 2-8

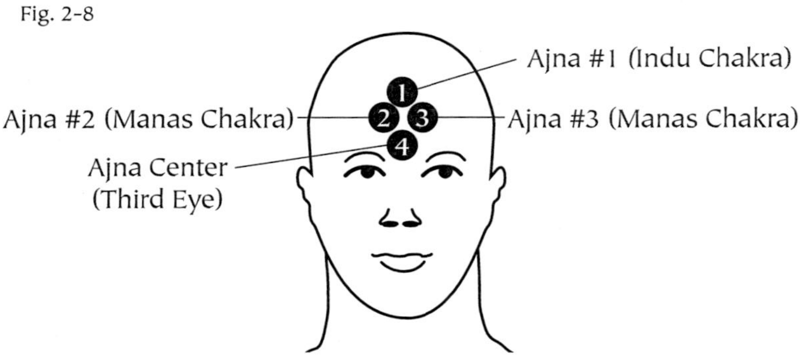


**Ajna Window Group**

The four acupuncture sites of the Ajna Group Window are used together as one larger, more encompassing group to strengthen, harmonize and access the information and latent energetics located at the Third Eye, as well as the information locked in the area surrounding and superior to the Third Eye Center at the acupuncture site of *Yintang*.

The two lateral sites (Ajna #2 and Ajna #3), located superiorly to the site of *Yintang,* will strengthen and access the Manas Chakra. The Manas Chakra is the seat and the gateway to what is known as our sense-consciousness and the perceptive mind. The Manas Chakra is also known as the Forehead Chakra.

The most superiorly located point, Ajna #1, will strengthen and access one's Indu Chakra. The Indu Chakra is the gateway to the upper Buddhic Planes and to the Atmic Planes. The Indu

Chakra is the seat of higher intelligence and holds the power to help us with discernment, mindfulness, Being in the Now and for acquiring and maintaining Wisdom.

The acupuncture site of *Yintang* is the access site of the Ajna Center. For Esoteric Acupuncture, these four acupuncture sites are called collectively the Ajna Window Group. The Ajna Center is the information storage area for the consciousness to open one's higher intuitive powers and to really understand how to move inward beyond the regions where the mental plane will take us. Initially opening the Third Eye will allow us an opportunity to enter the realms of the Causal Plane and beyond. The Causal Plane is the storage center plane of our higher abstract mind and is the gateway to the consciousness plane of the Buddhic Planes and higher.

You will notice that these four Ajna Window Group points are contained within several of the anterior New Encoding Patterns such as: The Extended Indigo Triangle Pattern, The Cube on Cube Window Pattern, The Crystalline Grid Pattern, The Crystalline Heart Grid Pattern and The Extended Crystalline Grid Pattern. The activation of the stored information at these sites may sometimes be transferred and connected to the Brahmarandra Chakra located within the cranium and directly inferior to the location of the Esoteric *Sishencong* Window Group of points. The goal, after connecting the energies of the Ajna Window Group to the Brahmarandra Chakra, is to next transform the frequency vibrations (information) within the Brahmarandra Chakra to resonate with the frequency of the Sahasrara (Crown Chakra) through the wisarga (power bridge). In this manner, one is able to link the inner head centers with the Sahasrara (Crown Chakra) located above the cranium.

One very important point to remember is that the highest frequency of the Divine Light between the eyebrows at the Ajna Center is known to devout, disciplined meditators as the frequency of "Light without Light." Even to most people working with and teaching the Hindu Chakra System, the concept of Light without Light and this fine level of frequency of light is not a very well known fact. Light without Light is a refined vibrational reality of extremely fine frequency consciousness and a reality usually only accessible by those who have done very serious inner plane work to Still the Mind. In the visualization sections of several of the posterior New Encoding Patterns, you will notice how the client mentally connects the energies at the *Feng Fu* (Du-16) acupuncture site to the energies at the Ajna Center site accessed through the acupuncture point *Yintang*. The Divine Light at the Ajna Center is the feminine or Mother aspect that communicates and is equally supported and strengthened by connecting with the Father aspect of "Sound without Sound" stored at the Taluka Chakra (Lalana Chakra/Alta Major Center). For those who have done the necessary inner plane work, the barrier that surrounds the field of Sound without Sound can be pierced by inserting an acupuncture needle at the acupuncture site of *Feng Fu* (du-16) on the posterior of the head, One reason why we have the client visually make the connection between those two very important "major" head centers is to connect the feminine "Mother" vibrations to the masculine "Father" vibrations so these two opposing, yet complimentary frequencies can be brought upward to communicate with "Celestial Fullness."

When inserting needles into the acupuncture sites of the Ajna Window Group in female clients with very sensitive or extremely thin facial skin, it may be wise to use slightly thinner needles than the Seirin .16 mm X 15 mm red colored handle needle that is usually recommended. Use the slightly thinner .14 mm X 15 mm gauge Seirin lime colored handle needles, In the higher spiritual teachings, it is often taught that we should not be so preoccupied with the physical plane, and a slight mark on the forehead or face made by an acupuncture insertion of a tiny needle should not be of any concern. We still live in a three-dimensional world with many worldly, social protocols of how things should be. Just be aware that many people, especially women in the United States, will not want a temporary tiny scar or mark on their forehead or face. If a person has toxin-laden blood with Liver Qi Stagnation and/or Liver Blood Stagnation, there is a high possibility that a small needle mark may turn brown and take a week or even longer to dissipate. Just be aware of the sensitivities of your client.

## Karmic Release Window Group

Fig. 2.9

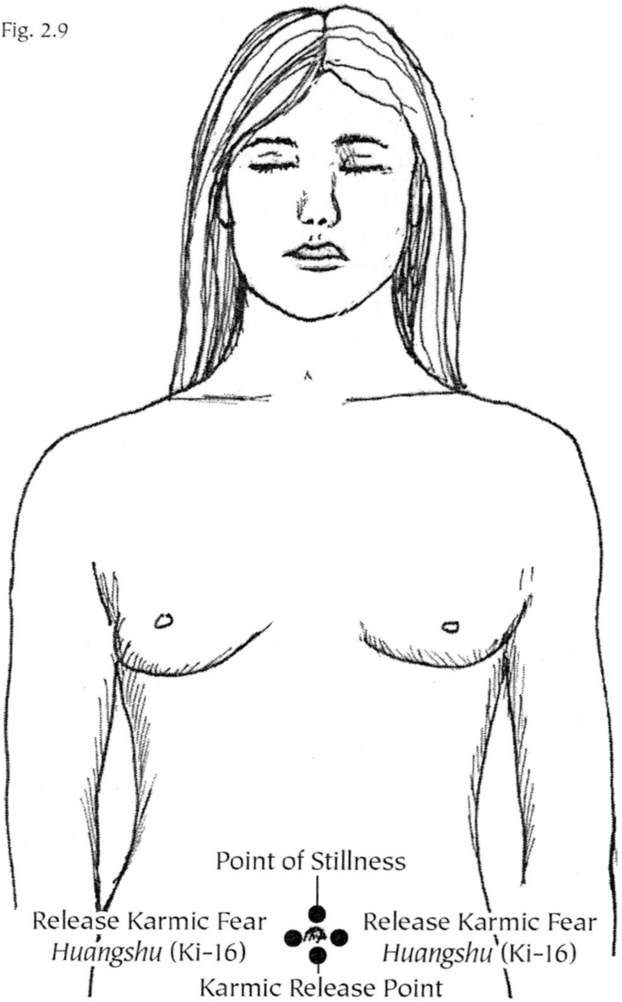

Point of Stillness

Release Karmic Fear *Huangshu* (Ki-16)

Release Karmic Fear *Huangshu* (Ki-16)

Karmic Release Point

## Karmic Release Window Group

The four acupuncture sites of the Karmic Release Window Group surround the umbilicus. The umbilical cord is the lifeline of nutrients and food for an unborn infant, as well as a direct transporter of consciousness from the mother to the child. After birth, the cells of the umbilicus (belly button) still retain memory of the experience in the womb and store information.

Because of the direct link of consciousness from your biological mother to both you and to her biological parents, you will inherent some portions of ancestral qi and some ancestral karma from your biological grandparents and others along this ancestral link. By inserting acupuncture needles in the four acupuncture sites of the Karmic Release Window Group surrounding the umbilicus, the consciousness (information) of one's ancestral qi can be accessed. If there is unwanted stress from ancestral karma, that energy can be alleviated with continued acupuncture treatments that utilize the Karmic Release Window Group of points.

You inherit both positive and negative information, as energy, from your parents, as well as from your biological ancestors. In the western modality of Homeopathic Medicine, some homeopathic physicians believe that everyone inherits one or more of three miasms. A miasm is thought to be the root cause of one or more of the underlying chronic diseases that afflict humanity. The three miasms are sometimes divided into: 1) the tuberculosis miasm; 2) a syphilis miasm; and 3) a cancer miasm. Sometimes the three miasms are broken down into: 1) a sycosis miasm; 2) the syphilis miasm; and 3) a psora miasm.

If you have certain tendencies or habits that you picked up from your biological mother that no longer suits who you are, then ask your practitioner to treat you with an Esoteric Acupuncture pattern that contains the four points of the Karmic Release Window Group.

The four points are all located approximately one *cun* (more or less) from the center of the umbilicus. The very top point is known as "The Point of Stillness." This is one of the heart points used in The Eight Heart Gates *Shaoyang* Pattern that is introduced in Chapter V.

Some younger women today may feel it is fashionable to have a metal jewelry piercing that punctures the umbilicus. Often the piercing is directly on the site of the Point of Stillness and goes through the skin into the umbilicus. In those cases, I will insert the acupuncture needle just slightly above the piercing with the needle angling toward the umbilicus. If there is a scar at this site from a previous piercing that was removed, I will insert the needle directly into the scar. I have seen several women who had had their piercing removed and the remaining scar was slightly off to the left or right of the site of the Point of Stillness. In those cases, I will still needle the scar. Do not think that the acupuncture needles have to always form a symmetrical design. Asymmetry affects consciousness in a different way than symmetry.

Although I usually perform freehand needling without a guide tube, I may use a guide tube when needling the scar above the umbilicus. The reason is because often the scar tissue is very tough, thus making it difficult to cleanly insert the acupuncture needle. When someone comes in for an Esoteric Acupuncture treatment and has an umbilicus piercing, I do not make comments or any suggestions about removing the piercing. But, if the person asks me first, then I will definitely suggest they remove the piercing.

The next two acupuncture points in the Karmic Release Window Group correspond to the traditional bilateral *Huangshu* (Ki-16) points. Insert the needle, approximately one *cun* from the center of the umbilicus, into the site of *Huangshu* (Ki-16) on the client's right side, followed by needling the *Huangshu* (Ki-16) point on the left side. The fourth and last point is known as the Lower Karmic Release Point. The point is located below the umbilicus on the vertical midline of the body and lined up directly below the Point of Stillness. These four acupuncture points comprise the Karmic Release Window Group.

## *Siman* Fourfold Fullness Window

Fig. 2.10-a

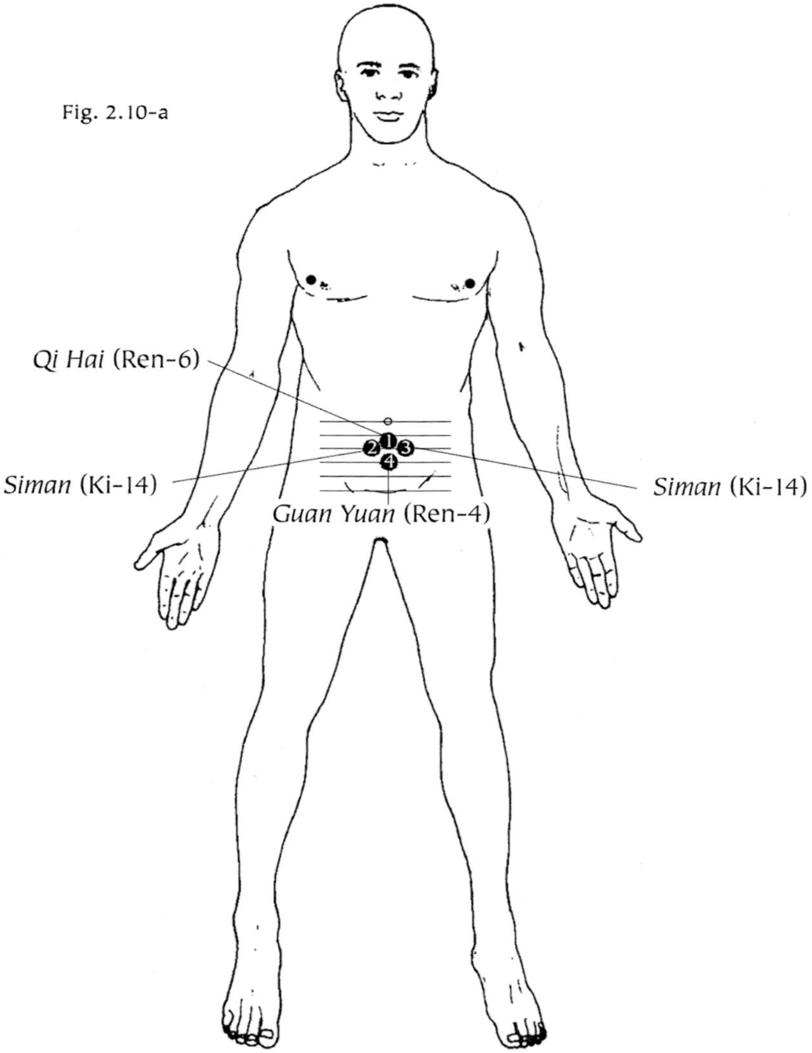

*Qi Hai* (Ren-6)

*Siman* (Ki-14)

*Siman* (Ki-14)

*Guan Yuan* (Ren-4)

The *Siman* Fourfold Fullness Window Group is located in the area sometimes called our Lower *Dan Tian* or our Lower Cinnabar Field. *Siman* (Ki-14) can be translated in to English as "Fourfold Fullness."

To correctly locate the four acupuncture sites of the *Siman* Fourfold Window Group, it is best to divide the vertical distance from the umbilicus to the upper border of the symphysis pubis (pubic bone) into five approximately equal parts by drawing imaginary horizontal lines. These five sections are considered one *cun* apart. (See figure 2.10-b below.)

### *Siman* Fourfold Fullness Window

Fig. 2.10-b

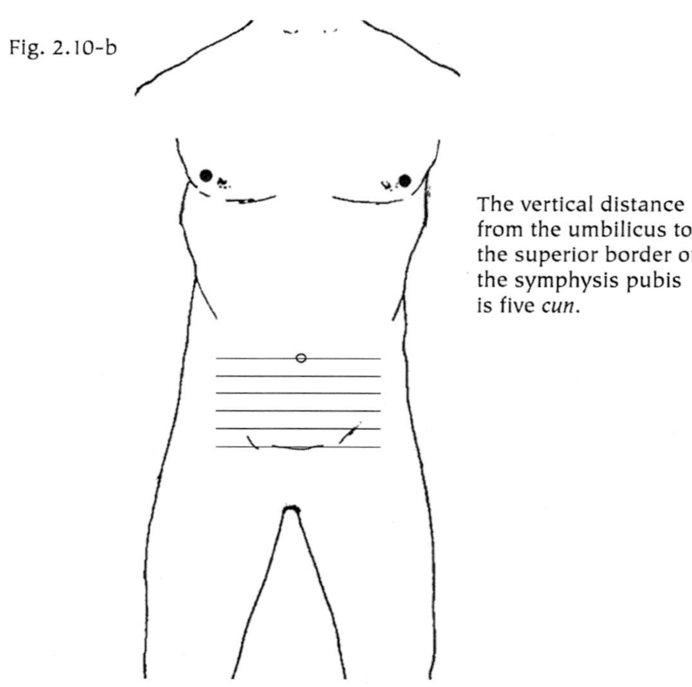

## Point Location for *Siman* Fourfold Fullness Window

The first acupuncture point needled in the *Siman* Fourfold Window Group is *Qi Hai* (Ren-6). *Qi Hai* is usually translated to mean "Sea of Qi." The translation of the name tells you how much power and importance the Chinese gave to this acupuncture point. *Qi Hai* (Ren-6) is located directly on the anterior vertical midline of the body approximately one and a half *cun* inferior to the umbilicus. (See figure 2.10-c.)

### *Siman* Fourfold Fullness Window

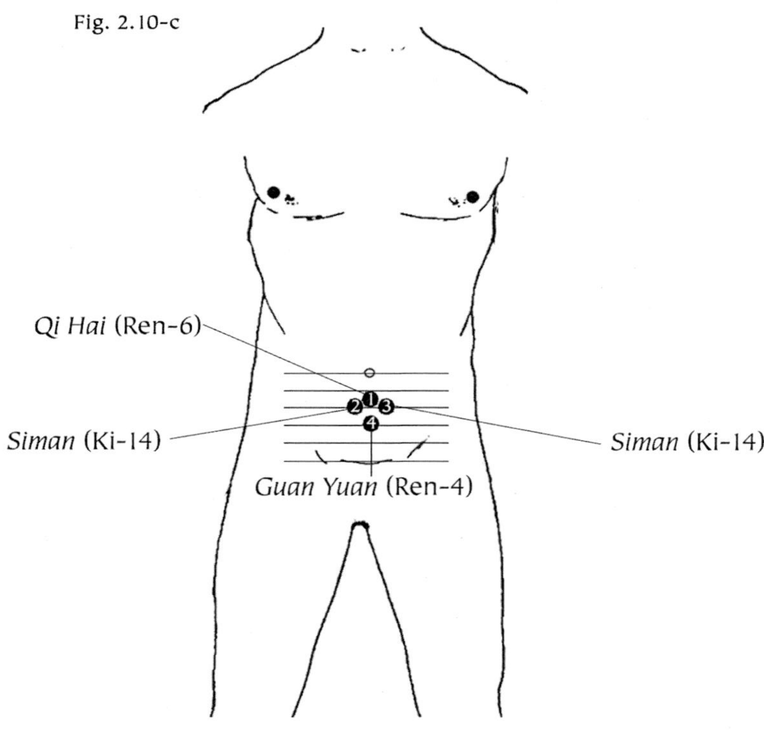

The next two acupuncture sites needled are the bilateral acupuncture points *Siman* (Ki-14). It is interesting to note that although these acupuncture point are rarely used in a clinical setting in the United States today, I feel they are very important gateways that can remove blockages within this lower *Dan Tian* region to allow one to move into higher realms of consciousness. The bilateral *Siman* (Ki-14) points will also strengthen the whole kidney meridian system.

For accessing and activating the qi in the *Siman* Fourfold Fullness Window Group, needle the *Siman* (Ki-14) point on the client's right side first, followed by the left side. *Siman* (Ki-14) is found approximately two *cun* inferior to the umbilicus and approximately one-half *cun* on either side of the imaginary anterior vertical midline. (***Grasping the Wind***[4] by Ellis, Wiseman and Boss states that *Siman* (Ki-14) is located one inch on either side of the anterior vertical midline. Both **A Manual of Acupuncture**[5] by Deadman and Al-Khafaji and ***Chinese Acupuncture and Moxibustion***[6] edited by *Cheng Xinnong* state that the bilateral *Siman* (Ki-14) points are one half *cun* from the anterior vertical midline of the body.)

The fourth and last acupuncture site needled in the *Siman* Fourfold Fullness Window is *Guan Yuan* (Ren-4). *Guan Yuan* is usually translated to mean "Original Pass" or "Original Gate" meaning that this point is the passageway for Original Qi. *Guan Yuan* (Ren-4) also activates our lower *Dan Tian* and is the anterior site of our Life Gate Fire.

The four acupuncture sites in the *Siman* Fourfold Fullness Window are located very close together so be very mindful when inserting the needles into the acupuncture sites. Needling the four sites of the *Siman* Fourfold Fullness Window will initiate the process to activate and release much inner qi to trigger consciousness expansion.

In Traditional Chinese Medicine, the Fourfold in the *Siman* name usually refers to the Fourfold physical nature of: 1) Blood; 2) Qi; 3) Food; and 4) Dampness. In Esoteric Acupuncture, we are not so interested in the physical aspects of the Fourfold nature. We are interested in the "Fullness" part of the Fourfold that refers to the esoteric "Fullness" of consciousness by the awakening of the lower to reach the higher.

The consciousness levels are divided into two parts each with four divisions. There is the Lower Quaternary of the Physical, Etheric, Astral and Mental Planes. The lower level connects with the Upper Quaternary consisting of the Buddhic, Atmic, Monadic and Logoic Planes. The two divisions are linked together through the Causal Plane. This is the esoteric meaning of "Fourfold Fullness." (See the chart below.) (For additional information about the Lower *Dan Tian* region, see Chapter III.)

**Esoteric Fourfold Fullness**
**Lower Quaternary Connects with The Upper Quaternary**

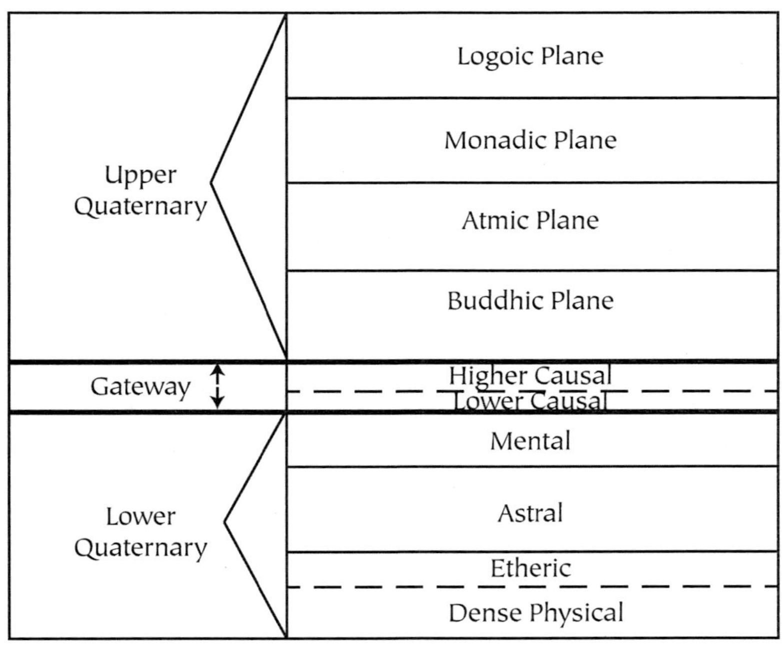

## Window Groups with Three Sites

### Jewel in the Lotus Window

Fig. 2.11

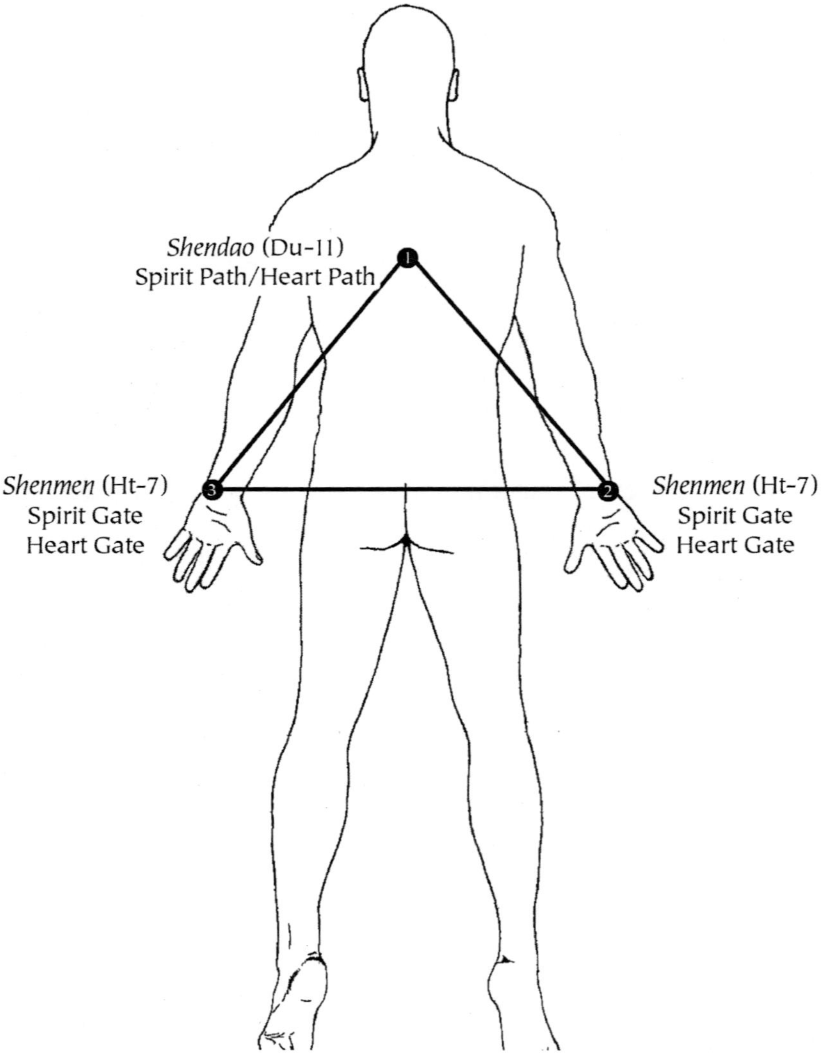

*Shendao* (Du-11)
Spirit Path/Heart Path

*Shenmen* (Ht-7)
Spirit Gate
Heart Gate

*Shenmen* (Ht-7)
Spirit Gate
Heart Gate

## Jewel in the Lotus Window

The concept of our Jewel in the Lotus was discussed in ***Esoteric Acupuncture: Gateway to Expanded Healing, Volume I*** and in ***Sea of Fire-Cosmic Fire: Esoteric Acupuncture, Volume IV***. The "Jewel" being discussed is a very fine, inner heart frequency of consciousness contained within the twelve closed petals of the Anahata Heart Chakra. Just because a person is nice, kind and an overall caring, gentle person, does not mean this inner Jewel will automatically reveal its contents and share its hidden wisdom. A person with those characteristics will probably have a few of the petals from one or perhaps two of the outermost groups of petals partially or fully opened. They will not have twelve petals fully opened.

If you are interested in opening the petals of your Anahata (Heart Chakra) to uncover the Jewel Within, you must do some form of inner plane work on yourself. You must learn how to Still your chaotic mind. It is best if a person is at least aware of the concept of the Jewel in the Lotus, then learn how to access its field. The Jewel in the Lotus Window will assist you in reaching that calm, quiet place sometimes called your Unified Field or your Higher, Inner, Spiritual Heart Center.

Figure 2.11 shows the figure with the palms facing upward. The palms represent the field of the heart. (The soles of the feet are controlled by the kidneys, the opposing, yet complimentary, force of the heart.) You must have your client place his or her palms upward in order to insert an acupuncture needle in the correct site.

The bilateral wrist points are called *Shenmen* in Chinese and Heart-7 (Ht-7) for English speaking practitioners. *Shenmen* is usually translated as either "Heart Gate" or "Spirit Gate." Remember spirit in Chinese Medicine refers to the heart system. There is one Heart Gate (Spirit Gate) point located on each wrist.

To locate the site of *Shenmen* (Ht-7), you will first locate the inner wrist crease that is the crease closest to the palms on each wrist. You will then feel for a slight depression that is toward the lateral side of the wrist (closer to the little finger). The location is found on the radial side of the tendon of the flexor carpi ulnaris muscle. Radial side means closer to the thumb. So although this acupuncture point is found toward the lateral side of the wrist crease closer to the little finger, the slight depression where *Shenmen* (Ht-7) is located will be next to the flexor carpi ulnaris tendon on the side closest to the thumb.

When acupuncturist needles are inserted into the sites of the bilateral *Shenmen* (Ht-7) points, the qi will flow through the acupuncture heart channel on the etheric level and eventually communicate with *Shendao* (Du-11) on the posterior of the body. By having your client make a visual connection between the bilateral *Shenmen* (Ht-7) points and bringing the qi upward from the bilateral points in a triangular formation to connect with the Heart Path at *Shendao* (Du-11), we are forming a grid on the Mental and Astral Planes that are of a finer frequency than the qi of the Etheric Plane where the acupuncture meridians flow. We are opening the qi of the two Heart Gates at the bilateral sites of *Shenmen* (Ht-7) and visually moving the energy on the Mental Plane to connect with the Heart Path at *Shendao* (Du-11), the Gateway to the Anahata (Heart Chakra). The visual connection means the movement of qi is not confined within the Etheric Plane of the acupuncture meridians.

The reason this triangular formation is called The Jewel in the Lotus Window Group is because of the special communication between the three acupuncture points. Although the field may look like any other triangular formation, the energies are being directed upward toward the central "Heart Path" or "Spirit Path." To reveal the mysteries of the Jewel in the Lotus, one must gently shower the heart with the correct frequencies to open the petals surrounding the Jewel. We have opened the Heart Gates and directed the energies to enter the Heart Path for the purpose of communicating with the Inner, Spiritual Higher Heart. With the proper dedicated inner plane work by the individual, the opportunity arises for the awakening of the Jewel in the Lotus.

## *Mingmen* Window

Fig. 2.12

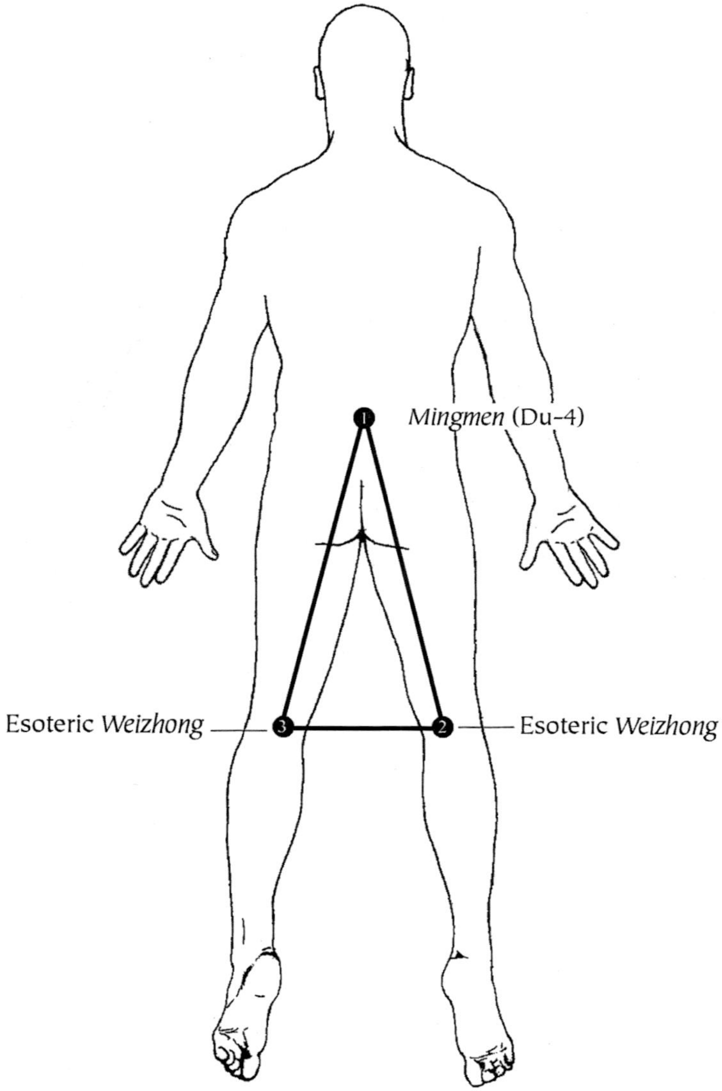

*Mingmen* (Du-4)

Esoteric *Weizhong*

Esoteric *Weizhong*

### *Mingmen (Du-4)*

The acupuncture site of *Mingmen* (*Du*-4) is known as "The Gate of Vitality" or "The Life Gate" and is a key acupuncture point for strengthening and tonifying the kidney qi of the physical body. This point is often used in traditional acupuncture treatments to rectify imbalances that are connected with the kidney system such as: lower back pain, irregularities with one's menstrual cycle, diarrhea, impotence and leucorrhea.

The Chinese have also stated that: "*The Gate of Vitality is the organ of Water and Fire, it is the residence of Yin and Yang, the Sea of Essence and it determines life and death.*"[7] Just by reading the description of the acupuncture point called *Mingmen* (Du-4), one is able to see the great importance the Chinese placed on the functions and energetics of the Gate of Vitality (Life Gate).

In the Chinese Five Element model, the heart is associated with the fire element of heat. But, the Chinese have also stated that the "*Gate of Vitality provides heat for all our bodily functions and for the Kidney-Essence itself.*"[8] The kidneys control water, as well as the *Mingmen* Fire, the Life Gate of the body. The fire controlled by the kidneys is not identical to the fire controlled by the heart. But, the fire from the *Mingmen* Fire of the kidney system gives us the physical life force and the willpower to move forward to initiate various tasks or goals we have. The qi created and stored at the posterior site of *Mingmen* (Du-4) is the "sister" site for the lower *Dan Tian* area in the anterior of the body below the umbilicus.

The *Mingmen* Fire of the kidneys and the acupuncture site known as both *Mingmen* and *Du*-4, along with the heart fire of *Shendao* (*Du*-11) are collectively known in Esoteric Acupuncture as our Lower Twin Flames Within. A more detailed description our Lower Twin Flames Within is given in ***Discern the Whisper: Esoteric Acupuncture, Volume II***, so no further depth of discussion will be included here.

One goal in an Esoteric Acupuncture treatment is to activate the qi at *Mingmen* (Du-4) to align and vibrate at a frequency that will blend and complement the frequency of a balanced, strong, harmonious *Shendao* (Du-11) field. In Esoteric Acupuncture, these two acupuncture sites are known as the gateways to accessing and activating our Lower Twin Flames Within. We all have two sets of Twin Flames Within, a lower set and a higher set. It is desirable to connect and harmonize our Lower Twin Flame Within before connecting and activating our Higher Twin Flame Within. One of the flames of the Higher Twin Flames Within resides in the Anahata (Heart Chakra) encapsulated within the twelve heart petals. The other flame of the Higher Twin Flame Within resides within the twelve petals of the Guru Chakra located directly below the Sahasrara (Crown Chakra).

In the Classics of Difficulties, Chapter 36 it states: "*The Gate of Vitality is the residence of the Mind and is related to the Original Qi.*" [9] This connection to the mind is another example of how the Chinese view the energetics of the kidneys, more specifically the *Zhi* of the kidney system, as another aspect of consciousness. More about the consciousness of the *Zhi* of the kidneys will be discussed in Chapter III of this book.

The bilateral Esoteric *Weizhong* points, one located in the posterior crease of each knee, are known as minor chakra locations. Do not confuse this acupuncture site with the traditional location of the traditional *Weizhong* (UB-40) points. The Esoteric *Weizhong* points are needled in the dimples on the posterior crease that are located medial to the traditional location of *Weizhong*. Have your client visually connect the bilateral Esoteric *Weizhong* points with the apex of the triangle at *Mingmen* (Du-4) located directly on the spine. Although all three points are water points directly connected to our Swadthisthana (Second Chakra), the upward pointing triangle that was made with the visual connection of the three acupuncture sites makes this connection an Esoteric *Shaoyin* connection. Again, we are balancing and strengthening our heart and kidney systems.

## Support The Mountain Window

Fig 2.13

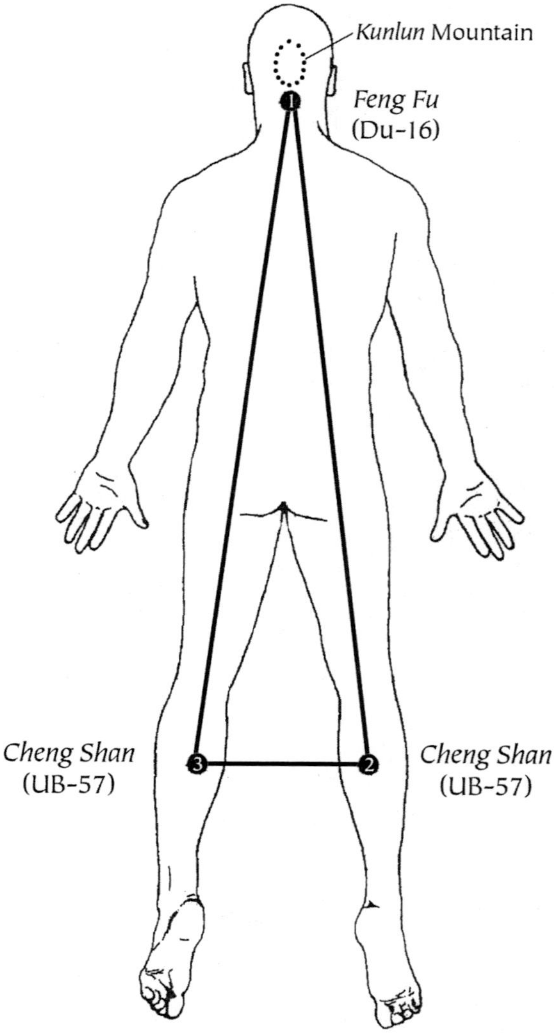

*Kunlun* Mountain

*Feng Fu*
(Du-16)

*Cheng Shan*
(UB-57)

*Cheng Shan*
(UB-57)

## Support the Mountain Window

When you have taken care of the lower energies of the Muladhara (Root Chakra), or at least they are not the main focus of your daily endeavors, you may choose to invest your energies on your true Inner Spiritual Journey. If you choose this path, you will now be able to shift and blend the lower energies with the energetics of the higher planes.

Inserting an acupuncture needle at the acupuncture site of *Feng Fu* (Du-16) activates the medulla oblongata of the brain. The medulla oblongata is connected to and influences the Muladhara (Root Chakra). This means that *Feng Fu* (Du-16) is also connected to the Muladhara (Root Chakra) and can be used to activate, tonify and align the energies of the Muladhara (Root Chakra). The information and energetics of Taluka Chakra (also known as the Alta Major Center, the Talu Chakra or the Lalana Chakra) is also activated when an acupuncture needle is inserted at the site of *Feng Fu* (Du-16).

There exists an Inner Sound that is also known as "Sound without Sound" that is stored at the site of the Taluka Chakra (Alta Major Center/Lalana Chakra/Talu Chakra). The Sound without Sound is the male or father aspect of an extremely fine vibration of consciousness that compliments the matching female or the mother frequency of "Light without Light" found at the Third Eye Center called the Ajna Center (*Yintang*).

When you make a mental triangular connection from the bilateral *Cheng Shan* (UB-57) points upward to meet at *Feng Fu* (*Du*-16) located in the depression inferior to the occipital protuberance on the back of the head/neck region, you are attempting to move the lower frequencies of the Muladhara (Root Chakra) into the higher frequencies of the Muladhara (Root Chakra). (See figure 2.13 on the opposite page.)

The two *Cheng Shan* (UB-57) acupuncture points will anchor and strengthen one's connection to the Muladhara (Root Chakra) and give energy to assist with our daily survival needs. Those two points will automatically activate stuck qi at the coccyx (tailbone). But, our intention and goal is to move the consciousness from the lower day-to-day energies of the Muladhara (Root Chakra) up into the finer frequencies of the head chakras. For this process to occur, it requires the Taluka Chakra (Alta Major Center/ Lalana Chakra/Talu Chakra) to be opened to allow energy to flow upward and can be accomplished by inserting an acupuncture needle into the acupuncture site of *Feng Fu* (Du-16).

One way to shift your focus from the realms of the lower consciousness planes to the higher consciousness planes is to work with the New Encoding Patterns. One of the more advanced techniques to awaken the higher head centers is to first mentally connect the qi at *Feng Fu* (Du-16) with the qi at the Ajna Center (*Yintang*). You will then visualize a triangular connection by bringing the energies from *Feng Fu* (Du-16) to the Ajna Center at *Yintang* and connect the energies from those two sites with the energy stored at the esoteric Du-20 site of *Tian Man*. This triangular visualization will initiate the building of one's Antahkarana, the "Rainbow Bridge" to our higher consciousness planes.

Using an acupuncture needle to activate *Feng Fu* (Du-16) will connect the etheric Du channel/meridian to the medulla oblongata of the brain. The inner Sound without Sound (Father) is located within a higher astral level of the medulla oblongata. By mentally connecting the qi stored at *Feng Fu* (Du-16) with the qi stored a *Yintang* (Ajna Center), you will be connecting the field of Sound without Sound to the field of Light without Light stored in the Ajna Center. For those who have done the proper amount of inner plane work, the planes of both the inner light and inner sound can be stimulated by needling *Feng Fu* (Du-16). For the Inner Sound without Sound and the Inner Light without Light to truly manifest, you must awaken the Ajna Center at *Yintang* by being Still. (The visualization connections for these head center points are shown in detail in Chapter V.)

## *Yuan Jian* Window Group

Fig. 2.14

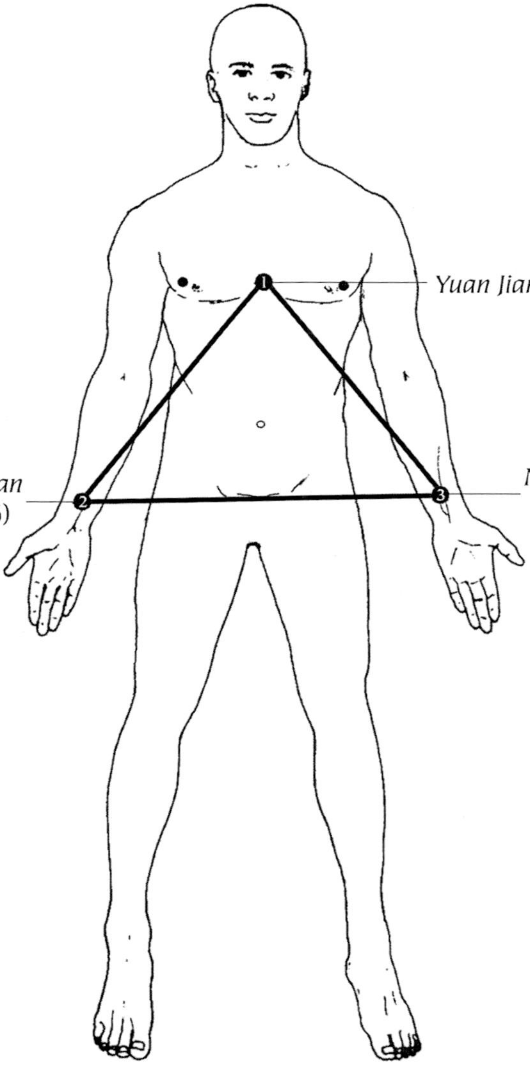

*Yuan Jian* (Ren-17)

*Nei Guan* (Per-6)

*Nei Guan* (Per-6)

## *Yuan Jian* Window Group

In Esoteric Acupuncture, the pericardium acupuncture meridian is used as a direct pathway to the Anahata (Heart Chakra). The *Yuan Jian* Window Group consists of three pericardium sites. The acupuncture site at *Yuan Jian* (Ren-17) is the direct anterior connection to the Anahata (Heart Chakra). In Esoteric Acupuncture, the Chinese name *Yuan Jian,* meaning "The Source," is used instead of the more commonly used Chinese name *Danzhong* meaning "Chest Center."

*Yuan Jian* is located on the anterior midline of the chest level with the fourth intercostal space. In younger males, *Yuan Jian* can be located by drawing an imaginary horizontal line that connects the two nipples. *Yuan Jian* (Ren-17) is located on the midline of the chest directly on this imaginary horizontal line. Locating *Yuan Jian* (Ren-17) by this method does not always hold true with women.

In Esoteric Acupuncture, *Yuan Jian* (Ren-17) is considered the "sister" point to the acupuncture point *Shendao* (Du-11) located on the posterior of the body directly on the spine below the spinous process of the fifth thoracic vertebra. These sister points are both direct gateways to the Anahata (Heart Chakra), one from the anterior and one from the posterior.

The bilateral acupuncture points located in the inner forearm are called *Nei Guan* (Per-6). *Nei Guan* is usually translated as "Inner Gate." Esoterically, this inner gate is the inner gateway to the Anahata (Heart Chakra). *Nei Guan* (Per-6) is found on the inside of the forearm approximately two *cun* from the transverse crease of the inner wrist. The acupuncture point is found between the tendons of the palmaris longus muscle and the tendon of the flexor radialis muscle. Sometimes there may be blood vessel directly between the two tendons at the site of *Nei Guan* (Per-6). In those cases merely use your non-needling hand and move the tendon to one side.

Visually connect the bilateral *Nei Guan* (Per-6) points and bring the energies upward from those two points to connect with

*Yuan Jian* (Ren-17) in the center. Again, a visual upward pointing Fire Triangle is formed, while simultaneously strengthening the Heart Qi. The strong overlaying of the Heart Qi on the Mental Plane reinforces the inner path to the Anahata (Heart Chakra).

## Window Group with Five Sites

### One Hand Clapping Window

Fig. 2.15-a

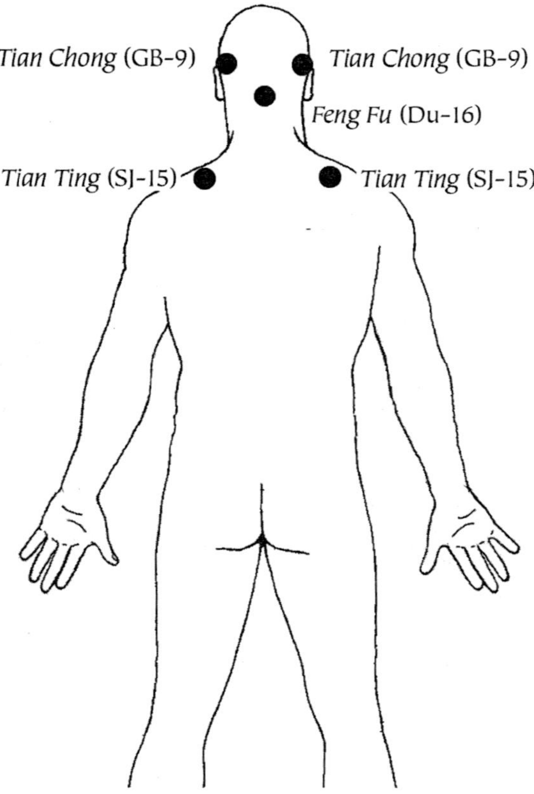

## One Hand Clapping Window

You will notice that the four outer acupuncture sites in the One Hand Clapping Window group consist of the bilateral *Tian Chong* (GB-9) points and the bilateral *Tian Ting* (SJ-15) points. In the Six Channel Theory of Chinese Medicine, the connection between the gallbladder channel and the *San Jiao* (Triple Burner) channel is known as a *Shaoyang* connection. In Esoteric Acupuncture, the interlinking of these specific bilateral pairs is known as an Upper *Shaoyang* Connection. These four acupuncture points connect a grid known as our "Celestial Hearing" grid.

If you learned the Chinese name of the acupuncture point known as SJ-15 in an acupuncture school in the United States, you most likely were taught the name *Tian Liao. Tian Liao* is often translated into English as "Celestial Bone Hole." In Esoteric Acupuncture, the acupuncture point SJ-15 is called *Tian Ting* and translated as "Celestial Hearing." We are interested in activating the Celestial Hearing aspect of our consciousness.

The *Tian Chong* (GB-9) points are gallbladder points. You may ask how can gallbladder points influence hearing, when physical hearing is controlled by the kidney system in Traditional Chinese Medicine? First of all, we must emphasize the difference between Celestial Hearing and normal three-dimensional hearing. Celestial Hearing is contained within the field of the Higher Heart System and controlled by this system. The concept of Celestial Hearing is not taught in any traditional acupuncture curriculum in the United States today. Although Celestial Hearing contains the fields of clairaudience and the various levels of clairaudient powers, Celestial Hearing also encompasses "hearing" realms above the clairaudient realms. What people think of as normal three-dimensional hearing is only one of the five "normal" senses. But, portions of humanity are now awakening and becoming aware to the fact that the old programs limiting humanity to only five senses is a constricting and controlling outdated program.

The esoteric meaning of the English translation of *Tian Chong* as "Celestial Hub" refers to the fact that celestial frequencies and extremely fine celestial matter gather at these bilateral acupuncture sites. Also, the proximity of the bilateral *Tian Chong* (GB-9) points to the physical outer ears implies closeness to the power of hearing.

The *Hun* of the liver of the wood element encompasses the gallbladder system that is also contained within the field of the wood element. Think of the various frequencies of *Hun* as fabrics of consciousness. (More is discussed about the *Hun* in Chapter III.) To understand how the bilateral *Tian Chong* (GB-9) points are part of the Celestial Hearing Field, you should know that at the state of heightened awareness the wood element, known as the general, "bows" to the Emperor of the heart system. This means that the fire element of the heart controls the wood element of the liver and gallbladder. If we think of *Shen* as consciousness, then we can surmise that the heart field controls the wood field.

It is important to remember that the Higher *Shen* of the heart field controls the power of Celestial Hearing. One of the New Encoding Patterns presented in Chapter V is called The *Hun* Follow the *Shen* Pattern. Our Original *Hun* is a tentacle from our Original *Shen* contained within our Monadic Ray. The celestial realms of consciousness are greatly influenced by the Higher *Shen* of the Higher Heart. Since the gallbladder system of the wood element follows the lead of an Awakened Inner Celestial *Shen*, these bilateral *Tian Chong* (GB-9) points are following and flowing into the lead of the Celestial Heart Field.

The bilateral *Tian Ting* (Sj-15) points are translated to mean "Celestial Hearing." The area around where the bilateral *Tian Ting* (Sj-15) points are located are often struck by a wooden stick for those Zen practitioners who are sitting in Zazen meditation. This striking of this area is to put the meditator back in his or her meditative state.

Those who have studied Traditional Chinese Medicine know that *sanjiao*, or the three burners, refer to three regions of the body. The upper *jiao*, or upper burner, consists of the heart and lungs. The fact that *Tian Ting* (SJ-15) is translated to mean "Celestial Hearing" tells us that this particular upper *jiao*, upper burner, point is a heart point. (See the Upper *Shaoyang* Gate hourglass connection of the bilateral *Tian Chong* (GB-9) points with the bilateral *Tian Ting* (SJ-15) points in figure2.15-b below.)

**One Hand Clapping Window**
**Upper *Shaoyang* Gate**

Fig. 2.15-b

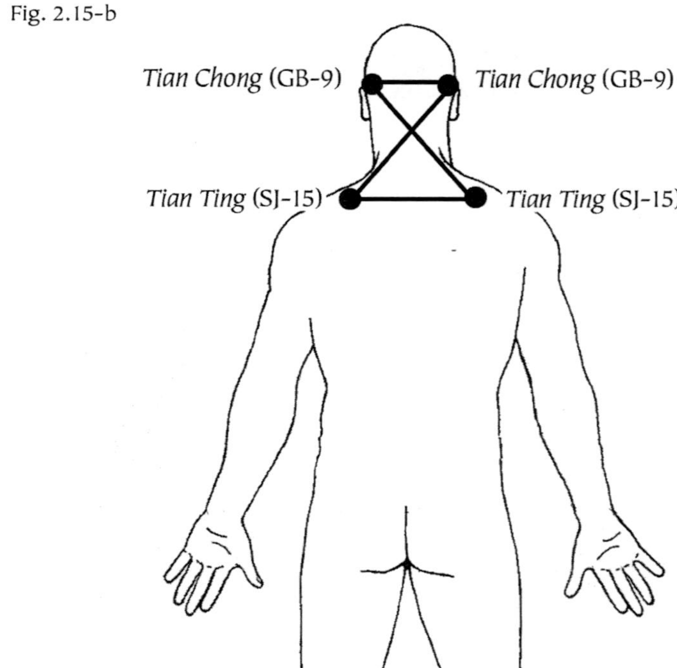


With the hourglass shaped polygon created by the Upper *Shaoyang* Gate connection, you will also notice a triangle with its apex pointing downward and a triangle with its apex pointing upward. The downward pointing triangle is a Water Triangle of the kidney system. The triangle with its apex pointing upward is a Fire Triangle of the heart system. The heart system with the kidney system creates an Esoteric *Shaoyin* connection. We now have both a *Shaoyang* and a *Shaoyin* field, with the *Shaoyin* field overlaid on top of the *Shaoyang* Field.

The fifth and last acupuncture site of the One Hand Clapping Window Group is *Feng Fu* (Du-16), the access site for the field of "Sound Without Sound." When the five sites are connected as shown in figure 2.15-c below, you notice a pyramid or one half of an octahedron.

**One Hand Clapping Window**
**Heart Field of Celestial Hearing**

Fig. 2.15-c

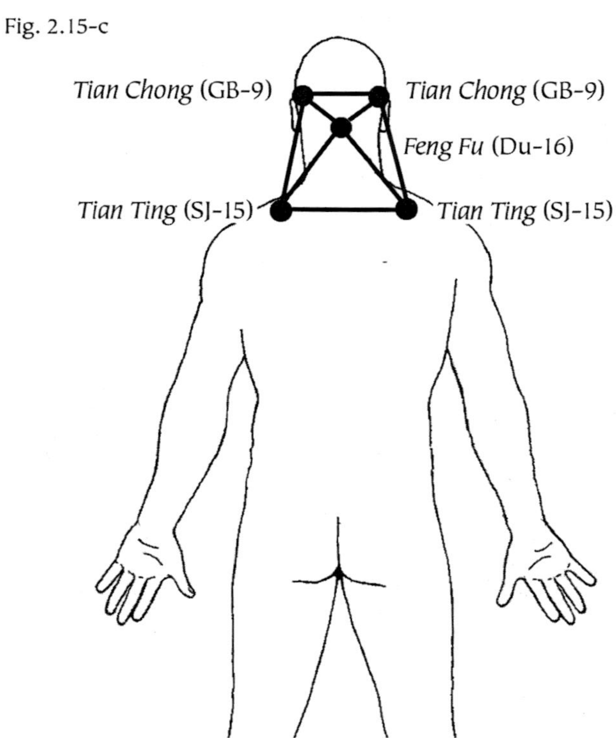

The One Hand Clapping Window Group is contained with the more complex New Encoding Pattern called The Esoteric *Shaoyin* Heart Window Pattern discussed in Chapter V. The Field of One Hand Clapping within the Esoteric *Shaoyin* Heart Window Pattern will allow the recipient of the treatment an opportunity to move into alignment with his or her frequency of Celestial Hearing of the Heart. This process is also dependent upon the amount of inner plane work done by the recipient of the Esoteric Acupuncture treatment. The Field of Celestial Hearing also includes levels of clairaudence. A clairaudient field allows the client to move into the higher field of clairsentience, that of "knowing things by heart." With continued dedicated inner plane work, you may reach the inner consciousness of your Higher Heart and unravel the mysteries of your Original *Shen* that contains the highest frequencies of consciousness connected to your heart system.

As mentioned earlier, these Window Groups of Esoteric Acupuncture offer a Window of Opportunity to delve into the Inner Spiritual Heart Realms.

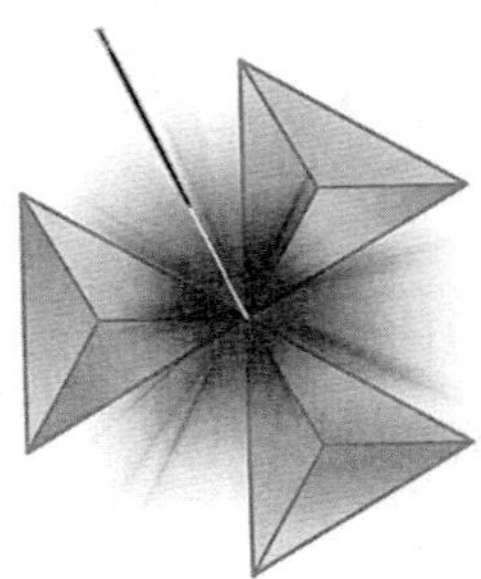

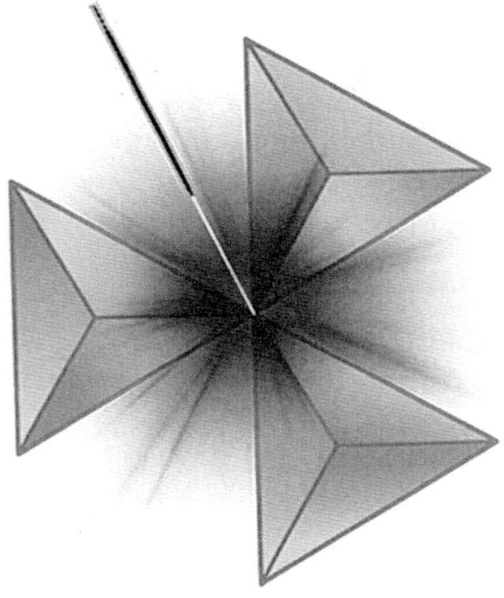

# Chapter III: Fabrics of Consciousness and Chinese Medicine

*The hun and the po are the yin and yang aspects of the shen.*[1]

Elisabeth Rochat de la Vallee

*"Moral and spiritual greatness is possible only for those who are above the competitive battle for existence."*[2]

Wallace Wattles

## Subtle Fields Within the Chinese Five Element System

It has been discussed many times how each individual element within the Five Element model of the Chinese system and the various properties and functional aspects contained in each of the five elements are intertwined and interdependent on each other. They all work together as a group within the larger system that helps to define an individual. One or more portions of this five element group may have more power or may require more attention, but the group as a whole, with this intricate, complex interweaving internet of energies, guides and shapes our daily lives. When the five elements and the systems within the elements are working in a harmonious manner within our energy fields, our lives will be more in tune and in harmony with nature and our Inner Spiritual Higher Heart Center.

When one or more of the systems start to function in a less than harmonious manner, eventually all the systems are influenced to some degree. We may then start to experience signs of mental, emotional or physical stress. The five elements in the Chinese system are: fire and the heart that control our *shen*; earth and the spleen that control our *Yi*; metal and the lungs that control our *Po*; water and the kidneys that control our *Zhi*; and wood and the liver that control our *Hun*. No single element or individual system operates fully independent from the other systems. Of the five elements within this theory, the fire element of the heart system is the ruler. The heart is considered the "emperor" and is supposed to rule over the other elements.

But the heart system of fire also requires energy and assistance from the other elements to "rule" or oversee in the most productive and beneficial manner. There is a push/pull energy field created by the interaction of the five elements upon each other. Each element can support and nourish the other systems, or can drain and possibly deplete qi from other the systems. No one system stands alone without interaction with the other elements. This is why it is so important to have all five systems working in a harmonious manner supporting and nourishing each other. It is advisable for each individual to understand his or her own path and how to best nourish and flourish that path. You must know what works best for you. The collective energetics of the five systems of the Five Element Theory will define who you are and how you choose to respect, pay attention or ignore what is best for your overall well being and expansion of consciousness.

Each of the five elements in the Traditional Chinese model has a corresponding color associated with that element. Three of the colors, green, red and yellow, are also colors associated with three of the chakras in the Hindu Chakra System. Just remember that the colors in the Chinese Five Element model denote abnormal physical, emotional or mental disorders. The colors associated with the Hindu Chakra System denote positive energy fields that will nourish and strengthen a particular chakra. (See figure 3.1 below.)

**Chinese Five Elements**

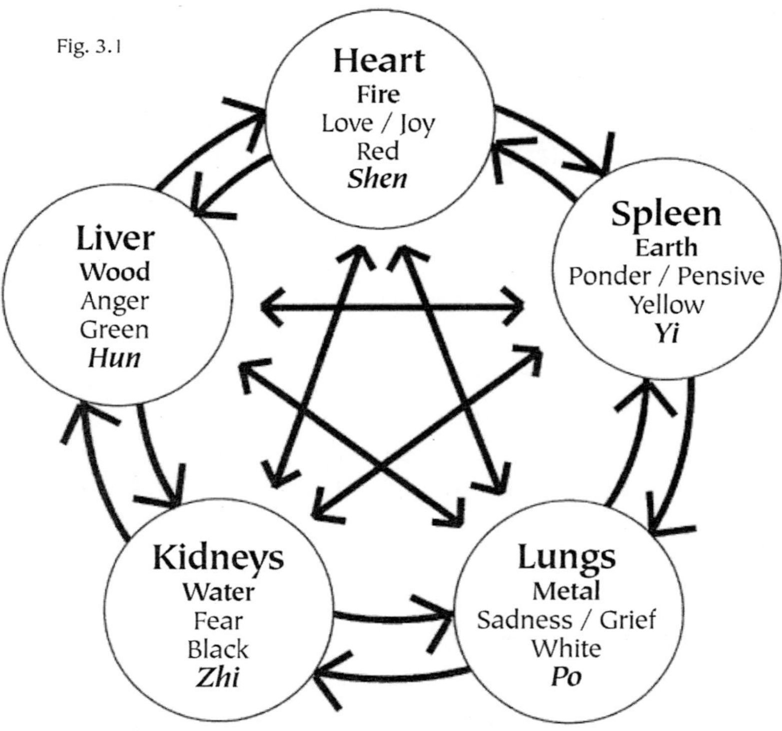


Within each of these five elements, there are physical, emotional and mental attributes connected to the various organs and the organ systems. There also exists the energetics of the specific meridians associated with specific organs. You will notice in the diagram of the wheel of the Chinese Five Element Theory that each of the five major organ systems in the Chinese medical model has corresponding Chinese names associated with each of the different five elements. The Chinese names within each of the Five Elements refer to some level of consciousness. This consciousness exists within smaller fields that are part of the larger field that contains our overall consciousness. In this chapter, these levels of consciousness connected to each of the five elements will be discussed in a slightly expanded format that was not available in the Age of Pisces.

In our three-dimensional world, and at the level of consciousness of humanity today, everything we know can be broken down into particles or waves. What came first, particles or waves? It is well known that waves came before particles. Think of waves as energy or qi. This means that energy existed before there existed what we call solid particles. Particles are in fact merely waves that have compactified to the point that we view this new compactified form of energy as particles. Pure consciousness is synonymous with waves.

Consciousness in an individual is not merely stored in the physical brain of the human being as some people may think. Consciousness does not need a specific physical location to exist. Consciousness is stored in every cell of the body, as well as the spaces between the cells and the space within the cells. Consciousness is not merely stored in the mind as taught in orthodox western thinking. Consciousness also exists outside of the dense physical vehicle. If over ninety percent of what we view as space is made up of waves and waves are synonymous with consciousness, then what we view as this vast nothingness we call space must contain consciousness.

Part of what we call consciousness is definitely stored in our physical brain. But in Chinese medical theory, it is stated that various other aspects of the mind are stored in the five major yin organs of the body. It was stated earlier that the five major yin organs of the body consist of: the liver, the heart, the spleen, the lungs and the kidneys. Just know that when the five elements are discussed, each element refers to much more than merely the name of the element. Wood of the liver system is not merely wood that you make into furniture. Fire of the heart system is not merely the type of fire that burns things or heats things. Earth of the spleen system is not merely soil and other things contained within the physical earth. Metal of the lung system is not merely metal that is used to make knives, pots and pans or engines. And water of the kidney system is not merely water that one drinks or uses to wash clothes..

This chapter will briefly discuss various aspects of our *Hun, Shen, Yi, Po* and *Zhi,* which are all fabrics of consciousness related to the five major yin organs. It is very important to understand that our *Hun, Shen, Yi, Po* and *Zhi* refer to energetic frequencies and that these wavelengths refer to various levels and densities of consciousness. Each of the five fabrics of consciousness connected with the Five Elements will be discussed starting with the *Shen* of the heart. More emphasis will be placed on the *Shen* of the heart and the *Hun* of the liver. Another way to view these five fabrics of consciousness is to think of them as fabrics of life force.

## *Shen*

*Shen* is a somewhat nebulous concept in Chinese Medicine and is connected to our heart and to our heart system of the fire element. *Shen* is loosely translated as spirit or mind. Those who have read about *shen* in Chinese medical texts may feel that the mind is only associated with the *shen* of the heart system and not with the other four yin organ systems. One confusing thought for those who only have a superficial understanding of Chinese medical philosophies, but do not understand the complexities and subtleties of Chinese medicine, may involve the idea that a certain aspect contained within each of the five element systems are actually a part of what we in the West know as the mind.

Rather than saying that various aspects of the mind are directly influenced by some factor stored in each of the five yin organs of the human body, it may be easier for the western trained practitioner to say that various aspects of consciousness are stored in the five major yin organs of the body. Think of consciousness rather than mind. What is stored in the mind is a portion of consciousness. But, consciousness is not limited to the cells of one's mind alone. It is the various aspects of consciousness that guide and directly influence the various brain centers of the mind. And various aspects of consciousness are controlled by the different five elements. It is very important to understand that the physical brain is not the sole residence of what we know as our mind.

Giovanni Maciocia states in his medical textbook ***The Practice of Chinese Medicine***:

> *"The word Shen is often translated as 'spirit' in Western acupuncture books and schools....I believe 'Mind' is a more accurate translation, while what we would call 'spirit' in the West is the complex of all five mental-spiritual aspects of a human being, i.e. Ethereal Soul (Hun), Corporeal Soul (Po), Intellect (Yi), Will-Power (Zhi) and the Mind (Shen) itself....Of all the organs, the Mind is most closely related to the Heart which is said to be the 'residence' of the Mind....The Heart controls all mental activities of the Mind."* [3]

There is another meaning to the word *Shen* that is frequently mentioned in relationship to diagnosing a patient in a clinical setting. In a medical context, Giovanni Maciocia states that the word *Shen* also indicates:

> *"an undefinable and subtle quality of 'life,' 'flourishing,' or 'glitter' which can be observed in health. This quality applies to the complexion, the eyes, the tongue and the pulse."*[4]

Ted J. Kaptchuk, O.M.D. states in his Chinese medical textbook ***The Web That Has No Weaver*** that:

> *"Shen is best described as spirit. It is an elusive concept, perhaps because, in the medical tradition, it is the Substance unique to human life....In a healthy person, Shen is the capacity of the mind to live life."*[5]

To summarize the idea of *Shen* in Chinese medical thought, the Chinese believe that *Shen* resides within the heart and is intimately connected to the heart and the heart system. Although *Shen* is most often translated to mean both the mind and spirit, I feel that *Shen* also includes the physical heart. When speaking of *Shen* within the context of Esoteric Acupuncture, *Shen* will include body, mind and spirit, or more correctly spirit, mind and body. Remember that *Shen* is merely an aspect of consciousness. But in this instance, the consciousness is a particular frequency that is closely associated with, and controlled by the heart system. When we refer to the heart in Chinese Medicine, we are referring of the totality of the physical, mental and spiritual aspects of the heart.

In Chinese medical thought, the mind does not only refer to the physical cells that make up the physical brain. If we think of *Shen* as a certain wavelength that is a part of consciousness, then it may be easier to understand what is being discussed within the framework of Esoteric Acupuncture.

The Chinese believe that the spirit connected to *Shen* is thought to reside in heaven and is connected to the heavenly realms. The frequency of *Shen* connected to the mind is of a denser quality than the *Shen* connected with our spirit.

Since the *Shen* that is connected to certain aspects of the mind is of a denser frequency than the *Shen* connected to spirit, it is said that the *Shen* of the mind is connected to more earthly matters, or at least connected to the realms of denser realities. In the context of treatments in Esoteric Acupuncture, we are interested in the various qualities of *Shen*, especially the various levels of a refined Inner *Shen*.

The broader concept of *shen* can be subdivided into two components comprising a yin and yang balance of opposing forces or qualities that are simultaneously complimentary forces or qualities to each other.

## *Shen Yin* and *Yang* Chart

| **Mind** | **Spirit** |
|---|---|
| *Yin* | *Yang* |
| Heavy | Light |
| Earthly | Heavenly |
| Feeling Aspects | Higher Intuition |
| Thinking | Knowing |

### The Monadic Ray and Original *Shen*

If we carefully study and understand the various levels of the planes of consciousness as we reach upward from the denseness of the Personality Plane into the finer density realms above the dense planes, we will eventually enter the level of our Monadic Plane, our Original Consciousness and our Original Encoding. Our Original Encoding at the Monadic Plane can be further subdivided into two extremely refined frequencies that are called our "Original *Shen*" and our "Original *Hun*." Both the Original *Shen* and the Original *Hun* are part of one's Original Encodings and are transported downward through a fabric of consciousness known as our Monadic Ray to the much denser three-dimensional physical vehicle on the Personality Plane.

At a certain stage, as the Original Encoding is being transported to a denser reality, the Original *Shen* becomes distinct from the Original Encoding. Sometime during this same densification process, the Original *Hun* splits from the Original *Shen*. This means that our Original *Hun* is "birthed" from our Original *Shen*. The Original *Hun* is a tentacle emanating from our Original *Shen*. This is the esoteric meaning of the "*Hun* follow the *Shen*." The *Hun* follow the *Shen* is also the name of an advanced New Encoding Pattern presented in Chapter V of this book. After the separation, the frequencies of the Original *Shen* and the Original *Hun* start to take on different vibratory rates. At the very initial stage of the separation of the fabric of consciousness of the Original *Hun* from the Original *Shen*, the information contained within both fabrics is still similar and very closely knitted together. As the frequencies of the Original *Shen* and the Original *Hun* move further downward through the Monadic Ray toward the denser Personality Plane, the fabrics of consciousness from the two frequencies separate even more. At the denseness level of the Personality Plane, much of the information in the two fabrics become more clearly defined with separate and distinct characteristics and properties, but are still intertwining, interdependent fabrics of consciousness.

Take note that the consciousness levels and the quality of information stored in both the Original *Shen* and the Original *Hun* are of a much finer frequency than the consciousness of either the *Shen* or the *Hun* talked about in Traditional Chinese Medicine and found on the denser Personality Plane. The Original *Shen* is the highest level of our Inner, Spiritual *Shen*. This is a level we are trying to activate and access with the more complex New Encoding Patterns of Esoteric Acupuncture.

Although the journey toward this level may not appeal to the masses, you are not a part of the masses and would not be reading this book unless your inner journey involved moving toward The Truth of your Inner Spiritual Higher Heart Center.

At the denser planes of existence, the *Shen* of the heart system is very distinct and separate from the *Hun* of the liver system. In the Chinese Five Element Theory, the *Hun* does not come from the *Shen* at this denser level. In fact, the Chinese Five Element Theory states the liver system of the wood element is the "mother" of the heart system of the fire element. The *Shen* of the heart system of the fire element in the Chinese Five Element Theory is not synonymous with the Inner Spiritual Higher *Shen* of our Original *Shen* as discussed in Esoteric Acupuncture. Although our denser *Shen* retains a fabric of consciousness of our Original *Shen*, the denser *Shen* comes from the Original *Shen* and not vice versa. The *Shen* of Traditional Chinese Medicine does not contain the fineness, the depth, the vastness or the expansiveness of the Esoteric, Ageless Wisdom contained within our Original *Shen*.

Our Original *Shen* eternally contains a "spark" or life force that is of a much more refined quality and a much finer frequency than the spark of life force of the *Mingmen* Fire of the kidneys. The life force contained within our Original *Shen* is part of our Original Encoding and returns to the Monadic Plane after the death of the physical vehicle to remain in a dormant state. Although this particular life force is in a dormant state, it still retains the vibrations or frequency of the "Original Spark of Life" to be transported into the next incarnation of a physical reality. The "Original Spark of Life," contained within our Original *Shen*, passes through and activates the lower life force within our *Mingmen* Fire on the dense physical plane at the moment the sperm and the egg from our biological parents unite. This begins the new life anchored in a physical vehicle.

The *Mingmen* Fire is contained within our Original *Zhi* of the kidney system. The acupuncture site of the acupuncture point known as Du-4 by English speaking practitioners is called

*Mingmen* by those who studied the Chinese name of acupuncture points. *Mingmen* is translated to mean "Life Gate" or "Gate of Vitality." The English translations of *Mingmen* showed how important this acupuncture point was to the ancient Chinese scholars who named this point. Although the life force and vitality of our *Mingmen* Fire are distinguished and dissolved on the Personality Plane at the time of the death of the physical vehicle, the *Zhi* on the Personality Plane de-compactifies into our *Original Zhi* and returns to the Soul Plane through our Monadic Ray. Just remember that although an individual does not carry the same *Mingmen* Fire in each new incarnation, the Original Spark of Life is the same for the same spirit no matter how many times the spirit inhabits a new physical vehicle.

From each monad on the Monadic Plane, there exists the possibility of twelve fabrics of consciousness forming. When the spark of life of the monad is ready to incarnate once again into a physical vehicle, the monad divides into subdivisions that descend to the Soul Plane. The largest number of subdivisions from any one monad is twelve. These twelve extensions from the same monad are called Soul Sparks or Monadic Extensions. Each of the twelve Soul Sparks/Monadic Extensions, now on the Soul Plane Level, has the potential to produce an additional twelve fabrics known as soul extensions that will descend into the Personality Plane.

Each of the Soul Sparks also carries a packet of information known as the Original Encoding. Since the Original Encoding is descending into a denser form as it is being transported by one's Monadic Ray, the Original Encoding starts to gather different information that will eventually be used to shape the personality and characteristics of an individual on the Personality Plane. (The Original Consciousness is the same for each of the twelve Soul Sparks that come from the same monad.)

The next separation is that each of the twelve sparks of consciousness on the Soul Plane has the possibility of subdividing into twelve different souls who will incarnate in the denser reality on the Personality Plane. If all twelve Soul Sparks form twelve extensions on the Personality Plane in a relatively similar timespan, this will create one hundred and forty-four separate people who have incarnated.

To find your Esoteric Soul Mate means that if you are one of the one hundred forty-four people living in the Personality Plane of physical reality, then there are one hundred and forty-three possible choices who could become your Esoteric Soul Mate. (See figure 3.2-a below.)

**Esoteric Soul Mate**

Fig. 3.2-a

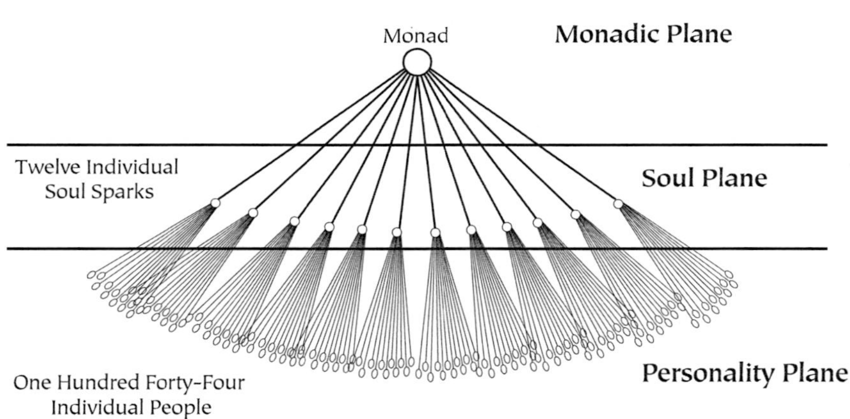


Since each of the twelve different sparks of life on the Soul Plane come from the same monad and share the same Original Consciousness, there will be some very basic, fundamental similarities in each of those twelve individual Soul Sparks. There will also be many different and varied qualities that each of you have because of other factors such as: bloodline and ancestral lineage, the location of your reincarnation and other factors.

Your Esoteric Soul Mate is different from your Esoteric Twin Flame Without. Your Esoteric Twin Flame Without has to come from the same Monad and also from the same Soul Spark on the Soul Plane. This means there are only twelve possible personalities that can extend to this denser reality from the same Soul Spark. If you are one of the people on the Personality Plane from a particular Soul Spark, then there are only eleven possible choices on the Personality Plane that could be your Esoteric Twin Flame Without. Your possibilities now become much more limiting than with your Soul Mate. (See figure 3.2-b below.)

## Esoteric Twin Flame Without

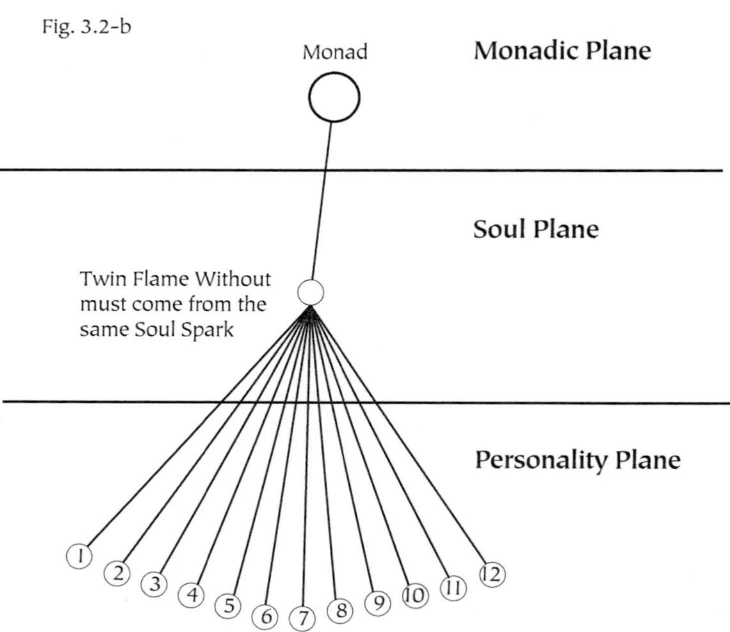


Fig. 3.2-b

In the rare instance that you find your Esoteric Twin Flame Without in this lifetime and both of you have done the proper inner plane work, you will instantly recognize each other. You will acknowledge the inner connectedness between the both of you without having to verbally share anything. You will identify and instantly recognize the connection by the knowing aspect of your hearts. Sharing the same Original Consciousness means that your puzzles pieces and other inner thoughts, inner ideas and goals in life will be very similar and very, very close. Although there may some similarities on the external realms, the close similarities and stronger ties will exist in the inner worlds.

You will not find your Esoteric Twin Flame Without by comparing notes on an internet dating service. Having many external similarities and liking the same foods, movies and enjoying the same physical sights and physical exercises could signal (but not necessarily) a Soul Mate connection, rather than an Esoteric Twin Flame Without connection. After the external similarities become uninteresting, unexciting and uninspiring, what happens to the supposed Soul Mate connection? Without the inner realm connections, the excitement and pleasures of the external world often do not have the power to sustain a meaningful, long-lasting relationship where both partners are spiritually advancing together.

If you happen to find your Esoteric Twin Flame Without in this lifetime, it will be a synchronistic event, not a planned, scheme by plotting out a game plan. Esoteric Twin Flames Without will also know things on the Monadic Plane level that are not necessarily readily identifiable on the Soul Plane Level or the Personality Plane.

Our Original *Shen* and our Original *Hun* are always with us throughout time and in each incarnation. Unless we are aware of this concept and are engaging in some sort of inner plane work to quiet and eventually still the chaotic, monkey-mind of our concrete mind of the left-brain, we will not just organically access these extremely high, inner levels of consciousness. Just because we are getting older and generating more life experiences does not mean that we will eventually reach these higher levels. If reaching and staying on these higher levels of consciousness are desirable goals, then the safest and recommended method is to be diligent with your inner plane work. Depending on one's tier density level of consciousness, regular acupuncture treatments with the proper New Encoding Pattern will align the recipient of the treatment with his or her spiritual center. The power of each Esoteric Acupuncture treatment and the resultant benefits are dependent on the consciousness level of both the practitioner and the person receiving the treatment.

The discipline and dedication required to reach these higher, inner plane levels may not appeal to the majority of people who are only interested in the activities of the lower three-dimensional world. Our Original *Shen* and Original *Hun* hold many of the keys to our puzzle piece in life. Tapping into both our Original *Shen* and our Original *Hun,* by way of our individual inner plane work, will help to unravel and unlock more doors of consciousness to allow us an opportunity to reach those expanded, higher realms of reality. The Original *Shen* and Original *Hun* have their genesis on the Monadic Plane. Tapping into one's higher self or communicating with one's Spirit Guides will usually only allow the person access to the Soul Plane Level.

According to the teachings of Esoteric Acupuncture, the inner plane work and the experiences on this individual pathway for the purpose of reaching the higher, inner realms are known as our Soul Journey. It is through our individual Soul Journey that we may experience a glimpse of returning home to our Inner Heart Center. This glimpse will occur while a person is still in the physical vehicle. A person's Soul Journey is also a "solo" journey. Although your partner may support and assist you (and vice versa) on your inner plane work and your journey, unless your partner is your Esoteric Twin Flame Without, your true inner journey will be a solo journey. Your true Soul Journey will not be an identical journey with another individual. There is a very specific requirement that is necessary before you can call an incarnated physical being your Esoteric Twin Flame Without. Remember that your Esoteric Twin Flame Without has to be the identical spirit that comes from the same monad extending downward to the same Soul Spark (Soul Extension) on the Soul Plane and further descending to the Personality Plane. If you are one of the twelve Personality Plane extensions from the same soul extension, then there are only eleven possible Esoteric Twin Flames Without available to you

Dedication and discipline to follow what is required on your individualized Soul Journey will eventually lead you to your Spirit Journey. The Spirit Journey is the higher aspect of one's Soul Journey. When someone is on his or her Spirit Journey, he or she will be vibrating with the frequencies of Tier Density Level V. (See Chapter V for details about the five Tiers of Density.)

With each different incarnation, we have encodings or fabrics of consciousness that shape various aspects of our character and influence our interests and personality later on in life. These Personality Plane Encodings are developed at the very beginning of each new journey in the newly formed physical vehicle, thus marking and shaping a new physical reality for that individual. The country where we are born, our particular ethnic group, the year we are born, the qi, *shen* and other qualities from our biological parents all factor into one's Personality Plane Encodings.

Remember this encoding gathered and developed on the Personality Plane is not our Original Encoding. Our Personality Plane Encodings are developed during the first years of our lives (including when we are in the womb) and most are set in place by the time we grow our permanent teeth (around age seven). Although these Personality Plane Encodings may remain with us for the duration of our physical existence, we are able to alter or release those undesirable encodings at the level of the Personality Plane. This requires an awareness of these traits and inner plane work to make the changes.

We carry a certain Original Consciousness and a certain Original Encoding that stays with us in each and every incarnation. These original encodings cannot be erased or released just because we wish to make alterations to the Original Encodings. Since most people remain unconscious and do not have a clue to the concept of one's Original Consciousness, there is generally no wish to become awakened to The All Field. The All Field is a term used in Esoteric Acupuncture that includes every level of consciousness in every dimension and no dimensions, throughout time and timelessness, throughout all the multiverses to the levels beyond the tiniest superstring to realities not presently comprehensible for the most advanced human minds of today.

If you are at the level of consciousness to understand some aspects of your Original Consciousness and Original Encodings, you will not only accept these facts, but you will embrace these revelations. We retain, sustain and transport this Original Consciousness through our Monadic Ray. This does not mean that everyone is able to access his or her personal Original Consciousness. Our Original Consciousness retains the clear vibrations that contain our puzzle piece in life, the true reason why we chose to reincarnate in this lifetime.

Our Original Consciousness encompasses much more than the Original Encodings associated with our many lifetimes on planet Earth. Do not confuse the Original Encodings, that are contained within the Original Consciousness, with the Personality Plane Encodings developed at the time of conception of the individual and the encodings developed through our acquaintances, our physical experiences and other outside influences during the first seven years of our life. Unless one develops and maintains a disciplined inner spiritual practice, the encodings that people may be consciously aware of are those encodings developed in our consciousness (and subconscious mind) during the first seven years of growth in the dense physical vehicle.

The Original Consciousness and Original Encoding do not include our Ancestral Qi or our Original *Jing* (essence). The fabrics of consciousness of one's Ancestral Qi and Original

*Jing* are gathered and "sprouted" on the Soul Plane and carried along the Monadic Ray as this ray extends further downward into the dense Personality Plane. One's Ancestral QI depends upon the family bloodline you incarnated into this particular lifetime and is dictated by your biological parents. You do not always reincarnate into the same family bloodline. One's Original *Jing* (essence) is contributed through the qualities and consciousness of both the sperm from your biological father and the egg of your biological mother.

Upon the death of one's physical vehicle, the Ancestral Qi and Original *Jing* (essence) return to the Soul Plane and dissolve. The Original Consciousness and Original Encoding remain with the non-physical spirit and return to the Monadic Plane. Both the Original *Shen* and the Original *Hun* are part of one's Original Encoding. When the spirit is ready to reincarnate into a denser, three-dimensional reality once again, the consciousness of both our Original *Shen* and Original *Hun* return to the physical vehicle through our Monadic Ray. Although the vitality, energetics and power of the Original *Shen* and the Original *Hun* start to gather momentum before the actual uniting of the sperm and the egg, at the very moment of the conception of the newly incarnated soul, the Monadic Ray at the Monadic Plane extends downward, through the Soul Plane and into the consciousness of the newly formed fetus.

Think of the Monadic Ray as a fabric of consciousness that holds and transports the Original Encodings of each and every individual from the Monadic Plane down through the Soul Plane to the newly incarnated individual. When the individual spirit no longer requires the use of a physical vehicle, certain consciousness reverts back to the Soul Plane or to the Monadic Plane. Like the different fingerprints on the fingers of a hand, or the information stored in the uniqueness of everyone's eye, each individual has his or her own Monadic Ray that retains one's individual Original Encodings and other information that makes each of us unique from everyone else. (See the Monadic Ray Connection Chart on the following page.)

## Monadic Ray Connections

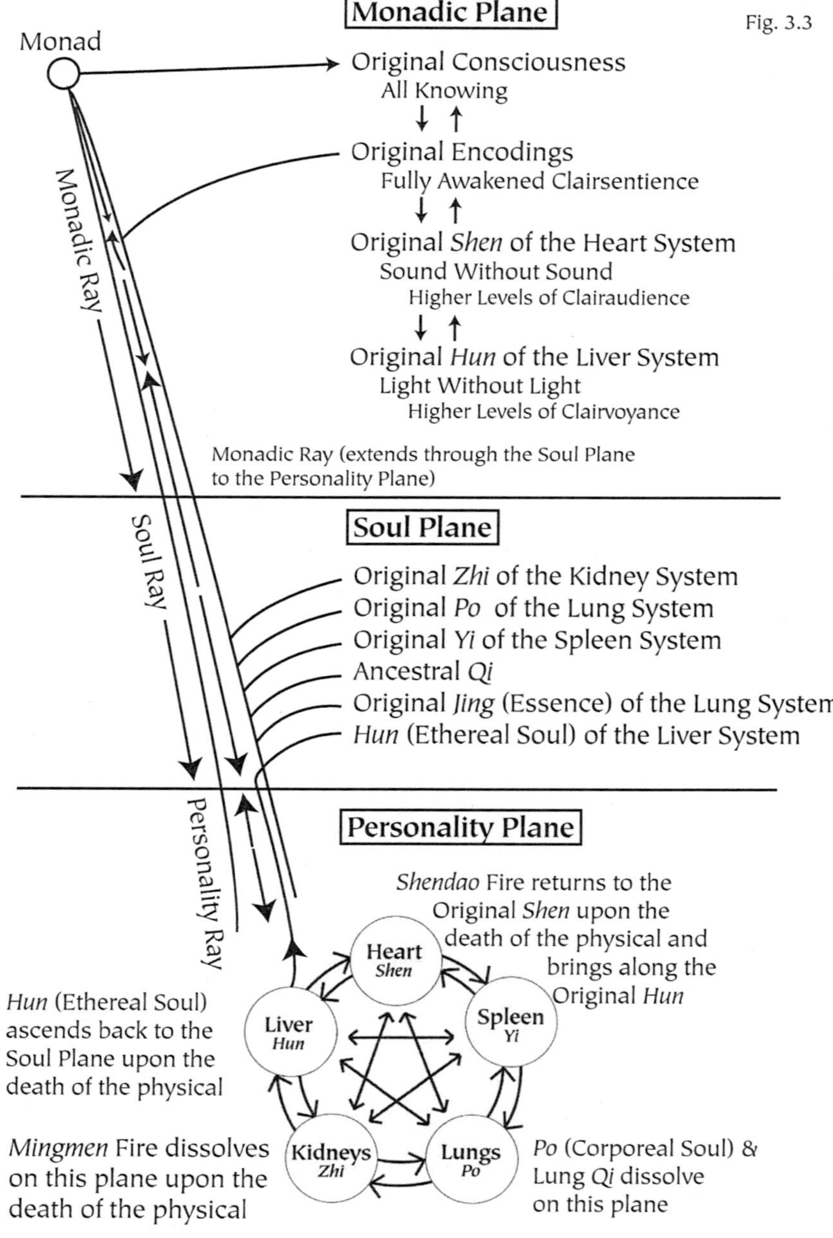

## Planes of Consciousness Within A Three Plane Model

|  |  |
|---|---|
| **Monadic Plane** | Logoic |
| | |
| | Monadic |
| | |
| | |
| | |
| | |
| **Soul Plane** | Atmic |
| | |
| | |
| | Buddhic |
| | |
| | |
| | Upper Causal |
| **Personality Plane** | Lower Causal |
| | Mental |
| | |
| | Astral |
| | |
| | Etheric |
| | Physical |

The chart on the preceding page lists the planes of consciousness divided into a Three Plane Model. There are seven planes of consciousness in a more expanded model. The seven planes of consciousness are listed to the right side of the chart to give the reader an idea how the Monadic Ray Connections fit into A Three Plane Model of human consciousness.

Although figure 3.3 on the page 199 shows the Monadic Ray as a linear projection from the monad on the Monadic Plane down through the Soul Plane and into the Personality Plane, the Monadic Ray is not really a linear projectile. The connection from the Monadic Plane to the dense Personality Plane is an instantaneous connection. I felt that drawing the Monadic Ray in a linear manner would help the reader to more easily visualize and understand the esoteric teaching that are being presented here about one's Monadic Ray.

You will also notice that the Original *Zhi* of the kidneys, the Original *Jing* of the lung system, the Original *Yi* of the spleen system and that part of the *Hun* that is connected to the Ethereal Soul all return to the Soul Plane upon the death of the physical vehicle. The Corporeal Soul usually dissolves upon the death of the physical vehicle and remains in the Personality Plane.

The New Encoding Patterns within Esoteric Acupuncture (specifically the higher tiered New Encoding Patterns) are designed to bring the recipient of a treatment back into alignment with his or her Inner, Spiritual Heart Center. This process will allow the client to enter a quiet, very tranquil frequency that creates an opportunity to open certain consciousness gateways. These gateways open into pathways of consciousness that allow the recipient of the treatment an opportunity to remember why he or she decided to reincarnate in a physical vehicle this time around. This process will then assist the client to enter the path of the journey of his or her puzzle piece in life. That choice is up to each individual.

There are other rays that descend into the Personality Plane to influence and shape a person's characteristics and qualities of expression. When an individual spark is ready to further descend into the Personality Plane and gather density along this journey, the Soul Ray on the Soul Plane will descend through one soul extension and activate the Ancestral Qi, the Original *Jing*, the *Mingmen* Fire, the Original *Zhi* of the kidney system, the Original *Po* of the lung system, the Original *Yi* of the spleen system and transport these fabrics of consciousness downward through the Soul Ray to eventually enter into a physical vehicle on the Personality Plane

Our Original *Shen* and our Original *Hun* are with us at the very beginning, even before the moment when the sperm and the egg first unite to spark the birthing of one's current physical vehicle. Each individual has his or her unique Original *Shen* and Original *Hun*. Some of the qualities and attributes within our Original *Shen* and Original *Hun* may seem to be broad, but nonetheless, everyone has his or her own unique Original *Shen* and Original *Hun*.

We have various qualities of consciousness within our *Shen*. We have both the thinking aspect and the feelings aspect. The feelings aspects are denser vibrations within our *Shen*. The "knowing" aspect and the Love/Wisdom frequencies are much finer vibrations of our Higher, Inner, Spiritual Heart. The knowing aspect of *Shen* is also known in theosophical philosophy as the field of Love/Wisdom. We may not be able to consciously access the information contained within our Monadic Ray (our Original Consciousness plus our Original *Shen* and our Original *Hun*), but nonetheless, each of us has our own individual Monadic Ray.. It requires aligning with the frequencies of both the Original *Shen* and the Original *Hun* to be able to access the Akashic Records. Then it requires the *Shen* of the heart system to be able to remember our past lives. The part of the *Yi* of the spleen that is responsible for the ability to recall things stored in one's mind dissolves at the Soul Plane. Although we may recall some past life information from the Soul Plane Level, it is the memory portion of the consciousness contained within the Original *Shen* that allows one the clearest pathway of recalling past life events.

## *Shen* Disturbance

A diagnosis of *Shen* Disturbance in Tradition Chinese Medicine often refers to some type of mental disorder or mental disharmony. Other typical symptoms of shen disturbance may include: insomnia, dream disturbed sleep, restlessness, anxiety, constant excessive mental chatter, hyperactivity, the inability to concentrate, incoherence and being startled very easily.

According to Dr. Joseph *Changqing Yang* in his book entitled ***Shen Disturbance, A Guideline for Psychiatry In Traditional Chinese Medicine***, he breaks down various types of *Shen* Disturbance Disorders into more distinct categories. Dr. *Yang's* categories include:

*Shen* Lassitude
*Shen* Insufficiency
*Shen* Tiredness (Weakness)
*Shen* Irritable
*Shen* Clouded
*Shen* Confused
*Shen* Inflexibility
*Shen* Numbness
*Shen* Oversensitivity
*Shen* Loss[6]

For those of you who are studying Traditional Chinese Medicine or are interested in the thinking behind *Shen* Disturbance Disorders from a Traditional Chinese Medicinal perspective, I would highly recommend that you purchase Dr. *Yang's* book. Dr. *Yang's* book is a thoroughly researched presentation on mental disharmonies from a more traditional Chinese perspective and covers the topic in a more complete format than you will receive in acupuncture school.

Esoteric Acupuncture is not concerned with the traditional concepts of *Shen* Disturbance Disorders. We are interested in awakening and expanding the various consciousness levels of our inner *Shen*. We are interested in the spiritual aspect of the heart and want to awaken both the Inner, Spiritual *Shen* and the knowing aspect of *Shen*. There are two interpretations of the phrase "I know it by heart." The exoteric meaning of "I know it by heart" refers to the fact that someone knows something by repetitive rote memorization. "I have done this task so many times that I know it by heart." The esoteric meaning of "I know it by heart" refers to the fact that a person knows something, but not because he or she has read, heard or been told that bit of information. They just know it by heart. This knowingness comes from within, not from without. Book learning or hearsay information is not a part of this knowingness of the heart. You must trust your own higher heart field. This is the beginning stage of clairsentience connected to our Original *Shen*.

There are five levels of consciousness called Tiers of Density in Esoteric Acupuncture that are listed below that will give the practitioner a guideline has how to select various New Encoding Patterns based on the client's consciousness level. Tier Density Level I is the densest tier. Tier Density Level V is the highest vibrating tier. The criteria for the density levels are based upon the level of awakening of one's Inner *Shen*. The Tiers of Density are discussed in Chapter Five.

Tier Density Level I: Our Inner *Shen* Asleep
Tier Density Level II: Arousal of Our Inner *Shen*
Tier Density Level III: Awakening of Our Inner *Shen*
Tier Density Level IV: Refining Our Awakened Inner *Shen*
Tier Density Level V: Our Supreme Balanced Inner *Shen*

The consciousness and frequencies of the heart and the *Shen* can be viewed within two triangles each with three separate, but connected, levels of density moving from the heaviest densities to the lightest densities of Right Heartedness and the Awakened Inner *Shen*. (See figure 3.4-a and figure 3.4-b on the next page.)

## Heart Triangle

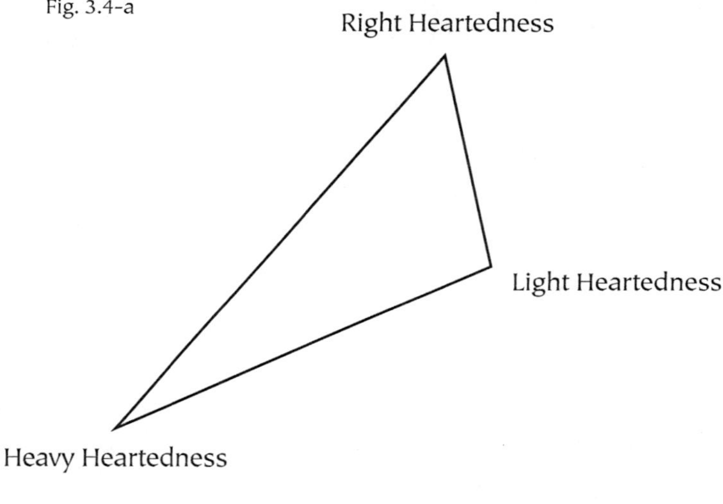

## *Shen* Triangle

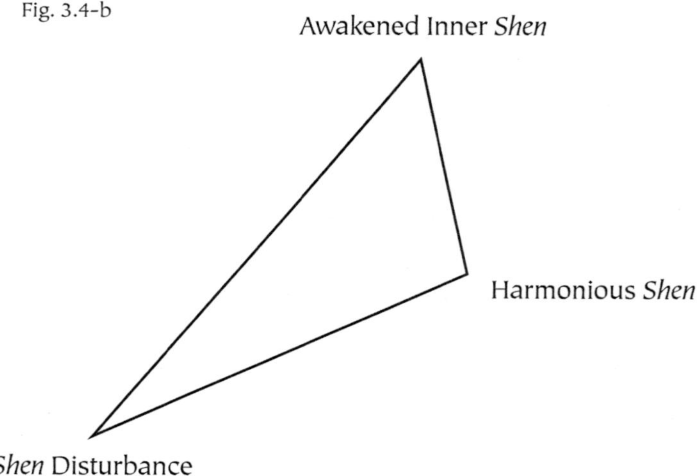

### *Hun*

The various aspects of consciousness of the *Hun* are connected to the liver and the liver system of the wood element in the Chinese Five Element Theory. It is important to understand what the Chinese mean when they discuss wood in a medical setting.

> *"Wood as a material is not wood as an element. Wood as a material is wood to make chairs and tables. Wood as an element is a kind of vibration."*[7]

Think of the phrase "a kind of vibration" to mean various fabrics of consciousness. Likewise, when discussing specific aspects of the other four elements such as: the *Shen* of fire, the *Yi* of earth, the *Po* of metal and the *Zhi* of water, think of those aspects associated with their respective elements as different fabrics of consciousness.

"*The Hun and the Po are the yang and yin expressions of the Shen.*"[8] The *Hun* of the liver system is considered the yang aspect. The *Po* of the lung system is the yin aspect. This particular division of the *Shen* into what the Chinese say are the yin and yang aspects of *Shen* is different than the chart shown previously under the *Shen* section. There are multiple ways to subdivide concepts. The concepts shown on the Yin and Yang *Shen* Chart on page 188 are not taught anywhere except through the Esoteric Acupuncture teachings.

The reason for placing the *Po* within the yin aspect of the *Shen* is because the *Po* is so closely linked with the Chinese aspect of *jing* translated to mean essence. (This is discussed later under the section on *Po*.) Both the *Hun* and the *Po* are connected to spirits, but the Chinese say they are spirits of the earth, not of the heavens like *Shen*. The *Hun* and the *Po,* with their relationship to yang and yin respectively, are merely aspects of the multitude of dualities in life.

Do not get confused by the Chinese saying that the spirit of the *Hun* is of the earth and not the heavens like *Shen*. The Traditional Chinese thinking did not and does not include the concept of Original *Hun*. Our Original *Hun* is contained within the denser fabrics of the *Hun*, but is of a much higher, finer distinct frequency than the Hun discussed in Traditional Chinese Medicine. Although the denser and finer fabrics of our *Hun* intertwine and interconnect, they are separate fabrics of the *Hun* and originate in different consciousness planes. Just remember that at the moment of the death of our physical vehicle when the spirit exists the body, both the Original *Hun* and the Original *Shen* return back to the level of the Monadic Plane in the higher spiritual realms.

Some of the ancient Chinese scholars have stated there are three different *Hun*. According to Claude Larre in his book ***The Liver***, it is stated:

> *"Since the Han Dynasty there have always been three hun....There is unity in the hun, but it is a unity of heaven, earth and man. For example in the texts of internal alchemy the three hun are placed in the three fields in the head at the level of the brain, in the chest and just below the umbilicus, and the liver has a special relationship with each of these areas."*[9]

According to the internal alchemy school of Chinese thought, the three Cinnabar Fields are located on the anterior vertical midline of the body at three specific locations. Some people feel that the lower Cinnabar Field is located approximately one and a half *cun* below the umbilicus at the location of the acupuncture point *Qihai* (Ren-6). In Traditional Chinese Medicine, the measurement of one *cun* is approximately the equivalent of one inch, but will vary depending on the individual and will even vary within the same individual depending on the location of the measurement on the body. This means that one *cun* on the same individual can be a different linear length depending on the location on the body where the measurement is being done. (For a more thorough discussion of the measurement of *cun*, please consult an acupuncture textbook.)

No matter how long the distance from the umbilicus to the superior border of the symphysis pubis (pubic bone) may be in inches, this distance is always considered to be five *cun*. Draw imaginary horizontal lines within this space to give you five equal segments between the umbilicus and the superior border of the symphysis pubis (pubic bone). (See figure 3.5-a below.)

**Lower Cinnabar Field**

Fig. 3.5-a

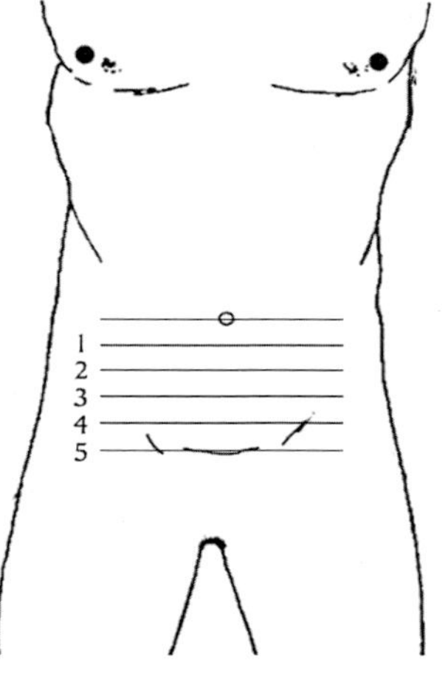


The vertical distance from the umbilicus to the superior border of the symphysis pubis is five *cun*.

It was mentioned that some people feel the Lower Cinnabar Field is located at the acupuncture site of *Qihai* (Ren-6). Since the acupuncture site of *Qihai* (Ren-6) is located approximately one and a half *cun* directly inferior to the umbilicus, you will find the location of this acupuncture site by finding the mid way spot between the first and the second linear section inferior to the umbilicus and directly on the vertical midline of the anterior of the body. (See figure 5.3-b below.)

**Lower Cinnabar Field**

Fig. 3.5-b

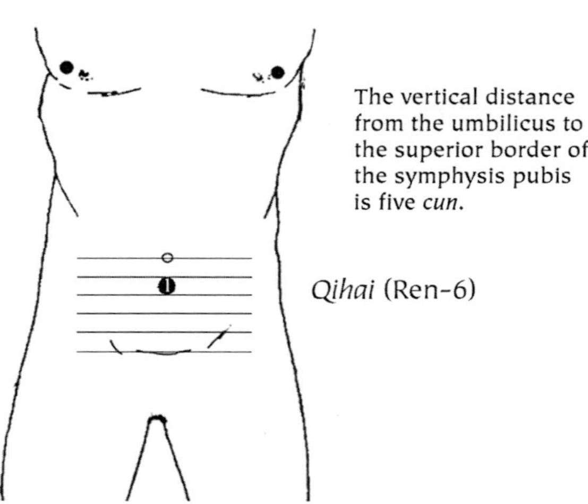


Other people feel that the location of the lower Cinnabar Field is either slightly inferior to the location of the acupuncture site of *Qihai* (Ren-6) at two *cun* below the umbilicus or located directly at the site of *Guanyuan* (Ren-4). *Guanyuan* (Ren-4) is translated as "Original Pass" and is located three *cun* below the umbilicus and lower than the acupuncture site of *Qihai* (Ren-6). An alternate name for the acupuncture point Ren-4 is

*Dan Tian* meaning "Cinnabar Field." In that school of thought, the lower Cinnabar Field is located at the acupuncture site of *Guanyuan* (Ren-4). (To view the location of *Guanyuan* (Ren-4) in relationship to one's umbilicus, see figure 3.5-c below.)

**Lower Cinnabar Field**

Fig. 3.5-c

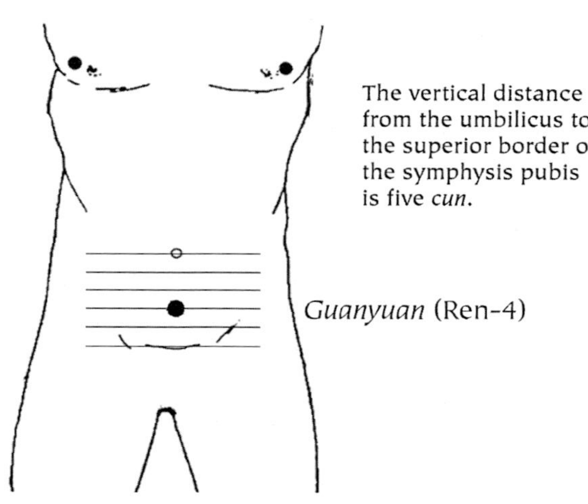


Although *Guanyaun* (Ren-4) was used as the activation site for the Lower *Dan Tian* in the 3-6-1 Antahkarana Visualization Pattern discussed in detail in ***Sea of Fire—Cosmic fire: Esoteric Acupuncture, Volume IV***, it is probably better to think of the lower Cinnabar Field as an area, or field, rather than merely a precise point. Just know that the first of the three *Hun*, starting from the lower Cinnabar Field is located on the vertical midline of the body below the umbilicus and above the upper border of the pubic bone. You are able to energize this area by placing your dominant hand on the body at this region below the umbilicus with the palm touching the body and mentally sending qi through your hand into this region. (See figure 3.5-d for the location of the Lower Cinnabar Field.)

**Lower Cinnabar Field**

Fig. 3.5-d

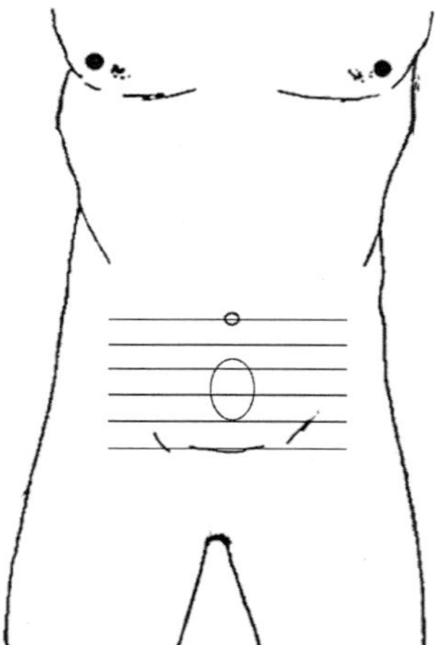

The vertical distance from the umbilicus to the superior border of the symphysis pubis is five *cun*.

Ruth Montgomery wrote a book published in 1973 entitled ***Born to Heal*** about a healer she called Mr. A. The basis of Mr. A's amazing ability to heal people revolved around Mr. A's power of being able to send tremendous amounts of healing energy to the region known as the Lower Cinnabar Field. Mr. A would energize the sexual qi of the kidney system. (Mr. A did not use the Chinese name of *Dan Tian* to refer to this area of the body.) He would place himself in a certain vibratory state of consciousness and place his hand on a person's lower abdomen at the area of the Lower Cinnabar Field. Mr. A felt that all problems arose because people had blockages in this region or had no energy or low energy coming into this region. Remember this is also the region known in Chinese Medical thought as the storage area of one's *Mingmen* Fire. It is the qi from the *Mingmen* Fire that gives one the willpower and the physical strength to accomplish things in life. The *Mingmen* Fire gives you that extra oomph in life. As mentioned earlier, *Mingmen* is translated as either "Life Gate" or "Gate of Vitality." The ancient scholars who named this point knew the importance of *Mingmen* (Du-4).

Those who have studied acupuncture theory in an accredited academic school know that the palms of both hands are under the influence and control of the heart qi. Sweaty palms usually suggest there is too much heat in the heart system and not enough cooling qi (water from the kidney system) to balance the heart field. Do not confuse heat in the palms and sweaty palms that is caused by a yin deficiency condition or caused by an excessive heat condition with powerful healers who are able to generate healing energy (heat) in the palms of their hands to energize their client/patient.

Energizing a weakened Lower Cinnabar Field is usually very beneficial to most people. Some people may feel that if your Lower Cinnabar Field is out of balance, then you should not send energy to that imbalanced area. Having a healer with very clean heart qi physically placing his or her energized palm on the Lower Cinnabar Field region will balance and strengthen the qi of the *Mingmen* Fire, not strengthen imbalanced energy in that area. Unless the client has a very weakened and depleted heart qi condition, the energy of love from the heart of the healer will harmonize any negative energy. If you are an energy healer working on the Lower Cinnabar Field of a very weak client/patient, be very mindful and proceed slowly.

To access and strengthen the Lower Cinnabar Field from the posterior side, you can needle or otherwise stimulate the acupuncture point *Mingmen* (Du-4). The site of this point is located directly on the posterior spine below the spinous process of the second lumbar vertebra. Those of you who have studied Traditional Chinese Medicine know that the acupuncture point *Mingmen* (Du-4) is associated with the kidney system of the water element and is a major acupuncture point.

In western academic thinking, especially in the western scientific model, everything has to fit into a box or a neat category. The western mind is trained in the concepts of reproducibility, constant repetitive categorizations and organizational abilities. A part of Chinese medical philosophy functions under the premise that there is no clear cut box or category where you can always place certain concepts or theorems. In eastern thinking, a particular theorem or idea may fit in a certain category sometimes and may fit equally well in another category at other times. This flexibility in philosophy of the eastern mind may turn some westerners off to accepting the strength and beauty of eastern thought. Knowledge of the flexibility inherent within eastern thinking allows one the ability to appreciate that although the lower *Dan Tian* area of the Lower Cinnabar Field is usually associated with the kidney system of water, an aspect of the *Hun* of the liver system of wood is also connected to this same lower region.

The second of the three *Hun,* that is the second of the three Cinnabar Fields, is the Central Cinnabar Field. The Central Cinnabar Field is located on the vertical midline of the chest at the area somewhat between the breast surrounding the acupuncture point *Yuan Jian* (Ren-17). (This acupuncture point is more often called *Tanzhong* or *Danzhong* in Chinese. I prefer to use the Chinese name *Yuan Jian* that can be translated as "The Source.") *Yuan Jian* (Ren-17) is located directly on the anterior vertical midline of the chest level with the fourth intercostal space of the ribs. In many younger males, *Yuan Jian* (Ren-17) is located at the junction where the anterior vertical midline intersects an imaginary horizontal line that connects both nipples. *Yuan Jian* (Ren-17) is one of the direct anterior pathways to activate the Anahata (Heart Chakra). To access the Central Cinnabar Field from the posterior of the body, you can needle the acupuncture point *Shendao* (Du-11) located on the spine directly below the spinous process of the fifth thoracic vertebra. Although the Central Cinnabar Field, as used in Esoteric Acupuncture, is associated with the heart field, a portion of the consciousness of the *Hun* of the liver system also "resides" in this area. Remember the heart controls blood, but the liver stores the blood. The denser *Hun* resides in the blood and resides in the Central Cinnabar Field. (See figure 3.6 below.)

**Central Cinnabar Field**

Fig. 3.6

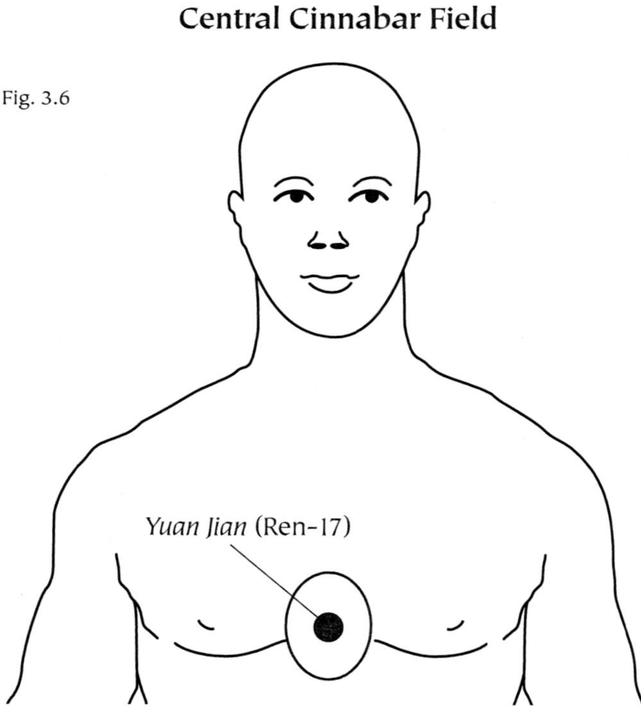


The third *Hun* of this particular three *Hun* grouping is located at the Upper Cinnabar Field. The Upper Cinnabar Field is located in an area of the brain that can be accessed through certain acupuncture sites on the forehead and the head. The Cinnabar Field is not directly on the exterior of the forehead, but rather in the astral spaces within the cranium. An alternative name for the Upper Cinnabar Field is the Brahmarandra Chakra, also known as the Nirwana or Nirvana Chakra. The area that houses the Brahmarandra Chakra is not physically a part of the physical brain. The Upper Cinnabar Field can be accessed and activated by three acupuncture sites: 1) Ajna #1; 2) *Shang Xing* (Du-23); and 3) *Shenting* (Du-24). *Shang Xing* (Du-23) has an alternative name *Shen Tang* that can be translated as "Spirit Hall."

To find Ajna #1, see the Cube on Cube Window Pattern in Chapter V. *Shen Tang/Shang Xing* (Du-23) is found on the vertical anterior midline of the head approximately one *cun* behind the natural hairline of the anterior of the head. *Shenting* (Du-24) is also located on the anterior midline of the head directly in front of *Shen Tang/Shang Xing* (Du-23) and approximately one half *cun* behind the anterior hairline of the head. (See figure 3.7 below.)

**Upper Cinnabar Field**

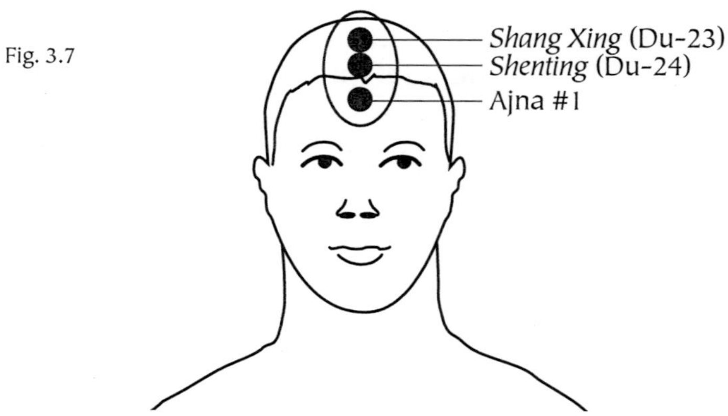


Fig. 3.7

Each of the three individual fabrics of the denser *Hun* of the liver has a slightly different function and will be discussed below.

### 1) *Hun* and Our Ethereal Soul

The Chinese believe that the *Hun* of the liver system is connected to our Ethereal Soul. The Ethereal Soul is different than the Corporeal Soul connected with the *Po*.

According to ***Webster's Third New International Unabridged Dictionary***, ethereal means: "of or relating to the regions beyond the earth; celestial; heavenly."[10] When the spirit of a person no longer has use for the physical vehicle, his or her Ethereal Soul separates from the physical body and returns to the Soul Plane.

Giovanni Maciocia in his very well written, well organized book called the ***Practice of Chinese Medicine*** states:

> *"There are three types of Ethereal Soul: a vegetative one common to plants, animals and human beings; an animal one common to animals and humans; and a human one which is present only in humans beings."*[11]

It is not of importance for the presentation of Esoteric Acupuncture to discuss in further detail the other two aspects of *Hun* related to a vegetative type or the animal *Hun*. For Esoteric Acupuncture, only the *Hun* known as our Ethereal Soul will be discussed. When talking about the three *Hun* within humans, it is important to understand that the three aspects are merely three different fabrics of consciousness with slightly different frequencies due to a minor change of resonance from energies (information) connected with each of the three aspects. The three aspects are all connected to a larger fabric of consciousness that is part of the total liver system. Claude Larre in the book ***The Liver***, which he co-wrote with Elizabeth Rochat De La Vallee, states:

> *"When talking of the three hun we usually have a tendency to try and separate out their different functions. But life itself is a unity and this unity is made when all parts of the body and emanations of the three hun are working together."*[12]

Just know that the three fabrics of *Hun* are merely different aspects all interwoven as one fabric connected with the liver system. The Ethereal Soul is that aspect of our soul that stays with us in each incarnation.

Acupuncturists and other seekers of the Esoteric Ageless Wisdom Teachings should know that the aspect of the *Hun* connected with our Ethereal Soul can be accessed and activated by gently inserting an acupuncture needle at the acupuncture site of *Hunmen* (UB-47). *Hunmen* is often translated as either "*Hun's* Door" or "*Hun* Gate."

### 2) *Hun*—Emotions: Anger and Judgment

This aspect of our *Hun* organizes and distributes the consciousness of our emotional body. One very important aspect that requires emphasis is that of judgment versus being non-judgmental. Many years ago I remember asking Nataraj Muni Baba Swami, a realized Spiritual Master currently residing in the Los Angeles area of California, about anger and judgment. At that time, Swami Nataraj said that he felt judgment was one of the most difficult aspects of our spiritual journey to work through and release. It is less of a challenge to work through and release anger than it is to release judgment.

I have noticed an aspect of judgment used by several light workers when dowsing or clairvoyantly making observations and decisions on certain people. I have met several of these light workers who claim that it is okay to remove hooks, cords and other attachments from people by merely asking that individual's higher self. In my opinion, that is black magic. I want to make it perfectly clear that I am not condemning all aspects of black magic. Black magic in the esoteric sense is merely working with moving or transforming energy. One of the esoteric criteria of black magic versus white magic is that in black magic, something is done to another individual or another group without that individual or group's permission. One fundamental principle of white magic is that you have to ask permission on all planes before you decide to take any action, and most importantly your actions must be based upon your heart.

With black magic, you act without permission and your actions reflect your lower ego that states that you know what is best for another person or another group. You are being judgmental. You feel that you know more than that individual, so it is justifiable to put your "trips" on someone else.

Some light workers have stated that they asked and received permission from the higher self of another individual. That seems devious and not in alignment with the higher heart vibrations. Asking permission to the another individual's higher self presupposes that the other person's higher self is immersed in light and that another person's higher self agrees with your opinions about life and good versus not so good. It is easy to "front load" your answer if you have not done adequate inner plane work yourself and have not integrated discernment into your daily heart field.

When I say you have to ask permission, this means on all levels of consciousness including the mental plane of the three-dimensional realms of consciousness. The times when it is in alignment to only ask that individual's higher self is when that individual is in a coma, too sick or too old to comprehend, or that individual is a young child or baby. In those times when an individual is unable to consciously comprehend your questions, those individuals must be within your immediate blood family, or you must receive a request for permission to perform your work by someone who is the legal or spiritual guardian of that individual who is not able to directly speak for himself or herself.

How do these particular light workers know the karma of the individual who is carrying those attachments? Maybe the individual that the light worker wants to clear of outside attachments needs more time with those hooks, cords, attachments or other energetic blockages to fully understand and learn from that challenge.

If you do not consciously ask permission of another individual before any type of energetic clearing, then you are performing black magic. One of the esoteric premises of black magic is that the practitioner feels that he or she knows what is best and does not need to ask permission. That is how wars begin. If you purposely change someone's energy field without permission, then you are what is know as a "twilight worker." This means you are utilizing energies from a denser aspect while claiming to be working with the light. Twilight workers walk and work in the realms between daylight and darkness. Many twilight workers do not carry enough light (high enough level of consciousness) to realize they are using the energetics of the dark.

If you are controlled by your lower ego, it is not easy to observe without judgment. When you are working with your higher heart, then you can observe without judgment. It is amazing how some people obtain small bits of esoteric knowledge and feel that mental work from the left-brain, without the inner plane heart work, is adequate to begin using that esoteric knowledge. Esoteric knowledge blended with the heart frequencies results in wisdom. Without the heart frequency, esoteric knowledge is merely more information to clog or clutter your mind.

The liver controls anger. Liver qi has a tendency to move upward and outward. If the liver qi is imbalanced in an excessive way, then the energy of the *Hun* may manifest as headaches, shouting at someone, arguing with someone or wanting to punch or kick someone. These are typical movements of an imbalanced liver that negatively affects the *Hun*.

The opposite of the outward movement is an imbalanced *Hun* shrinking inward. You see this condition when a person is depressed and does not want to do anything except sleep, forget the world and all the problems he or she is facing and not wanting to see or talk to anyone. During this inward process, a person may also cry excessively. In Chinese Medicine, tears are the fluids of the liver controlled by the *Hun* that controls crying. Crying excessively or very frequently is a *Hun* imbalance. The extreme opposite end of the *Hun* field is when a person is contemplating suicide, wanting to end all the despair, hopelessness and helplessness that is overwhelming that person's life. To override this extreme end of the *Hun* requires movement toward the *Shen* of the heart and the various aspects and branches of love such as: happiness, playfulness, joy, laughter, excitement to do things again and the enthusiasm to live life to its fullest. The situation of extreme despair within the *Hun* field and needing to be assisted by, or "rescued" by the heart is another example of the *Hun* follow the *Shen*.

3) ***Hun* and Three Levels of Eyesight**

Those of you who have studied or read about Chinese Medicine know that the liver system is connected to and controls the physical eyes. This means that on the physical level, if you have physical seeing issues, several protocols according to traditional Chinese Medicine may include: moving stagnant liver qi, reducing fire in the liver or strengthening a deficient liver blood system. From a naturopathic viewpoint, some suggestions may include: purging the liver of toxins, juice fasting, colonics or enemas, or ingesting liver cleansing herbs. Another liver connection to our physical eyesight is that tears are the fluids of liver. (Perspiration is the fluid of the heart.)

There is a more refined level of the physical eyesight connected to an aspect of *Hun* possessed by those known as trackers. (Another outward aspect of the liver system is the ability to see clearly.) Sometimes a person can see far distances without the aid of binoculars or any other type of telescopic instrument. People known as trackers have this ability to see clearly for many miles. This is possible because trackers are able to access the highly developed, finely tuned vibration of the denser *Hun* system of the liver so that system is locked into one's intuitive powers of the Ajna Center and Sahasrara (Crown Chakra). This type of unique vision is known as intuitive eyesight.

Trackers are also able to notice and physically see things with their three-dimensional eyesight that those who are not trackers would ordinarily overlook. I am not talking about someone with 20-15 eyesight or even 20-10 eyesight vision. Those people may have a slight ability to see more minute details than the ordinary physical eyesight of those with 20-20 vision. But, even someone with the eyesight of 20-10 vision usually does not have the same eyesight or visionary capabilities as those possessed by trackers. Trackers have a very refined inner vision and very refined intuitive nature that is connected with a function of their *Shen*. It is the combination of gifted physical eyesight with the psychic, intuitive powers always present that distinguish trackers from those with better than average eyesight.

Trackers have an inherent sensitivity that is very refined and a special ability to notice things that would be missed by those with a less expanded consciousness. Although sometimes investigators of crime scenes may have some of the same abilities as trackers, most investigators do not have the highly intuitive and psychic abilities inherent with true trackers. For example, trackers can see the most minute details and beauty in a small weed growing by the sidewalk. They notice the activity of bees and small insects when a person with ordinary vision and common consciousness would miss those details. They notice the slightest change in a person's facial expression that may reveal something different than what the person is verbally saying. Trackers notice when there is a slight shift in cloud formations. They notice the aura and the "feelings" emanating from plants, trees and other natural surroundings. They notice the slightest differences in any situation. Trackers are astutely observant. It is the attention, awareness and inherent intuitive powers in all situations that differentiate trackers from those with merely 20-15 or 20-10 eyesight.

On a slightly more refined level from the tracker level is

the person with the ability to see auras and other non three-dimensional images with the physical eyesight. Although some trackers can see auras, many of the trackers possess the fine line of sight just below those with the ability to see auras. People at the level of an awakened *Hun* are slightly more refined than trackers who are able to see colors emanating from people, plants and animals. Even inanimate objects emanate colors. On the other hand, most people who are able to distinguish auras do not possess the ability of trackers. This type of awakened *Hun* that encompasses seeing auras is available to anyone who is able to move out of his or her programmed perception that says this reality is not possible.

There is an even more refined level of the *Hun* related to "seeing," known as inner sight or a deeper Insight. At this level of inner sight, you are moving from "seeing" with two eyes to "seeing" with one eye. Some people say that the one eye is your Third Eye of the Ajna Center. Others say that the "true" Third Eye is an awakened Sahasrara (Crown Chakra). You are able to see without the use of your physical eyesight.

Clear clairvoyants go inward to "see" in the mind with a highly refined inner sight, rather than relying on the ability of a refined system of physical eyesight. This inner vision is a much deeper, more refined frequency than seeing with the physical eyesight of certain types of clairvoyants. Those with the clearest mind-sight that are not bound by space/time are utilizing some level of the consciousness of their Original *Hun*. This level of being able to see in the mind also requires being able to at least access the lower levels of one's Original *Shen*. The truly gifted remote viewers go inward and use their inner sight or insight and are not bound by space/time. They do not use or rely on their physical eyesight for their remote viewing work.

The *Hun* is associated with a type of movement that is connected to thinking, imagination and the ability to quickly visualize thoughts in the mind. The movements such as imagination and thoughts can travel very rapidly through both long linear distances, as well as span great non-linear distances in very a short time. How fast and how far away can your mind and your imagination travel?

Since the *Hun* is now also associated with the mind, this means that the *Shen* of our heart system is not the only aspect of consciousness that affects the mind. Another aspect of the denser *Hun* helps to shape and guide our dreams and is present in our thoughts and when we practice meditation. Everything that we consider intellectual, pedagogic or anything to do with the mind are heavily influenced by the *Hun*. The denser *Hun* needed for imagination plays a part in our ability to access the right-brain of our abstract mind. The *Hun* are also very much connected to the left-brained thinking and are needed for us to have a single-pointed mind for concentration and focus. In order to solve complex questions or complex problems or to create new ideas require a strong, balanced *Hun*. The fact that the *Hun* influences and can strengthen both sides of the mind means that the strong, balanced *Hun* will allow one to become and stay bicameral. Being bicameral is the true nature of the consciousness of the New Humanity of the 21st Century.

## *Po* of the Lungs

To understand how *Po* is defined in Esoteric Acupuncture, it is best to think of *Po* as a level or type of consciousness related to the lung system. There are seven types or levels of *Po* that are slightly different than the older thinking of Traditional Chinese Medicine. The Chinese believe that the *Po* is connected to our Corporeal Soul. According to ***Webster's Third New International Unabridged Dictionary***[13] corporeal is defined as: "having, consisting of, or relating to a physical material body." In the same dictionary, soul is defined as: 1) "the immaterial essence or substance, animating principle, or actuating cause of life or of the individual life; 2) the psychical or spiritual principle in general shared by or embodied in individual human beings or all beings having a rational and spiritual nature."[14]

There is a substance known in Traditional Chinese Medicine as *Jing*. The closest translation of *Jing* for those studying Traditional Chinese Medicine in the West would be the word essence. Our *Po* are closely connected to our *Jing* (essence), especially to the idea of structure. The Chinese concept of *Po* states that it is the essence, or that part of our soul that is connected to our physical existence. The *Jing* (essence) has substance (some level of denseness) and is connected to the yin aspects of our lives versus the various *Hun* that are associated with movement and to the yang aspects of our lives.

Within the Chinese concept of yin and yang, *Jing* (essence) is considered a heavier substance. It is the quality of the *Jing* (essence) of the *Po* that makes the *Po* yin versus the finer frequency of the *Hun* of our Ethereal Soul.

Ted Kaptchuk states in his medical textbook on Traditional Chinese Medicine ***The Web That Has No Weaver*** that:

> *"Essence is a kind of deep, 'soft,' 'juicy' potential inherent in living beings which forms and fills the life cycle as it unfolds. In the usual Chinese way that defies categories, it is the potential, guidance, and actuality that shapes birth, development, maturation, decline, and death....Essence's transformation is noticed most easily in reflection and contemplation."*[15]

Some ancient Chinese scholars felt that in order for the fetus to survive from the union of the sperm and egg, the *Po* of the lungs had to come before the Hun of the liver.

> *"There are non medical texts which say that the po come first and then the hun, but this is just to say that the jing has to be there in order to produce the structure and to bring together all the constituents for a being."*[16]

Some Chinese scholars believe that the *Hun* of the liver come before the *Po* of the lungs. A translation from the Chinese medical ***Nei Jing Texts*** states:

> *"The hun means to nourish and infuse with life. The po do not make life, they just serve life....If the shen and the hun are really the powers which direct the movement necessary for life within the unity of being which emerges from the void, then they must be there at the beginning of that being.*[17]

When certain ancient Chinese scholars said that *Jing*, or essence, had to be present to produce the structure of the newly formed fetus, the promoters of this type of thinking did not understand the holographic nature of consciousness and did not understand, or know about, Original *Shen* and Original *Hun*. The most fundamental forms of our Original *Shen* and our Original *Hun* have always been with us and both are contained within the Original Consciousness. One's individual Key Codes are stored within our Original *Shen* that is a tentacle of our Original Encodings.

The fabrics of consciousness from one's Original *Shen* and one's Original *Hun*, along with the denser *Shen* of the heart and the *Hun* of the liver, all appear within the soul at the moment of the unification of the physical sperm and the physical egg. Consciousness does not require particles, such as brain cells, blood cells or other cells, in order to exist. Likewise, our fundamental Original Consciousness does not require a denser plane of reality, such as *Jing* or essence to have a place to survive or exist. The fundamental Original Consciousness is always in existence. But the heavier quality of *Jing* (essence) and the *Po* of the lungs allow the fundamental Original Consciousness a denser dwelling place, so the fundamental consciousness can occupy and diffuse throughout the physical cells and throughout the space confined within the boundary of the physical vehicle of the newly formed fetus. It is the denseness of *Jing* (essence) and *Po* that allows *Shen, Hun, Zhi, Yi* and *qi* to interconnect within the fetus, thus creating physical platform for the growth and eventual birthing of a newborn physical entity.

In other words, the fundamental aspects of Original *Shen* and Original *Hun* do not necessarily require the denseness of *Jing* (essence) and the *Po* to exist. But, it is with the aid and the presence of both the *Jing* (essence) and the *Po* of the lungs that allow both the fundamental Original *Shen* and Original *Hun* to become part of a denser, physical, three-dimensional reality. Remember, the *Po* resides within qi. So it is the intimate interconnectedness of *Jing* (essence) with the *Po* of the lungs that now form the interconnectedness between the *Shen, Hun, Zhi* of the kidneys *and the Yi of the spleen system* within the newly created fetus.

The etheric organs of the body are formed prior to the development of the cells of the denser physical organs. At the time of conception, there must be qi. Since the *Po* exist within qi and houses the *Jing* (essence), *Po* and *Jing* must also be present at the time of conception. This also means that during the very initial stages of the Original *Shen* and Original *Hun* interconnecting with the *Po* of the lungs, other fabrics of consciousness are also beginning to enter into this magnificent design and process of human birthing. The *Zhi* of the etheric kidneys and the *Yi* of the etheric spleen have now come forth and have interlinked with the Original *Shen*, the Original *Hun* and the denser *Shen* and *Hun* and the *Po* to begin the genesis of a journey that creates a unique, distinct soul inhabiting a dense physical vehicle. The fabrics of consciousness from each of the five element organ systems, the *Shen* of the heart system, the *Hun* of the liver system, the *Po* of the lung system, the *Zhi* of the kidney system and the *Yi* of the spleen system all combine to create a unique life force within a newly created fetus

Correct breathing is so important to our overall health, and the lungs control our breathing. This may be a challenge in the 21st Century cities of today because of the chemical spraying of our skies. To keep our Corporeal Soul in the best shape possible means that we must take care of our lungs. Lung problems are very prevalent in the United States, not only because of smoking and the chemicals in the air, but also because of the large variety of unhealthy foods available to the uninformed public. The toxicity of living in the 21st Century combined with the overall poor choices of foods and drinks by the masses have put extreme stressors on our lung system. Foods and drinks that block our qi flow, such as dairy and processed sugars, often create dampness that can further hamper proper qi flow throughout the body. For many individuals, consuming alcoholic beverages often causes histamine reactions that challenge the lungs, spleen and liver system. This may in turn eventually overburden or even damage our qi.

At the time of death of the physical vehicle, the *Po* and *Hun* usually dissociate and go in separate directions. The natural movement for the *Hun* is to rise, to expand and to diffuse. The *Hun* travel outward. The *Po* are denser frequencies with the natural characteristic to merge with the *Jing* (essence) within our dense physical body. The *Po* remain inward.

The *Po* control an interesting cycle for each human that has incarnated in three-dimensional reality. At the very moment of conception when the egg and sperm unite, a unique characteristic of the *Po* has its genesis. This unique characteristic is the concept of breathing within the womb. When the fetus is in the womb of the mother, the "breathing" of the fetus is a circular movement with the breathing contained within the body of the fetus. At the very moment of the birth of the newborn baby, the baby takes an outward breath to signal a new life cycle. Often the baby will cry trying to gasp for more air in this new life.

At the other end of the cycle of life, another event takes place. At the very moment that the soul leaves the physical vehicle during the deathing process, the body tries to take in one last gasp of air. This completes the cycle for that spirit/soul. At birth the breath goes outward with the first cry. At the time of death, the breath goes inward with the last gasp of physical life. This signals the completion of the physical cycle for that individual. This is the completion of one cycle only, not the end of the spirit.

> *"All life is absorbed with time. A life is the cycle of existence between birth and death... Death does not end the life of any man. It only marks the separation of a fulfilled portion from an unfolding principle."*[18]
>
> Noble Drew Ali

Sometimes the dissociation between the *Hun* and the *Po* does not occur. When this happens, the Ethereal Soul (*Hun*) does not leave the earthly plane. The *Hun* and the *Po* have not disconnected. These types of events lead to a discarnate soul roaming the lower fourth dimensional realms. These discarnate souls have been called ghosts. (In fact, in traditional Chinese acupuncture there is a set of acupuncture points known as "ghost points.") The discarnate entities are still attached to the earthly plane, but do not have a dense physical body to occupy. Perhaps, the lack of dissociation between the *Hun* and the *Po* at the time of the death of the physical vehicle in individuals is more numerous than we think. There have been many sightings of ghosts throughout history and throughout this planet at this present time.

One denser aspect of our *Po,* known as our Corporeal Soul, does not survive the death of the physical vehicle and usually dissipates on the physical plane. There is a much finer frequency aspect of our *Po* that is called Original *Po* in Esoteric Acupuncture that is not the Corporeal Soul aspect. The Original Po returns back to the Soul Plane upon the death of the physical vehicle to remain until the next incarnation.

On the other hand, one aspect of our *Hun* returns to the higher Causal Sub Plane of the Soul Plane at the time of death of the physical vehicle and stays with us in each incarnation. Another much finer fabric of consciousness, known as our Original *Hun*, is transported by way of our Monadic Ray through the Soul Plane back to the Monadic Plane.

## *Yi* of the Spleen

The *Yi* is that portion of consciousness that is connected to the spleen system. The *Yi* reinforces our ability to concentrate and therefore assists the *Hun* of the liver in this endeavor. A strong and balanced *Yi* will benefit one immensely to memorize and store numerous amounts of information that can later be recalled. Although both the *Shen* of the heart and the *Zhi* of the kidneys are also connected to memory, it is the *Yi* of the spleen that is most responsible for one's ability to recall endless amounts of information on the normal-dimensional planes. This ability for recall is hindered by what the Chinese call dampness. Dampness in western terminology is called candida that can refer to a yeast infection. A damp condition is most often caused by sugars, dairy, refined starches, alcohol, excessive oil intake and both emotional and mental stressors.

It was mentioned earlier that the *Hun* of the liver system controls dreaming, while asleep, while daydreaming and during the lucid state known as Dreamtime. Usually most people cannot remember their dreams, partially because excessive dampness and/or lack of inner plane development. The *Yi* gives us the ability to recall information, to recall memories and to recall our nightly dreams. The lack of recall of one's dreams is an indication that the part of the *Yi* connected to the astral realms of dreams is not fully awake and functioning properly. The more clearly we are able to recall dreams is an indication that the consciousness associated with the *Yi* of the spleen system is active, very strong and is infused with certain frequencies of both our *Shen* of the heart and our *Hun* of the liver.

Although all of us have had many past lives, most people

cannot remember any previous lifetimes. When a higher aspect of the *Yi* of the spleen system is communicating with the higher aspects of the *Hun* of the liver system and both these levels of consciousness are able to tap into the Stillness of the *Shen,* then an opportunity may arise to recall past life experiences. Although some aspects of the *Yi* of the spleen system are required for recalling past life experiences, the Higher *Shen* has more power to assist persons in the recall of memories of past life experiences.

## *Zhi* of the Kidneys

Since some of the properties and powers of the *Zhi* of the kidney system have been discussed in other sections of this book, only a brief overview will be given here.

It is necessary to know about the qualities and the powers of the *Mingmen* Fire of the kidneys and how important this fire is to a person's well being and to the strength and quality of one's *Zhi.* The acupuncture point known as *Mingmen* (Du-4) is translated to mean either "Life Gate" or "the "Gate of Vitality." When one's *Mingmen* Fire is strong and vibrant, the *Zhi* will likewise be strong and vibrant. This condition will mean that the individual will have clarity of thinking, strong willpower to accomplish goals and will be full of life. *Mingmen* Fire directly feeds the consciousness of one's *Zhi* of the kidney system.

If you observe the physical vehicle in the transformational state of the deathing process, you will notice that the *Zhi* of the kidneys are weakening. The *Zhi* gives us our willpower and determination in life. During the deathing process, the life force of that person and willpower to do things start to diminish. The vitality of life starts to diminish. The laughter and sparkle of life in the eyes start to fade. If a dying person is not spiritual, that person will mostly likely be immersed in fear and the other tentacles and offshoots of fear.

You will also notice that in a dying person the knees start

to relax outwardly. The *Zhi* is weakening and cannot "hold things in." Defecation and urination are not controllable with an extremely weakened *Zhi* of the kidney system. Remember in the Five Element model, the kidneys are considered the mother of the liver system, meaning the kidney system has much influence over the liver and the *Hun*. *Di Chong* (Ki-1) is located on the soles of each foot. *Di Chong* can be translated as "Earth's Thoroughfare," expressing the idea that the qi from Mother Earth is allowed to enter at these acupuncture sites. The bilateral *Di Chong* (Ki-1) points also allow the physical vehicle a direct "grounding" pathway to connect with Mother Earth.

As the *Zhi* of the kidneys further weakens, this process communicates to the Ethereal Soul aspect of the *Hun* of the liver that the time is approaching for a new journey to begin. When the spirit no longer requires the use of a physical vehicle, the *Mingmen* Fire of the kidneys extinguishes itself on the Personality Plane and the Ethereal Soul (*Hun*) departs and returns to the Soul Plane. At the moment of the death of the physical, higher aspects of both the *Zhi*, known as Original *Zhi*, and the Original *Po* return to the Soul Plane.

## Summary of the Five Fabrics of Consciousness

There are many facets of consciousness connected to the five major rays of consciousness associated with each of the five elements of the Chinese Five Element System. A certain aspect of the *Hun* controls our dreams. If lower aspects of the *Shen* are infused with the frequencies of the *Hun*, then we will have more pleasant dreams. If the lower aspects of the *Zhi* of the kidneys are infused with the frequencies of *Hun*, then we will have more frightening dreams, even nightmares. If these dreams (either pleasant or not so pleasant) are vivid, then certain frequencies of the *Yi* of the spleen are also infused with the *Hun*.

One of the major functions of the liver system is to allow the qi to flow smoothly throughout the body and through the acupuncture meridians and the thousands of finer nadi pathways. This movement of qi helps to set things in motion. The *Hun* have an expansive and diffusive nature and have a tendency to move outward. An imbalanced outward movement of the liver system is seen when an angry person wants to punch someone, punch the wall, kick someone or yell or scold someone. An angry person may point his or her finger toward you and direct their hostilities at you. These outward actions are part of an agitated *Hun*. If the *Hun* is over abundant with hostilities, it is very difficult to be able to Still the mind

The liver, through the *Hun,* is able to also assist us in analyzing and seeing all situations clearly and help us to move toward acting on those situations. Procrastination is the field of the gallbladder system and is what is known in Esoteric Acupuncture as "The Thief of Life," the "I'll do it later syndrome." A strong, well-balanced *Hun overrides* procrastination and assists us in manifesting our goals. When a balanced, harmonious *Shen* is also infused and integrated with the *Hun,* one is able to have clarity and discernment when moving forward in completing tasks, overcoming challenges, fulfilling commitments and in manifesting one's goals.

If a person has done the proper amount of inner plane work, then on certain occasions, that individual is sometimes able to enter into a realm of consciousness known as the "Dream State." Some individuals are also able to enter this Dream State during meditation and also while in an awakened state during the day or night. When we are able to access information during these states of consciousness and later are able to clearly remember the information when we come back into a three-dimensional reality, this means that the higher aspects of the *Yi* of the spleen, the higher consciousness of both the *Hun* of the liver and the *Shen* of the heart are all infused into one fabric or stream of consciousness. If that individual is also engaged in spiritual work to uplift humanity, then this particular fabric becomes a higher refined aspect of the Thread of Active Creativity. These are all parts of the Antahkarana, the bridge of higher consciousness.

The *Zhi* of the kidney system is connected to our Swadthisthana (Sacral Chakra). This second chakra field controls relationships, sexual energies (sexual power), self-esteem and ego issues, as well as controlling our need for power and money. If a person works to develop certain powers for selfish reasons, he or she will not be activating the higher aspects of the *Shen* of the Higher Heart. That individual has infused more of the fear aspects of the *Zhi* of the kidneys with the *Hun*, the *Yi* and the *Po*. If we are developing psychic abilities for power to control and/or impress others, then we are still at the level of our lower *Zhi* and not the higher aspects of *Zhi*.

In my opinion, the desired states or levels of consciousness that we should be striving to activate and incorporate as part of our daily lives are the higher aspects of all five fabrics of consciousness, described in the Chinese systems that include: the *Zhi*, the *Po*, the *Yi*, the *Hun* and the *Shen*. Of these five aspects of consciousness, it is especially important to work on the higher aspects of our *Shen*. When a person does service work to uplift humanity, then the vibrations of this thread resonate at a much higher, lighter frequency. That person will have tapped into and anchored the frequencies of the Higher Heart. This thread of consciousness is a part of the Sutratma of the Antahkarana (talked about in the next chapter) and the Monadic Ray. This indicates that all of the finer frequency fabrics of consciousness from the five major organ systems of the body are all intertwined, interconnected and working harmoniously as one unified stream of consciousness.

When a person is able to reach the highest state of awareness on a steady and consistent basis through inner plane work, he or she will have entered a realm known esoterically as reaching immortality. Immortality in the esoteric sense does not mean the physical body does not decay and that a person is able to retain the same physical vehicle forever. Esoterically, immortality refers to the continuity of consciousness throughout all of one's many lifetimes. The more you are able to receive and interpret the frequencies coming from your Monadic Ray, your Inner Wisdom becomes clearer. This esoteric definition of immortality may not appeal to the masses. Because of fear of the unknown, those people who are interested in immortality would most likely want to keep the same physical vehicle.

If you review the Monadic Ray Chart in this chapter, you will notice that the Original *Hun* is a branch coming from the Original *Shen*. This is the esoteric meaning of the *Hun* follow the *Shen*. At this level, it is very difficult to separate the *Hun* from the *Shen*. If one is able to enter into the state of consciousness to fully bathe in the vibrations emanating from one's Original *Shen*, Original Encodings and one's Original Consciousness, then that person has reached one level of esoteric immortality.

Blood is both the transporter of physical and non-physical nutrients to the various parts of the body. I mentioned in ***Support the Mountain: Esoteric Acupuncture, Volume V*** the importance of always being discerning when it comes to selecting the types of food and drink you choose to ingest. The foods and drinks with the highest life-force and enzymes and with the least amount of chemicals, preservatives, and other artificial flavorings or chemical food enhancements (such as monosodium glutamate, aspartame, artificial dyes, artificial moisturizers, nuclear fallout or other airborne toxic chemicals) will allow your physical and non-physical bodies to grow and develop in the most natural and beneficial manner to keep you in your heart center. Eating and drinking foods that are below your normal standards are indications that your consciousness is not at a high enough level to override the demands of your lower chakras. I have heard this statement many times: "I normally do not eat that type of food, but there was nothing else to eat." If you know that something is not healthy for your body and you are truly vibrating in your own highest heart field, then you cannot ingest those types of foods or drinks. And, you definitely would not be buying those types of foods to store in your house or apartment. We all have choices in life. If staying true to your heart is important, than you will have the discipline to refrain from unwise choices. No one ever dies from going hungry for one meal or even a few meals.

It has been mentioned that blood is the transporter of both physical and non-physical nutrients to various parts of the body. The non-physical nutrients include consciousness in the form of energy information. The blood is controlled by the fire element of the heart and the Heart Master, the pericardium.

The heart is the realm of the "Emperor" and controls calmness, tranquility and harmony. When the liver, sometimes known as the General, can "bow down" to the Emperor, then one's spiritual alignment and spiritual awakening is allowed to blossom in a more harmonious and rapid manner. One of the desired goals for allowing the Emperor to take control is to be able to quiet our chattering mind. The process of working toward being quiet may eventually lead us to a place of Stillness. The idea of the activity of the liver system giving way to the superior frequencies of the heart is the genesis of the acupuncture pattern The *Hun* Follow the *Shen* Pattern discussed in Chapter Five. We are aligning and harmonizing the chakras to move into our inner, Spiritual Heart Path and eventually strengthening this center path of our Higher Heart.

There is another aspect of our *Hun* that is not mentioned in the Chinese texts and is known in Esoteric Acupuncture as our Original *Hun*. Our Original *Hun* has been with us since the very beginning within our monad and is a slightly denser fabric emanating from our Original *Shen*. The Original *Hun* survives after the death of the physical vehicle and returns by way of one's Monadic Ray back to Monadic Plane. An aspect of our Original *Hun* and the denser *Hun* of the liver system are both present at the very beginning of the life of a newly created soul.

The five fabrics of consciousness connected to the five organ systems are heavily influenced by the choices of foods and drinks we choose to ingest. Only eat the purest, organically grown foods. Try to stay away from chemicals, genetically modified foods and heavily sugar-laden drinks. Make those choices from your centered heart.

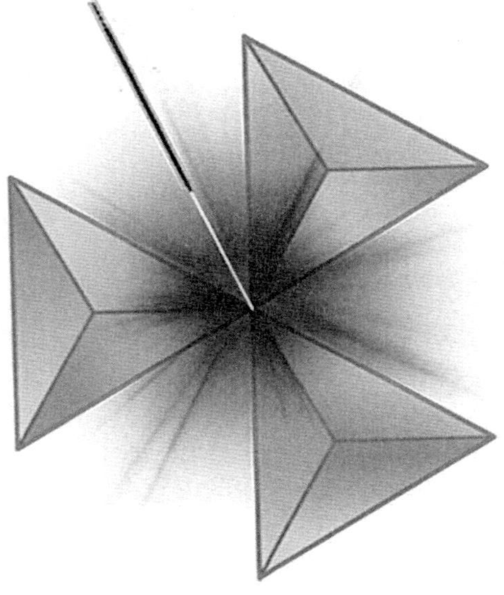

# Chapter IV: What is the Antahkarana?

> *Working diligently and perseveringly in each mind-moment "to let everything go," no longer engaging thoughts, to just breathe and be clear mind, body-mind begins its healing.*
>
> Jikun Kathy Sankey, O.M.D., L.Ac.

> *Universe constantly communicates with you. If you are very Still, you may "hear." The greatest block to this inner interconnection with Universe is your cluttered, concrete mind.*
>
> M.S.

You will notice that the definitive article "the" was not used in front of Universe in the above quote. I first noticed this type of thinking from the writings of the magnificent mind of R. Buckminster Fuller in his geometric-mathematical-philosophical books on topology and geometric shapes. R. Buckminster Fuller has been one of the individuals who has changed my life and helped to shape my way of thinking about the importance of geometrical fields, systems and the interconnected relationship of everything to everything. When R. Buckminster Fuller talks about Universe, he does not use the definitive article "the" in front of Universe. He merely writes Universe, not <u>the</u> Universe. At first, the omission of the definite article preceding the concept of Universe seemed a little awkward to me. You will usually see "the" in front of any discussion of Universe, such as the Universe such and such. Much later it dawned upon me why R. Buckminster Fuller wrote about Universe without writing "the"

Universe. Placing the definite article "the" in front of Universe creates a limiting field, implying that "the" Universe refers to one specific Universe, the one that encompasses the Milky Way Galaxy where we reside. Universe is a much greater field than the Universe. The Universe is not synonymous with Universe.

When we say the Universe, we are referring to a vast space that encompasses our present understanding of how galaxies, black holes and solar systems are interconnected within what is a nebulous field called "the" Universe. Astrophysicists have now written about the existence of multiple universes. Some people refer to the collection of universes as the Multiverse. "The" Universe is one specific field and is contained within Universe, which is a bigger all encompassing field. When R. Buckminster Fuller says Universe, rather than the Universe, he is talking about a much larger field that not only encompasses our Universe, but is much greater and much more expansive with no borders. I used the term The All Field in the book ***Sea of Fire, Cosmic Fire: Esoteric Acupuncture, Volume IV*** that is synonymous to R. Buckminster Fuller's idea of Universe. We exist in "the" Universe that, in turn is contained within Universe or The All Field. The All Field contains all dimensions and no dimensions, all things and no thing, all fields both explained and unexplainable, all fields known and unknown and all fields seen and unseen or unseeable.

## In Search of the Lost Chord/Cord

According to some teaching of the Siddha (Hindu) lineage, Om or AUM is considered "The" primordial vibration of The Universe. It is this inner frequency that is more readily accessible to those who can Still the Mind. Although this sound is available to all and can be vocally created by everyone, unfortunately most of humanity is not even aware of the concept of OM or AUM. In Esoteric Acupuncture, the "lost chord" is the sound of AUM. The sound of A-U-M is slightly different than the sound of O-M. I mentioned in an earlier book that AUM has a higher vibratory frequency than OM. The three parts to A-U-M are of a different frequency with a finer vibratory rate than the two parts of O-M.

I used to go outside at night around midnight or a little after midnight several times per month (before the chemical spraying in the sky became extremely dense) and just meditate while sitting on a bench in the backyard. The neighborhood where I live in the Los Angeles area is very quiet and extremely peaceful at night. The backyard is relatively small but has many plants, a small koi (fish) pond and trees and tall hedges that emit very soothing negative ions. Although I live several miles from the ocean, sometimes on a very still night I could actually hear the faint sounds of waves from the Pacific Ocean.

I remember one particular night a few years ago. It was very foggy and the moisture in the air caused the electrical wires from the streets to emit a loud, erratic electrical sound that I initially interpreted as noise. When the air is dry at night, there are very little audible sounds from the electrical and telephone wires on the streets. The noise on that particular night seemed to be extremely loud, chaotic and slightly disruptive. As I tried to shut out the noise from the electrical wires, I remember thinking to myself: "Welcome to life in a big city." Eventually I was able to quiet my mind and delve into a deep meditation. The "noise" did not enter my consciousness. As I was coming out of the meditative state, I remember that the "soft sounds" emanating from the electrical wires became one harmonious AUM. As my consciousness had shifted to a higher, calmer state, the electrical sounds that I first interpreted as chaotic noise became a beautiful outpouring of a very calm, soothing rhythm. My perception of the sounds transmitted from the electrical wires had changed to the point that these sounds became One with the surrounding environment and blended harmoniously into the energetics of city life.

I then realized that no matter where you are, if you are able to find that quiet center in your heart/mind and remain in that deep, inner center of calmness within, even for just a moment, then you will be able to shape and transform the outer world to resonate with your inner world. This is accessing the space within your Inner Spiritual Higher Heart Center. The goal is to first obtain some level of peacefulness, then a level of Stillness may appear.

If you can adjust the physical outer world to be in harmony with your inner physical world, then your whole world becomes more peaceful and calm. It is the calmness that allows you an opportunity to more readily access those expansive places in the abstract part of the mind. Eventually you may enter those realms of Love-Wisdom.

When I was a teenager living in Okinawa, Japan, many years ago, I remember one summer day going with my father to the homes of two of his political/business associates. Those of you who have ever lived or visited southern Japan during the summertime know how hot and humid the weather can be. I remember this particular day to be very hot and very humid. When we reached the first destination, I was offered a cold soda. I remember gulping down the delicious, ice-cold soda thinking how great it was to have refrigerated, cold drinks. I noticed that my father's associate offered my father hot, green tea, which they both sipped very slowly. Being a teenager, I thought that was strange to be drinking hot tea on a hot day. But, I was not too inquisitive why they would drink hot tea on a hot day. It wasn't until the second visit when again my dad and the host sipped hot green tea that my curiosity was aroused. On the way home, I asked my dad how they could drink something hot on a hot day. My father said the idea was to sip the hot tea very slowly and in very small portions to bring his inside temperature closer to the hot temperature on the outside. By sipping the hot tea very slowly, he could bring his internal environment closer in temperature (frequency) to the outer temperature and therefore would not feel the hot, humid weather as much. I also remember how calmly and slowly both my father and his associates drank the hot tea. I thought that was interesting because even after I had gulped down the ice-cold soda, I was soon very hot again. The key is to try to be in alignment with your surroundings at all times.

The silent, yet eternal emanating sound of A-U-M is "The Lost Chord." The internal AUM is the chord that connects us to "All That Is." The sound of AUM can be consciously vocalized so that its frequency is able to bring your consciousness to that inner, peaceful space of Oneness. For those who are very diligent and have done the necessary inner plane work, the internal AUM may be a vibration that has no sound, the "sound without sound."

Although this internal, eternal sound never leaves and this musical chord is not actually lost, most of humanity is not aware of its existence. The chord (sound) stays well hidden. Most of humanity is not at a state of consciousness where they are able to quiet the mind, let alone Still the Mind. Today with so many outer distractions, some very interesting and attracting, many people may never find a need or a reason to want to Still the Mind. "Why should I quiet my mind when there are so many things to do and there is so much information on the internet. And besides, I also have Twitter and Face Book." However, if you wish to effectively balance the chaos and stress inherent to city life in the 21st Century, one way is to find that inner, quiet heart space. Finding that Inner Spiritual Higher Heart Center will nudge, or perhaps quickly propel you toward the path of discovering your true puzzle piece in life.

There is another "Lost Chord" intertwined within the ever-present, eternal sound of A-U-M. According to the Divine Grace Acharya Keshav Dev in his book ***A Mystery***, it is stated:

> *"According to the Yoga, the indestructible Cardiac Plexus (anahat chakra), which is present in the center of the human body within the heart, reverberates constantly with the perpetual, infinite sound called Brahmnaad. It is a mystery as to the genesis of this sound and for how long it will*

*continue cannot be said. It was for this reason that it has been termed as Anantnad (infinite universal sound)."* [1]

In Search of the Lost Cord (not chord) refers to the building of one's Antahkarana. The Antahkarana can be thought of as an energetic consciousness cord sometimes resembling a stream of various colored lights that emanate from the top of one's head. Think of the Antahkarana as a spiritual antenna. Clairvoyants who are able to see the outpouring of the multitude of colored lights flowing from the top of the head gave birth to another name for the Antahkarana now also known as the "Rainbow Bridge" or the "Rainbow Bridge of Colored Light."

In the past, this consciousness cord emanating from the top of one's head usually had to be consciously built by the individual working with extremely fine mental matter. Today, there are other methods to build the Antahkarana. All of the New Encoding Patterns in Esoteric Acupuncture that contain the Six Surrounding One needling pattern (synonymous with the 3-6-1 configuration) are designed to assist the recipient of the treatment to build this consciousness cord known as the Antahkarana. One beauty of receiving an Esoteric Acupuncture treatment using a New Encoding Pattern with the 3-6-I configuration is that the recipient of the treatment does not have to consciously be aware of the concept of the Antahkarana. The initial building of one's Antahkarana will take place with the correct sequencing of the acupuncture sites of any of the New Encoding Patterns with the Six Surrounding the One configuration, whether the recipient of the treatment is aware of the Antahkarana or not. Building one's Antahkarana by receiving Esoteric Acupuncture treatments is merely another method to assist in the connection to the Source of "All That Is."

When the Antahkarana is strongly and distinctively constructed, you will have both the inseparable "Lost Chord" and the "Lost Cord" merged as a single integral part of your daily waking consciousness. But the recipient of an Esoteric

Acupuncture treatment must still do some level of inner plane work to notice the benefits of building his or her Antahkarana.

When the Antahkarana (spiritual antenna) has been built through Esoteric Acupuncture treatments, the recipient of the treatment can choose to maximize more efficiently this benefit by refining his or her lifestyle and choosing to meditate on a more consistent basis. Some people may choose to ignore the building of this esoteric foundation for inner spiritual growth process. The choice for the recipient of the treatment will depend on the level of consciousness he or she is presently at. If the recipient of an Esoteric Acupuncture treatment with the 3-6-1 encoding sequence contained in the treatment later chooses not to use the newly formed Antahkarana, there will be no negative effects such as qi leakage or susceptibility to outside energy attacks.

What is the Antahkarana exactly and what are its functions? Why is the Antahkarana important? Is the Antahkarana a necessary component of one's daily existence in the 21st Century? Very often there is a large gap between interesting and/or esoteric knowledge or information that may be beneficial to one's internal growth and what the average person defines as a necessity in his or her daily reality in a fast-paced, three-dimensional world. In most cases, esoteric knowledge is merely stored in one's mind as an interesting tidbit of information to be shared at certain gatherings or discussions with friends or students. The esoteric knowledge has not been converted into wisdom that becomes integrated as a part of one's daily existence.

If an inner spiritual awakening and development are important to you, then building the Antahkarana is one method to assist you in this endeavor. An inner spiritual awakening is not always synonymous with a religious experience. Although a religious experience may also be an inner spiritual awakening, more often a true, inner spiritual awakening is not tied into a specific religion. The inner spiritual awakening that is referred to here occurs on the Soul Plane or the Monadic Plane. A religious experience takes place on a level of the Personality Plane.

I have heard some individuals say that the Chakra System, Kundalini and systems related to those fields, including building one's Antahkarana, are outdated programs that are not necessary today. Most of the things we learn are actually programs in one form or another. Speaking different languages, religions, mathematics, learning skills such as playing sports, learning the rules of a game or system, learning how to write, playing an instrument, dancing, martial arts and countless other things and activities we have learned are all programs. Working with the Antahkarana, chakras and Kundalini may have been programs instilled in our consciousness many eons ago. Who is the judge to say one program is no longer needed, while another program is okay to implement and keep today? If you believe that the chakra system and working with Kundalini are old systems, then why should we discard these particular "old" systems yet retain an old system such as language or addition and multiplication? You are the judge as to whether the chakra system and working with Kundalini and building the Antahkarana are important to you. It is not wise to merely discard an old programmed system just because you might not resonate with that system.

Old systems do not necessarily make those systems outdated and useless for the needs of today. The systems of communicating to others by speaking or writing in a certain language are old, slow programs. Humanity has not yet evolved as a group to be able to instantaneously and telepathically communicate with each other. Does that mean that we should abandon these old methods of communication of writing or speaking to others?

Those individuals whom I have heard or read about who say that Kundalini, the chakra system and the Antahkarana are outdated and unnecessary systems claimed to have had extraterrestrial experiences and have said they themselves are not from this planet or have had a very traumatic physical and mental experience or experiences. Those may be true claims. Some individuals claim to have had a near-death experience and feel that they no longer have to utilize a slow and outdated system such as the chakra system or work with raising Kundalini. They have now awakened certain levels of consciousness that they had not been aware of before their near-death experience or extraterrestrial encounters. But the majority of individuals living on planet Earth today who may be interested in the esoteric knowledge and the Ageless Wisdom Teachings presented in this book and elsewhere, have not had extraterrestrial contacts or experienced a near-death trauma that has elevated the individual to a heightened state of awareness. For most people, it may be more desirable to have a slower, organic, more controlled method of consciousness expansion, rather than an abrupt, unexpected and accelerated expansion of reality

The key point to be emphasized is that it is usually more beneficial to have a firsthand, organic (slower), natural experience of a heightened spiritual awakening, not merely an experience that has expanded your reality abruptly. We are interested in Esoteric Acupuncture to develop heightened awareness on all levels, including eating healthily to bring your physical vehicle to a lighter, finer frequency that is in alignment with your expanded emotional, mental and spiritual levels.

Although certain individuals may have awakened various levels of clairvoyance or clairsentience, those types of siddhis (powers) do not necessarily make a person more spiritual. Being familiar with or experiencing extraterrestrial or inner-terrestrial abductions, having knowledge of the pyramids and other spiritual vortexes or merely reading about esoteric teachings does not mean that the individual has had a firsthand spiritual awakening to discover his or her true Inner Spiritual Higher Heart. They have just expanded the horizons of the mind and opened more mental compartments to be able to store more information. Some of the information may be interesting and even very fascinating. Nonetheless, acquiring those tidbits of information and repeating that information to others are merely exercises of left-brained, intellectual acuity. Most often, those types of very abrupt or uninvited experiences will cause much fear, anger and paranoia. Will the information move you along your true Inner Spiritual Higher Heart pathway, so you may be of service to others?

Besides those people who had traumatic life experiences, there are many young souls who may think that the old methods and older ways of thinking are outdated for the newer, expanded and accelerated energetics of the Age of Aquarius. These same people may feel that old systems are not in alignment with the rapid changes that are occurring today and may not be aware of the need to organically develop and strengthen their Inner Spiritual Higher Heart.

In every age throughout the history of humanity, there has been a small group of advanced, awakened souls who have assisted in keeping the masses aware of the need to explore and develop their Inner Spiritual Higher Heart Center. It is important to understand the distinction between spiritual and religious. Being a member of some organized religion does not automatically qualify you as being spiritual. Spirituality is not synonymous with religious. There are many religious people who are very spiritual. But, there are also many very religious people who are not very spiritual. A spiritual person, as defined within the scope of Esoteric Acupuncture, is someone who has done some level of personal inner plane work to awake and align the various aspects of his or her inner heart in order to live in the field of goodness, kindness, love and compassion. A spiritual person is an aware person with an awakened inner heart who tries to maintain this higher frequency as much as possible to be able to help and share with others. The act of helping others must come without any expectations of monetary benefits or other types of payments from those actions unless, of course, your current work to make a living is in the service work field.

This Inner Plane Heart Awakening becomes a part of the fabric of who you are and is not a valve that is turned on and off depending upon who you meet or who you are with. The truly awakened, spiritual person has touched this inner path and strives to stay on this Inner Heart Path.

To those that "know," the Ageless Wisdom will never be outdated. There is a fundamental fabric of wisdom that holds the vibrations of goodness, spiritual integrity, honesty and a genuine concern for your fellow brothers and sisters. This fabric of wisdom flows through the consciousness of each succeeding generation to keep humanity connected to its true Inner Spiritual Higher Heart Center. This fundamental fabric of consciousness also flows through and is connected to our Planetary Consciousness, as well as being connected to a greater Cosmic Consciousness. This fundamental energy thread is the spiritual fabric of consciousness, interwoven into the teachings of the Ageless Wisdom schools. Although the method you choose to access this spiritual path may change with different generations, the "true" path and journey do not change. The journey is your "Soul Journey" and is also a "Solo Journey." Those that do not understand will most likely decline the opportunity to attempt their individual Soul Journey. It may seem like too much work and may feel like a lonely journey. It is not the case for those who have found their inner heart space and their puzzle piece in life and are journeying on their path. One's true puzzle piece is also your "puzzle peace." For these people, the Soul Journey is not lonely and is filled with abundance, contentment, joy and love.

The consciousness fabric of the Ageless Wisdom teachings has always survived. It is the responsibility of the Light Workers of every generation to keep the light of the Ageless Wisdom Teachings alive and to spread these teachings to those who are ready and willing to receive. Those of you reading this work who resonate with what is being said are the current Light Workers of today. The idea of "do not cast pearls before swine" means that those who are not at a certain level of light quotient will not understand or truly appreciate the Pearls of Wisdom of the Ageless Wisdom Teachings. When the student is ready, the teacher will appear.

Your point of view on any subject can change and either evolve or devolve depending on the amount of light you are carrying and maintaining. As your inner light quotient increases, your interpretation and understanding of any information or knowledge usually changes. The Ageless Wisdom Teachings carry a truth that is also "The Truth." "The Truth" never changes. Your understanding or interpretation of a truth may change, but know that various interpretations of The Truth by those with lesser light quotients are only partial understandings and may or may not be correct. "A truth" can have different interpretations. "The Truth" is singular. The Truth is the Truth. There is no right or wrong with The Truth. The Truth just is. Now, depending upon your light quotient, you may have a very strong opinion on a specific topic and because of a strong ego, you may insist that your interpretation is "The Truth." That will be "your truth" heavily influenced by the amount of light, or lack of light you carry. It might not be The Truth, which is singular with no alternative interpretations. Those who want to know "The Truth" of their true purpose for incarnating this lifetime on planet Earth will greatly benefit by building their Antahkarana, one's spiritual antenna. Building one's Antahkarana and using this bridge to higher consciousness will assist that individual to discover his or her true puzzle piece in life.

Possessing or acquiring powers such as clairvoyance, clairaudience and clairsentience are inherent rights for an awakened, multi-sensorial New Humanity. But acquiring those types of siddhis (powers) or similar powers without a very strong spiritual center and spiritual foundation will often be used solely to display powers from one's lower ego. Acquiring telekinetic powers without a strong spiritual center usually leads to wanting to display one's powers to others, much like some of the fakirs in India. "Let me show you my powers." This is the world of glamour, Maya and delusion.

Working with building one's Antahkarana/antenna is merely another method to assist one in discovering his or her true puzzle piece in life. When you have found your true puzzle piece, your reality of who you are and your true focus pulls or pushes you to stay on your path. Assisting you in discovering your true puzzle piece in life is the focus and foundation of this book and all of the books in the **Esoteric Acupuncture** series. The frequencies and the spin field created by an Esoteric Acupuncture treatment will allow the recipient of the treatment to move toward his or her Inner Spiritual Higher Heart Center with more calmness and more clarity.

Be Still and move into your heart space. If you feel that working with the Antahkarana is not part of your journey, then do not work with building the Antahkarana. (You would not be reading this book unless you were at least curious about the Antahkarana and the Ageless Wisdom Teachings.) If the idea of creating and maintaining a productive, yet calm and peaceful, centered, harmonious lifestyle is important to you, then working on building and refining your Antahkarana will help you achieve and maintain that goal. If you only desire to "feel" safe and not participate in any work you feel is not necessary for your three-dimensional existence, then the discipline required for working on the inner planes and developing and strengthening your Inner Spiritual Higher Heart Center may not be for you. I am not referring to being a kind, understanding, loving individual. Those attributes are already expected to be in place for those on their individual Soul Journey to reach and stay in their Inner Spiritual Higher Heart Center.

If a person's only requirements revolve around the Muladhara (root chakra) demands of one's day-to-day basic survival needs or basic daily routines (buying and preparing food, earning money to pay rent or mortgage, paying bills, raising a family), then most likely that person would not be interested in building and working with his or her Antahkarana. A person may be interested in building his or her spiritual antenna, but due to the heavy pull and commitments to the realms of the Root Chakra field, will not have the necessary time for working on building and refining his or her Antahkarana. If you have a family to take care of, that must be your first priority, your most urgent obligation and duty. If one's focus is on making money, enjoying entertainment and having a good time in life, resolving relationship issues and finding one's "perfect" partner, then that person most likely will not be interested in building his or her Antahkarana.

For some people, but not everyone, there may come a time when they may ask: "What is life all about?" "What is my true purpose in life?" For a question like that to manifest in one's consciousness, that person would have to be vibrating, at least temporarily, at a heightened level of consciousness. Working with Kundalini and building one's Antahkarana will assist in finding answers to your inner, spiritual questions. You have a purpose in this lifetime above the level to carve out a living or making more money to buy more things.

One definition of the Antahkarana is that it is a word that describes a vertical astral beam of consciousness (as streams of light) that emanates from the top of one's head allowing a level of consciousness to move upward, as well as energy to descend into the individual's head chakras by way of entering through *Tian Man* (Du-20) and the surrounding *Sishencong* Window Group. This vertical beam of astral energy reveals various colored lights. The density of the vibrations or the refinement of the vibration of the emanating stream of light is directly dependent on the consciousness level of the individual. The consciousness level of the client determines the actual colors for the emanating light stream.

The Antahkarana is sometimes known as the "Rainbow Bridge" because of this very reason of radiating gradations of various colors of light. I mostly see violets, lavenders, pinks, blues, greens, golden shades, ashen white and sometimes silver in the Antahkarana of my clients after they have received an Esoteric Acupuncture treatment from me. The silver color is usually infused with shades of darker blue. The golden light often has shades of darker green infused within the gold colored light. Although during mental visualizations I like to work with the shade of gold that is the color of a gold coin, the gold light

I see within the Antahkarana of my clientele is usually a more yellowish-gold and not the golden hue of a gold coin.

Building one's Antahkarana is one method that allows an individual to tap into the Akashic Records. Having a fully formed Rainbow Bridge and using the Bridge gives you a pathway that allows you access to consciousness levels above the normal three-dimensional realms of reality. The field where the Akashic Records are kept is a very fine vibrational field that exists in the very subtle causal energy fields and above, is not an actual physical location or a physical storage center like that found in computers. The term Akashic Records refers to stored information of an extremely fine frequency that is gathered from every known age and kept in an extremely fine field of consciousness that is not a physical location. The Akashic Records contain every action and thoughts that have ever been performed, spoken, written, seen, felt, recorded, dreamed or imagined.

Although the consciousness field containing the Akashic Records is available to everyone, there is one major barrier that has been set in place to prevent access to the information in the Akashic Records. A majority of the masses may not be spiritually awakened enough to properly use the information in a positive manner that is not harmful or detrimental to others. There is a safety shield that surrounds each individual known as an atomic shield. The atomic shield divides the Astral Plane from the etheric levels. This atomic shield exists to deny those with a lower vibrational consciousness from accessing the information stored in the higher Akashic Records field. Those who are able to Still the Mind, have a greater possibility of reaching the plane of the Akashic Records. To Still the Mind is not synonymous with quiet thinking where you sit in meditation without physical movement, yet your mind is in the chattering mode, constantly moving. You are also able to reach some level of the Akashic Records during certain "ah ha" moments when thoughts just come to you. Where do these thoughts come from? Sometimes the thoughts may come from your subconscious mind. Other times, those thoughts may appear because you have accessed a certain level of the field of the Akashic Records.

I have observed, without judgment, the energy field above the heads of many long-time meditators without seeing any remnants or traces of an Antahkarana. The teachers and practitioners of most forms of meditation are not aware of this consciousness bridge that can be formed and refined by mental matter and with an Esoteric Acupuncture treatment by a practitioner who knows the correct New Encoding Patterns to use on the client. If there are no higher, spiritual factors involved in wishing to reach the plane of the Akashic Records, then one's desire to access seemingly obscure and esoteric information can become purely ego-based motives to exhibit academic and mental prowess.

Knowing the existence of the Antahkarana, the bridge to higher consciousness, and wishing to build this bridge, are benefits of understanding and receiving an Esoteric Acupuncture treatment. At least the initial frequencies connected to your Antahkarana will be activated and formed by receiving an Esoteric Acupuncture treatment. The ability to mentally connect the triangular acupuncture sites in a specific order, while receiving the Esoteric Acupuncture treatment, will further assist the recipient of the treatment to obtain a deeper, more meaningful and a stronger spiritual connection. The procedure of visually connecting the triangular formations within the New Encoding Patterns is designed to give the recipient of a treatment an opportunity to implement an accelerated procedure for the building of the Antahkarana, our spiritual antenna. The connections to your deeper, spiritual realms will also occur in a more timely fashion with the conscious intent of building your Antahkarana, versus the more commonly followed path of hoping "something" will happen by the mere process of sitting in quiet meditation. This means that a serious and dedicated meditator will sometimes, over a period of time, gradually develop an Antahkarana. Other meditators may not have or display any aspect of the bridge, even after years of meditating. The knowledge of the existence of one's Antahkarana and the ability to construct its foundation with an Esoteric Acupuncture treatment will hasten the formation of the Rainbow Bridge.

One real beauty of receiving an Esoteric Acupuncture treatment is that the New Encoding Patterns are specifically designed to build and refine one's Antahkarana. Even if your client is a first time recipient of an Esoteric Acupuncture treatment and has never heard of the Antahkarana, the needling process of a New Encoding Pattern with the Six Surrounding the One configuration, plus the triangular visualizations that the client will connect with the guidance of the practitioner, will automatically begin the building process of the client's Antahkarana, the Rainbow Bridge of Consciousness.

Repeated Esoteric Acupuncture treatments over a period of time will help the client to strengthen and refine his or her own Rainbow Bridge. Treatments with the New Encoding Patterns will not cause one to have a premature Kundalini awakening. One benefit for those people who decide to build their Antahkarana is that they will find a smoother pathway to be able to quiet the chattering, concrete mind. This in turn will assist in centering oneself to be able to move into the field of his or her own Inner Spiritual Higher Heart Center and to strengthen the functions of the abstract mind.

For those who choose the path of building the Antahkarana, I recommend that you enjoy the journey. As long as you keep refining your Inner Spiritual Higher Heart Center and keep working with the strengthening and expansion of your Antahkarana, you will obtain a greater understanding of your individual Soul Journey. You will begin to "know in your heart" your interconnectedness to other people, to other places and to other realities outside of your own personal three-dimensional world. This process will greatly broaden your various planes of consciousness. Consciousness has no borders or no limiting boundaries except to those who are not able to recognize and move out of the realities of a heavily programmed three-dimensional concrete mind. The expansion of consciousness will in turn assist you in uncovering who you are and why you are here on planet Earth for this particular incarnation. By going inward with focus and discipline, you will eventually move from your Soul Journey to your Spirit Journey. Although this process may take some linear time, the object is to enjoy the journey and not to merely focus on getting somewhere or finding something quickly. When you have found the calling of your Spirit Journey and are moving forward on your Journey, you will be following the path of your puzzle piece in life. Everyone has a different puzzle piece in life. Although all Spirit Journeys are different for each of us, there is no one Spirit Journey superior to another.

It was mentioned earlier that some people might feel that building the Antahkarana is an old, outdated method of trying to obtain some level of spiritual awakening and is not a necessity for a spiritual awakening. Of course, it is not a necessity for a spiritual awakening. Everything is moving so rapidly nowadays that all the requirements and discipline needed in the building process of the Antahkarana may seem too slow for the fast paced society of today. One thing is definitely true. Planet Earth, as a whole, has very rapidly shifted into a higher frequency reality. Since we are living in such a complex, modern society that is so different from only a few years ago, some people may feel there are newer, quicker, better methods that override the necessity of having to rely on older methods. Some people may feel that one day they will be able to merely take a pill, ingest a "magic" plant or plug into a new electronic or computerized gadget to reach a specific desired level of spiritual awakening. There are many thoughts and theories about the best or most efficient method to reach a certain level of spiritual awakening. Although many theories sound interesting and convincing, do these theories work and are those methods able to harmoniously connect one to the higher realms of spiritual consciousness?

The real "reward" is uncovering the various complex and multi-layered, hidden layers you will discover. You will overcome any and all the challenges encountered during your individual journey toward spiritual awakening. You will experience opportunities for many awakenings. The journey itself will assist you in unraveling the mysteries that are hidden from you now on your present adventure of discovering your true puzzle piece in life. Stepping onto the path of your own individual Soul Journey is one reward. Another will be moving from your Soul Journey to your Spiritual Journey. The "reward" is the journey itself and not necessarily the moment of the awakening. Enjoy the ride!

## Window to the Sky Points

There is a set of acupuncture points known as the Window to the Sky Points or the Window of Heaven Points. Most of these acupuncture points are on the neck or near the neck, except the bilateral *Tianfu* (Lu-3) points on the upper biceps of the lateral aspects of both arms along the lung meridian and the bilateral *Tian Qi* (Per-1) points that are located approximately one *cun* lateral from each nipple in the fourth intercostal space.

In Esoteric Acupuncture, the acupuncture point known as Ren-24 is also called *Tian Qi*. Do not confuse the *Tian Qi* name referring to the first acupuncture point on the pericardium meridian that are bilateral Window to the Sky points with the Ren-24 located in the center of the mentolabial groove superior to the chin and inferior to the lower lip.

Those of you who are familiar with Esoteric Acupuncture will note that those New Encoding Patterns that start with The Crown Infinity Pattern all contain *Feng Fu* (Du-16), an important Window to the Sky Point in the Esoteric Acupuncture work. The anterior New Encoding Patterns that contain The Extended Indigo Triangle Pattern contain the bilateral Window to the Sky Points called *Tianrong* (SI-17).

Why are the majority of these Window to the Sky points or the Window of Heaven points located on or near the neck? Think of the head as the region that houses the upper chakras in the Thirteen Chakra System. The trunk of the body houses the lower chakras. As qi, prana and Kundalini travel upward, these energetic frequencies will ascend through the neck into the head chakras. Think of the Window to the Sky points as specific gateways along a bridge (your neck) that offer you the possibility of moving qi from the denser chakras on the trunk of the body upward through the acupuncture meridian on the neck to connect with and activate the head chakras. This process moves along at a slightly accelerated pace when used in a New encoding Pattern of Esoteric Acupuncture.

If you have formally studied acupuncture in an accredited Acupuncture and Asian Medical College or University and are presently a licensed acupuncturist, you will be able to safely activate these very specific gateways by inserting small acupuncture needles at certain Window to the Sky acupuncture sites in a specific order within your treatment. When inserting acupuncture needles into any of the Window to the Sky Points, I recommend using the Seirin red handled .16 by 15 mm needle. On a sensitive client, I recommend using the Seirin lime handled .14 mm by 15 mm needle. If a male has a full beard or your client has a weathered neck from too much sun, then I recommend the Seirin light blue handled .20 mm by 15 mm needle. I usually insert the needle perpendicularly or at a slight oblique angle for the points on the neck.

If you are a practitioner of another modality besides acupuncture and wish to use Esoteric Acupuncture patterns on your clientele, you can activate the gateway points on the neck by many means. There are many health tools available today such as: Esoteric Acupuncture Astral Oils by Dr. Yury Kronn (the founder of Energy Tools), very small magnets, Selenite wands by Tom Ledder of Colorado (USA), Korean hand pellets, crystals, photon beam machine, prana from your hands or finger or any other appropriate tools of energy activation.

The neck is a bridge that contains acupuncture sites that may act as pathways to allow a person a chance to move from a denser level of consciousness to a higher level of consciousness. Think of the Window to the Sky points as gateways or "shortcuts" to move from density to a lighter, more refined level of consciousness. When specific Window to the

Sky points are needled in the correct sequence within a New Encoding Pattern, then the possibility arises to more rapidly strengthen, transform and open the gateways from denseness to a higher frequency field. (See figure 4.1-a below.)

**Window to the Sky Points**
**Gateway from Denseness to a Higher Frequency Field**

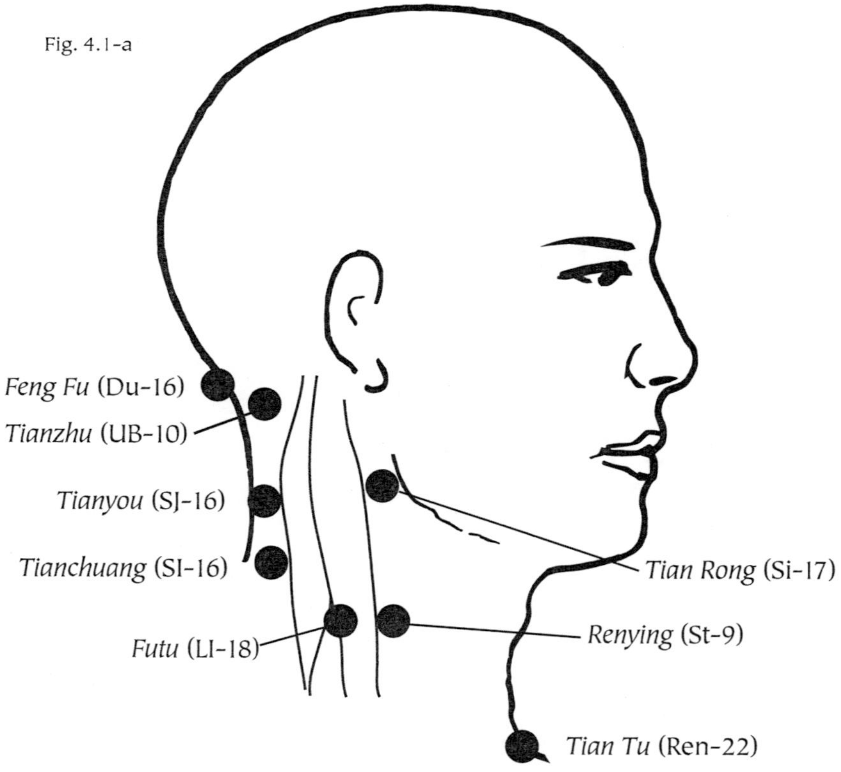


The initial construction of one's Antahkarana is somewhat expedited through mental visualizations. Remember that visualization is a right-brain activity of the abstract mind. If one is able to visually connect the energies at the three Major Head Centers in a triangular formation, the creation of the initial Antahkarana will occur more rapidly. The three major head centers are: the Sahasrara/Crown Chakra, the Ajna Center at the acupuncture site of *Yintang* and the Taluka Chakra at the acupuncture site of *Feng Fu*/Du-16).

**Three Major Head Centers**
**Connected in a Triangular Formation**

Fig. 4.1-b

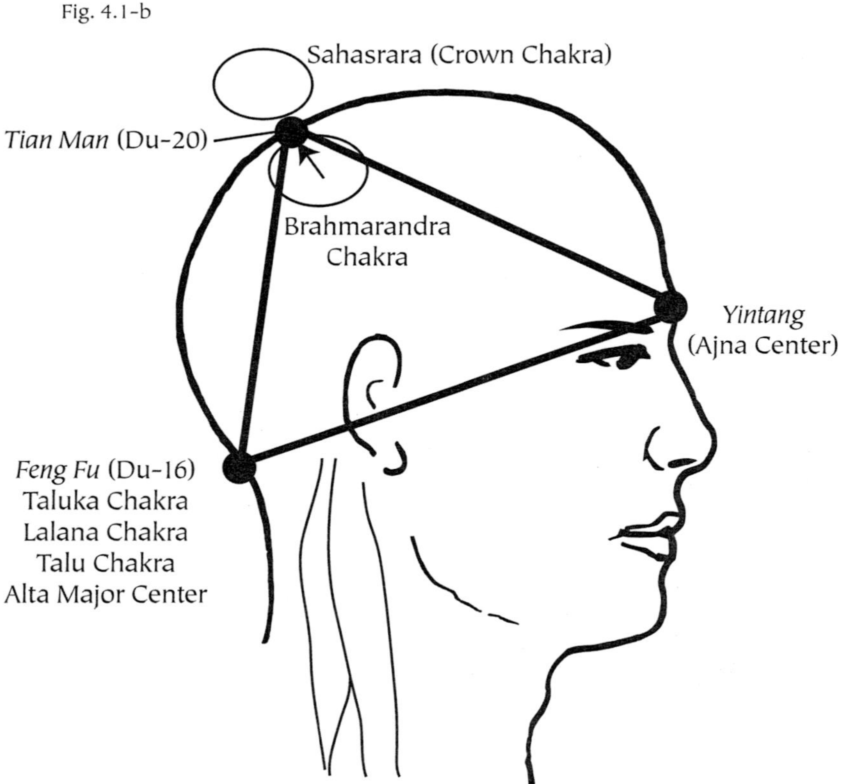


The chakra at the site of the acupuncture point called *Feng Fu* (Du-16) is also alternately known as the Taluka Chakra,

Lalana Chakra or Talu Chakra by various Hindu systems or the Alta Major Center in Djwhal Khul's (the Alice Bailey books) system. The connection and communication of these three Major Head Centers partially occurs through a process known as morphic resonance, an instantaneous, nonlinear consciousness connection. Although a broken-lined linear connection is shown in figure 4.1-c for clarity purposes, the connection is completed by way of a morphic resonant, nonlinear, instantaneous connection. After the acupuncture site of *Dazhui* (Du-14) is needled, the stored information (as qi) from *Dazhui* (Du-14) instantaneously communicates with the qi (information) at the acupuncture site of *Feng Fu* (Du-16).

**Morphic Resonant Connection**

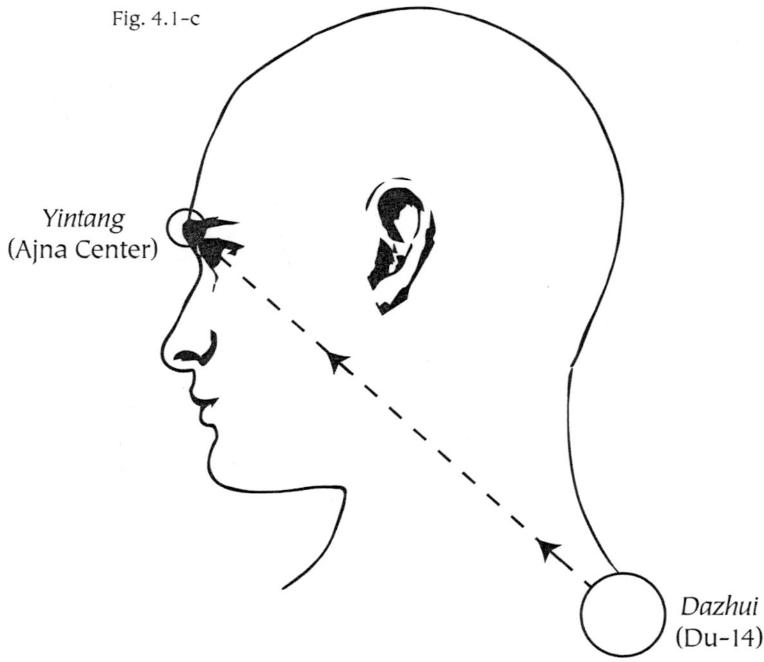

There is a little known "secret" related to the connection of the three Major Head Centers that will make the results from the connection stronger and more lasting. When you make the visualization connections of specific acupuncture sites on the head and neck in The Discern the Whisper Pattern or any of the variations of the Esoteric *Shaoyin* Patterns, you will notice that there is a visual connection from *Dazhui* (Du-14) to *Yintang* (Ajna Center). *Dazhui* (Du-14) is located directly on the posterior spine below the lower border of the seventh cervical vertebra where the neck attaches to the upper back/shoulder region. *Yintang* (Ajna Center) is located on the vertical midline of the forehead between the eyebrows and superior to the bridge of the nose. The Chinese acupuncture point *Yintang* is the access site for the head chakra known as the Ajna Center in the Hindu chakra system. The Ajna Center is also sometimes called the Third Eye. To obtain the most benefits from an Esoteric Acupuncture treatment using the Discern the Whisper Pattern or any of the variations of the Esoteric *Shaoyin* Patterns, it is important to have your client make a mental activation of *Yintang* and see that point being energized after the action of first inserting a needle at the acupuncture site of *Dazhui* (Du-14). Next have your client move the energy upward from the acupuncture site of *Dazhui* (Du-14) to the acupuncture site of *Feng Fu* (Du-16).

When Djwhal Khul, the ascended Tibetan Master, discussed in his massive text ***Treatise on Cosmic Fire*** the importance of connecting the three major head centers, he did not mention this particular step of first activating *Dazhui* (Du-14) so the qi at that site would instantaneously activate the information stored in the Ajna Center located at the acupuncture site of *Yintang*. It is very important to understand and make this connection from *Dazhui* (Du-14) to *Yintang* first, then move the qi upward from *Dazhui* (Du-14) to *Feng Fu* (Du-16) prior to visually connecting the three major head centers.

The Chinese name of the acupuncture point *Dazhui* is often translated as "The Big Hammer." Some Chinese medical scholars say that the moniker, "The Big Hammer," merely refers to the fact that often the seventh cervical vertebra is the largest protruding spine in that region of the lower neck. Go back to figure 4.1-c to see the relationship of the point locations of *Dazhui* (Du-14) and *Yintang* (Ajna Center) to each other.

The particular step of having your client visually connecting *Dazhui* (Du-14) to *Yintang* (Ajna Center) creates the morphic resonant vibrations for the whole grid of that posterior New Encoding Pattern. The esoteric meaning of the name "The Big Hammer" refers to a metaphor for the idea of striking lightly to produce "big results. When an acupuncture needle is inserted at the site of *Dazhui* (Du-14) prior to asking your client to visually see an activation at *Yintang* (Ajna Center), the needle symbolizes a hammer that subtly "pounds" and releases information stored at this site to form an Axiatonal Grid into the energy bodies of the individual receiving the treatment. This grid encompasses not only the acupuncture meridians of the Etheric Plane that communicates with the Dense Physical, Astral and Lower Mental Planes, but this morphic resonant event also connects the Buddhic, Atmic, Monadic and Logoic Planes of consciousness to the Axiatonal Grids of our Solar, Galactic and Cosmic fields. The subtle "hammering" of qi (information) stored at the site of *Dazhui* (Du-14) releases esoteric information. It is the idea of striking a hammer at a certain point to open up this connection to hidden aspects of one's higher, spiritual consciousness planes. This is the concept of small energy input producing great energy output.

This same visualization consisting of asking your client to mentally see *Dazhui* (Du-14) activating *Yintang*, then moving the energy upward from *Dazhui* (Du-14) to *Feng Fu* (Du-16) before mentally connecting *Feng Fu* (Du-16) with *Yintang* (Ajna Center) and connecting both of those points in a triangular formation to *Tian Man* (Du-20) is used in the Discern the Whisper Pattern, the Esoteric *Shaoyin* Heart Pattern, the Esoteric *Shaoyin* Kidney Pattern, the Esoteric *Shaoyin* Heart Window Pattern, the *Hun* Follow the *Shen* Pattern and the *Wei QI* Grid Strengthening Pattern. For a more complete description of the step-by-step visualization diagrams and instructions for activating all the acupuncture sites in these patterns, go to Chapter Five under the Visualization section.

According to Swami Satyeswarananda Giri Babaji Maharaj discussing Mahamuni Babaji's Kriya Yoga system, Swami Satyeswarananda states that the Inner Divine Light between the eyebrows at the Ajna Center is the Mother. The Inner Sound at the medulla oblongata is the Father.[2] It was mentioned in ***Sea of Fire-Cosmic Fire: Esoteric Acupuncture, Volume IV*** that needling the acupuncture site of *Feng Fu* (Du-16) will activate the medulla oblongata. The medulla oblongata is the part of the brain that connects with, and has the capabilities to stimulate, the multiple levels of the Muladhara (Root Chakra). Remember each chakra has at least seven levels of consciousness that store different qualities and densities of information. Activating *Feng Fu* (Du-16) with the purpose of connecting the three major head centers will access and open up the gateways to the higher levels of the Muladhara (Root Chakra), not the lower day-to-day activities or the survival mode realities. In Esoteric Acupuncture, we are interested in balancing the lower chakras in order to move smoothly into aligning and activating the fine frequency waves of the higher, head chakras and those chakras superior to the cranium.

Visually connecting *Feng Fu* (Du-16) to the Ajna Center at *Yintang* will merge the Inner Divine Light of the Mother with the Divine Inner Sound of the Father. When we say Mother and Father, we are not talking about an external consciousness of a male and female frequency, such as a personal god. We are talking about your own inner, higher *yin* and *yang* realms of higher consciousness. The Mother and Father being discussed are Within, not Without. This higher realm of spiritual consciousness is dormant in most people. In fact, most people are not even aware of the concept of a higher spiritual male and female consciousness. One of the best ways to access these higher realms of consciousness is to quiet the busy mind. Eventually the higher Mother and Father Within merge to become One with no differentiation between female and male or yin and *yang*. There is only consciousness at that level.

After the harmonious higher frequency is set up by the visual connection of the qi of Taluka Chakra (at Du-16) and the qi at the site of Ajna Center (at *Yintang*), we then visually connect both *Feng Fu* (Du-16) and *Yintang* to connect with the qi stored at *Tian Man* (Du-20). Remember that the esoteric location of *Tian Man* (Du-20) is located posteriorly to the traditional location of *Bai Hui* (Du-20) in a triangular formation. There are multiple levels of the Sahasrara (Crown Chakra) and the lower levels can be activated quite easily. When the three major head centers are interacting in this triangular connection, you will have created and activated the correct inner qi to open the "hidden" Thirteenth Gate, which is *Tian Man* (Du-20). The esoteric location of Du-20 (*Tian Man*) is the gateway to activate the higher realms of the Sahasrara (Crown Chakra). The fact that you are aware of the esoteric gateway and that you are activating the esoteric gateway means that you are working with the frequencies necessary to open up the inner planes of this chakra. Reaching the higher inner planes of consciousness stored within *Tian Man* (Du-20) is what is known in Esoteric Acupuncture as being in the field of "Celestial Fullness." You will have completed the inner circuit of Stillness allowing you an opportunity to reach the plane of the Akashic Records and to go beyond into the higher realms of consciousness of The All Field. The All Field is the multiverse of everything and No-thing, all dimensions and no dimensions, all realms and no realms. The All Field has no boundaries, no limitations, no beginning and no ending.

There is a small gap from the top of the cranium to the location of the Sahasrara (Crown Chakra) above the cranium. It requires a bridge, known as the wisarga, to link the Brahmarandra Chakra within the cranium to the Sahasrara (Crown Chakra) located above the cranium. If you insert an acupuncture needle at the site called *Bai Hui*, then the qi will exit from the inner pathway of the Du channel through *Bai Hui* and continue to traverse along the etheric Du channel, never connecting with the Sahasrara (Crown Chakra). It requires the specific triangular connections and needling the acupuncture site at *Tian Man* (Du-20) that will form the wisarga to allow the energies (information) from the intracranial Brahmarandra Chakra to flow into the Sahasrara (Crown Chakra) located above the cranium. (See figure 4.1-d below.)

**Building The Wisarga (Power Bridge)**

Fig. 4.1-d

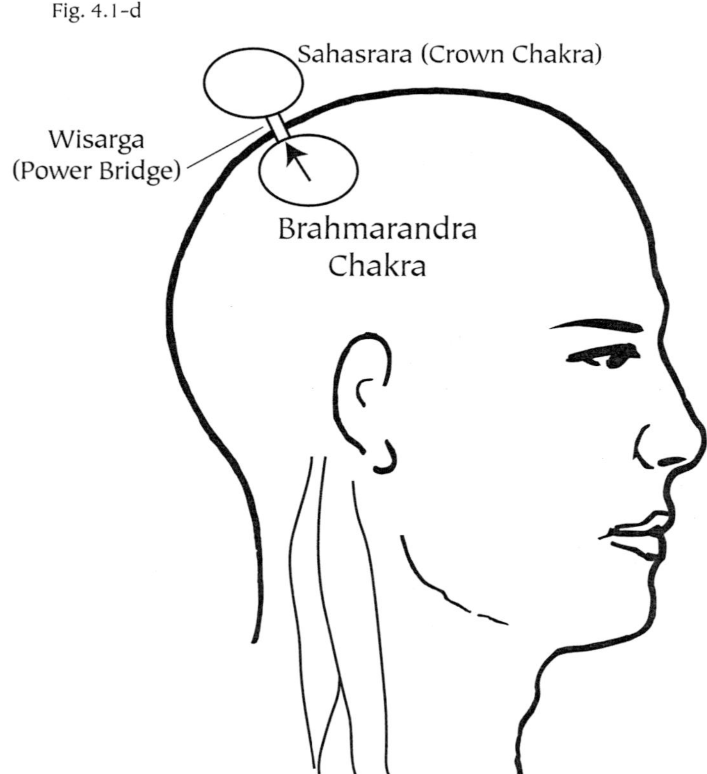


Retrieving information through the information highway known as the internet is a convenient method to quickly access much knowledge, and it is one method to expand one's consciousness. But, just because something is written or shown on the internet does not mean the information is true. Gathering external written or oral transmissions are not synonymous with achieving Inner, Spiritual Wisdom through Stillness. It is through Stillness, and not a massive collection of information and clutter, that another level of Wisdom begins to reveal itself.

Unfolding the Inner Ageless Wisdom has an inherent time lock that exists to safeguard the information from being misused by the undeveloped soul. Sometimes a severe trauma to the head may initiate an unusual, very deep spiritual awakening. Often a premature Kundalini awakening caused by chanting, pranayama (breathing techniques) or other methods will cause immediate access to the inner, hidden Wisdom. In most cases, a premature Kundalini awakening will cause fear and much anxiety in the unprepared individual. If you are interested in accessing the Inner Ageless Wisdom, it is my opinion that the best way to achieve this objective is to reach some level of inner Stillness first. Ingest only the cleanest, organic, fresh foods and drinks as possible. Then try to achieve some level of inner calmness, inner peace and inner, spiritual alignment. In this manner, "that which is concealed will be revealed," but in a more gentle fashion. There will not be such an abrupt change in your lifestyle and not too much stress placed on your emotional and mental bodies.

The Antahkarana is not merely the vertical visible spiritual antenna and the rainbow-colored Light of Wisdom. The most important point to understand about the Antahkarana is that it is one vehicle that allows an individual an opportunity to enter into a heightened, altered state of inner consciousness without having to ingest something or go outside of his or her own field. You are able to stay within your own field, but now have the opportunity to access a more refined stream of inner consciousness. You can think of the Antahkarana as one pathway that allows a higher refined stream of consciousness with unlimited levels to download into your various planes of denser consciousness, including your three-dimensional world. C.W. Leadbetter states in his book ***The Monad***:

> *We used to think of raising "ourselves" till we could unite "ourselves" with that glorified higher being, not realizing that it was the higher that was the true self, and that to unite the higher to the lower really meant opening out the lower so that the higher might work in it and through it.*[3]

Being aware of our Antahkarana, then consciously working with building the Antahkarana, are tools that will "open the lower so that the higher might work in it and through it" as stated it the quote above. This is one goal of Esoteric Acupuncture we are attempting to obtain by moving into and staying in our Inner, Spiritual Higher Heart Center. The Stillness that is constantly referred to in this work is the frequency that allows the higher to move into merging and working with the lower. It is through Stillness that the chaotic mental chatter is eliminated to allow the refined frequencies of discernment to appear. If you want to Discern the Whisper of your Heart, it is best to try and rid your "monkey mind" of the excess chatter of the outside world. Our "monkey mind" refers to the endless amounts of mental clutter and mental chatter that acts as heavy baggage creating blockages to the path of the finer frequency Still Mind.

As your inner spiritual world unfolds through dedicated inner plane work and as you are able to hold increased levels of light for longer periods of time, your Antahkarana will also unfold to expose greater depths of light frequencies. The Antahkarana is an ageless, open system, not an outdated, closed system. Just because there may be multiple choices to reach a certain level of heightened consciousness, does not mean that building the Antahkarana is no longer necessary.

When one is discussing the various levels or planes of consciousness, Astral Plane refers to the plane directly above the Etheric and the Dense Physical Planes. Astral in this context refers to the emotional body and the field of Maya, which is that of glamour and illusion. Illusion does not mean non-existent in the same manner as when someone is imagining something or making something up. Illusion in the context of Maya means being swayed by materialistic things and endeavors and allowing the lower ego of fame, fortune and accumulating things to take precedence over the inner spiritual work. But there are also other definitions of astral.

Astral can also mean "of or pertaining to the stars." According to Ramacharaka in his book ***The Life Beyond Death***, he stated that this definition of astral originally came into use in connection with occultism by reason of the common idea of men that "the other side is up in the skies; among the clouds or in the region of the stars."[4]

### The Six Strands of the Primary Antahkarana

For a somewhat simplified explanation of the Antahkarana, our personal spiritual antenna, think of the Antahkarana as requiring two distinct, but interconnected and very closely intercommunicating sections. The first section involves building the wisarga, the power bridge from the intracranial Brahmarandra Chakra to the Sahasrara (Crown Chakra) located above the cranium. This we have already constructed by inserting acupuncture needles in specific locations during any of the Esoteric Acupuncture treatments that have the 3-6-1 Encoding Group of acupuncture points located on the posterior of the head.

The second section consists of three distinct components. It is best to have all three components acting in concert as one unified, complete Antahkarana that extends upward from where the wisarga (power bridge) has been constructed to activate the chakras above the cranium. There is the Primary Antahkarana and two other bridges known as the Esoteric Antahkaranas. Although you may feel that all the branches of the Antahkarana are esoteric in nature, in Esoteric Acupuncture the unified, complete Antahkarana is explained in three distinct sections.

There are basically three ways for the unified, complete Antahkarana to be built. In the future, there will probably be other quicker methods using electromagnetic, microwave, scalar or other types of wave technology. But, for the informed spiritual aspirants today that are either spiritual disciples, spiritual initiates or spiritual leaders, I know of only three natural methods to build one's Antahkarana.

1) One way the Antahkarana was built in the past was using refined mental manner to visually build the rainbow bridge. This particular aspect of the Antahkarana is the bridge that extends upward from the region of the esoteric location of the *Sishencong* Window Group and the esoteric location of Du-20 known in Esoteric Acupuncture as *Tian Man*. In the past, in order to achieve the ability to utilize and manipulate refined mental matter for making the wisarga, known as the power bridge, it was required from the aspirant to obtain some level of Stillness within his or her inner world. This meant that he or she was able to shut off the excessive mental chatter (known as our "monkey mind") and achieve a tranquil state of inner calmness, inner peace and eventually Inner Stillness. In Chinese Medicine, excessive mental chatter is an indication of an imbalance within our heart system. This heart imbalance, sometimes known as *Shen* Disturbance in Chinese Medicine, often means that we are not totally honest with ourselves. Instead of looking inward, we are constantly looking outward. Mental chatter and always finding something to do to keep the mind occupied are ways of not having to deal with our own "stuff." "I do not have time to truly examine my life, because I am always busy dealing with other issues."

Moving away from The Truth brings us closer to chaos and the inability to quiet the mind. As mentioned in other Esoteric Acupuncture books, merely sitting in quiet meditation without physical movement is not synonymous with Stillness. You may be able to sit quietly without movement of the physical body, but your mind may be galloping at a nonstop pace. Silent thinking without physical movement is not what is considered Stillness. It is when one is in a state of Stillness, that one of the best opportunities appears for that individual to build the Antahkarana. The individual must be aware of the concept of the Rainbow Bridge and then must have the desire and discipline to go about trying to mentally create and strengthen the Antahkarana, our spiritual antenna.

Some individuals, but not all, who practice quiet mind meditation without being aware of the concept of the Antahkarana may, nonetheless, eventually unlock and later unblock the frequencies needed to build one's Antahkarana. This means that the consciousness (energy) from the Ajna Center will move to the Brahmarandra Chakra and later communicate with the Sahasrara (Crown Chakra). This process will initiate the building the Antahkarana. Stillness creates the opportunity to go inward to a profound depth. If one consciously works on building the Antahkarana with refined mental matter first, before entering the state of Stillness, then the bridge will form more easily and at a more expedited fashion than by merely meditating without the knowledge of one's Antahkarana.

2) A second way in which the Antahkarana may appear is that sometimes an individual may have past life karma that allows him or her to carry over a subconscious memory or imprint of a built Antahkarana from that person's past life. That person may not even be aware of the concept of the Antahkarana in this present incarnation. I have treated several clients who exhibited a partially built Antahkarana without being aware of the Rainbow Bridge or the term Antahkarana. These individuals had not even meditated in this current incarnation. Nonetheless, I could see the Antahkarana even before I inserted any acupuncture needles in those individuals.

On the other hand, I have treated individuals who have meditated regularly over many years, even decades, without being able to see the energy of their Antahkarana until after they received an Esoteric Acupuncture treatment. Perhaps those meditators could not reach the frequency necessary to Still the Mind during their regular meditation sessions.

You will observe that the non-meditator who has a partially built Antahkarana before an Esoteric Acupuncture treatment will be a very selfless individual who is very giving and helpful to others, especially in his own community. These individuals are usually very kind, generous and have genuinely caring and giving hearts. Sometimes these same individuals may not even take time for themselves because they are always helping others. They are very dedicated service workers. One major prerequisite for the Antahkarana to appear for those who do not meditate or are not conscious of how to build the Antahkarana is that the individual must be doing some sort of service work to uplift humanity. If you are a very kind and nice person but think only of yourself, unless you are meditating and working on strengthening your inner plane reality, your Antahkarana will not automatically appear because of your positive karma. For a service worker to have a partially built Antahkarana without even being aware of the concept of the Antahkarana and without meditating in this lifetime usually requires that he or she did much inner plane work in a previous lifetime. The karmic work carries over into this lifetime.

3) The third method for building the Antahkarana is to be treated by a practitioner of Esoteric Acupuncture who has a certain high frequency of light quotient and who is intimately aware of the Rainbow Bridge. The recipient of the Esoteric Acupuncture treatment does not need to be aware of the Antahkarana. By utilizing certain posterior New Encoding Patterns for the purpose of creating specific grid systems that have certain inherent energetic frequencies, the practitioner is able to lay the foundation through an Esoteric Acupuncture treatment to assist the client in building his or her Antahkarana. During the course of inserting acupuncture needles into specific acupuncture sites, while following a specific sequencing in the posterior New Encoding Patterns, it is very beneficial to ask the client to make certain triangular visualization connections.

These triangular visual connections are specifically designed to assist with the creation of a specific frequency called a Spin Field in Esoteric Acupuncture. A Spin Field, created by receiving a New Encoding Pattern of Esoteric Acupuncture, will place the recipient of the treatment into a higher vibrational frequency allowing that person a more conducive energy field in which to build his or her Antahkarana. (See the visualization sections in the posterior patterns in Chapter V.)

### Collective Thread of Active Creativity

The Thread of Active Creativity has three separate, but interconnected frequency rays that are slightly different aspects of the Antahkarana. The three separate threads joined as one thread make up the Thread of Creative Activity and will be called the Collective Thread of Active Creativity. The Collective Thread of Active Creativity is anchored in the throat and can be accessed and activated by inserting an acupuncture needle at the acupuncture site *of Tian Tu* (Ren-22) known as "Celestial Chimney." When the three separate fibers of the Thread of Active Creativity are harmoniously ascending together as a unified cord, this cord will exit from the top of one's head.

These three separate threads of energy are different aspects of the Chinese concept of the *Po*. Remember that the *Po* are connected to the lungs and that the lungs control the throat. Secondly, remember that the lungs are connected to the Vishuddha of the Hindu Chakra System. The Vishuddha is also known as the Throat Chakra and is the fifth chakra in the Seven Chakra System. In the Thirteen Chakra System, the Vishuddha is the sixth chakra. The Throat Chakra has influence over our creative endeavors and being able to express. Expression means much more than merely being able to speak out. The energy field of the Thread of Active Creativity allows one the opportunity to create a new idea or a new expression. The expression does not mean taking someone else's idea(s) and merely adding a new slant to something that has already been created. You will be able to create a new expression for the benefit of the planet. You will bring life into a new creation.

For the purpose of visualizing the connections within this portion of the Antahkarana, it may be easier to think of the three distinct vibrational frequencies of the Thread of Active Creativity as threads of light or threads of energy. The visualizations of the three distinct fabrics of consciousness are shown separately. It is recommended to make the mental visualizations one at a time. After the three individual cords have been visualized in your mind, then visualize the three distinct fabrics merging into one unified thread or cord.

These visualizations are included for those who may wish to do a very simplified guided visual meditation. A complex visual meditation called 3-6-1 Antahkarana Meditation was given in ***Sea of Fire-Cosmic Fire: Esoteric Acupuncture, Volume IV***. The simpler visualizations given here can be done before a quiet meditation or before the 3-6-1 Antahkarana Meditation.

Remember the lungs control the Throat Chakra. On this first visualization of the Thread of Active Creativity, the first strand travels from the anterior throat region at the acupuncture site of *Tian Tu* (Ren-22) downward to the anterior astral heart region at the acupuncture site of *Yuan Jian* (Ren-17). After the connection is completed, extend the qi from the heart region slightly downward to the region of the astral spleen. The spleen being referred to is the astral spleen, not the physical spleen. The astral spleen is located just inferiorly to the physical heart region. After the heart qi is thoroughly blended in with astral spleen qi, move the qi from the region of the astral spleen located on the center of the vertical midline of the body slightly to the left side of the ribcage to communicate with the qi contained within the region of the physical spleen. Hold the energies in this region for a few moments.

An aspect of the *Po* of the lungs located at the acupuncture site of *Tian Tu* (Ren-22) connects with an aspect of *Shen* at *Yuan Jian* (Ren-17) and combines with a higher aspect of the

*Yi* of the astral spleen. When these three particular aspects of consciousness of the *Po*, the *Shen* and the *Yi* combine properly with frequencies of Wisdom, the person will have opened the lower vibrations of Clear Mind Recall to access information from some levels of the Akashic Records. (See figure 4.2-a below.)

**Thread of Active Creativity**
**Thread #1**

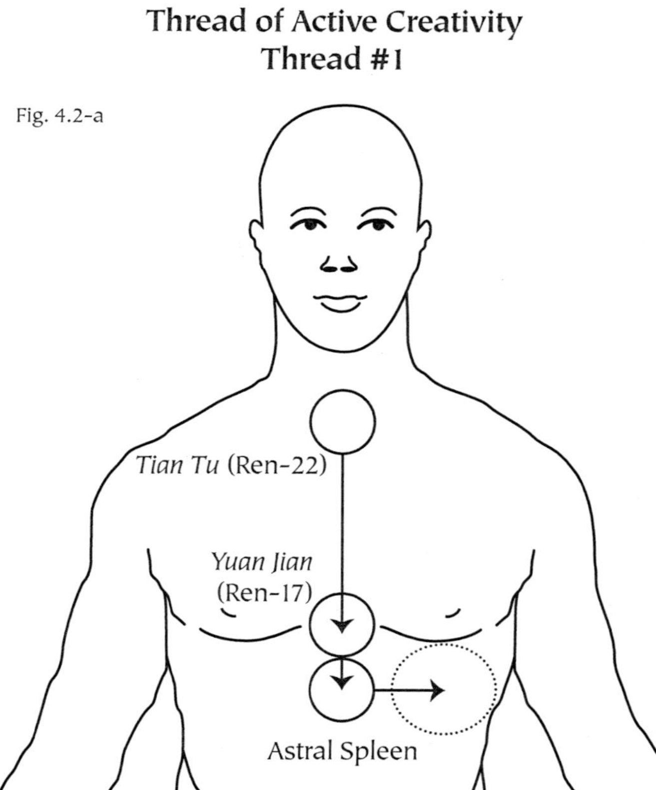


Fig. 4.2-a

The second cord of the Thread of Active Creativity travels upward from the solar plexus region to connect and communicate with the qi at the heart region. Both the astral spleen and the astral liver are contained within this solar plexus region. The vibrational connection from the solar Plexus to the heart region combines an aspect of the *Yi* of the spleen with the *Hun* of the liver and a higher aspect of *Shen*. It is in this field that the individual begins to resonate with the inner spiritual aspects of *Shen*. An aspect of *Hun* assists the individual to maintain discipline and devotion to this center pathway of the heart. (See figure 4.2-b below.)

**Thread of Active Creativity**
**Thread #2**

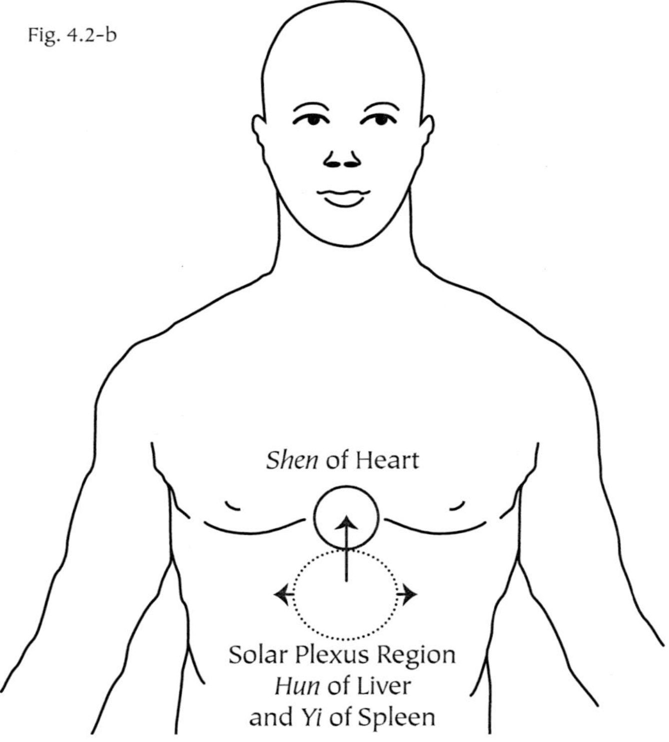


Fig. 4.2-b

The visualization with the third of the three cords of the Thread of Active Creativity begins from the throat region at the acupuncture site of *Tian Tu* (Ren-22) and moves upward to communicate with *Yintang* (Ajna Center). We are also bringing the Po of the lungs to connect with the Ajna Center. From the Ajna Center, also known as the Third Eye, bring the energy into the brain and the Brahmarandra Chakra located within the cranium directly below the esoteric site of *Tian Man* (Du-20). Remember than we are interested in the location of *Tian Man* and not the location of *Bai Hui*. (See figure 4.2-c below.)

**Thread of Active Creativity**
**Thread #3 (Part I)**

Fig. 4.2-c

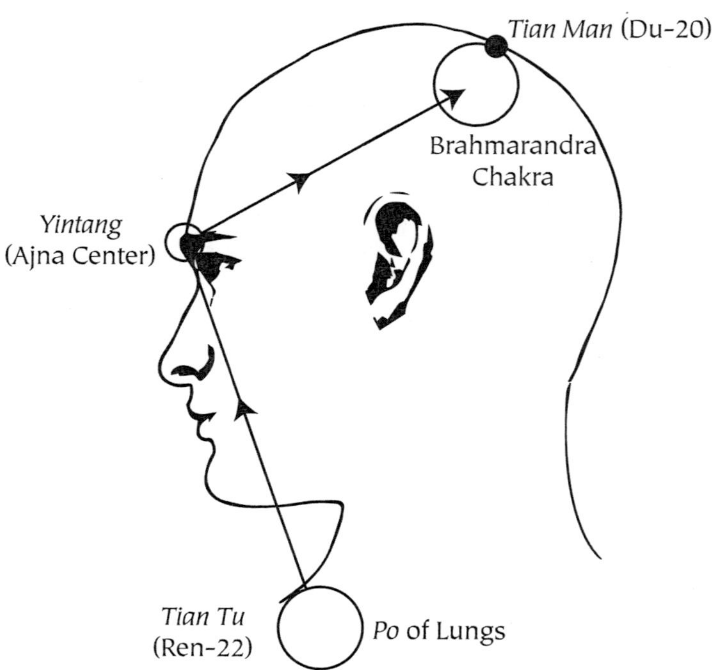

Just because qi exits the Brahmarandra Chakra at Du-20, does not mean that this qi will communicate with the Sahasrara (Crown Chakra). The energy from the Brahmarandra Chakra must exit through the esoteric location of *Tian Man* (Du-20). When this event occurs, it sets in motion an opportunity to activate the Guru Chakra that sits directly below the Sahasrara (Crown Chakra) fitting somewhat like a glove. (See figure 4.2-d below.)

**Thread of Active Creativity**
**Thread #3 (Part II)**

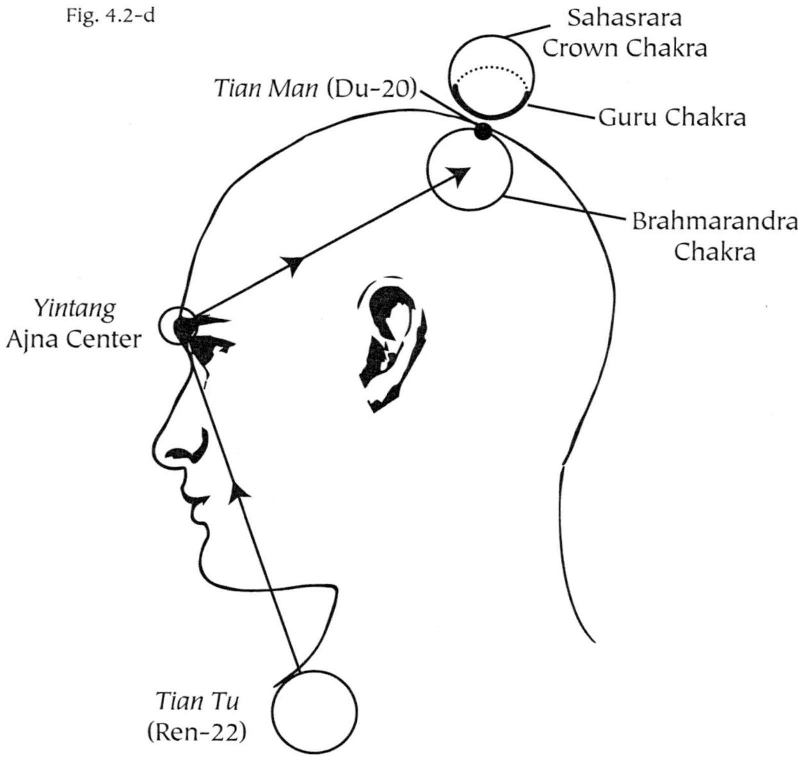

Notice that the gap above the skull to the Guru Chakra and the Sahasrara (Crown Chakra) now has a bridge that has been constructed by mental matter connecting the intracranial Bramarandra Chakra to the Sahasrara (Crown Chakra) situated superiorly to the cranium. This connective bridge called wisarga, is one of the Esoteric Antahkarana. (See figure 4.2-e below.)

**Thread of Active Creativity**
**Thread #3 (Part III)**

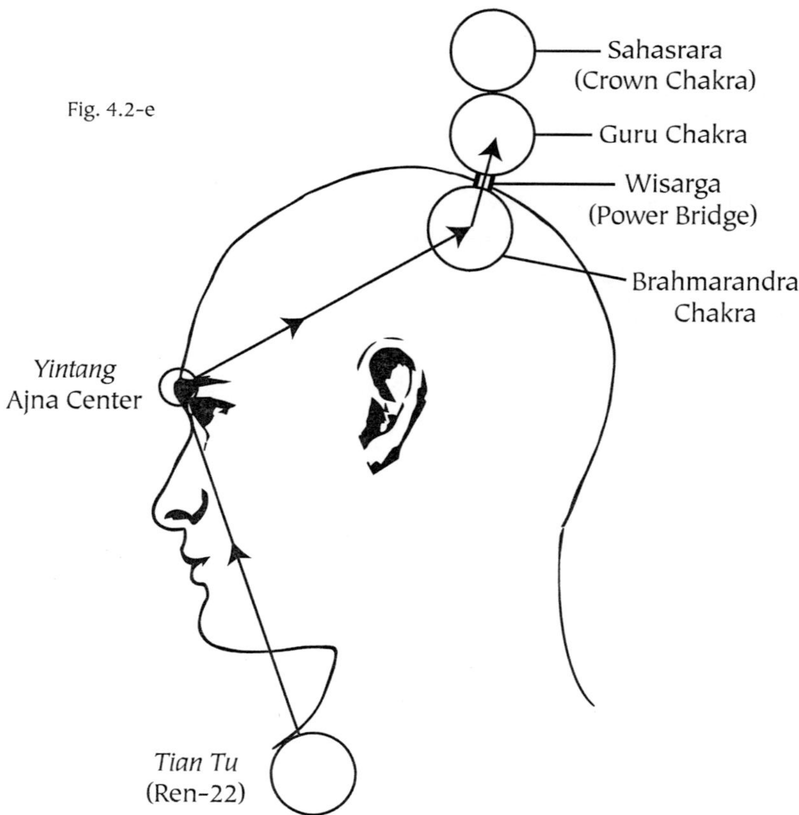


Fig. 4.2-e

The wisarga is the Hindu name for this power bridge. In the Tibetan teaching of Djwhal Khul, this same bridge is known as the Antahkarana. This may be confusing because the overall energy field extending upward from the cranium and called our "Rainbow Bridge" is also called the Antahkarana. Think of the wisarga as one of the two Esoteric Antahkarana.

The main function of this portion of the Antahkarana is to be able to move Kundalini upward from the Brahmarandra Chakra to communicate with the Sahasrara (Crown Chakra). The Brahmarandra Chakra is located within the cranium beneath the esoteric location of the *Sishencong* Group that surrounds *Tian Man* (Du-20). Those of you consciously working with Kundalini trying to make it rise will know that Kundalini only ascends to the region of the Brahmarandra Chakra. It is by way of the wisarga (power bridge) that Kundalini will move from within the cranium to the Sahasrara (Crown Chakra) outside of the cranium.

There is a "dormant" chakra that lies beneath and tightly connected to the Sahasrara (Crown Chakra). When this particular Esoteric Antahkarana (wisarga) has been built and fully activated, an opportunity arises for the Guru Chakra to "split" from the Sahasrara (Crown Chakra). (See figure 4.2-e on page 275.) If the Guru chakra separates from the Sahasrara (Crown Chakra), then an opportunity arises for the twelve petals of the Guru Chakra to begin to open and "mature." As an individual continues to work on refining the frequencies of his or her Anahata (Heart Chakra), the process will help to activate the blossoming and maturing of both sets of twelve petals, one set within the Anahata (Heart Chakra and one set of twelve petals within the Guru Chakra. The simultaneous opening and communication of the twelve petals of both chakras will eventually create a frequency field to allow the Jewel in the Lotus of the Anahata (Heart Chakra) to communicate with the Jewel within the Guru Chakra. If this event occurs, it is the beginning stage of uniting your Higher Inner Twin Flames Within.

These esoteric connections do not occur for souls

who are not vibrating at a certain higher frequency. Those individuals stuck in the lower chakras of glamour, Maya and physical denseness will not consciously experience the higher connections of the various higher, finer frequency aspects of the *Po* of the lung system, the *Zhi* of the kidneys, the Yi of the spleen system, the *Shen* of the heart system and the *Hun* of the liver system. For those who have done the necessary inner plane work, along with some level of service work to uplift humanity, one will eventually build a complete unified Antahkarana, spiritual antenna system. This means they will always be aligned with their inner spiritual center. That individual may experience emotional, mental or physical challenges, but he or she will have the tools necessary to handle any situation because of their spiritual alignment and spiritual strength. Although a clairvoyant may be able to see the Antahkarana above the head of that individual, the antenna is really an inner antenna to your Inner, Spiritual Higher Heart.

### Sutratma, Our Life Thread

The second portion of the Antahkarana ("Rainbow Bridge") consists of the Sutratma that is also known as "the life thread." There are two distinct vibrations, or distinct threads, that make up the Complete Sutratma. The Sutrama Proper is one portion of the Complete Sutratma and is the main fabric of the Complete Sutratma. The other fabric is usually just called Sutratma. The two fabrics together make up the Complete Sutratma or what is also called "the life thread." The Sutratma Proper does not have to be built because it already exists in each individual, but at such a low vibrational frequency that the Sutratma Proper is almost nonexistent in the masses. When discussing the life thread, be aware that it requires both heart fabrics to make the Complete Sutratma.

When Sutratma is mentioned in Esoteric Acupuncture, it refers to the Sutratma Proper only. It is only when both threads are collectively joined as one, that the term Complete Sutratma will be used. To help alleviate some of the confusion concerning the Sutratma, the second thread of the Complete Sutratma will be called Sutratma #2. This single strand of consciousness known as Sutratma #2 has to be built for it does not exist in most of humanity.

Although the kidneys in Chinese medicine are associated with water, there is a portion of the kidney system known as *Mingmen* Fire. There is an acupuncture point with the name *Mingmen* (Du-4) that is located directly on the posterior spine below the spinous process of the second lumbar vertebra. *Mingmen* can be translated to mean "Gate of Vitality" or "Life Gate" indicating the importance of sustaining and keeping alive this very special energy field, our "Lower Fire of Life." The flames of the *Mingmen* Fire must be fanned and energized to reap the benefits of this special powerhouse of energy. The *Mingmen* Fire gives us vitality, sexual drive, physical power and the willpower to do things and to accomplish goals in life.

In the concept of the Antahkarana, the dual cords of the Complete Sutratma are directly connected with the heart system. The concept of Esoteric *Shaoyin* involves the dynamics and interaction between the heart system and the kidney system. Without the Life Thread of our Sutratma, we no longer have physical life here on Earth.

Notice the name "Life Gate" associated with the acupuncture site *Mingmen* (Du-4). The Life Gate of the *Mingmen* Fire site of the kidneys is a direct link to the Life Thread of the Sutratma Proper of the heart. Strong balanced qi from the Gate of Vitality is needed to energize our Heart Flame of our Sutratma Proper. This is another example of the esoteric connection between various systems and acupuncture theory. (The theory of our Antahkarana and the Sutratma are not known in Traditional Chinese Medical Theory.)

The energy (consciousness) from the *Mingmen* Fire communicates with the *Shendao* Fire of the heart system. A finer frequency of our Heart Fire initiates an inner movement toward discovering one's Inner Spiritual Higher Heart. It was mentioned earlier in this section that although the Sutrama Proper does not have to be built because it already exists in each individual, the desire and the knowledge of striving to unlock the treasures within our Inner Spiritual Higher Heart are almost nonexistent in the masses. This means that for most of the masses, especially here In the United States, most people are not interested in going inward and being Still. "The fun is out there somewhere."

There is a frequency field of consciousness in Chinese medicine known as *Zhi* that is connected with the kidney system. The aspect of *Zhi* containing the *Mingmen* Fire integrates with, and becomes a part of the fabric of the Sutratma Proper of the heart without any conscious effort. This means that the frequency of one's *Mingmen* Fire of the kidneys automatically integrates with a portion of one's *Shendao* Fire of the heart first, then communicates with the Sutratma Proper. Our *Mingmen* Fire is our Life Gate to vitality and energy. Inserting an acupuncture needle into the acupuncture site of *Mingmen* (Du-4) strengthens and harmonizes our kidney qi. Our overall qi and willpower to do things and our zest for life and all of its mysteries, adventures and challenges depend upon the strength of our *Mingmen* Fire. Nothing out of the ordinary has to be done to sustain life, because the *Mingmen* Fire, the initiator of qi through our Life Gate, is connected to the Life Thread of our Sutratma Proper and sustains this vital life force within us.

There is an extremely fine frequency of our *Shendao Fire* that is of a much more refined frequency than other portions of our *Shendao* Fire of our heart. The very finest frequencies of our *Shendao* Fire are known in Esoteric Acupuncture as the "Upper Fire of Life." Our Upper Fire of Life is contained within our Sutratma #2. Remember that the Sutratma #2 is the other portion of our Complete Sutratma, our Life Thread. Unlike the Sutratma Proper that does not have to be built, the Sutratma #2 has to be consciously constructed of mental matter.

When you have consciously constructed your Sutratma #2 and have further refined this frequency through meditation or other methods to Still the Mind, this then becomes the consciousness that has a connection to your Original *Shen*. The Original *Shen* follows us into each new incarnation, but for most people is not activated. (Do not confuse our *Shen* taught in Traditional Acupuncture with the Original *Shen*.) The Original *Shen* remains with that soul in every incarnation and withdraws into the Monadic Plane upon death of the physical body.

It was mentioned in Chapter III that the *Mingmen* Fire, also known as our Lower Fire of Life, extinguishes its flame at the moment the physical vehicle expires and the soul leaves the body. The *Mingmen* Fire dissolves and remains extinguished in the Personality Plane. On the other hand, the Upper Fire of Life never extinguishes and returns to a higher plane along the path of our Monadic Ray and remains until one's next incarnation in a physical vehicle.

Through the individual's inner plane work of Stillness, the higher *Zhi* permanently bonds with the higher *Shen* frequencies and the combined frequencies are not distinguishable from one another. This is an initial step known as the process of the Esoteric *Shaoyin* merging into Oneness. One level of our Lower Twin Flames Within has merged as one.

When visually building the part of the Antahkarana known as the Thread of Active Creativity, you will notice there are other aspects of consciousness that are associated with the Chinese Five Element Theory that are also connected to the Sutratma. In figure 4.2-a, the consciousness at the lung/heart site of *Tian Tu* (Ren-22) is connected with the heart frequency at *Yuan Jian* (Ren-17). The Po of the lung system is linked to the Sutratma Proper.

In figure 4.2-b, you will notice that both the Hun of the Liver system and the Yi of the spleen system both connect to the Sutratma Proper. Traditional Chinese Medical Theory is combined with the Theosophical (Hindu/Tibetan theories) within Esoteric Acupuncture Theory. Nothing stands alone.

Figure 4.2-f on the next page shows a simplified diagram of the very basic level of one's Complete Sutratma ascending above the head to form part of one's Antahkarana.

## Complete Sutratma, Life Thread has Two Distinct Threads

Fig. 4.2-f

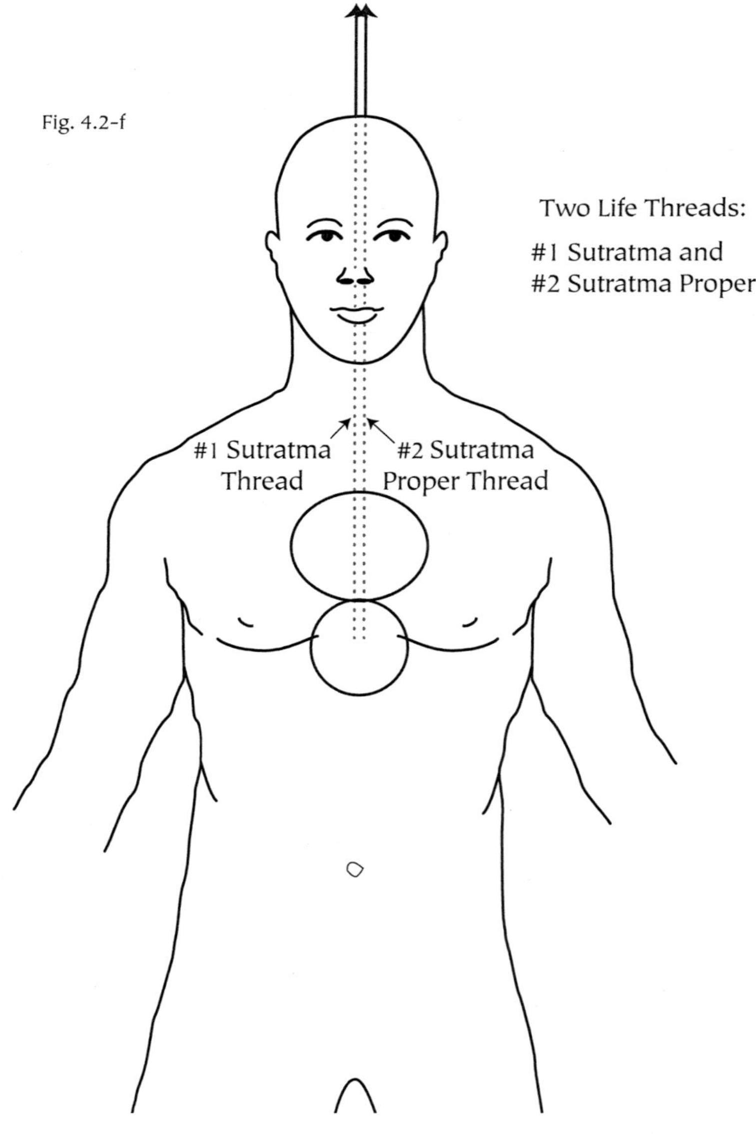

## Thread of Consciousness

The third portion of the Antahkarana Rainbow Bridge is the Thread of Consciousness. This thread consists of only one part and does not have to be built because it already exists in everyone. The Thread of Consciousness is anchored in the pineal gland of the brain. For most of humanity, the pineal gland is dormant. The frequencies emanating from the pineal gland from most people are so weak as to make the Thread of Consciousness also very weak and of very low density. Past life events are accessed through the Thread of Consciousness. (See figure 4.2-g below.)

**Thread of Consciousness**

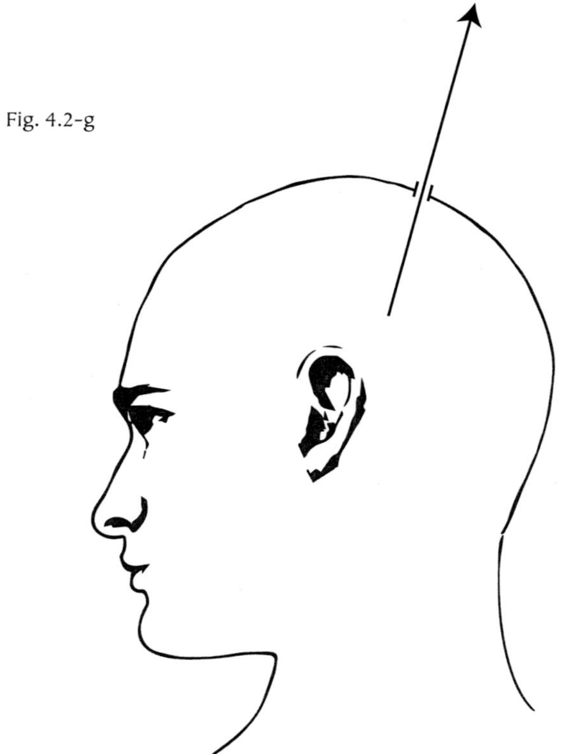

Fig. 4.2-g

## An Esoteric Antahkarana

There are very specific sparks of consciousness contained within each individual called permanent atoms. These permanent atoms are tiny centers of force that assist in the shaping of the various planes of consciousness within the newly incarnating soul. There are two groups of permanent atoms with three permanent atoms in each group. There is a lower triad of permanent atoms and an upper triad of permanent atoms.

The three permanent atoms of the lower triad are found in the petals that surround the Jewel in the Lotus of the Anahata (Heart Chakra) and are intimately connected to one another. There are three outer sets of petals with three petals in each group. The outermost set of petals house the Physical Permanent Atom. The set of petals next to this outermost group houses the Astral Permanent Atom. The next set of petals house the Permanent Mental Unit. These three outer sets of petals surround a very tightly close set of three petals that enclose the Jewel in the Lotus (the twelve petals).

For most people, the Astral Permanent Atom is very active. It is the activity from the Astral Permanent Atom that attracts and gathers the necessary astral energy to form the chakras on the astral plane.

In the past, the Upper Triad of Permanent Atoms, existing in the non-physical realms, were usually very well hidden from most people. Humanity, as a group, has evolved very rapidly these past few decades, and today more individuals are able to access and activate the Upper Triad of Permanent Atoms consisting of: the Manasic Permanent Atom, the Buddhic Permanent Atom and the Atmic Permanent Atom.

There are seven planes of consciousness in the planetary scheme for each individual. Each of the seven planes of consciousness is further subdivided into seven sub planes. The highest sub plane within each of the seven planes is called the Atomic Sub Plane. The Mental Plane is unique in that the fourth sub plane is the Atomic Sub Plane for the Mental Plane. The three higher sub planes are called the Causal Plane. The seventh sub plane of the Mental Plane is the Atomic Sub Plane of the Causal Plane. There are no permanent atoms on the top sub planes of the Monadic or Logoic Planes. The seven planes, the sub planes and the Atomic Sub Planes are shown below.

## Seven Levels of Consciousnes
### with Seven Sub-Planes within each Plane

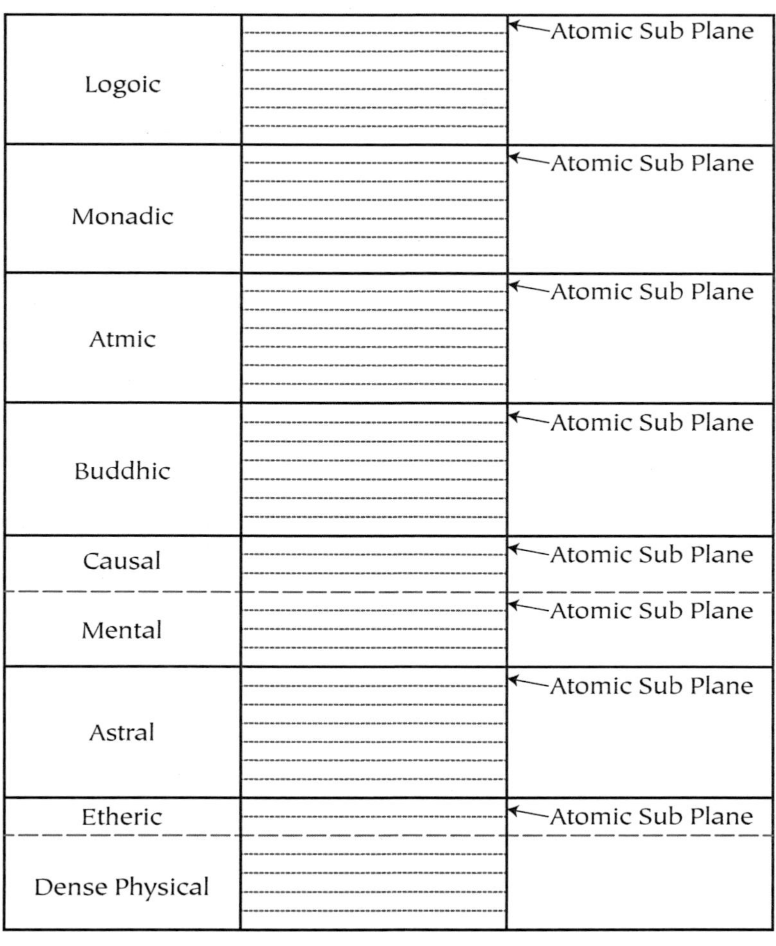

In the chart below, there are two levels of permanent atoms. Notice how the six permanent atoms are located within the Atomic (Highest) Sub Plane of each plane.

The connection between the Lower Triad and the Upper Triad is another portion of one's Esoteric Antahkarana and often the last bridge to form. (See the chart below.)

**Antahkarana Connecting the Upper Triad with the Lower Triad**

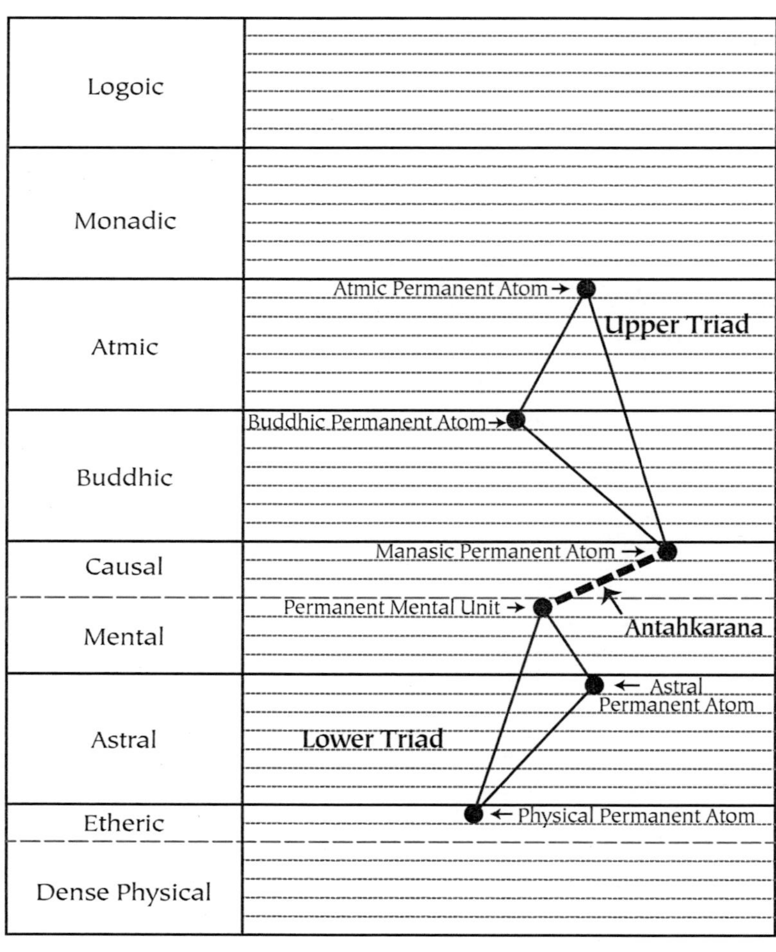

If you are able to form this bridge between the Lower and Upper Triad, the next step to reach a more advanced level of the Inner Spiritual Higher Heart will be to connect your Atmic Permanent Atom to the apex of your 3-Fold Monad.

## Connection to Your 3-Fold Monad

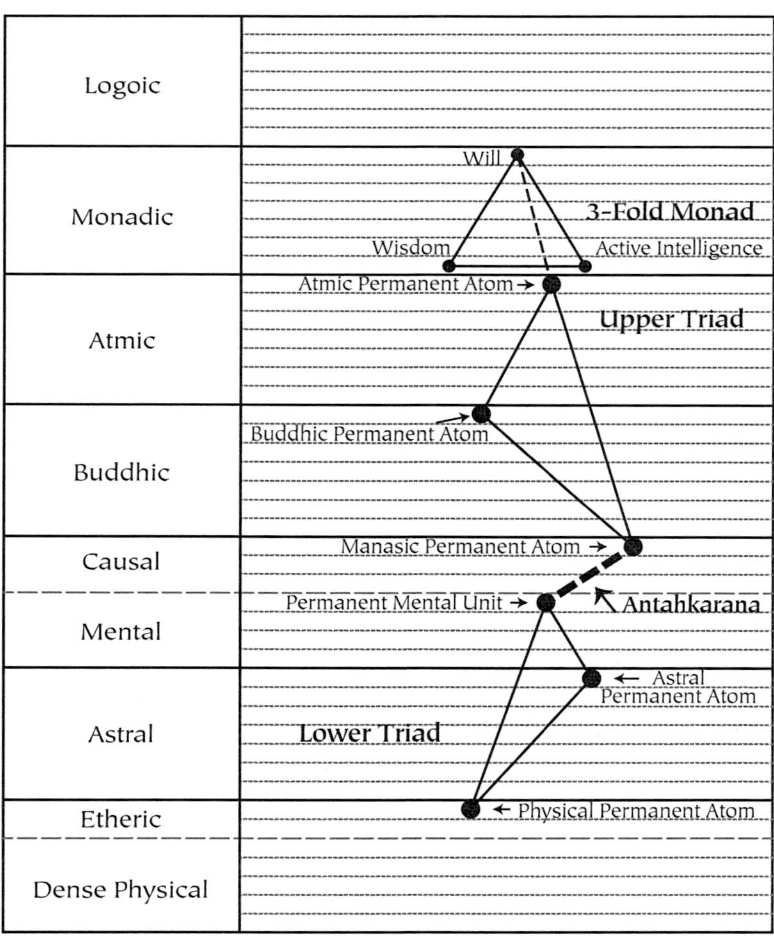

Having three distinct, yet interconnected esoteric bridges all known as the Antahkarana, plus a main bridge emanating from the top of one's head also called the Antahkarana may be confusing. Just remember that when speaking of the Antahkarana, one is generally talking about the energy field of the Rainbow Bridge emanating above the region of the esoteric *Sishencong* and *Tian Man* (Du-20).

In order to build the Antahkarana in the past, a person had to first be conscious of the concept of the Antahkarana. Then the individual had to create a certain vibrational state of consciousness and use refined mental matter to form the energetic structure for the building of the Antahkarana. One of the advantages of receiving an Esoteric Acupuncture treatment utilizing any of the New Encoding Patterns in this book is that the procedure itself (the acupuncture treatment) will start the process of constructing the Rainbow Bridge of Consciousness in the recipient of the treatment. The recipient of the Esoteric Acupuncture treatment does not have to know of the existence of the Antahkarana. If the practitioner is aware of building the Antahkarana and is doing some level of inner spiritual work, the bridges will automatically start to form while the acupuncture needles are being inserted in the client with any of the New Encoding Patterns in this book.

Just because you have assistance for anchoring the frequencies of the Antahkarana within your field does not mean that you will automatically begin to develop extrasensory perceptions or become fully awakened. But your awareness becomes refined and more acute. In many people, the building of the Rainbow Bridge is a beginning phase for an awakened state of consciousness to unfold and to uncover the mysteries of his or her Inner Spiritual Higher Heart. These Esoteric Acupuncture treatments will help the recipient of the treatment to unravel the mysteries and help to discover his or her puzzle piece in life.

## A Brief Overview of the Antahkarana

1) The six strands of energy that emanate upward from the top of the head as one thread and extending from the region of the esoteric location of Sishencong Group and Tian Man (Du-20) is the Antahkarana, our Rainbow Bridge. In Esoteric Acupuncture, this portion of the Antahkarana is known as The Primary Antahkarana and our personal spiritual antenna. When there is any reference to The Rainbow Bridge, it refers to this portion that extends upward from the top of one's head. The six strands of consciousness of the Antahkarana consist of: 1) the three strands of consciousness from the Thread of Active Creativity; 2) the two strands of consciousness from the Complete Sutratma; and 3) a single strand of consciousness from the Consciousness thread.
2) There is a portion of the Antahkarana that is known as the Power Bridge or the Wisarga that extends from the Bramarandra Chakra located within the cranium to connect to the Sahasrara (Crown Chakra) located outside of the cranium. This power bridge portion of the Antahkarana is known as the one of the three Esoteric Antahkarana.
3) The second Esoteric Antahkarana is the bridge that connects the Sahasrara (Crown Chakra) to the chakras above the Crown Chakra.
4) The third Esoteric Antahkarana is the bridge that connects the Lower Triad of Permanent Atoms to the Upper Triad of Permanent Atoms.

Think of the Antahkarana as your personal inner spiritual antenna to assist you on your individual Soul Journey and/or your Spirit Journey. There are six strands of consciousness, plus three Esoteric Antahkarana that make up your fully built Antahkarana, our Rainbow Bridge. When your Antahkarana is built, your "ah ha" moments become more frequent and the answers to our inner spiritual questions become clearer.

Building the Antahkarana is merely the first step. You must still go inward and quiet the mind.

There are only a handful of clients who have requested to have an Esoteric Acupuncture treatment while sitting up. In this manner, I am able to needle both the anterior and posterior of the client as one treatment, instead of the more traditional method of needling the posterior first, followed by needling the anterior. By sitting up for the entire treatment, the process will initiate a more rapid activation and centering of one's Inner Heart to hasten the building of the Antahkarana. The main criterion is that the client has to be a strong sitter (meditator). You do not want the client falling off the stool with needles in his or her face and head. Some clients will sit on a stool. Others have chosen to be activated while sitting in a lotus or half lotus position on the treatment table. I use the 3-6-1 Antahkarana Meditation pattern discussed in the ***Sea of Fire-Cosmic Fire: Esoteric Acupuncture, Volume IV*** for these treatments.

There is one person who has been coming for regular Esoteric Acupuncture treatments for a number of years. His name is Kenneth Klee. He is a unique person because on one hand, he is a professor of law at UCLA in Westwood, California and is a practicing lawyer. This makes him very left-brained. Yet on the other hand, he is a dowser and very gifted energy healer making him right-brained. Kenneth was the first person to have twenty-two opened chakras above his head after treatments with the 3-6-1 Antahkarana Meditation Grid. After several additional treatments, the twenty-two chakras disappeared leaving a flowing stream of light above his head that disappeared into the ceiling. The twenty-two separate chakras (pathways of the Tree of Life) had become one unified pathway above his head. Kenneth has activated and balanced the bicameral aspects of the mind and is now meditating on a very high frequency. Sometime this year, I started to notice a very large energy ball several feet above his head after the needles were inserted. We both said that the energy ball was a "Way Station" to allow the higher frequency information to download into a denser reality to be able to make conscious sense of the information. It will be exciting to see what transpires next for Kenneth Klee from the 3-6-1 Antahkarana Meditation Grid.

Below are several diagrams of how I see various Antahkarana after an Esoteric Acupuncture treatment. Even with clients who come on a regular basis, the Antahkarana changes shapes, colors and sizes depending on the energy of the client on a particular day. Others who can see chakras and auras may see differently than the few diagrams presented here.

**Typical Antahkarana With Chakras**

Fig. 4.3-a

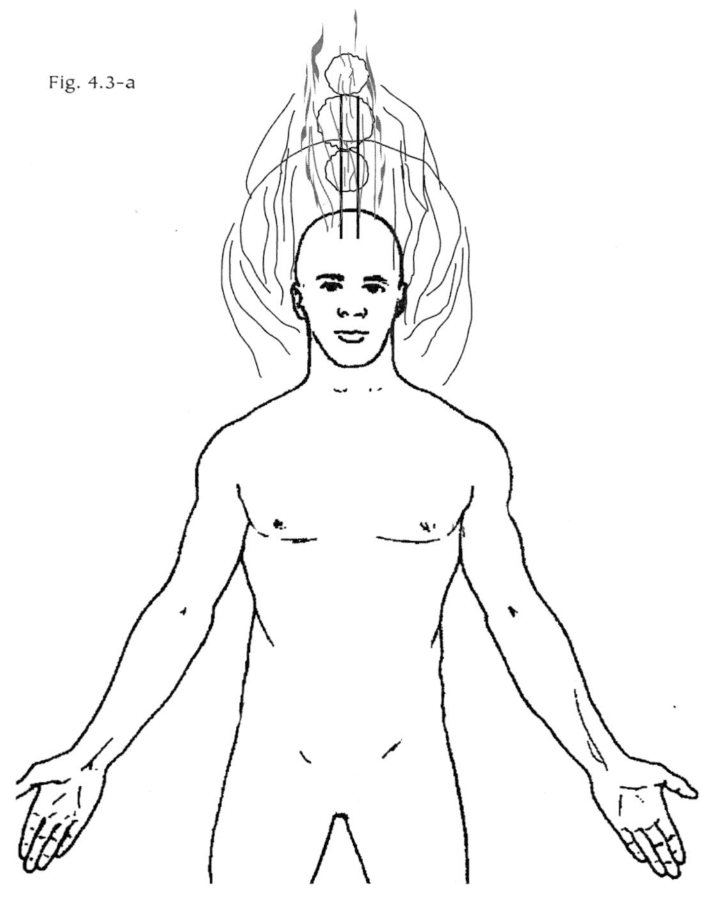

## Antahkarana with Inner Flame

Fig. 4.3-b

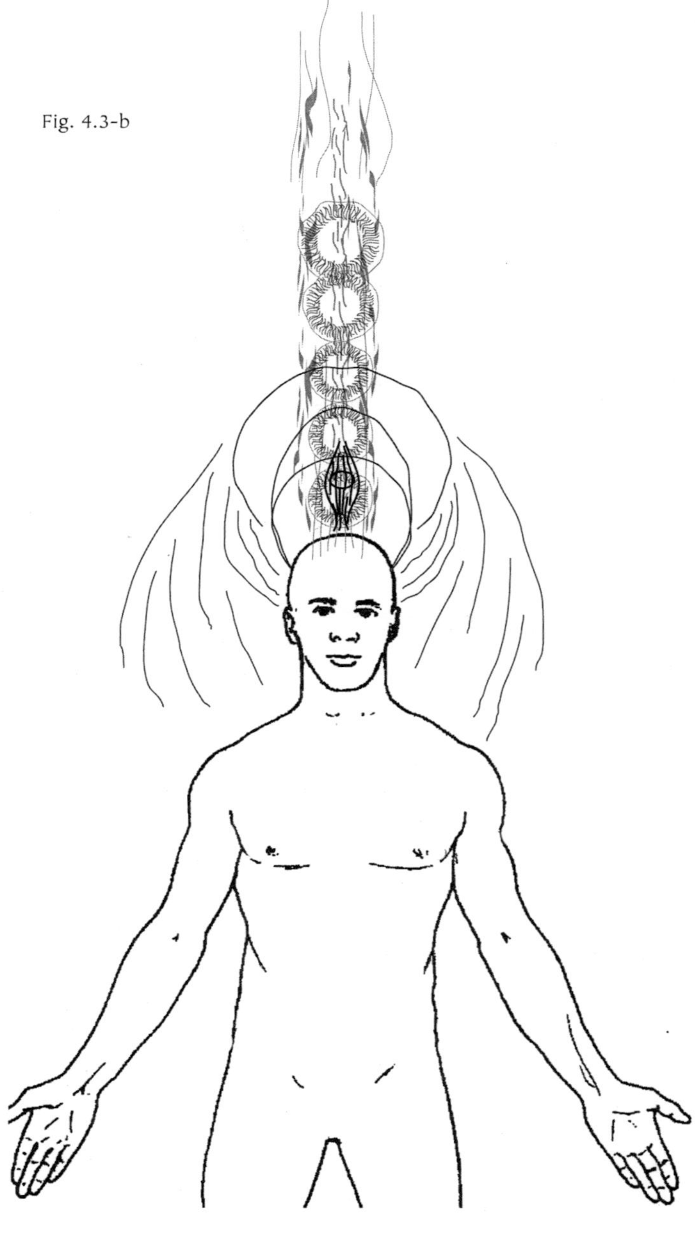

## Antahkarana With Chakras

Fig. 4.3-c

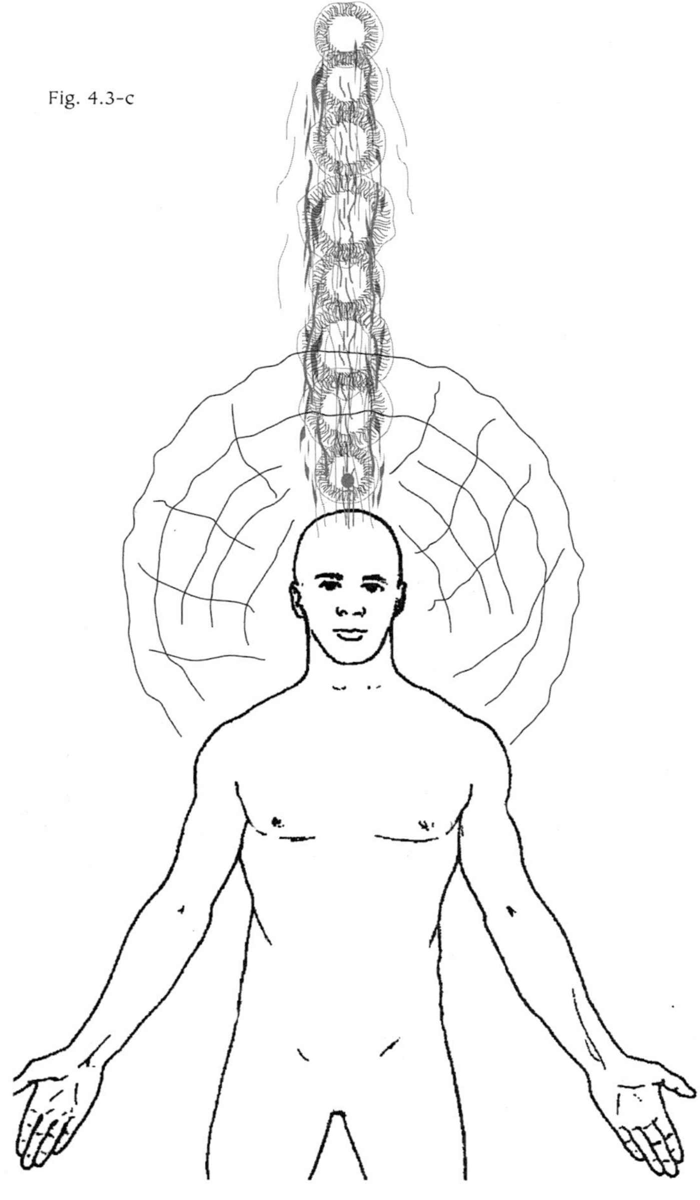

# Chapter V: Tiers of Density and New Encoding Patterns

*Never be afraid to love*
*Never be afraid to just be*
*Cast away your chains of doubt*
*Have the courage to be free*
*Open your eyes, you can fly*
*Open your eyes, you can fly*[1]

***Open Your Eyes***
sung by Flora Purim

Open your eyes refer to being able to go inward and awakening to our inner realms. When we are able to embrace our inner world, we can "fly."

Over the years of lecturing, most acupuncture practitioners, as well as energy workers from other modalities have asked me which New Encoding Pattern(s) or Chakra Balancing Pattern(s) to use on their clients/patients and how to determine which patterns would be the most beneficial for their clients/patients. Although I have tried to encourage practitioners of Esoteric Acupuncture to be very quiet and use their higher, intuitive heart to determine which New Encoding Pattern to use for a particular treatment, it seems like their academic schooling and rational, left-brained indoctrination have been too deeply entrenched in most of the practitioners who have attended my workshops and seminars for them to be comfortable relying on their intuitive powers of the heart.

In my search for The Truth, I have always been drawn to try and find the most fundamental source for all things. The most fundamental source means that there are no other known levels beyond that point. I feel that the most fundamental source of imbalance for humanity starts with imbalances within the heart field. It does not matter if there is a physical, emotional or mental challenge. We will eventually end up at the heart level to try and rectify the imbalance or imbalances. There are many levels of the heart. If this thinking is true, then we as the practitioners/healers should try to balance the frequencies at the most fundamental level. This is the Inner Spiritual Higher Heart Field.

I have mentioned in earlier Esoteric Acupuncture books that receiving an Esoteric Acupuncture pattern will not automatically bring a person into a heightened level of awareness or spiritual awakening. But, all treatments using the New Encoding Patterns will align and strengthen the Inner, Spiritual Higher Heart Center of the recipient of the treatment. This is the alignment with our higher *Shen*. Although some clients will experience a very heightened level of inner awareness at an accelerated pace, the results of any Esoteric Acupuncture treatment are dependent upon the level of inner plane work done by both the practitioner and the recipient of the treatment. The various New Encoding Patterns of Esoteric Acupuncture are designed to unlock the locks of the recipient of the treatment. I can unlock the locks for you, but you must take the locks off the doors, open the doors then go through the doors by yourself. This requires that you have the desire and discipline to move into your inner world and do a certain amount of inner plane work. This means that you must find some way to begin the journey of first quieting the mind, then Still the Mind.

It is very important that the practitioner is doing some sort of service work to uplift humanity. Just because a practitioner is working in the healing field does not automatically mean that the individual is performing service work from the heart. Often a practitioner in the healing field may merely think of his or her work as a job to pay the bills. But, receiving a New Encoding Pattern from an acupuncturist who is intimately knowledgeable with the subtleties of the totality of what Esoteric Acupuncture offers, will create a high frequency spin field which allows the recipient to move into heighten awareness and expanded consciousness much more readily than a treatment with a more traditional style of acupuncture.

If the recipient of an Esoteric Acupuncture treatment wishes to advance his or her spiritual awakening or to gather more inner spiritual consciousness, then it is equally as important for the recipient of the Esoteric Acupuncture treatment to also be doing some sort of service work for the uplifting of humanity. If the recipient of the treatment is doing work for lower selfish reasons and is not interested in helping others, then the recipient of the treatment becomes a drain on the energy of the practitioner and actually pulls qi from the practitioner. If the practitioner is also vibrating on a dense frequency, then treating a client who has a dense vibrational field will not seem to have much effect on the practitioner. But, those of you who are reading this book will most likely be vibrating at a fairly high frequency, and you will definitely notice if your client has a low or dense energy field.

Have you ever treated a person who "drained" your qi making you feel extremely tired after the treatment session? Have you noticed how sometimes at the end of the day after treating a number of clients you are not tired at all? Other times you are utterly exhausted after a day of treating your clients. We all know of, or have met, people who make you tired, agitated or even make you angry just by being around that person. Those types of people disrupt and/or drain your qi and can actually leave remnants of negative energy clinging to your astral field. These attached negative energy remnants will negatively affect you and may make you exceedingly tired throughout the day or very lethargic, disrupt your sleep giving you insomnia, and over a period of time can make you physically, emotionally and mentally challenged even to the point of you becoming very physically ill.

On the other hand, those recipients of an Esoteric Acupuncture treatment who work with the higher vibrational light frequencies and focus on service to others will augment the practitioner's energy and life force by giving the practitioner more positive, "energized" qi. Those individuals who work from a lower selfish level are most likely working from the levels of the lower Swadthisthana, second chakra, kidney field of fear. (There are also higher levels of the Swadthisthana Chakra.) Those who work from the levels of giving and others who do service work are working from the Anahata, Heart Chakra field of love. Those are the opposites, the lower kidney field versus the heart field. They are the takers versus the givers. This is again what is known as Esoteric *Shaoyin*, the heart opposing the kidneys, or love opposing fear.

Remember the kidney field of the second chakra is not a negative field. Much of the kidney field and especially the upper levels of the field of *Mingmen* Fire are very desirable frequencies. We need the kidney field to be balanced. I am only referring to the densest kidney frequencies of fear and the other dense tentacles protruding from fear such as: anger, hatred, pity, "poor me," insecurities, greed, selfishness and other frequencies of that nature. Which type of healer or person are you? Are you a giver or a taker?

People that are very left-brained and feel they have an extensive academic foundation may feel threatened by The Truth. There is no right or wrong with The Truth. The Truth just is. If a person's consciousness is limited to only the fields he or she is familiar with, they often challenge the statement about a search for The Truth by saying, "Whose truth is that which you are speaking?" "Who told you that?" "Where did you hear or read about that?" It is not only the words, but also the frequency of the words that can reveal to you the level of consciousness of an individual. It is okay for those not wanting to change. It is his or her prerogative to remain safe in the level of awareness and consciousness they are familiar with.

In my opinion, all the challenges we face, which have been called problems, are due to not being in our center. Our center is our Heart Center. Sometimes we may be confronted with a challenge that we did not consciously call upon. If we are in our Heart Center, then we will understand that the challenge is there to teach us a lesson and this particular phase will make us stronger and more understanding of our own personal journey here on planet Earth.

Only the most stubborn, rigid, angry, emotionally or mentally challenged person will not at least be open to hearing another viewpoint. Esoteric Acupuncture will assist a person to open his or her consciousness to other possibilities. Remember, there are infinite quantities and infinite levels with infinite qualities of possibilities. Being open to new possibilities is an attribute of the heart field of expansion. Not wanting to change, or being stuck in the old ways (like tradition) are attributes of the kidney field of contraction and its offshoot of stubbornness related to the liver system. You only have one time around in your present physical vehicle with your present emotional and mental bodies. Why not try, or at least be open to all possibilities that manifest before you? One way to awaken is to be open to possibilities. You may discover that many things you were taught and that you accepted as truth, may only be a partial truth, may be an untruth or might even be an outright lie or deception. It requires the combined heart and small intestine systems to be communicating harmoniously to be able to truly Discern the Whisper of your Heart.

## Tiers of Density

With Esoteric Acupuncture, I suggest that you first use a certain New Encoding Pattern on the posterior of the client followed by a complementary New Encoding Pattern on the anterior of the client. As your level of inner plane development expands, along with a heightened level of consciousness from your clientele, you will start to gravitate toward "knowing" which specific New Encoding Patterns to use on your clientele with a few variations depending on the individual energy field of that particular day. There will be a section later on in this chapter that makes suggestions on how to use specific New Encoding Patterns depending on the level of consciousness of your client. These levels of consciousness are known as Tiers of Density. Until you get to the point where you trust your "knowing sense," you can use the chart that is given in this section to determine which treatment protocol to use with each of your individual clients. When in doubt about which treatment protocol to use, and unless your client is a very fear-based person, use a higher tiered treatment protocol. If your client is feared based and you are not sure of which Tier Density Level he or she is at, choose the recommended treatment protocol from a lower tiered density level.

When Tiers of Density are mentioned, this refers to specific levels of consciousness with some individuals having a denser energy field versus others who may have a lighter or less dense energy field. For those who are interested in the teachings of Esoteric Acupuncture, the lighter energy fields should be a goal to attain. The lighter or less dense energy fields do not necessarily refer to the heaviness or thickness of the physical body. (Although in most cases, it may be more desirable to also have a less dense physical vehicle to move around in.) The lighter or less dense energy fields refer more to the ability to create and maintain an expansive mental and spiritual outlook on life with an understanding and appreciation of both the inner and outer worlds.

The Tiers of Density concept was first introduced in Esoteric Acupuncture by the book ***Support the Mountain: Esoteric Acupuncture, Volume V***. Some of the same information from ***Volume V*** will be repeated later in this chapter with additional criteria given. Your treatment protocol, consisting of your choice of which New Encoding Patterns to use on your client, will be determined by the level of consciousness of that individual. The criteria used for determining the various Tiers of Density involves the various levels of *shen* awakening for each client. *Shen* is a level of consciousness or awareness connected to the heart field. The more the *shen* of the heart is awakened, the lighter the energy field, and therefore the higher the Tier of Density.

The criteria used for constructing the five density levels,

and therefore the level of *shen* awakening, was determined by understanding the basic consciousness that shapes the habits and lifestyle of the general population. The general population refers to those people who live in cities or the surrounding suburban areas of the technological world of the 21st century. The criteria for determining the Tiers of Density do not apply to yogic practitioners who live solitary lives in the mountains or caves far from society, or to the monks, rishis, sadhus or other recluses who seclude themselves from the general population and retreat into their monasteries, temples, caves or other havens of solitude.

We have been taught in the West to think linearly. We are born on such and such a date. We live our lives from this age to this age. Then we die. Everything is linear. We are also accustomed to organizing people or groups in a hierarchic order according to status or some type of authority. Some people in the New Age Movement have ranked people's consciousness by assigning a number. If you are assigned a higher number, supposedly you are of a higher consciousness. The higher up the totem pole you go, the more prestige or reward you will receive. But, that is merely glamour of the astral realms.

The Tiers of Density are presented here to assist the practitioners of Esoteric Acupuncture in determining which New Encoding Patterns to use on their clientele. The one question I have been asked over and over again in my lectures and workshops is: "How do I choose which New Encoding Pattern to use?" In my earlier works, I have tried to encourage the practitioner to go inward to his or her higher intuitive center to determine the treatment protocol for the client. Esoteric Acupuncture encourages us to develop and feel comfortable with using our right brain. Since most of the licensed acupuncturists and other healthcare professionals have had years of schooling to be able to practice the modality of their choice, they have been heavily polarized to rely on their rational, left-brain.

I want to adamantly say that one level of density is not necessarily better than another level of density. A finer, lighter frequency level of density may be a goal to try to obtain for some. Others may feel perfectly content in a denser level of existence. A person going to college is not a better person than someone who is going to high school. They are merely at different levels of consciousness and different levels of the human experience along their own individual journey of life. At some point in his or her life, that high school level student may come to the point where he or she will decide whether to continue on to a higher plane of education, pursue another level of existence or stay in the consciousness of the high school experience. One choice is not better than another--merely different experiences. I do not want the readers of Esoteric Acupuncture to fall into the old thinking of higher up the totem pole is better.

Going to college (literally speaking) does not factor into what level of density you are at this moment. Consciousness is not only dependent upon one's left-brain activity. The right side of the brain that controls creativity, higher intuition, imagination, exploration and most importantly, the Inner Spiritual Higher Heart has to be activated to a certain level to move into the higher realms of spiritual consciousness. The higher realms of the spiritual heart and abstract consciousness are different from the higher realms of the concrete, mental consciousness. A person can be very dedicated in his or her work or research program while accessing the higher aspects of the left-brain, yet that person may be ignoring the higher aspects of the right brain, the domain of creativity, expansion and the Inner Spiritual Higher Heart. The criteria used in Esoteric Acupuncture for the assessment of the levels of *Shen* Awakening involves developing the finer frequency levels and having the individual consciously moving toward becoming fully bicameral. To access the realm of the Inner Spiritual Higher Heart requires a level of being able to Still the Mind. It takes discipline and dedication to move into the higher Tiers of Density, and that is a choice you may wish to make, or you may choose to follow another pathway. Moving to the higher levels of the Tiers of Density means you will ultimately connect with less people than if you stayed in the more comfortable lower levels. The masses prefer to stay in a denser comfort zone.

There are many teachers and lecturers trying to reach the masses and have become very well known. Those who choose to move into higher, inner, spiritual levels of consciousness usually accept the fact that they will be more isolated from the masses and the general public. Being more isolated from the masses does not in any way mean you will have to deal with loneliness or exclusion from society. You made the choice not to participate in many of the mindless, denser functions and activities of the masses. There is much excitement, joy and deep levels of heart experiences that are available to those who are quiet and can be honest with themselves and connect to their own Inner Spiritual Higher Heart. Merely finding things to do to have fun is functioning at a lower heart frequency. Joy, happiness and love are higher heart frequencies in comparison to fun and excitement. Stillness is an even higher heart frequency. The only thing above Stillness is The Truth.

Many people might prefer remaining in a lower density level because that particular level is where the fun and excitement exists for them. What people consider fun and exciting and what they consider important will dictate what level of consciousness they choose to remain in. They will focus their energies on those activities that meet the needs of their consciousness level. It is not necessarily a goal for most people to move into the higher levels of the Tiers of Density. We all have our own karmic journey during this particular incarnation. When our emotions and the goal of having fun dictate our choices, those are indications that we are not on the path of our individual Soul Journey. At the Soul Journey level, emotions do not control our decisions.

The New Encoding Patterns that are listed with each level of the Tiers of Density levels are those Esoteric Acupuncture Patterns that have the vibratory frequencies that will best assist your clients to smoothly move into their balanced spiritual chakra centers at their particular levels of density. The specific

New Encoding Patterns will harmonize and strengthen the higher heart frequencies for that level of consciousness. If you choose the patterns that best fit your client's consciousness level for that particular time period in his or her life, then the alignment from the Esoteric Acupuncture treatment will allow a more gradual, smooth transition into a higher realm of Energy Consciousness.

It is best not to move energy too quickly for your client, especially one who might be more fear-based. Since treatments using the New Encoding Patterns of Esoteric Acupuncture usually move qi more quickly than that of a more traditional acupuncture treatment, pay close attention to the level of consciousness of your client to avoid any emotional or mental challenges that may arise from a heightened surge of energy with an Esoteric Acupuncture treatment. In most cases, you do not want to blast your client with too much qi, or open the doors to higher spiritual awakenings too abruptly. Esoteric Acupuncture has a built in mechanism that does not allow for a premature Kundalini awakening, but will allow Kundalini to ascend in a more harmonious flow for those who have done the inner plane work. Those on psychotropic drugs, or who are experimenting with ayahuasca or other psychedelic enhancers, may not be able to handle the surge of qi with an Esoteric Acupuncture treatment. Even if your client comes to you requesting a treatment with a New Encoding Pattern, it is up to you the practitioner to decide which type of acupuncture treatment will be the most beneficial for your client on that particular day. In some instances, those new to the world of acupuncture may benefit the most by receiving a mild traditional form of acupuncture first instead of receiving an Esoteric Acupuncture treatment. It is best to allow your client to learn patience and to enjoy the heart alignment and awakening process as it organically unfolds.

Those of you who are practitioners that use dowsing or kinesiology (muscle testing) will be able to determine the number of chakras that are balanced or out of balance. We are only interested in the seven major body chakras for this analytical process and are not concerned at this point with determining the status of the other higher head chakras such as: the Taluka Chakra (Lalana Chakra), Manas Chakra, Indu Chakra, Brahmarandra Chakra or the Guru Chakra. The number of blocked or imbalanced chakras, along with the criteria listed in the five Tiers of Density levels, will give you a guideline for selecting the Tier of Density level of your clientele. Use the following information as a very loose guideline for assisting you in determining which of the five levels of density fit your client the closest. The number of chakras that are imbalanced can be used as a guideline for determining the tier density level of your client. If you are dowsing using a pendulum in the northern hemisphere following the Esoteric Acupuncture protocol, then balanced chakras will spin clockwise. Imbalanced chakras will spin counterclockwise. If you have your own system for determining an answer for a yes or no question, please use the system that is most comfortable to you. In the southern hemisphere, a balanced chakra will spin counterclockwise with a pendulum in the Esoteric Acupuncture System.

Both the Chinese and Tibetan pulse diagnostic systems are used to determine imbalances in the physical vehicle. The chakras are located in the astral plane. That is the reason why pulse or tongue diagnoses are not recommended in determining a balanced or imbalanced chakra. Some systems will teach that certain chakras will spin differently for males and females. With the New Encoding Patterns within Esoteric Acupuncture, we are interested in aligning the highest levels of the various chakras. We are not interested in dividing the male spin from female spin like some of the older systems. We are not so interested in the lower emotional spin of males and females. We are trying to activate and utilize the consciousness of the higher spiritual realms. These higher realms do not divide male energy from female energy. This is the reason in Esoteric Acupuncture that the balanced chakras spin in the same direction for both males and females. In the higher spiritual realms, there is no differentiation or separation between males and females, or yang and yin. The rotational spin of the pendulum may indicate an imbalance on the levels below the higher spiritual realms, but nonetheless we are striving to balance and strengthen the consciousness at those higher levels.

The chart below is a guideline for helping the practitioner choose the desired Esoteric Acupuncture treatment protocol.

| Tiers of Density | Number of chakras imbalanced |
|---|---|
| Level 1 | Five, six or seven chakras. |
| Level 2 | Four of five chakras. |
| Level 3 | Three or four chakras. |
| Level 4 | Two or three chakras. |
| Level 5 | One chakra or none. |

The practitioner must utilize the information given in each Tier of Density Level, as well as determine the number of imbalanced chakras. The number of imbalanced chakras by itself is not the best gauge for determining which New encoding Patterns to use. A person may be a dedicated meditator, a vegetarian and is on a path of spiritual practice to uplift the planet. Yet, maybe he or she may have had a rough week and five or six chakras may dowse as being imbalanced. Do not merely use the number of imbalanced chakras as the sole gauge for determining the Tier Density Level of your clientele.

After identifying the Tier Density level of your client, you may then select the New Encoding Patterns that will be the most beneficial for your client for this particular treatment. This means that the New Encoding Patterns listed for that particular Tier of Density are those patterns that have a very close vibratory frequency for that density level, and will assist the client to move into the highest levels of his or her Inner Spiritual Heart Center with the least amount of disturbance to the client's level of consciousness. The New Encoding Patterns move energy at the subtlest levels more quickly than treatments with a more traditional framework. The practitioner must be sensitive to the consciousness level of the client. You do not want to move too much energy, or too quickly, with a client that exhibits an excessive amount of fear. Those clients exhibiting certain tentacles of fear such as: tension, anger, "poor me," jealousy, envy, confusion, helplessness or not being able to release grief or loss will need to be brought along in a slower, more gentle manner. In those instances, do not use any of the more complex New Encoding Patterns.

The New Encoding Patterns listed in each level of density are only suggestions. You, as the practitioner, may feel that another New Encoding Pattern or Patterns may be more appropriate for your client on that particular day. It is highly recommended that you, the practitioner, follow the choice of your heart when deciding upon your treatment protocol for each of your clients.

There are two New Encoding Patterns (or more) with each of the density levels. There is at least one posterior pattern and one anterior pattern. It is best to balance both the *yin* (anterior of the body) and *yang* (posterior of the body) aspects of your client within one treatment. It is suggested to first treat your clients in the prone position leaving the acupuncture needles in for approximately forty to forty-five minutes. Then ask the client to turn over in a supine position. With your client in a face up position, needle the anterior of the body. Leave the client for an additional twenty to thirty minutes. Most people prefer a longer treatment while in the prone (face down) position. If you decide to leave your client face down for any length of time, make sure the client does not have sinus congestion. You want to make sure that the energy flows smoothly during the treatment.

Sinus congestion indicates an excess of dampness. In Chinese medicine, dampness usually slows the flow of qi. The bottom goal of the treatment plan is to balance as much as possible any *shen* disturbance.

Any level of mental or emotional inability to relax and/ or quiet the mind is considered *Shen* Disturbance in Chinese medical thought. How many of your clients have excessive mental chatter? Quieting the mind is not an easy task, especially today with all the wireless electromagnetic frequencies buzzing around in the airwaves. Most of the Esoteric Acupuncture treatments will help to relax your clientele. Remember we are trying to bring the client's energy field into his or her Inner Heart Center. If a person cannot relax, that person will not be in his or her true Inner Heart Center.

I want to make it perfectly clear once again that one level of density is not superior or inferior to another level of density. We are spiritual consciousness residing in a physical vehicle with one purpose: experiencing the human life journey. Most people may prefer to reside in a denser level of existence. Those same people are not aware of the need to explore the inner world of Stillness, and may feel that certain denser activities and materialistic accumulations are more attractive at that stage in his or her human life journey. The lower Tiers of Density contain more frequencies of fear that may include: anger, being more judgmental, more emphasis on sexual and money issues and having more attachments to the lower ego. As was stated before, we are all experiencing the human life journey from our own level of consciousness. Some people may have been on their Inner Spiritual Journey a little longer than others. Some of you "older souls" who have been on this journey, and acknowledge your Inner Spiritual Light, may choose to strive for a finer frequency Tier of Density level. The choice is strictly up to you.

## Tiers of Density with New Encoding Patterns

### Tier Density Level I
### Our Inner *Shen* Asleep

A person at this first Tier of Density Level One, cannot quiet his or her chaotic mind. This kind of mind is sometimes called the "monkey mind" where your head is filled with constant mental chatter making it difficult to focus or to concentrate on one subject for any length of time. This is the densest tier of any client who may seek an Esoteric Acupuncture treatment from you. If a person is on a lower, denser level than Tier Density Level One, that person will definitely not seek your advice and assistance for an Esoteric Acupuncture treatment.

An individual's reality at the Tier Density Level One does not include the idea of cultivating the Inner Spiritual Higher Heart Center. A person at this level might be aware of the concept of higher spiritual energies, but are unable to utilize these energies to come forth and assist in the blossoming of his or her Inner Spiritual Higher Heart. Stillness and finding time to cultivate the inner, peaceful places within are not part of his or her reality at Tier Density Level One. There is an urgency to keep busy.

How many people do you know that are always on their cell phone, I-pad, computer or other electronic gadget either talking, texting or tweeting messages, searching the web or constantly playing computer games? This is the level of the restless mind. "I am always on the go." "Even when I am waiting in the waiting room for my acupuncture treatment, I cannot relax my mind." If you are the type of person who is on a cell while walking to an appointment, shopping at a store, or constantly talking or texting while waiting in line somewhere, then you are in this Tier Density Level One. I have treated several people who are still texting or checking their emails on their phone while they are lying on the treatment table waiting for me to enter the room. They cannot quiet their mind until I start the acupuncture treatment. They are in Tier Density Level One. If your client leaves your treatment room and is immediately on his or her cell phone, they are definitely at the Tier Density Level One. They may think they are spiritually advanced because they do hatha yoga or that they are very intelligent and up-to-date on the most recent spiritual topics. If they cannot embrace the quiet, healing frequencies after their Esoteric Acupuncture treatment and are not aware that the microwaves from the cell phone are changing their vibratory rate, they are still in Tier

Density Level One. It does not matter if they have a microwave diffusing electromagnetic device on the cell phone. The act of not allowing the heart-centering frequencies from an Esoteric Acupuncture treatment to settle into their field is an indication of the lack of awareness and clearly shows they are still in Tier Density Level One.

People who reside in Tier Density Level One feel that time is money. Time is not money. Time is art. (This was discussed in Chapter One.) They feel that they must maximize their time to reap the most benefits. If they relax or meditate to quiet and center their mind, they somehow feel that they are wasting precious time. They have no idea of the concept of inner *shen* or the "real" benefits of relaxing and quieting the mind. If they are aware of the idea of inner *shen*, people at this level usually dismiss that concept and do not allow themselves the luxury of being Still.

Often people at this level will find worthy causes to keep busy. They are always doing things for other people. In this way, they do not have to review their own lives. They will not make the time to take an inventory of their own lives and their deeds, because they are always busy with other people's lives and other people's issues. The Chinese medical diagnosis for a person who cannot quiet his or her chaotic, busy mind is called *Shen* Disturbance.

Tier Density Level One is the level where one's day-to-day existence is very important. Survival is the most important factor. "Since I work for someone else, I must be sure to get to work on time so I do not get fired." "I do not have the freedom or luxury to make my own work schedule. Therefore, I must take orders from someone else."

A person at this level does not meditate or take the time to do other forms of mental centering such as: pranayama (breath work), *qi gong* or *tai qi*. They may be curious about Esoteric Acupuncture, but everything they do revolves around their daily regiment of survival or their daily routine revolving around "me" and how can I help myself? There are certain criteria, which "rule," or at least heavily influence those factors that decide what their priorities are on a daily basis. The factors include: one's work or lack of work, things revolving around the home, your daily food consumption and the need to play or find something that is fun that is separate from your work.

A person who is always late for an appointment or a meeting is stuck in Tier Density Level One. This does not include those individuals who may be late once in a while, or to those who occasionally might be late due to a traffic jam or other outside forces that delay them from being on time. But, there are some people who are constantly late. This is an indication of selfishness and is in the root chakra realms of Me, I come first and no one else matters. Some people who are constantly late may be very nice people, eat only organic foods and are very ecologically minded. A person who is constantly late may have attributes assigned to a higher Tier of Density, but the fact that they are constantly late keeps that individual in Tier Density Level One. Also, by the fact that they are not considerate of those whom they keep waiting shows not only disrespect, but that the person does not tell the truth. If you agree to be somewhere at a certain time and date and are constantly late, you are dishonest at the core. There is something wrong with your truth mechanism.

At this Tier Density Level One, one group may make lots of money, while another group has a difficult time making financial ends meet. The amount of physical wealth that one has does not necessarily mean that you will move upward into a higher, finer frequency level of density. The main difference between these two groups is that the group with the money is more in the controller realm. The group having a hard time meeting all of their financial obligations is in the controlled group. Those with more money usually have more influence and options, therefore they can control more things in their daily existence. But, many of those same people who are making money become slaves to the energies within the Swadthisthana (second chakra) that controls finances and money. It is one thing to make money and be content in the field that is created by the energy of the money you have gathered. It is another thing to always be in need of money, or feel like you need more money. Money sometimes creates a strange energy field. Do you control the money? Or does the money control you? When money starts controlling you, you become a slave to the second chakra field of power.

In this Tier Density Level One, a great portion of energy is used to feed the physical and emotional aspects of your lives. How much time per week do you spend going to restaurants or fast food establishments, going shopping for food, cooking your meals, eating, cleaning the dishes, then putting the dishes away? There is absolutely nothing wrong with the amount of time and energy you spend around food. At this density level, this is normal. When you are in a family setting, especially with children, it is your responsibility as an adult to take care of the daily needs of your children and other dependents.

Taking care of the physical vehicle with some sort of physical movements is very important. Some of the more typical types of physical exercises for those in the Tier Density Level One group include: playing organized sports, weight lifting, martial arts, boxing, pilates, aerobics, running, hiking, mountain climbing, skiing, using a treadmill and bicycling. The emphasis at this level is on developing and strengthening short muscles and building your cardiovascular system. Try to keep your physical body trim and in shape. At this level of density, these goals are normal and in alignment with the level of their consciousness.

At this level, socialization is very important. You must be, or at least want to be, where the action is. You love throwing parties, going to parties, going to nightclubs, restaurants, and attending various social events. You utilize Facebook, Twitter or the latest social media service. You enjoy being around people. You love to mingle and meet new people. Social gatherings usually include alcoholic beverages, drinks with white sugar and for many people, recreational drugs. Some may not be drawn to lively events such as nightclubs, but are still drawn to smaller, quieter social settings. If you do not enjoy social gatherings where you actually mingle with people, you still socialize but through the latest social media networks.

In Tier Density Level One, it is very important to have a partner to share things. This Swadthisthana (second chakra) attribute of relationships is a driving factor in your daily existence. Your lower ego will not allow you to feel secure by yourself. You need a partner. You explore and have multiple intimate relationships at this level. You do not know of the existence of your own Inner Twin Flames Within. Twin Flame to you means a sexual partner with similar tastes for the things in life you desire and finding the partner with a matching sexual drive. (For the esoteric meaning of Twin Flames Within and Twin Flames Without, see ***Discern the Whisper: Esoteric Acupuncture, Volume II***.)

You love convenience and enjoy all the electronic gadgets that make life easier. These include everything from cell phones and portable computers, to garage door openers, wireless devices for opening and locking your car door, microwave ovens and other remote control devices. You appreciate the convenience of fast foods and choose not to think about the lack of quality or nutrition in fast foods. You also drink canned sodas and other drinks in aluminum cans and eat microwaved and pre-packaged foods. You prefer anything that is quick and easy.

Going out to lunch and dinner are very important events for you. It is during these types of settings that you feel you can relax while you socialize and gossip. This is a big part or your weekly routine. At this level, the nutritional quality of foods is not as important as the setting and the presentation of the foods. You may enjoy a fancy restaurant with a peaceful ambience and impressive presentation of the meal, even though the food is not organic or vibrating at a high vibrational frequency level. Those of you who cannot afford fancy restaurants are more interested in the cost of the foods instead of the nutritional quality of the foods. You do not care what you eat, as long as it is cheap. You look for bargains, such as the all-you-can eat buffets. By the way, leave room for dessert!

The energy of bargaining carries an interesting vibration.

The word bargain can be broken into two words: bar and gain. Look at the Third World countries where it is accepted and even expected that customers looking to purchase something must bargain for the price. Look at the low energy created by bargaining. Those Third World countries with the bargaining mentality stay poor. The elite classes in those Third World bargaining countries may be extremely rich, but the masses remain poor. If you bargain too often in your life or are constantly looking for a bargain, you are actually saying to yourself that you are not worthy of purchasing or obtaining something expensive or something really special. You wait for sales, or look for the brand name "seconds" that are actually factory rejects. You are carrying a vibratory frequency that is calling out to the universe that you are looking to bar gains in your life.

In Tier Density Level One, everything important is outside of you. You are working a job for financial reasons and have not found what you really want to do in life. You do not feel adequate or understand your true spiritual nature. Therefore you feel you need outside heroes. You have your latest guru or worship movie and music stars, sports heroes and other celebrities. For those of you into sports, you can recite the statistics of all of your favorite sports stars. For those of you into movie or television stars, you are able to recite all the movies and awards that your favorite stars have received. The gossip magazines and tabloids seem to interest you. You want to know the latest scoop on what is going on with the celebrities. You may spend many hours weekly searching the internet for the latest celebrity gossip.

At this level, work and play are very distinct. You need a way to recharge yourself from the daily grind at work. You need to find something that will help you to de-stress. You might indulge yourself in alcohol, recreational drugs, sugar, emotional foods, television, texting or the internet. You need vacations and look forward to the yearly days off from work. You want to have fun. You are always looking for new fun things to do. Emotions rule at this level. There is absolutely nothing wrong with having fun. Just understand that within the frequency range of the many tentacles of love, fun is a much lower vibrating frequency field than other frequency fields such as joy, happiness or compassion. Merging the opposites of work and play is not even a remote reality at this level of density.

Those in Tier Density Level One do not like to make decisions and would much rather follow orders given by somebody else. You do not want to be responsible for any decision-making situation because a higher authority might challenge your decision. You do not have confidence in yourself. You are programmed to be afraid of making a wrong decision. Many people today are programmed not to think, but rather to follow orders. Even in schools today, people are not taught to think. They are programmed to only recite what is being taught in order to get a good grade from the teacher or professor. You have not quite learned how to be a true thinker and to challenge authority when your views differ. Even when, within your heart, you have a different opinion, you do not challenge the popular or accepted version. Do not be afraid to voice your opinion. You have the right to have an opinion, even if your opinion is different from the mainstream version.

Many people in Tier Density Level One have a victim mentality, or at least do not take responsibilities for things that happen to them. The blame game is prevalent at this stage. "I caught a cold or the flu from someone, and therefore it is not my fault. I am not responsible." At this level, they are looking to blame someone else or something else for their own lack of knowledge. We do not catch the flu or catch colds from the outside. We build those types of conditions through bad diets, lack of sleep, lack of exercise and a multitude of things that weaken our immune system. Colds and flus are built from the inside. When some triggering factor sets off the viruses and bacteria that we have been feeding all along, we then blame someone or something else so we do not have to take responsibility for our ignorance. The triggering factor that may set off your flu or cold systems is not the cause.

For you the practitioner, I recommend that you slowly introduce the concept of Esoteric Acupuncture to your clientele. The New Encoding Patterns move a lot of qi, so remember to not inject too much energy in the initial introductory treatments. Select the patterns from the lower density levels. If your client has a lot of emotional insecurities, much confusion in his or her life or other types of tentacles of fear, the New Encoding Patterns may exacerbate those fears much more than from a more traditional acupuncture treatment.

Each of the Tiers of Density will have specific New Encoding Patterns with a diagram of that pattern followed by the needling sequence for that particular pattern. In this practical section of recommended New Encoding Patterns to use on your client according to his or her tier of density, the specific needling sequence is given after the diagram of the acupuncture points. Many of the point location descriptions are given in the Master Points chapter, so some of the point location descriptions may not be repeated again. In those instances where acupuncture points are used that were not discussed in the Master Points section, a description of the point location will be given.

There will be a visualization section after each of the posterior needling sequence sections. The only anterior New Encoding Patterns that have visualization connections are the two anterior patterns in Tier Density Level One, the Integration Synthesis Pattern and the Merkabah Spin Pattern. The visualizations are to be directed by the practitioner with the recipient of the treatment making the actual mental visual connections. The mental visual connections are exercises to strengthen the abstract mind of the right brain.

The acupuncture meridians are on the etheric plane. The etheric plane is the gateway to the dense physical plane, as well as the gateway to the astral (emotional) plane. The mental plane is the connection to the lower astral plane and the gateway to the higher causal planes. The causal planes are the beginning levels of allowing one to move into the hyperspatial realms above the three dimensional realties of our daily existence.

It is recommended to insert the needles in the posterior patterns first before turning the client over and needling the anterior pattern. Only the guidelines for the visualization connections for the posterior patterns are given except for the two anterior patterns just mentioned. I do not have the client make any mental visualization connections on the anterior patterns after being needled on the posterior side first. Most of the time your client will be so relaxed and in an altered or a Dreamtime reality after receiving needles on a posterior pattern making it is very difficult for your client to make any mental visualizations on the anterior side.

Two exceptions for having your client make mental visualization connections on an anterior treatment would be the Integration Synthesis Pattern or the Merkabah Spin Pattern. In either of those two patterns, the visualizations would be recommended if either pattern is the sole pattern for the acupuncture treatment. For example, your client may want to receive an Esoteric Acupuncture treatment but has never had any type of acupuncture treatment previously. Since the Integration Synthesis Pattern has only four acupuncture points and the Merkabah Spin Pattern has only six acupuncture points, either of those two patterns will be a gentle, but effective, introduction to both acupuncture and to Esoteric Acupuncture. You will notice that the Merkabah Spin Pattern with six acupuncture points contains the same four points and the same needling sequence as the four points in the Integration Synthesis Pattern. Use needles of 15mm (approximately one-half inch) in length with a quick insertion and no twisting or aggressive, repeated thrusting technique once the acupuncture needle has been inserted.

If your client cannot make the triangular visualization connections on the New Encoding Pattern you are needling within a reasonable time span (a few seconds), have your client relax and you (the practitioner) should make the visual connections for your client. You do not want to spend ten or fifteen minutes waiting for your client to make all the visual connections within the particular New Encoding Pattern that you chose to needle. Also, the insertion of the acupuncture needles release endorphins in the client's body making the client more relaxed. The longer the time elapses from the insertion of the first acupuncture needle, the chances increase that your client will become more and more relaxed and not able to make the visualization connections.

If your client cannot make the visual connections relatively quickly, it is an indication that his or her right brain is not as well developed as it could be. That person is a left-brained individual. Visualization and imagination are right brain functions. We are attempting to strengthen our bicameral hemispheres of the brain. The right brain controls the whole. The left-brain controls the parts. Academia teaches the left-brain to understand the parts to make sense of the whole. A spiritually awakened person will understand the totality of the subject, yet may not be able to explain all the individual parts,.

You will notice that most of the posterior New Encoding Patterns that are being presented in this chapter have The Crown Infinity Pattern (seven acupuncture points) as the first section needled, followed by additional acupuncture sites in the more complex patterns. It is important to remember that the seven acupuncture sites of the Crown Infinity Pattern symbolizes the concept of Six-Surrounding-the One and 360 surrounding the One that was discussed in Chapter One under a Brief Treatise on the Law of 3-6-1

The visualization connections are the same for the first seven acupuncture sites regardless of the rest of the pattern. Even though several of the patterns include The Crown Infinity Pattern as part of a more complex pattern, I have decided to include these particular visualizations for both The Crown Infinity *Shaoyin* Pattern and the Discern the Whisper Pattern for the benefit of those who have not memorized the visualizations. This visualization of the seven points of the Crown Infinity Pattern will not be repeated in the more complex Esoteric *Shaoyin* Patterns that follow.

## Tier Density Level 1 Posterior Position

### Crown Infinity *Shaoyin* Pattern
(11 Points)

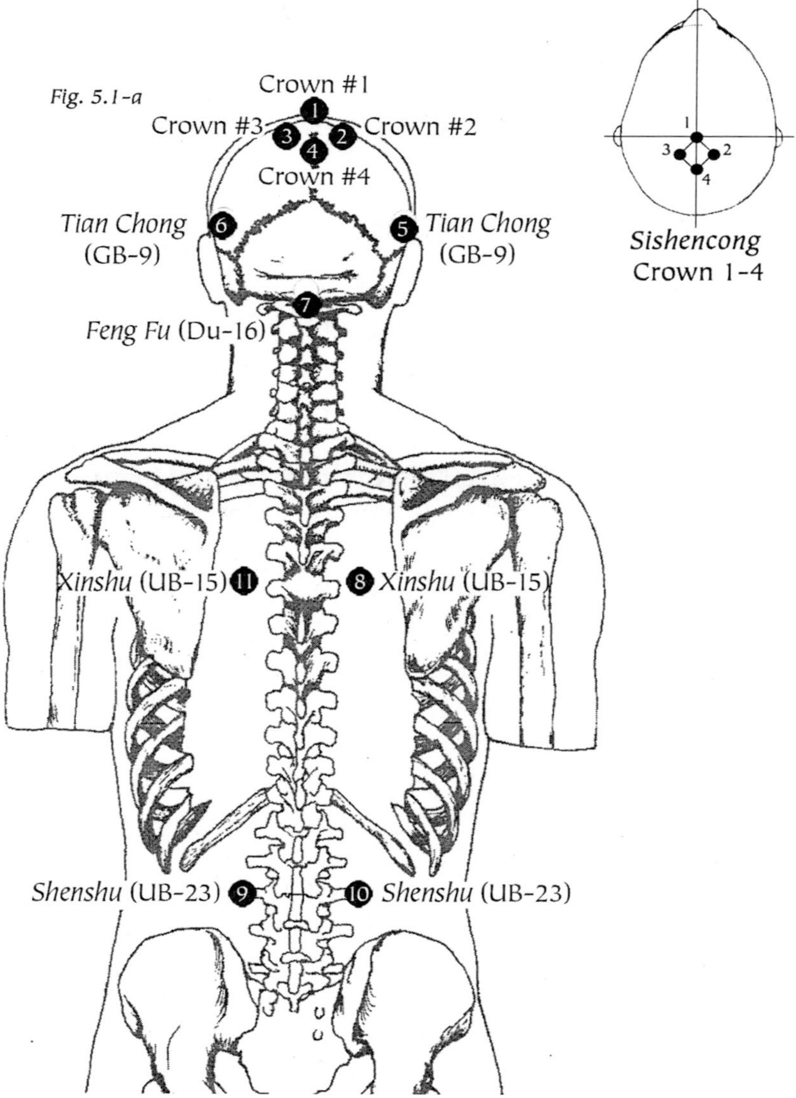


*Fig. 5.1-a*

## Needling Sequence for The Crown Infinity *Shaoyin* Pattern

1 to 4. *Sishencong* — "4 Spirits"
Crown # 1 Crown #2 Crown #3 Crown #4
5. *Tian Chong* (GB-9) Right
6. *Tian Chong* (GB-9) Left
7. *Feng Fu* (Du-16)
8. *Xinshu* (UB-15) Heart Transporter Point—Right
9. *Shenshu* (UB-23) Kidney Transporter Point—Left
10. *Shenshu* (UB-23/ Kidney Transporter Point—Right
11. *Xinshu* (UB-15) Heart Transporter Point—Left

### Point Locations for The Crown Infinity *Shaoyin* Pattern

The first seven acupuncture points in The Crown Infinity *Shaoyin* Pattern are the same acupuncture points used in the Discern the Whisper Pattern and in the various Esoteric *Shaoyin* Patterns. The first four acupuncture points are part of a group known as *Sishencong*. In traditional acupuncture treatments, these four points are almost always needled as a group. In Esoteric Acupuncture, the four *Sishencong* points are always needled as a group.

You will notice that there are two diagrams for the *Sishencong* group. (Figures 5.1-b and 5.1-c.) Although we are interested in the esoteric location of the *Sishencong* Group, it is easier to first determine the site of the traditional Du-20 known as *Bai Hui*. Find the apex of each ear. Now draw an imaginary line from the apex of one ear to the apex of the other ear going over the top of your client's head. Next draw an imaginary vertical midline going over the top of your client's head. Where this imaginary vertical midline intersects the imaginary horizontal line that connects the apex of both ears is the location of the traditional Du-20 (*Bai Hui*). The esoteric Du-20 known as *Tian Man* is located approximately one inch posteriorly to the traditional Du-20 (*Bai Hui*). (See figure 5.1-c.) One point I would like to emphasize is that points #2 and #3 of the *Sishencong* group are not always on the same horizontal line as shown in figure 5.1-c. This means that usually one of these points is either higher or lower than the other point. We are not trying to needle a perfect four-sided polygon. Look for the qi, or feel for the qi. Remember, locating the acupuncture points is NOT an academic, mechanical procedure as taught in acupuncture schools. Finding the location of the qi is an art. We must not forget in our profession that a key element to being a true energy worker is to locate the energy. Besides the academic training necessary to learn acupuncture and Chinese Medicine, the working portion (diagnosis and the needling) requires accessing the heart. Acupuncture is an art form, not merely a left-brain system.

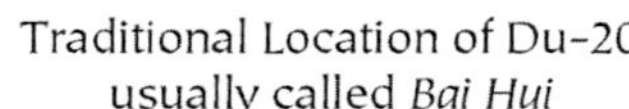

Traditional Location of Du-20
usually called *Bai Hui*

*Fig. 5.1-b*

1
2
3
4
*Bai Hui*
(Du-20)

Esoteric Location of Du-20
now called *Tian Man*

*Fig. 5.1-c*

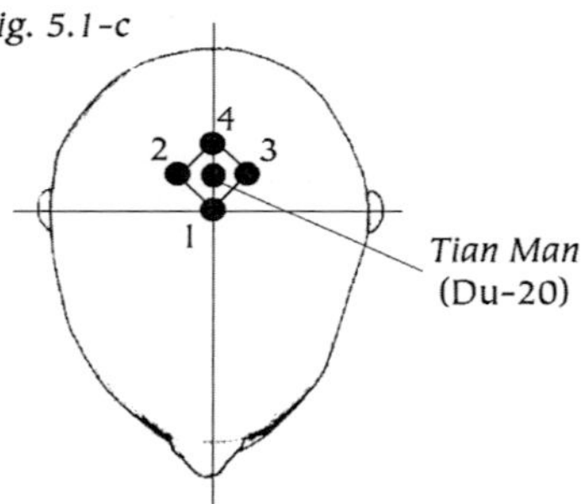


It is important that you locate *Tian Man* (Du-20) so you can correctly needle the four esoteric *Sishencong* points. Remember that the location of the esoteric *Sishencong* Group is more toward the back of the head than the traditional location of *Sishencong*.

Headaches on the top of the head are often referred to as *Jueyin* headaches referring to the liver system. With Esoteric Acupuncture, we are not interested in the *Jueyin* function of the *Sishencong* Group. *Sishencong* is often translated as "Four Spirits" or "Spirit Brightening." The use of the word spirit in Chinese Medicine refers to its connection with Shen of the heart system. That is the reason that the esoteric *Sishencong* Group is connected to the heart system and not the liver system. We are interested in the esoteric *Sishencong* Group to activate and balance the Higher Heart System, not necessarily the physical heart.

The first acupuncture point needled in the esoteric *Sishencong* Group is called Crown #1. Crown #1 is located directly on the vertical midline of the head approximately one inch anteriorly to *Tian Man* (Du-20). When your client is in a prone position with his or her face in a face cradle, I will usually angle the needle slightly upward. I will needle the other three points in this group with the same upward angle.

The second acupuncture site needled in the *Sishencong* Group is the point located on the client's right side approximately one inch lateral to the right of the location of *Tian Man* (Du-20). This acupuncture point of the *Sishencong* Group is known in Esoteric Acupuncture as Crown #2.

The third acupuncture site needled in the *Sishencong* Group is the point located on the client's left side approximately one inch lateral to the left of the location of *Tian Man* (Du-20). Although on figure 5.1-c the second and third points look like they are both on the imaginary horizontal line that connects the apexes of both ears, in reality one of the points is almost always anterior or posterior to the imaginary horizontal line. You must look for or feel for the qi. We are not interested in needling a perfectly symmetrical four-sided polygon. This acupuncture point of the *Sishencong* Group is known in Esoteric Acupuncture as Crown #3.

The fourth acupuncture site in the *Sishencong* Group is located approximately one inch (2.54 cm) posteriorly to *Tian*

*Man* (Du-20) and located directly on the vertical midline that is the Du channel. It is very important that you feel comfortable with locating and needling these four points of the esoteric *Sishencong* Group. This last acupuncture point of the *Sishencong* Group is known in Esoteric Acupuncture as Crown #4. The *Sishencong* group is the heart gateway to the Sahasrara (Crown Chakra) located superiorly to the cranium. Remember that one translation of *Sishencong* is "Four Spirits." The concept of *Shen* in Chinese philosophy includes the interconnectedness of body, mind and spirit. And *Shen* resides in the heart.

The fifth acupuncture point needled in The Crown Infinity *Shaoyin* Pattern is *Tian Chong* (GB-9) on the client's right side. To determine the location of *Tian Chong* (GB-9), it is best to first locate *Shuaigu* (GB-8). *Shuaigu* (GB-8) is located approximately one *cun* directly superior to the apex of each ear. The traditional location of *Tian Chong* (GB-9) is found approximately one-half *cun* posteriorly and superiorly to *Shuaigu* (GB-8) and in a slight depression. The *Tian Chong* location that is being suggested for Esoteric Acupuncture is found slightly more than one half *cun* posteriorly to *Shuiagu* (GB-8) and slightly higher. There is a very distinct depression at this acupuncture site. In many cases, this point is tender, so mention this to your client before inserting the acupuncture needle. Needle *Tian Chong* (GB-9) on the right side first, followed by *Tian Chong* (GB-9) on the left side.

The seventh and last acupuncture point of the Crown Infinity section of this pattern is *Feng Fu* (Du-16). *Feng Fu* (Du-16) is located directly on the vertical midline of the posterior of the head in a depression inferior to the occipital protuberance. This is a very important acupuncture site in Esoteric Acupuncture. The acupuncture point *Yamen* (Du-15) is located on the same vertical midline on the posterior of the head approximately one half *cun* superior to the posterior hairline. Sometimes description for locating *Feng Fu* (Du-16) is found by measuring one *cun* above the posterior hairline. Just make sure that *Feng Fu* (Du-16) is not needled too closely to the bottom of the posterior hairline. (See *Feng Fu* in Chapter 2.)

## Crown Infinity *Shaoyin* Pattern

*Fig. 5.1-d*

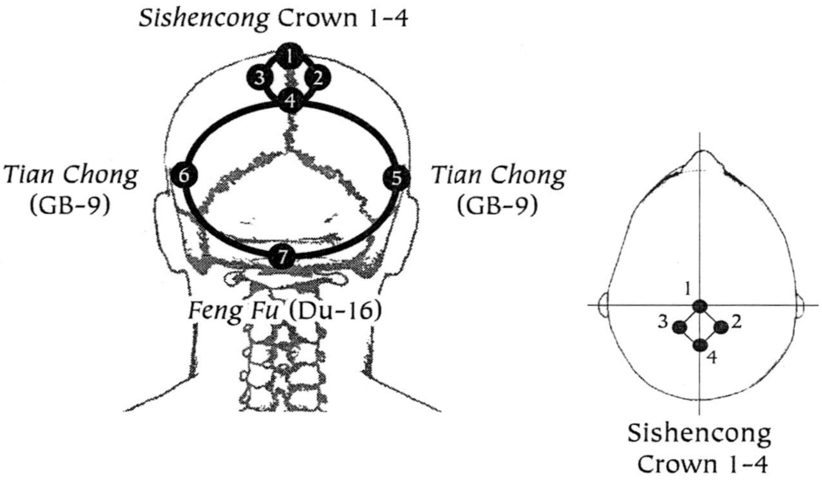


If you start at one note in any western scale and either move upward or downward on that scale, the eight note is either half or twice the frequency of the first note in that same scale. The figure 8 symbolically represents infinity. If you look at figure 5.1-d above, you will notice an asymmetrical figure 8. This is why the sequencing of these seven acupuncture points is known as The Crown Infinity Pattern. The *Sishencong* group surrounds the gateway to the Crown Chakra (Sahasrara), and the seven acupuncture points in this particular order will create the asymmetrical figure 8. Additionally, the number eight esoterically represents the number that allows one to be able to go into hyperspace or move into hyperspatial realities above our three-dimensional realities. (For a more detailed description on six surrounding one, see ***Climbing Jacob's Ladder: Esoteric***

***Acupuncture, Volume III*.)**

Acupuncture points number eight through number eleven in the Crown Infinity *Shaoyin* Pattern strengthen the *Shaoyin* portion of this pattern. I mentioned in ***Esoteric Acupuncture: Gateway to Expanded Healing, Volume I***, that one of the basic principles in Esoteric Acupuncture is the concept of Esoteric *Shaoyin*. In Chinese medicine, *Shaoyin* consists of the heart and kidneys channels.

The bilateral *Xinshu* (UB-15) points are heart qi transporting points. The bilateral *Shenshu* (UB-23) points are kidney qi transporting points. Transporting points are those points that move energy to and from a particular organ system. Esoteric *Shaoyin* involves balancing the heart system of love with the kidney system that encompasses fear. Esoteric Acupuncture is not as interested in the physical heart and kidneys as with the finer, higher frequencies of the heart and kidney systems. The heart and the fire element versus the kidneys and the water element are the opposing forces. Love and fear are the opposites that balance each other, as well as allow expanded consciousness to develop.

The distance from the center of the spine to the medial border of each scapula is considered to be three *cun* in Chinese medicine. To locate *Xinshu* (UB-15), first locate the lower border of the spinous process of the fifth thoracic vertebrae. Then find the medial border of the right scapula. *Xinshu* (UB-15) is located on the imaginary vertical line that is halfway between the center of the spine and the medial border of the right scapula. Since it was mentioned that the distance from the middle of the spine to the medial border of either scapula was considered to be three cun, the midpoint where *Xinshu* (UB-15) is located is considered to be one and one-half *cun* lateral to the spine. This first *Xinshu* (UB-15) point is needled on the client's right side. This is the eighth acupuncture point in The Crown Infinity *Shaoyin* Pattern.

The ninth acupuncture point needled in The Crown Infinity *Shaoyin* Pattern is *Shenshu* (UB-23) on the client's left side.

Feel for the superior borders of the iliac crest on both side of the body. If you draw an imaginary horizontal line connecting the superior borders of both iliac crests and intersecting the spine, you will locate the fourth lumbar vertebra (L-4) where the imaginary horizontal line crosses the spine. We are looking for the second lumbar vertebra. *Mingmen* (Du-4) is located at the lower border of the spinous process of the second lumbar vertebra. *Mingmen* (Du-4) is a major kidney point. The bilateral kidney transporting points are known as *Shenshu* (UB-23) and are located bilaterally from the second lumbar vertebra and approximately one and one half *cun* from the center of the spine. *Shenshu* (UB-23) on the client's left side is needled first, followed by *Shenshu* (UB-23) on the client's right side. These two acupuncture points are the ninth and tenth acupuncture points in The Crown Infinity *Shaoyin* Pattern.

The eleventh and last acupuncture point in the Crown Infinity *Shaoyin* Pattern is needled on the client's left side lateral to the lower border of the spinous process of the fifth thoracic vertebrae and approximately one and one half *cun* from the center of the spine. Both of the *Xinshu* (UB-15) points should be on an imaginary horizontal line that crosses the lower border of the spinous process of the fifth thoracic vertebrae.

Notice the needling sequence from *Xinshu* (UB-15) on the client's right side crisscrossing to *Shenshu* (UB-23) on the client's left side followed by *Shenshu* (UB-23) on the right side and ending with *Xinshu* (UB-15) on the client's left side. The needling sequence of these four acupuncture sites forms an hourglass shape figure that is also a figure eight. Remember in Esoteric Acupuncture, the number eight signifies a frequency that will allow one to have the possibility to enter into hyperspatial realities. Hyperspatial is used in Esoteric Acupuncture to mean the realms of consciousness above our three-dimensional world.

Besides using the transporter acupuncture points of the urinary bladder system corresponding to the heart and kidney systems that comprise what the Chinese call *Shaoyin,* we have also created two intersecting triangles. The triangle pointing upward is a fire triangle of the heart system. The triangle pointing downward is a water triangle of the kidney system. Once again, we are working with Esoteric *Shaoyin* that consists of the heart system of love opposing, yet simultaneously` harmonizing, the kidney system of fear.

The Crown Infinity *Shaoyin* Pattern is the suggested posterior New Encoding Pattern to use on a first time client, or for an existing client that has not quite embraced the shift into his or her Inner Heart Space. This particular pattern contains the very basic Crown Infinity Pattern, plus the fundamental *shaoyin* principle of complimentary and opposing systems of life. The heart controls love and fire. The kidneys control fear and water. The heart system versus the kidney system are the opposing forces, as well as the complimentary and tonifying forces.

The Crown Infinity *Shaoyin* Pattern is both a powerful, yet gentle pattern at the same time. It will shift the client who has done the proper amount of inner plane work into a higher vibratory rate of consciousness, but with a harmonious frequency, so as to make the shift organic and gentle.

## Energetics of The Crown Infinity *Shaoyin* Pattern in Esoteric Acupuncture

If you truly want to understand the energetics of Esoteric Acupuncture, the most important group of Esoteric Acupuncture points to become intimately familiar with is the first seven acupuncture points in this pattern. These first seven acupuncture points make up The Crown Infinity Pattern that was introduced in ***Gateway to Expanded Healing: Esoteric Acupuncture, Volume I***. Sacred Geometry and sacred numbers, as used in Esoteric Acupuncture, revolve around understanding the concept that six signifies beginnings, creation and expansion. In Hebrew, Bereshith means "In Beginning," or more grammatically correct, "In the beginning." Bara Shith or Bara Sheth means "created six." This is interpreted as meaning: "In the beginning, created six."

According to R. Buckminster Fuller, six is the minimum number required for one minimum-structural system. The six vectors of a tetrahedron make up one structural quantum. The tetrahedron is a minimum-structural system. Six refers to a tetrahedron that is the simplest structure that we know with our present level of consciousness that has both insidedness and outsidedness. A tetrahedron has six vectors that outline its structure. A tetrahedron has four triangles. Triangles are the signature for tetrahedrons. The property of insidedness and outsidedness of the minimal-structural system of a tetrahedron represents the esoteric symbol for consciousness. A tetrahedron is the signature for consciousness. A tetrahedral structure also reveals "As Within, so Without," as well as "As Above, So Below." Working with triangles and tetrahedrons will assist us in working with consciousness to raise our vibratory rate to that of a higher frequency. Remember that when you sequence your acupuncture needles in a triangular fashion, you are also creating a field that allows for qi to move more quickly than needling in the Asian traditional fashion of not paying attention to triangles.

In Esoteric Acupuncture, Six Surrounding One is a key to unlocking the secrets of sacred geometry as it relates to healing, wellness and raising one's level of consciousness. Six Surrounding One is a major esoteric code that will allow you to smoothly enter the world of the Ageless Wisdom teachings, also known as the mystery school teachings.

Six Surrounding One also means there is a number seven. Look at the Crown Infinity Pattern in figure 5.1-e on the following page. You will notice six acupuncture sites surrounding one acupuncture site. You will also notice the seven separate but connected acupuncture points. Esoterically, seven refers to harmony and is the esoteric number for completion. (Some people feel that the number nine represents completion, but that is for a lower plane of consciousness). Why do you think Pythagoras used seven notes in the musical scale? Was it just by chance, or was it because there is an underlying rhythmical wave pattern connected to the number seven that also creates order out of chaos? The esoteric understanding of seven states that the that the seven emanates from three, and that three comes from one.

## Six Surrounding One

*Fig. 5.1-e*

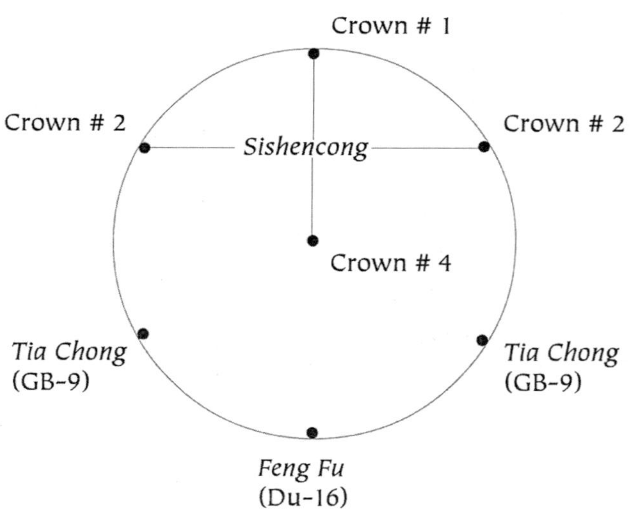


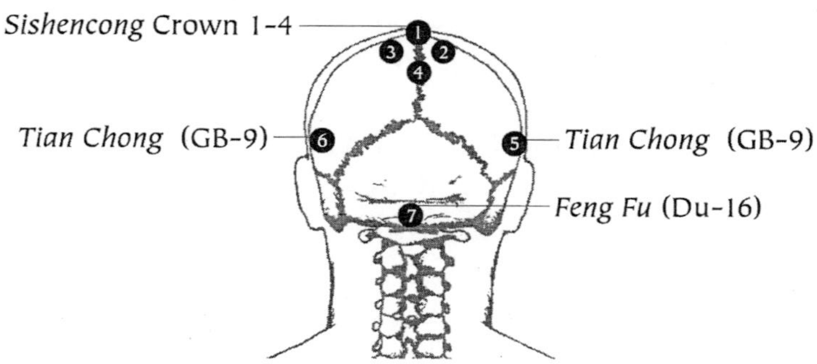

Djwhal Khul also states in his massive book ***Treatise on Cosmic Fire*** that: "7 is the number that governs evolution of substance and form-building in our solar system."[2]

The number eleven symbolizes a gateway (11) or an opening to somewhere or to something. There are eleven acupuncture points in the Crown Infinity *Shaoyin* Pattern. The Crown Infinity *Shaoyin* Pattern is designed to allow your client to open an initial gateway into the realms of his or her Inner Spiritual Higher Heart. The seven acupuncture points of the Crown Infinity Pattern within this pattern will begin the activation process to open up the higher head centers. Then the next four acupuncture points on the posterior body will allow the client being needled to gently move into his or her heart center by balancing the frequencies of the kidney system and the heart system, which is Esoteric *Shaoyin*. This is a very gentle, but effective initial treatment for your clientele at this first Tier of Density.

Over the years, many people have told me that they are constantly seeing the numbers 11-11, especially on a digital clock. They keep seeing this sequence over and over again. In Esoteric Acupuncture, double elevens is an indication there is a double gateway (11 and 11), or twin gateways, opening up in your life that may require your attention. Think of each of the elevens as a pathway. This is an indication that your lower double flames are starting to become activated with a similar frequency. These double gateways are another expression of Esoteric *Shaoyin* that comprise the interconnectedness of the heart and kidney energies. The double elevens mean that the opposing frequencies are now starting to blend into a more complimentary and harmonious frequency. If you ignore these signs, you may miss an opportunity for a more accelerated ascension to your higher, inner planes of consciousness. The double elevens will assist you in your process of going inward to access your higher consciousness, which will in turn give you more clues and guidance on the next steps to take.

These same people have asked me the meaning of 11-11.

The two elevens signify that the Inner Spiritual Higher Heart is ready to be activated and wants to open and align one's Inner Twin Flame Within. At this level, constantly seeing a representation of the Twin Gateways, signifies the lower Twin Flames Within are wanting to open and connect, but as yet, the two flames are disconnected. (See figure 5.1-f below.) These two lower flames consist of the flame of *Shendao* of the heart and the flame of the *Mingmen* Fire of the kidney system. (For more on the esoteric meaning of Twin Flames, see ***Discern the Whisper: Esoteric Acupuncture, Volume II.***)

If you are quiet and do your inner plane work, then you will see that the 11-11, or the two (twin) gateways are starting to merge. The twin gateways are merely another way to express your inner Twin Flames. When viewing the disconnected twin gateways from a different angle, the double 11-11's line up differently and reveal one gateway instead of two. This "hidden" gateway is an opening to your One True Path, that of your Higher, Inner, Spiritual Heart. (See figure 5.1-g below.)

## Significance of 11-11

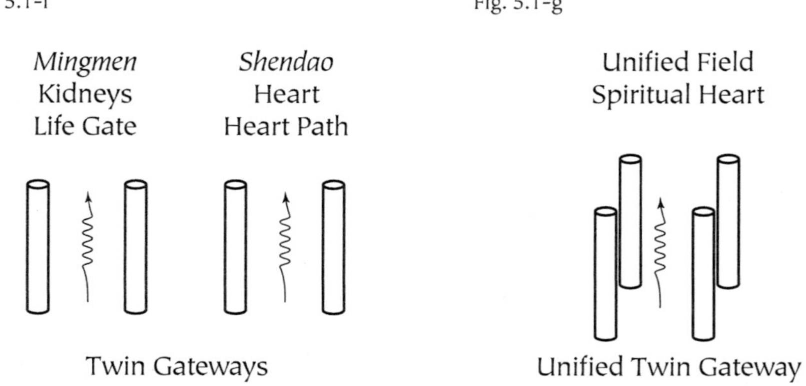

## Visualization Connections for The Crown Infinity *Shaoyin* Pattern

First of all, remember that one of the basic concepts in Esoteric Acupuncture involves Esoteric *Shaoyin*. In Esoteric Acupuncture, we are not interested in the *shaoyin* discussed in the Chinese medical text ***Shang Han Lun*** that explains various symptoms with a yang deficiency (cold) condition. Esoteric *Shaoyin* consists of the kidney system of water and fear opposing the heart system of fire and love. A triangle with its apex pointing upward symbolizes the heart system of love. A triangle with its apex pointing downward symbolizes the kidney system of fear. The two opposing triangles represent the conflict between love and fear. When the two opposing triangles are imposed one on top of the other, we have a six-pointed figure that unites the *yin* with the *yang*, the female with the male, the upper with the lower. The six-pointed figure with the superimposed fire and water triangles symbolize the unity and cooperation between the two opposing forces. They are now complimenting each other. (See figure 5.1-h.) When this same two-dimensional diagram is expanded into a three-dimensional double tetrahedron, we are expanding the complimenting fields of love and fear. (See figure 5.1-i.)

*Fig. 5.1-h*

*Fig. 5.1-i*

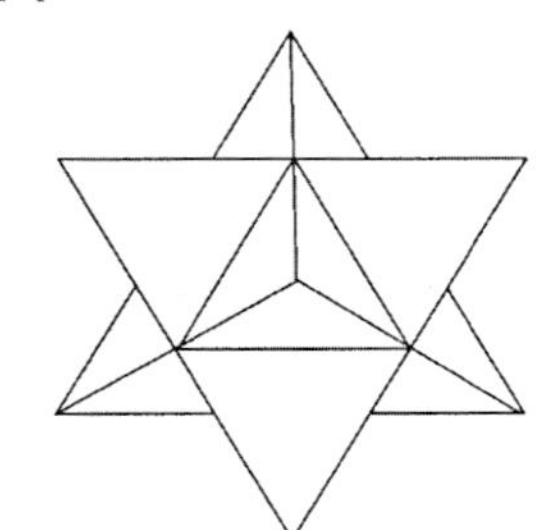

Have your client visually connect the acupuncture points Crown # 2 and Crown #3 in his or her mind. These two acupuncture points are the second and third points needled in the *Sishencong* group. Next have your client connect the qi from these two points to Crown #1 forming a triangle pointing toward the front of the client's head. (See figure 5.1-j below.) It does matter if you have your client connect Crown #2 to Crown #3 before connecting those two points to Crown #1, or if you have your client connect Crown #3 to Crown #2 before connecting those two points to Crown #1. The triangle will be pointing toward the front of the client's head. When your client is in a prone position, the triangle will be pointing downward. Since the triangle is pointing toward the front of the head, this triangle is still a fire triangle of the heart.

## *Sishencong*

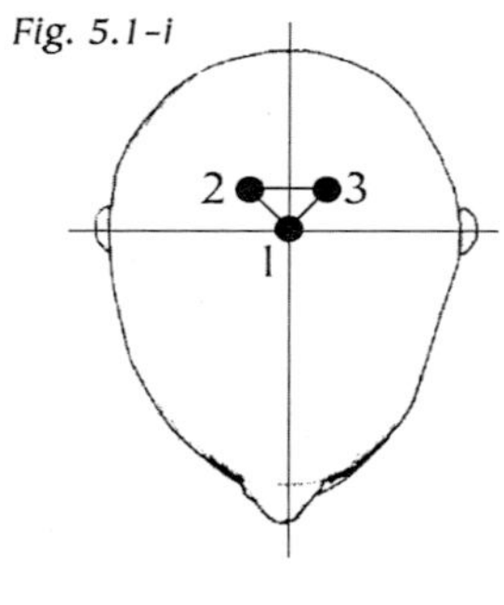


Fire Triangle

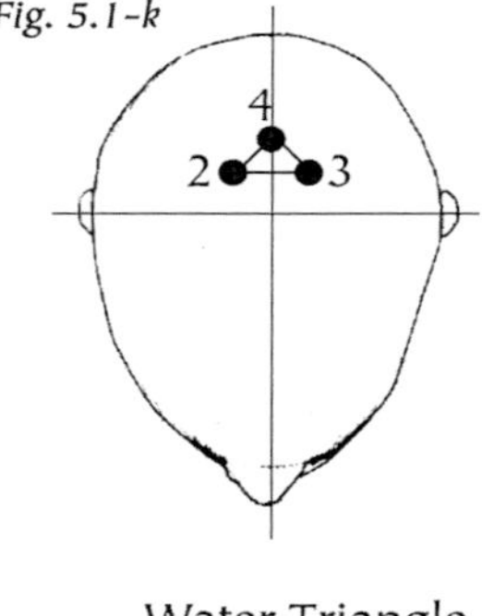


Water Triangle

Next have your client again connect the acupuncture points Crown #2 to Crown #3. This time have the client connect the qi from those two acupuncture sites toward the back of the head connecting with Crown #4. (See figure 5.1-k on p. 333.)

Again, it does not matter if you have your client visually connect Crown #2 to Crown #3 or have your client connect Crown #3 to Crown #2. Next have your client bring the energy from the points Crown #2 and Crown #3 downward to connect with the point Crown #4. The connection of these three points creates a water triangle of the kidney system. The energetic line connecting the acupuncture points at the sites of Crown #2 and Crown #3 is called the platform and is the platform for both the fire triangle and the water triangle. The visual formation of the first triangle plus the visual formation of the second triangle creates two opposing triangles (fire and water) of an Esoteric *Shaoyin* field consisting of the heart system and the kidney system.

Does this configuration look familiar? This is an example of the four pillars of an 11-11 configuration surrounding an inner pathway. Although Tian Man (Du-20) is not needled in this pattern, the four *Sishencong* points surround the inner gateway of *Tian man* (Du-20). (See figure 5.1-l below)

### *Sishencong*

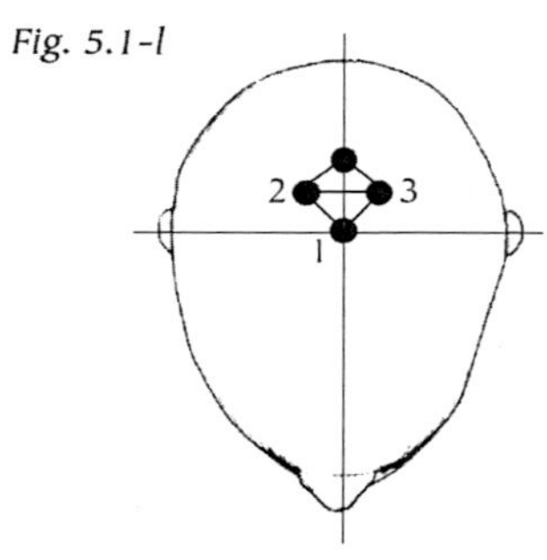


*Fig. 5.1-l*

Next visually connect the bilateral *Tian Chong* (GB-9) points (points #5 and #6), located behind and above the ears, with each other. (See figure 5.1-m below.)

Crown Infinity *Shaoyin* Pattern

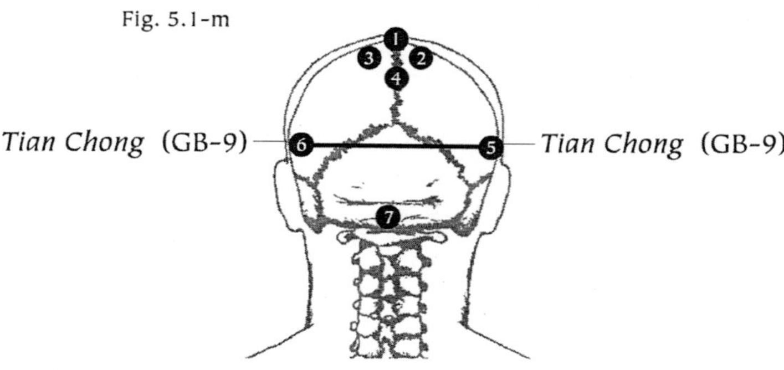


After the bilateral *Tian Chong* (GB-9) points have been visually connected, bring the qi from these two acupuncture points upward to Crown #4 to form an upward pointing fire triangle. (See figure5.1-n below.)

Crown Infinity *Shaoyin* Pattern

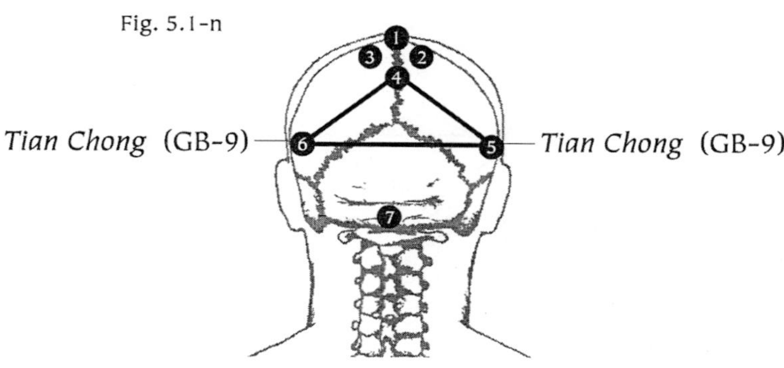

The purpose of needling the bilateral *Tian Chong* (GB-9) in Esoteric Acupuncture is to activate the dormant gateway to the cosmic hearing aspect of the Higher, Inner, Spiritual Heart. Although the *Tian Chong* points are part of the gallbladder meridian of the wood system, when we later make a specific visual connection with the bilateral *Tian Ting* (SJ-15) points, we will be initiating a *shaoyang* connection. A *shaoyang* connection consists of the *san jiao* (triple burner) channel communicating with the gallbladder meridian. Although we will not be making this particular *shaoyang* connection in The Crown Infinity *Shaoyin* Pattern, I wanted the practitioner to understand that in Esoteric Acupuncture, the bilateral *Tian Chong* (GB-9) points are use to activate the hearing aspect of the Higher, Inner, Spiritual Heart system.

Now visually have your client bring the qi from these bilateral *Tian Chong* (GB-9) points downward to connect with *Feng Fu* (Du-16) the seventh acupuncture point. This downward pointing figure is a water triangle. (See figure 5.1-o.) We have now created an additional Esoteric *Shaoyin* field with this visual connection of points in The Crown Infinity *Shaoyin* Pattern.

**Crown Infinity *Shaoyin* Pattern**

*Fig. 5.1-o*

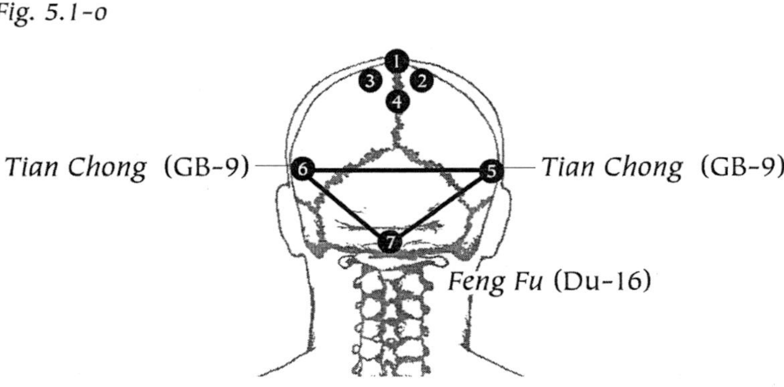

With these last visual connections, we again have an Esoteric Shaoyin Field. There is a balancing of the heart field with the kidney field. (See figure 5.1-p below.)

**Crown Infinity *Shaoyin* Pattern**

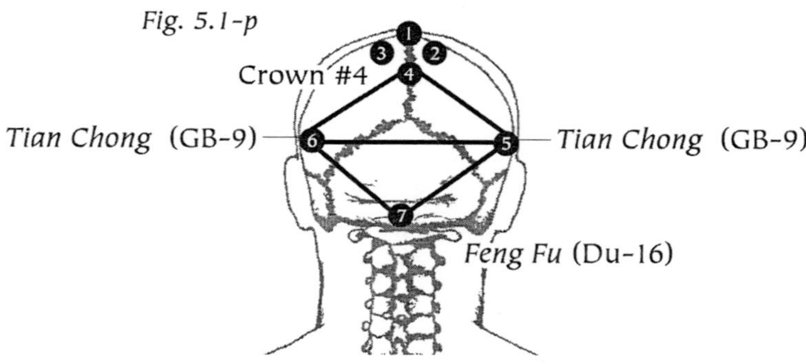


This particular Esoteric *Shaoyin* Field is very important in Esoteric Acupuncture because the visual connections initiate the beginning stage of activation and realization of the inner, higher realms. The acupuncture site of *Feng Fu* (Du-16) is the area that has the possibility of triggering the realms of the Inner Wind Mansion. The Inner Wind Mansion will raise your consciousness to understand and be able to utilize the realms of "Sound with no Sound" and the "Light Without Light." This four-sided polygon encompasses the field of our *Kunlun* Mountain, as well as our inner Mountain within the Mountain. The Brahmarandra Chakra within the cranium is our Inner Mountain within the Mountain.

The eighth acupuncture point needled in the Crown Infinity *Shaoyin* Pattern is *Xinshu* (UB-15) on the client's right side of the spine. The ninth acupuncture point needled is *Shenshu* (UB-23) found on the left side of the spine. Have your client connect the *Xinshu* (UB-15) point on his or her right side to the *Shenshu* (UB-23) point on his or her left side. (See figure 5.1-q below.)

### Crown Infinity *Shaoyin* Pattern

*Fig. 5.1-q*

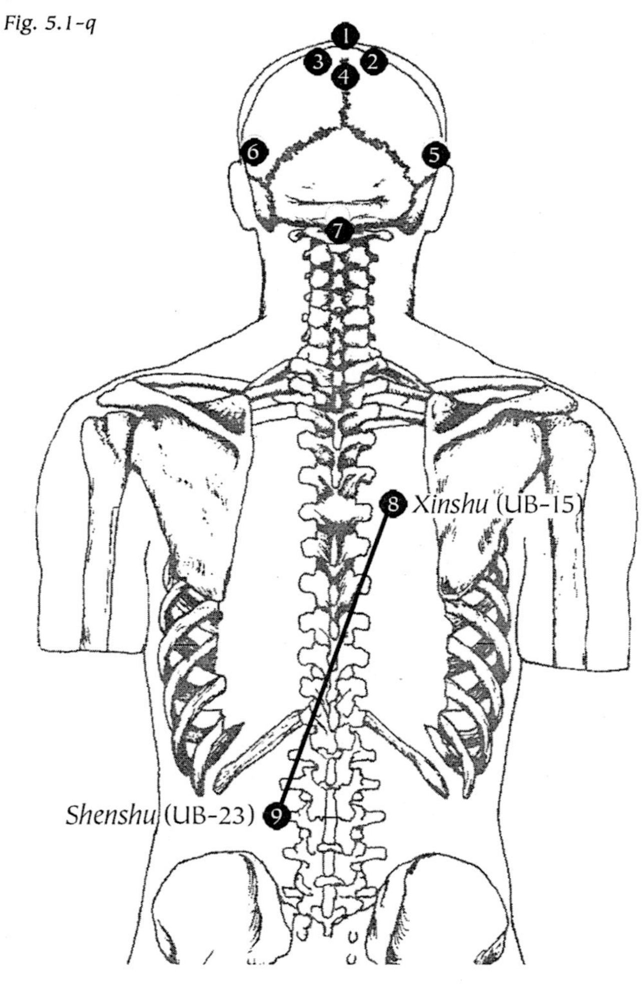

The tenth acupuncture point needled in The Crown Infinity *Shaoyin* Pattern is the kidney point *Shenshu* (UB-23) on the client's right side. (See figure 5.1-r below.)

## Crown Infinity *Shaoyin* Pattern

*Fig. 5.1-r*

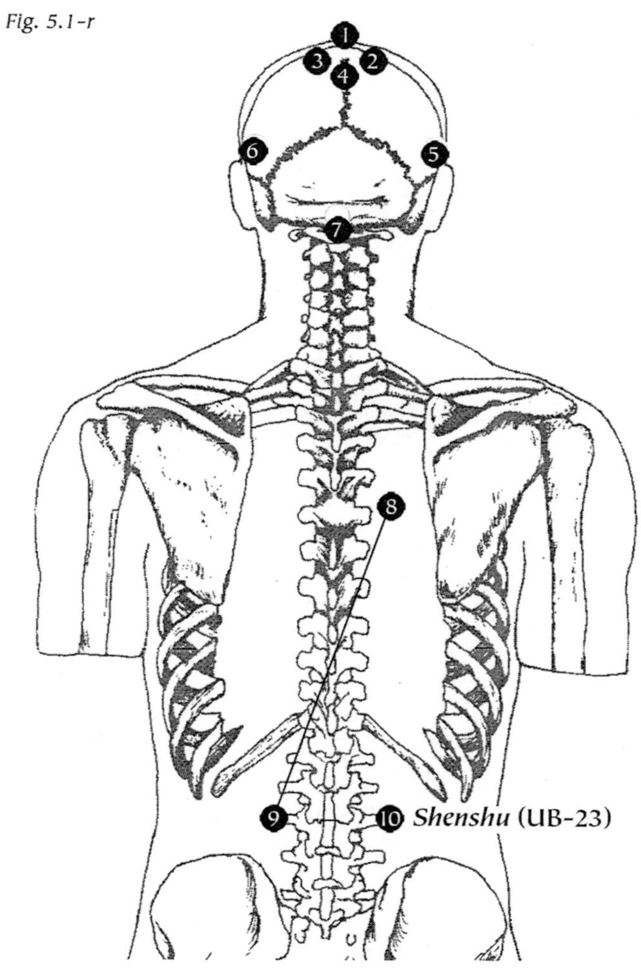

Now have your client visually connect the *Shenshu* (UB-23) point on the left side of the spine to the *Shenshu* (UB-23) point on the right side of the spine. (See figure 5.1-s below.)

## Crown Infinity *Shaoyin* Pattern

*Fig. 5.1-s*

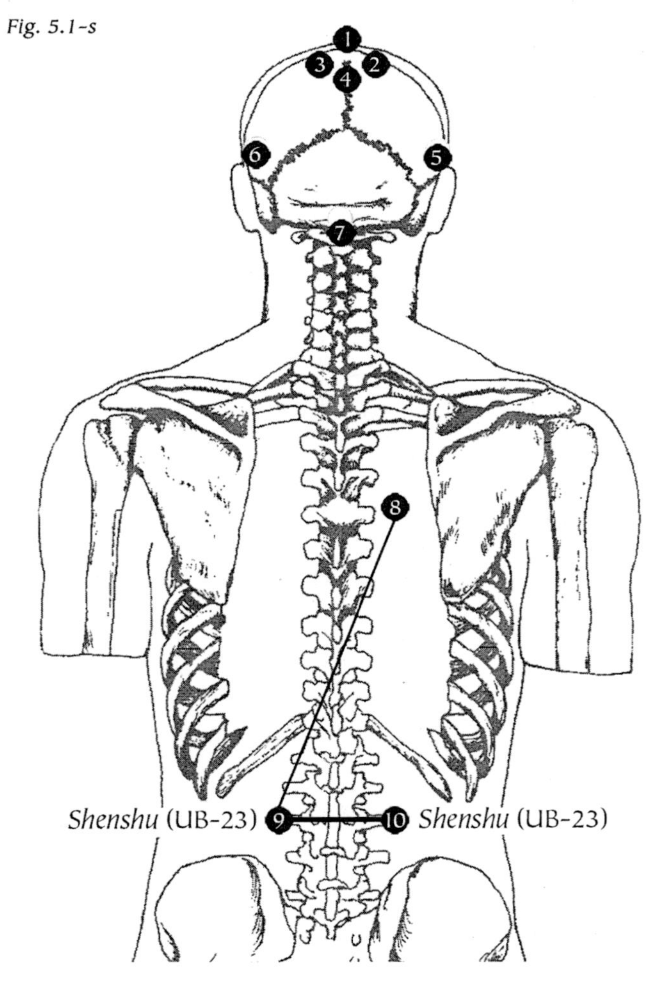

The eleventh and last acupuncture point needled in the Crown Infinity *Shaoyin* Pattern is *Xinshu* (UB-15) on the client's left side. (See figure 5.1-t below.)

## Crown Infinity *Shaoyin* Pattern

*Fig. 5.1-t*

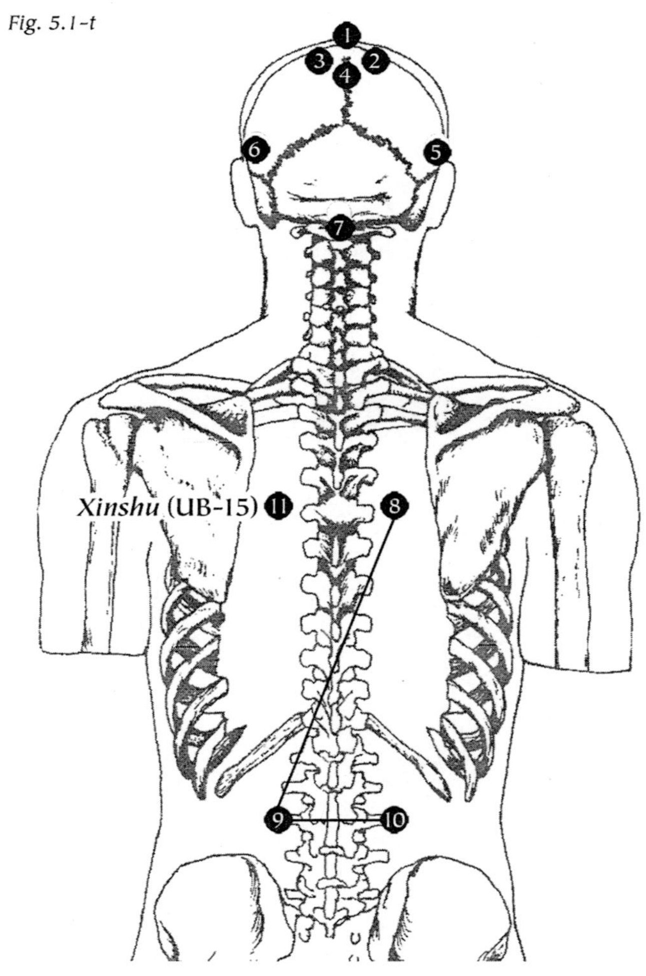

You will now ask your client to bring the energy upward from the *Shenshu* (UB-15) point on his or her right side and make a crisscross connection to the *Xinshu* (UB-15) on the client's left side. (See figure 5.1-u below.)

## Crown Infinity *Shaoyin* Pattern

*Fig. 5.1-u*

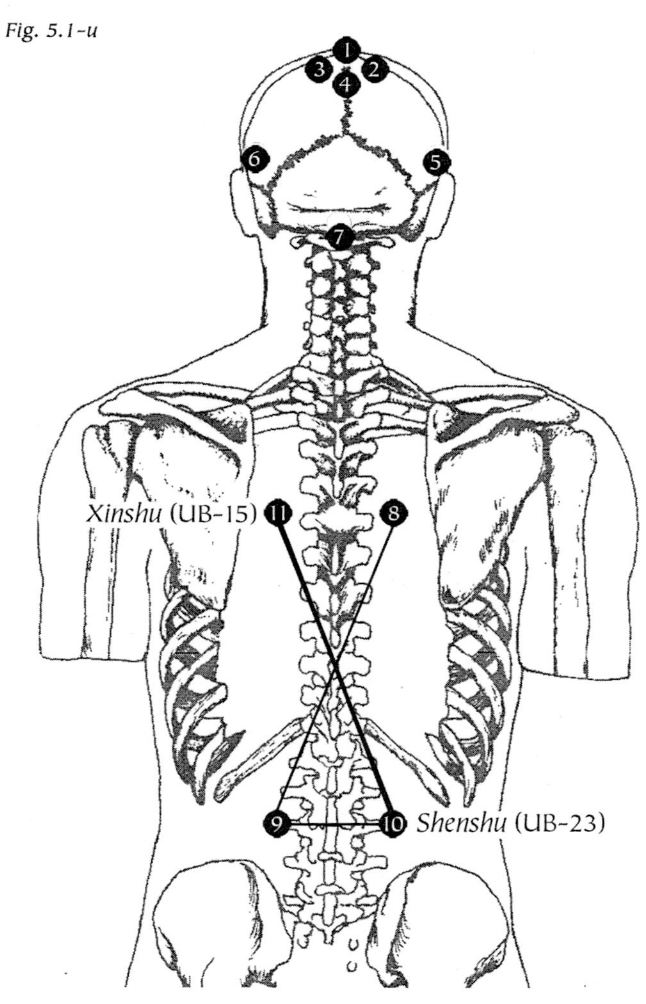

Next visually connect the bilateral *Xinshu* (UB-15) points. The geometric figure created by the needling sequence of these four acupuncture points on the body forms an hourglass shaped polygon. You will notice a water triangle pointing downward and a fire triangle pointing upward opposing and harmonizing each other. Since the four acupuncture sites needled are also heart and kidney-transporting points of the urinary bladder meridian, this hourglass formation creates a very strong *Shaoyin* field. (See figure 5.1-v below.)

## Crown Infinity *Shaoyin* Pattern

*Fig. 5.1-v*

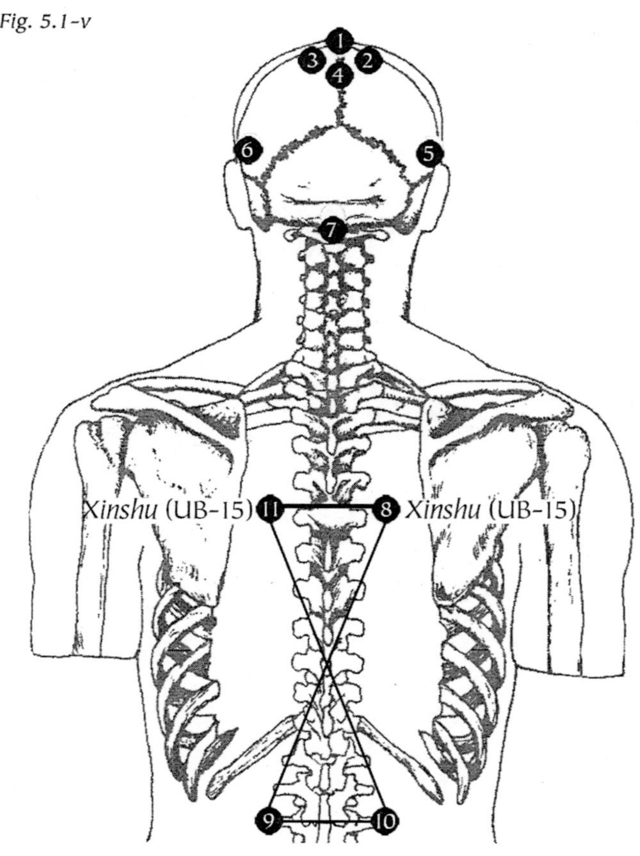

The last visualization in The Crown Infinity *Shaoyin* Pattern is to bring the energy upward from both of the *Xinshu* (UB-15) heart points and connect these bilateral points with The Wind Mansion at *Feng Fu* (Du-16). This triangle with the upward pointing apex is a fire triangle. (See figure 5.1-w.

**Crown Infinity *Shaoyin* Pattern**

Fig. 5.1-w

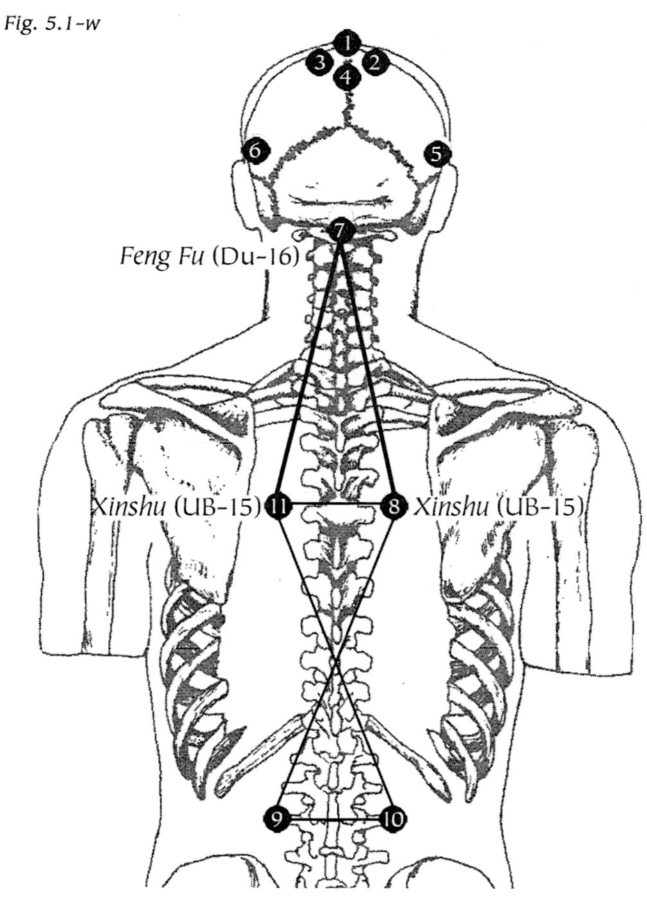

The number eleven, which is the number of points used in this pattern, is symbolic of a pathway. Think of 11 as a gateway or portal to some place. The acupuncture points used in this pattern will assist the recipient of this treatment to activate his or her connection to a portal to higher consciousness. This is a very "gentle" pattern to allow the recipient to slowly unfold into a higher, lighter frequency of density.

**Crown Infinity *Shaoyin* Pattern**
**Complete Grid**

*Fig. 5.1-x*

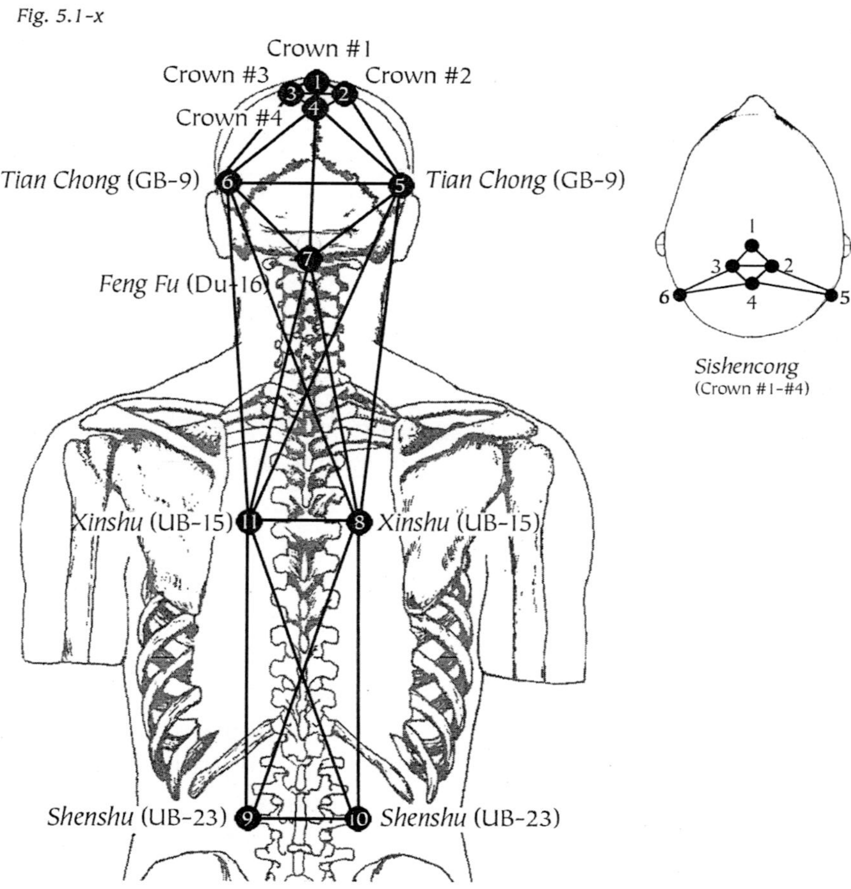

## Tier Density Level 1 Supine Position: Integration Synthesis Pattern

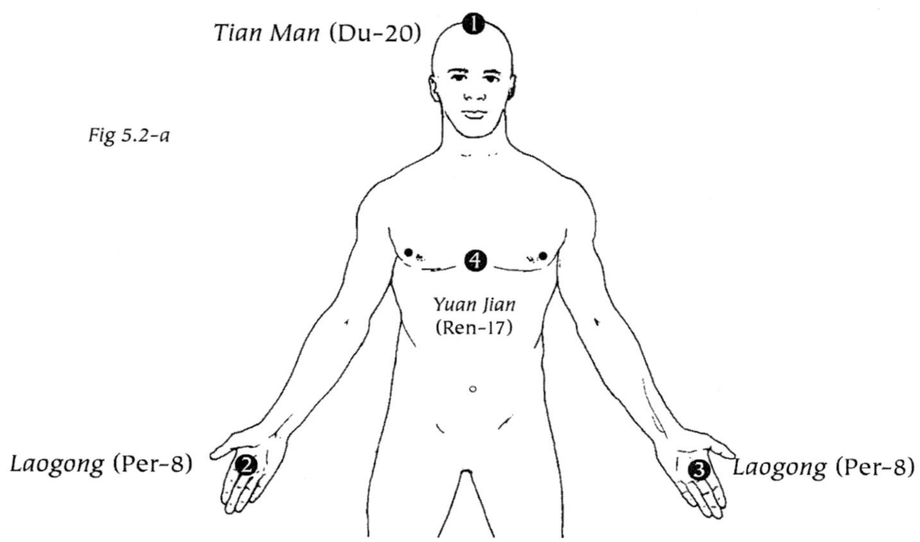


The Integration Synthesis Pattern is a very simple, yet very effective pattern to treat a client who has difficulty shutting down the mental chatter, a symptom sometimes known as Restless *Shen* or *Shen* Disturbance. I have had many practitioners express their appraisals for the results obtained by needling the four acupuncture sites of The Integration Synthesis Pattern.

Dr. Alexander Joannou, whom I first met in Melbourne, Australia in 2010, started using The Integration Synthesis Pattern after attending my workshops in Australia. I became friends with Dr. Joannou during the course of his attending my Esoteric Acupuncture intensive workshops during 2011 and 2012. Dr. Joannou is a medical doctor who had been practicing western medicine for over thirty years. He became interested in alternative modalities to the western role model and had been practicing acupuncture for approximately twelve years when I met him. Dr. Joannou has a deep understanding of the esoteric world and has an intense desire to understand the subtle intricacies of Chinese Medicine. He tries to attend as many acupuncture workshops and seminars presented in Australia as his time will allow.

Dr. Joannou said it wasn't until incorporating Esoteric Acupuncture into the acupuncture portion of his practice that he started to see noticeable positive mental and emotional results from his patients who received acupuncture treatments from him. Dr. Joannou specifically said that he had positive results involving various levels of imbalanced *Shen* from his patients when they were needled with The Integration Synthesis Pattern. This pattern is a very effective pattern for your client who is in a Tier Density Level 1 consciousness state.

For a more detailed explanation of The Integration Synthesis Pattern, see ***Gateway to Expanded Healing: Esoteric Acupuncture, Volume I.***

### Needling Sequence for the Integration Synthesis Pattern

1) *Tian Man* (Du-20)
2) *Laogong* (Per-8) Right palm
3) *Laogong* (Per-8) Left palm
4) *Yuan Jian* (Ren-17) more commonly known as *Tan Chong*

### Point Locations for The Integration Synthesis Pattern

The first acupuncture site in The Integration Synthesis Pattern is *Tian Man* (Du-20). It is important to know that we are looking for the location of the esoteric Du-20 that is known as *Tian Man* and not the location of the traditional Du-20 that is known as *Bai Hui*. Find the apex of each ear. Now draw an imaginary line across the top of your client's head connecting the apex of each ear. Where this imaginary horizontal line, going across the top of the head, intersects the vertical midline at the top of the head is where *Bai Hui* (Du-20) is located. Now look or feel for a slight depression located approximately one *cun* or one inch posteriorly to the traditional *Bai Hui* (Du-20). This is the location of the esoteric Du-20 (*Tian Man*). Sometimes the scalp does not have much flesh, so the needle insertion is very superficial and at a slight angle. Do not insert the needle perpendicular to the scalp. Insert a .20 mm X 15 mm blue handled Seirin needle at this site, angling the needle slightly toward the front of the client's head. I recommend the .20 mm X 15 mm blue handled Seirin needle over the slightly thinner .16 mm X 15 mm red handled Seirin because on some people the palms may have a thicker layer of skin, and the red handled .16 mm needle may not penetrate the palm as well as the slightly thicker .20 mm gauge.

Points #2 and #3 are the bilateral *Lao Gong* (Per-8) points located on the client's palms. Point #2 is *Lao Gong* (Per-8) located on the right palm and is needled first, followed by needling the *Lao Gong* (Per-8) point on the left palm.

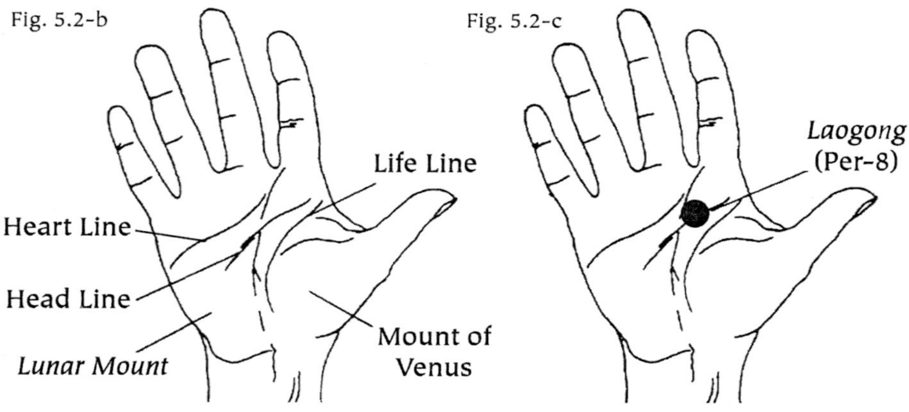

The acupuncture site of *Laogong* (Per-8) is located between the index finger and middle finger on the palm and usually on the headline of the palm. Although this acupuncture point is a point of the pericardium channel, in Esoteric Acupuncture this acupuncture point is used to activate the Anahata (Heart Chakra). (See figure 5.2-b.) The palms are usually sensitive so use a quick but gentle straight insertion with no twisting motion upon insertion.

The fourth and last acupuncture point in The Integration Synthesis Pattern is *Yuan Jian* (Ren-17). This acupuncture point is more commonly known as *Tanzhong* or *Danzhong* and is translated as "Chest Center." I prefer to use an alternate name *Yuan Jian* that is translated as "The Source." In Esoteric Acupuncture, this acupuncture point is the stimulus site to access, tonify and harmonize the Anahata (Heart Chakra). *Yuan Jian* (Ren-17) is located directly on the vertical midline of the chest level with the fourth intercostal space. In men, *Yuan Jian* (Ren-17) is often level with an imaginary horizontal line drawn between the nipples.

## Visualizations for The Integration Synthesis Pattern

This is the one of only two anterior New Encoding Patterns that will include a visualization connection of the acupuncture points by the client who is receiving this treatment. The only other anterior pattern with a visualization connection is The Merkabah Spin Pattern that is an extension of The Integration Synthesis Pattern. I always recommend doing a posterior New Encoding Pattern first, followed by an anterior New Encoding Pattern. After retaining needles in the posterior of the body, your client will most likely not be in the mindset to visualize complex connection of points on the anterior of the body.

If you have a client who would like to experience an Esoteric Acupuncture treatment for the first time, needling only the Integration Synthesis Pattern or the Merkabah Spin Pattern without a posterior pattern may be recommended for that client.

After the four acupuncture needles have been inserted in the proper sequence, have your client visually connect the bilateral *Laogong* (Per-8) points on the palm of your hands. (See figure 5.2-d below.)

## Integration Synthesis Pattern

*Fig 5.2-d*

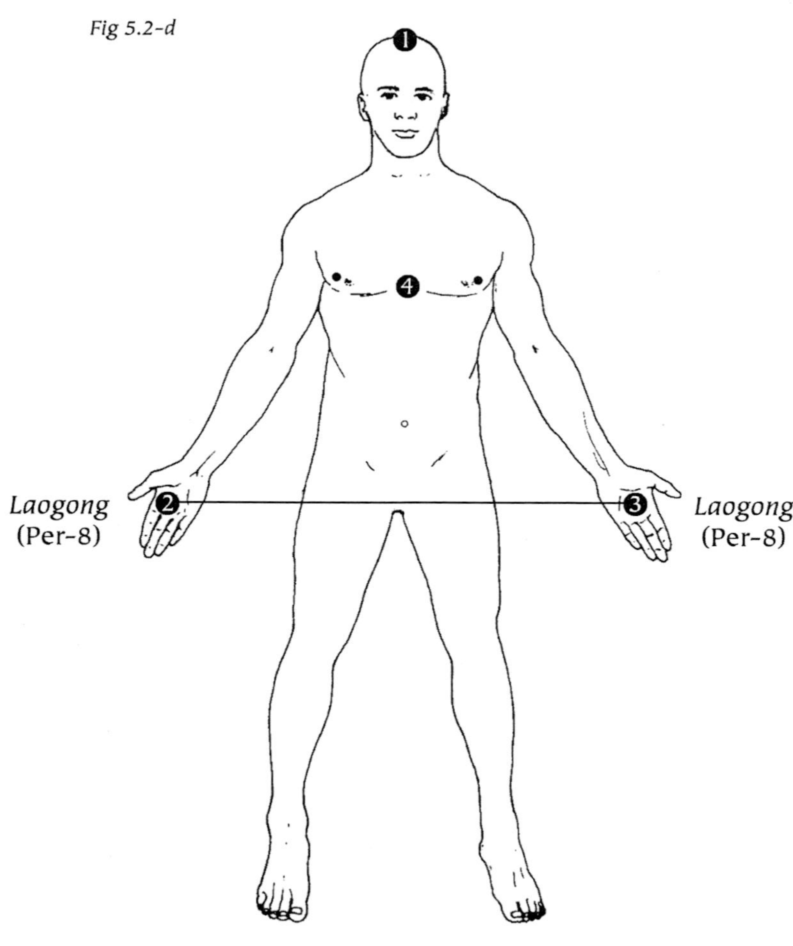

Next bring the qi from the bilateral *Laogong* (Per-8) points upward simultaneously from both palms to connect with *Tian Man* (Du-20) on the top of the head. This connection forms a Fire Triangle of the heart system. (See figure 5.2-e below.)

## Integration Synthesis Pattern

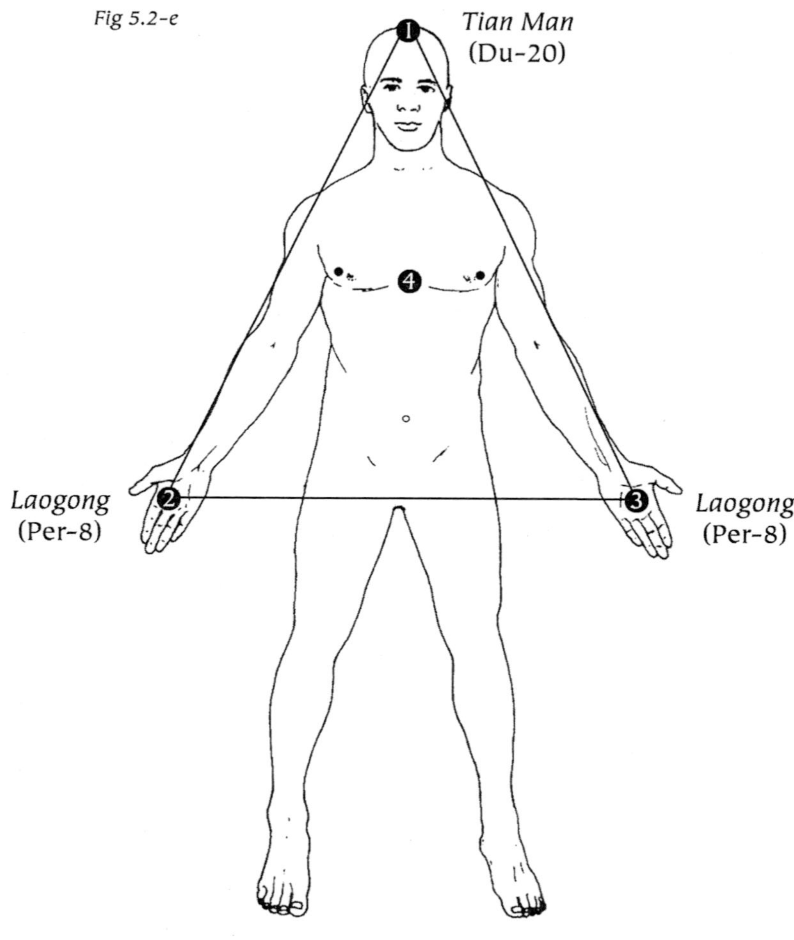

Now have your client connect those three acupuncture points simultaneously with *Yuan Jian* (Ren-17) on the chest as shown in figure 5.2-f below.

**Integration Synthesis Pattern**
**Complete Visualization and Grid**

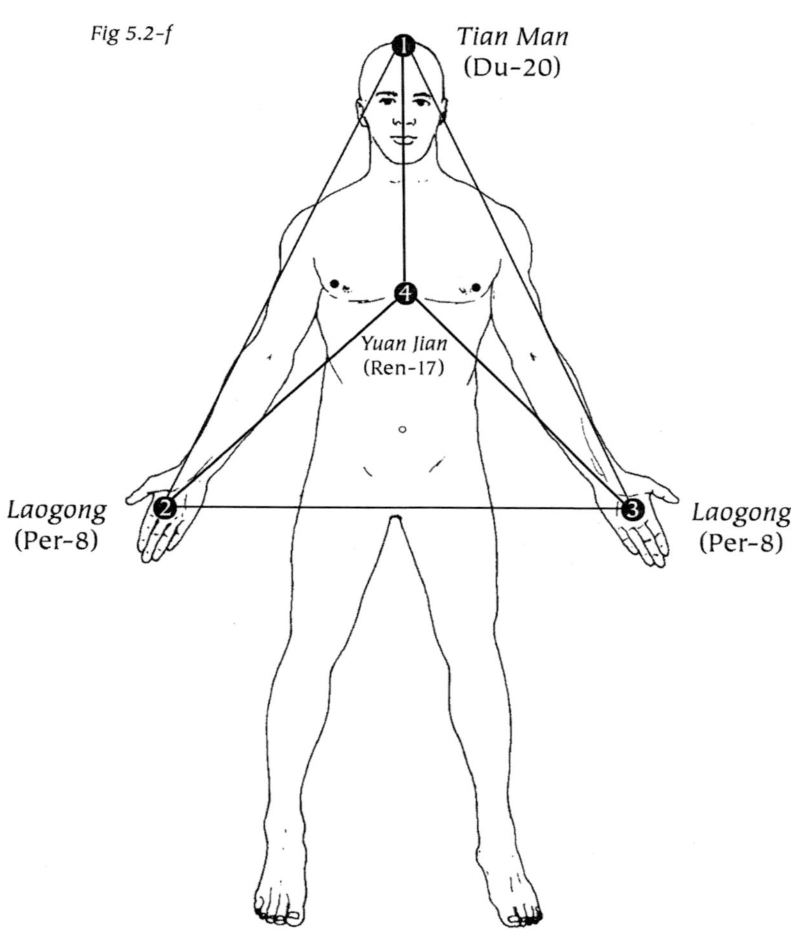

Next have your client visualize *Yuan Jian* (Ren-17) rising a foot or more above his or her chest. This visualization creates a tetrahedron that is a signature of a Merkabah, a light vehicle for potential hyper spatial, expanded consciousness exploration.

If you closely examine the visual tetrahedron, you will notice six vectors with four triangles. The six vectors and the four triangles form a structure. According to R. Buckminster Fuller, "A structure is omnitriangulated. A system divides Universe into an outsidedness and an insidedness—into macrocosm and microcosm." [3]

It was mentioned in the preceding pattern, that six is the smallest number of vectors that can create a structure in our three dimensional world. Six is the minimum number required for one minimum-structural system. The six vectors of a tetrahedron make up one structural quantum. Six refers to a tetrahedron.

> *"In addition to possessing inherent insidedness and outsidedness, a system is inherently concave and convex and finite. A system must consist of a plurality of subsystems.... At minimum, it takes four triangular planes having inherent fourness of vertexes to constitute differential withinness and withoutness."* [4]

Fig. 5.2-g

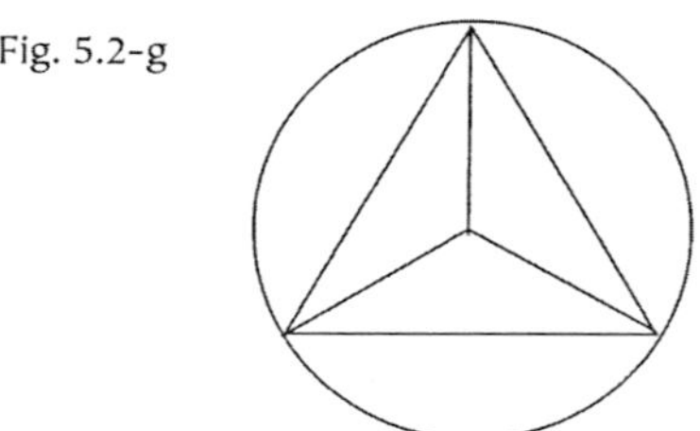

## Merkabah Spin Pattern

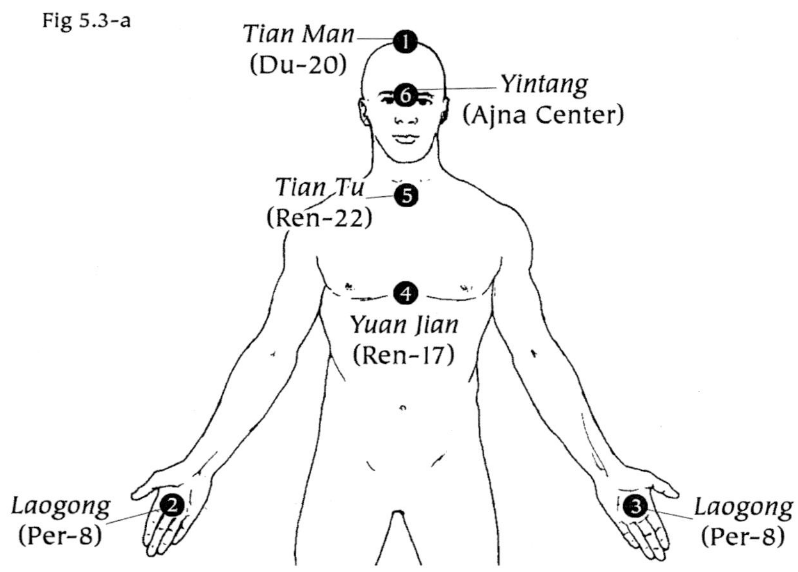


Fig 5.3-a

### Needling Sequence for the Merkabah Spin Pattern

1) *Tian Man* (Du-20)
2) *Laogong* (Per-8) Right palm
3) *Laogong* (Per-8) Left palm
4) *Yuan Jian* (Ren-17) more commonly known as *Tan Chong*
5) *Tian Tu* (Ren-22)
6) *Yintang* (Ajna Center)

### Point Locations for The Merkabah Spin Pattern

The Merkabah Spin Pattern is similar to The Integration Synthesis Pattern, except that The Merkabah Spin Pattern is a slightly more advanced pattern with a higher frequency.

The Integration Synthesis Pattern is used for those at the Tier Density Level #1. The Merkabah Spin Pattern is an alternate anterior pattern for those at Tier Density Level #1, but who want to work on aligning with the higher head frequencies. This is still a very simple, but powerful pattern. You would most likely use The Merkabah Spin Pattern instead of The Integration Synthesis Pattern for your clientele who meditate or utilize other modalities to center the Inner Spiritual Higher Heart.

For the point location and needling sequence of the first four acupuncture sites in the Merkabah Spin Pattern, please refer to The Integration Synthesis Pattern.

The fifth acupuncture point in The Merkabah Spin Pattern is *Tian Tu* (Ren-22). This point is located on the vertical midline of the anterior of the body in the sternal notch. (See figure 5.3-b below.)

## Merkabah Spin Pattern

Fig 5.3-b

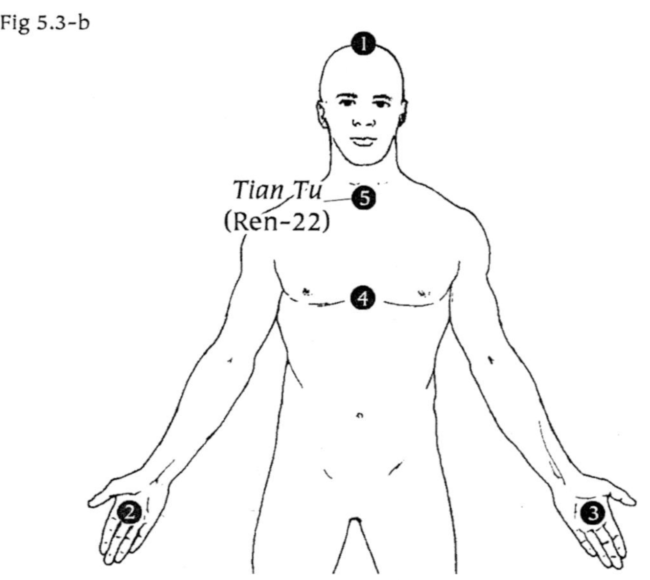

The sixth and last acupuncture point in The Merkabah Spin Pattern is *Yintang* (Ajna Center). *Yintang* (Ajna Center) is located on the vertical midline of the forehead directly between the eyebrows and above the bridge of the nose. (See figure 5.3-c below.)

## Merkabah Spin Pattern

Fig 5.3-c

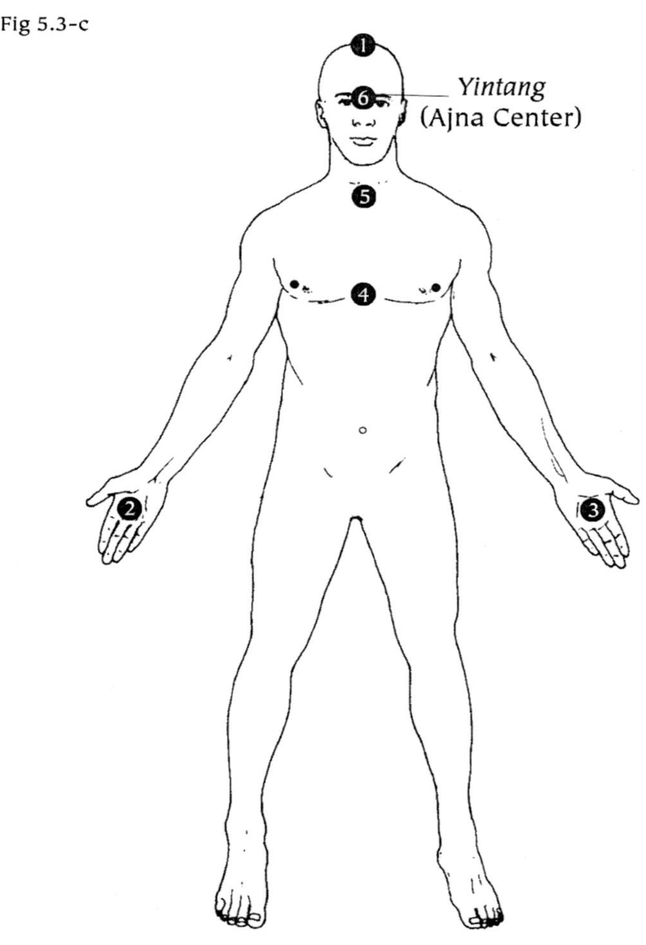

## Visualization of The Merkabah Spin Pattern

First have your client make the initial connections that we did in The Integration Synthesis Pattern. (See figure 5.3-d below.)

### Merkabah Spin Pattern

Fig 5.3-d

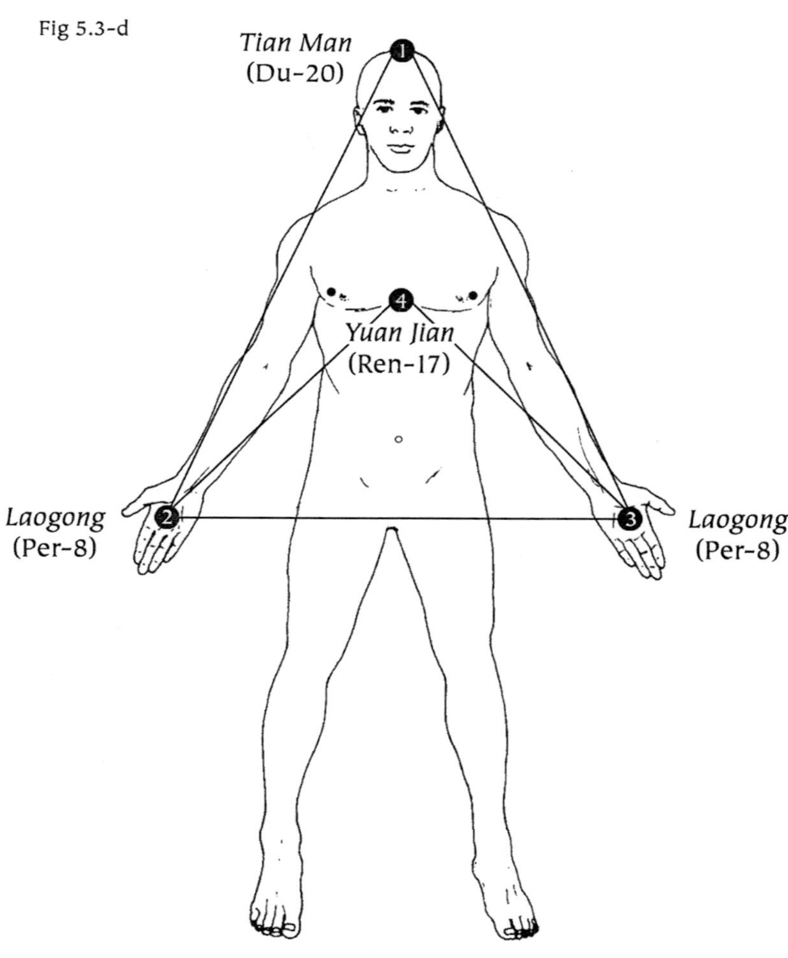

Now have your client visualize a simultaneous upward connection from the bilateral *Laogong* (Per-8) points to *Tian Tu* (Ren-22) and from *Yuan Jian* (Ren-17) straight upward to *Tian Tu* (Ren-22). You have again created another upward pointing Fire Triangle. (See figure 5.3-e below.)

## Merkabah Spin Pattern

Fig 5.3-e

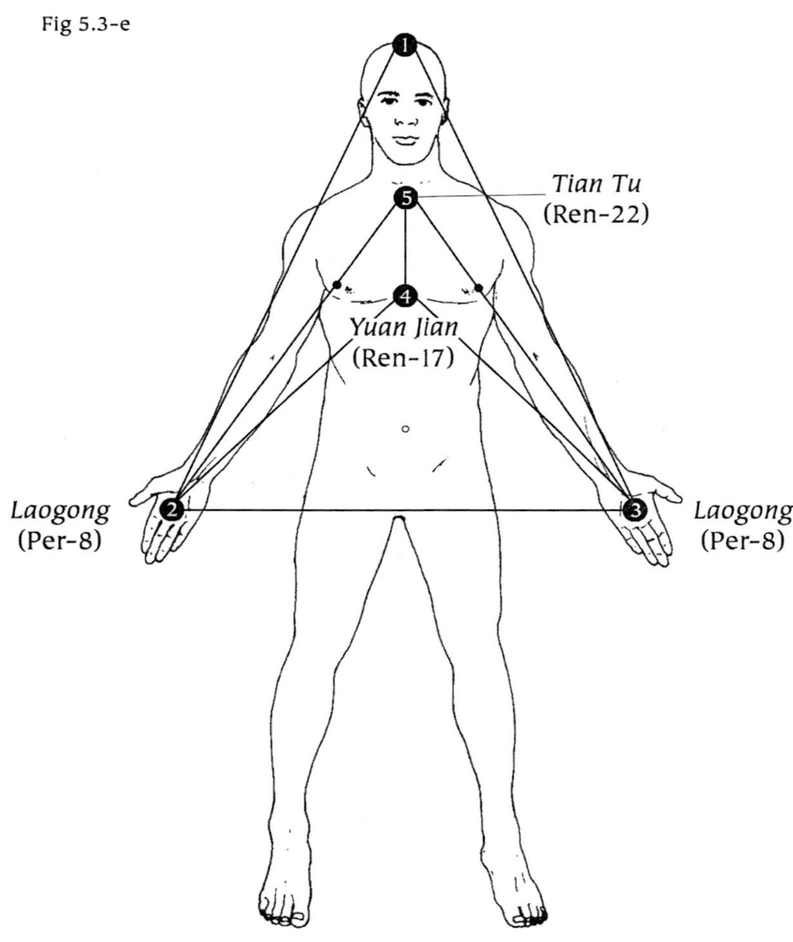

The last visualizations is to have your client bring the qi from the bilateral *Laogong* (Per-8) points upward to connect with *Yintang* (Ajna Center) between the eyebrows and to bring the qi straight upward from *Tian Tu* (Ren-22) to connect with Yintang (Ajna Center). Once again we have created an upward pointing Fire Triangle. (See figure 5.3-f below).

## Merkabah Spin Pattern

Fig 5.3-f

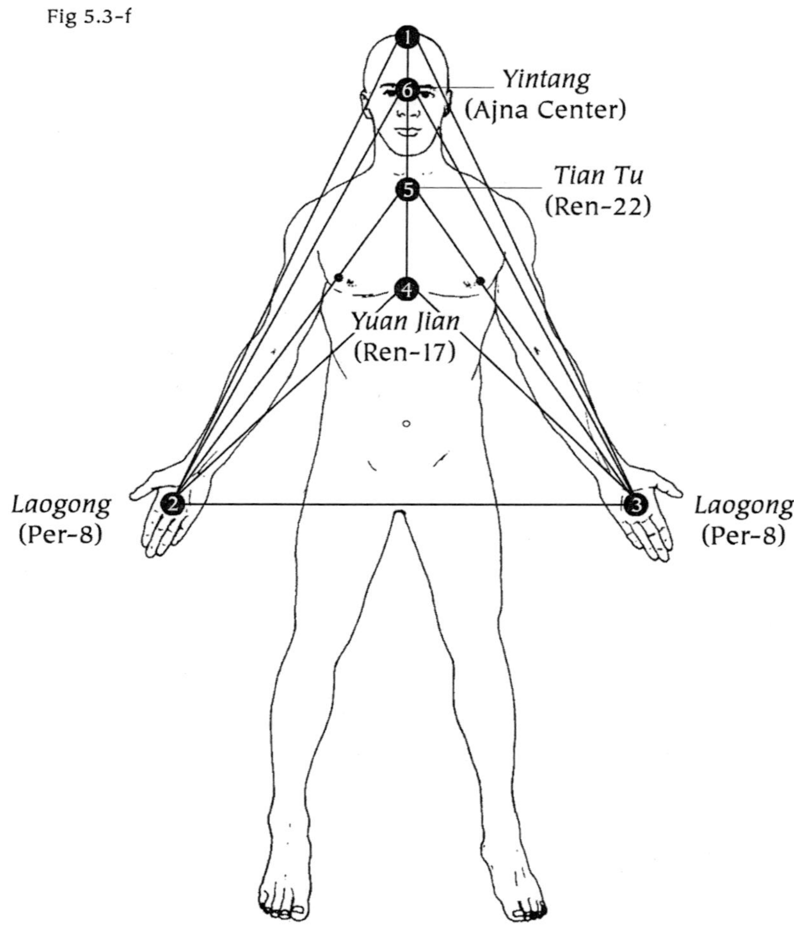

## Merkabah Spin Pattern
### Complete Visualization and Grid

Fig 5.3-g

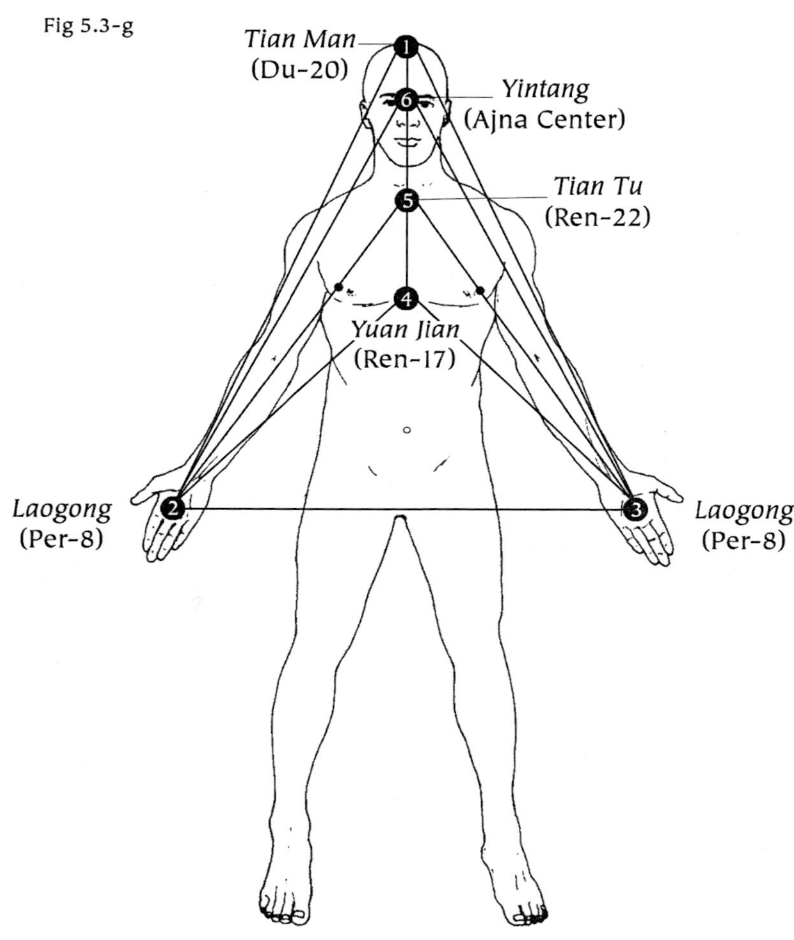

## Tier Density Level II
## Arousal of Our Inner *Shen*

At Tier Density Level II, you are starting to become aware of choices in foods and beginning to buy organic produce. Those of you who eat meat are now trying to buy cleaner meats with no antibiotics or hormones. You are now more aware that everything you eat becomes your new cells that alter your various bodies from the dense physical to the etheric, astral and mental planes. You may still eat fast foods on rare occasions, but you are now much more aware of what you put into your body. You are starting to endorse the idea of quality over quantity. All you can eat buffets no longer interest you.

There is a slight urge to explore the possibility of meditation or other forms of inner spiritual growth, such as pranayama (breathing). At this stage it is still difficult to quiet the mind, so you might be more interested in guided meditation or some form of visual meditation. Instead of any type of formal meditation, you might merely want to sit still for a few minutes without disturbance from exterior noise. Soothing, gentle music may help you to enter into a more relaxed state of mind.

As you further your practice of trying to quiet the mind and find inner peace, your choice of physical exercises may start to change. Instead of merely muscular building exercises, toning exercises, cardiovascular and fat reduction exercises such as; aerobics, pilates, karate, taikwondo, or other martial arts, jogging or weight lifting, you may start to consider other forms of gentler physical movements such as: the various types of hatha yoga, *tai qi* or *qi gong*. Gentler physical forms do not necessarily mean easier on the physical body. There are many difficult poses in the various types of Hatha Yoga. Depending on your instructor, *tai qi* can be very taxing on the legs and lower abdomen. Those who like to dance are now slowly starting to move from hip hop and rap, ballroom and line dancing to a more free form, creative type of dancing. (Although many of the moves in hip hop are very creative, the energy and movements within that type of expression are too locked into a very heavy second chakra sexual energy field. There is nothing wrong with hip hop at all and many of those who choose that expression are very athletic and very creative. It is merely a denser form of movement because of its heavy ties to the lower sacral chakra due to the music itself, especially the drum machine used to keep the rhythm and beat.

At Tier Density Level II, your work and play are still very distinct. For most people, work is still depleting. You may feel good about the monetary aspects and feel thankful and happy to be able to support yourself and your family. But, most people still need some energy boost or excitement that relieves them of the stress of work. So much energy is put into television, going to movie theaters, sporting events, concerts and other forms of entertainment to help you find that balance outside of work. You still need something outside of yourself to recharge your soul so you can go back to work the next day. You look forward to the weekend and those government holidays such as President's Day, Memorial Day, the Labor Day and other events that give you one more day away from your work.

Many people at this Tier Density Level II may have more money, so they can afford more enjoyable vacations and buy more "toys." Socialization is still very important at this level. Instead of merely frequenting nightclubs, restaurants and bars, the socialization may start to include spiritual gatherings and metaphysical workshops. Some may organize small intimate spiritual gatherings, or merely small intimate social gatherings.

You now are aware of how humans are rapidly depleting resources from Mother Earth. You are recycling and starting to move away from being so wasteful. You understand that chemicals in foods, drinking water and products are negatively changing the energies of Earth. You are aware of conservation and will reuse things such as grocery bags. You are trying not to be so wasteful, like you had been in the past.

At this level, you also realize the importance of wearing clothes made from natural fibers. You try to stay away from synthetic fibers, even if the clothing is very lightweight and feels very soft. Some of the lightweight microfibers are made to feel very soft and are usually less expensive than the natural fibers such as: wool, cotton, silk and linen. The polyesters, microfibers and other synthetic materials attract the unwanted positive ions into your field. The natural fibers attract the beneficial negative ions into your field. You try to buy the natural fibers, if possible.

Instead of always relying on following orders from someone else, you are now starting to make your own decisions. You are beginning to raise your consciousness and are now at least aware of trying to get in touch with your Inner Heart Center. You are starting to trust yourself. You are not afraid to make minor decisions that affect others like you were in the past. Still at this level, you are not so forthright to volunteer your input or opinion in making major decisions that may have a major impact on yourself, as well as involving other people.

You may be in your second, third or fourth intimate relationship, but you now desire a more meaningful relationship with more communication, rather than merely having a partner. Some people may rather stay single because they are searching for their "soul-mate." If you do not have an intimate partner, it is okay. At this tier level, you would rather be alone than be with someone that is not your equal, or who is not moving in the same direction as you.

Some people at this Tier Density Level II have the urge to teach and to give advice, even if someone does not ask for their advice. Those types of teachers are not the higher leveled teachers who teach from their heart. The lower level teachers merely display their knowledge and are working from their lower ego. Teachers that are aware of the Esoteric Ageless Wisdom do not give advice unless they are asked. You do not "put your trips" on others without permission or without being asked first. In reality, most people do not want to hear unasked for advice.

## Level II Posterior: Option #1
## The Discern the Whisper Pattern

The Discern the Whisper Pattern is the basic complete posterior pattern upon which the more complex Esoteric *Shaoyin* Patterns are built. Those of you interested in Esoteric Acupuncture should familiarize yourself with the Discern the Whisper Pattern. Discernment in one's life is a key step into trusting yourself and your decisions. The acupuncture points that are used for the activation and strengthening of discernment are the bilateral *Tian Zong* (SI-11) points located within each scapula. The bilateral *Tian Zong* (SI-11) points are directly connected to *Shendao* (Du-11) through the visualization that the client will do after the acupuncture needles have been inserted.

The Crown Infinity Pattern that is contained within the Discern the Whisper Pattern is the foundation for all of the posterior patterns. But, the Discern the Whisper Pattern is the key fundamental posterior New Encoding Pattern that is the building block pattern for other more complex New Encoding Patterns. (The Crown Infinity *Shaoyin* Pattern is a very effective pattern, but is not as complete a grid pattern as The Discern the Whisper Pattern.) You will notice that the Esoteric *Shaoyin* Kidney Pattern, the Esoteric *Shaoyin* Heart Pattern, the Esoteric *Shaoyin* Heart Window Pattern and the *Wei Qi* Grid Strengthening Pattern are all built upon the Discern the Whisper Pattern. You will first needle the Discern the Whisper Pattern followed by needling additional acupuncture sites depending on which New Encoding Pattern you decide to use for your client at that particular treatment. If you are interested in Esoteric Acupuncture and are only able to remember one posterior New Encoding Pattern, then become intimately familiar with the Discern the Whisper Pattern. Although we do not needle the Muladhara (Root Chakra) in the Discern the Whisper Pattern, you will see that in the visualization section we connect the acupuncture point *Mingmen* (Du-4) with the coccyx (tailbone).

This particular visualization connects the Swadthisthana (second chakra) with the Muladhara (Root Chakra).

I have had many practitioners ask me if they could also use a more traditional type of acupuncture treatment along with the New Encoding Patterns or the Chakra Balancing Patterns. If you wish to do both, an Esoteric Acupuncture treatment and augment with a more traditional type of treatment, then the main New Encoding Pattern that I suggest is The Discern the Whisper Pattern. If your client comes in for an Esoteric Acupuncture treatment but says to you that he or she also has a physical problem that needs to be addressed, first needle the acupuncture sites of The Discern the Whisper Pattern. While the needles are still inserted, you can needle additional acupuncture sites using whichever traditional style you prefer to address the physical problem. It does not matter if you wish to use any of the various Chinese, Korean, Japanese or European systems with an Esoteric Acupuncture treatment. After the treatment is complete and it is time to remove the acupuncture needles, remove the needles you used for the traditional treatment first, followed by removing the needles from the Discern the Whisper Pattern.

The feedback that I have received from acupuncturists who work primarily with pain management is that when they used the New Encoding Patterns along with a more traditional approach for relieving pain, the patients felt more pain relief than the traditional approach itself without the New Encoding Pattern. I have also heard from a couple of supervisors at acupuncture clinics in two acupuncture schools that when they experimented with Esoteric Acupuncture and incorporated it with a more traditional approach, they had better results than merely using a traditional approach by itself. Remember that even though Esoteric Acupuncture is designed to open and align higher consciousness, the mere fact that you are inserting acupuncture needles at acupuncture sites means that you will be working on the *Ying Qi* level (nutritive, deeper level) and the *Wei Qi* level (outer, protective level) of your client/patient.

## Tier Density Level II: Posterior Option #1

## Discern the Whisper Pattern

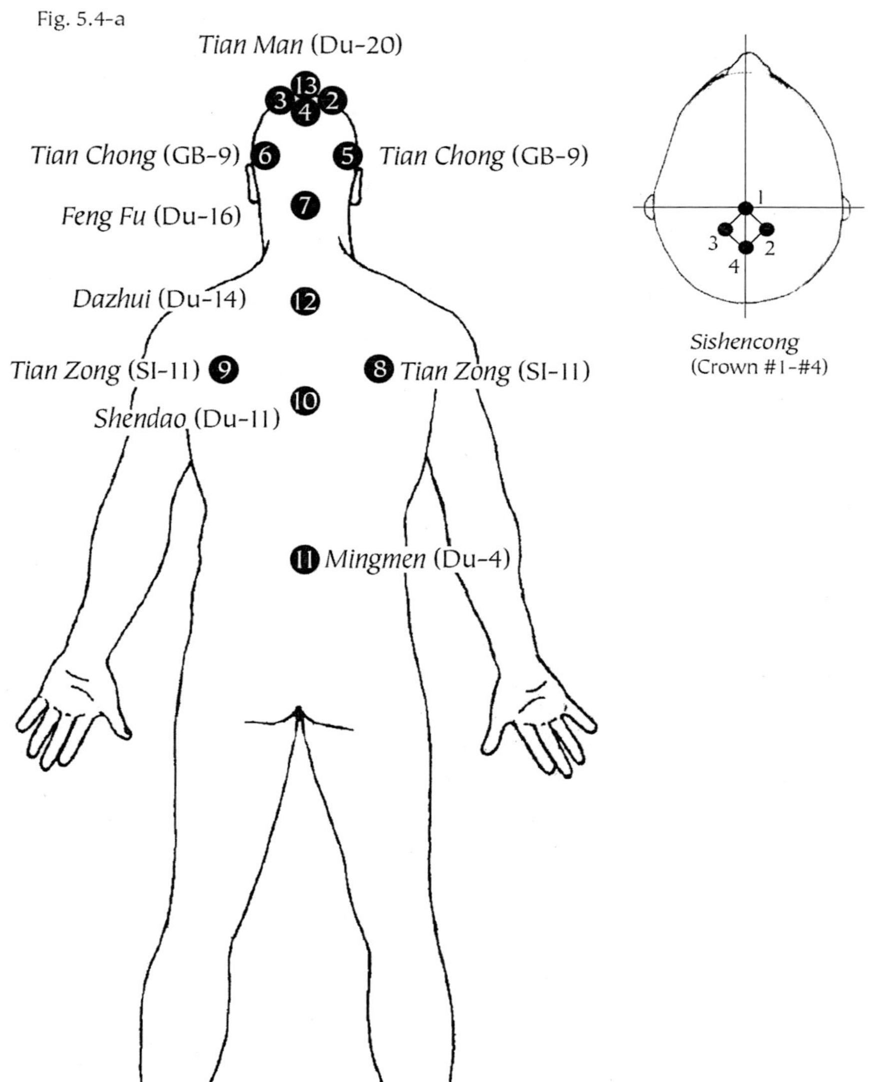

## Needling Sequence for the Discern the Whisper Pattern

1 through 4) *Sishencong* -- "4 Spirits"
Crown # 1: Frontal site; Crown #2: Right side (client's right side); Crown #3: Left side; Crown #4: Closest to back of the head
5) *Tian Chong* (GB-9) Right side
6) *Tian Chong* (GB-9) Left side
7) *Feng Fu* (Du-16)
8) *Tian Zong* (SI-11) Right side
9) *Tian Zong* (SI-11) Left side
10) *Shendao* (Du-11)
11) *Mingmen* (Du-4)
12) *Dazhui* (Du-14)
13) *Tian Man* (Du-20)

## Point Locations for The Discern the Whisper Pattern

Although the location of the first seven acupuncture points in the Discern the Whisper Pattern were discussed in The Crown Infinity *Shaoyin* Pattern, the location of these first seven points will be repeated. The first ten acupuncture points in The Discern the Whisper Pattern are the same acupuncture points used in the various Esoteric *Shaoyin* Patterns. The first ten points will not be repeated in the various Esoteric *Shaoyin* Patterns. It is important that you become intimately familiar with the sequencing and location of these first ten acupuncture points in the Discern the Whisper Pattern.

Even though we will not be needling any acupuncture points on the arms or wrist, it is best to have your client place his or her arms on the treatment table with the palms facing upward. In this particular position, the area between both scapulae will be more exposed than if the client's arms were place upward toward the head or top of the treatment table. The positioning that I am recommending will open "The Wings of Your Heart," which are the scapulae.

The first four acupuncture points are part of a group known as *Sishencong*. These four points are almost always needled as a group. You will notice that there are two diagrams for the *Sishencong* group. (Figures 5.4-b and 5.4-c.) Although we are interested in the esoteric location of the *Sishencong* Group, it is easier to first determine the site of the traditional Du-20 known as *Bai Hui*. Find the apex of each ear. Now draw an imaginary line from the apex of one ear to the apex of the other ear going over the top of your client's head. Next draw an imaginary vertical midline going over the top of your client's head intersecting the imaginary horizontal line that connects both apexes of the ears. Where this imaginary vertical midline intersects the imaginary horizontal line that connects the apex of both ears is the location of the traditional Du-20 (*Bai Hui*). The esoteric Du-20 site known as *Tian Man* is located approximately one inch posteriorly to the traditional Du-20 (*Bai Hui*). (See figure 5.4-b and 5.4-c.)

Esoteric Location of Du-20
now called *Tian Man*

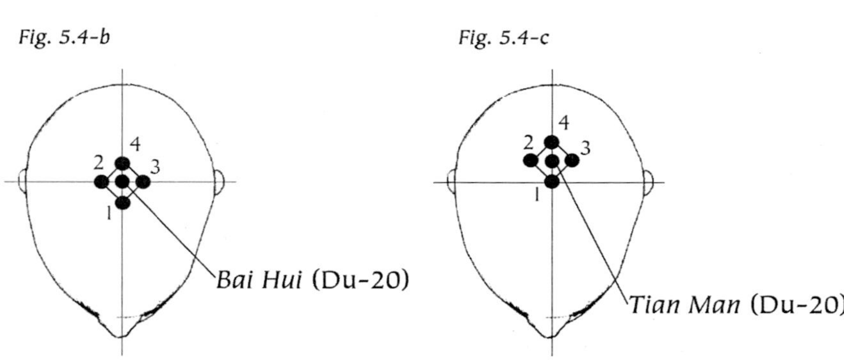


It is important that you locate *Tian Man* (Du-20) so you can correctly needle the four esoteric *Sishencong* points. Remember that the locations of the four acupuncture points in the esoteric

*Sishencong* Group are found more toward the back of the head than the traditional location of *Sishencong*.

Headaches on the top of the head are often referred to as *Jueyin* headaches related to the liver system. With Esoteric Acupuncture, we are not interested in the *Jueyin* function of the *Sishencong* Group. The esoteric *Sishencong* Group is connected to the heart system and not the liver system. Remember that *Sishencong* can be translated as "Four Spirits." It is the *Shen* of the heart system in Traditional Chinese Medicine that is related to spirit or spirits. The main function of the esoteric *Sishencong* Group in Esoteric Acupuncture is to assist in the activation and balancing of the Inner Spiritual Higher Heart System.

The first acupuncture point needled in the esoteric *Sishencong* Group is called Crown #1. Crown #1 is located directly on the vertical midline of the head approximately one inch anteriorly to *Tian Man* (Du-20). When your client is in a prone position with his or her face in a face cradle, I will usually angle the needle slightly upward. I will needle the other three points in this group with the same upward angle.

The second acupuncture site needled in the *Sishencong* Group is the point located on the client's right side approximately one inch lateral to the right of the location of *Tian Man* (Du-20). This acupuncture point of the *Sishencong* Group is known in Esoteric Acupuncture as Crown #2.

The third acupuncture site needled in the *Sishencong* Group is the point located on the client's left side approximately one inch lateral to the left of the location of *Tian Man* (Du-20). Although on figure 5.4-b the second and third points look like they are both on the imaginary horizontal line that connects the apexes of both ears, in reality one of the points is almost always anterior or posterior to the imaginary horizontal line. You must look for or feel for the qi. We are not interested in needling a perfectly symmetrical four-sided polygon. This acupuncture point of the *Sishencong* Group is known in Esoteric Acupuncture as Crown #3.

The fourth acupuncture site in the *Sishencong* Group is

located approximately one inch posteriorly to *Tian Man* (Du-20) and directly on the vertical midline that is the Du channel. It is very important that you feel comfortable with locating and needling these four points of the esoteric *Sishencong* Group. This last acupuncture point of the *Sishencong* Group is known in Esoteric Acupuncture as Crown #4. It is important that you locate the esoteric Du-20 known as *Tian Man* rather than the traditional Du-20 known as *Bai Hui*.

The fifth acupuncture site needled in The Discern the Whisper Pattern is *Tian Chong* (GB-9) on the client's right side. To determine the location of *Tian Chong* (GB-9), it is best to first locate *Shuaigu* (GB-8). *Shuaigu* (GB-8) is located approximately one *cun* directly superior to the apex of each ear. *Tian Chong* (GB-9) is found approximately one-half to one *cun* posterior and superior to *Shuaigu* (GB-8). Feel for a slight depression in this area. Sometimes one or both of the *Tian Chong* (GB-9) may be tender. Although this point is on the gall bladder meridian, in Esoteric Acupuncture *Tian Chong* (GB-9) is part of the "Celestial Hearing" group meaning that these bilateral acupuncture sites are connected to the Higher, Spiritual Heart System. (See figure 5.4-d.) Needle *Tian Chong* (GB-9) on the right side first, followed by *Tian Chong* (GB-9) on the left side.

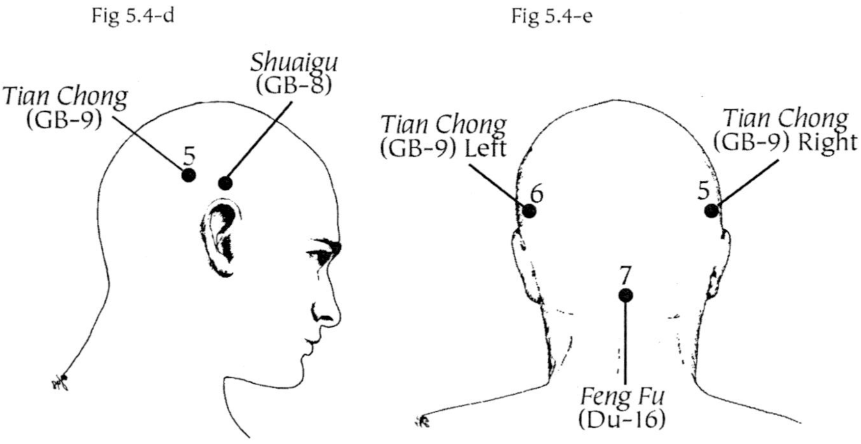

The seventh and last acupuncture point of the Crown Infinity section of The Discern the Whisper Pattern is *Feng Fu* (Du-16) often translated as "Wind Mansion." *Feng Fu* (Du-16) is located directly on the vertical midline of the posterior of the head in a depression inferior to the occipital protuberance. Feel for the slight depression at this area. (See figure 5.4-e.)

Acupuncture points #8 and #9 in The Discern the Whisper Pattern are the bilateral *Tian Zong* (SI-11) points located on each of the scapula. First locate the superior and inferior borders of the right scapula. Draw an imaginary horizontal line one at the superior border and the other at the inferior border of the scapula. Next draw two imaginary horizontal lines dividing the scapula into three equal sections from the superior border to the inferior border. We now have three sections on the right scapula divided horizontally. (See figure 5.4-f below.)

**Celestial Gathering Site**

*Fig. 5.4-f*

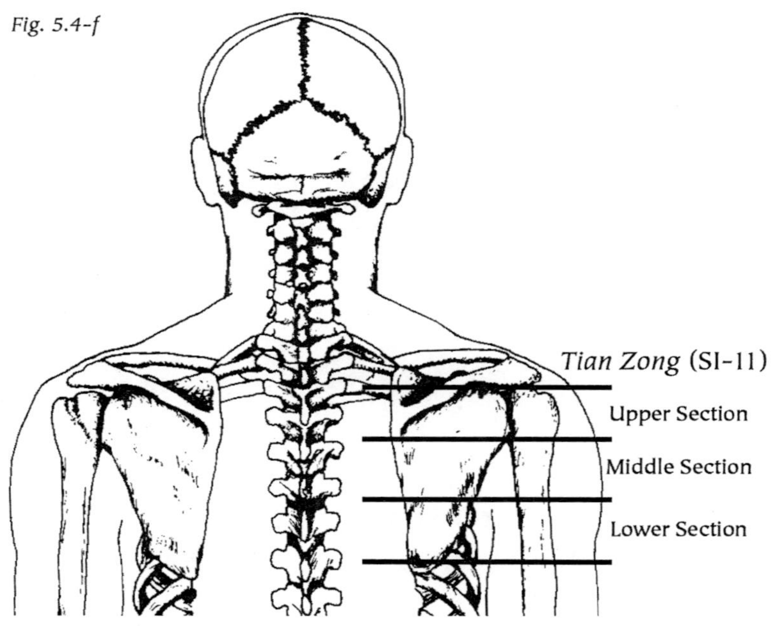

Next locate the medial and lateral borders of the right scapula. Draw an imaginary vertical line at both the medial and lateral borders of the scapula. Draw an additional imaginary vertical line in the center of the imaginary vertical lines on the medial and lateral borders of the scapula. (See figure 5.4-g below.)

**Celestial Gathering Site**

*Fig. 5.4-g*

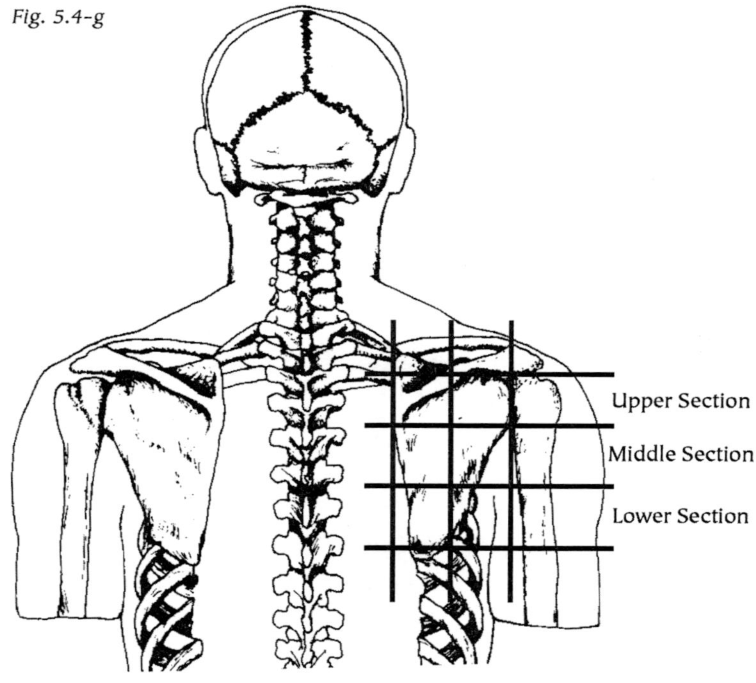


In some people, the imaginary vertical lines may be slightly angled outward from the spine at the superior borders of each scapula. The spot where the central vertical line intersects the horizontal line that divides the upper one-third of the scapula from the middle one-third of the scapula is the location of *Tian Zong* (SI-11). Feel for the depression in this area. Sometimes the depression may be slightly medial or lateral to where the imaginary vertical and imaginary horizontal lines intersect. Insert a .20 mm X 30 mm Seirin L-gauge needle at this site angling slightly downward. (See figure 5.4-h below.)

**Celestial Gathering Site**

*Fig. 5.4-h*

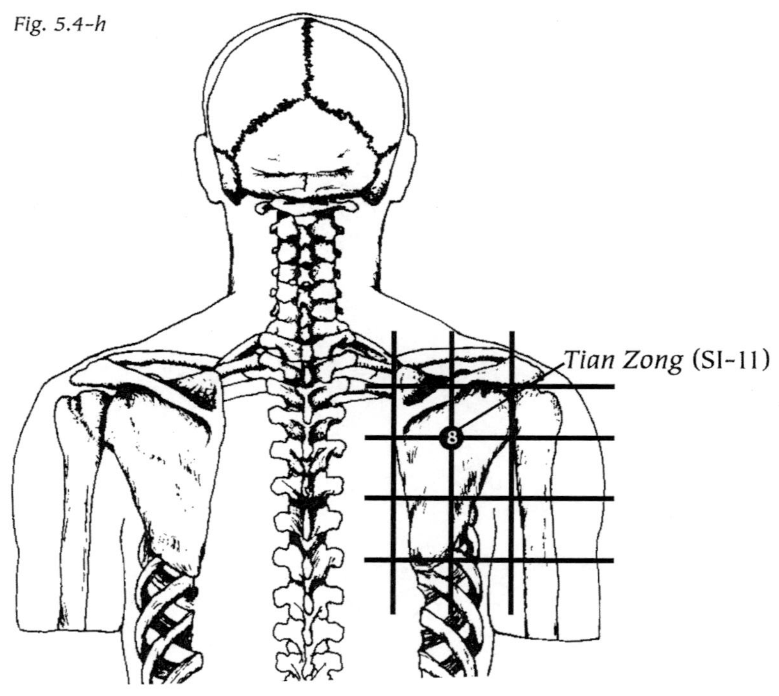


Needle the client's right scapula first, followed by needling the site of *Tian Zong* (SI-11) on the left scapula. These bilateral *Tian Zong* (SI-11) points on the scapulae are known in Esoteric

Acupuncture as the gateways that assist you to open the "Wings of your Heart. (See figure 5.4-i below.)

**Celestial Gathering Sites**
**The Wings of Your Heart**

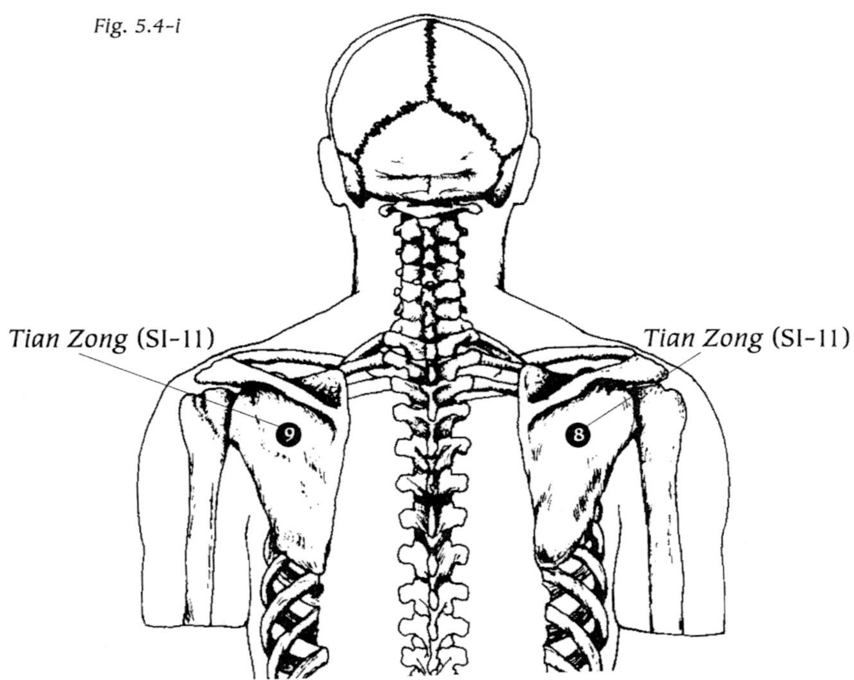


*Fig. 5.4-i*

There is an alternative method for locating *Tian Zong* (SI-11) that may place the location at a slightly different spot. One method of locating *Tian Zong* (SI-11) is not more academically correct over the other method. Remember that the guidelines for locating any acupuncture sites are merely guidelines. Everyone's physical body and the terrain of the body are different. I have tried to encourage practitioners to not rely solely on an acupuncture book as the definitive source for locating points, but to "look" for the qi or to feel for the qi. I have had acupuncture doctors (only Asian males) challenging my location of certain points. When I would ask those Asian male doctors to tell me which location (theirs or mine) had the most qi, they would have no idea what I was talking about. Again, look for the acupuncture location with the most qi and not just the measurements or anatomical landmarks you learned in acupuncture school.

This alternate method requires that you first locate *Jianzhen* (SI-9) and *Naoshu* (SI-10). *Naoshu* (SI-10) is found on the posterior aspect of each shoulder. With the arms adducted, *Naoshu* (SI-10) is found in the depression inferior to the scapular spine. These two acupuncture sites are not needled, but used only as "landmarks" to locate *Tian Zong* (SI-11). (See figure 5.4-j below.)

**Celestial Gathering Site**

*Fig. 5.4-j*

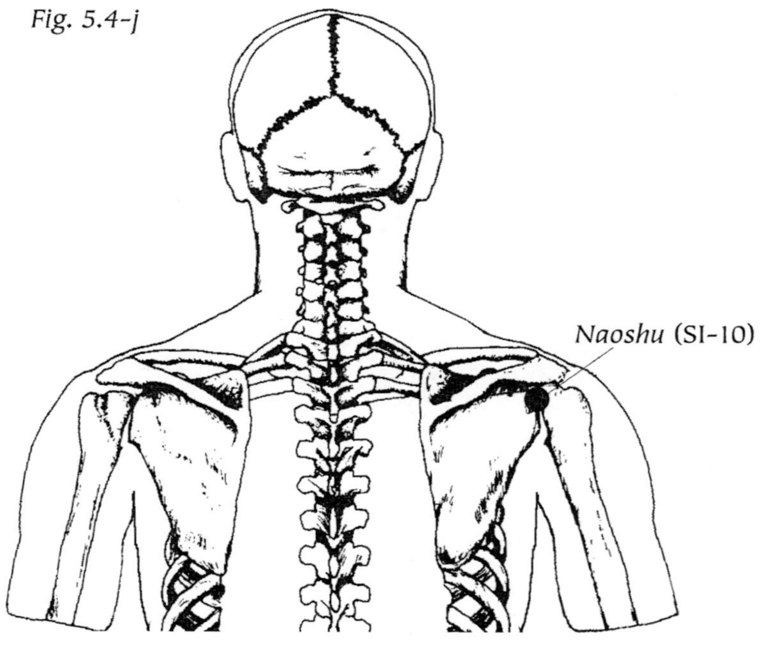

*Jianzhen* (SI-9) is located on the posterior aspect slightly superior to the crease of each armpit. When the client is face down with the arms next to the body, *Jianzhen* (SI-11) is found approximately one *cun* superiorly to the posterior axillary crease. (See figure 5.4-k below.)

**Celestial Gathering Site**

*Fig. 5.4-k*

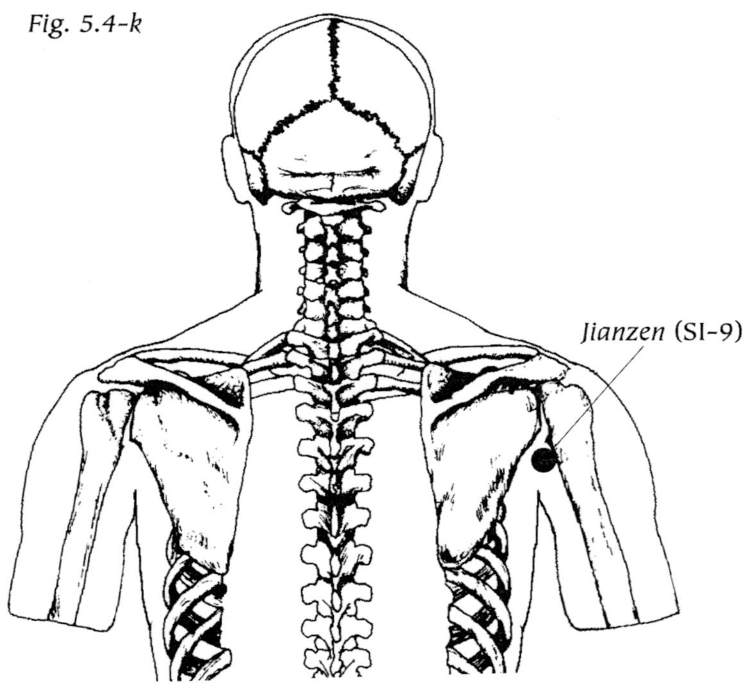


When both *Jianzhen* (SI-9) and *Naoshu* (SI-10) are located on your client, form an imaginary equilateral triangle using *Jianzhen* (SI-9) and *Naoshu* (SI-10) as two of the three corners. Equilateral means that the three sides of the triangle should be of equal lengths. Sometimes when you palpate to locate *Tian*

*Zong* (SI-11) within the scapula, the location may be slightly off from an equilateral triangular location. Figure 5.4-l shows the location of *Tian Zong* (SI-11) using the equilateral triangle method. If your client's arms are further out from the body and you are using the equilateral triangle as the guide, then *Tian Zong* (SI-11) will be more lateral than shown on the figure below. Depending on the terrain of the body (especially the scapular spine), often *Tian Zong* (SI-11) may be located slightly closer to the center of the body and not exactly at the location of the third angle of the equilateral triangle. (See figure 5.4-l below.)

**Celestial Gathering Site**

Fig. 5.4-l

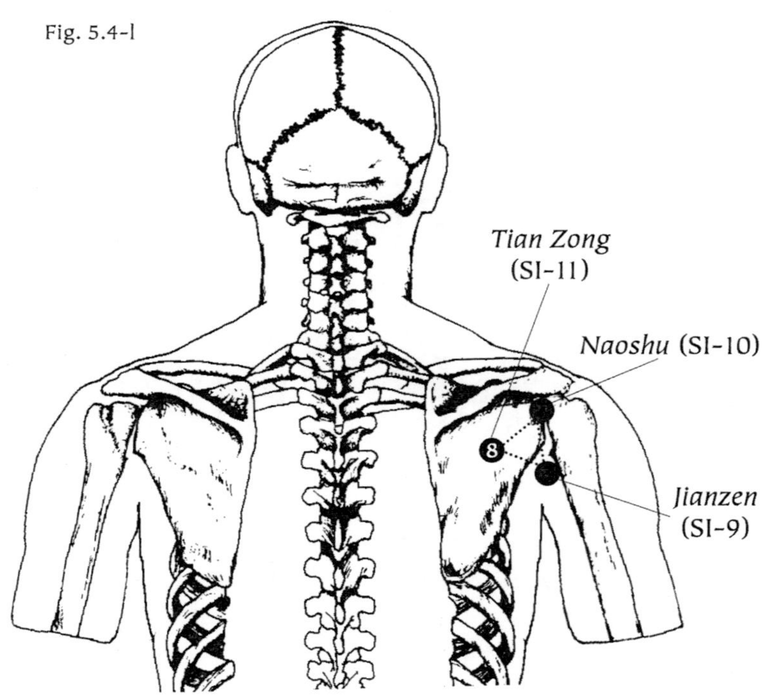

The tenth acupuncture point in The Discern the Whisper Pattern is *Shendao* (Du-11) translated as "Spirit Path," "Heart Path," or "Path of the Evolved Person". The Chinese translation of *Shendao* reveals the importance of this particular acupuncture point. The activation of dormant qi at this site will also give the person direct access to his or her Anahata (Heart Chakra). *Shendao* (Du-11) is located directly on the posterior spine directly below the lower border of the spinous process of the fifth thoracic vertebrae. I usually needle this site with the needle angling downward. (See figure 5.4-m below.)

**Discern the Whisper Pattern**

*Fig. 5.4-m*

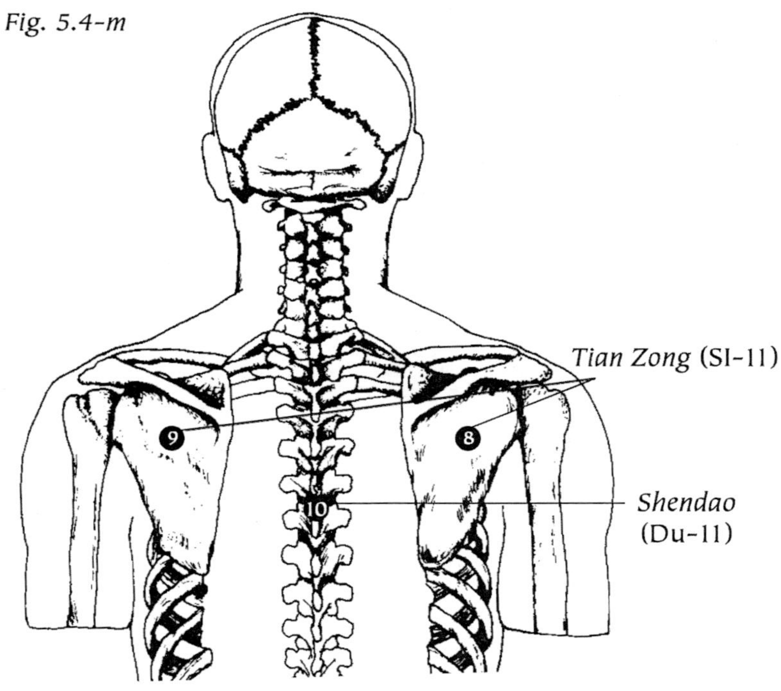


The eleventh acupuncture site needled in the Discern the Whisper Pattern is *Mingmen* (Du-4) that is located on the posterior spine directly below the spinous process of the second lumbar vertebrae. Find the highest point on both iliac crests (hip bones) on your back. Draw an imaginary horizontal line connecting these two points. This imaginary line usually intersects the spine at the fourth lumbar vertebra. Count upward two vertebra from this point and that will be the second lumbar (L-2) vertebra. Make sure you insert the needle at the lower border of L-2 and not directly on the spinous process. Again, I usually needle *Mingmen* (Du-4). with a sight downward angling of the acupuncture needle. On many people, the spine is very sensitive. I only insert the acupuncture needles on the spine to a depth less than one-half of an inch. (See figure 5.4-n below.)

### Discern the Whisper Pattern

Fig. 5.4-n

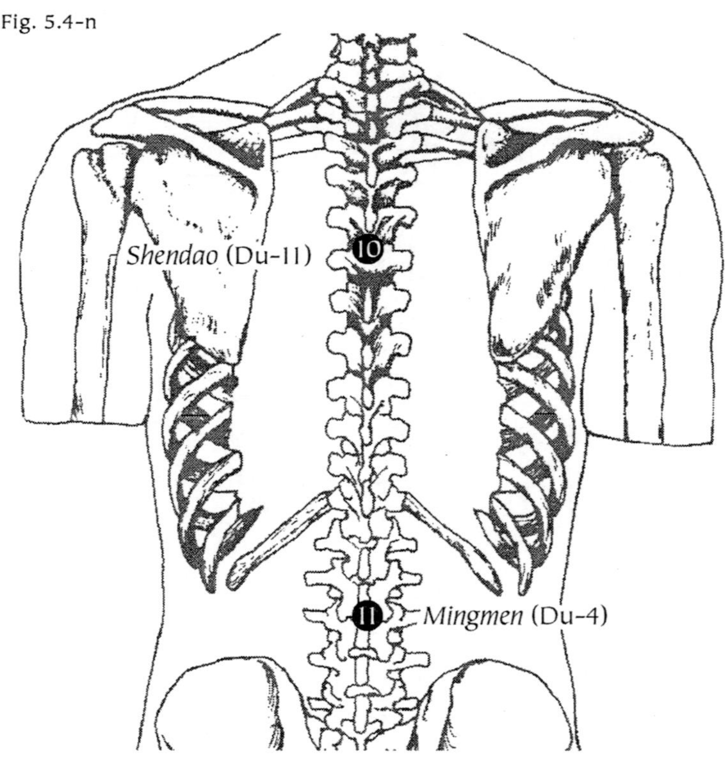

The twelfth acupuncture site needled in The Discern the Whisper Pattern is known as *Dazhui* (Du-14) and is often translated as the "Big Hammer." *Dazhui* (Du-14) is located on the posterior spine directly below the lower border of the spinous process of the seventh cervical vertebrae (C-7). (See figure 5.4-0 below.)

**Discern the Whisper Pattern**

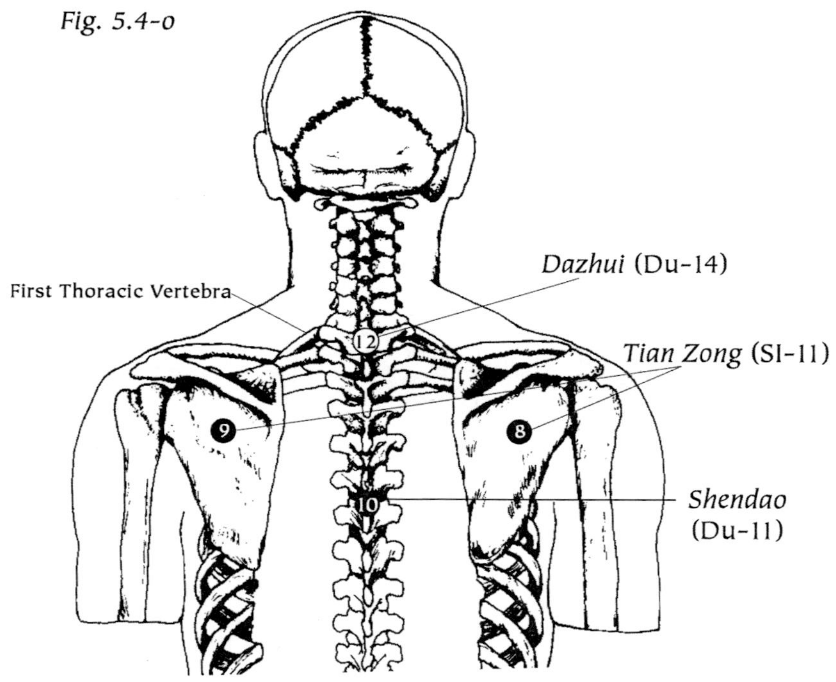


Often *Dazhui* (Du-14) is the largest protruding vertebra in this region, but not always. Sometimes the first thoracic vertebra (T-1) may protrude higher than *Dazhui* (Du-14). Other times both T-1 and C-7 do not protrude at all. When in doubt, place one finger on the vertebra that you think is the seventh cervical vertebra and place another finger on the vertebra above it (closer to the neck). Have your client move his or her head directly backward up off of the face piece of the treatment table. The sixth cervical vertebra will go inward, while the seventh cervical vertebra will not. Do not just assume that the largest protruding vertebra is automatically "The Big Hammer."

The thirteenth and last acupuncture point in The Discern the Whisper Pattern is *Tian Man* (Du-20) often translated as "Celestial Fullness." *Tian Man* (Du-20) is located on the vertical midline on the head in the center of the four esoteric *Sishencong* points that were the first four points needled in this pattern.

The Discern the Whisper Pattern has thirteen acupuncture points that is a number that signifies power, not bad luck like we have been told in the West. In ***Climbing Jacob's Ladder: Esoteric Acupuncture, Volume III***, it was stated that the twelve directions surrounds the thirteenth "hidden" gate. The thirteenth gate is *Tian Man* (Du-20). But, Du-20 is only the "hidden gateway" if we insert an acupuncture needle at the site of *Tian Man* and not the traditional location of the Du-20 called *Bai Hui*. Needle *Tian Man* (Du-20) as shown on figure 5.4-q.

Traditional Location of Du-20 usually called *Bai Hui*

*Fig. 5.4-p*

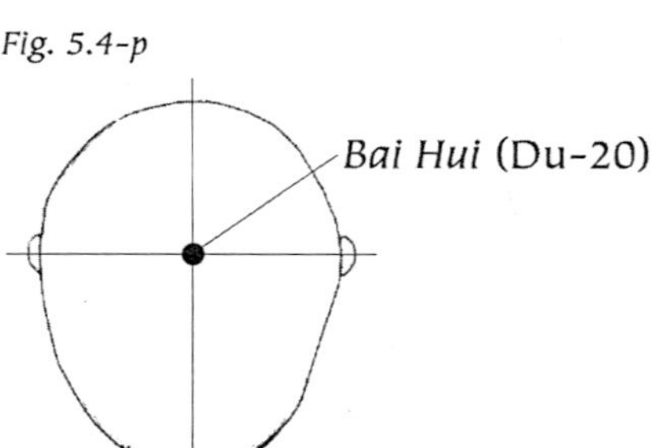


13th "Hidden" Gateway called *Tian Man*

*Fig. 5.4-q*

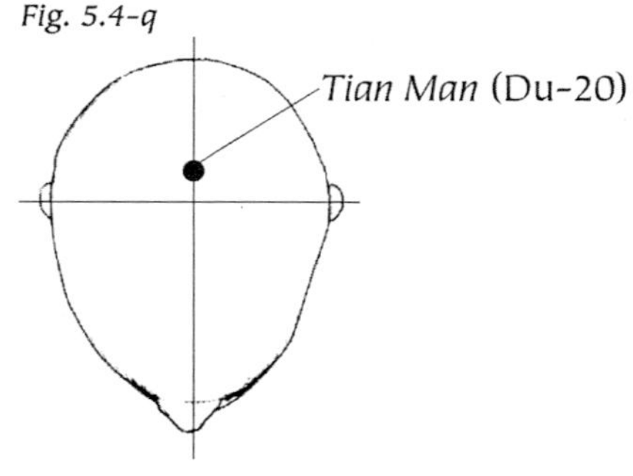

## Visualization Connections for The Discern the Whisper Pattern

If you feel as a practitioner that you would like to incorporate Esoteric Acupuncture into your treatment protocol, then it is very important to memorize this visualization of the thirteen acupuncture points of the Discern the Whisper Pattern. The Discern the Whisper Pattern and the same sequencing of the thirteen points are contained within several of the more complex patterns such as: The Esoteric *Shaoyin* Heart Pattern and The Esoteric *Shaoyin* Kidney Pattern.

The visualization of The Discern the Whisper Pattern begins after the first ten acupuncture needles have been inserted in the correct acupuncture sites and with the correct sequencing of the acupuncture points. We begin by first having your client visualize a gold colored light, then bringing the gold colored light down through the four *Sishencong* points and directly down the spine to the client's tailbone. Ask your client to energize the Muladhara (Root Chakra) with the gold colored light. We will not be needling the Muladhara (Root Chakra), but want to activate the chakra to connect with the upper six chakras. Next ask your client to breathe in gold colored light slowly through the nostrils and exhale through the mouth. Have your client do this for three or four breaths. Pay close attention to how your client is breathing. Those with a closed or guarded heart will take very small, shallow breaths. Sometimes with a male client, I do not see the back at the chest region move at all with the breathing. When a person is more secure with him or herself, then the client will take deep breaths. This is an indication that the client is more open. When your client does not take deep breaths, you do not have to mention this to the client. This is just so the practitioner will have a rough gauge as to how spiritual open the client is. In order to be spiritually centered and spiritually strong, you must work with your Inner, Spiritual Heart and not merely the physical heart.

We begin the visualization by asking your client to visually connect the acupuncture points Crown # 2 and Crown #3. After the acupuncture needles have been inserted, I recommend that you touch the skin near the point to assist your client in making the visual connections. The visual connection should only take a few seconds. If your client cannot make the visual connections within a few seconds, then tell your client to relax and you will make the visual connections for them. Often after several acupuncture needles have been inserted, your client may start to become very tired and will not be able to make any visual connections. (See figure 5.4-r below.)

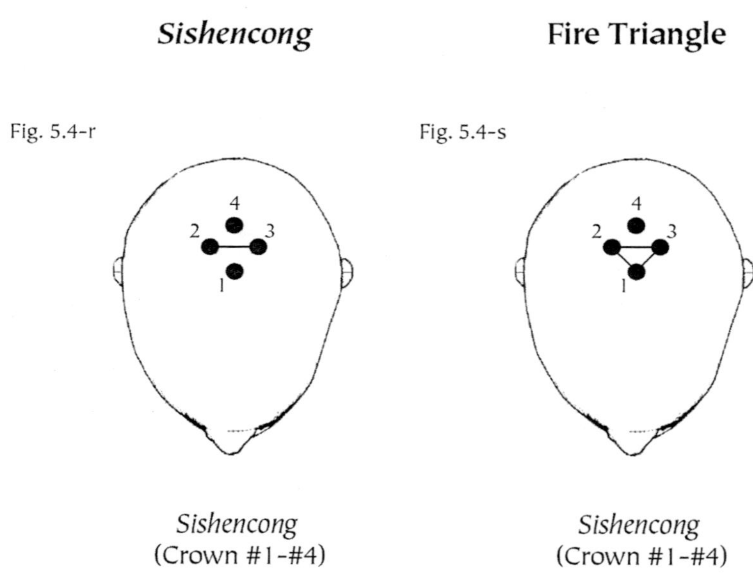


*Sishencong* (Crown #1-#4)

*Sishencong* (Crown #1-#4)

Then ask your client to connect both of these *Sishencong* points (Crown #2 and Crown #3) to Crown #1 forming a triangle pointing toward the front of the client's head. (See figure 5.4-s above.) This triangle is a fire triangle of the heart system. Since your client will be lying face down, the triangle may seem to be pointing downward. But, this triangle is in fact a fire triangle of the heart system.

Again have your client again connect the acupuncture points Crown #2 to Crown #3. I lightly touch the scalp next to these two acupuncture points. (See figure 5.4-t.) This time have your client connect the qi from both Crown #2 and Crown#3 points to Crown #4. Although this visualization forms a triangle that looks like it is pointing upward, it is still a Water Triangle pointing toward the back of the head. (See figure 5.4-u below.)

***Sishencong***

Fig. 5.4-t

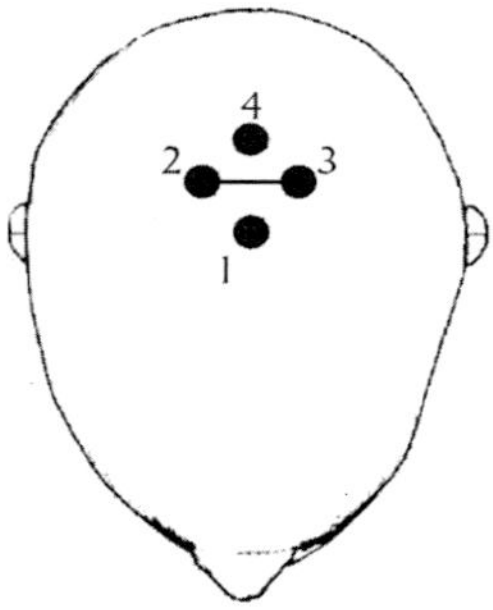

*Sishencong*
(Crown #1-#4)

**Water Triangle**

Fig. 5.4-u

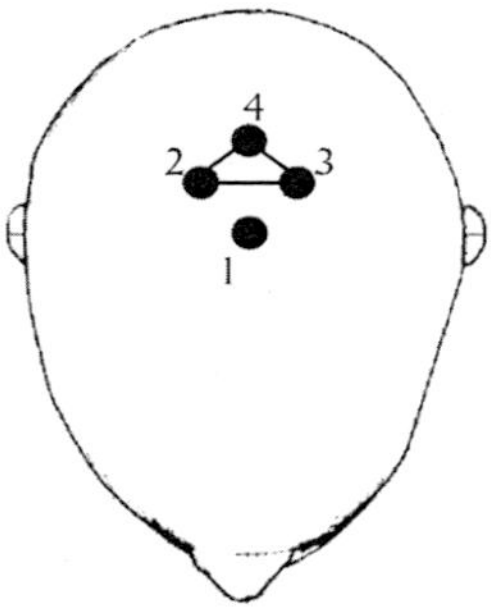

*Sishencong*
(Crown #1-#4)

The visual formation of the opposing energetics of the Fire Triangle versus the Water Triangle has created an Esoteric *Shaoyin* Field. There is a triangle pointing toward the anterior of the body that is the Fire Triangle of the heart system opposing, yet simultaneously enhancing, the Water Triangle of the kidney system that is pointing toward the posterior of the body. (See figure 5.4-v below.)

### Esoteric *Shaoyin* Field

Fig. 5.4-v

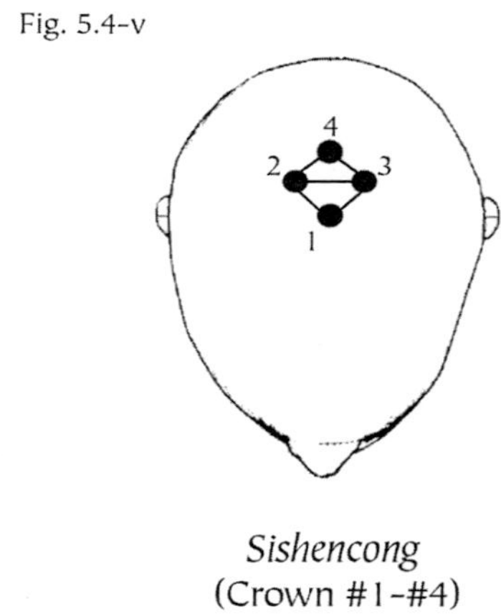


*Sishencong*
(Crown #1-#4)

Next visually connect the bilateral *Tian Chong* (GB-9) points that are located superiorly to the apex of the ears and slightly posteriorly to the ears. (See figure 5.4-w below.)

Fig. 5.4-w

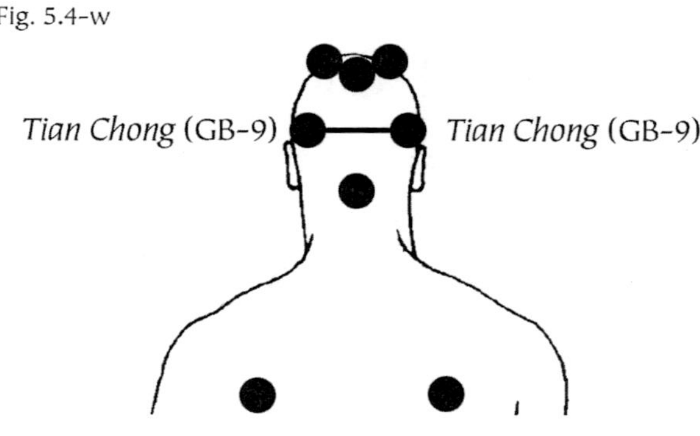

Then have your client visualize the qi from these bilateral *Tian Chong* (GB-9) acupuncture points moving upward to connect with Crown #4 to form an upward pointing Fire Triangle. (See figure 5.4-x below.)

Fig. 5.4-x

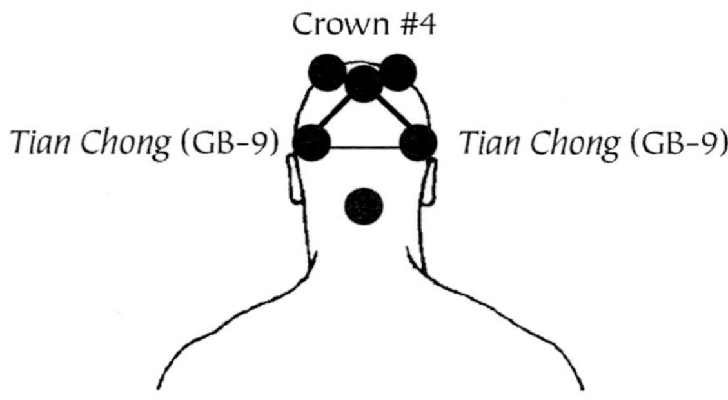


After your client has made the Fire Triangle connection, have your client once again connect the bilateral *Tian Chong* (GB-9) points with each other. (See figure 5.4-y below.)

Fig. 5.4-y

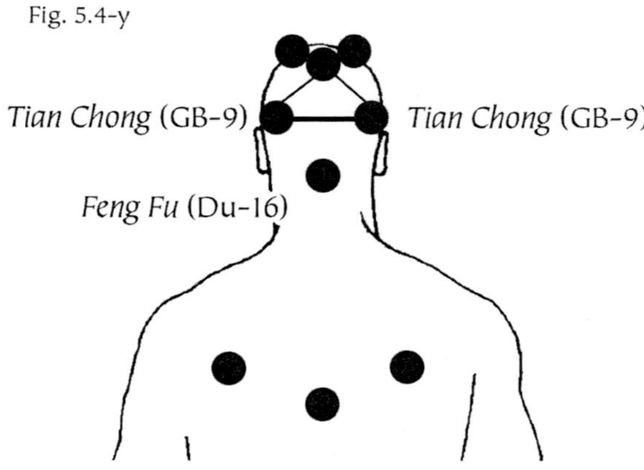

This time have your client visualize the qi from the two *Tian Chong* (GB-9) points flowing downward to connect with the energies at the acupuncture site of *Feng Fu* (Du-16). This visualization forms a downward pointing Water Triangle of the kidney system. (See figure 5.4-z below.)

**Water Triangle**

Fig. 5.4-z

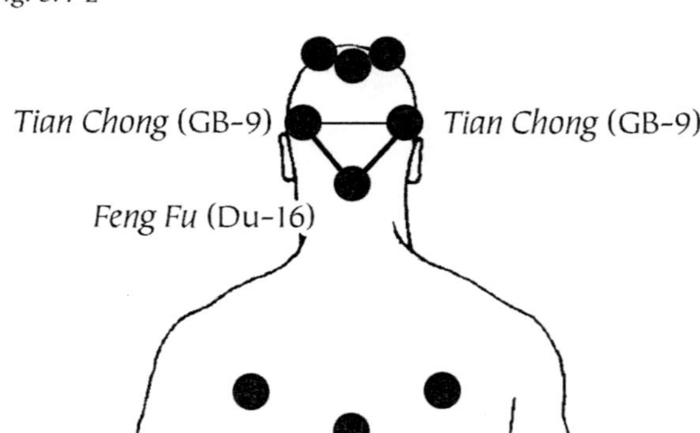


We have now created an additional Esoteric *Shaoyin* Field of the heart and kidney systems with this visual connection of these last four acupuncture sites. First the bilateral *Tian Chong* (GB-9) points connect upward to Crown #4. Then the bilateral *Tian Chong* (GB-9) connect downward to *Feng Fu* (Du-16). The first seven acupuncture points of The Discern the Whisper Pattern make up the seven acupuncture sites of The Crown Infinity Pattern. If there is only one New Encoding Pattern that should be called the most important pattern in Esoteric Acupuncture, then it would most likely be The Crown Infinity Pattern. This pattern is the key posterior New Encoding Pattern that sets up and reveals the secrets of 3-6-1. This also connects acupuncture's profound relationship to Sacred Geometry, the Hindu Nadi and Chakra Systems, tetrahedral geometry, the Hebrew Qabbalah/Kabbalah, Platonic Solids, Pythagorean theories, spin fields and even creation itself. (See figure 5.4-aa below.)

## Additional Esoteric *Shaoyin* Field

Fig. 5.4.aa

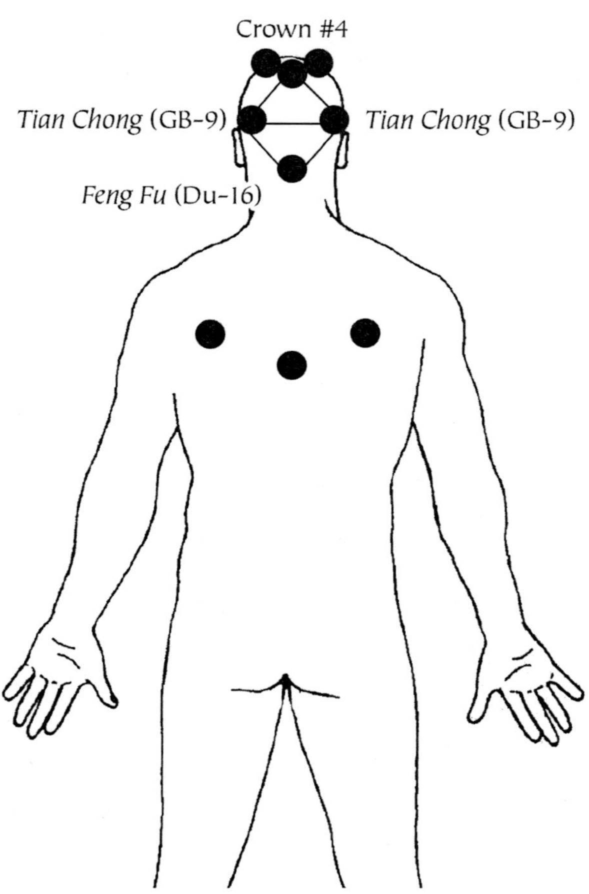

Next have your client visualize an energy connection between the bilateral *Tian Zong* (SI-11) points that are located in both scapulae. (See figure 5.4-bb below.)

Fig. 5.4-bb

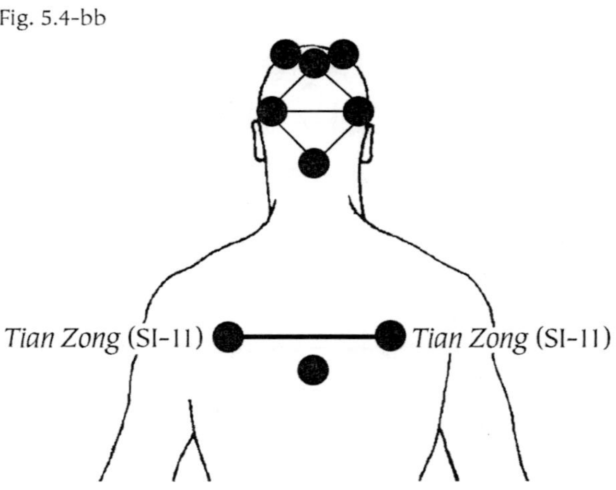


Now have your client move the qi from both of these acupuncture sites upward to connect with the acupuncture site of *Feng Fu* (Du-16). This visualization will create an upward pointing Fire Triangle. (See figure 5.4-cc below.)

**Fire Triangle**

Fig. 5.4-cc

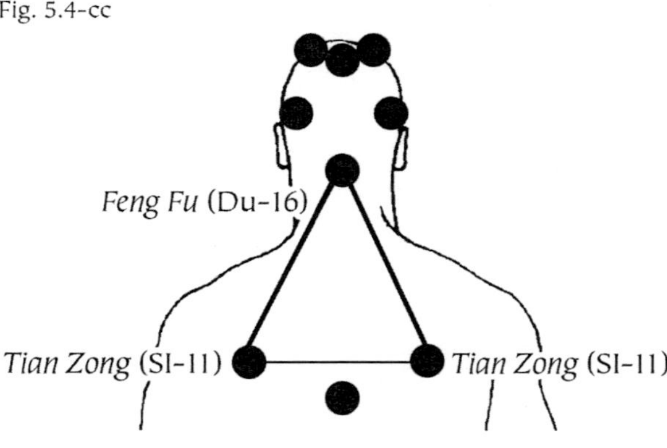

Again, connect the bilateral *Tian Zong* (SI-11) points that are located in both scapulae. (See figure 5.4-dd below.)

Fig. 5.4-dd

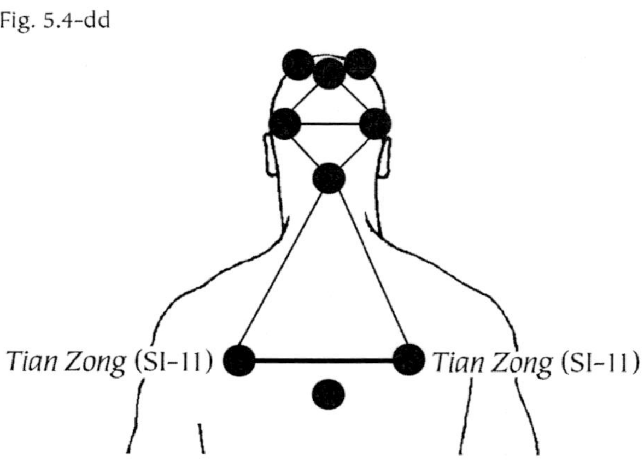


Now have your client visualize the energies from the bilateral *Tian Zong* (SI-11) points moving downward to connect with the acupuncture site of *Shendao* (Du-11) located directly below the spinous process of the fifth thoracic vertebra. This forms another Water Triangle. (See figure 5.4-ee below.)

**Water Triangle**

Fig. 5.4-ee

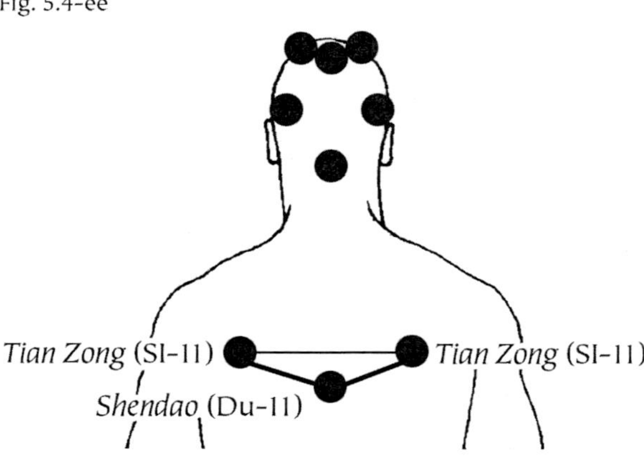

With this last set of visual connections, we have again formed both an upward pointing fire triangle and a downward pointing water triangle in this area of the body. This is another Esoteric *Shaoyin* formation balancing the fundamental human emotional frequencies of love and fear. But, this field also encompasses what is known as our Wing Maker Field. (See figure 5.4-ff below.)

### Additional Esoteric *Shaoyin* Field

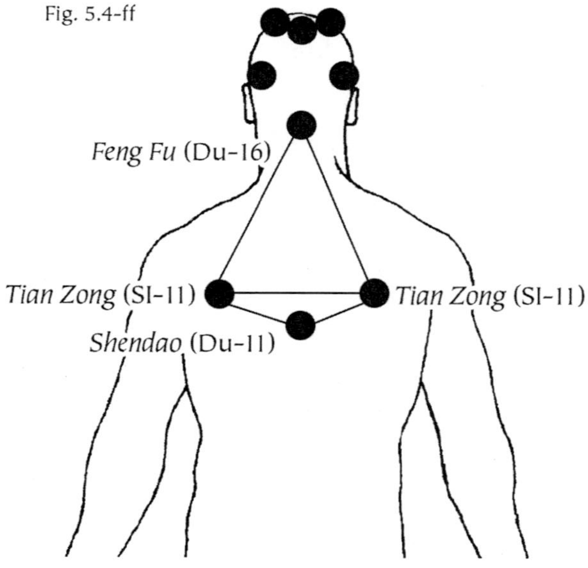


Have your client visually connect these last four acupuncture points to make a four-sided polygon without the horizontal connection between the bilateral *Tian Zong* (SI-11) points. Make a visual connection from *Feng Fu* (Du-16), downward and to the client's right scapula at the site of *Tian*

*Zong* (SI-11). Now connect *Tian Zong* on the right scapula to *Shendao* (Du-11) located directly on the spine below the spinous process of the fifth thoracic vertebra. Move the energy upward to the acupuncture site of *Tian Zong* (SI-11) on the left scapula. The final connection to complete this polygon is to move the energy from *Tian Zong* (SI-11) on the left scapula back to the first point *Feng Fu* (Du-16).

The area enclosed by this polygon is an area that I call The Wing Maker Frequency. (See figure 5.4-gg below.) The scapulae are considered the "Wings of Your Heart." The Wing Maker

**Wing Maker Frequency within an Esoteric *Shaoyin* Field**

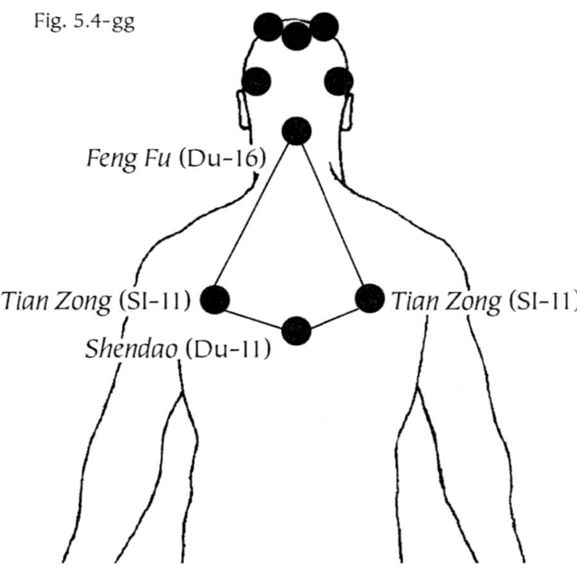


Frequency is a level of your Higher Heart frequency. If I am ever in a situation where the energy is not quite what I would like it

to be, I say to myself: "Bring me into Wing Maker Frequency." Merely saying this phrase to myself will instill my centered Higher Heart frequency within my fields. I often say "Bring me into Wing Maker Frequency" when I enter a lecture hall or classroom where I will be teaching. Remember, it is usually not in alignment with the universal principles of truth to go changing "things" outside of you without permission. (Of course there are exceptions such as being a parent gives you the right to guide and mold your children without asking their permission.) If I change the energy of a lecture hall or classroom, without the permission of the owner of that space, I will be in fact practicing black magic. One of the basic esoteric principles of black magic is to initiate changes to something or someone outside of yourself because you think you know better that the other person. That is how wars and disputes arise because one side wishes to dominate. But, when I bring myself into Wing Maker Frequency, I am not changing anything outside of myself.

If you put yourself into Wing Maker Frequency, then when you enter a space with a dense vibrational field, the light you carry from your heart frequency will automatically change the frequency of that dense space. By working on yourself and uplifting your own frequency, you will be practicing white magic. (For more on the esoteric definitions of white magic versus black magic, read ***The Sea of Fire-Cosmic Fire: Esoteric Acupuncture, Volume IV***.)

After your client has visually formed the Wing Maker Frequency polygon, have your client concentrate qi at the Heart Center gateway of *Shendao* (Du-11) located below the spinous process of the fifth thoracic vertebra. Very often at this stage of the visualization, I will first have the client bring additional gold colored light through the region enclosed by the four *Sishencong* points and down the spine to *Shendao* (Du-11) before I ask the client to connect *Shendao* (Du-11) to *Mingmen* (Du-4).

After there is adequate energy formed at *Shendao* (Du-11), have your client bring the energy straight down the spine from *Shendao* (Du-11) to *Mingmen* (Du-4). This visualization signifies the connection of one set of our Twin Flames Within, our Lower Twin Flame Within. (See figure 5.4-hh below.)

### Connecting Our Lower Twin Flames Within

Fig. 5.4-hh

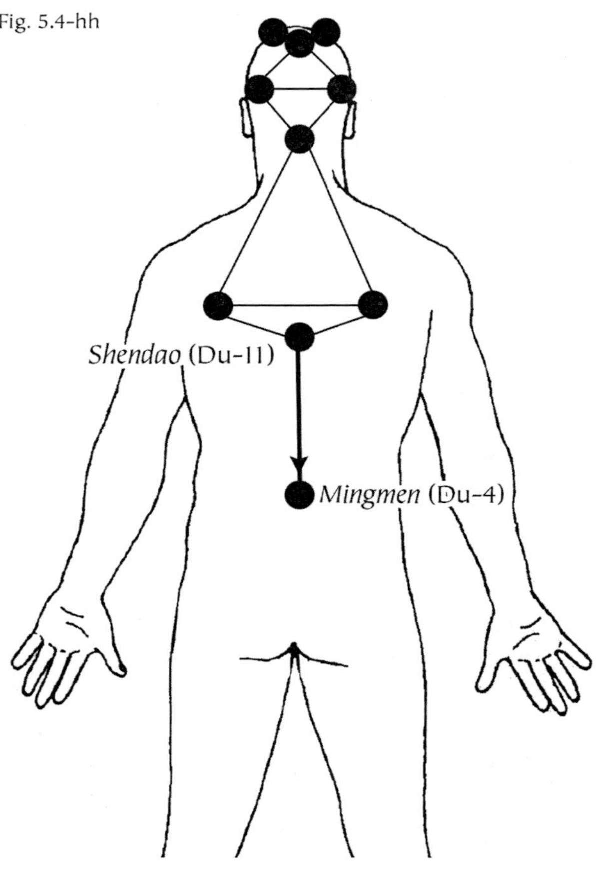


Pay close attention to the level of difficulty or ease at which your client makes this mental connection of the Lower Twin Flames Within. (The connection of the lower Twin Flames

Within is made when the flame of *Shendao* of the Heart Fire communicates and blends with the flame of the *Mingmen* Fire of the kidney system. Approximately one third of the clientele that come to me for an Esoteric Acupuncture treatment seem to have a very difficult time making this vertical connection between the Twin Flames. The visual connection is merely moving the qi down the spine from *Shendao* (Du-11), located at the fifth thoracic vertebrae, to *Mingmen* (Du-4) at the second lumbar vertebra. The same clientele may be able to very quickly connect the triangular formations, but may have difficulty with this straight downward connection from *Shendao* (Du-11) to *Mingmen* (Du-4).

If your client has difficulty with making the connection of his or her Lower Twin Flames Within, then this is an indication that there is still a wide gap between the Lower Twin Flames Within. A desired goal may be to have the Lower Twin Flames Within resonating with frequencies that are compatible to each other. When this is the case, then visualizing this connection between these two acupuncture sites is usually very easy and very rapid.

It was mentioned in an earlier volume of ***Esoteric Acupuncture*** that the heart system included love and all its tentacles such as: expansion, compassion, forgiveness, relaxation, fun, laughter, happiness, joy and others. The kidney system encompasses the many levels of fear and its tentacles such as: constriction, anger, hatred, revenge, envy, regret, pity and others. The heart is the gateway to the spiritual realms. The kidneys are the gateway to the grounding and strengthening of physicality.

Within the kidney system is a field known as our *Mingmen* Fire. The actual acupuncture point known as *Mingmen* (Du-4) has been called "The Gate of Vitality" and also "The Life Gate." It is from this region that we generate and regenerate our willpower and the physical energies to accomplish things in life. This is our physical power base. As we age, the qi from this power base declines.

The heart system encompasses playing, playfulness and wisdom. The kidney system encompasses work, seriousness and seeking information and knowledge. In your own life, how close are your Lower Twin Flames Within?

Ask yourself this question: "How close are the frequencies of your work connected to the frequencies of what you consider playtime?" "Do you really enjoy your work, and is your work really your puzzle piece in life?" We all have a certain puzzle piece in life. Have you found your specific puzzle piece and know exactly how your path and work fit into the larger picture of society or the planet. Are you actively delving within your particular puzzle piece?

As long as we are still residing in a three-dimensional reality with a dense physical body, we need the strength and harmony of both of the Lower Twin Flames Within. If you dread going to work or your work is constantly draining you of energy, then that is a distinct indication that the job or career you are employed in is not your puzzle piece in life. Your daily work that you perform for a living should give you energy, not drain you of energy. Those with a larger gap between their work time and playtime, really enjoy days off from work and look forward to vacations. Those same people may be the ones who have difficulty making the visual connection from *Shendao* (Du-11) to *Mingmen* (Du-4). Visualization is a right brain function that is very often obscured by those relying strictly on the left-brained rational aspect of the brain. The interesting point of this straight vertical connection between *Shendao* (Du-11) and *Mingmen* (Du-4) is that the same people who have had difficulty with this particular visual connection had no difficulty with making the other triangular connections that preceded this visual connection.

You will notice in the needling sequence for The Discern the Whisper Pattern that we are not inserting an acupuncture needle into the coccyx (tailbone) that will directly stimulate the Muladhara (Root Chakra). The Discern the Whisper Pattern is designed to gently open the higher head centers and to assist in the communication and unification of the Lower Twin Flames Within. But, it is best to connect the basic grounding chakra our Muladhara (Root Chakra) to The Discern the Whisper grid in this visualization process.

Although we are not going to insert an acupuncture needle at the site of the Muladhara (Root Chakra) in the Discern the Whisper Pattern, we are still going to activate the Muladhara (Root Chakra) by visually connecting the Swadthisthana (Sacral Chakra) to the root. Have your client concentrate qi at the site of *Mingmen* (Du-4). Then have your client visually bring energy straight down the spine from the site of *Mingmen* (Du-4) to the coccyx. Have your client concentrate energy at his or her tailbone. (See figure 5.4-ii below.)

**Activating the Muladhara (Root Chakra)**

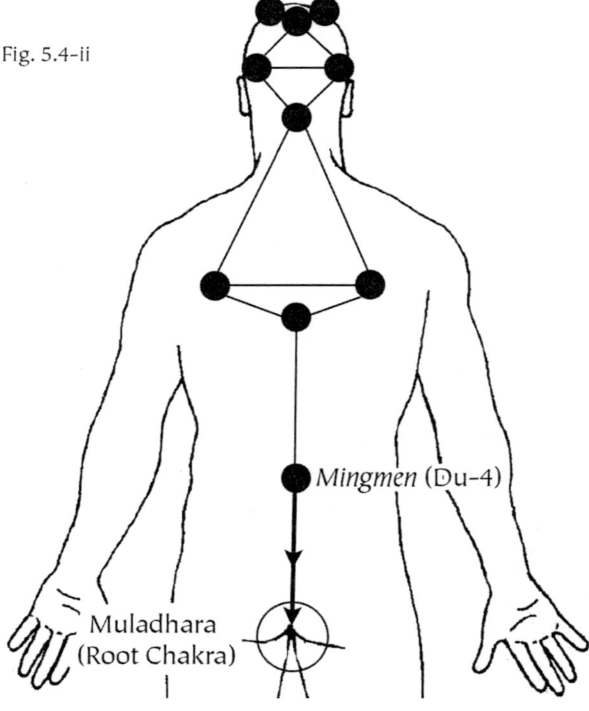


Fig. 5.4-ii

When the client feels that the Muladhara (Root Chakra) has been adequately activated and energized with enough mental energy, have the client visualize bringing the energy straight up the spine from the coccyx area back to the second chakra site of *Mingmen* (Du-4). We are reinforcing the energy connection from the Muladhara (Root Chakra) back to the Swadthisthana (second chakra). (See figure 5.4-jj below.)

### Discern the Whisper Pattern

Fig. 5.4-jj

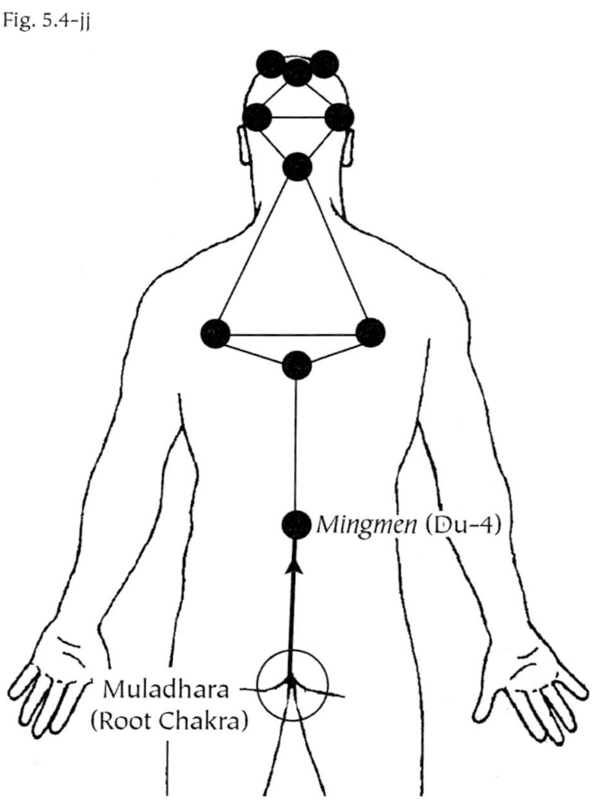

After briefly connecting and gathering the qi at the site of *Mingmen* (Du-4), again visually move the energy straight up the spine to the site of the acupuncture point *Shendao* (Du-11) that activates the Anahata (Heart Chakra). (See figure 5.4-kk below.)

## Discern the Whisper Pattern

Fig. 5.4-kk

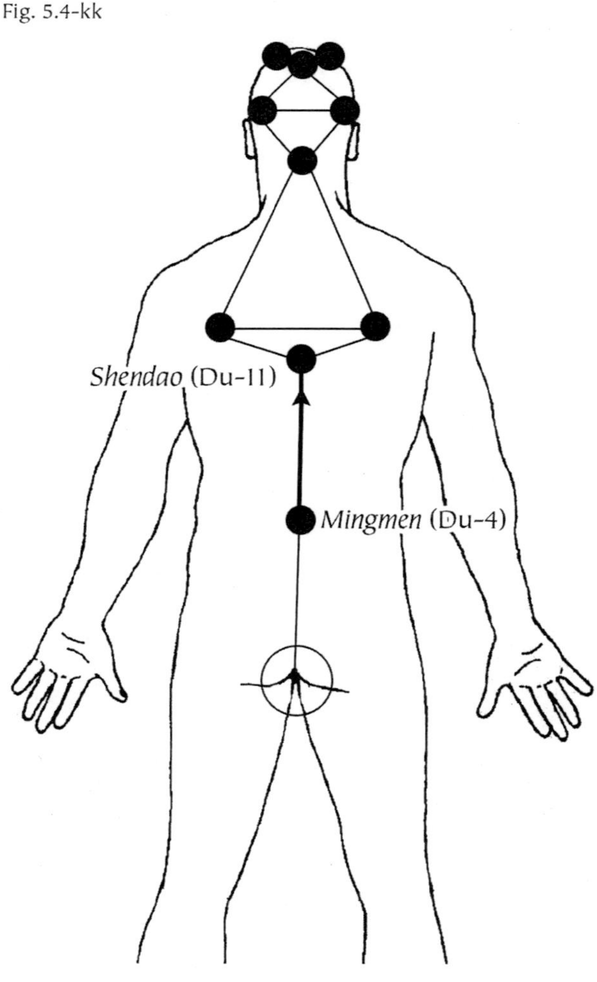

Now from the acupuncture site of *Shendao* (Du-11) that is the activation point for the Anahata (Heart Chakra), have your client visually move the qi upward to connect with Vishuddha (Throat Chakra) at *Dazhui* (Du-14). (See figure 5.4-ll below.)

## Discern the Whisper Pattern

Fig. 5.4-ll

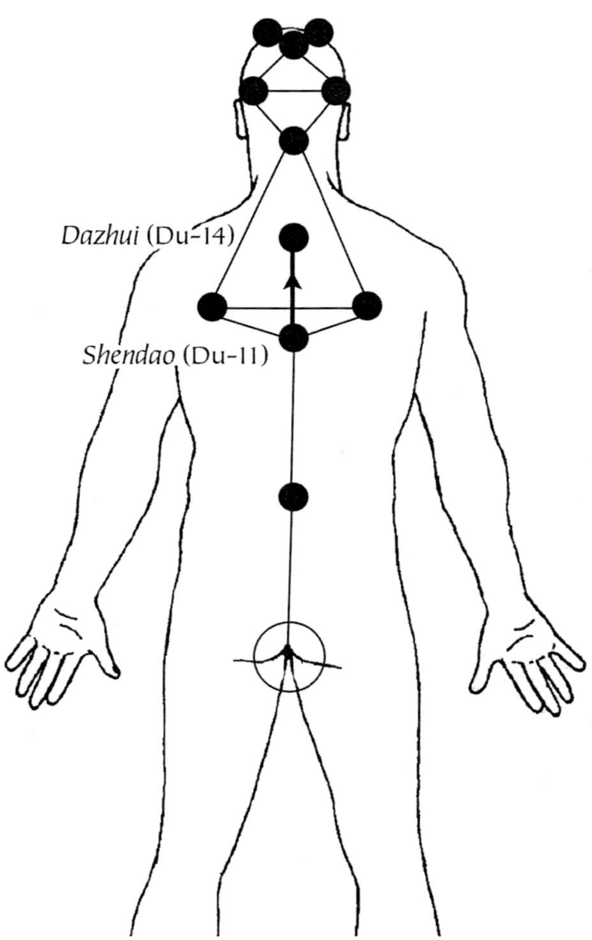

When the qi is sufficiently gathered and energized at the acupuncture site of *Dazhui* (Du14), have your client next visually see *Yintang* being activated. *Yintang* is located on the vertical midline of the forehead between the eyebrows and just superior to the bridge of the nose. Although figure 5.4-mm shows a straight connection from *Dazhui* (Du-14) on the spine to *Yintang* located between the eyebrows on the forehead, this connection is not a linear connection. Notice that it was said earlier to visualize *Yintang* being activated. The connection between *Dazhui* (Du14), and *Yintang* (Ajna Center) is a morphic resonant, consciousness connection. This means that the connection is not a typical linear connection, but occurs simultaneously in a non-linear fashion. (See figure 5.4-mm below.)

**Discern the Whisper Pattern**
**Morphic Resonant Connection**

Fig. 5.4-mm

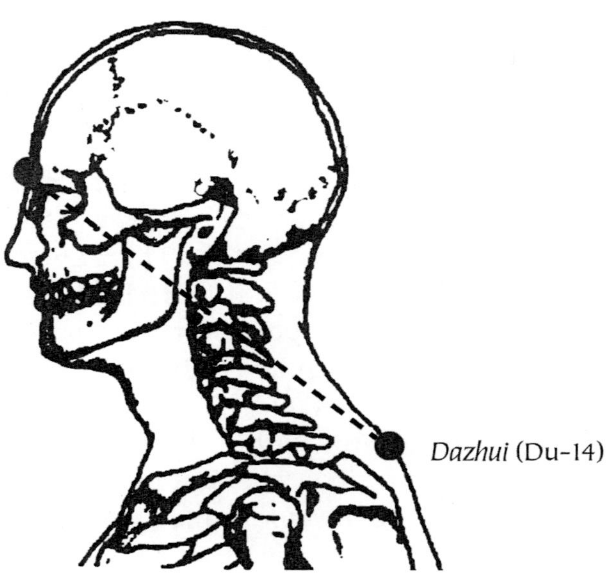

If you are treating a licensed acupuncturist, do not assume that the acupuncturist knows where *Yintang* is located. *Yintang* is not often needled in a traditional clinical setting by acupuncturists using traditional protocols. You do not want to embarrass your acupuncturist client by assuming he or she knows the correct location of *Yintang*. Unless an acupuncturist is treating a patient for sinus or allergy problems, frontal headaches or possibly eye problems, *Yintang* is not an acupuncture point that is commonly used in a clinical, medical setting. Always try to make your clients feel as comfortable as possible. When acupuncture needles are inserted into the client, he or she will usually become very relaxed. You do not want to place unnecessary stress on the client, who happens to be an acupuncturist, by making him or her try to remember where that acupuncture point is located. When I am treating a client who happens to be an acupuncturist and I ask the client to move the qi from *Dazhui* (Du-14) to *Yintang,* I always describe the location of *Yingtang* to all of my clientele, even the acupuncturists. I will say something like: "Now move the qi from this location (*Dazhui*/Du-14) to the Third Eye point that is located on the vertical midline of your forehead between your eyebrows and directly above the bridge of your nose. Most people who are asking for an Esoteric Acupuncture treatment will know approximately where the Third Eye is located. Make sure that the client is activating *Yintang* (Ajna Center). That is why I say "the point directly above the bridge of your nose." Some people may think that the Third Eye point is on the vertical midline of the forehead, but more in the center of the forehead. This would place the point location superior to *Yintang* (Ajna Center). But, the morphic resonant connection is stronger and clearer from *Dazhui* (Du-14) to *Yintang* (Ajna Center) than to any of the other sites within the Ajna Window Group.

After the morphic resonant consciousness connection from *Dazhui* (Du-14) to *Yintang* (Ajna Center) has been completed in your client's mind, have your client visualize the energy upward from *Dazhui* (Du-14) to the site of the "Wind Mansion" known as *Feng Fu* (Du-16). This is also the activation point for the Alta Major Center, also known as the Taluka Chakra, the Talu Chakra or the Lalana Chakra. Although *Dazhui* (Du-14) will automatically connect with *Feng Fu* (Du-16) because they are both on the Du meridian, it is important to have your client make the upward visual connection between these two acupuncture points. (See figure 5.4-nn below.)

**Discern the Whisper Pattern**
**Etheric Channel Connection**

Fig. 5.4-nn

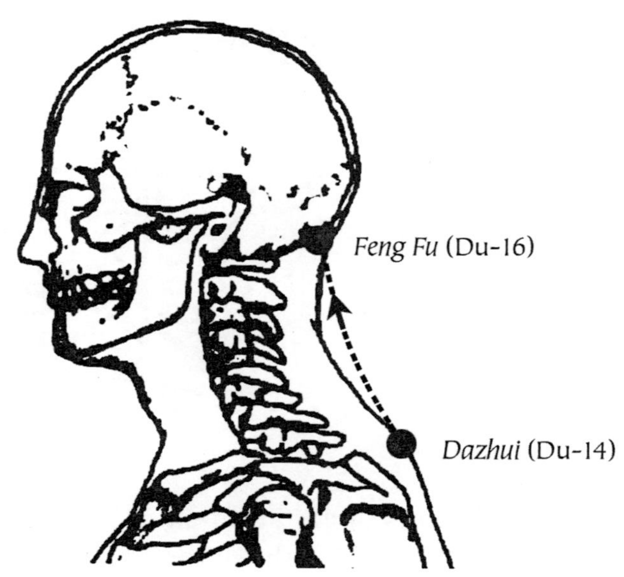


Now, from the acupuncture site of *Feng Fu* (Du16), have the client make a visual linear connection to *Yintang* (Ajna Center). This connection is a linear connection and not a morphic resonant connection. This mental connection is very important for the building of one's Antahkarana. (See figure 5.4-oo below.)

## Discern the Whisper Pattern
### Linear Visual Connection

Fig. 5.4-oo

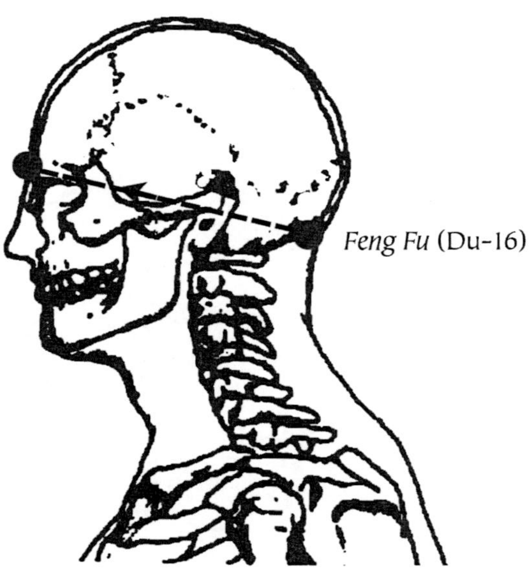


The various meditation styles and the various groups within each of the styles have their own ideas and own opinions on the form or forms that are most beneficial to the meditator of that particular style. Some of the more traditional styles of meditation are very attached to the "form." You have to sit a certain way, wear a particular kind of robe or certain style of garment, repeat a very specific chant or concentrate on your breathing.

If you are interested in building your Antahkarana, the

only "form" that is needed to be able to mentally visualize specific connections within certain New Encoding Patterns that are discussed in this book. If the three major head centers are connected and resonating together as one group, then the building and smooth flow of energy to and from the Antahkarana is more likely to occur. We are building our Axiatonal Grid System that is our central consciousness connection to everything and everywhere.

The last visualization connection in The Discern the Whisper Pattern is to have your client bring qi upward from both *Feng Fu* (Du-16) and *Yintang* to simultaneously meet at *Tian Man* (Du-20). This visualization will make a triangular connection with these three acupuncture sites. (See figure 5.4-pp below.)

**Discern the Whisper Pattern**
**Triangular Visual Connection**

Fig. 5.4-pp

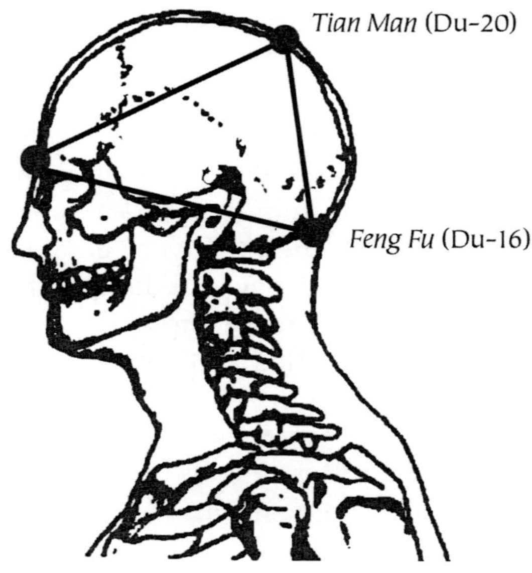

The Taluka Chakra (also known as the Talu Chakra, the Lalana Chakra or the Alta Major Center) is located at the acupuncture site of *Feng Fu* (Du-16). The Taluka Chakra, along with the Ajna Center at the acupuncture site of *Yintang* and the Sahasrara (Crown Chakra) at the acupuncture site of *Tian Man* (Du-20) are collectively known as the three major head centers in the Djwhal Khul Tibetan system. Once again do not forget that the esoteric location of Tian Man (Du-20) is not the same location as the location of Bai Hui (Du-20).

Being aware of these three major head centers and actually making the visual or mental triangular connections of these three centers, after the three centers have been activated by the insertion of acupuncture needles at the specific acupuncture site, will help you in the building of your Antahkarana. The needling of the sites followed by the visual connections of the three head centers will greatly assist in maintaining the continuity of qi flow to and from the Antahkarana to your higher realms of consciousness above the three-dimensional realities and above the Sahasrara (Crown Chakra).

The thirteen acupuncture points in the Discern the Whisper Pattern are the exact same thirteen acupuncture points and have the exact sequencing order as the first thirteen acupuncture points of The Esoteric *Shaoyin* Heart Pattern and The Esoteric *Shaoyin* Kidney Pattern, The Esoteric *Shaoyin* Heart Window Pattern and the Psychic Protection Grid Pattern. If you intimately know and understand the energetics of the Discern the Whisper Pattern, then it is very easy to familiarize yourself to the other mentioned New Encoding Patterns.

It is very important for those of you who intend to delve deeper into the mysteries of Esoteric Acupuncture to become intimately familiar with The Discern the Whisper Pattern. This pattern is the posterior New Encoding Pattern that lays the foundation for the rest of the various posterior Esoteric *Shaoyin* Patterns. The posterior New Encoding Patterns usually have more power to align the client to his or her Inner Spiritual Higher Heart Center than the anterior New Encoding Patterns.

## Discern the Whisper Pattern
### Complete Visualization and Grid

Fig. 5.4-qq

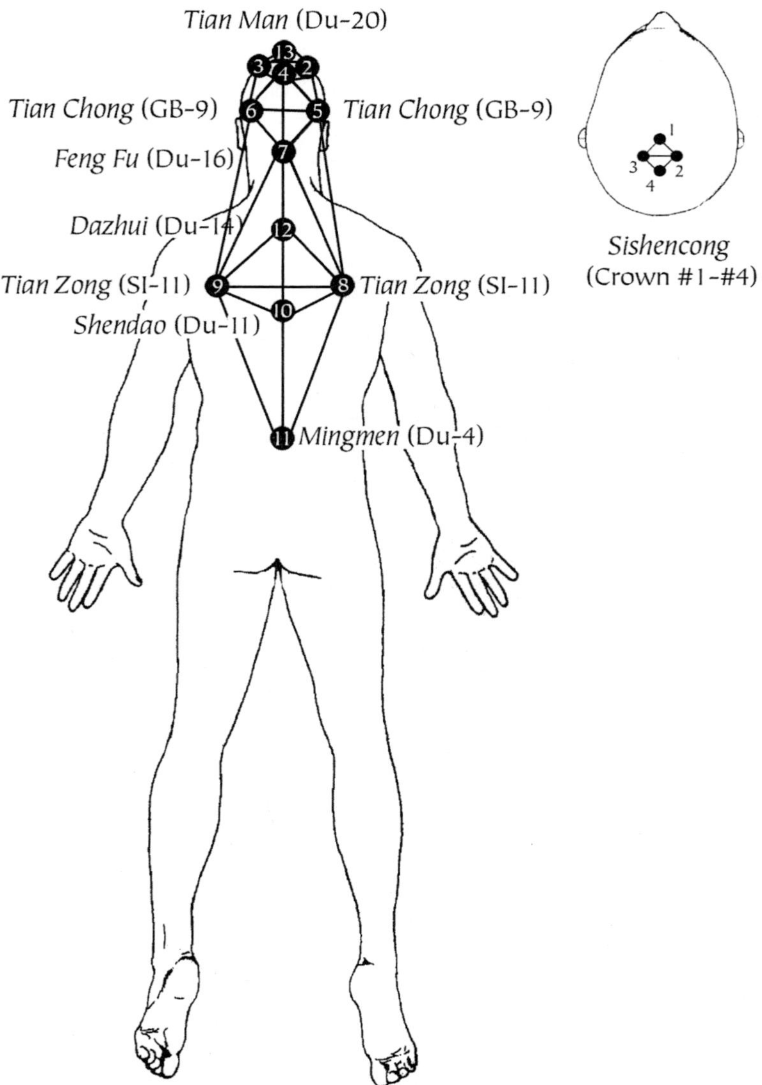

## Level II Anterior: Eight Heart-Gates *Shaoyang* Pattern (12 Points lead to a "hidden" 13th region)

### Eight Heart-Gates *Shaoyang* Pattern

*Fig 5.5-a*

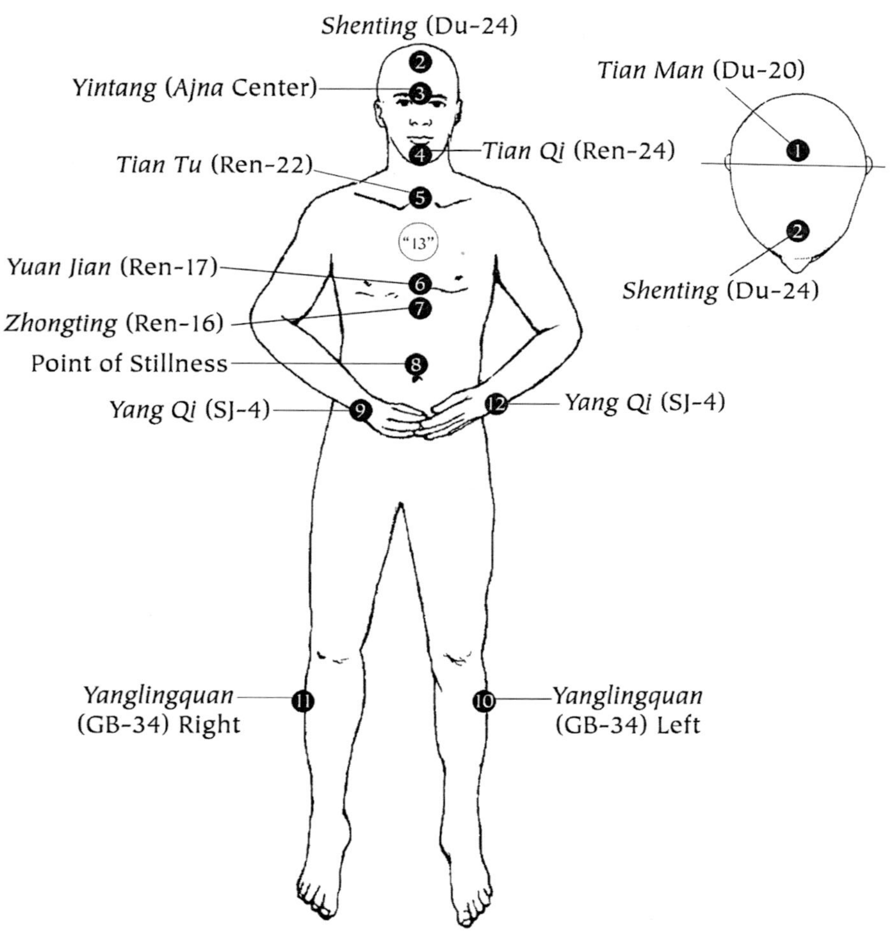

### Needling Sequence for The Eight Heart-Gates *Shaoyang* Pattern

1) *Tian Man* (Du-20)
2) *Shenting* (Du-24) "Celestial Court" or "Heavenly Court"
3) *Yintang* (Ajna Center) "Third Eye" Point
4) *Tian Qi* (Ren-24) "Celestial Pool"
5) *Tian Tu* (Ren-22) "Celestial Chimney"
6) *Yuan Jian* (Ren-17) More commonly called *Danzhong* or *Tanzhong,* "Chest Center"
7) *Zhongting* (Ren-16) "Center Palace" (Gateway to the Central Cinnabar Field)
8) Point of Stillness
9) *Yang Qi* (SJ-4) Right
10) *Yanglingquan* (GB-34) Left
11) *Yanglingquan* (GB-34) Right
12) *Yang Qi* (SJ-4) Left
13) "Hidden Heart Center"

It was mentioned in an earlier edition of ***Esoteric Acupuncture*** that as we evolve in consciousness, while simultaneously staying focused on our inner plane work, then our Inner, Spiritual Higher Heart Center becomes refined and will incrementally (sometimes very rapidly) evolve to a higher, more refined frequency. Some schools of thought in Chinese medicine place the Earth element of the spleen and stomach at the center of existence for humans. This school of thought states that everything revolves around the foods and drink we ingest. That school of thought feels that the foods and drinks and the whole process of digestion and transformation of the multitude of food products into the various types of qi for the body are at the very center of our existence. Without physical foods and drinks, most people would not be able to transform those products into qi, blood, muscles and other physical and mental components.

Although the connection between diet and spiritual consciousness was discussed in ***Support the Mountain: Esoteric Acupuncture, Volume V,*** this topic will be briefly touched upon again. Everything we eat and drink alters all of the planes of existence that make up who we are. Cleaner (no genetic modification or chemicals) and vibrationally lighter foods will allow for the qi (energies) of the foods and drinks to move to the higher head centers. If your choice of foods is of a heavier and denser vibration, then the qi will benefit the lower chakras first. If you have difficulty processing raw, organic foods, then that is an indication that you have some challenges to your Manipura (solar plexus chakra) that controls digestion. This is the third chakra and considered part of the lower chakras. This is not to imply that you must be a raw foods vegan to activate your higher head centers. But, vibrationally cleaner and lighter foods and drinks will transform into lighter, higher vibrational qi/prana. It is already difficult to quiet the mind and advance along our spiritual journey without succumbing to the lower pleasure of the tastes buds of your tongue. It is up to each individual along his or her own individual spiritual journey to decide what foods and drinks to ingest. I suggest that you ask yourself: "Will this food or drink assist or hinder my spiritual journey." "Will these foods and drinks help me stay in my spiritual center, or pull me off my central spiritual path?"

According to Elisabeth Rochat de la Vallee's translation of the Chinese medical classics in her book ***A Study of Qi*** she states:

> *"The tastes activate and guide the qi. There is a strong primitive link between food and qi. It is vitally important to eat carefully because it is not only a question of good health but a question of good qi and its regulation. The qi is able to make the will solid, and the will is able to direct and form the inner disposition that determines what you say."* [5]

If we examine the United States today, one of the biggest challenges we have as a society and as a nation is digestion. The field of digestion not only involves how we are digesting physical foods, but also how are we digesting life?

Looking at the number of obese and overweight individuals in the United States today, will convey a general sense that, as a whole, we are not digesting foods or emotionally digesting life very well. The widespread use of mind-altering drugs, alcohol and chemically laced foods is quite prevalent in the United States today.

In Esoteric Acupuncture, the center is always the heart. Remember that there are multiple levels of the heart, not merely the physical and emotional levels. The Inner, Spiritual Heart is a finer vibrating frequency than the Anahata (Heart Chakra).

The fire element of the heart is a much higher vibrational center than the frequencies of the earth element of the stomach and spleen. Everything revolves around the heart, including the choices of foods and drinks we choose to ingest. The heart controls our tongue in Chinese Medicine, and is an important component in the selection of the foods and drinks we ultimately decide to ingest.

In acupuncture school, we are taught the concept of *Shen* disturbance. *Shen* is often translated into English as mind or spirit. In Chinese medical thought, our *shen*, or the mind and spirit, is controlled by our heart. *Shen* disturbance covers many conditions related to some sort of abnormal challenges with the spirit or mind. These conditions may range from excessive mental chatter, where we cannot still the mind, to something more severe such as being diagnosed as manic-depressive or bipolar.

Other conditions may include: not being able to relax, not being able to concentrate and experiencing insomnia. The use of *Shen* in a Chinese clinical setting involves the fields of the Physical, Etheric, Astral (emotional) or Mental Planes.

In Esoteric Acupuncture, we are including consciousness fields above the concrete mental plane that involve the Causal, Buddhic, Atmic, Monadic and Logoic Planes. As we evolve with our physical and spiritual work simultaneously, sometimes the heart center will ascend from the Anahata (Heart Chakra) to the area of Sahasrara (Crown Chakra).

With more dedication, discipline and karmic ripening, the Spiritual Heart Center will move from the Sahasrara (Crown Chakra) to the Mahan Chakra above the Sahasrara (Crown Chakra). With continued dedication, devotion and discipline through diet and inner plane work (meditation), the Spiritual Heart Center will become more refined and will again ascend to a higher chakra.

### Point Locations for The Eight Heart-Gates *Shaoyang* Pattern

The first acupuncture heart point needled in the Eight Heart-Gates *Shaoyang* Pattern is *Tian Man* (Du-20). Although *Tian Man* (Du-20) is not considered a heart point in traditional Chinese medicine, it is a higher heart point in Esoteric Acupuncture. As we refine and strengthen our inner, Higher, Spiritual Heart Center, the heart energies ascend from the Anahata region around *Yuan Jian* (Ren-17) at the center of the chest at the level of the intercostal space of the fourth rib to the Sahasrara (Crown Chakra) above the cranium. The gateway to the Sahasrara (Crown Chakra) is through *Tian Man* (Du-20). Remember the esoteric Du-20, known as *Tian Man,* is approximately one inch posterior to the traditional Du-20 known as *Bai Hui*.

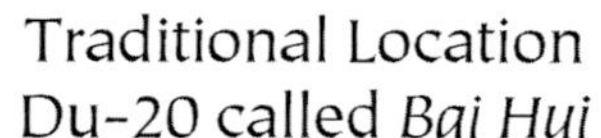
Traditional Location
Du-20 called *Bai Hui*

Fig. 5.5-b

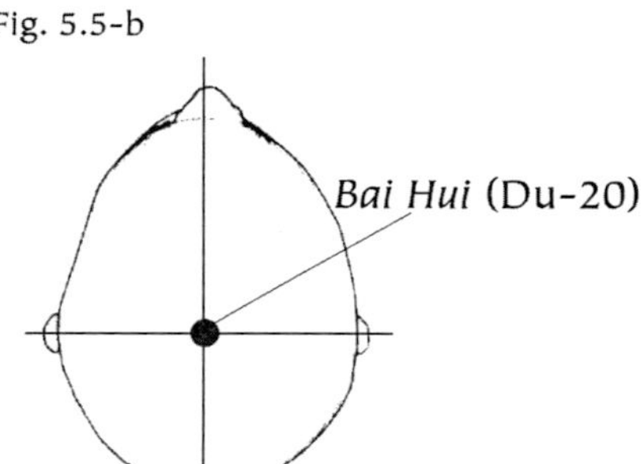


Esoteric Location
Du-20 called *Tian Man*

Fig. 5.5-c

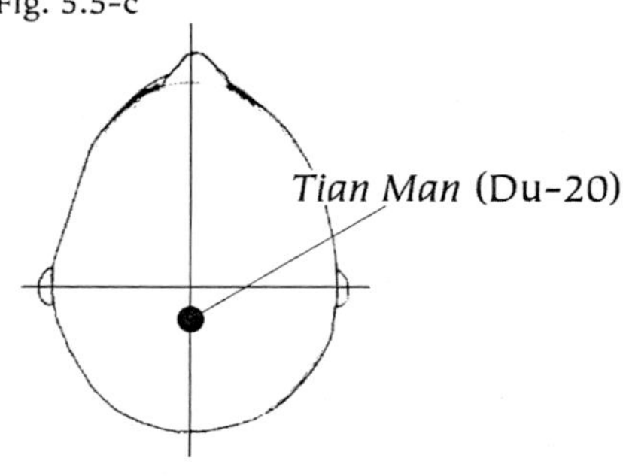

The second acupuncture heart point needled in the Eight Heart-Gates *Shaoyang* Pattern is *Shenting* (Du-24) located directly on the anterior vertical midline of the head approximately one-half *cun* behind the anterior hairline. *Shenting* can be translated as "Celestial Court." Inserting an acupuncture needle at the site of *Shenting* (Du-24) and activating the energies at that site will automatically activate and strengthen The Celestial Court that consists of the *Sishencong* group along with *Tian Man* (Du-20).

A practitioner once asked me: "How do I find the original frontal hairline on a bald man?" An older bald male practitioner who was taking the same course I was teaching pointed to his head and said: "All bald men intuitively know exactly the end of their original frontal hairline." So as a practitioner, if you cannot determine the frontal hairline of a bald client, just ask that client to point to his original anterior hairline.

### Eight Heart-Gates *Shaoyang* Pattern

Fig. 5.5-d

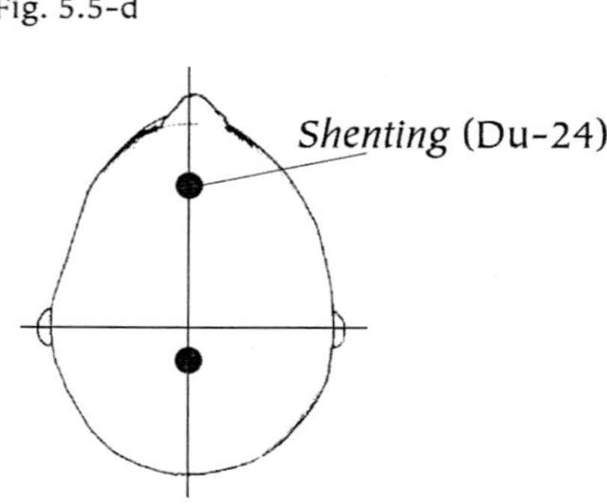


The third acupuncture heart point needled in The Eight Heart-Gates *Shaoyang* Pattern is the Chinese acupuncture point *Yintang* also known as the Ajna Center in the Hindu Chakra

System. A more common name for this acupuncture site is the Third Eye Point. In the Hindu chakra system, this site is sometimes called the Brow Chakra. To understand how this acupuncture point is called a heart point you must understand *Shen* and consciousness. *Shen* is often translated as both spirit and mind. I feel that *Shen* includes mind, spirit, as well as the body. Mind is not merely the western version of the physical brain. Mind is also consciousness. The focus of Esoteric Acupuncture is to expand our limited three-dimensional realities and to do so necessitates the awakening to a higher heart consciousness. The Ajna Center is the gateway to higher intuition and the expansion into hyperspatial realties.

The acupuncture site of *Yintang* (Ajna Center) is located on the imaginary vertical midline of the forehead directly between the eyebrows and superior to the bridge of the nose. On some individuals who have sinus issues, inserting an acupuncture needle into this site may be a little sensitive. (See figure 5.5-e below.)

## Eight Heart-Gates *Shaoyang* Pattern

Fig 5.5-e

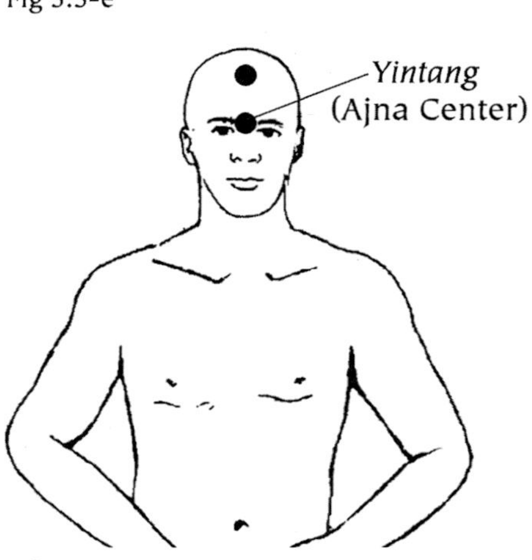

The fourth acupuncture heart point of The Eight Heart-Gates *Shaoyang* Pattern is *Tian Qi* (Ren-24) located directly on the anterior midline of the face in the horizontal cleft below the lower lip. Most of the acupuncture books in the United States use the Chinese name of *Cheng Jiang* for Ren-24. I do not like the translation of *Cheng Jiang* that is "Sauce Receptacle." (In my opinion, that is a very non-medical explanation for an acupuncture point.) The name used in Esoteric Acupuncture is translated as "Celestial Well" and is more in alignment with working on one's celestial heart frequencies.

On some people, this acupuncture point is located very close to the lower lip. On others, the indentation is farther from the lower lip. This acupuncture site is usually very sensitive on most people, so be aware to insert the needle shallowly with no twisting. I usually tell the client that this point may be sensitive in advance of inserting the needle. In Esoteric Acupuncture, needling *Tian Qi* (Ren-24) strengthens one aspect of the heart that controls the tongue. Remember in Chinese Medicine, the heart system is one of the systems that control the tongue. (See figure 5.5-f below.)

## Eight Heart-Gates *Shaoyang* Pattern

Fig 5.5-f

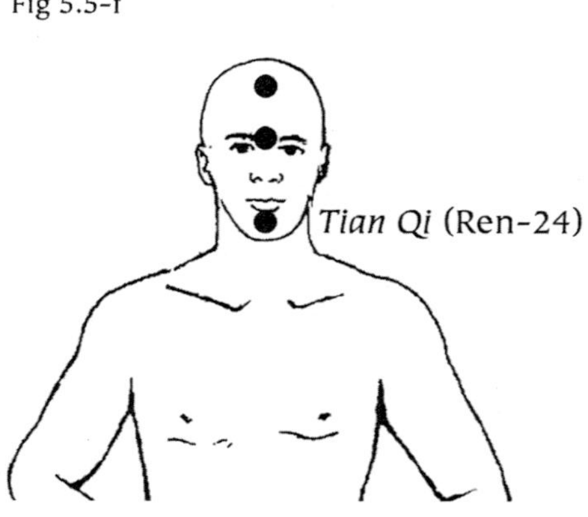

The fifth acupuncture heart site needled in the Eight Heart-Gates *Shaoyang* Pattern is *Tian Tu* (Ren-22). *Tian Tu* can be translated as "Celestial Chimney." Although most acupuncturists who adhere to the more traditional Chinese view of this acupuncture point may feel that *Tian Tu* (Ren-22) is more closely related to the throat and the lungs, in Esoteric Acupuncture the *Tian Tu* (Ren-22) point is used to harmonize and align the upper *jiao* (the Upper Burner) to the frequencies of the heart. (See figure 5.5-g below.)

## Eight Heart-Gates *Shaoyang* Pattern

Fig 5.5-g

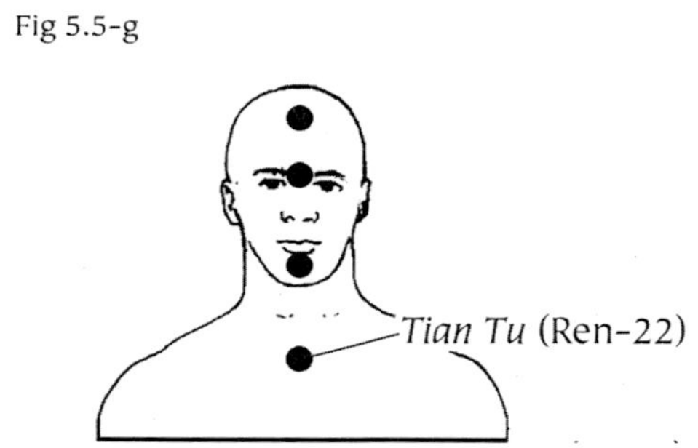


The upper *jiao* consists of the heart and lungs and are both located in the upper chest region. The physical closeness of these two organ systems means that those two systems are able to communicate very intimately if they are in harmony. As an individual becomes more aligned with his or her Higher Spiritual Heart Center, needling *Tian Tu* (Ren-22) in the Eight Heart-Gates *Shaoyang* Pattern will allow the lungs and heart systems to blend into one united frequency of the heart. The "Celestial Chimney" of *Tian Tu* (Ren-22) allows the correct qi to flow into the heart center of the chest at *Yuan Jian* (Ren-17).

*Tian Tu* (*Ren*-22) in Traditional Chinese Medicine is usually used for throat disorders. Since *Tian Tu* (*Ren*-22) is known as a "Window of Heaven" or "Window to the Sky" point, the traditional thinking may be to needle this point to treat symptoms such as: dizziness, blurry vision, hearing problems or sudden loss of speech. The esoteric function of *Tian Tu (Ren*-22) when needled in any of the New Encoding Patterns of Esoteric Acupuncture is to move qi to the heart region first, then to assist in opening the gateways to the Inner Spiritual Higher Heart.

In Esoteric Acupuncture, the energetics at the acupuncture site of *Tian Tu* (Ren-22) have two main functions. One of the functions of *Tian Tu* (Ren-22) is that it is used as an anterior gateway to activate and harmonize the Vishuddha (Throat Chakra). The more important function of *Tian Tu* (Ren-22) is that this acupuncture site is used as an adjunctive heart point. In other words, *Tian Tu* (Ren-22) communicates and strengthens the Anahata (Heart Chakra) that is activated at the anterior acupuncture site of *Yuan Jian* (Ren-17). One way that *Tian Tu* (Ren-22) communicates with *Yuan Jian* (Ren-17) is due to the fact that they are on the same acupuncture meridian. They are both a part of the Ren meridian/channel. *Yuan Jian* (*Ren*-17) is a chakra site that is the gateway to access the Anahata (Heart Chakra) from the anterior side of your client. The acupuncture point *Shendao* (*Du*-11) is the posterior access site and gateway to the Anahata (Heart Chakra) from the posterior side of your client. If you look at figure 5.5-h, you will notice that there is also another connection from *Tian Tu* (Ren-22) to *Yuan Jian* (Ren-17) by way of the subcutaneous/cutaneous *shaoyin* regions. "*The cutaneous regions explain how treatment applied at the level of the skin (for example medical ointments, massage, cupping, plum blossom needling, skin scraping and dermal needling) is able to have a deep therapeutic effect.*" [6]

Although Esoteric *Shaoyin* has been discussed in earlier volumes of the Esoteric Acupuncture series, I would like to emphasize its importance once again. Esoteric *Shaoyin* refers to the opposing, yet often harmoniously interacting, forces of the kidney and heart systems. The heart system encompasses the fire and love components in life. The kidney system encompasses the water and fear components in life. Just remember in the Traditional Five Element Theory, the heart system is connected to joy and happiness and not love like in Esoteric Acupuncture. Joy and happiness are branches of love and not the other way around. Love and fear are the two fundamental emotions of humans. Joy and happiness are not strong enough to offset the energies of fear. Only love has the strength to offset and balance fear.

Since the energies located at *Tian Tu* (Ren-22) connect to the energies located at *Yuan Jian* (*Ren*-17) by way of the cutaneous *shaoyin* region connection, *Tian Tu* (*Ren*-22) is also connected to *shaoyin* by this pathway. In the bigger picture of *shaoyin*, the Chinese believe that "*the shaoyin is the Heart vessel.*"[7] This *shaoyin* connection between these two acupuncture points shows from a more traditional Chinese medical viewpoint that *Tian Tu* (Ren-22) is indeed connected to the Heart Field.

The acupuncture needle only has to be inserted to a very shallow depth at site of *Tian Tu* (*Ren*-22). I use Seirin .16mm X 15mm red handled needles with no insertion tube. The needle is inserted approximately one half the length of the needle shaft. Those Seirin needles are slightly longer than one half inch, so the needle insertion is only approximately one quarter of an inch or just slightly longer.

A chimney is thought of as a pathway that allows smoke to escape. But, a chimney has both ascending and descending pathways. *Tian Tu* (Ren-22), "The Celestial Chimney," is viewed in Esoteric Acupuncture as the thoroughfare to allow qi to enter through the lungs-throat area (upper *jiao* region) and descend to the heart region to connect with the gateway to the Anahata Heart Chakra) *at Yuan Jian* (*Ren*-17). Activating the energies at *Tian Tu* (Ren-22) and unblocking any stuck qi in the Vishuddha (Throat Chakra) allows the energies to flow from the Anahata (Heart Chakra) to ascend to the higher head centers. If *shaoyin* is the heart vessel, then *Tian Tu* (Ren-22) is a heart point because of its location on the Subcutaneous/Cutaneous *Shaoyin* Region shown in figure 5.5-h below.

## Subcutaneous/Cutaneous *Shaoyin* Regions

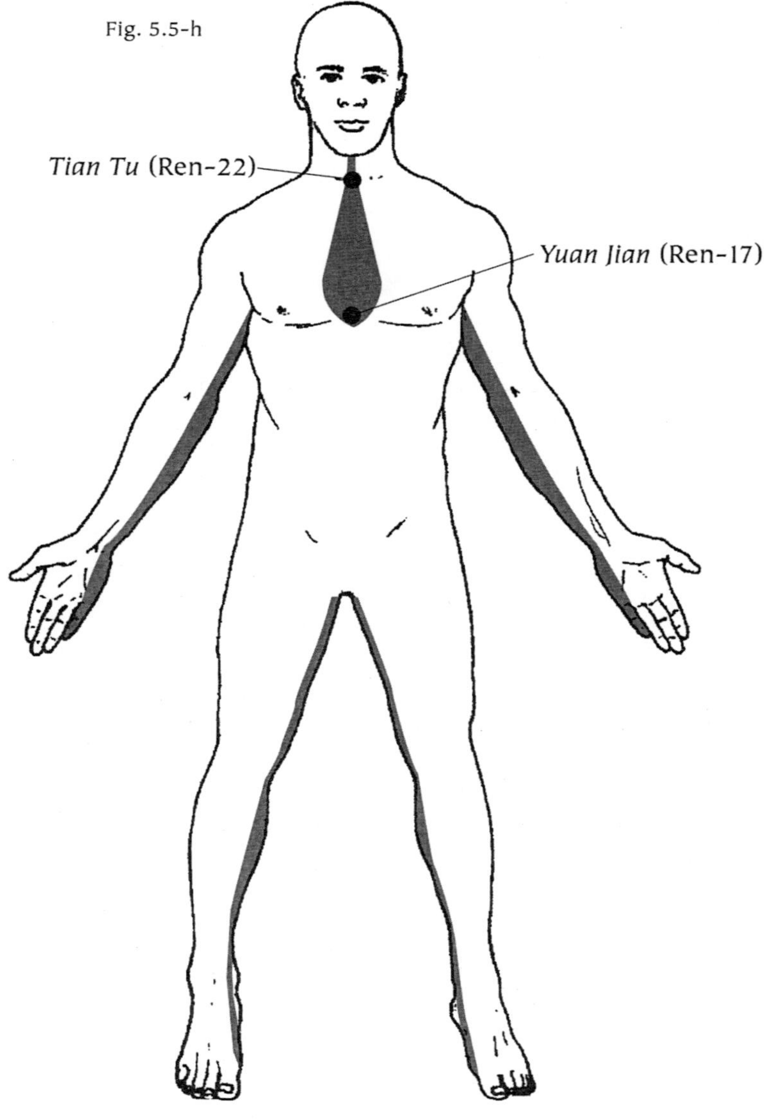

The sixth acupuncture Heart Gate point in the Eight Heart-Gates *Shaoyang* Pattern is *Yuan Jian* (Ren-17). *Yuan Jian* can be translated as "The Source." A more common Chinese name for Ren-17 is *Tanzhong* or sometimes spelled *Danzhong*. *Yuan Jian* (Ren-17) is located on the anterior midline of the body level with the fourth intercostal space. In most young men, this point can be found by first drawing an imaginary horizontal line between the nipples. Where this imaginary horizontal line intersects the anterior midline is where *Yuan Jian* (Ren-17) is needled. This acupuncture site is the location of a pericardium point that has direct anterior access to the Heart Chakra. *Yuan Jian* (Ren-17) is the anterior access point of the Anahata Chakra. (See figure 5.5-i below.)

**Eight Heart-Gates *Shaoyang* Pattern**
**Direct Access Site to the Anahata (Heart Chakra)**

*Fig 5.5-i*

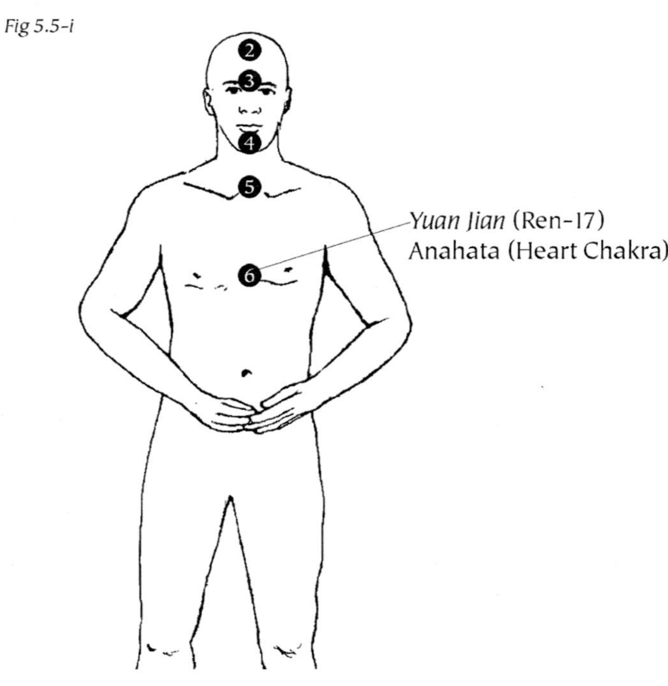

The seventh acupuncture heart point in The Eight Gates *Shaoyang* Pattern is *Zhongting* (Ren-16) located in the sternum level with the fifth intercostal space. *Zhongting* (Ren-16) is located directly inferior to *Yuan Jian* (Ren- 17). *Zhong Ting* can be translated as "Center Palace." *Zhong Ting* (Ren-16) corresponds to the Hindu Hrit Chakra. The distance between *Yuan Jian* (Ren-17) and *Zhong Ting* (Ren-16) in males is very often farther apart than in women. I insert the acupuncture needle in the depression just superior to the xiphoid process. In men, the xiphoid process is more prominent and usually longer than in women. (See figure 5.5-j below.)

**Eight Heart-Gates *Shaoyang* Pattern**
**Hrit Chakra (Broken Heart)**

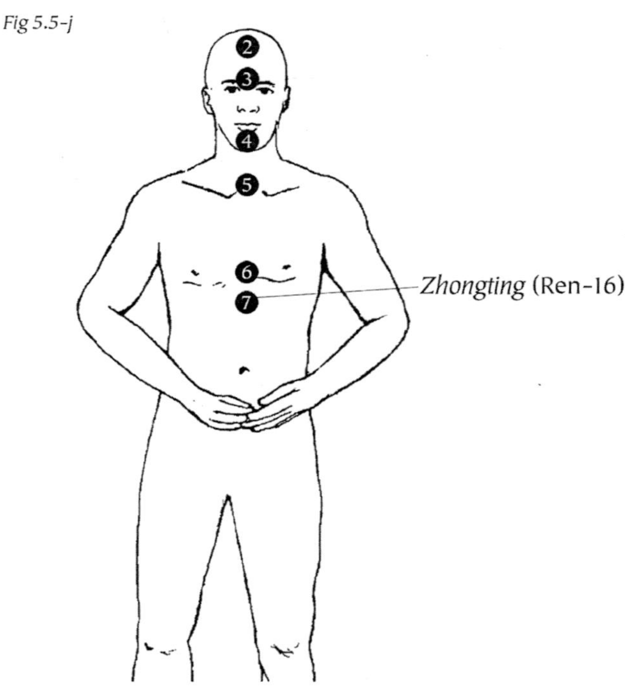


*Fig 5.5-j*

It was mentioned in ***Sea of Fire-Cosmic Fire: Esoteric Acupuncture, Volume IV*** that the Hrit Chakra symbolically represented the "broken Heart," or the splitting apart the denseness of the emotional heart into a finer frequency vibration to allow the Inner Spiritual Heart to open. In some Hindu schools of thought, the Hrit Chakra is located in the same location as the Anahata (Heart Chakra).

Most people think of a broken heart as an incident or event that occurs when someone or something outside of yourself greatly impacts your emotional body to have you react in a certain way that reflects sadness, betrayal, mistrust, disappointment, tragedy or other emotions with similar vibrational frequencies. When broken heart is used in Esoteric Acupuncture in connection with the Hrit Chakra, it refers to an opportunity to explore or move into a consciousness plane that will further the development of your higher, Inner, Spiritual Heart. The esoteric meaning of a broken heart requires that you have "cracked through" to a deeper level and a deeper, more profound understanding of the heart frequency. You have now started to move above the emotional frequencies of the Heart Chakra and are now in the plane of the knowing aspect of your heart. If you are able to rise above the sadness and pain of the emotional broken heart, then this allows you an opportunity to truly move into the realms of your higher, Inner, Spiritual Heart space. You will automatically "know things by heart."

This process of going through and understanding the esoteric broken heart usually means that the twelve petals of the Anahata have opened to a certain degree. This may mean that each of the twelve petals have opened outward from the chest revealing an opened petaled flower, or that the twelve petals will now be opening upward to communicate with the twelve petals of the Guru Chakra.

The eighth Heart Gate point in the Eight Hearts *Shaoyang* Pattern is located directly on the vertical midline of the anterior of the body approximately one inch superior to the center of the umbilicus, or approximately one-half inch superior to the outer upper edge of the umbilicus (depending on the size of the umbilicus). This is not a traditional acupuncture point and is not used in traditional types of acupuncture treatments. In Esoteric Acupuncture this point is named "Point of Stillness." This is another of the esoteric heart points, another Heart Gate or Heart Gateway. Since the umbilicus is Ren-8 in traditional Chinese acupuncture, an alternate name for the Point of Stillness used in Esoteric Acupuncture is Ren-8.5. I prefer to call this point the Point of Stillness. (See figure 5.5-k below.)

**Eight Heart-Gates *Shaoyang* Pattern**
**Point of Stillness**

*Fig 5.5-k*

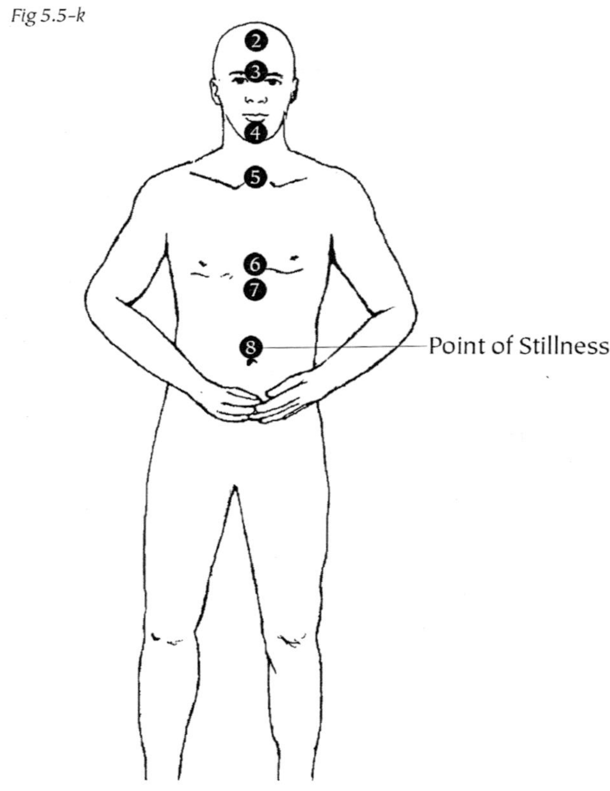

The heart syndrome known in Chinese Medicine as *Shen* Disturbance was discussed earlier. One of the major symptoms of *Shen* Disturbance is not being able to quiet the mind. This condition may lead to restlessness, irritability, being very aggressive or combative, extreme agitation and/or insomnia. This condition is also known as excessive mental chatter. The Point of Stillness is a catalytic point to move the multiple heart centers into alignment with each other and to assist in quieting a chattering mind. The Point of Stillness is an anchoring point to allow the mind to settle down and eventually enter the space of Stillness. It is much more difficult to experience silent meditation if your mind is wandering. Being in a quiet place of Stillness is not synonymous with silent thinking. You may be able to still the physical vehicle, but if your mind is chattering you will not be able to enter the higher realms of the still heart/mind. If you are able to really quiet your mind, your frequency will change to a vibration that will allow you to enter into a space or realm known in Esoteric Acupuncture as "The Center of the Center." This is accessing your Inner Spiritual Higher Heart.

In Chinese medical theory, the name for the combination of the *san jiao* (triple burner) meridian with the gallbladder meridian is known as *Shaoyang*. For Esoteric Acupuncture, the concept of *Shaoyang* is not the same as theory taught in the Chinese text *Shang Han Lun*. The idea of *Shaoyang* in Esoteric Acupuncture is to utilize a certain combination of acupuncture points in a specific needling sequence to raise the vibrational frequency of the recipient of the treatment to the vibratory rate that will allow the recipient to move into his or her Inner Spiritual Higher Heart space. There are four specific *Shaoyang* points used in The Eight Heart Gates *Shaoyang* Pattern that will assist in the harmonious movement of heart qi to the Spiritual Center. The first of the acupuncture *Shaoyang* points needled is located on the dorsum (back) of the client's right wrist directly on the crease. Locate the *san jiao* (triple burner) meridian at the posterior wrist crease of your client. Now feel for the depression at the crease on the dorsum of the hand. There is actually a deep depression. Make sure you insert the needle in this hole. This is the location of *Yang Qi* (SJ-4). (See figure 5.5-l below.)

**Eight Heart-Gates *Shaoyang* Pattern**

*Fig 5.5-l*

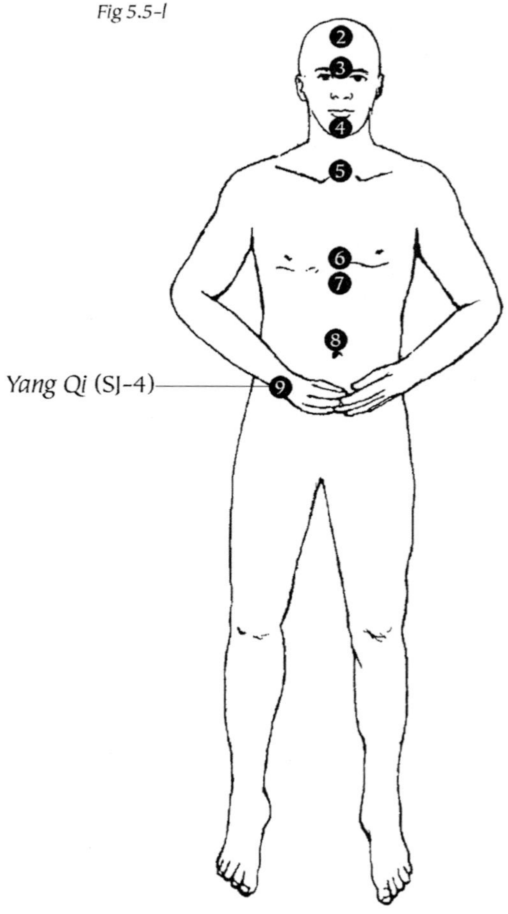

The next *Shaoyang* point and the tenth acupuncture point needled in The Eight Heart Gates *Shaoyang* Pattern is *Yanglingquan* (GB-34) on the client's left side. You will look for the head of the tibia bone on the client's left leg. The point is located inferiorly to the head of the tibia bone and slightly anteriorly. (See figure 5.5-m below.)

**Eight Heart-Gates *Shaoyang* Pattern**

*Fig 5.5-m*

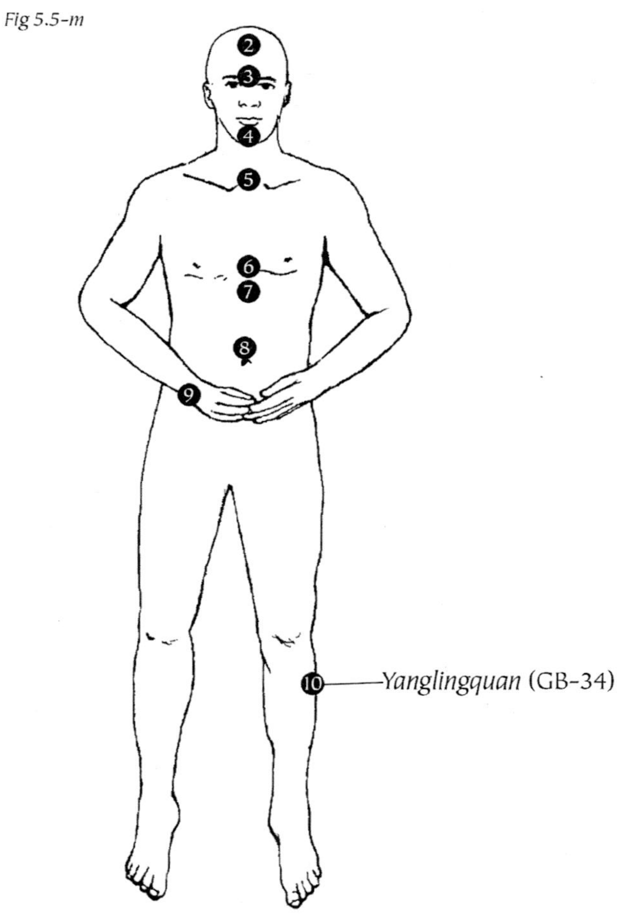

The next *Shaoyang* point and the eleventh acupuncture point needled in The Eight Heart Gates *Shaoyang* Pattern is the bilateral *Yanglingquan* (GB-34) on the client's right side (See figure 5.5-n below.)

## Eight Heart-Gates *Shaoyang* Pattern

*Fig 5.5-n*

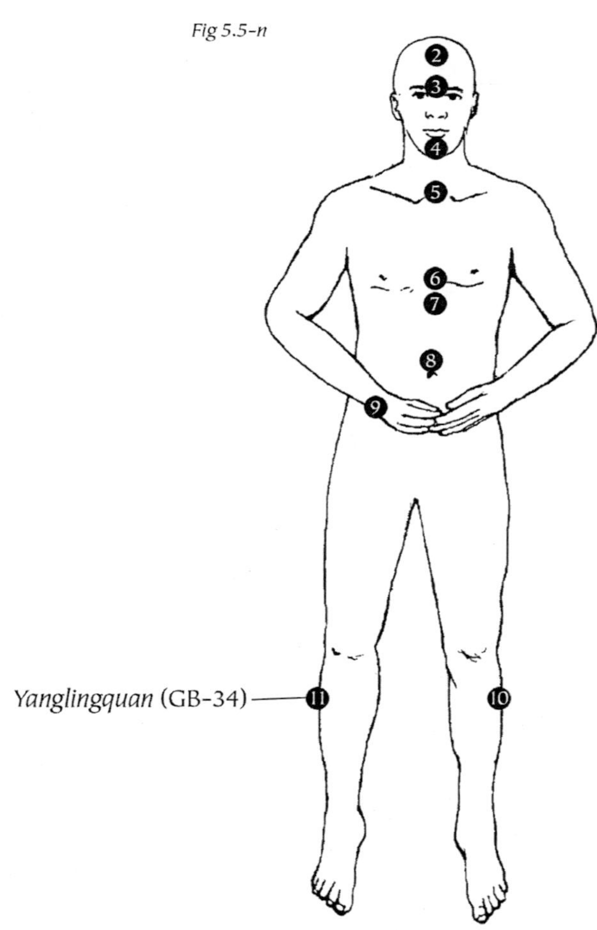

The twelfth and last acupuncture point needled in The Eight Heart-Gates *Shaoyang* Pattern is *Yang Qi* (SJ- 4) located on the dorsum of the left wrist. (See figure 5.5-o below.)

**Eight Heart-Gates *Shaoyang* Pattern**

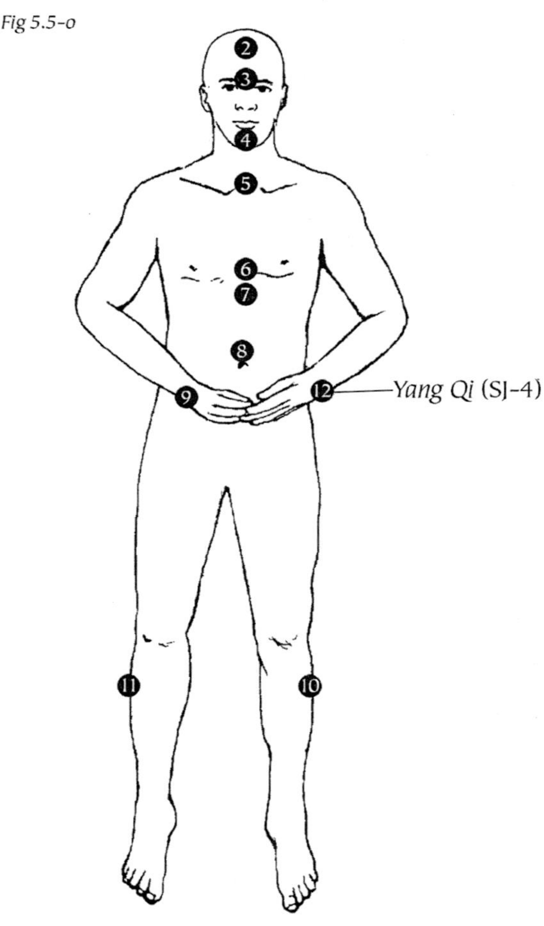

If you notice the needling sequence on these last four acupuncture points, you will again observe an hourglass shaped geometric connection. The bilateral *Yang Qi* (SJ-4) points plus the bilateral *Yanglingquan* (GB-34) points give us the *Shaoyang* connection. But, since we also have an upward pointing fire triangle and a downward pointing water triangle, we have also added an additional Esoteric *Shaoyin* Field. We now have both the *Shaoyang* and *Shaoyin* fields. (See figure 5.5-p below.)

**Dual *Shaoyang* and *Shaoyin* Fields**

*Fig 5.5-p*

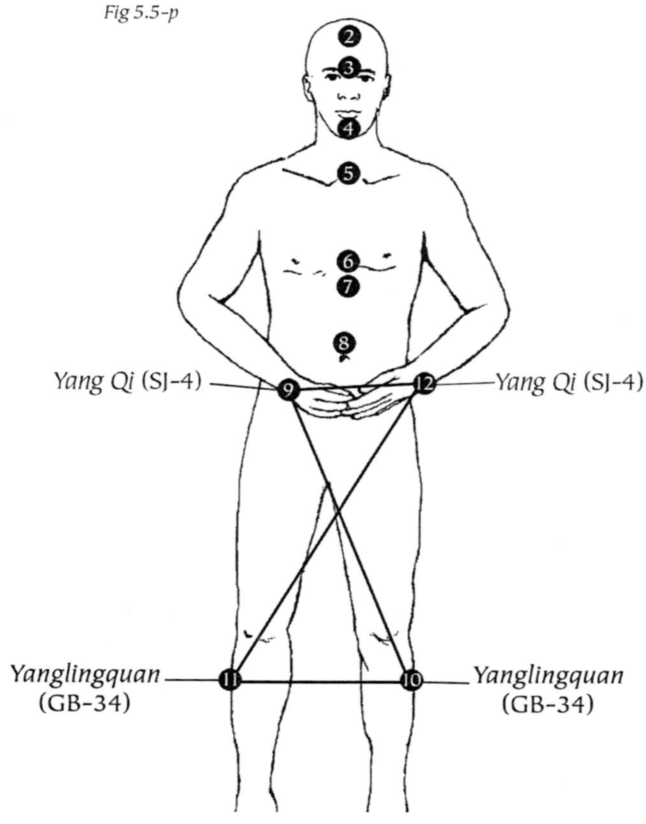

When the twelve acupuncture points of The Eight Heart-Gates *Shaoyang* Pattern are needled in the correct sequence, the Heart Center ascends slightly upward along the anterior midline of the body from the area of the Anahata (Heart Chakra) at the location of *Yuan Jian* (Ren-17) to a slightly higher location. When people tenderly tap this region and say: "I feel it here," or "I feel it in my heart," they are giving acknowledgement to the Inner, Higher Spiritual Heart. But remember, the Inner, Higher spiritual Heart is not located in this region. (See figure 5.5-q below.)

**Eight Heart-Gates *Shaoyang* Pattern**
**Hidden Heart Gate**

Fig 5.5-q

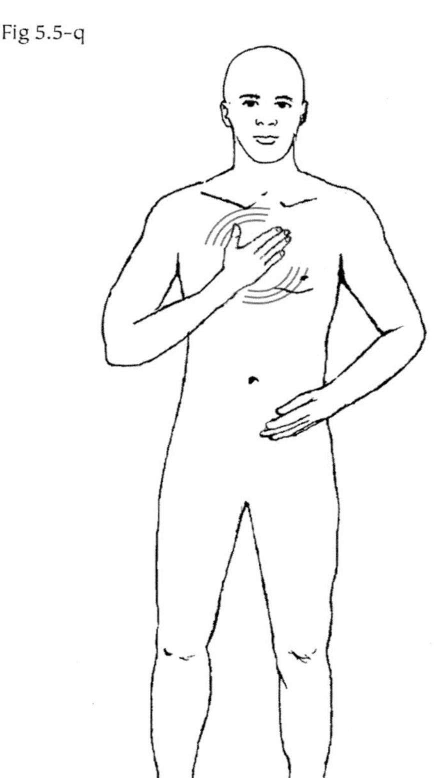

## Eight Heart-Gates *Shaoyang* Pattern
**Complete Grid**

*Fig 5.5-r*

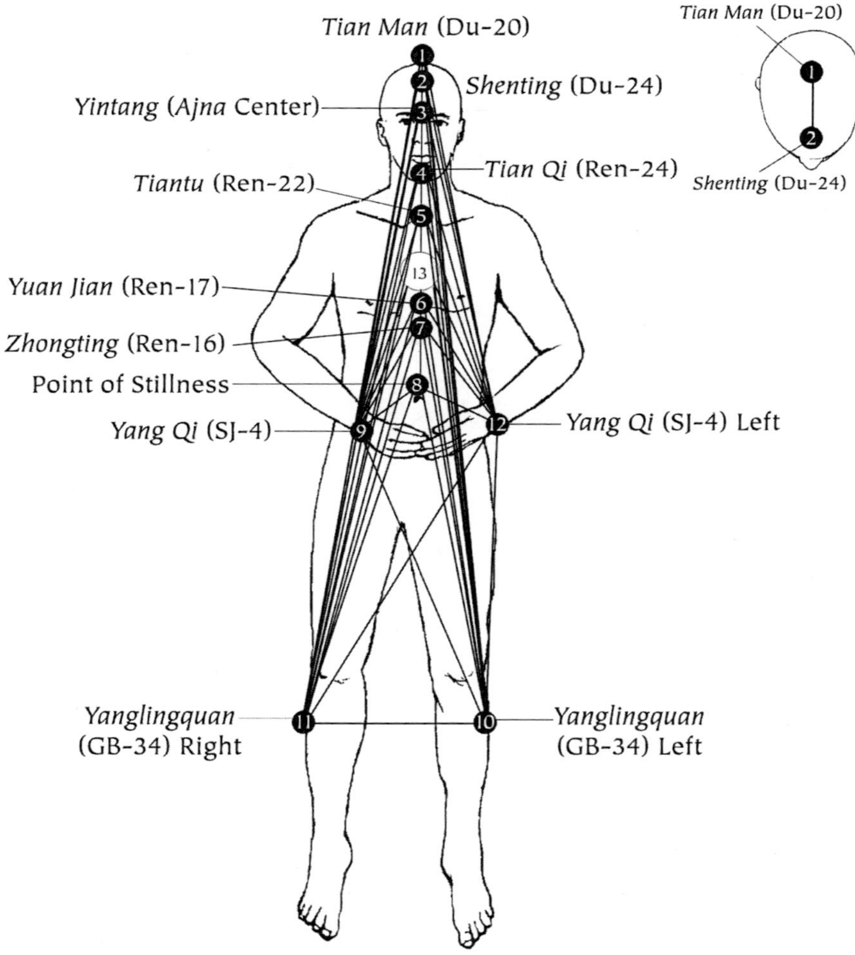

*Tian Man* (Du-20)
*Shenting* (Du-24)
*Yintang* (*Ajna* Center)
*Tian Qi* (Ren-24)
*Tiantu* (Ren-22)
13
*Yuan Jian* (Ren-17)
*Zhongting* (Ren-16)
Point of Stillness
*Yang Qi* (SJ-4)
*Yang Qi* (SJ-4) Left
*Yanglingquan* (GB-34) Right
*Yanglingquan* (GB-34) Left

*Tian Man* (Du-20)
*Shenting* (Du-24)

## Level II Posterior: Option #2
## The Crystalline Waters Pattern

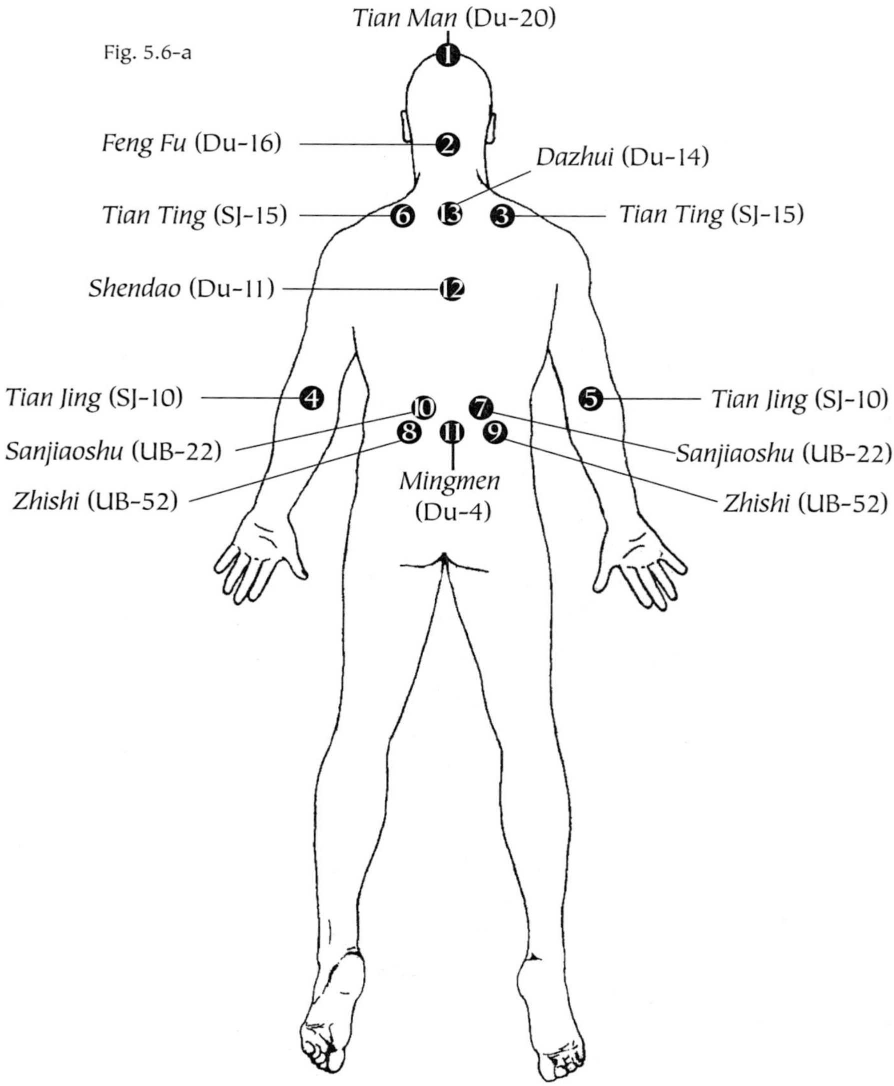

Fig. 5.6-a

**Needling Sequence for The Crystalline Waters Pattern**

1. *Tian Man* (Du-20) "Celestial Fullness"
2. *Feng Fu* (Du-16) "Wind Mansion"
3. *Tian Ting* (SJ-15) "Celestial Hearing" Right side
4. *Tian Jing* (SJ-10) "Celestial Well" Left side
5. *Tian Jing* (SJ-10) "Celestial Well" Right side
6. *Tian Ting* (SJ-15) "Celestial Hearing" Left Side
7. *Sanjiaoshu* (UB-22) "Triple Burner Transporting" Right side
8. *Zhishi* (UB-52) "Will's Dwelling," Left side
9. *Zhishi* (UB-52) "Will's Dwelling," Right side
10. *Sanjiaoshu* (UB-22) "Triple Burner Transporting" Left side
11. *Mingmen* (Du-4) "Gate of Vitality" or "Life Gate"
12. *Shendao* (DU-11) "Spirit Path" or "Heart Path"
13. *Dazhui* (Du-14) "The Big Hammer"

You will notice with the Crystalline Waters Pattern, I have used several *sanjiao* (triple burner) points, along with kidney points and certain specific points to align the Inner, Spiritual Higher Heart Centers. *Sanjiao* is the Chinese term for an acupuncture meridian (channel) that is known to the acupuncturists who prefer the English name as the triple burner or triple heater meridian. There is an upper burner, a middle burner and a lower burner all with various duties that assist in our daily physical functions.

The *sanjiao* meridian and the kidney meridian both influence and exert a level of control over the water pathways of the body. The Crystalline Waters name of this New Encoding Pattern implies that we are working on some level of the kidney system that is associated with the water element in the Chinese Five Element Theory. The idea of water suggests that we are working with form and on a denser plane of consciousness.

Both The Crystalline Waters Pattern and The Discern the Whisper Pattern have thirteen acupuncture sites. Both patterns are also included as options within Tier Density Level 2. Although the similarity of both New Encoding Patterns having thirteen acupuncture points may suggest from one's knowledge and the understanding of the esoteric meaning of sacred numbers, that both New Encoding Patterns are equal in value. But, the Discern the Whisper Pattern has a slightly higher vibrational frequency and is designed to activate a slightly higher plane of consciousness. The Discern the Whisper Pattern is designed to move the *Mingmen* Fire of the kidney system that greatly influences the Swadthisthana (second chakra) to move upward to connect with the Anahata (Heart Chakra). Then qi from both of these centers are able to move upward to connect and communicate with the higher head centers and the centers beyond the head centers.

I have used a bilateral set of acupuncture points called *Sanjiaoshu*. In Chinese, *shu* means transporting. The bilateral *Sanjiaoshu* acupuncture points are on the urinary bladder meridian system and are often referred to as UB-22, which means the twenty-second points on the urinary bladder (UB) meridian. The name UB-22 is the moniker of this *SanJiaoshu* point as taught to the English-speaking students in the acupuncture schools in the United States.

In Chinese medicine, both *sanjiao* and the kidneys control water in the body. They are referring to the physical aspects of water. "The *sanjiao* is the passage of water and food....The *sanjiao* is the official who builds waterways." [8]

The bilateral acupuncture points *Zhishi* (UB-52) are on the urinary bladder meridian, but needling those bilateral urinary bladder acupuncture points stimulates some of the functions of the kidney system. *Zhishi* can be translated as "Will's Dwelling" or "Will Chamber." In Chinese medicine, the kidney system controls our willpower. Thus, *Zhishi* refers to the area that houses the energy that controls or has the capabilities to activate or strengthen one's willpower. Needling these bilateral acupuncture points in an Esoteric Acupuncture session will not only help to strengthen our willpower or motivational energies, but also assist in releasing the constricting energies of fear.

The upper burner or upper *sanjiao* is intimately connected

to the heart. When activating the Sahasrara (Crown Chakra), it is necessary to pass through the Anahata (heart chakra). The Sahasrara is the dormant yang or father aspect. The higher frequencies of the Anahata (heart Chakra) correspond to the yin or mother aspect. You must go through the mother to activate the dormant father. The bilateral acupuncture meridians known as the *sanjiao* pathways are not really a physical system. The *sanjiao* system as described by the Chinese states: "It has a name, but no form." [9] The idea of "That which has no form," means that one has entered into some level of the state of Stillness and Oneness. Having no form is similar to what Taoists believe. This idea of "no form" an attribute of the *sanjiao* (three burner) system in acupuncture that is important in the deeper understanding of the Crystalline Waters Pattern. We are aligning the frequencies to move into the higher levels of the heart to enter into the higher areas of the Sahasrara (Crown Chakra) domain. We are interested in awakening. Disease is the field of constriction. Healing is expansion. Awakening into the expansive field of consciousness is the real healing.

In the Chinese Five Element Theory, it is stated that the kidneys control the water element. In the Esoteric teachings, the kidneys represent the number 2. This does not merely refer to the fact that there are two kidneys in the body.

Water has very unique properties. When water is frozen, it takes on a very a dense quality in the form of ice. In this dense form, water is very constricted. Water in its more normal state, requires some sort of container to hold its form. Water in this state will conform to any shape of the container. This means that water is controlled and shaped by the container. If something is controlled, it is not free. In a more refined state, water becomes steam and will take on any shape. If steam is within a container, steam will take the shape of the container. If there is open space, steam will expand without any constricting boundaries. The ability of water to be able to change into various physical states of denseness or refinement represents the idea that consciousness can stay in its present state and remain stagnant, become more constricted and move into a denser state of existence, or transmute its denseness into a more refined state. This is the concept of fear transmuting its dense frequencies and eventually moving into a more refined state of love and the heart.

Another property of water is its ability to reflect objects. The esoteric attachment of the number 2 with the kidneys partially refers to waters ability to reflect. The Chinese say that the kidneys control fear. The other aspect of the kidneys being esoterically connected to the number 2 is that fear is connected to the number 2. Fear has a more chaotic energy field than the calmness of a harmonized heart. Water is esoterically related to chaos. But, from chaos comes order. This is the concept of having to experience certain levels of fear and chaos then learning from those challenges to eventually opening up one's heart and moving into the higher heart space. The heart is esoterically related to the number 1.

Water also has the property of being able to receive light. When the energy is of a more dense nature, you will see a reflection corresponding to the number 2. When both the energy surrounding water and the water itself becomes more refined, water will receive the light. This state corresponds to the number 1, which is the esoteric number of the heart and love. Instead of reflecting the light, the light merges with the water to esoterically symbolize Oneness. When you are in your true heart space, you do not need or require anything outside of you. If you feel that you need something or someone to make you complete, you are resonating in the kidney frequency of the number 2.

### Point Locations for The Crystalline Waters Pattern

The first acupuncture point needled in The Crystalline Waters Pattern is *Tian Man* (Du-20). Just a reminder that the esoteric location of Du-20 is located approximately one inch posteriorly to the traditional location of the Du-20 known as

*Bai Hui*. It is important to activate the esoteric Du-20, instead of activating the traditional Du-20.

The second acupuncture site needled is *Feng Fu* (Du-16). *Feng Fu* (Du-16) is located directly on the posterior vertical midline on the back of the head in the depression below the occipital protuberance where the head meets the neck. *Feng Fu* (Du-16) is approximately one *cun* superior to the posterior hairline on the back of the head.

The third acupuncture point needled in The Crystalline Waters Pattern is *Tian Ting* (SJ-15) on the right shoulder. First locate *Jianjing* (GB-21) on the highest part of the shoulder midway between the center of the spine and the acromial end. (See figure 5.6-b below.)

**Crystalline Waters Pattern**

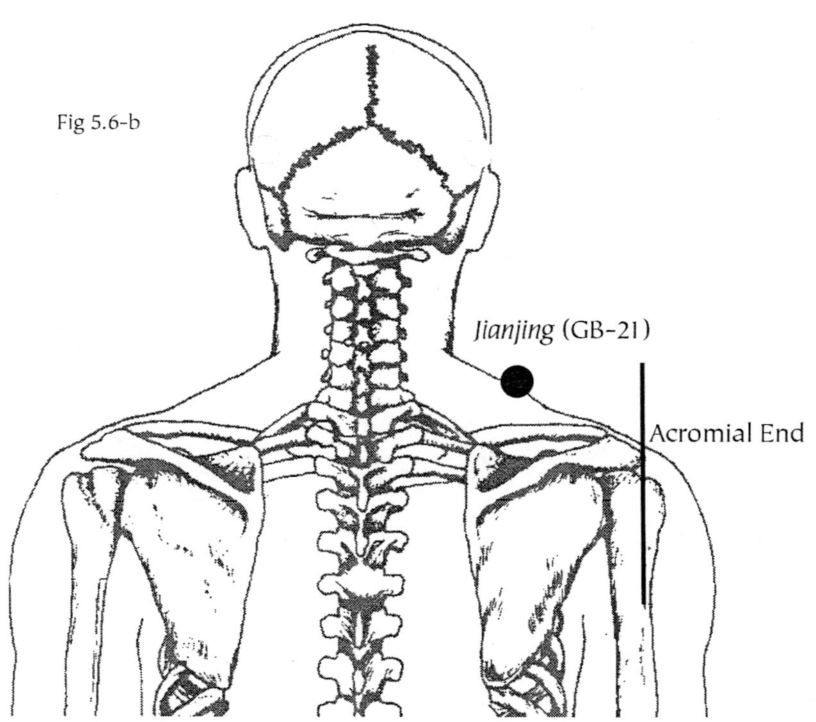

Next feel for the medial end of the suprascapular fossa. *Quyuan* (SI-13) located in the slight depression superior to the medial end of the scapular spine. (See figure 5.6-c below.)

## Crystalline Waters Pattern

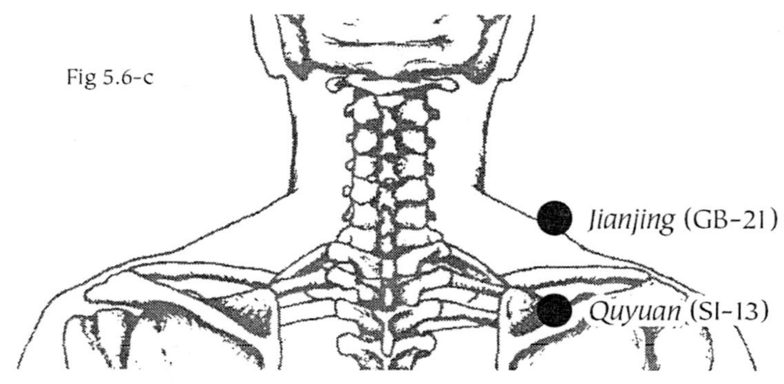


*Tian Ting* (SJ-15) is located posteriorly to *Jianjing* (GB-21) and is found approximately halfway between *Jianjing* (GB-21) and *Quyuan* (SI-13). (See figure 5.6-d below.)

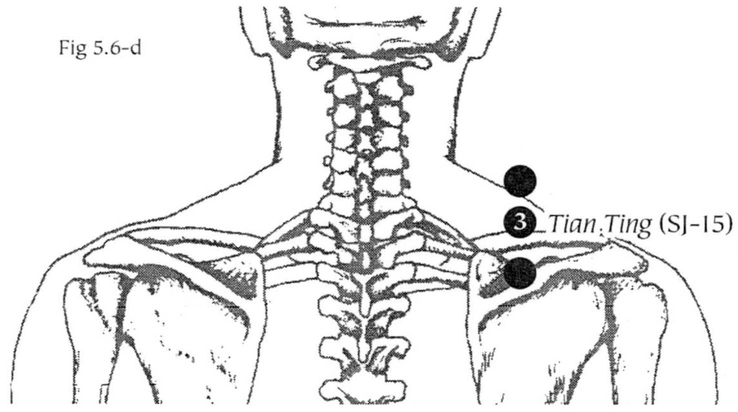

The fourth acupuncture site needled is the bilateral *Tian Jing* (SJ-10) point on the left arm located in the slight depression approximately one *cun* from the olecranon (elbow bone) when the arm is slightly bent. (See figure 5.6-e below.)

**Crystalline Waters Pattern**

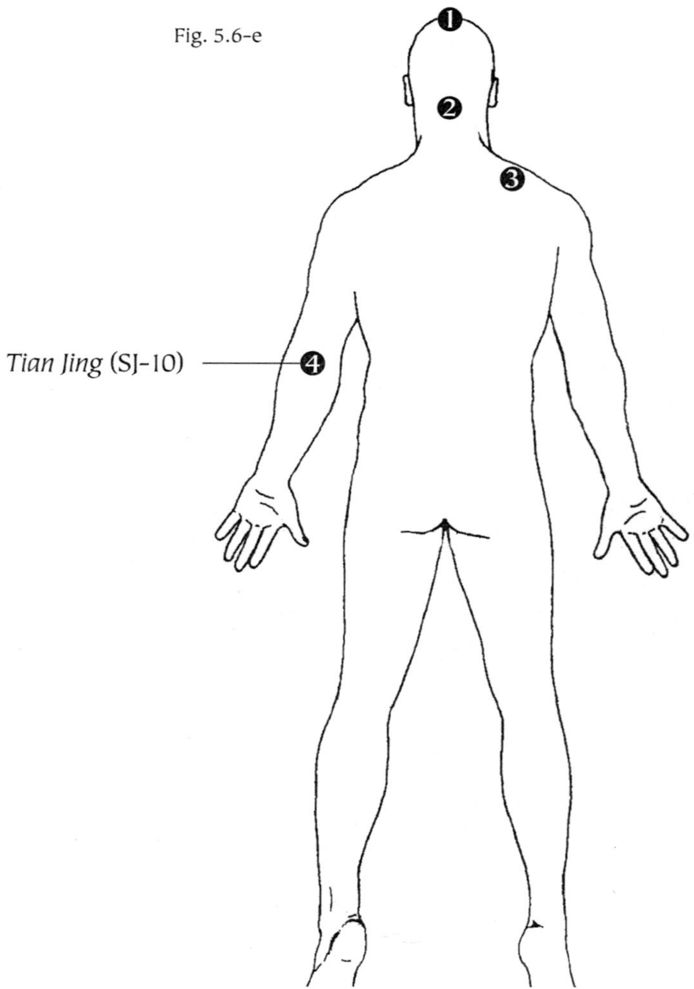

The fifth acupuncture point needled in the Crystalline Waters Pattern is *Tian Jing* (SJ-10) on the right arm. (See figure 5.6-f below.)

## Crystalline Waters Pattern

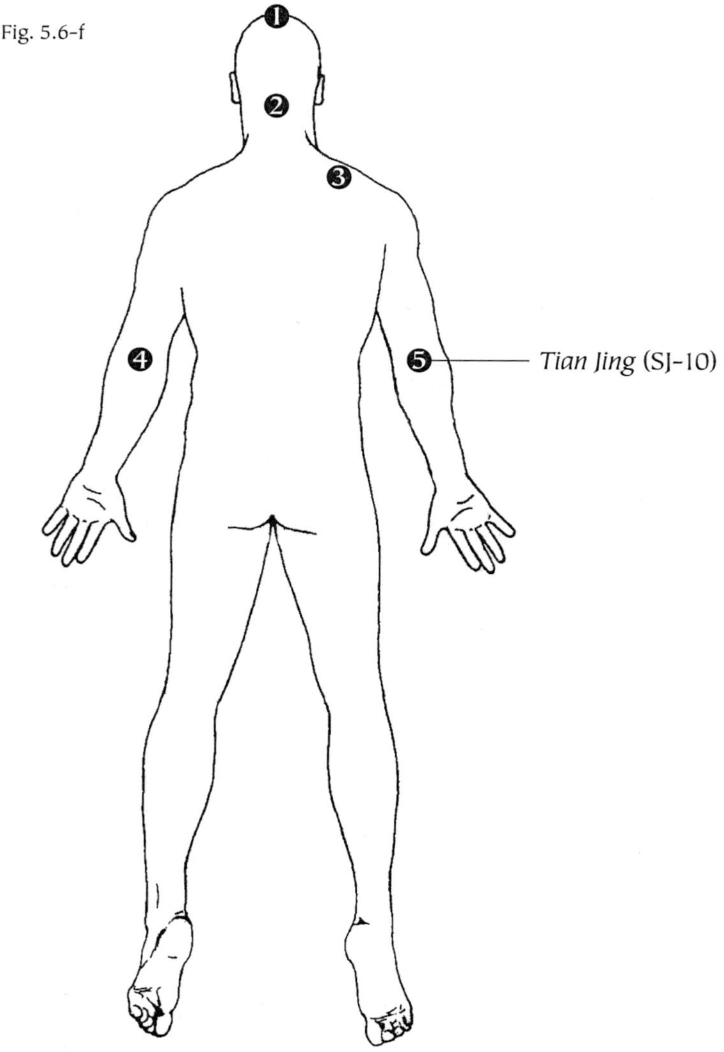


Fig. 5.6-f

The sixth acupuncture point needled in the Crystalline Waters Pattern is *Tian Ting* (SJ-15) located on the client's left shoulder. (See figure 5.6-g below.)

## Crystalline Waters Pattern

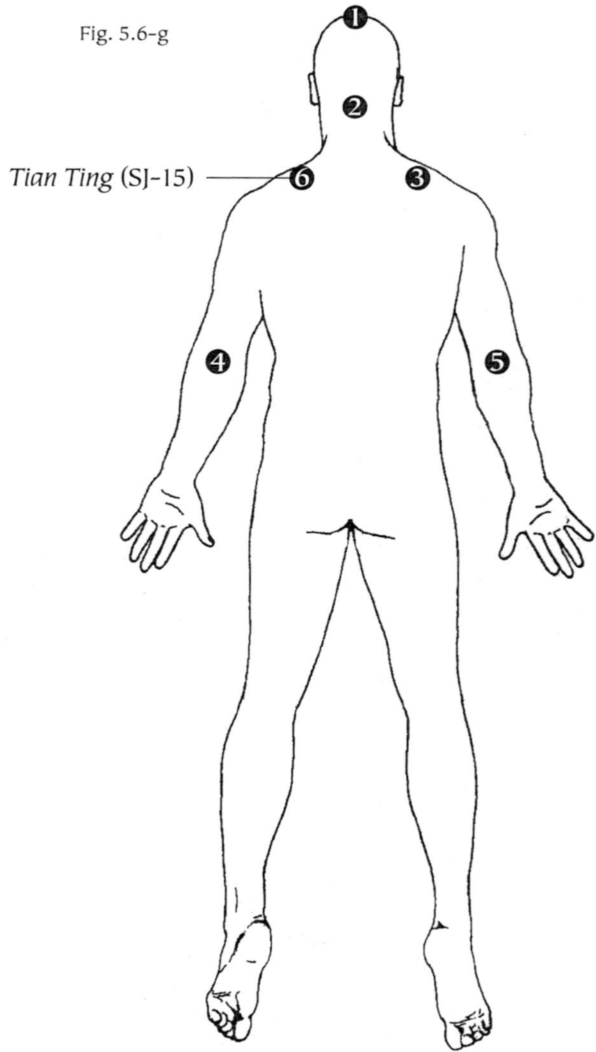

The seventh acupuncture site needled in the Crystalline Waters Pattern is *Sanjiaoshu* (UB-22) on the right side. The bilateral *Sanjiaoshu* (UB-22) points are located approximately one and one-half *cun* from the center of the spine and level with the lower border of the first lumbar vertebrae. (See figure 5.6-h below.)

**Crystalline Waters Pattern**

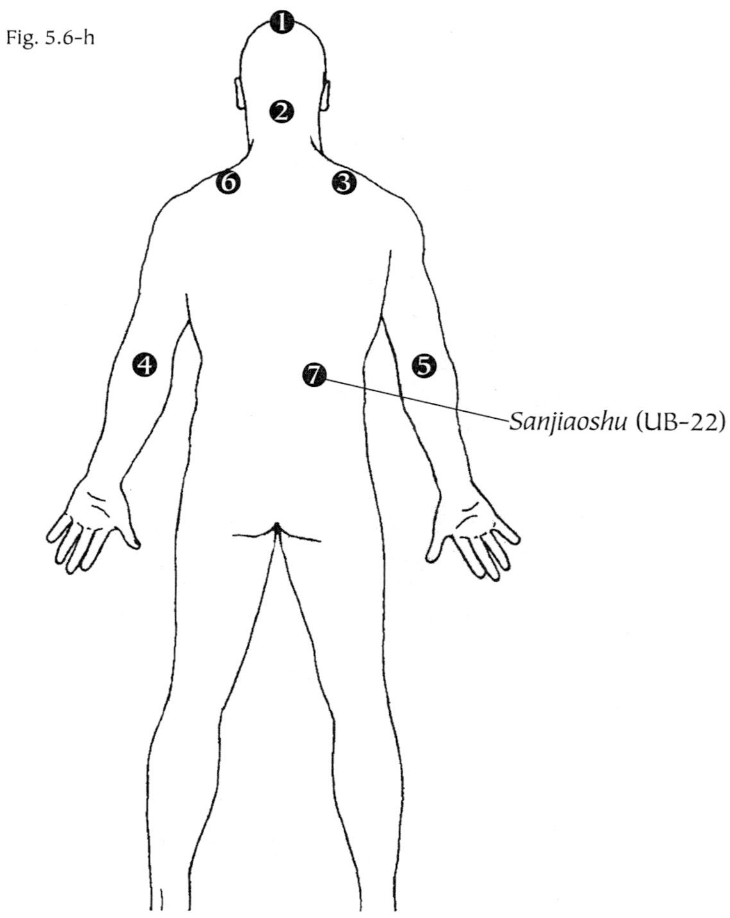


Fig. 5.6-h

The eighth and ninth acupuncture points needled in the Crystalline Waters Pattern are the bilateral *Zhishi* (UB-52) points. *Zhishi* (UB-52) is found approximately three *cun* bilaterally on each side of the spine level with the lower border of the spinous process of the first lumbar spine. The bilateral *Zhishi* (UB-52) points are on the outer bladder meridian versus the bilateral *Sanjiaoshu* (UB-22) points that are on the inner bladder meridian. Needle the client's left side first. (See figure 5.6-I below.)

## Crystalline Waters Pattern

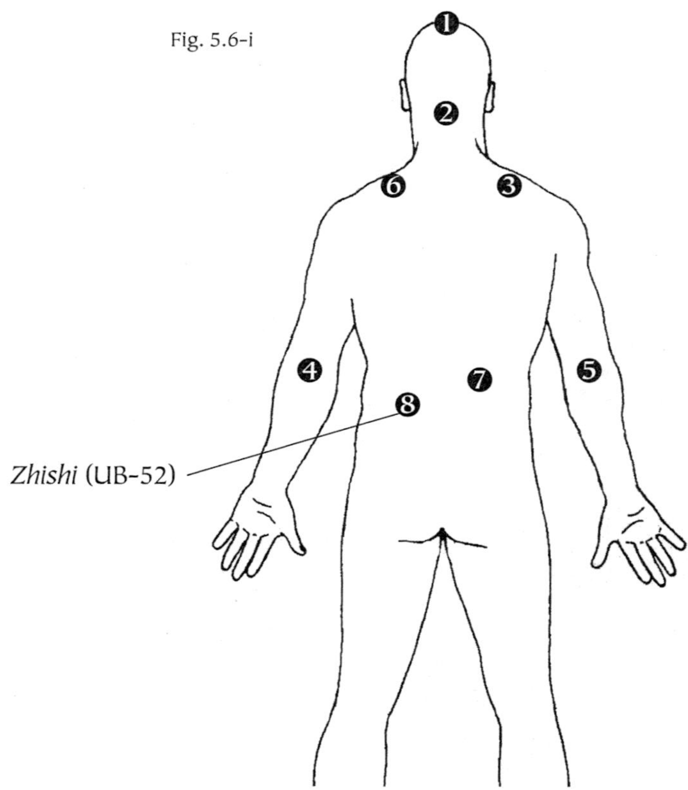

The ninth acupuncture point needled in the Crystalline Waters Pattern is the *Zhishi* (UB-52) point found on the client's right side. (See figure 5.6-j below.)

**Crystalline Waters Pattern**

Fig. 5.6-j

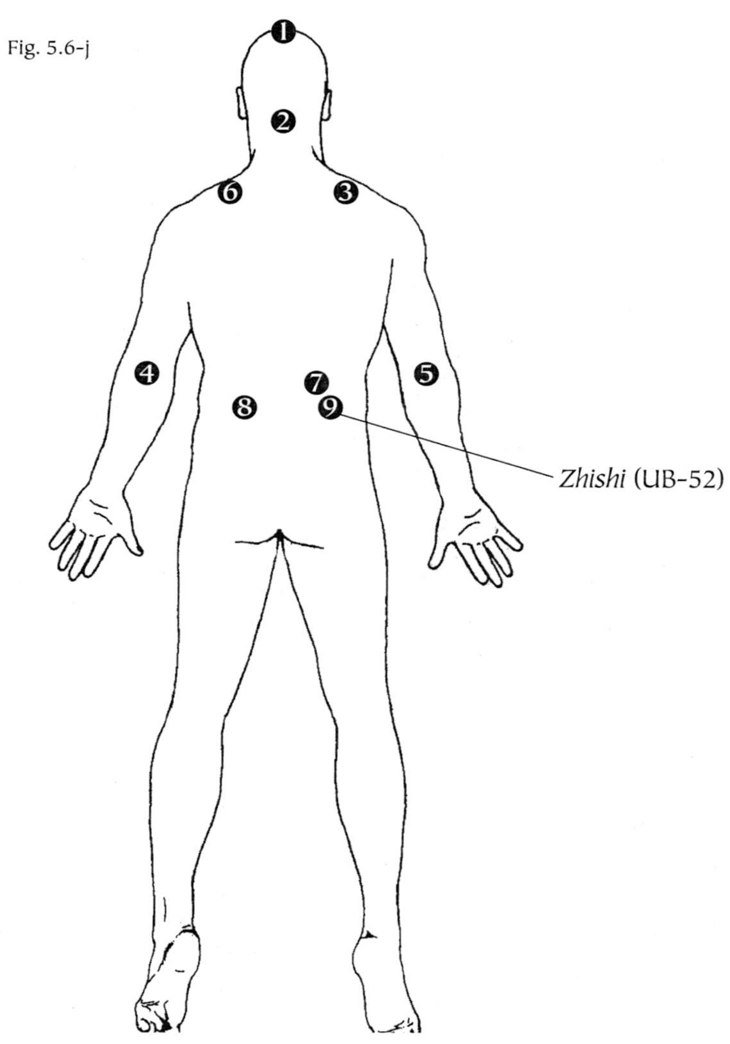

The tenth acupuncture point needled in the Crystalline Waters Pattern is *Sanjiaoshu* (UB-22) on the client's left side. (See figure 5.6-k below.)

## Crystalline Waters Pattern

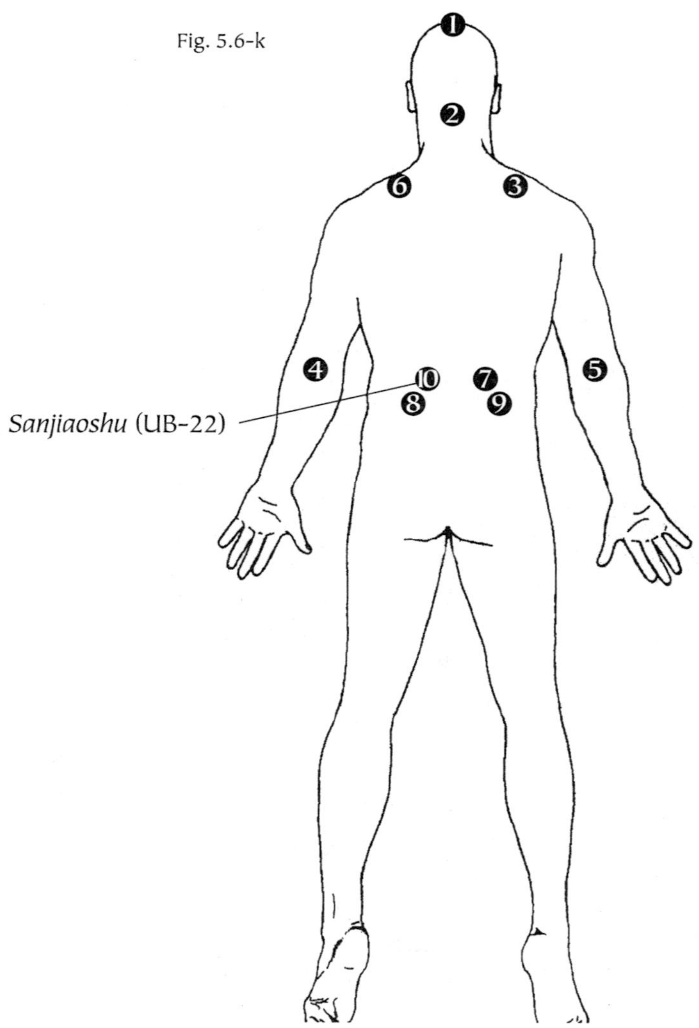

The eleventh acupuncture point needled in The Crystalline Waters Pattern is *Mingmen* (Du-4) located directly on the spine below the lower border of the spinous process of the second lumbar vertebrae. *Mingmen* (Du-4) should be on the imaginary horizontal line that is level with the bilateral *Zhishi* (UB-52) points. (See figure 5.6-l below.)

## Crystalline Waters Pattern

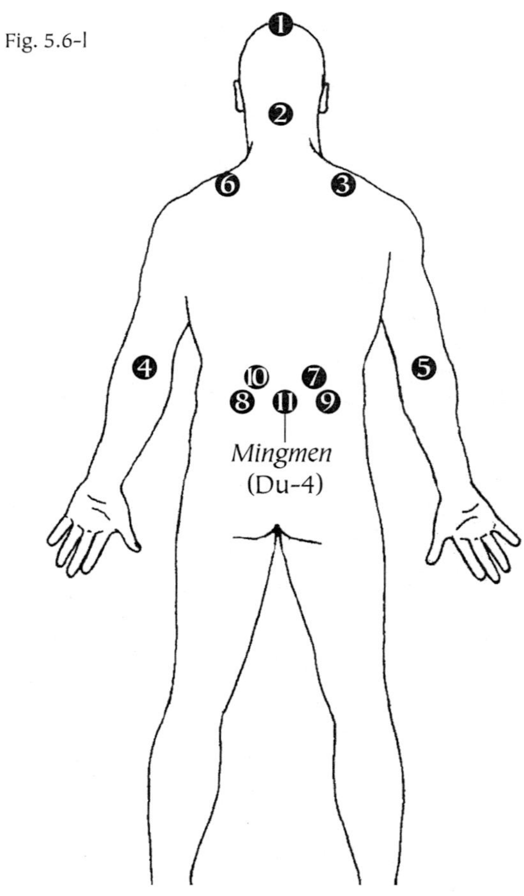

The twelfth acupuncture point needled in the Crystalline Waters Pattern is *Shendao* (Du-11). *Shendao* (Du-11) is located directly on the spine below the lower border of the spinous process of the fifth thoracic vertebra. *Shendao* (Du-11) is translated to mean "Spirit Gate," "Heart Gate," or "Path of the Evolved Person." (See figure 5.6-m below.)

## Crystalline Waters Pattern

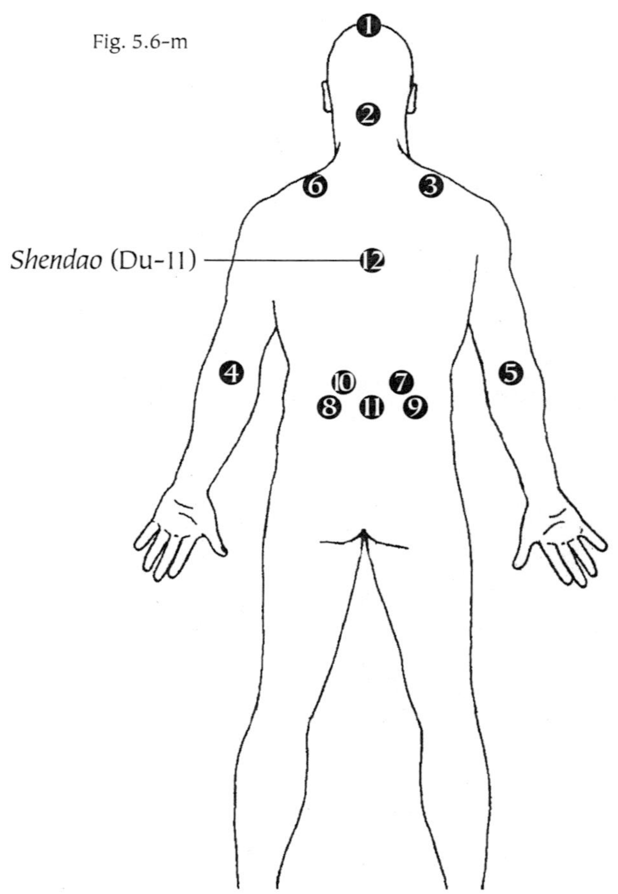

The thirteenth and last acupuncture point needled in the Crystalline Waters Pattern is *Dazhui* (Du-14.) (See figure 5.6-n below.)

## Crystalline Waters Pattern

Fig. 5.6-n

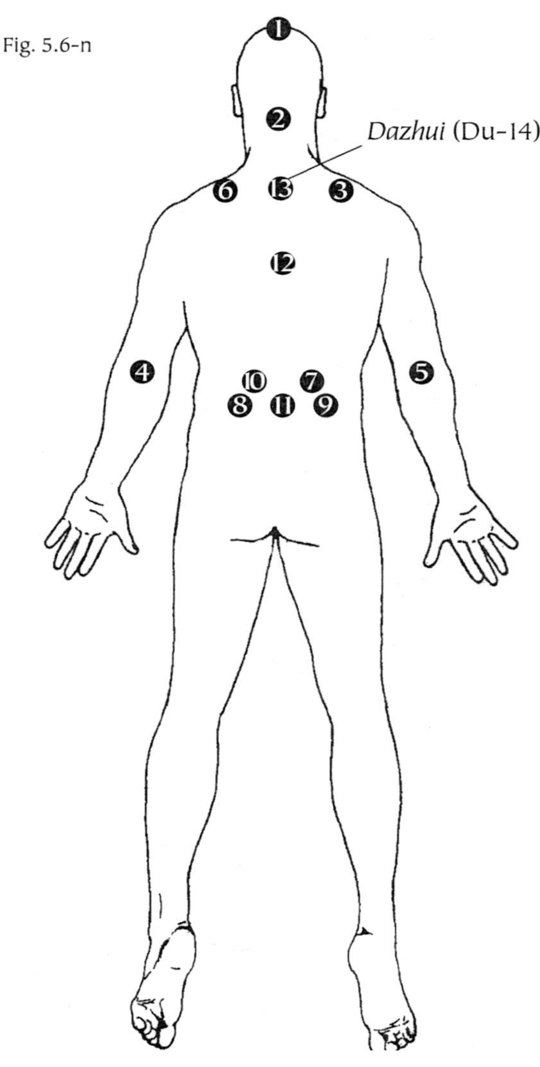

## Visualizations for The Crystalline Waters Pattern

The first point needled in The Crystalline Waters Pattern is *Tian Man* (Du-20) on the top of the client's head. Remember that the esoteric location of *Tian Man* (Du-20) is posterior to the traditional Chinese location of *Bai Hui* (Du-20). The second acupuncture point needled is *Feng Fu* (Du-16). We start the visualization process after needling only these first two points. Visually bring qi from *Tian Man* (Du-20) downward to connect with the qi of *Feng Fu* (Du-16) following the Du channel flow. (See figure 5.6-o below.)

### Crystalline Waters Pattern Visualizations

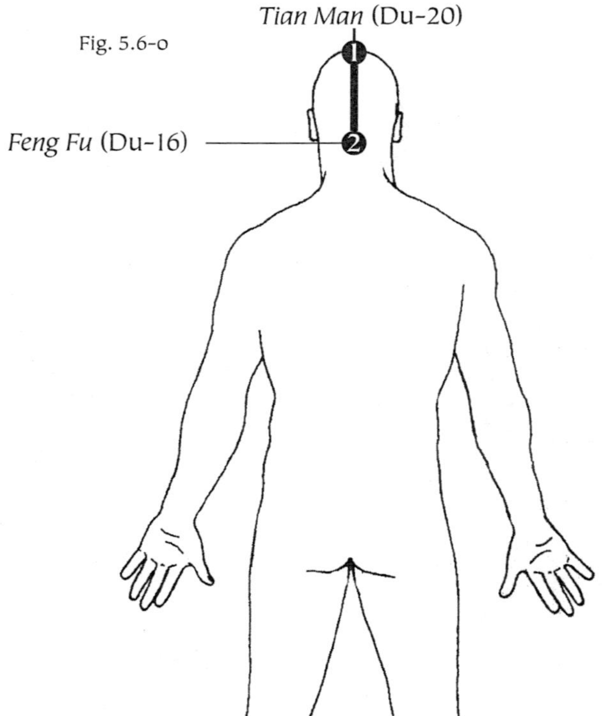

Needle the next four acupuncture sites and resume the visualization process. Have your client visualize the energies from *Tian Ting* (SJ-15) on the right shoulder area connecting with the *Tian Jing* (SJ-10) point on the left elbow. (See figure 5.6-p below.)

## Crystalline Waters Pattern Visualizations

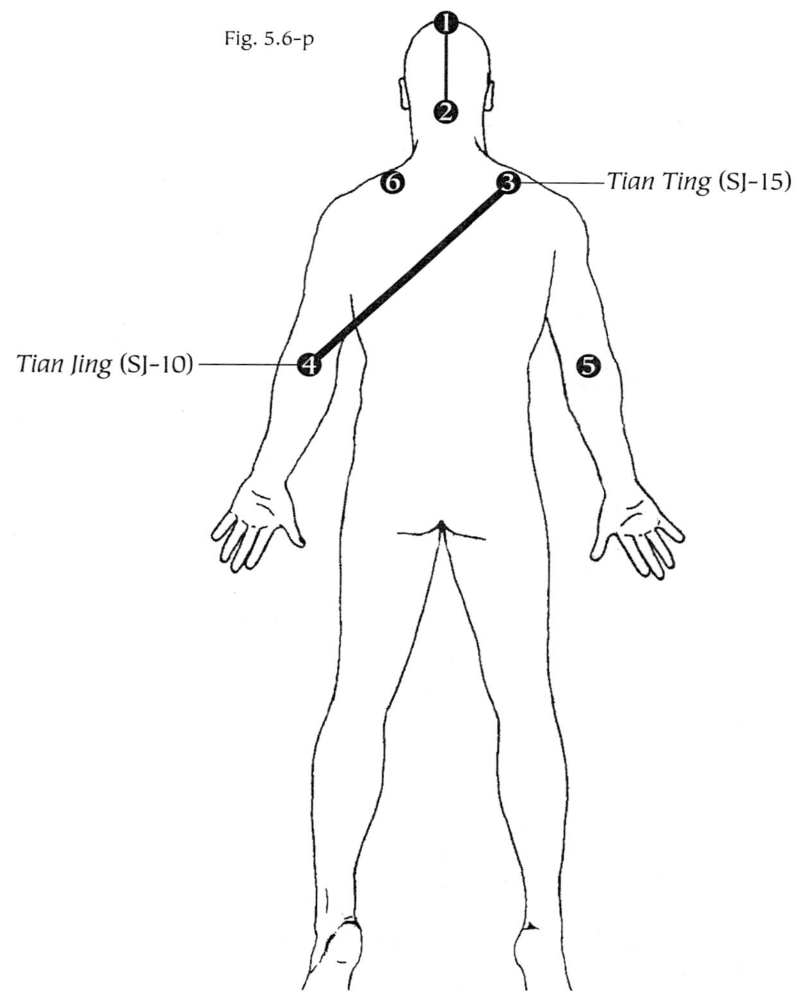

Next visually have your client connect the left *Tian Jing* (SJ-10) point to the *Tian Jing* (SJ-10) point on the right elbow. (See figure 5.6-q below.)

## Crystalline Waters Pattern Visualizations

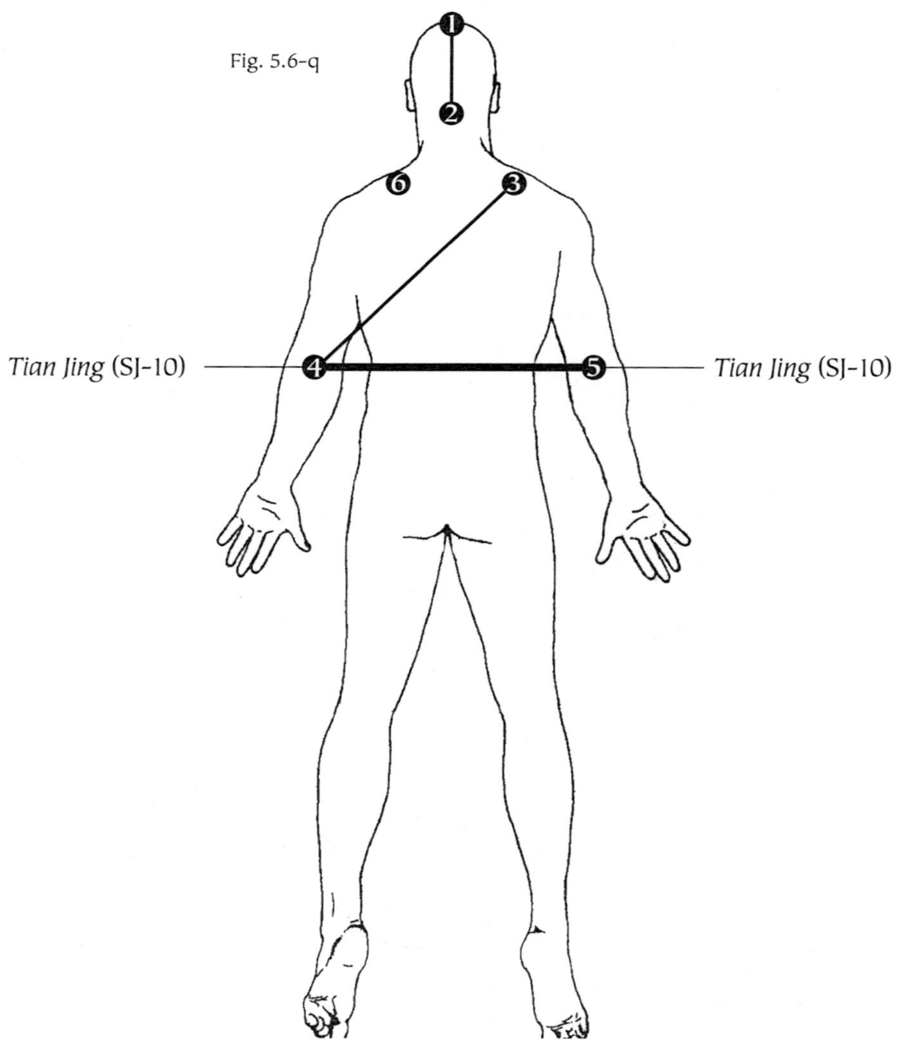

Now have your client visually connect the *Tian Jing* (SJ-10) point on the right elbow with the *Tian Ting* (SJ-15) point on the left shoulder. (See figure 5.6-r below.)

## Crystalline Waters Pattern Visualizations

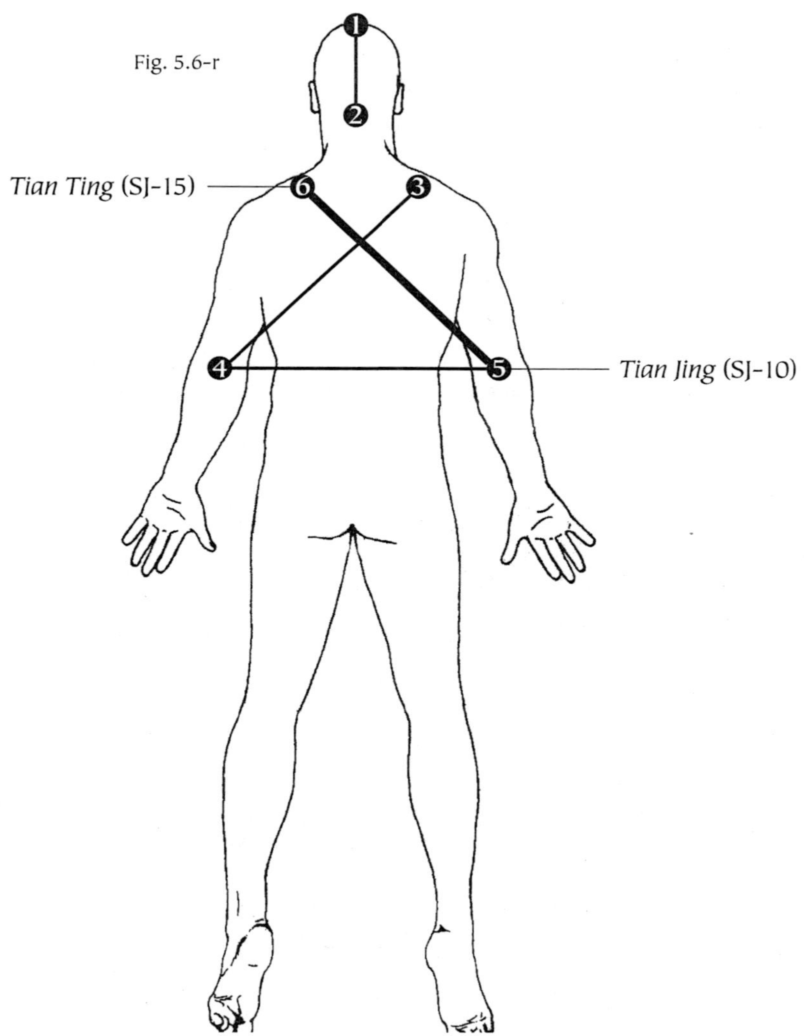

You will now connect the bilateral *Tian Ting* (SJ-15) points with each other. Have you client visually connect the *Tian Ting* (SJ-15) point on the left shoulder with the *Tian Ting* (SJ-15) point on the right shoulder. (See figure 5.6-s below.)

## Crystalline Waters Pattern Visualizations

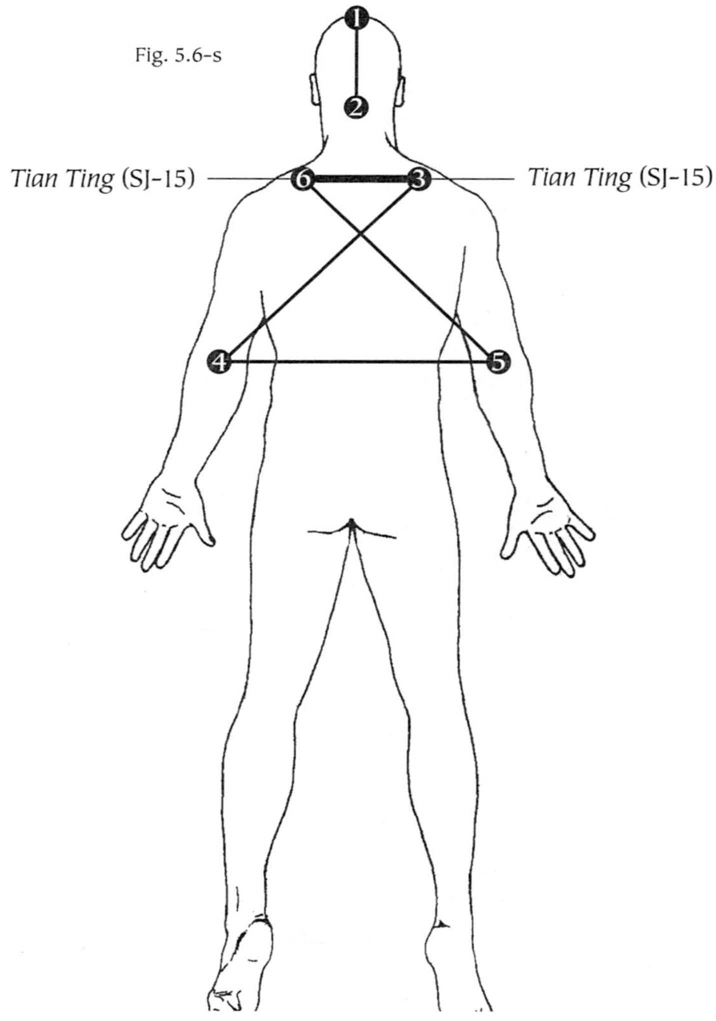


Fig. 5.6-s

After the hourglass shaped visualization has been made, bring the energies from the bilateral *Tian Ting* (SJ-15) points upward to connect with *Feng Fu* (Du-16). We have created another Fire Triangle. (See figure 5.6-t below.)

## Crystalline Waters Pattern Visualizations

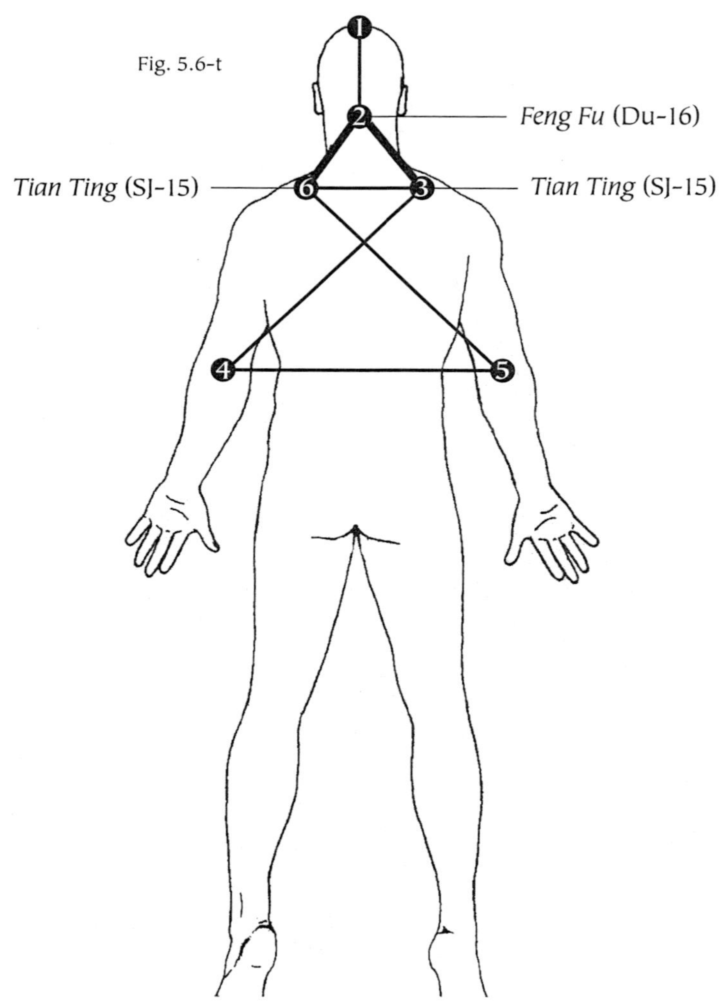


Fig. 5.6-t

Have your client now bring the energies upward from *Tian Jing* (SJ-10) on the right side to connect with *Tian Ting* (SJ-15) on the right side. (See figure 5.6-u below.)

### Crystalline Waters Pattern Visualizations

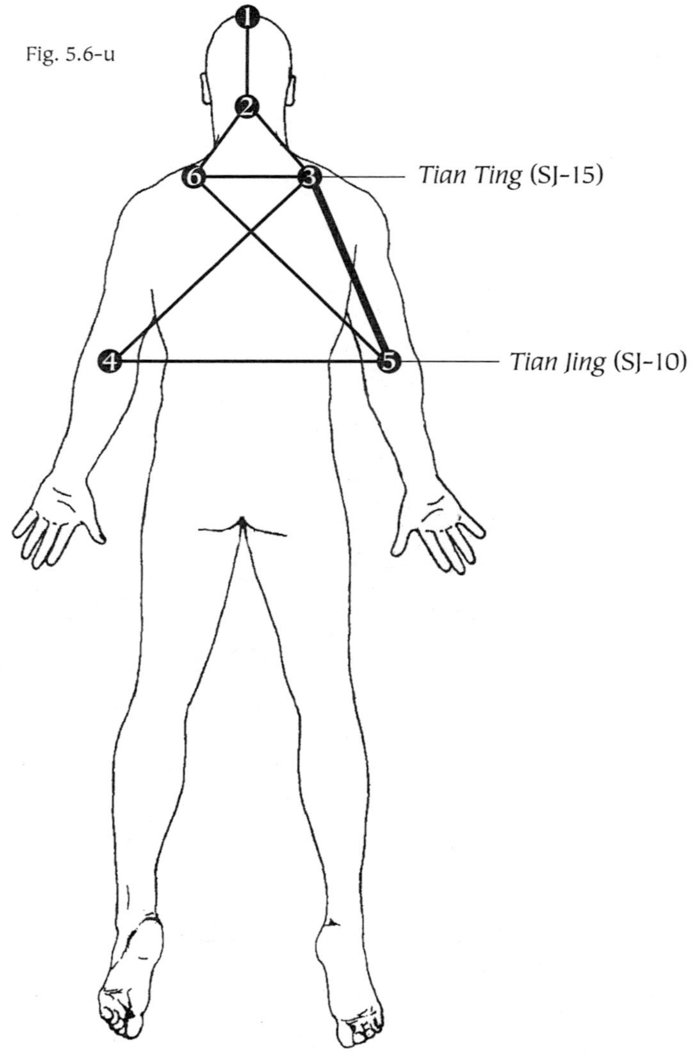


Fig. 5.6-u

Next have your client now bring the energies upward from *Tian Jing* (SJ-10) on the left side to connect with the acupuncture point *Tian Ting* (SJ-15) on the left side. (See figure 5.6-v below.)

**Crystalline Waters Pattern Visualizations**

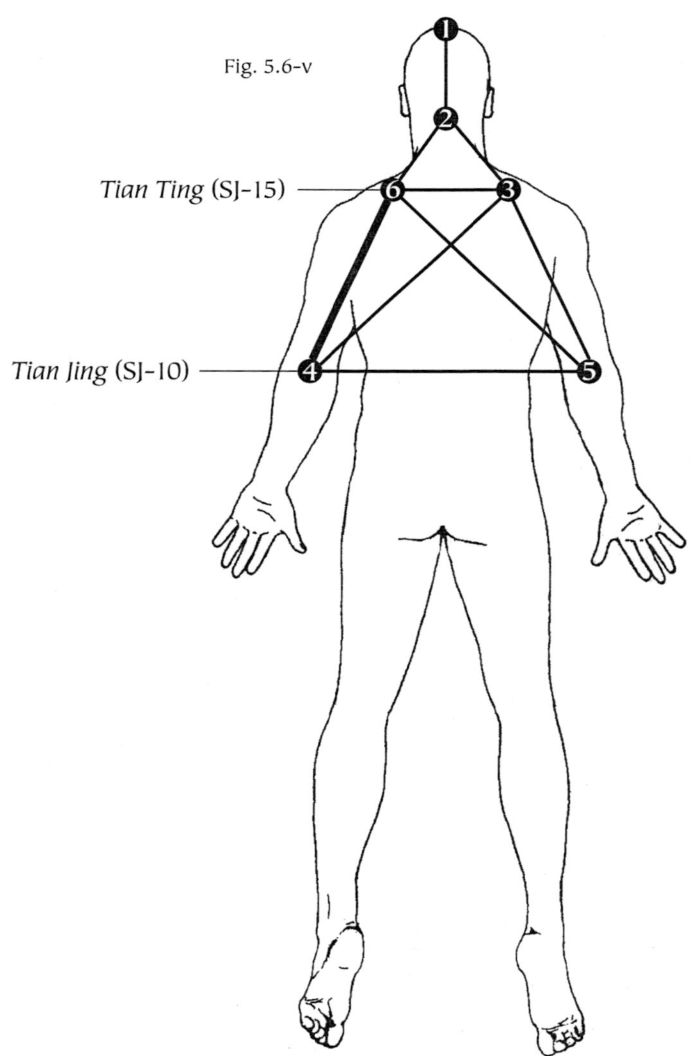


Fig. 5.6-v

Needle the next four acupuncture sites. Have your client visually connect *Sanjiaoshu* (UB-22) on the right side to *Zhishi* (UB-52) on the left side. (See figure 5.6-w below.)

## Crystalline Waters Pattern Visualizations

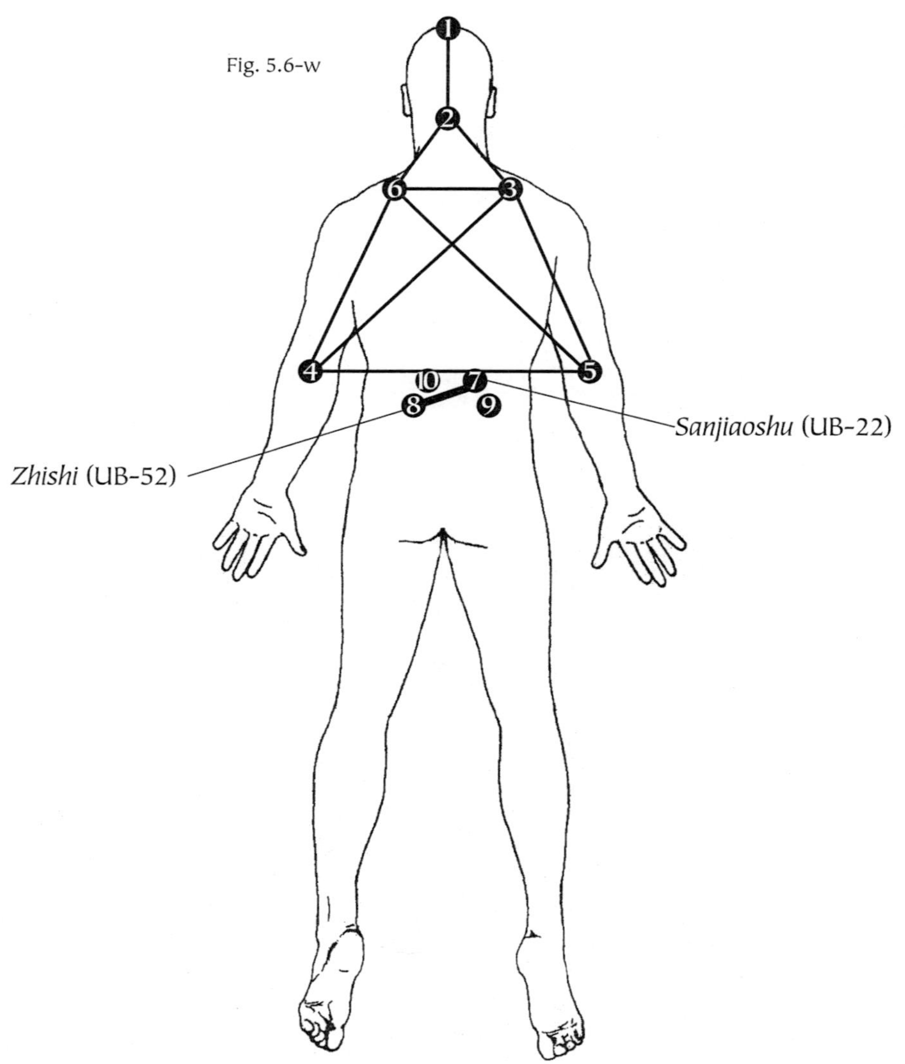


Fig. 5.6-w

Next have your client visually connect the bilateral outer bladder kidney points *Zhishi* (UB-52) to each other. Visually connect *Zhishi* (UB-52) on the left side to *Zhishi* (UB-52) on the right side. (See figure 5.6-x below.)

**Crystalline Waters Pattern Visualizations**

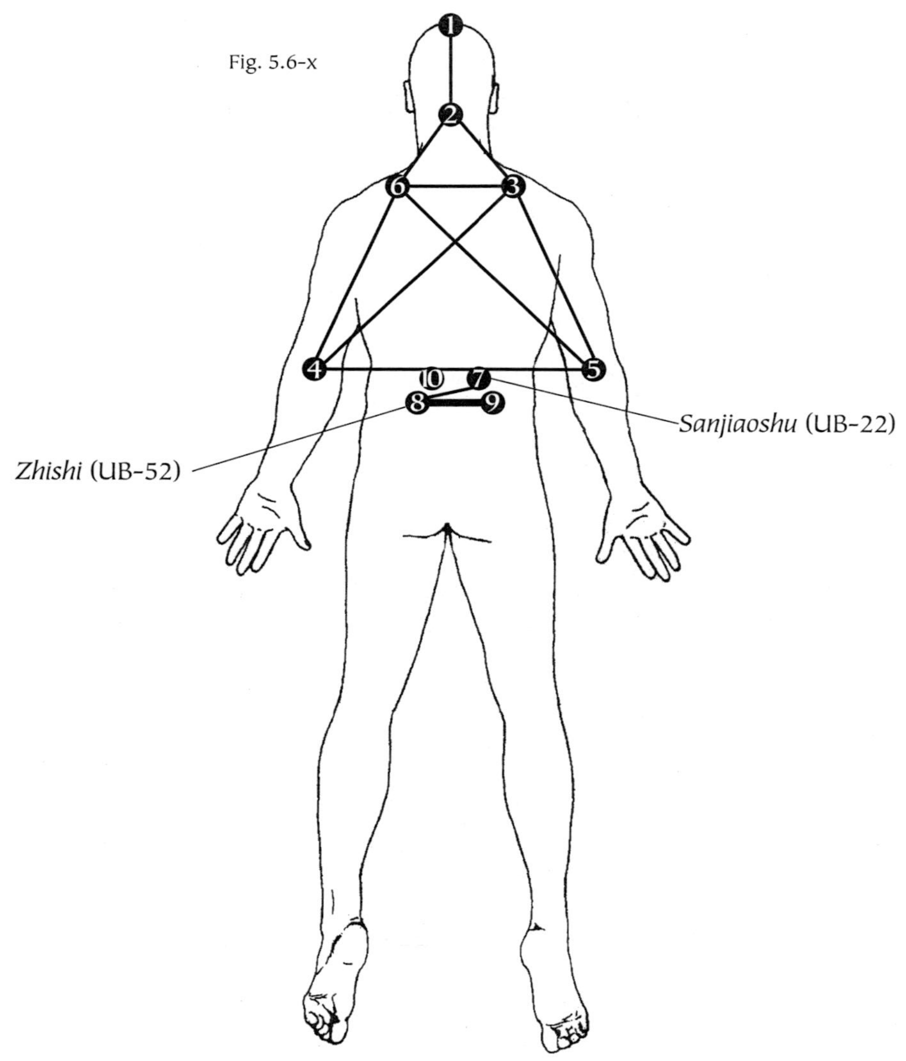

Fig. 5.6-x

Now have your client visually connect the *Zhishi* (UB-52) point on the right side with the *Sanjiaoshu* (UB-22) point on the left side. (See figure 5.6-y below.)

## Crystalline Waters Pattern Visualizations

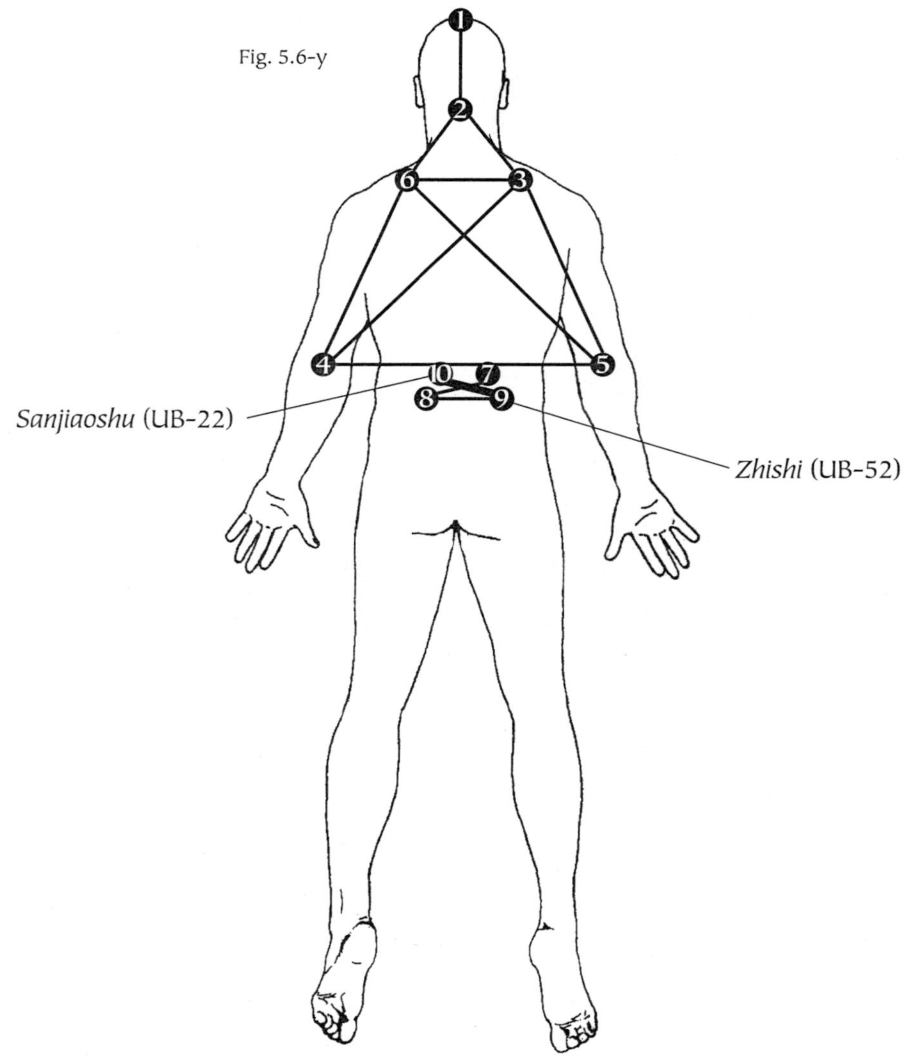


Fig. 5.6-y

Next have your client visually connect the bilateral *SanJiaoshu* (UB-22) points together. (See figure 5.6-z below.)

**Crystalline Waters Pattern Visualizations**

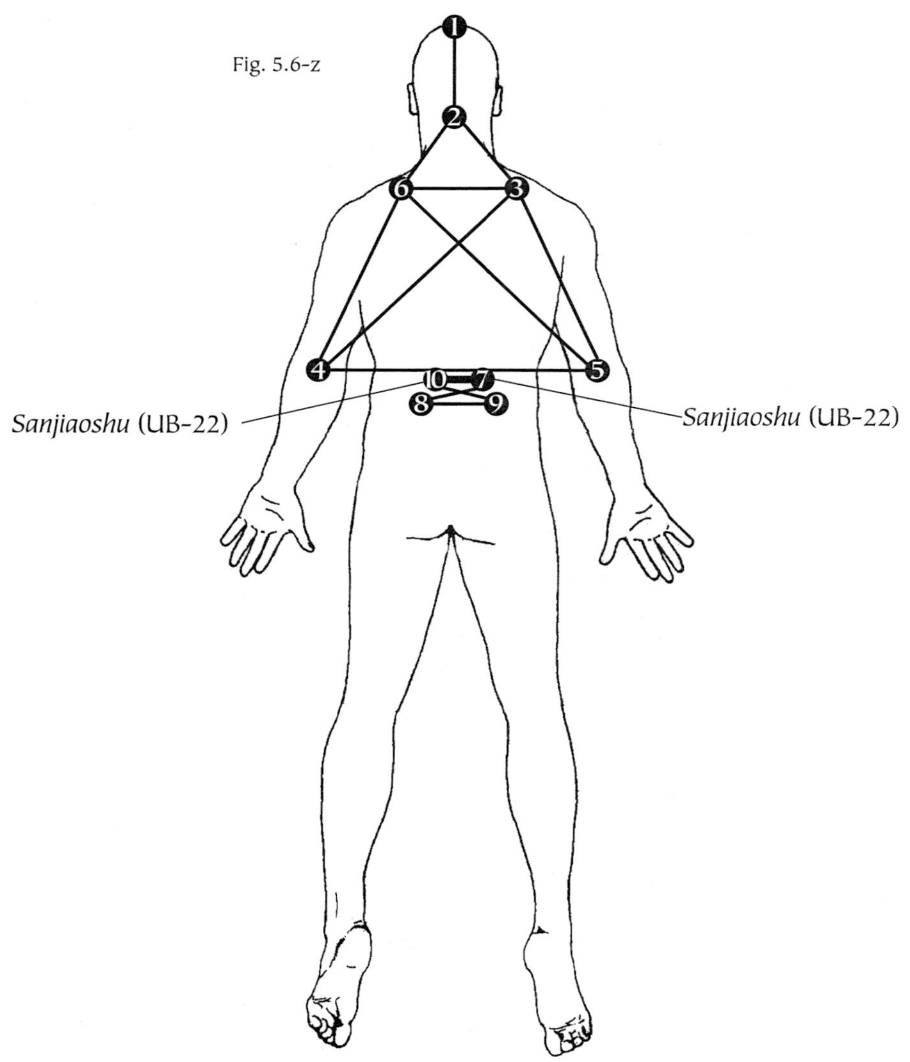


Fig. 5.6-z

Insert an acupuncture needle into the site of *Mingmen* (Du-4) located directly on the spine between the bilateral *Zhishi* (UB-52) points. (See figure 5.6-aa below.)

## Crystalline Waters Pattern Visualizations

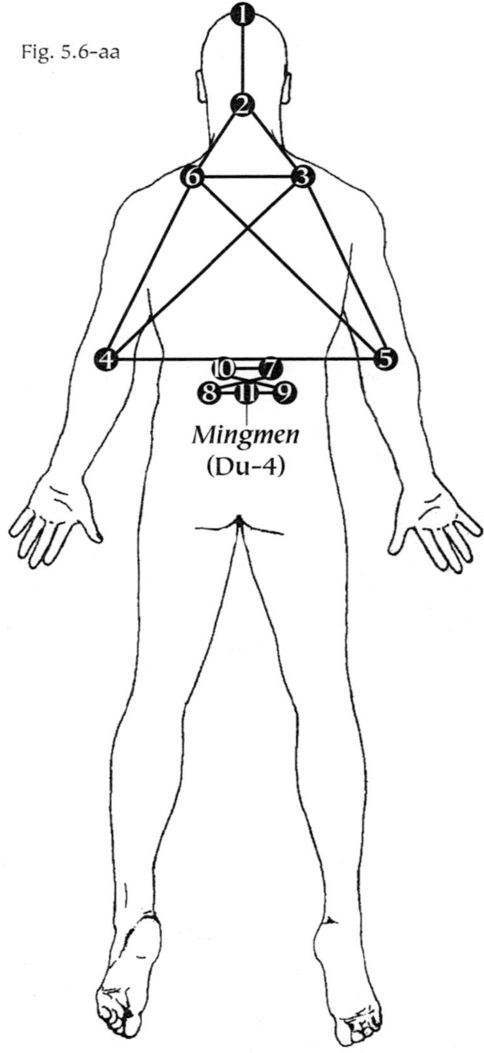


Fig. 5.6-aa

Now have your client bring the energies from the bilateral *Sanjiaoshu* (UB-22) points (#7 & #10) downward to connect to *Mingmen* (Du-4). We have again formed a Water Triangle pointing downward. (See figure 5.6-bb below.)

## Crystalline Waters Pattern Visualizations

Fig. 5.6-bb

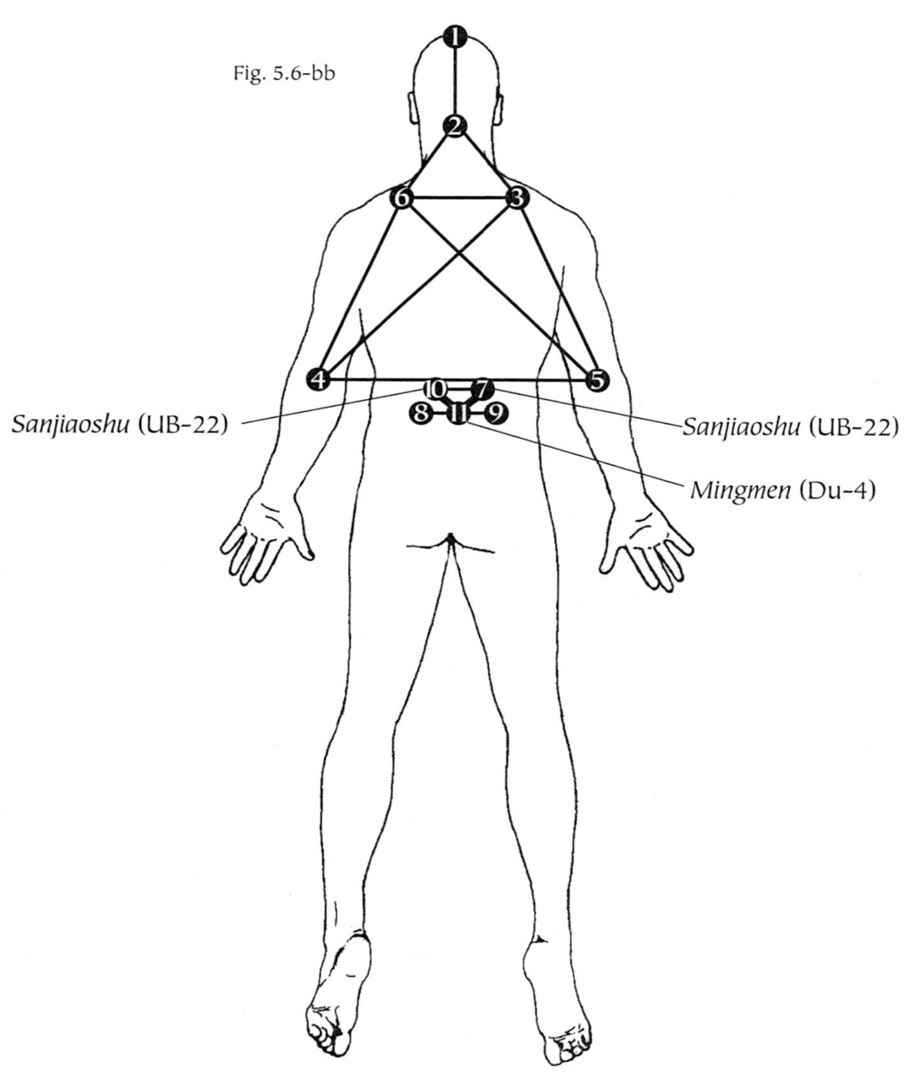

Now insert an acupuncture needle at the site of *Shendao* (Du-11) directly on the spine below the spinous process of the fifth thoracic vertebra. (See figure 5.6-cc below.)

**Crystalline Waters Pattern Visualizations**

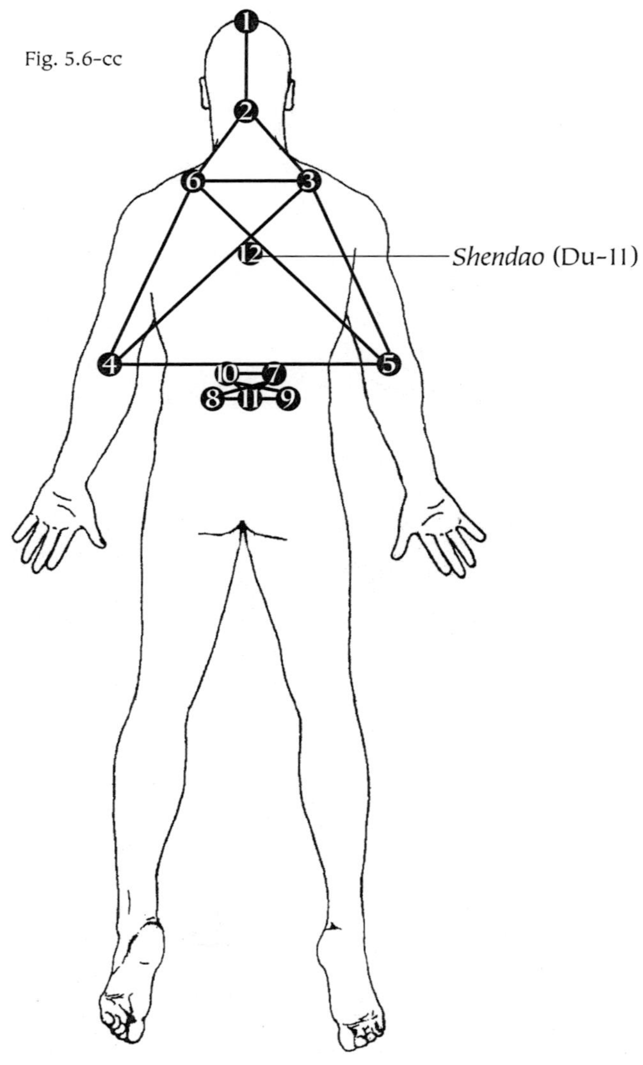


Fig. 5.6-cc

After the acupuncture needle has been inserted at the site of Shendao Du-11), have your client bring the qi upward from *Mingmen* (Du-4) with *Shendao* (Du-11). (See figure 5.6-dd below.)

## Crystalline Waters Pattern Visualizations

Fig. 5.6-dd

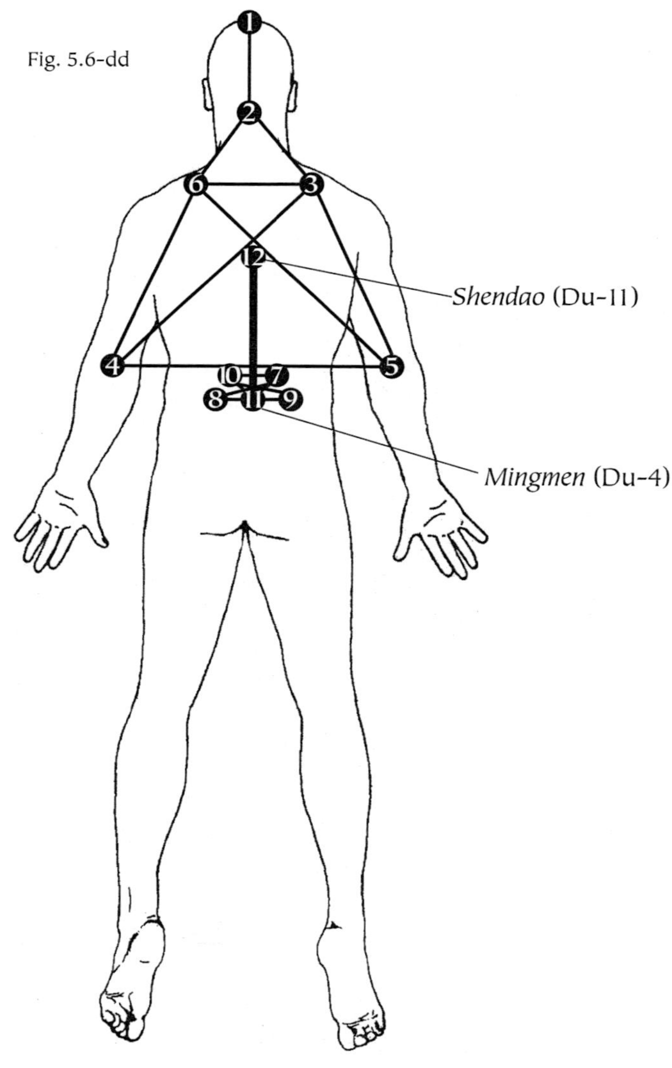

Next have your client visually bring the energies upward from the bilateral *Sanjiaoshu* (UB-22) points to connect with *Shendao* (Du-11). This visual connection creates a Fire Triangle with the apex pointing upward. (See figure 5.6-ee below.)

## Crystalline Waters Pattern Visualizations

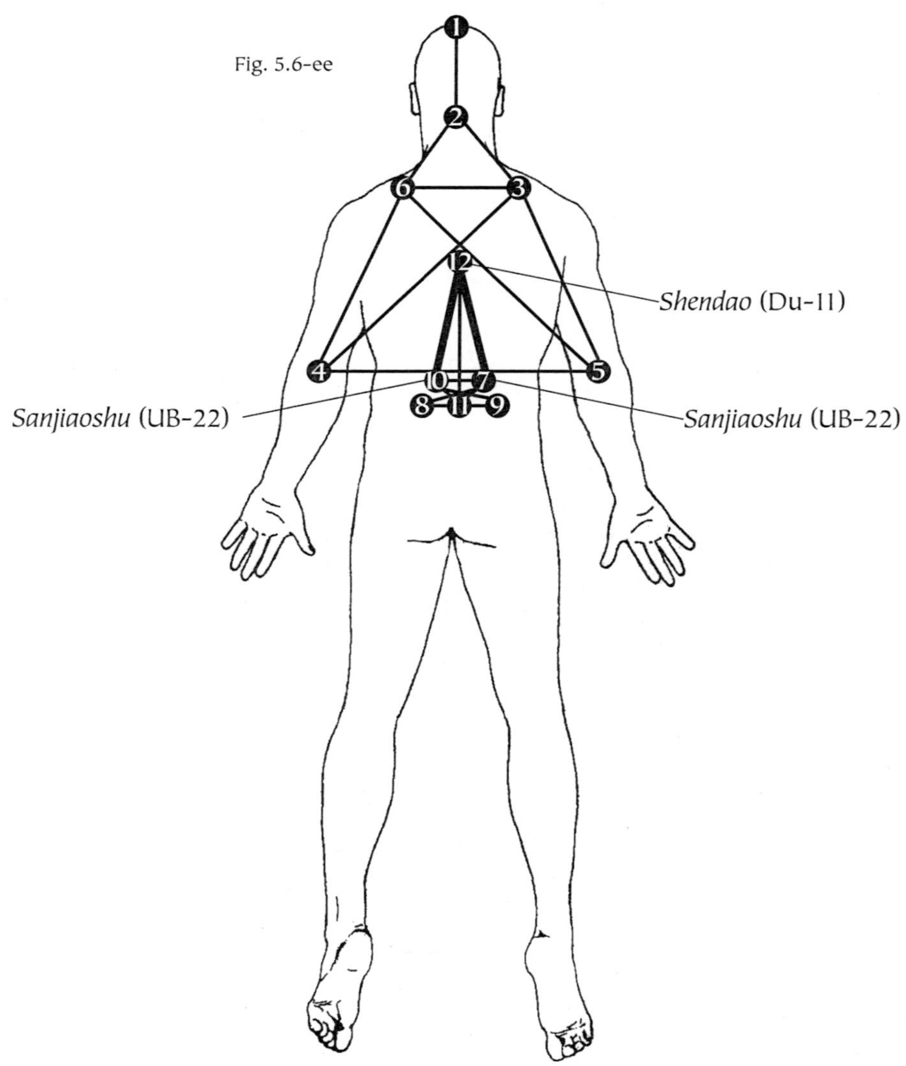


Fig. 5.6-ee

Next have your client visually connect the bilateral *Tian Jing* (SJ-10) points to *Shendao* (Du-11). This process again forms an upward pointing fire triangle of the heart system. (See figure 5.6-ff below.)

## Crystalline Waters Pattern Visualizations

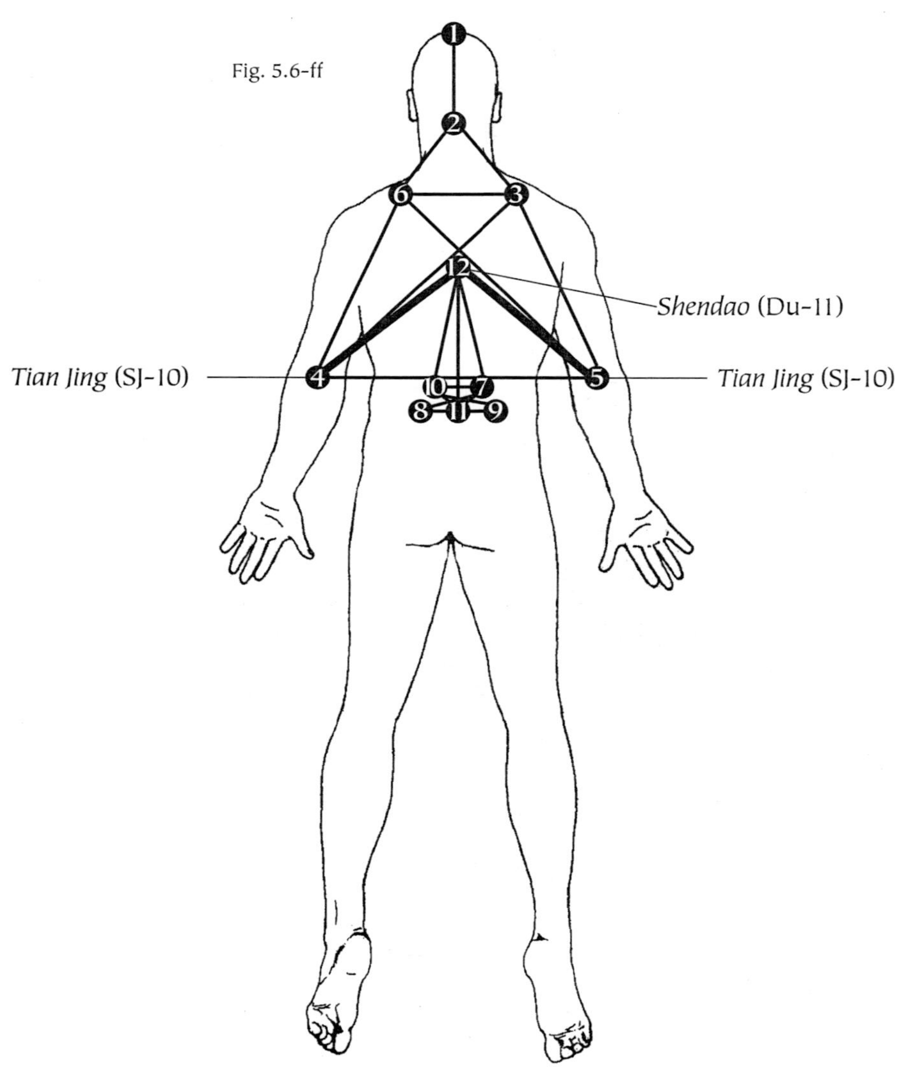

Fig. 5.6-ff

Now insert the last acupuncture needle in The Crystalline Waters Pattern at the site of *Dazhui* (Du-14) located below the lower border of the spinous process of the seventh cervical vertebra. (See figure 5.6-gg below.)

## Crystalline Waters Pattern Visualizations

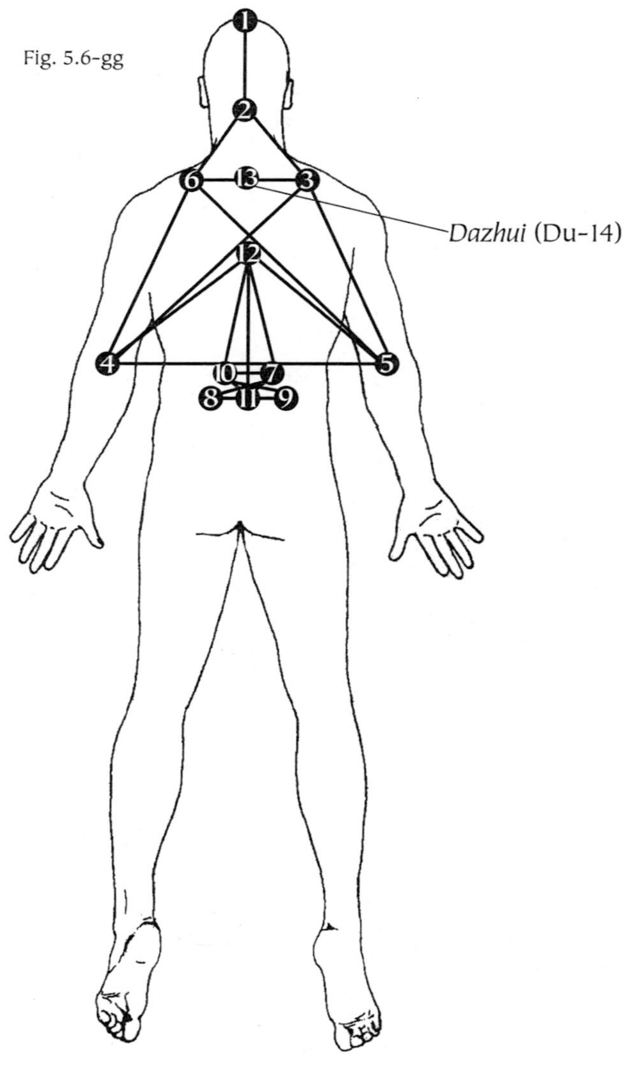

Fig. 5.6-gg

Now bring the qi upward from *Shendao* (Du-11) to connect with the qi at *Dazhiui* (Du-14). (See figure 5.6-hh below.)

## Crystalline Waters Pattern Visualizations

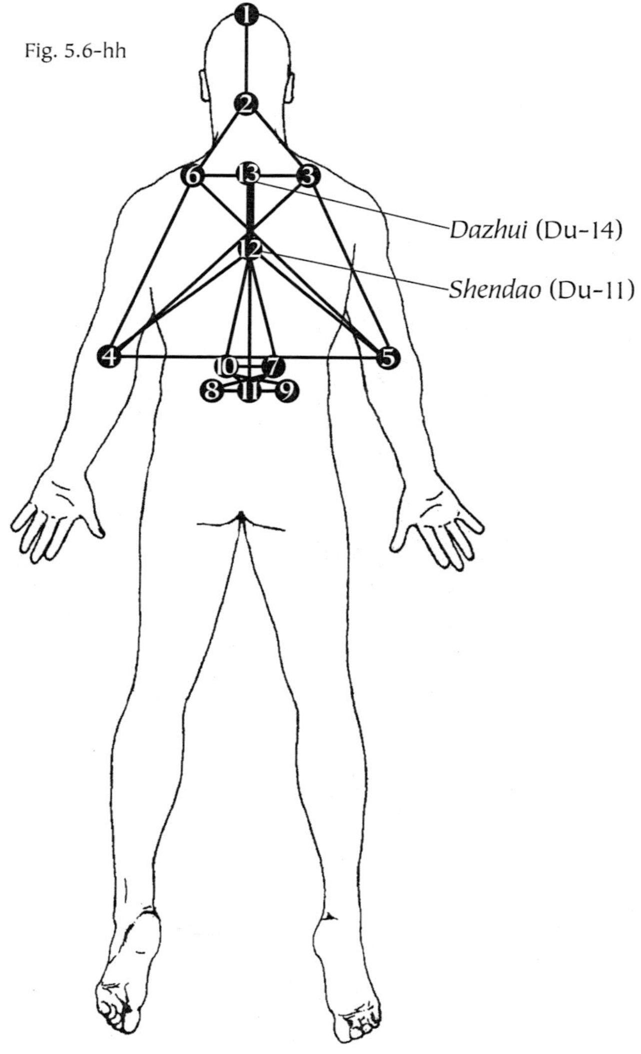


Fig. 5.6-hh

This next visual connection is not a linear connection but a non-linear consciousness connection known as a morphic resonant connection. A morphic resonant connection is the terminology used by Rupert Sheldrake who presented the idea of morphogenetic grids and morphogenetic fields to the world.

Have your client gather qi at *Dazhui* (Du-14) located below the lower border of the spinous process of the seventh cervical vertebra. Next have your client visually activate *Yintang* (Ajna Center), but without a linear connection from *Dazhui* (Du-14) to the Third Eye (*Yintang*) point. Your client will still be lying in a prone position when you ask him or her to make this morphic resonant connection. Remember that *Yintang* (Ajna Center) will not be needled in The Crystalline Waters Pattern. (See figure 5.6-ii below.)

**Crystalline Waters Pattern Visualizations**
**Morphic Resonant Connection**

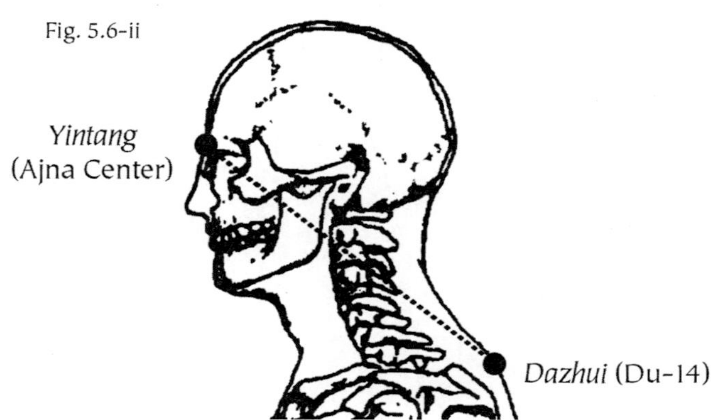

Now have your client visually bring the qi upward from the bilateral *Tian Jing* (SJ-10) points to form a Fire Triangle with the apex at *Dazhui* (Du-14). (See figure 5.6-jj below.)

## Crystalline Waters Pattern Visualizations

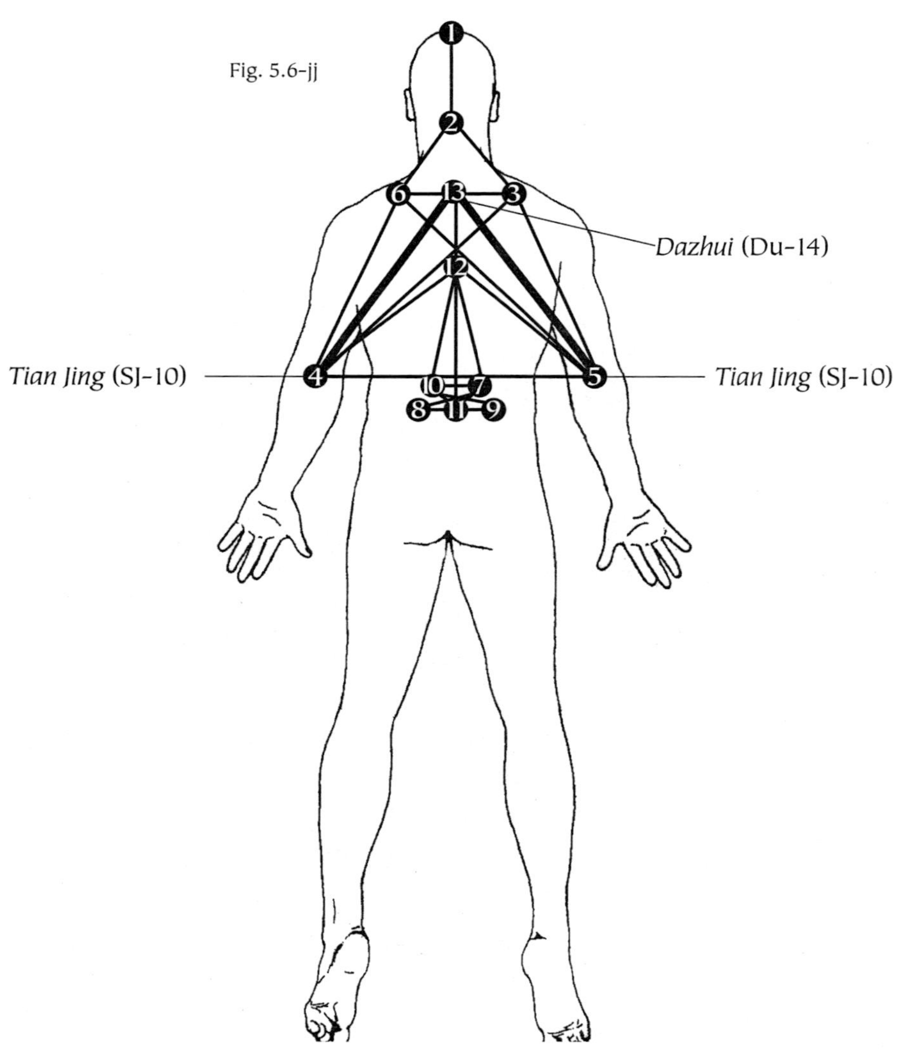

Have your client bring the qi upward from *Dazhui* (Du-14) to connect to the qi stored at *Feng Fu* (Du-16). (See figure 5.6-kk below.)

## Crystalline Waters Pattern Visualizations

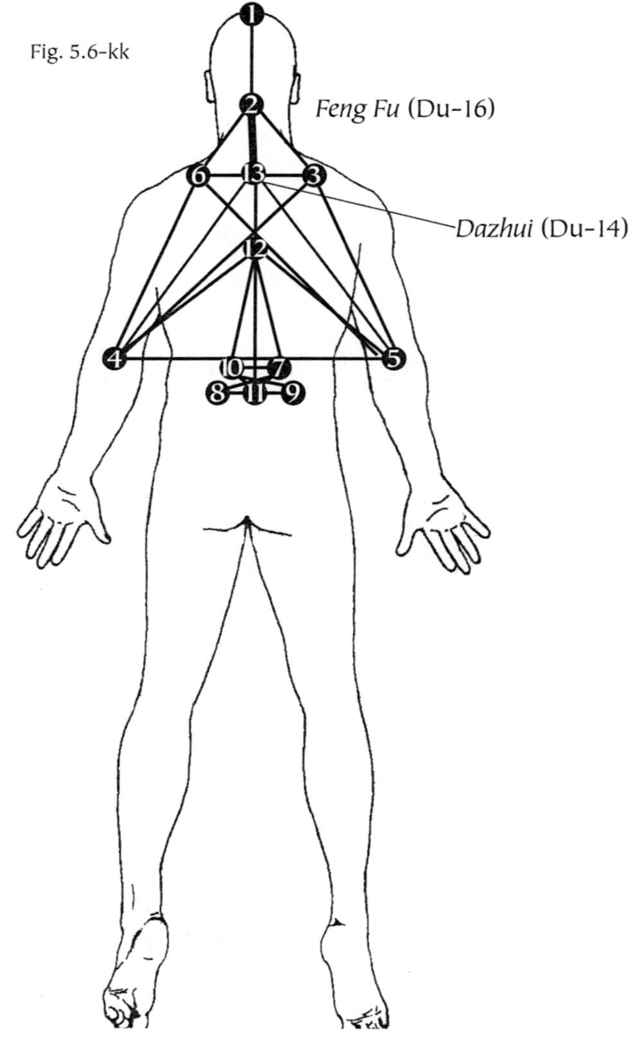


Fig. 5.6-kk

Next have your client bring the qi upward from the bilateral *Tian Jing* (SJ-10) points to form another Fire Triangle with *Feng Fu* (Du-16). (See figure 5.6-II below.)

**Crystalline Waters Pattern Visualizations**

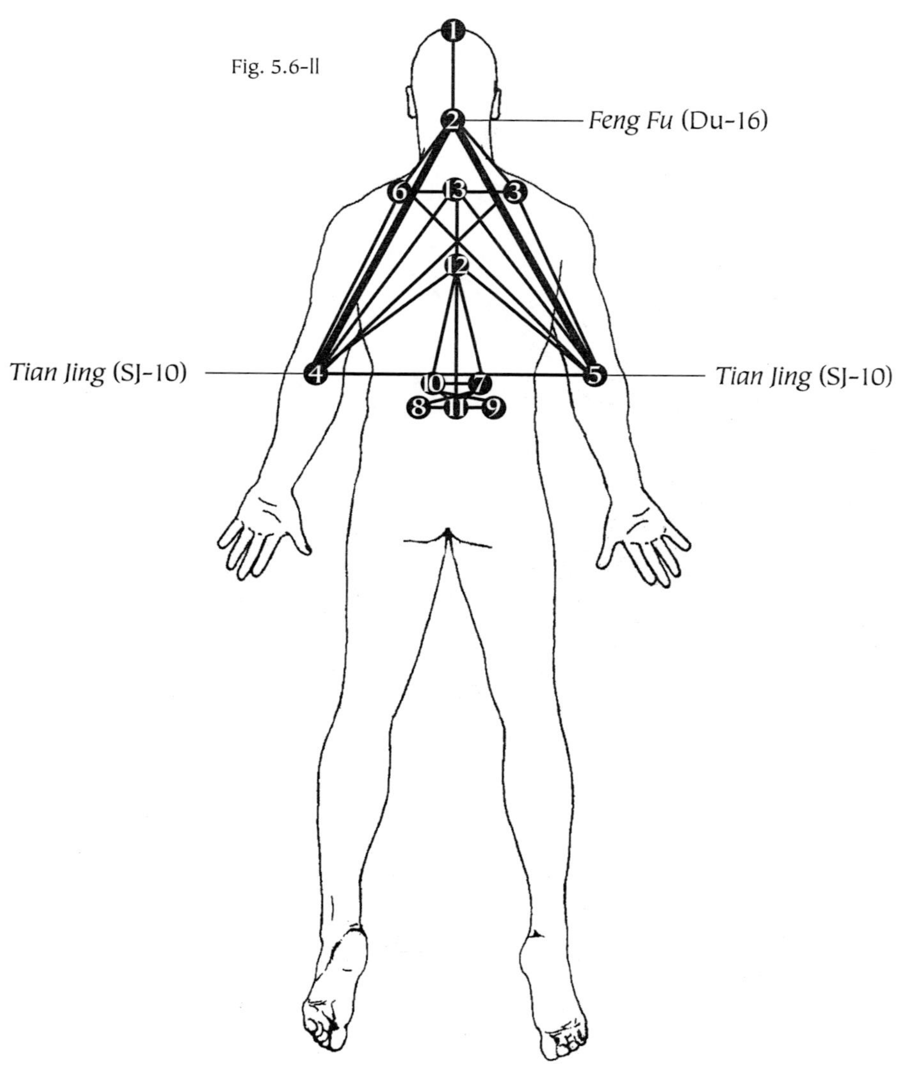

Now ask your client to visually connect the qi at the acupuncture site of *Feng Fu* (Du-16) linearly to the qi at *Yintang* (Ajna Center) as shown in figure 5.6-mm below.

## Crystalline Waters Pattern Visualizations

Fig. 5.6-mm

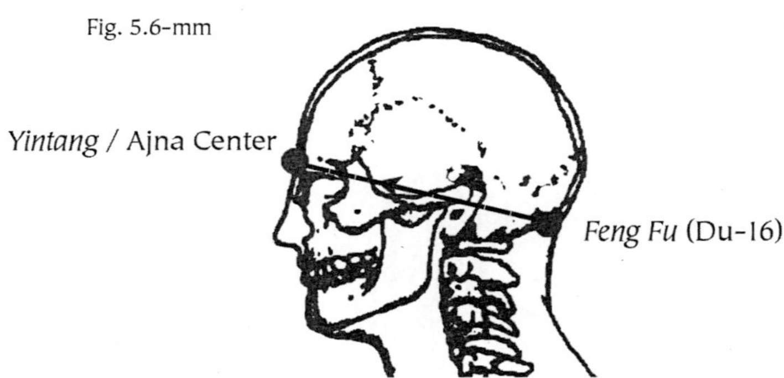


Next have your client simultaneously bring the energies upward from both *Feng Fu* (Du-16) and *Yintang* (Ajna Center) to connect with *Tian Man* (Du-20) to form a Fire Triangle. The three centers are the Three Major Head Centers. Remember the Sahasrara (Crown Chakra is above the cranium. (See figure 5.6-nn below.)

Fig. 5.6-nn

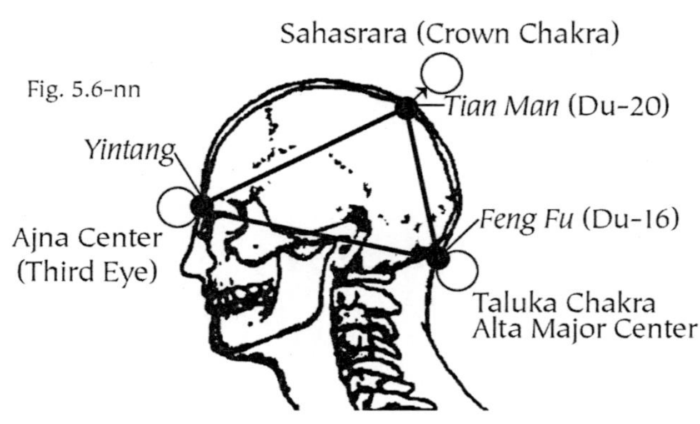

The last visual connection in the Crystalline Waters Pattern is to ask your client to simultaneously bring the qi upward from the bilateral *Tian Ting* (SJ-15) points to connect with the apex point *Tian Man* (Du-20). (See figure 5.6-oo below.)

## Crystalline Waters Pattern Visualizations

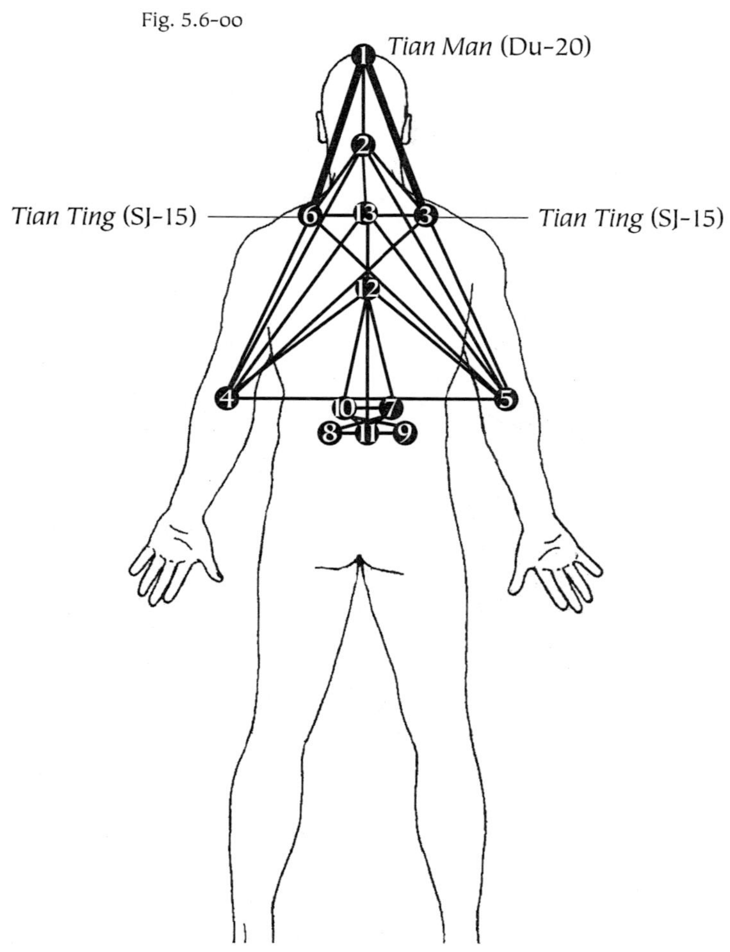

## Crystalline Waters Pattern
### Complete Grid

Fig. 5.6-pp

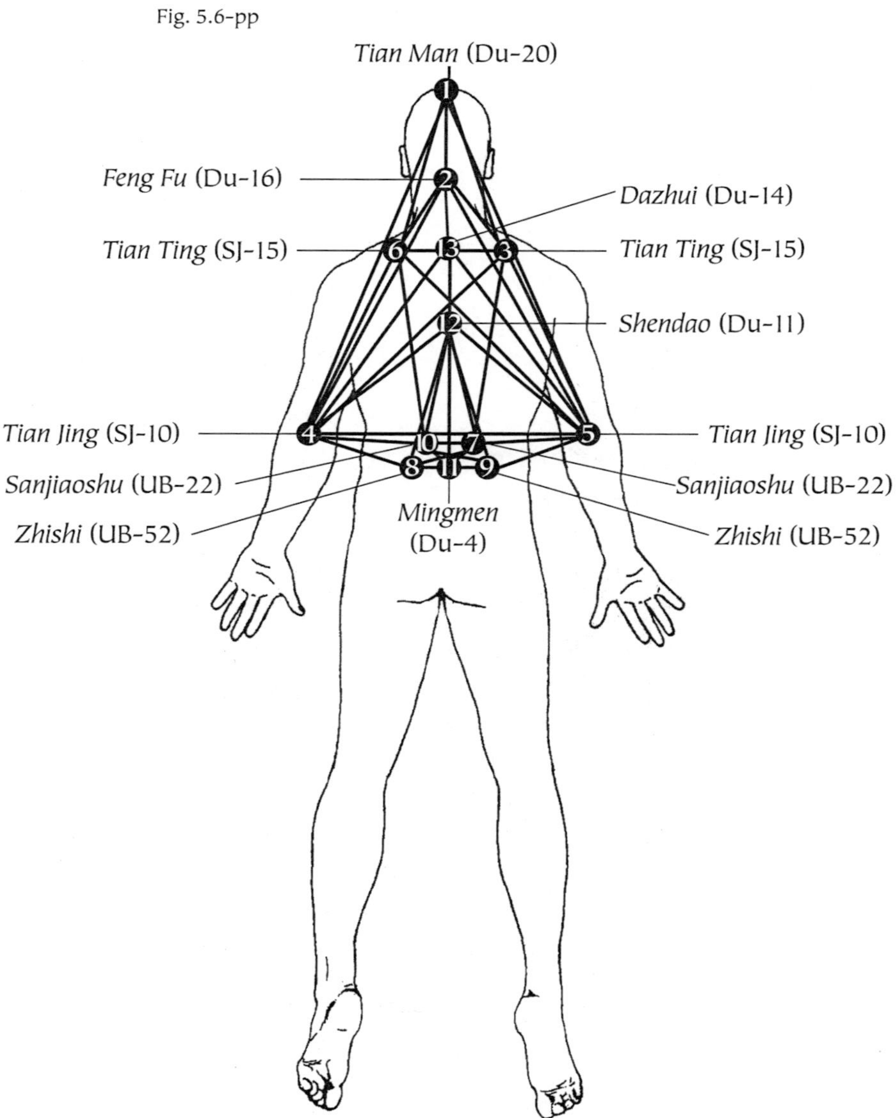

The idea of creating a crystalline water vibration in your client's energy field, means you are transforming the denser frequencies of the kidney and water systems into a higher vibrating frequency. We are transmuting fear into a frequency more in alignment with our heart qi. A crystalline frequency means moving closer to a light frequency.

> *"Fear is the most limiting of all beliefs and states of being because it causes people to "freeze" vibrationally and withdraw into a dense vibrational shell."* [10]
>
> David Icke

**Tier Density Level III**
**Awakening of Our Inner *Shen***

Those of you who are at Tier Density Level 3 are now eating strictly organic, fresh foods. You know the importance of eating raw foods and are incorporating fresh raw foods into your daily regiment whenever possible. At Tier Density III you are fully aware of how the things you ingest shape all of your various bodies, as well as the different planes of consciousness. You do not eat any of the types of foods that are considered junk foods. In fact, junk foods are not even considered foods to you who are at this level of consciousness.

You are now starting to understand how the higher, subtle levels of movement of various styles of Hatha Yoga, *tai qi* and *qi gong* affect your inner world. You are not so interested in exercising for merely the sake of the physical, but are beginning to become one with the inner spiritual qi flow. Your hatha yoga practice now involves aligning your spiritual center and not merely working on physical flexibility as before. Your *tai qi* and *qi gong* work have opened a new inner world of awareness that has heightened your sensitivity and has given you more clarity in recognizing how your center physical alignment is connected to the center spiritual alignment and how these alignments are connected to that of the Earth. You are now mentally attempting to work with your Kundalini so you will be able to communicate with the Kundalini of Mother Earth. You are more in tune with the higher frequencies of the Earth field. You have been shown a glimpse of this inner power and inner connectedness to everything around you. You are beginning to truly understand Oneness, but have not quite anchored that consciousness into your day-to-day consciousness.

At this tier level of density, those times of extreme challenges and crises are seen as opportunities to leap forward. You do not shrink into a despondent shell and ask "why me?" You do not sink into the "poor me" mode. For the true seeker on his or her spiritual path, the challenging events will produce two results:

1) *The intensification of the aspiration to move forward.*
2) *The achievement of a more stabilized attitude of detachment from all that the personality holds dear.*[11]

To find your home, you must leave home. This means it is usually necessary to leave the comforts and the routine structure of your daily life and to experience other realities to assist you in moving into alignment with your Inner Spiritual Higher Heart Center. Leaving home means getting out of your programmed, robotic daily existence. Often "leaving home" means you may face extreme difficulties at certain times in your life. The difficulties are outside of those mundane, routine chores that you had become accustomed to. Each of your most challenging events produced a subsequent reaction where you may have experienced your darkest moments. At the soul level, you needed those dark moments and extreme challenges to help catapult your forward into another level of consciousness on your own individual Soul Journey. "To find your home" means you have discovered your true Inner Spiritual Higher Heart Path. From the depths of your darkest, most trying experiences will birth your brightest, lightest and most intense awakenings. The darkest challenges afford you an opportunity to rapidly accelerate your inner, spiritual growth.

At this Tier Density Level III, you are beginning to question if your work is in alignment with your heart. Besides the need to earn money for your daily basic three-dimensional needs, you are now questioning if your present work is what you really want to do. More importantly, does your work help others and benefit higher planetary alignment? Does your work energize you, or does your work deplete your physical, emotional, mental and spiritual qi? You now understand that no matter how you choose to make money to earn a living, the results of the work must not harm others. In other words, you are not working at an occupation that makes or does things to harm others or are harmful to the planet as a whole.

An important question will arise at Tier Density Level III. That question is: "What is your puzzle piece in life?" Your heart is alerting you to the fact that your daily activities must be in alignment with your heart. You will not find or know your puzzle piece in life without being in alignment with your higher heart.

At this tier level, second chakra events such as relationships and financial matters are not such issues for you. You may make lots of money or just a little. The amount of money does not matter because you are perfectly satisfied with whatever amount you make. You may be in a stable relationship or be by yourself. Whatever the situation, you are fine with the ways things are. If you are by yourself, you are not looking on the internet dating sites to try and find your "soulmate."

Your social life is changing and social events are not such a priority as they used to be when you were on a lower density tier. Special occasions such as holidays and birthdays may still be of great interest to you, but not the frivolous socialization and gossip that consumed your time in the past.

As you continue to evolve at this density level, you are starting to become aware that the physical movements of Hatha Yoga, *tai qi* or *qi gong* may not be enough for what you want to achieve. You are seeking some level of quietness or stillness. Your inner plane world is starting to awaken more and you are becoming less interested in physical movement. Inner plane work through meditation is becoming more a part of your daily routine. You are now cultivating inner dedication. Your quiet time is now a very important part of your daily, or at least your weekly routine.

Although sports, news and entertainment may still interest you, you are now moving more and more into the metaphysical world. You are not so interested in what other people are doing. Your favorite sports heroes or sports team are not so important in your daily life at this density level. You do not need aspirations or inspiration from the outside. You are starting to carve your own niche in your life journey and seeking your own truths. You are beginning to think and connect more globally rather than just locally. Your consciousness and responsibilities are growing. Both your inner and outer worlds are now expanding very rapidly. You are starting to become more interested in the esoteric world and are being more drawn into exploring and understanding the Ageless Wisdom Teachings. You are now beginning to feel that urgency to move into something more important to your soul development. You have not quite found your puzzle piece in life and are not quite on your Soul Journey, but your inner guides are pushing you to find that path.

One of the most important attributes at this level is that you should always keep your word! You do not make frivolous promises. You understand that the heart controls your tongue. You follow your heart. The way you speak and the intonation of the words that come out of your mouth are directly connected with your heart. If you make a promise, you do not make excuses why you cannot or did not keep that promise. No matter what, you always keep your word. Your Spiritual Heart Path is to be truthful, trust worthy and a person of the highest integrity.

The first option for the posterior pattern in Tier Density Level III is the Esoteric *Shaoyin* Heart Pattern followed by the anterior pattern Cube on Cube Window Pattern.

## Level III Posterior: Option #1
## Esoteric *Shaoyin* Heart Pattern

Fig. 5.7-a

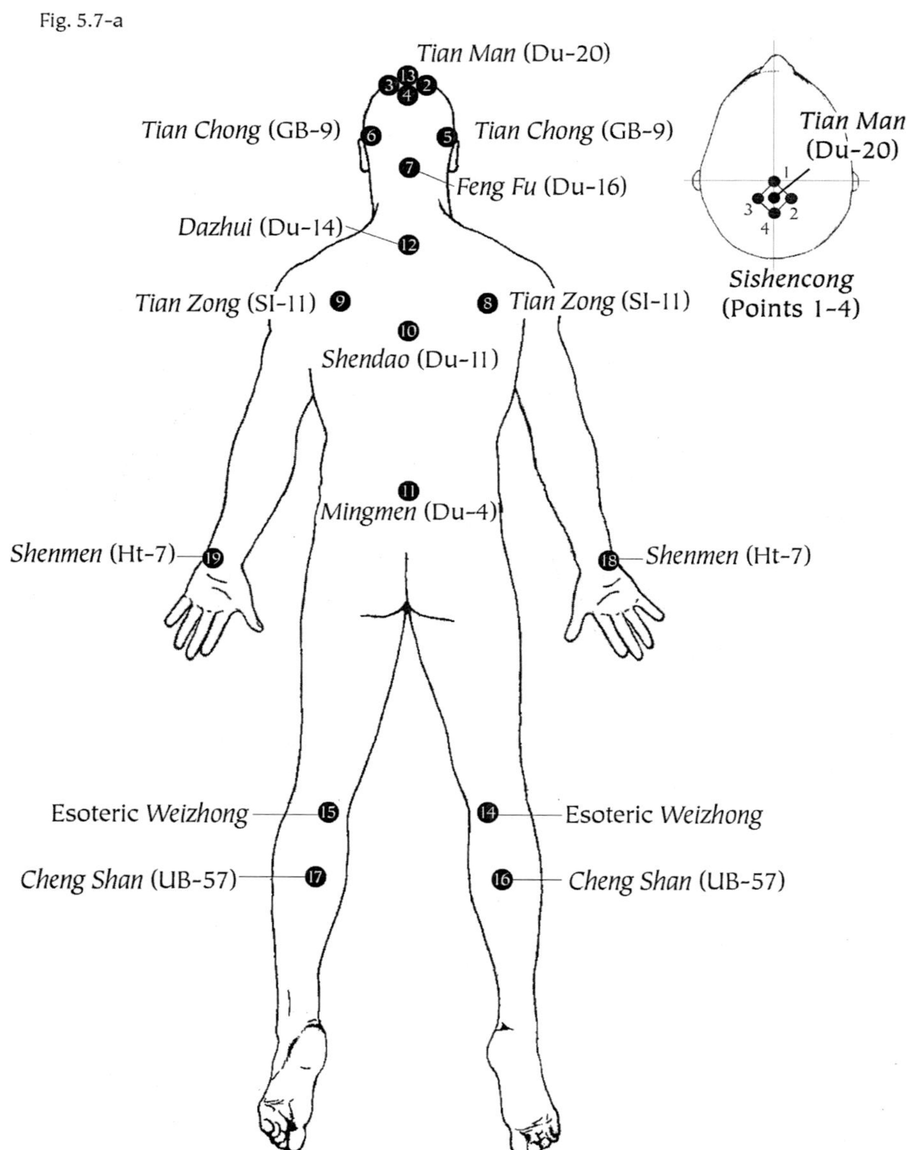

**Needling Sequence: Esoteric *Shaoyin* Heart Pattern**
**Think of this pattern having three sections.**

First Section:
1) to 4) *Sishencong* -- "4 Spirits"
5) *Tian Chong* (GB-9) Right side
6) *Tian Chong* (GB-9) Left side
7) *Feng Fu* (Du-16)

Second Section:
8) *Tian Zong* (SI-11) Right side
9) *Tian Zong* (SI-11) Left side
10) *Shendao* (Du-11)
11) *Mingmen* (Du-4)
12) *Dazhui* (Du-14)
13) *Tian Man* (Du-20)

Third Section called The Three Fire Triangle Group
14) Esoteric *Weizhong*--Right side
15) Esoteric *Weizhong*--Left side
16) *Cheng Shan* (UB-57)--Right side
17) *Cheng Shan* (UB-57)--Left side
18) *Shenmen* (Ht-7)--Right side
19) *Shenmen* (Ht-7)--Left side

**Point Locations for The Esoteric *Shaoyin* Heart Pattern**

For the point locations of the first thirteen acupuncture points (First and Second Sections) in The Esoteric *Shaoyin* Heart Pattern, please refer back to The Discern the Whisper Pattern. The thirteen acupuncture sites in The Discern the Whisper Pattern are the exact same thirteen acupuncture points, with the same sequencing order, as The Esoteric *Shaoyin* Heart Pattern.

**Third Section:**

Points fourteen and fifteen are part of the third section. This grouping of six acupuncture points is called The Three Fire Triangle Group.

The third section of the Esoteric *Shaoyin* Heart Pattern consists of six acupuncture points. Because of the sensitivity of the needling the bilateral Esoteric *Weizhong* points and the bilateral *Shenmen* (Ht-7) points on some individuals, this is the phase where I sometimes use the red handled Seirin needles. The red handled Seirin needles are .16 mm by .15mm in length. These needles are shorter and slightly thinner than the .20 mm by 30 mm Laser Seirin needles that are used for the first thirteen acupuncture points in The Esoteric *Shaoyin* Heart Pattern.

The fourteenth and fifteenth acupuncture points are the bilateral Esoteric *Weizhong* points in the right leg followed by Esoteric *Weizhong* in the left leg. The Chinese name for UB-40 is *Weizhong* and is often translated as "Bend Middle." Traditionally *Weizhong* (UB-40) is found on the posterior side of the knees at the midpoint of the transverse crease of the popliteal fossa between the tendons of the biceps femoris muscle and the semitendinosus muscle. For Esoteric Acupuncture, Esoteric *Weizhong* is used instead and is often needled at a slightly different location. Instead of being located at the midpoint of the transverse crease, the point is usually found closer to the tendon of the semitendinosus muscle that is toward the medial aspect of the transverse crease. The key is to look for the dimple in the transverse crease behind the knees. The dimple is almost always closer to the medial aspect of the knee, and away from *Wei Yang* (UB-39). *Wei Yang* (UB-39) is found closer to the lateral aspect of the transverse crease of the popliteal fossa. The point location of the Esoteric *Weizhong* may be very close to *Yin Gu* (Ki-10) which is located at the medial aspect of the knee between the tendon of the semitendinosus muscle and the tendon of the semimembranosus. If the dimple is located close to *Yin Gu* (Ki-10), make sure that you needle the Esoteric *Weizhong* point on the lateral aspect of the tendon of the semitendinosus muscle and not in the location of *Yin Gu* (Ki-10). (See figure 5.7-b below.)

## Esoteric *Shaoyin* Heart Pattern

Fig. 5.7-b

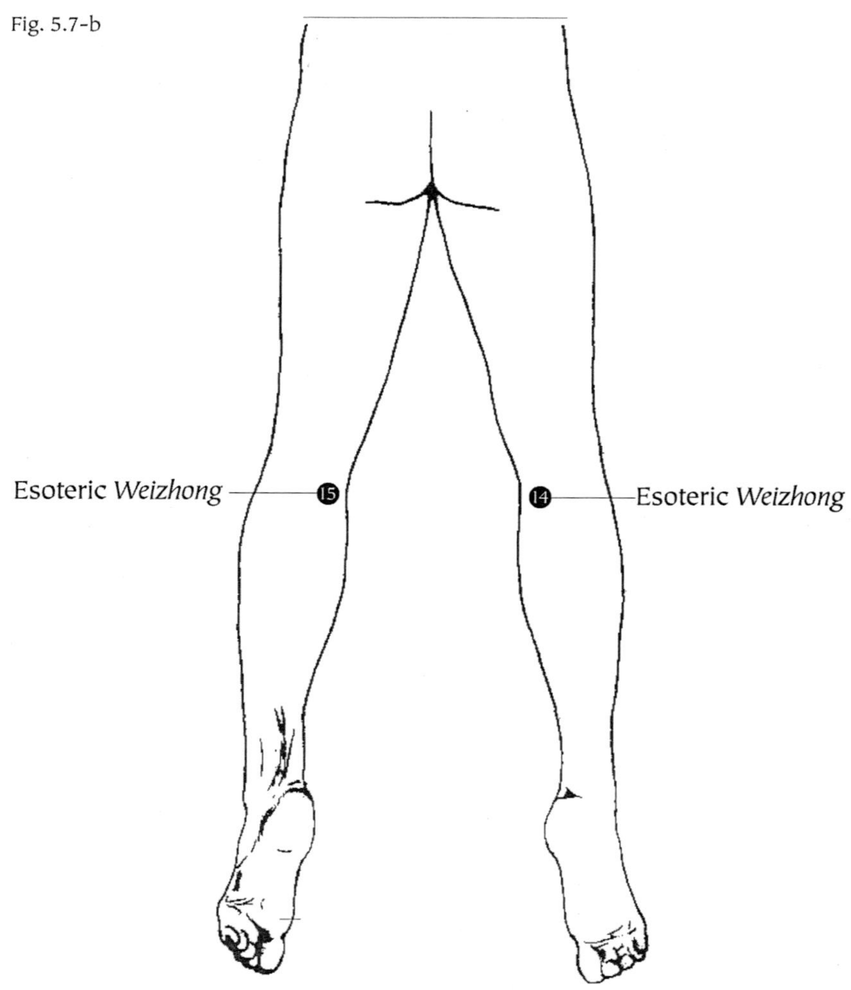

The next two points needled in this Three Fire Triangle Group are the bilateral *Cheng Shan* (UB-57) points. These bilateral points are the Support the Mountain points that reinforces energy at the *Feng Fu* (Du-16) site to support the "Inner Mountain" Chakra known as the Brahmarandra Chakra. (See figure 5.7-c below.)

**Esoteric *Shaoyin* Heart Pattern**

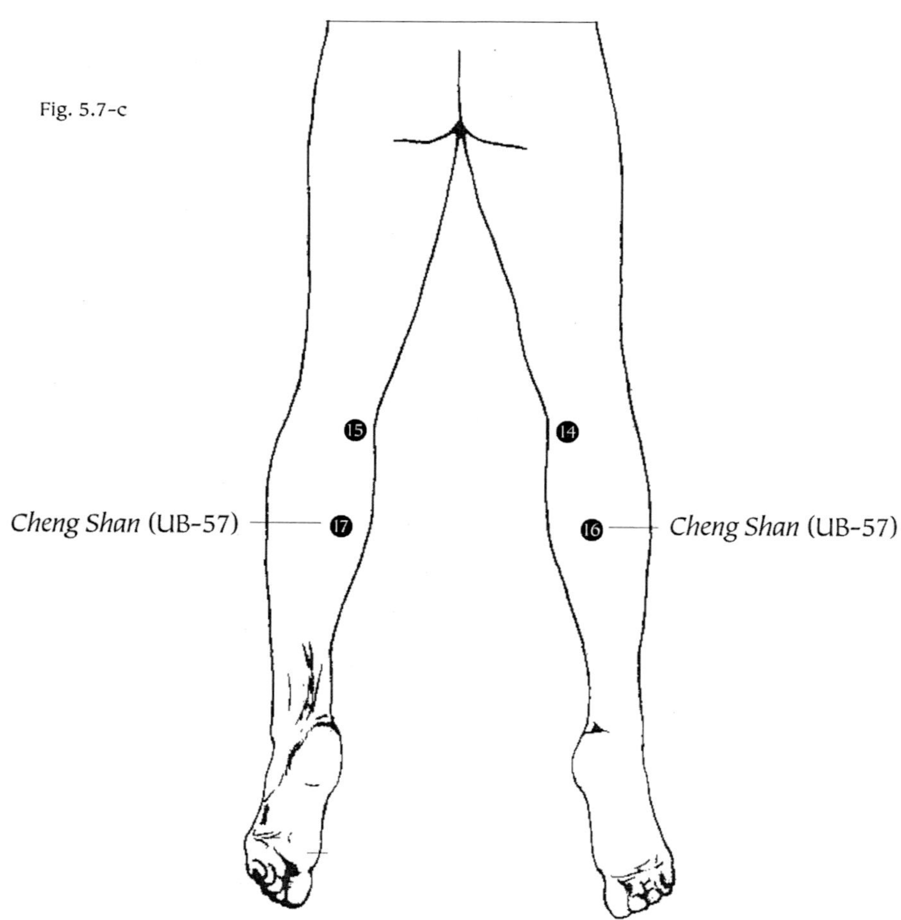


Fig. 5.7-c

## Esoteric *Shaoyin* Heart Pattern

Fig. 5.7-d

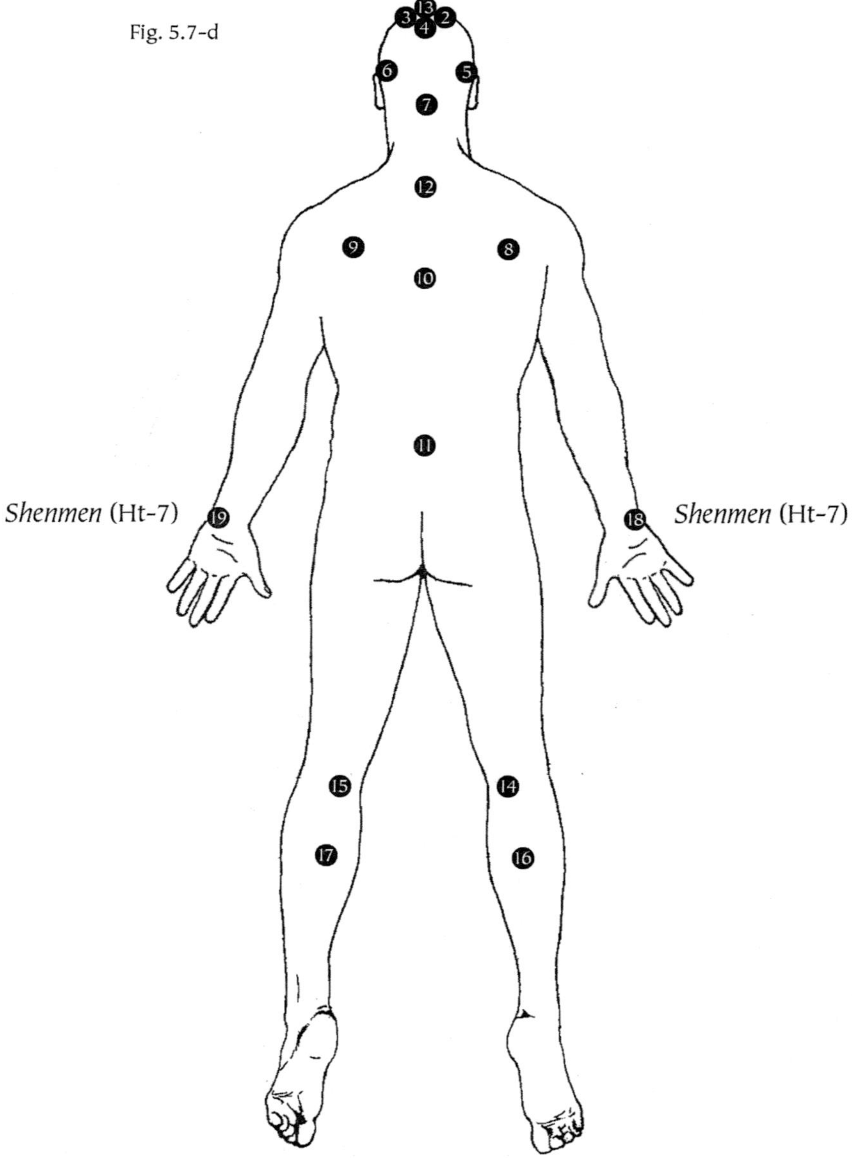

## Visualizations for The Esoteric *Shaoyin* Heart Pattern

Since the visualizations for the first thirteen acupuncture points in the Esoteric *Shaoyin* Heart Pattern are the same as the visual connections in the Discern the Whisper Pattern, we will only discuss the visualizations for the last six acupuncture points in this pattern. In fact, the first thirteen acupuncture points in the *Esoteric Shaoyin* Heart Pattern are exactly identical to the thirteen acupuncture points and have the same needle sequencing as the Discern the Whisper Pattern. To visually connect the first thirteen points in The Esoteric *Shaoyin* Heart Pattern, refer back to the Discern the Whisper Pattern in Tier Density Level II.

The Esoteric *Shaoyin* Heart Pattern is a slightly more complex grid pattern than the Discern the Whisper Pattern. The Esoteric *Shaoyin* Pattern has six additional acupuncture points that are minor chakra sites. Instead of merely gridding the upper portion of the body as was done in the Discern the Whisper Pattern, we are now going to connect and grid the lower extremities to the upper parts of the body. Two of the upward pointing Fire Triangles using four of the last six acupuncture points bring the energies upward from the minor chakra sites on the lower extremities. The last visual Fire Triangle connection is very important, and it connects the bilateral acupuncture points *Shenmen* (Ht-7) called the "Heart Gates" to the central "Heart Path" known as *Shendao* (Du-11). Instead of having the bilateral *Shenmen* (Ht-7) points travel through the heart meridian on the etheric level to connect with *Shendao* (Du-11), the visual connection works on the higher Mental Plane rather than the lower Etheric Plane.

Notice how the Esoteric *Shaoyin* Heart Pattern has nineteen acupuncture points. The number nineteen was discussed in Chapter One in the Brief Treatise on the Law of 3-6-1. The number nineteen has the encoding of "All That Is." Nineteen is a very high vibrating and very powerful number. Remember it was mentioned earlier that nineteen multiplied by nineteen results in 361. That is the Esoteric 3-6-1 Encoding for all modalities of acupuncture, not just Esoteric Acupuncture.

The first visual connection in this Three Fire Triangle section is to connect the bilateral Esoteric *Weizhong* points. (See figure 5.7-e below .)

## Esoteric *Shaoyin* Heart Pattern Visualization

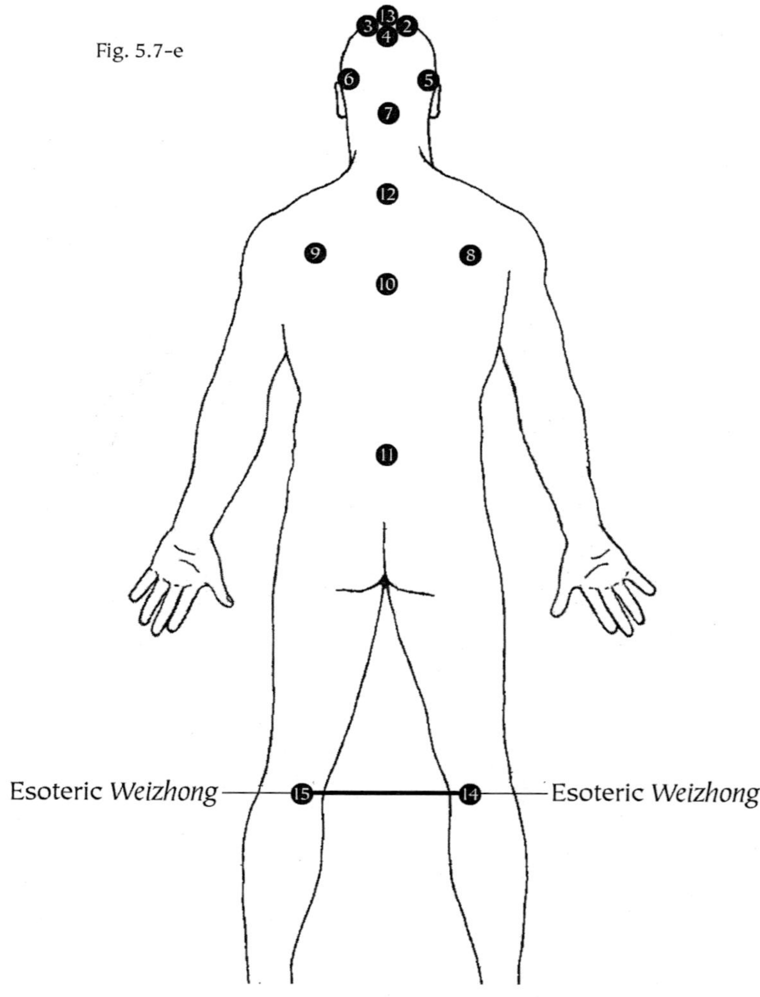


Fig. 5.7-e

Now visually bring the qi upward from the bilateral Esoteric *Weizhong* points (minor Swadthisthana Chakra sites) to connect with the central Swadthisthana Chakra site *Mingmen* (Du-4) located on the spine below the spinous process of the fourth lumbar vertebra. (See figure 5.7-f below.)

## Esoteric *Shaoyin* Heart Pattern Visualization

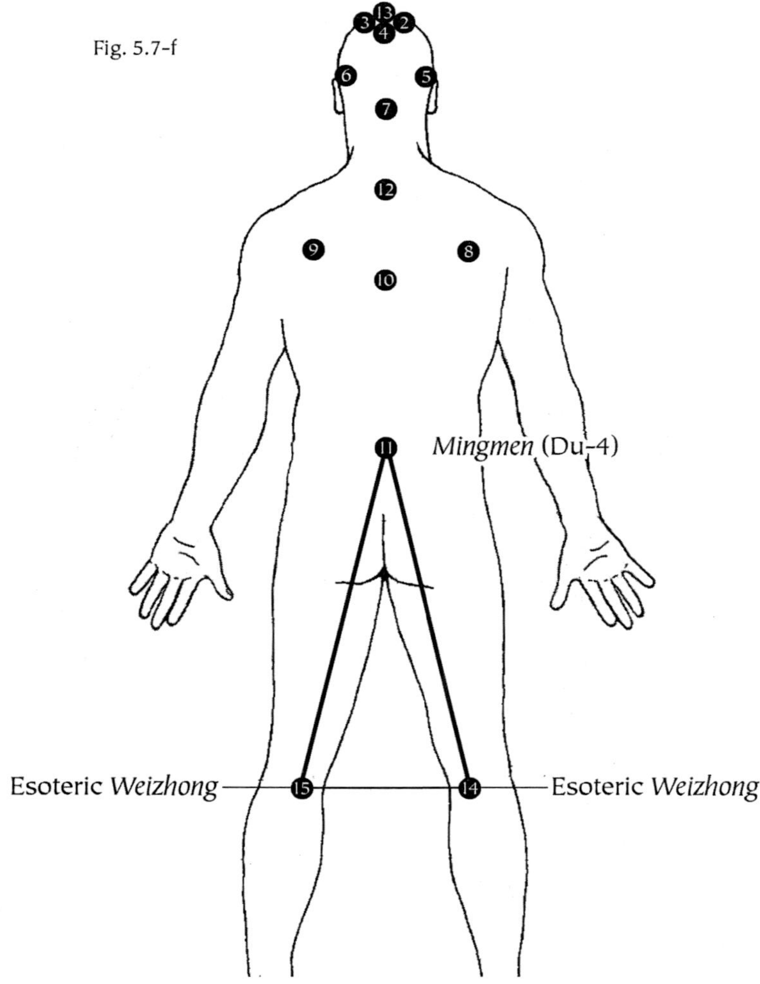

The next visualization in The Three Fire Triangle section is to connect the bilateral *Cheng Shan* (UB-57) points with each other. These are Muladhara (Root Chakra) points and also known as the Support the Mountain points. (See figure 5.7-g below.)

## Esoteric *Shaoyin* Heart Pattern Visualization

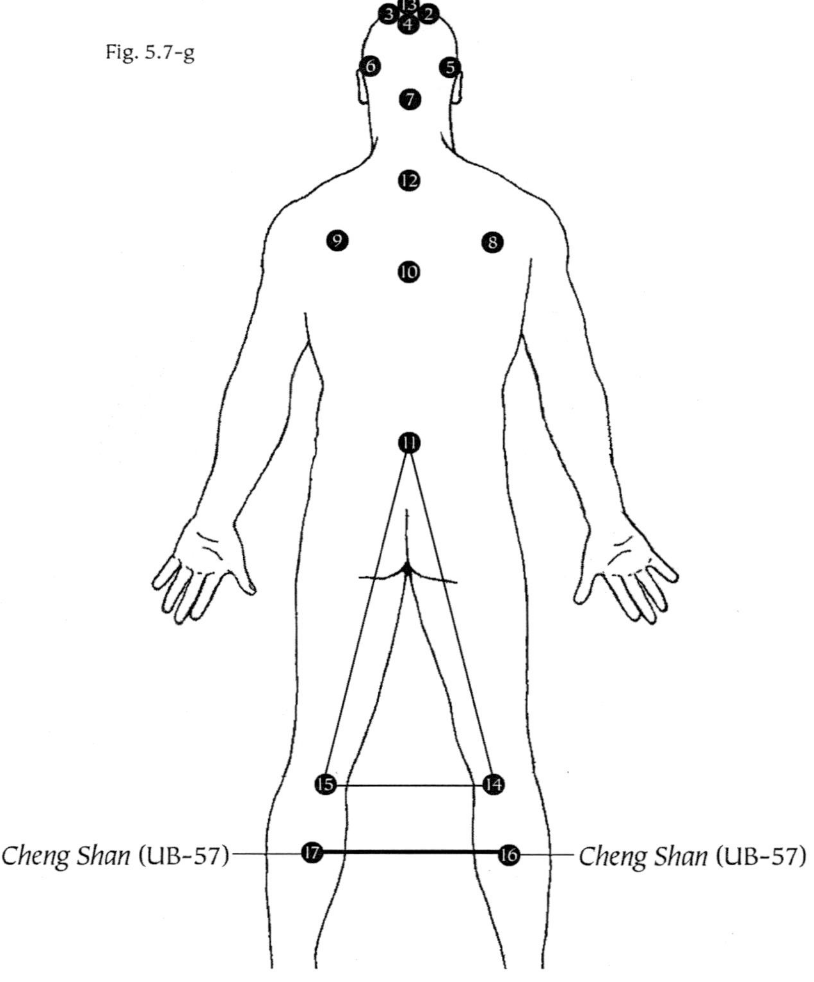

Now bring the qi upward from the bilateral *Cheng Shan* (UB-57) points to connect with the Taluka Chakra (Lalana Chakra) at the acupuncture site of *Feng Fu* (Du-16). Remember that *Feng Fu* (Du-16) activates the medulla oblongata that is the part of the brain connected with the Muladhara (Root Chakra). (See figure 5.7-h below.)

### Esoteric *Shaoyin* Heart Pattern Visualization

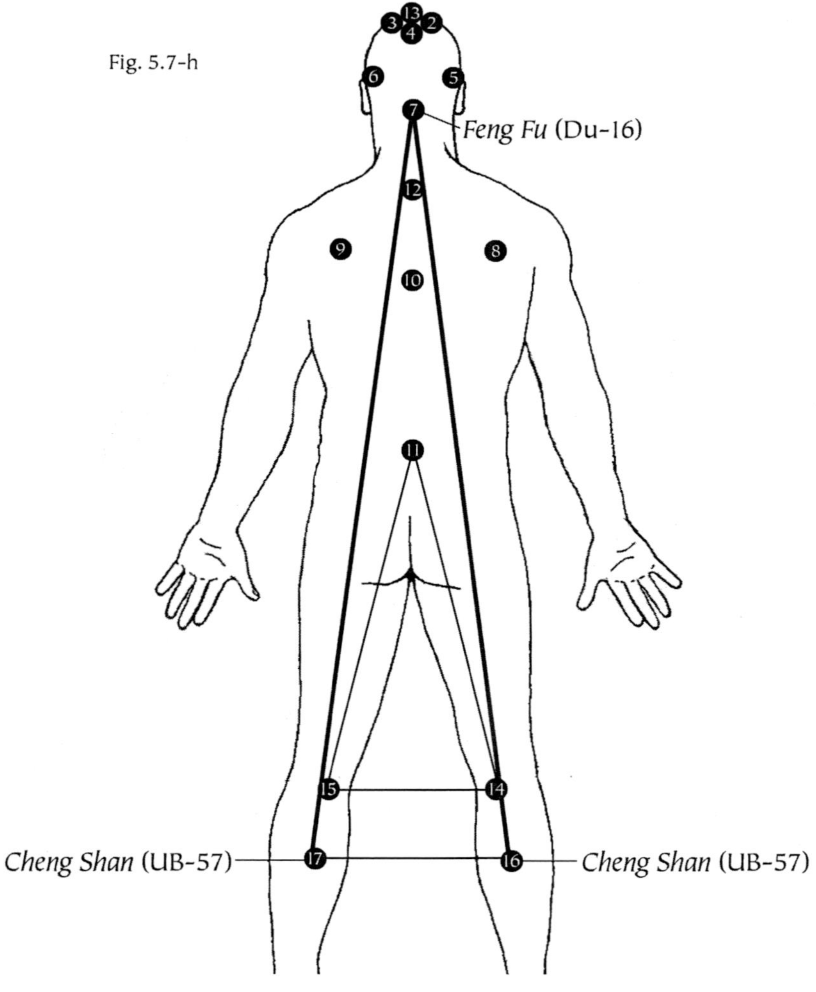

The next visualization is to connect the bilateral Heart Gate points *Shenmen* (Ht-7) on the wrist to each other. (See figure 5.7-I below.)

## Esoteric *Shaoyin* Heart Pattern Visualization

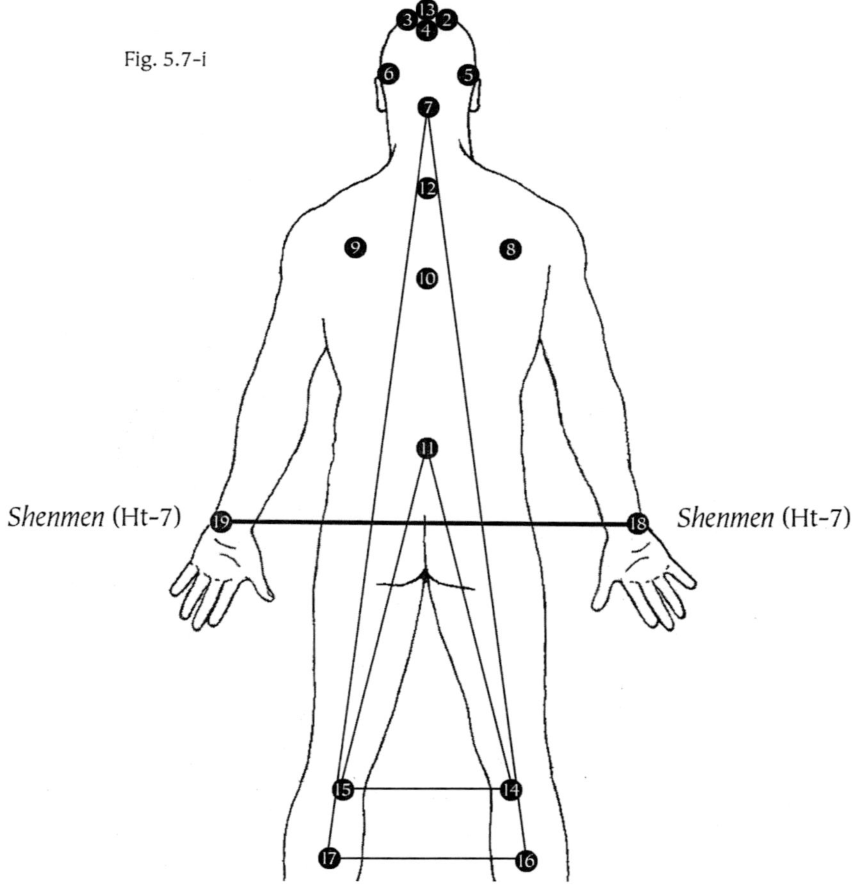


The last visualization in the Esoteric *Shaoyin* Heart Pattern is to visually bring the qi upward from the bilateral Heart Gate points *Shenmen* (Ht-7) to connect to the central Heart Path *Shendao* (Du-11). We are opening the gates of the heart (Heart Gates) and mentally making sure the qi flows directly to the Heart Path at *Shendao*. Mentally visualizing the qi moving in a triangular motion from the wrists to the spine creates is a quicker connection than merely allowing the qi to move through the regular etheric acupuncture pathways. (See figure 5.7-j below.)

**Esoteric *Shaoyin* Heart Pattern Visualization**

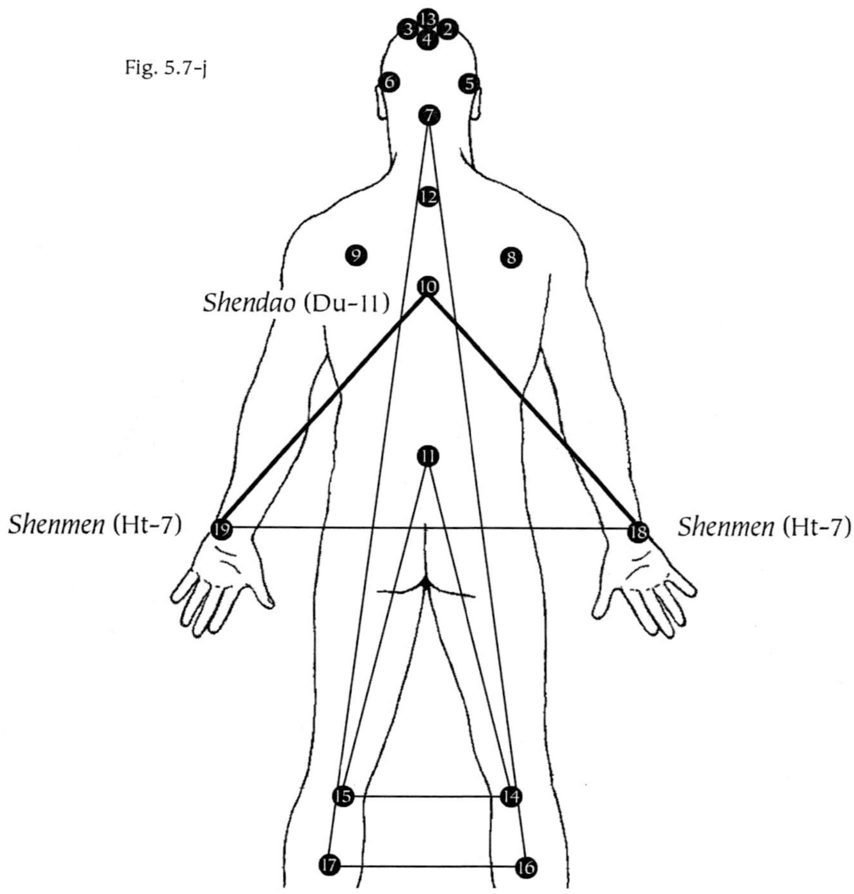

## Esoteric *Shaoyin* Heart Pattern
### Complete Grid

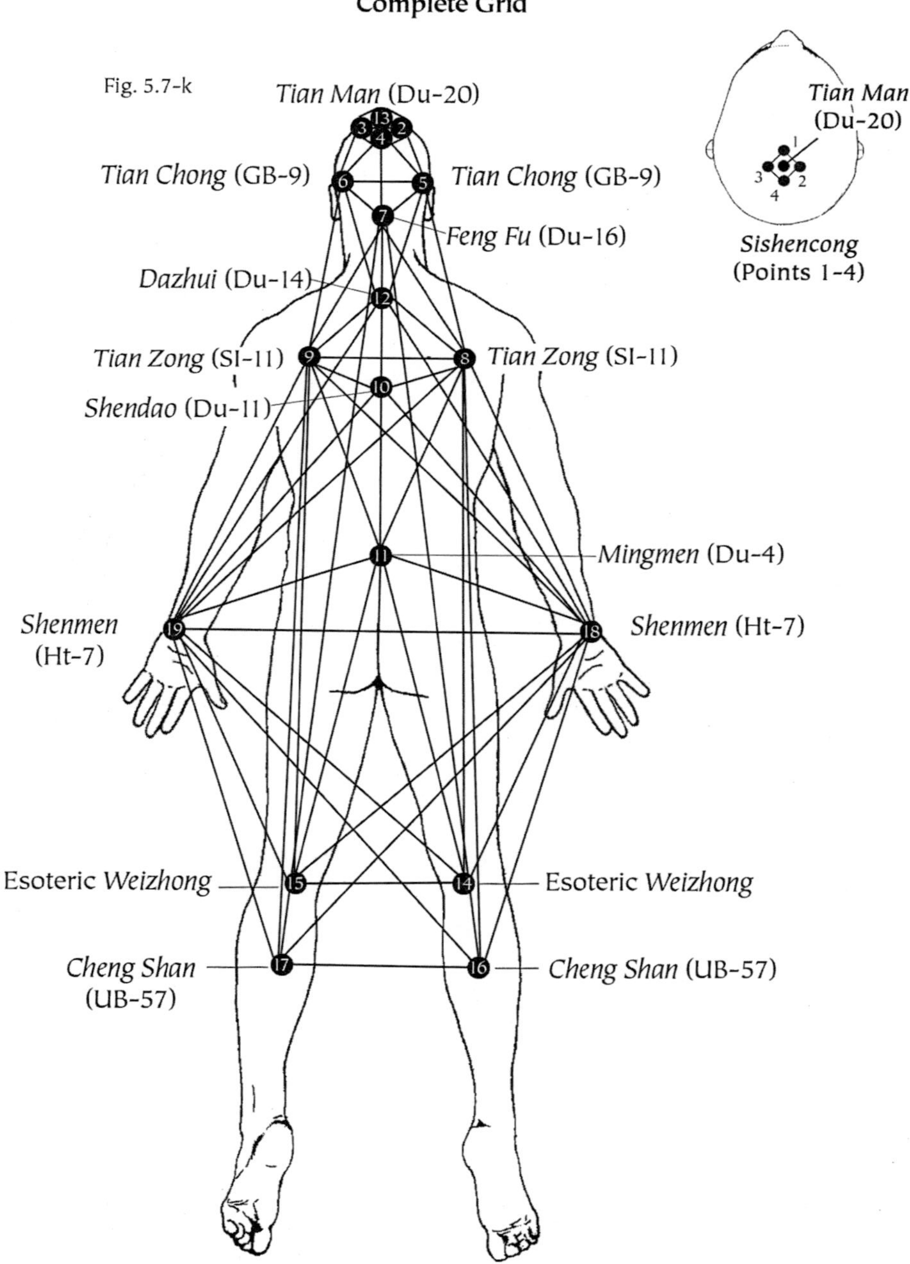


Fig. 5.7-k

## Level III Posterior: Option #2
# Esoteric *Shaoyin* Kidney Pattern

Fig. 5.8-a

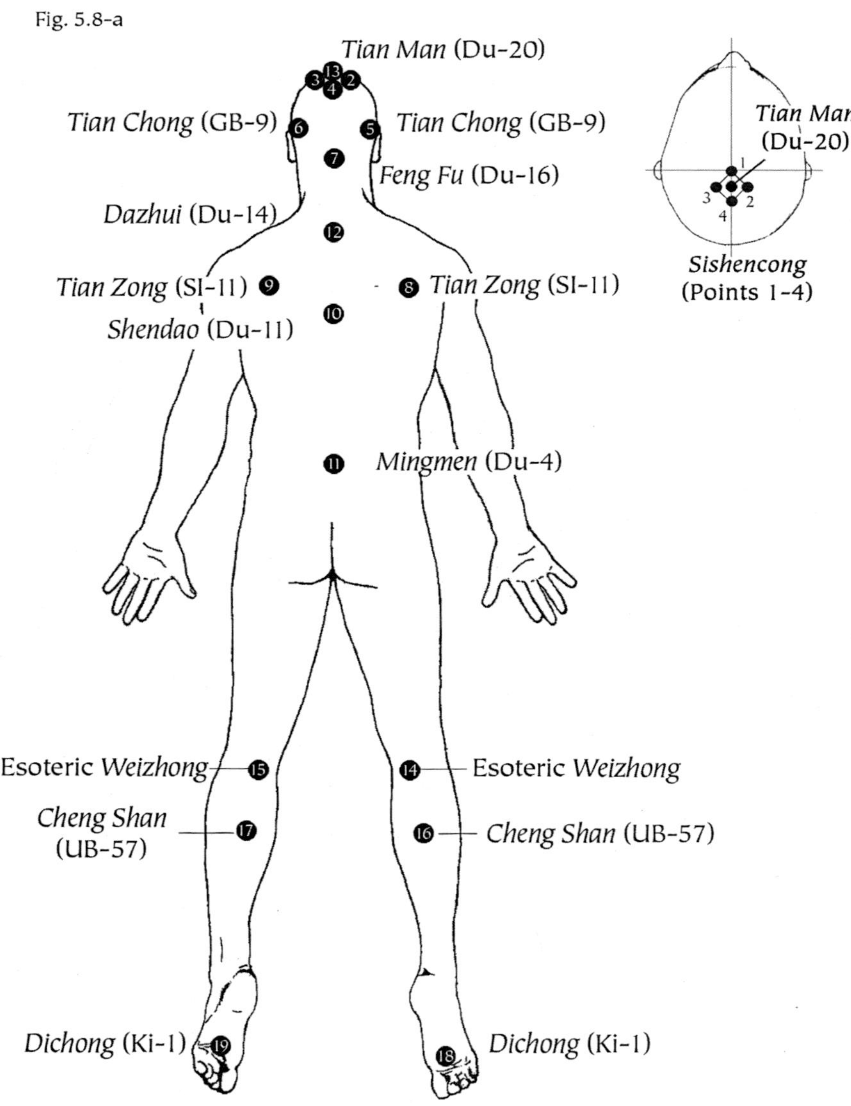

## Level III Posterior: Option #2
## Esoteric *Shaoyin* Kidney Pattern

The Esoteric *Shaoyin* Heart Pattern and the Esoteric *Shaoyin* Kidney Pattern seem to be very similar. The locations of the first seventeen acupuncture points in both patterns are the same with the exact same needling sequence. The difference between the Esoteric *Shaoyin* Heart Pattern and The Esoteric *Shaoyin* Kidney Pattern is the last two points. In the Esoteric *Shaoyin* Heart Pattern, the last two acupuncture points are the bilateral *Shenmen* (Ht-7) points on the wrist. In the Esoteric *Shaoyin* Kidney Pattern, the last two acupuncture points are the bilateral *Dichong* (Ki-1) points located on the soles of each foot. The more commonly used Chinese name (at least in the United States) for Ki-1 is *Yongyuan*. In Esoteric Acupuncture an alternative name *Dichong* is used. *Dichong* can be translated as "Earth's Thoroughfare." This alternative Chinese name for Ki-1 suggests that there is some connection from the Earth to the human body through these bilateral kidney points on the soles of the feet.

When would you choose one pattern over the other pattern? You would choose The Esoteric *Shaoyin* Kidney Pattern when your client has more Muladhara (Root Chakra) and Swadthisthana (Sacral Chakra) issues. This can be determined by dowsing with a pendulum or by asking questions. In the Esoteric *Shaoyin* theory, the kidney system refers to physicality. The heart system connects with spirituality. This means that the Esoteric *Shaoyin* Kidney Pattern is designed more for strengthening and grounding your Earth Energies, while simultaneously aligning and strengthening your spiritual frequencies.

The Esoteric *Shaoyin* Heart Pattern is designed specifically to strengthen and align your spiritual heart energies with less emphasis on the physical grounding energies of the physical vehicle. This pattern is designed to open the pathways to the higher head chakras to give the client an opportunity to move into an alignment with his or her Inner Spiritual Higher Heart.

**Needling Sequence for The Esoteric *Shaoyin* Kidney Pattern;** Think of this pattern as having three distinct sections.

**First Section:**
1) to 4) *Sishencong* -- "4 Spirits"
5) *Tian Chong* (GB-9) Right side
6) *Tian Chong* (GB-9) Left side
7) *Feng Fu* (Du-16)
8) *Tian Zong* (SI-11) Right side
9) *Tian Zong* (SI-11) Left Side
10) *Shendao* (Du-11)

**Second Section:**
11) *Mingmen* (Du-4)
12) *Dazhui* (Du-14)
13) *Tian Man* (Du-20)

**Third Section called Fire Triangle Group**
14) Esoteric *Weizhong*--Right side
15) Esoteric *Weizhong*--Left side
16) *Cheng Shan* (UB-57)--Right side
17) *Cheng Shan* (UB-57)--Left side
18) *Dichong* (Ki-1)--Right side
19) *Dichong* (Ki-1)--Left side

### Point Locations for The Esoteric *Shaoyin* Kidney Pattern

For the location of the first seventeen acupuncture points in the Esoteric *Shaoyin* Kidney Pattern, please refer back to preceding New Encoding Pattern the Esoteric *Shaoyin* Heart Pattern. The first seventeen acupuncture sites in both patterns have the same sequencing order.

The eighteen and nineteenth acupuncture points in The Esoteric *Shaoyin* Pattern are the bilateral *Dichong* points one point on the sole of each foot. You will notice that the Ki-1 points in Esoteric Acupuncture are called *Dichong* and is found in a different location than the traditional location of Ki-1 that is known as *Yongquan*. To find the traditional location of Ki-1 (*Yongquan*), you divide the bottom of the foot into three horizontal sections excluding the toes. Then draw an imaginary vertical line through the center of the sole. *Yongquan* (Ki-1) is found at the point where the vertical midline of the sole intersects the horizontal line that divides the top one third of the foot from the middle one third of the foot.

To find the location of the Ki-1 point called *Dichong*, you will look for a slight upward crease on the bottom of the foot slightly lateral to the ball of the foot. If this crease is not readily visible, then gently pinch the sides of the client's foot just slightly. Insert the needle where the uppermost indentation shows. (See figure 5.8-b below.) Unless your client likes to walk around barefooted, the bottom of the foot is usually very sensitive. I will usually use a Seirin light blue handled .20 mm X 15mm needle. Make one gentle straight insertion with the needle to a depth of approximately one quarter of an inch (.64 cm).

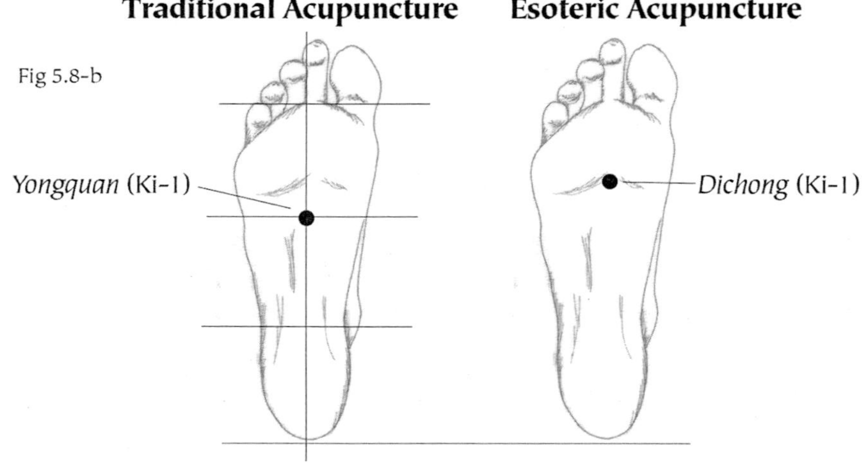


Fig 5.8-b

## Visualization of The Esoteric *Shaoyin* Kidney Pattern

The mental visualization connections for the first seventeen acupuncture points of the Esoteric *Shaoyin* Kidney Pattern are the same as the first seventeen points of the Esoteric *Shaoyin* Heart Pattern. For the visualization of the first seventeen acupuncture points, please refer back to the Esoteric *Shaoyin* Heart Pattern and to the Discern the Whisper Pattern.

The main difference between the Esoteric *Shaoyin* Heart Pattern and the Esoteric *Shaoyin* Kidney Pattern is that the latter pattern is more grounding. We are strengthening the physical (kidney system) to anchor into the Earth's qi, while simultaneously bringing the Earth qi into the body through the bilateral "Earth's Thoroughfare" *Dichong* (Ki-1) points. In the Esoteric *Shaoyin* Heart Pattern, we visually connected the bilateral Heart Gates at *Shenmen* (Ht-7) to the Central Heart Path at *Shendao* (Du-11). Basically, the practitioner is replacing the bilateral Heart Gate points of the Esoteric *Shaoyin* Heart Pattern and needling the bilateral *Dichong* (Ki-1) points in the Esoteric *Shaoyin* Kidney Pattern. The Anahata (Heart Chakra) is a higher chakra than the Swadthisthana (second chakra) of the kidneys.

Many people may have sensitive feet and may be apprehensive about having acupuncture needles inserted into the soles of the feet. Although licensed acupuncturists generally do not have problems needling their own clients/patients, those same acupuncturists are often the most squeamish about having needles inserted into the soles of their own feet. I will usually switch to a slightly thicker gauge acupuncture needle when needling *Dichong* (Ki-1). I will use the blue handled Seirin .20m X .15 needle at this site, rather than the red handled .16m X .15 needle. Also, some people may wear sandals in the areas with a warmer climate and will have thicker callouses on the soles of their feet. In those clients, the thin red handled Seirin needles may be too thin and will bend when you try to insert the needle. Use a firm, but quick insertion technique with no turning or thrusting after the initial insertion of the needle.

Start the last visualization of the Esoteric *Shaoyin* Kidney Pattern by needling the bilateral *Di Chong* (Ki-1) points on the bottom of both feet, (See figure 5.8-c below.)

## Esoteric *Shaoyin* Kidney Pattern Visualization

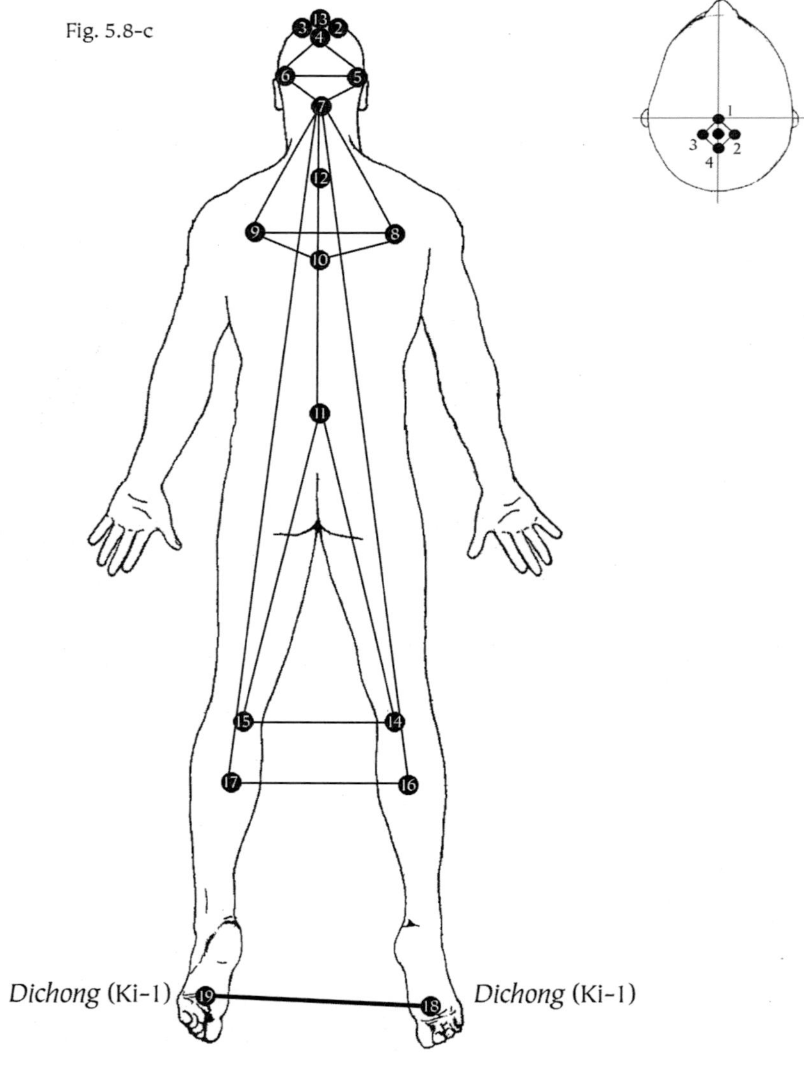

Have your client bring the qi upward from the bilateral *Dichong* (Ki-1) points to connect with *Tian Man* (Du-20). This triangular connection is longest Fire Triangle on the body that connects acupuncture points to each other. (See figure 5.8-d.)

## Esoteric *Shaoyin* Kidney Pattern

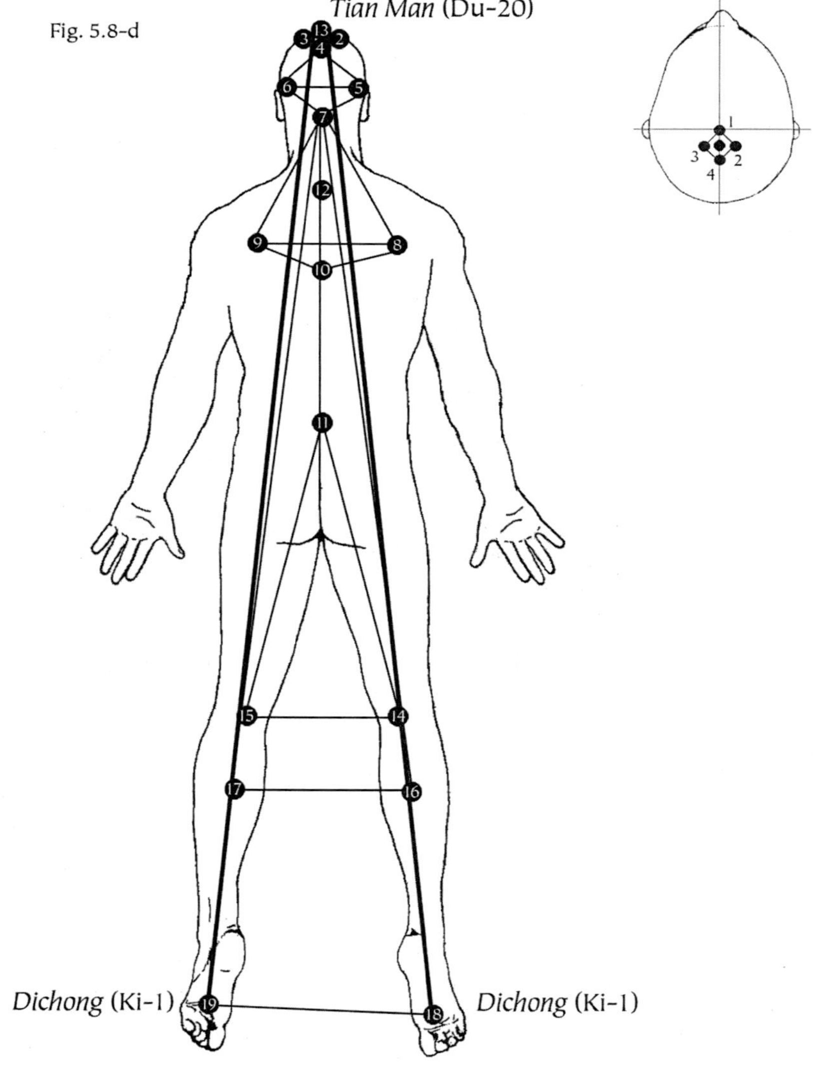

## Esoteric *Shaoyin* Kidney Pattern
### Complete Grid

Fig. 5.8-e

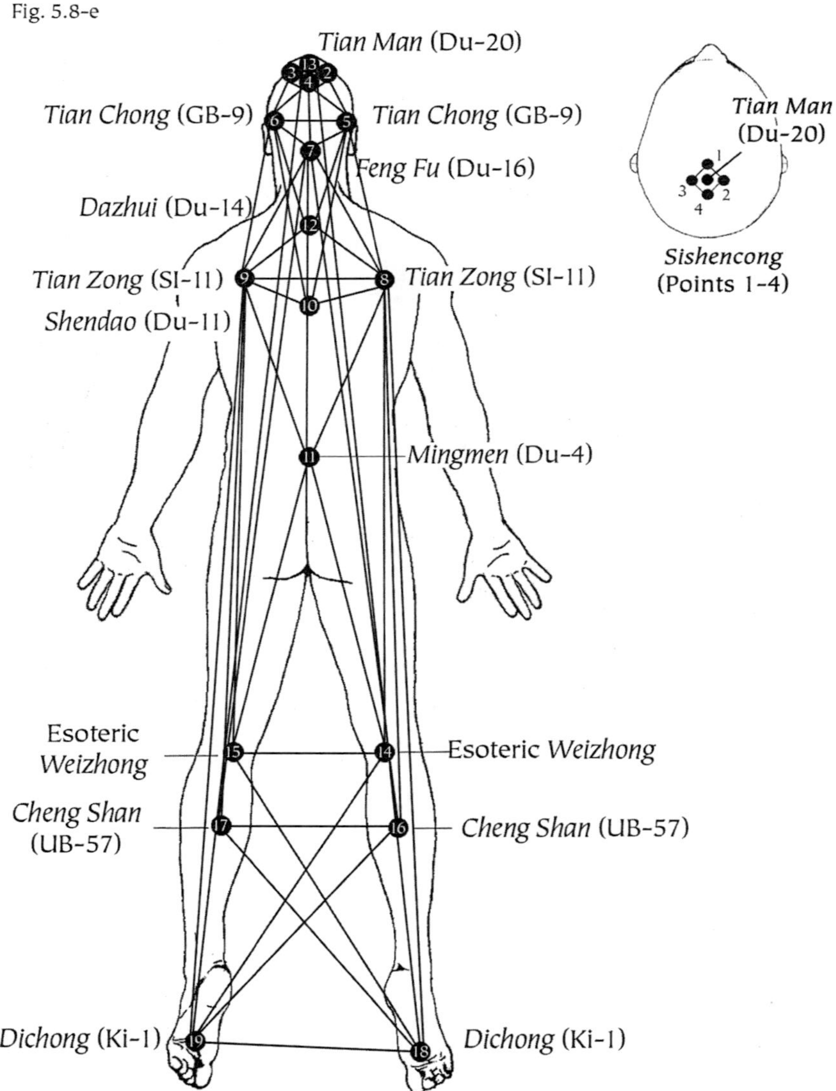

## Cube on Cube Window Pattern

Fig. 5.9-a

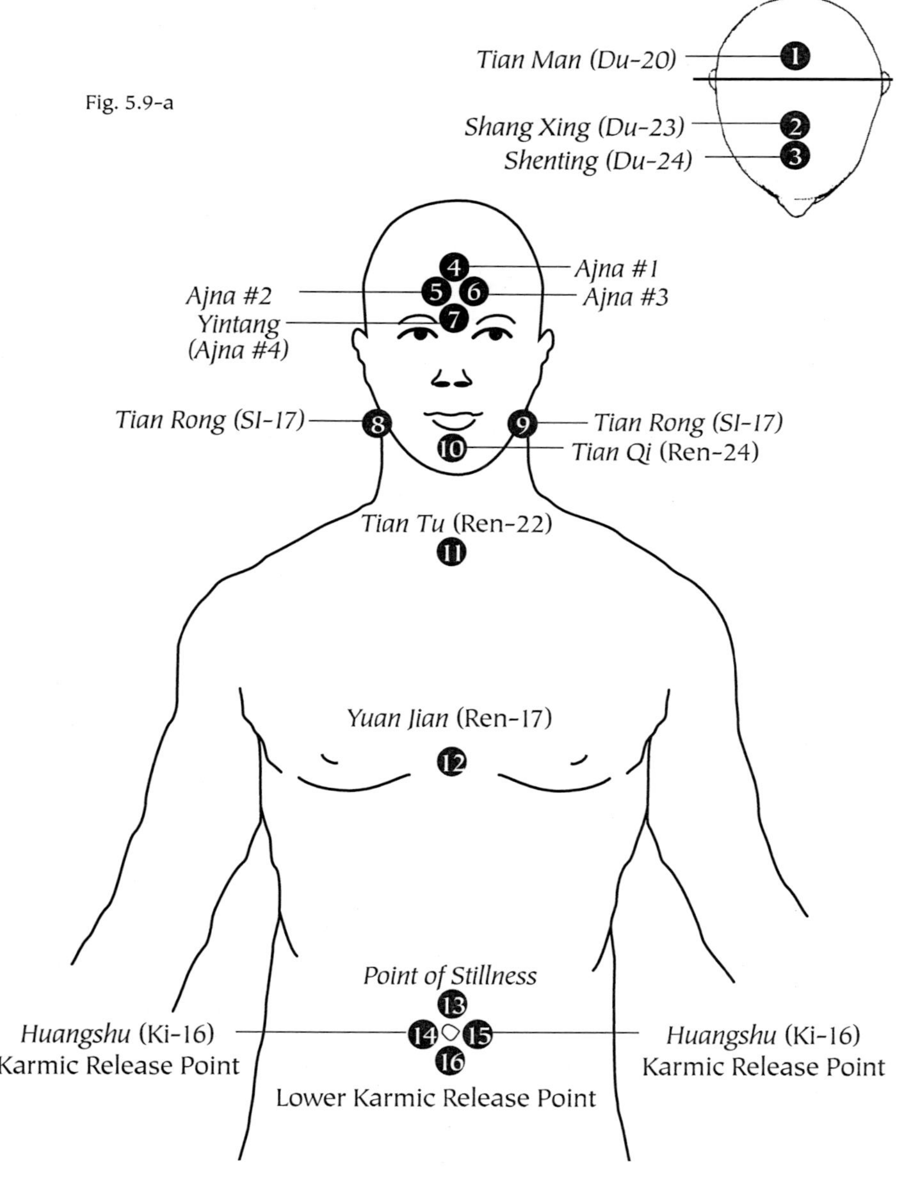

## Cube on Cube Window Pattern

The Cube on Cube Window Pattern is again another Esoteric *Shaoyin* balancing pattern energizing and aligning both the heart and kidney systems. The concept of the "cube on cube" means that you are in control and working on strengthening and refining both the physical and spiritual phases of your life. The top cube symbolizes the heart field of spirituality. The bottom cube represents the kidney field of physicality. The bottom cube must hold and stabilize the top cube. The physical must support the spiritual.

The grouping of four acupuncture points on the forehead is designed to activate, balance and strengthen the Ajna Center and the related chakras. Thee four acupuncture points are known as the Ajna Group. These points are the "window" to the higher spiritual planes.

The sister group to the upper Ajna Group consists of four acupuncture points surrounding the umbilicus and is known as the Karmic Release Points. These four acupuncture points are the grounding and balancing "window" for the Swadthisthana (Sacral Chakra) and the Muladhara (Root Chakra).

The sixteen acupuncture points in this pattern reflect the two cubes. Each of the cubes has eight stars or eight corners. It is important to become intimate with the Cube on Cube Window Pattern, because this pattern is the foundation for the Crystalline Grid Pattern and the Crystalline Heart Grid Pattern.

## Needling Sequence

There are sixteen acupuncture points in the Cube on Cube Window Pattern. Each cube contains eight corners. The sixteen acupuncture points in this pattern representing a cube on top of a cube. The top or upper cube presents spirituality. The bottom or lower cube represents physicality.

The eighth note in a western musical scale is an octave above or below the starting note in the scale. The number eight esoterically represents the possibility of moving into hyperspatial realities. Placing eight on top of eight represents an expanded, balanced spiritual consciousness being in alignment with an expanded, balanced physical consciousness. Since cubes are merely triangles arranged in a certain geometric format, the cube on cube concept is another version of Esoteric *Shaoyin*—the heart balanced with the kidneys, or spirituality in harmony with physicality.

Think of the Cube on Cube Window Pattern as having two needling sections. The first section consists of ten acupuncture points. The second section consists of six acupuncture points. First Section:

1) *Tian Man* (Du-20) "Celestial Fullness"
2) *Shang Xing* (Du-23) "Upper Star"
3) *Shenting* (Du-24) "Celestial Court" or "Heavenly Court"
4) Ajna #1 (Indu Chakra)
5) Ajna #2 (Manas Chakra) Right side
6) Ajna #3 (Manas Chakra) Left side
7) *Yintang* (Ajna Center) "Third Eye" Point
8) *Tian Rong* (SI-17) "Heavenly Appearance;" Right side
9) *Tian Rong* (SI-17) "Heavenly Appearance;" Left side
10) *Tian Qi* (Ren-24) "Celestial Pool"

Second Section:

11) *Tian Tu* (Ren-22) "Celestial Chimney"
12) *Yuan Jian* (Ren-17) More commonly known as *Danzhong* or *Tanzhong*.

### Four Karmic Release Points #13 to #16

13) Point of Stillness (Ren-8.5)
14) Karmic Release Point; *Huangshu* (Ki-16) Right side
15) Karmic Release Point; *Huangshu* (Ki-16) Left side
16) Lower Karmic Release Point

## Point Locations for The Cube on Cube Window Pattern

The first acupuncture point needled in the Cube on Cube Window Pattern is *Tian Man* ("Celestial Fullness"). Remember this acupuncture point is found at the esoteric location for Du-20 and not the traditional location for *Bai Hui* (Du-20). The esoteric location for Du-20 is found approximately one *cun* posteriorly to the traditional location for *Bai Hui* (Du-20). (See figure 5.9-b below.)

## Cube on Cube Window Pattern

Fig. 5.9-b

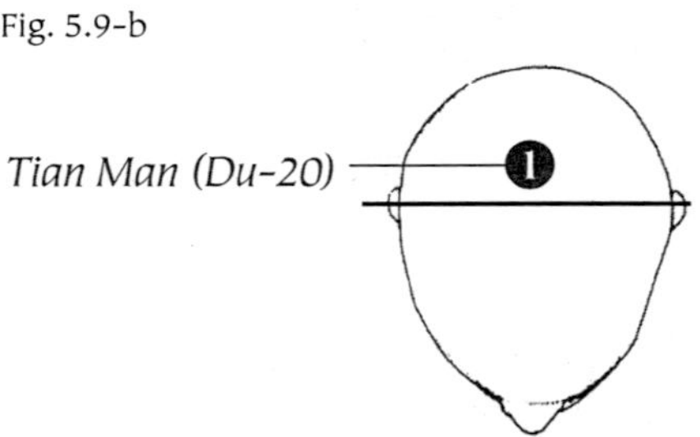


The second acupuncture point needled in the Cube on Cube Window Pattern is *Shang Xing* (Du-23) "Upper Star." To find the needling location for *Shang Xing* (Du-23), it is best to first locate *Shenting* (Du-24). *Shenting* (Du-24) is located directly on the vertical midline of the body on the top of the anterior of the head one-half *cun* behind the anterior hairline. You are only going to locate the site of *Shenting* (Du-24) and will not be inserting a needle at this site yet. The second acupuncture point needled is *Shang Xing* (Du-23). *Shang Xing* (Du-23) is one of the stars of a double tetrahedron located on the top of one's head. This particular double tetrahedron is flopped and twisted.

*Shang Xing* (Du-23) is also found on the same vertical anterior midline at the top of the anterior head approximately one-half *cun* posteriorly to *Shenting* (Du-24). (See figure 5.9-c below.)

**Cube on Cube Window Pattern**

Fig. 5.9-c

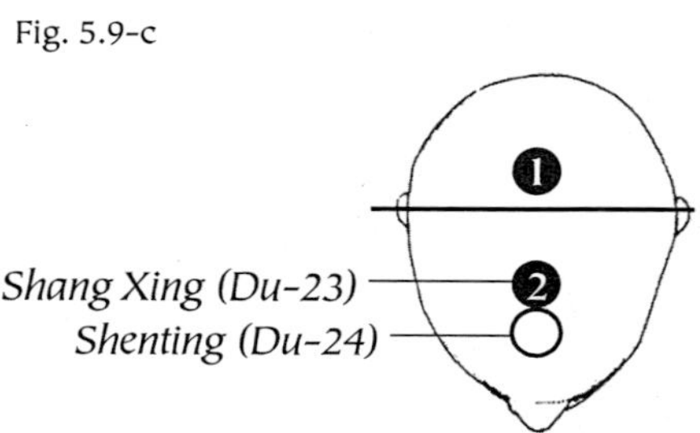


After inserting an acupuncture needle at the site of *Shang Xing* (Du-23), next insert an acupuncture needle at the location of *Shenting* (Du-24). You located this acupuncture site previously. (See figure 5.9-d below.)

**Cube on Cube Window Pattern**

Fig. 5.9-d

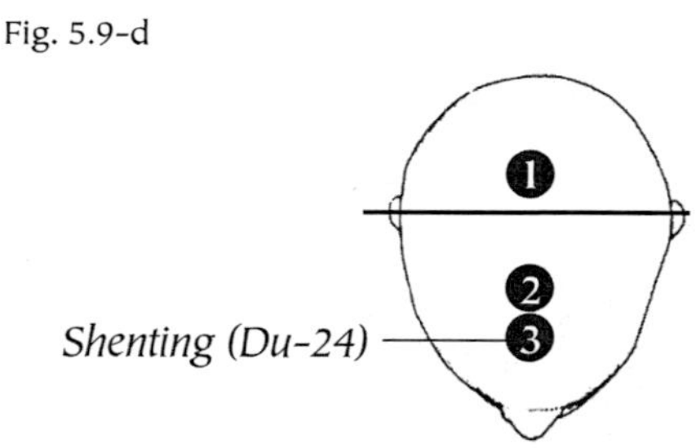

The fourth acupuncture point needled in the Cube on Cube Window Pattern is Ajna #1. To locate Ajna #1, you must first find the acupuncture site of *Yintang* located between the eyebrows and above the bridge of the nose. (See figure 5.9-e below.)

**Cube on Cube Window Pattern**

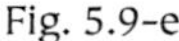

Fig. 5.9-e

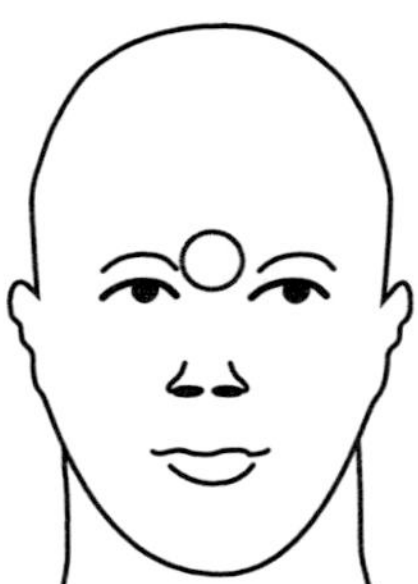

Next determine the horizontal distance between the inner canthi of both eyes. Ajna #1 is located on the vertical midline of the forehead directly superior to *Yintang* and the same distance from *Yintang* as the distance between the two inner canthi of the eyes. (See figure 5.9-f below.)

**Cube on Cube Window Pattern**

Fig. 5.9-f

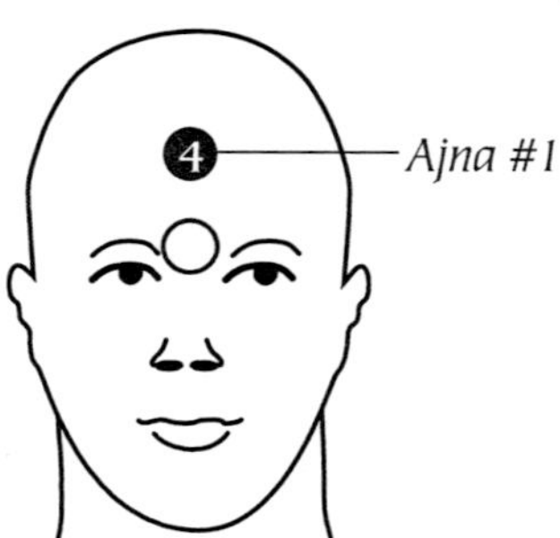

Now find the mid point between Ajna #1 and *Yintang*. Draw an imaginary horizontal line dissecting the mid point between Ajna #1 and *Yintang*. (See figure 5.9-g below.

**Cube on Cube Window Pattern**

Fig. 5.9-g

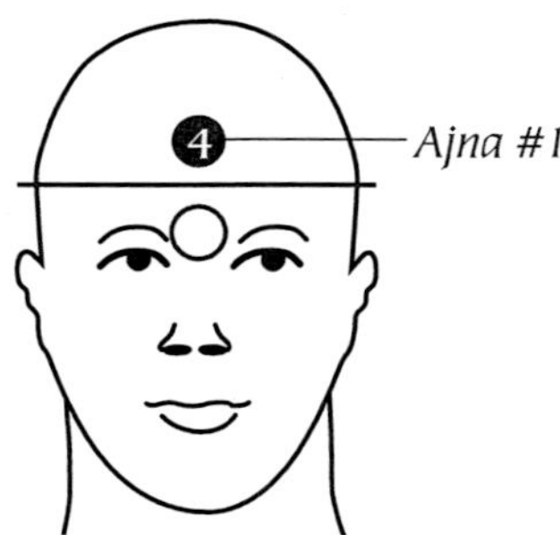


Next draw an imaginary vertical line upward from the inner canthi of the right eye to intersect with the imaginary horizontal line. (See figure 5.9-h below.)

**Cube on Cube Window Pattern**

Fig. 5.9-h

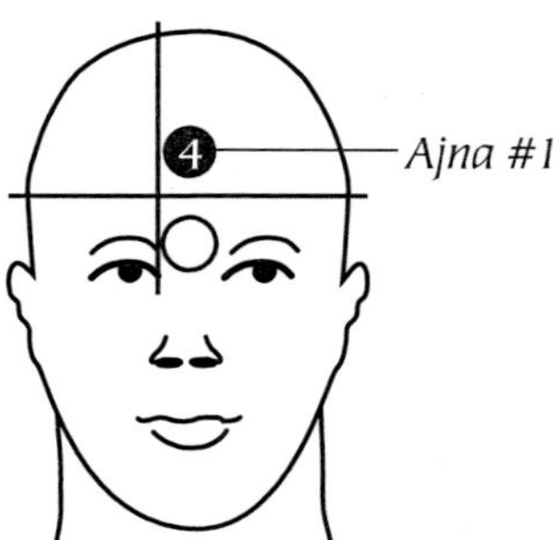

Where this vertical line intersects the imaginary horizontal line is the site of the fifth acupuncture point Ajna #2. (See figure 5.9-i below.)

## Cube on Cube Window Pattern

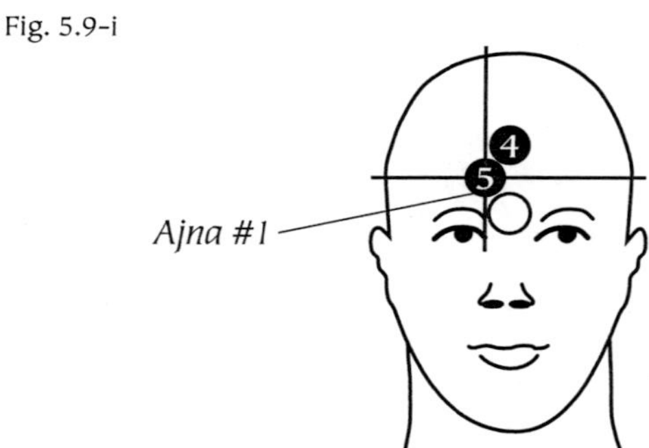

Fig. 5.9-i

Draw an imaginary vertical line from the inner canthus of the left eye again intersecting with the imaginary horizontal line that dissects the mid point between Ajna #1 and *Yintang*. (See figure 5.9-j below.)

## Cube on Cube Window Pattern

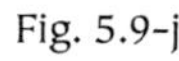
Fig. 5.9-j

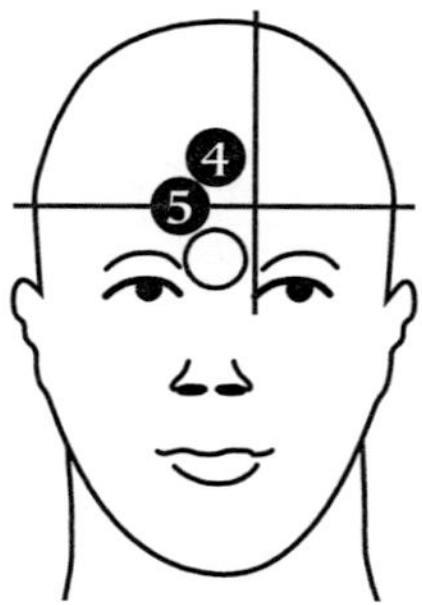

Now insert an acupuncture needle into this last location on the client's left mid forehead. This point is known as Ajna #3. (See 5.9-k below.)

**Cube on Cube Window Pattern**

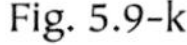
Fig. 5.9-k

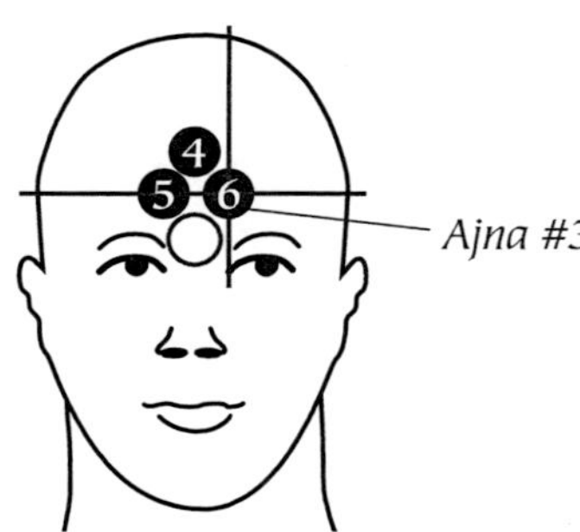


After acupuncture needles have been inserted in the first three upper Ajna points, you will now insert an acupuncture needle at the site of *Yintang*, the first site you located in the Ajna Group of four points. This is the seventh acupuncture point. (See figure 5.9-l below.)

**Cube on Cube Window Pattern**

Fig. 5.9-l

The eighth acupuncture point in the Cube on Cube Window Pattern is a Window to the Sky/Window of Heaven point known as *Tian Rong* (SI-17). *Tian Rong* can be translated as "Heavenly Appearance," "Heavenly Countenance" or "Heaven's Reception" depending on the source. In Esoteric Acupuncture, the bilateral *Tian Rong* (SI-17) points activate the heart system. On one level, these bilateral acupuncture points connect to the tongue that is controlled by the heart system. On a higher level, the bilateral *Tian Rong* (SI-17) points send qi to one's Inner Spiritual Higher Heart Field to activate that energy field.

Find the angle of the mandible on the right side. You are looking for the angle of the client's right jawbone. Next try to feel the client's sternocleidomastoideus muscle in the neck. Insert the acupuncture needle in the neck posteriorly to the angle of the right jawbone, but anteriorly to the sternocleidomastoideus muscle. Insert the acupuncture needle in the slight depression in the neck, but in front of the sternocleidomastoideus muscle. Try not to insert the acupuncture needle directly into the client's sternocleidomastoideus muscle. (See figure 5.9-m below.)

**Cube on Cube Window Pattern**

Fig. 5.9-m

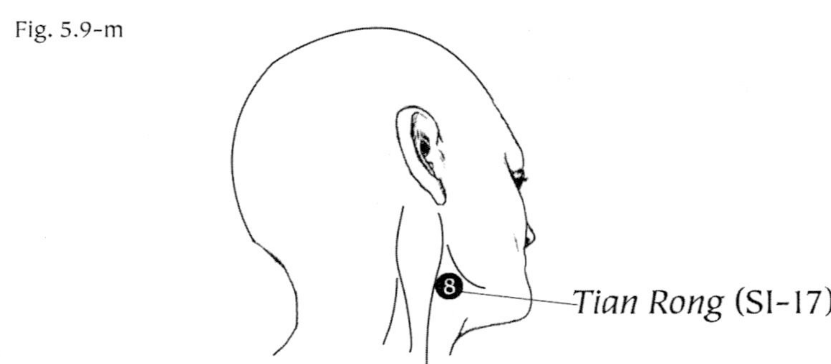

Find the acupuncture site of *Tian Rong* (SI-17) on the client's right side and insert an acupuncture needle at this site followed by needling the same point on the left side. (See figure 5.9-n below.)

**Cube on Cube Window Pattern**

Fig. 5.9-n

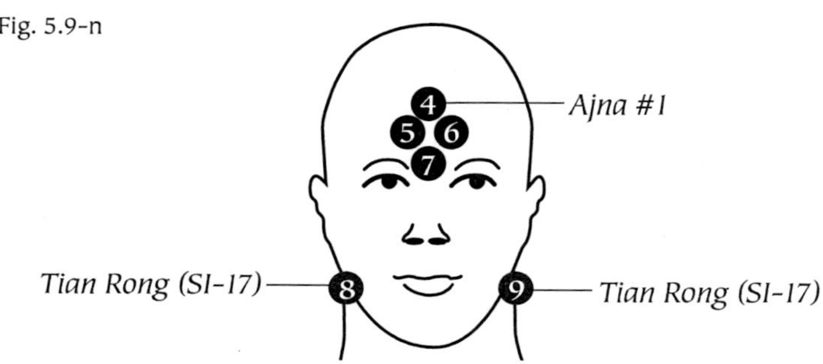


The tenth acupuncture point is called *Tian Qi* (Ren-24) and is located between the lower border of the lower lip and above the chin directly on the vertical midline of the face. Insert the acupuncture needle at the horizontal crease below the lower lip. The location of this cease will vary depending on your clientele. (See figure 5.9-o below.)

**Cube on Cube Window Pattern**

Fig. 5.9-o

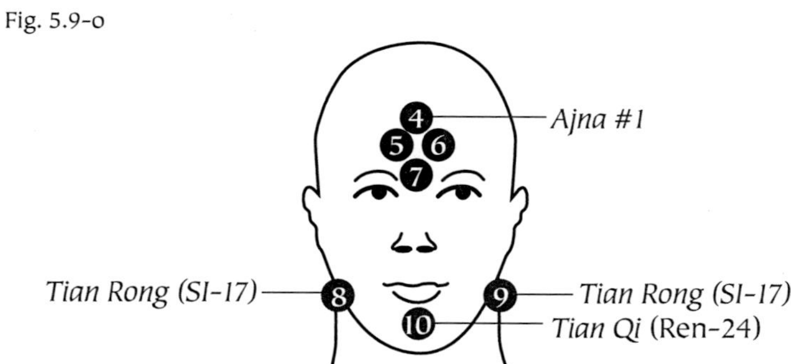

The eleventh acupuncture in the Cube on Cube Window Pattern is called *Tian Tu* (Ren-22) and is located in the suprasternal notch directly on the vertical midline of the anterior of the body. (See figure 5.9-p below.)

**Cube on Cube Window Pattern**

Fig. 5.9-p

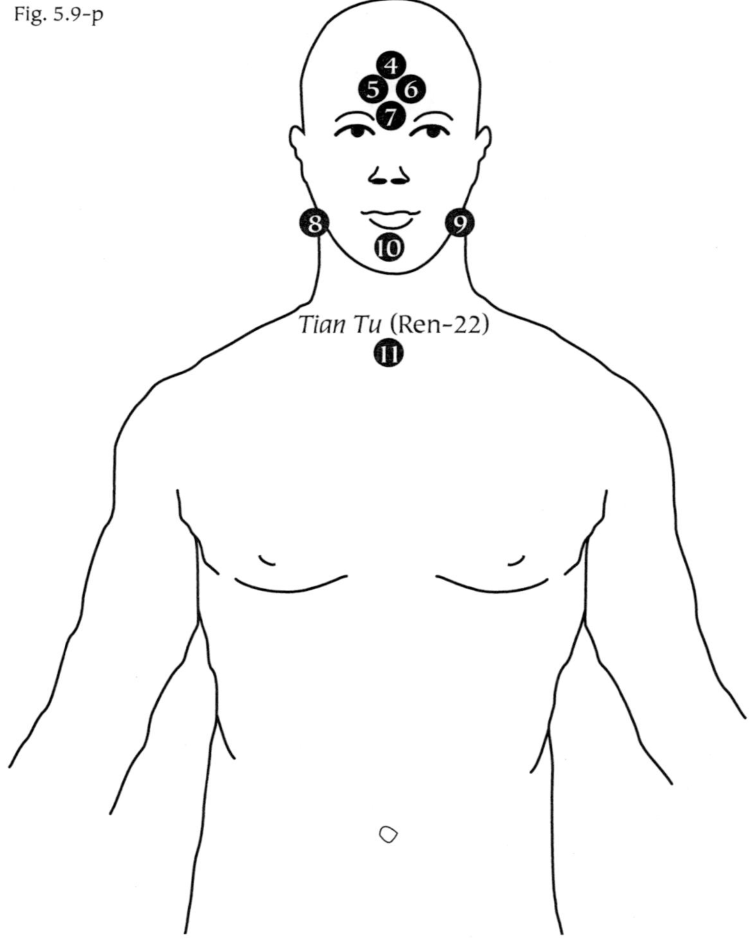

The twelfth acupuncture point in the Cube on Cube Window Pattern is called *Yuan Jian* (Ren-17) in Esoteric Acupuncture. This point is located directly on the anterior vertical midline of the chest in the fourth intercostal space. This acupuncture point is often level with the nipples on younger males. (See figure 5.9-q below.)

## Cube on Cube Window Pattern

Fig. 5.9-q

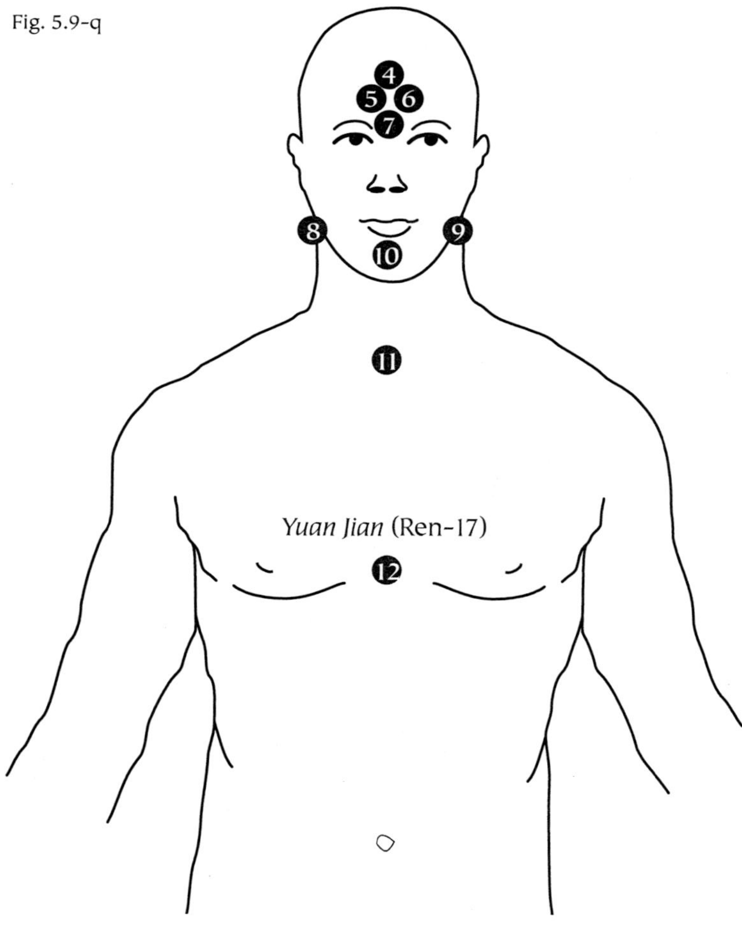

These next four acupuncture sites are collectively called the "Karmic Release Points" in Esoteric Acupuncture and are located in four sites all approximately one *cun* from the center of the umbilicus. The first point in this group is called "Point of Stillness" and is a heart point. The Point of Stillness in located superior to the center of the umbilicus and directly on the vertical midline of the anterior body. (See figure 5.9-r below.)

## Cube on Cube Window Pattern

Fig. 5.9-r

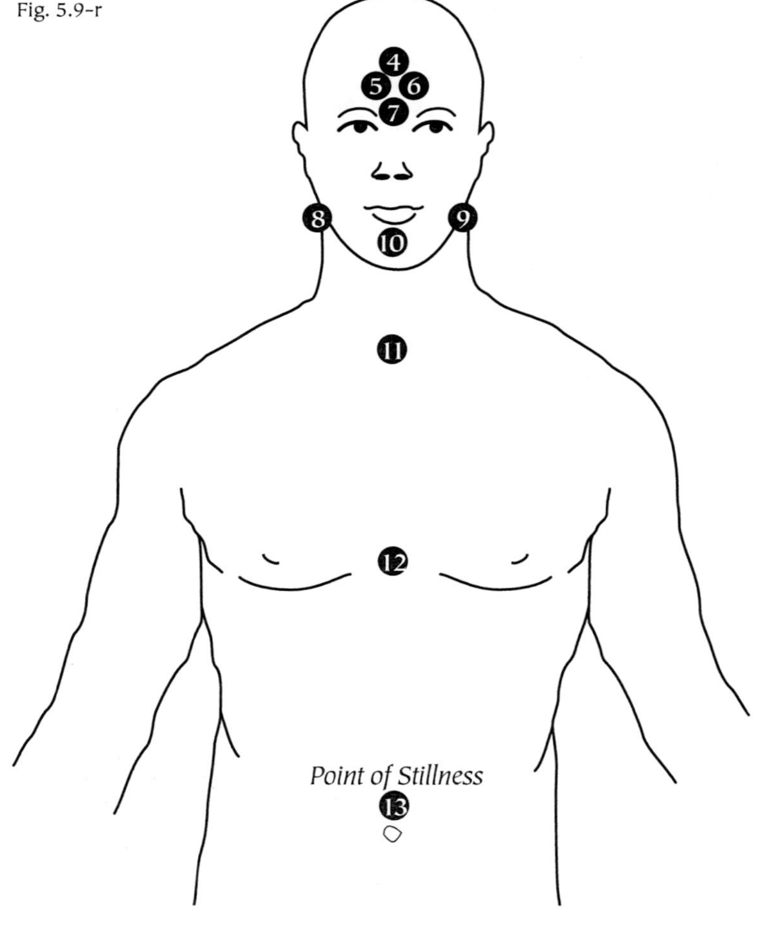

The fourteenth acupuncture point in the Cube on Cube Window Pattern is *Huangshu* (Ki-16) on the client's right side. This acupuncture point is found approximately one *cun* from the center of the umbilicus on the horizontal line that intersects the center of the umbilicus. (See figure 5.9-s below.)

**Cube on Cube Window Pattern**

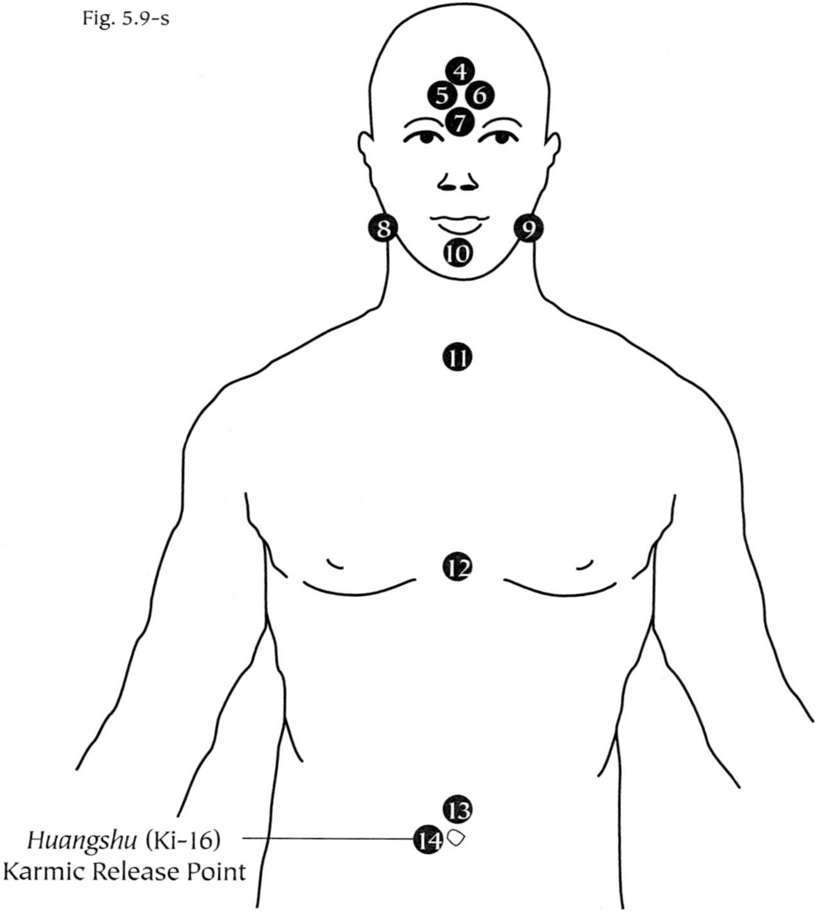


Fig. 5.9-s

The fifteenth acupuncture point and the third point within the Karmic Release Group is *Huangshu* (Ki-16) on the client's left side. Again, insert the acupuncture needle approximately one *cun* from the center of the umbilicus and on the imaginary horizontal line that dissects the center of the umbilicus. (See figure 5.9-t below.)

**Cube on Cube Window Pattern**

Fig. 5.9-t

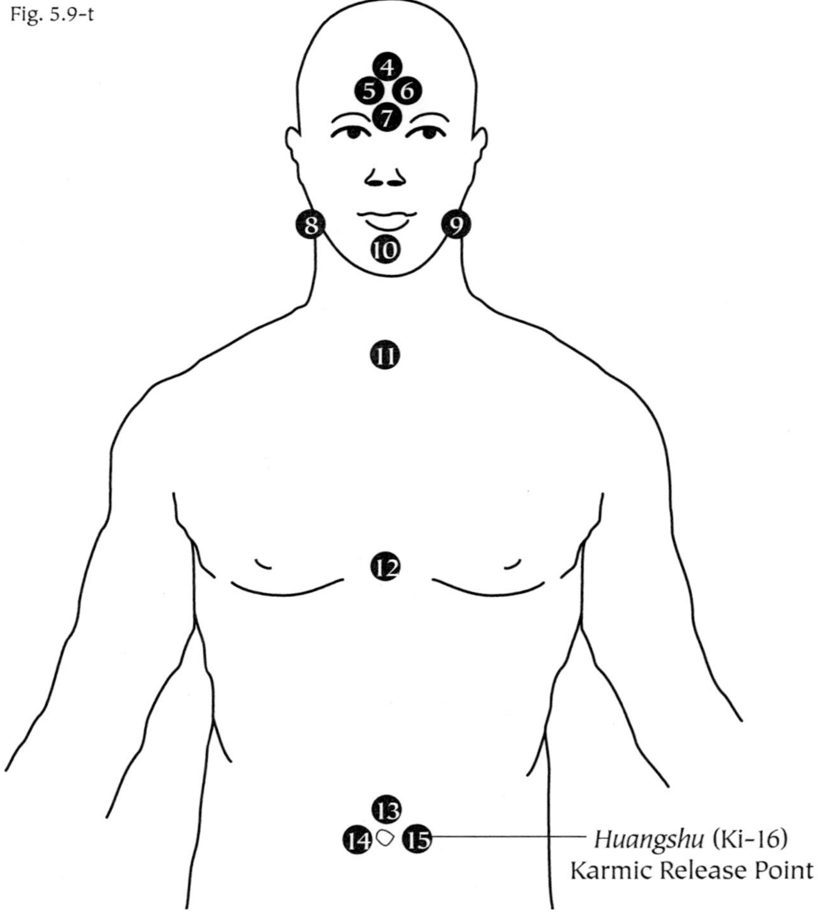

The sixteenth and last point in the Cube on Cube Window Pattern is located directly on the vertical anterior midline of the body approximately one *cun* inferiorly to the center of the umbilicus. (See figure 5.9-u below.)

## Cube on Cube Window Pattern

Fig. 5.9-u

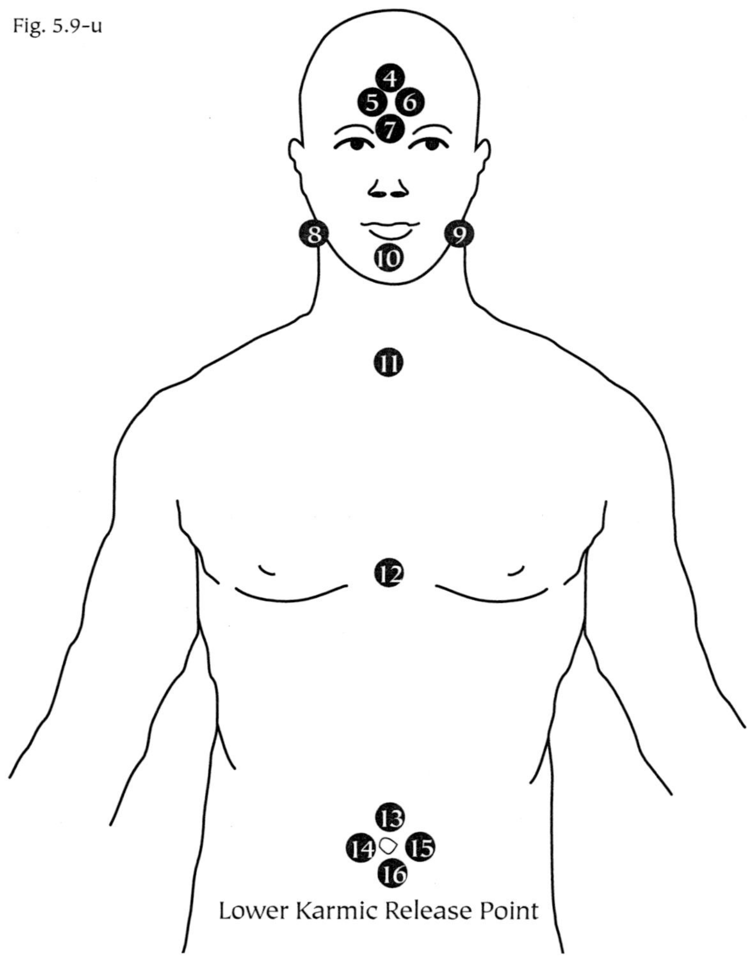

## Cube on Cube Window Pattern
### Complete Grid

Fig. 5.9-v

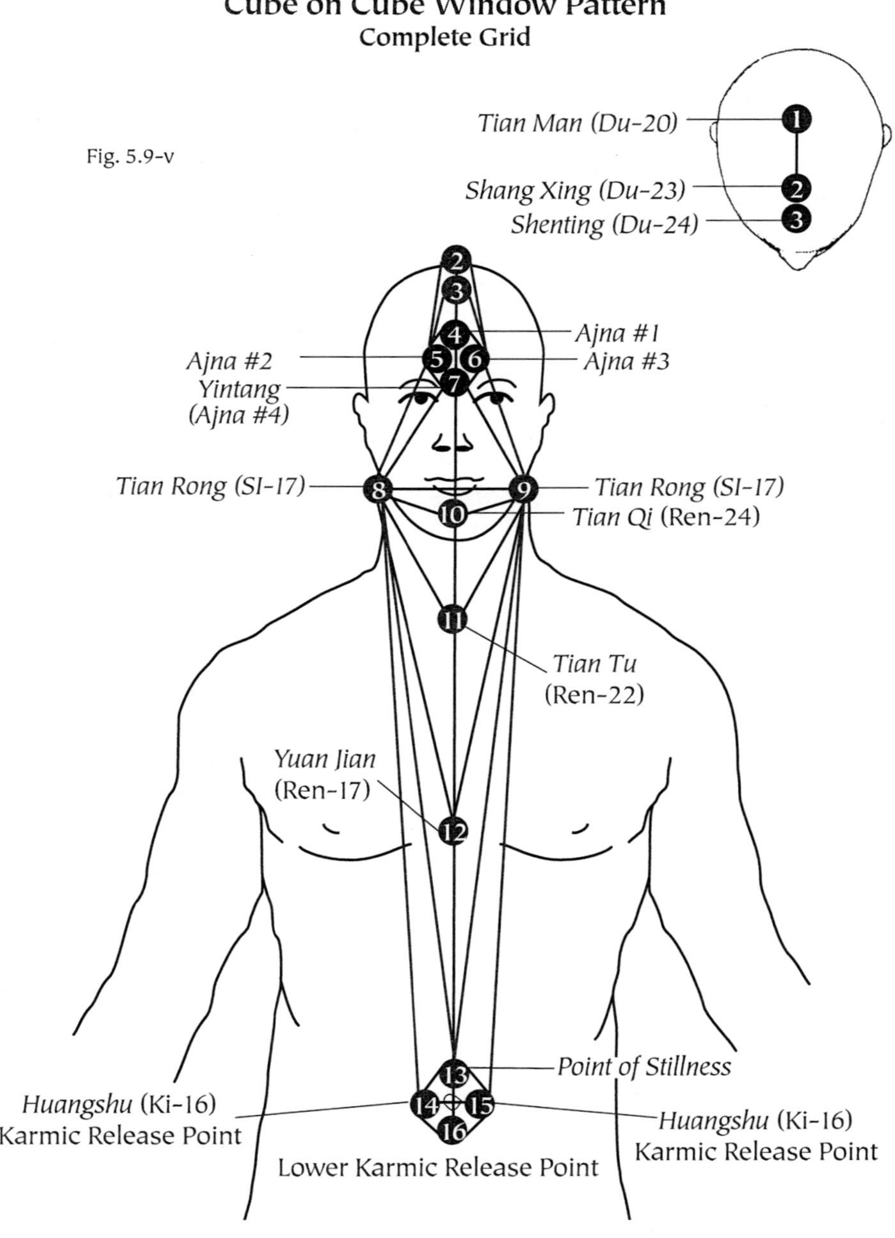

## Tier Density Level IV
## Refining Our Awakened Inner *Shen*

At Tier Density Level IV, you are either a serious meditator or practice some form of inner plane work on a consistent basis. Inner plane work does not mean meditation only, but you are aware and are able to meditate, or have other methods to quiet and still the mind when needed. You may be doing some version of advanced pranayama (breathing exercises) or advanced inner visualizations to bring you to your place of quietude, your place of very deep, inner peace.

The "true" teachers of the Ancient, Ageless Wisdom are on this tier density level or on the higher density levels. The Ancient, Ageless Wisdom Teachings will resonate with those of you who are ready to "hear" the teachings. In actuality, your Higher, Inner Heart will know the teachings as the truth. There is an old saying: "Don't cast pearls before swine." This means that it is not advisable for a teacher to share rare or very highly esoteric teachings with those who are not at the level to fully understand and appreciate those teachings. Those pearls of wisdom may create arguments and even generate dense, negative energies to drain your energy field. Be discerning with those you share your wisdom with.

At Tier Density Level IV you radiate a certain frequency that attracts students to you. You do not need to look for students. The students will find you. There are many initiates and students searching for the right teacher from whom to learn. Truth seeks its own level. When a true teacher of the Ancient, Ageless Wisdom Schools address those who have come to hear the teacher, those in attendance with know from their hearts that the teachings carry a vibration of truth.

At Tier Density Level IV, you do not give advice unless someone asks you first. This is very important. You do not need to put your "trips" (advice or opinions) on others. Even if you think you know better, you do not preach to others who may be on a different level of density. You let things be. You allow the natural flow of both nature and that person's karmic lessons to move at their own pace. You do not interfere, unless asked. The "true" nature of the advanced heart frequency allows things to be without judgment. If you carry some answers to "the truth" a person is seeking, that person will find you and come to you.

You may now be an advanced teacher of *Tai Qi, Qi Gong* or various types of yoga other than Hatha. Yoga may now include Bakti, Laya or Raja. You allow things to be. You observe rather than judge. You do not stick your nose into other people's issues. You conserve and utilize your qi for you realize how much discipline and inner strength it takes to refine your inner awakened *Shen* to further your own Soul Journey and your Spirit Journey. You do not blame others for any challenges or obstacles that you encounter. You take full responsibility for all your karmic debts and all the challenges that come to you. Your puzzle piece is now unfolding and your work is assisting you with some answers of why you are here in this incarnation.

At Tier Density Level 4, you are not ruled by food. Food is not an issue. You can eat or not eat. You do not eat foods that are of a lower vibration than your standards. At Tier Density Level 4, you never say: "Well I normally do not eat that type of food, but I was hungry and there was nothing else to eat." You have trained your inner discipline to be able to skip meals, especially when the foods available to you are not vibrating at a high enough frequency to be nourishing to your own vibratory rate. You only eat the highest, cleanest vibrating food. You are bicameral. You are now accessing information from your abstract mind.

Some of you may wish to delve into the higher realms of the lunar, nature devas. This is the world of the sangomas, curanderos/curanderas, shamans and the santaristas. Those of you who are called into this realm must become very aware of the lower fourth dimension astral beings. Not all entities in the fourth dimensional are spiritually enlightened beings of light. This realm also contains the dark side.

## Treatment #4 Posterior Pattern
## Esoteric *Shaoyin* Heart Window Pattern

Fig. 5.10-a

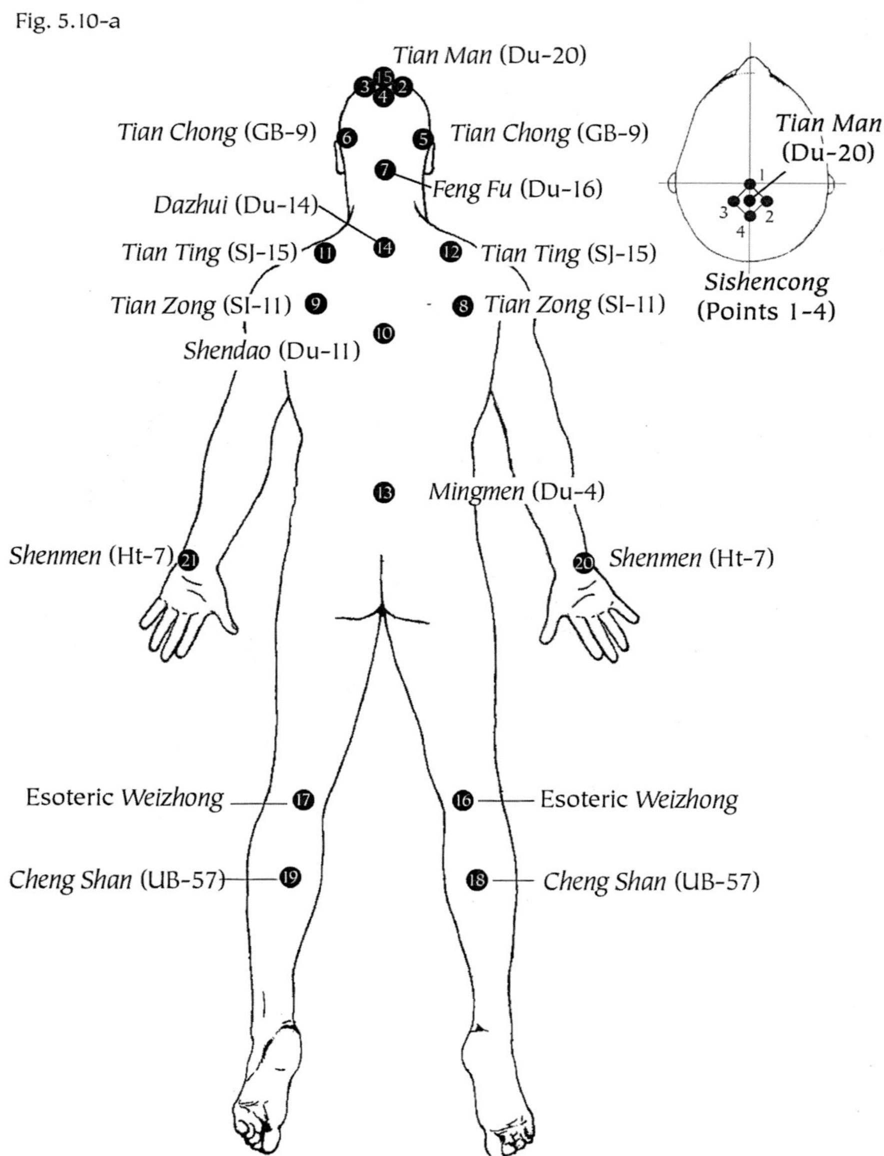

## The Window of One Hand Clapping

The difference between the Esoteric *Shaoyin* Heart Window Pattern and the other two Esoteric *Shaoyin* New Encoding Patterns that have the same first ten acupuncture points is that the Esoteric *Shaoyin* Heart Window Pattern has two additional acupuncture points that create a unique field or a specific window. This specific field is a more expansive and finer frequency plane and is known in Esoteric Acupuncture as the Window of One Hand Clapping. A window can be thought of as an opening that allows things to pass through, or as an interval or an opportunity for some action to occur. The "window" that is created in this pattern allows the recipient of the treatment an opportunity to move into this particular field of One Hand Clapping. The Esoteric *Shaoyin* Heart Window Pattern is the major posterior New Encoding Pattern that I use on a majority of my current clientele.

For the Esoteric *Shaoyin* Heart Window Pattern, the two additional acupuncture points added are the bilateral *Tian Ting* (SJ-15) points on the posterior of both shoulders. One thing to take note of is the needling sequence for these two acupuncture points does not follow the normal right side first followed by the left side. After the first ten acupuncture points in the Esoteric *Shaoyin* Heart Window Pattern have been inserted, the practitioner will needle the left *Tian Ting* (SJ-15) point (point number eleven) first followed by the *Tian Ting* (SJ-15) point on the right side. The only other New Encoding Pattern that has a left side first sequence when inserting the acupuncture needles is Spirit Path presented in ***Esoteric Acupuncture: Gateway to Expanded, Healing, Volume I.***

When the bilateral *Tian Ting* (SJ-15) points in the Esoteric *Shaoyin* Heart Window Pattern are visually connected in an hourglass geometrical configuration with the bilateral *Tian Chong* (GB-9) points, an esoteric "window" is created. In Traditional Chinese Medical Theory, *san jiao* is known as "that which has no form." (SJ, as in the acupuncture point SJ-15 stands for the fifteenth point on the *san jiao* acupuncture channel.) From an exoteric viewpoint, "that which has no form" this could refer to the fact that although there is a *san jiao* (triple burner/triple heater) channel, there is no physical organ that is directly associated with the *san jiao* channel.

The *San Jiao* (*Tian Ting*/SJ-15) pairing with the Gallbladder channel (*Tian Chong*/GB-9) creates an Upper *Shaoyang* Four Gates connection. This particular hourglass connection also contains the acupuncture point *Feng Fu* (Du-16) within the field. In Traditional Chinese Medicine, *Shaoyang* treatments often refer to a condition in a patient who has a syndrome that is considered partly inside and partly outside. From a physical treatment protocol, the healer should address both the inner and outer disharmonies.

From an esoteric viewpoint (not exoteric), "that which has no form" and the connection with the *san jiao* meridian refers to working with spirit and the energetic, spiritual realms. The physical realm has form. The spiritual realms have no form. When we are working with an Upper *Shaoyang* Field like the field created by the bilateral *Tian Ting* (SJ-15) points being connected with the bilateral *Tian Chong* (GB-9) points, we are entering the realms of the Higher, Inner, Spiritual Heart Field that has no definite form.

In the acupuncture meridian system, *san jiao* refers to the triple burner or triple warmer system. In the school of Chinese Acupuncture Theory, the triple burners/warmers refer to: 1) the lower burner of elimination: 2) the middle burner of digestion; and 3) the upper burner of the lungs and heart. In this system, the upper burner, that includes the bilateral acupuncture points *Tian Ting* (SJ-15) refers to the heart system. Another point of view by certain Taoist groups has the heart as the middle burner and the Third Eye region as the upper burner. In the Esoteric *Shaoyin* Heart Window Pattern, we will follow the theories of both the Traditional Chinese Acupuncture School of thinking and the Taoist's point of view. Just know that the *Tian Ting* (SJ-15) points are part of the upper *jiao*/upper burner portion of the triple burner system. The physical location of the bilateral *Tian Ting* (SJ-15) points place these points in the physical vicinity of both the physical heart and the head centers. The Inner Spiritual Higher Heart Center is not located in the physical heart region. As we evolve during our inner spiritual journey, the heart center ascends to the head centers and later to the chakras above the head. Also remember that in the Chinese Five Element Theory, *san jiao* is part of the fire element of the heart.

Those of you who are familiar with the traditional Chinese names of the acupuncture points will notice that in Esoteric Acupuncture, SJ-15 is called *Tian Ting* and not the more commonly used Chinese name *Tian Liao*. *Tian Liao* is often translated as "Celestial Bone Hole" or "Heavenly Bone Hole." *Tian Ting* can be translated as "Celestial Hearing." In the Traditional Chinese Medical model, the kidneys and kidney system control one's physical hearing. Celestial Hearing is not one of the lower five senses and is not part of our physical hearing system. Celestial Hearing is awakened by the stillness of the heart and is controlled by the Inner Spiritual Higher Heart. Celestial Hearing is hearing without 3-D sound.

The bilateral *Tian Chong* (GB-9) points, as used in Esoteric Acupuncture, are not merely acupuncture points to influence imbalances associated with the gallbladder system of the wood element. The bilateral *Tian Chong* (GB-9) points are used to reinforce the activation power of the Inner Spiritual Higher Heart. Although the name *Tian Chong* is usually translated as "Celestial Hub," 'Celestial Surge" or "Celestial Thoroughfare,"[12] within the context of Esoteric Acupuncture, the bilateral *Tian Chong* (GB-9) points are considered to be "Celestial Hearing" sites that are connected to the higher heart.

Just remember that *Tian Ting* (SJ-15) is part of the upper burner or upper *jiao* that is associated with the heart. Even with the New Encoding Patterns that do not use the bilateral *Tian Ting* (SJ-15) points, the *Tian Chong* (GB-9) points are still closely connected to the higher heart system.

When the client makes the visual connections in the Crown

Infinity Pattern, he or she is connecting the bilateral *Tian Chong* (GB-9) points to the acupuncture point Crown #4 that is the fourth point in the *Sishencong* Group. It was mentioned earlier that *Sishencong* is often translated to mean "Four Spirits," or "Spirit Brightening." In Chinese Medicine, spirit refers to the *Shen* that is a part of the heart system. We are visually connecting the bilateral *Tian Chong* (GB-9) "Celestial Hearing" points to another heart point (Crown #4).

In Traditional Chinese Acupuncture, the four *Sishencong* points are often used to treat *jueyin* (liver) headaches at the top of the head. We are not interested in treating *jueyin* headaches. Just remember that the esoteric location of *Sishencong* surrounding *Tian Man* (Du-20) is the esoteric gateway to one's Higher, Inner, Spiritual Heart Center. In Esoteric Acupuncture, the insertion of acupuncture needles at the four acupuncture sites of *Sishencong* is always done to activate various levels of one's heart field. The level of one's heart that can be activated depends on the amount of inner plane work done by the recipient of the Esoteric Acupuncture treatment.

We are also connecting the bilateral *Tian Chong* (GB-9) points in a downward pointing triangle to the acupuncture site of *Feng Fu* (Du-16). *Feng Fu* (Du-16) is known as the "Wind Mansion" in traditional acupuncture theory. Wind is usually associated with some liver imbalance. We are not interested in a liver imbalance in this particular New Encoding Pattern. Inserting an acupuncture needle into the site of *Feng Fu* (Du-16) activates the medulla oblongata of the brain, as well as activating and harmonizing the Taluka Chakra (also known as the Lalana Chakra, Talu Chakra and the Alta Major Center). This activation process allows the prepared individual to possibly enter the field known in Hindu philosophy as "sound without sound." In Esoteric Acupuncture, the five acupuncture points (the bilateral *Tian Ting*/SJ-15 and bilateral *Tian Chong*/GB-9 points plus *Feng Fu*/Du 16) activate a field of consciousness known as the "Window of One Hand Clapping." This is the window of opportunity that occurs when receiving a treatment with the Esoteric *Shaoyin* Heart Window Pattern.

The outer acupuncture points on the head, the bilateral *Tian Chong* (GB-9) points plus *the bilateral Tian Ting* (SJ-15) points on the shoulders, are visually connected to form a geometric hourglass shaped polygon. This field may lead to the genesis of one level of clairaudience. This means being able to tap into the higher realms of consciousness where there is "sound without sound," "hearing without hearing" and the field of One Hand Clapping. But, you must be able to reach some level of Still Mind Consciousness in order for this field to open up for you.

### Esoteric *Shaoyin* Heart Window Pattern Point Location and Visualizations

To begin the needling sequence of the Esoteric *Shaoyin* Heart Window Pattern, mentally separate the Esoteric *Shaoyin* Window Pattern into four separate needling sections.

First Section:

The first section consists of the ten acupuncture points found in both the Esoteric *Shaoyin* Heart Pattern and in the Esoteric *Shaoyin* Kidney Pattern. The first seven acupuncture points make up the Crown Infinity Pattern that is contained in a number of posterior New Encoding Patterns. There are three additional acupuncture points on the posterior of the upper body: the bilateral *Tian Zong* (SI-11) points located in each scapula and *Shendao* (Du-11) located directly on the spine below the spinous process of the fifth thoracic vertebra. The point locations and needling sequence of the first ten acupuncture points were discussed in the Discern the Whisper Pattern and will not be repeated here. This first section consists of the same ten acupuncture points with the same visualization connections as The Discern the Whisper Pattern.

The Second Section:

This section begins by inserting acupuncture needles in the bilateral acupuncture points *Tian Ting* (SJ-15). This acupuncture point is more commonly known as *Tian Liao* to those who have studied the Chinese names of acupuncture points in the schools in the United States. In order to determine the acupuncture site of *Tian Ting* (SJ-15), one method is to first find the location of *Jianjing* (GB-21). It is found on the highest point of the trapezius muscle midway between the spine at the acupuncture point *Dazhui* (Du-14) and the lateral tip of the acromion. If you are trying to locate the acupuncture site of *Jianjing* (GB-21), do not press with a lot of force. On many people, this acupuncture point is very tender, so use your sensitivity to locate this point. (See figure 5.10-b below.)

### Esoteric *Shaoyin* Heart Window Pattern
**Locating *Jianjing* (GB-21)**

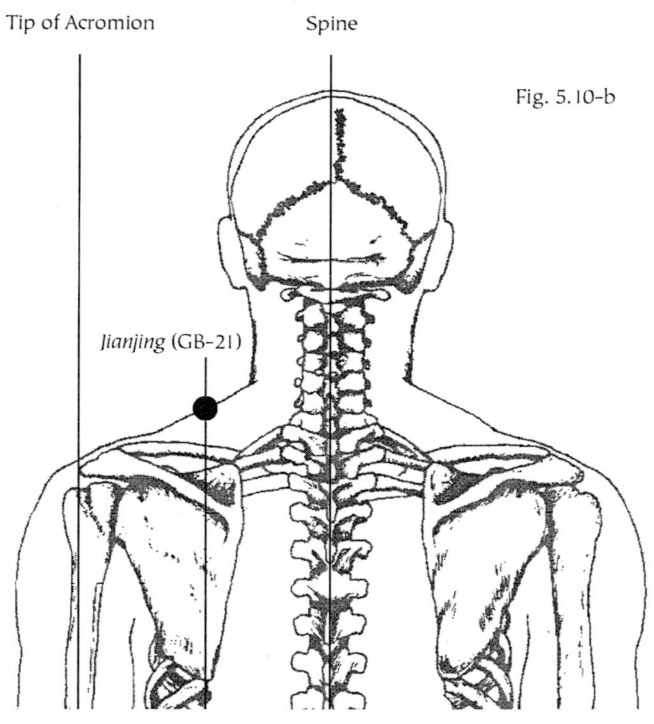


Fig. 5.10-b

The next step is to determine the location of *Quyuan* (SI-13). *Quyuan* (SI-13) is found in a slight depression superior to the medial end (closer to the spine) of the scapular spine. On some people, the scapular spine may be slightly difficult to locate. Find the medial end of the left scapula at the superior edge using one of your fingers, then move that same finger slightly lateral until you are able to locate a slightly tender depression lateral to the innermost border of the scapula. (See figure 5.10-c below.)

**Esoteric *Shaoyin* Heart Window Pattern**
**Locating *Quyuan* (SI-13)**

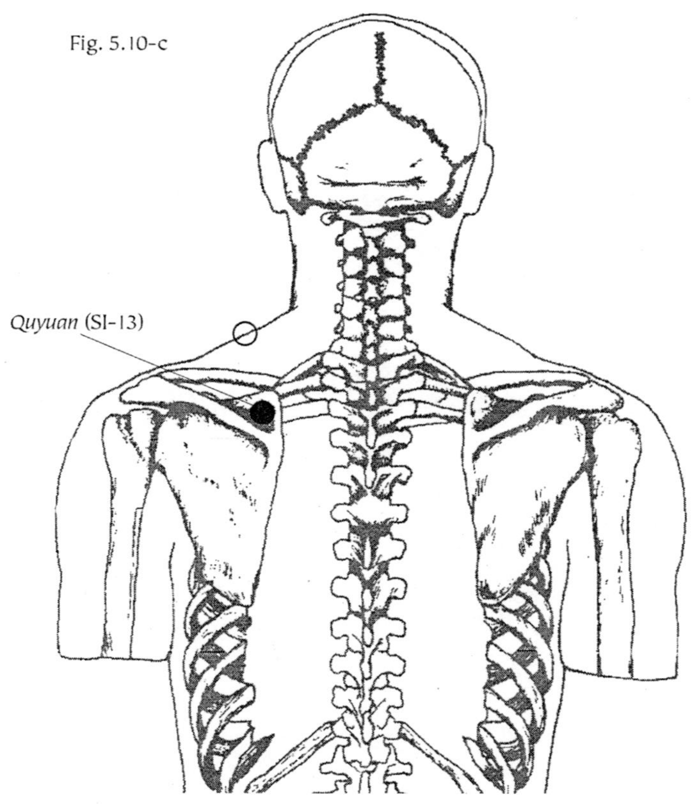

Fig. 5.10-c

The acupuncture site of *Tian Ting* (SJ-15) is located midway between *Jianjing* (GB-21) and *Quyuan* (SI-13). Remember that the translation of *Tian Ting can* be read as "Celestial Hearing." Celestial Hearing refers to the heart system and not to the kidney system of physical hearing. Needle the left Tian Ting (SJ-15) point first. (See figure 5.10-d below.)

**Esoteric *Shaoyin* Heart Window Pattern**
**Locating *Tian Ting* (SI-15)**

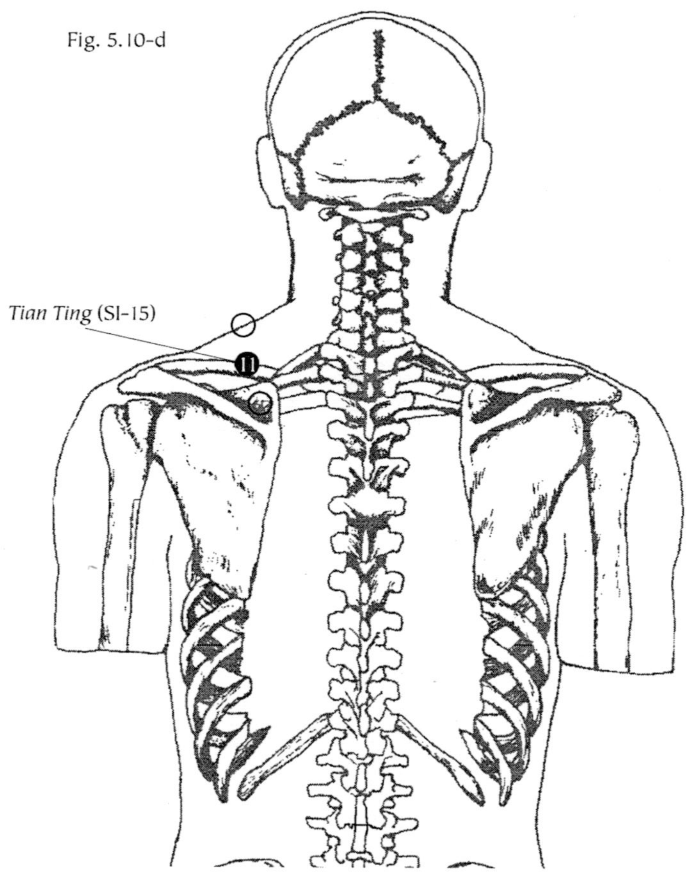

Next you will insert an acupuncture needle into the site of *Tian Ting* (SJ-15) on the right side. Follow the instructions given to locate *Tian Ting* (SJ-15) on the left side to find the correct acupuncture site of *Tian Ting* (SJ-15) on the right side. (See figure 5.10-e below.)

## Esoteric *Shaoyin* Heart Window Pattern

### Locating *Tian Ting* (SI-15)

Fig. 5.10-e

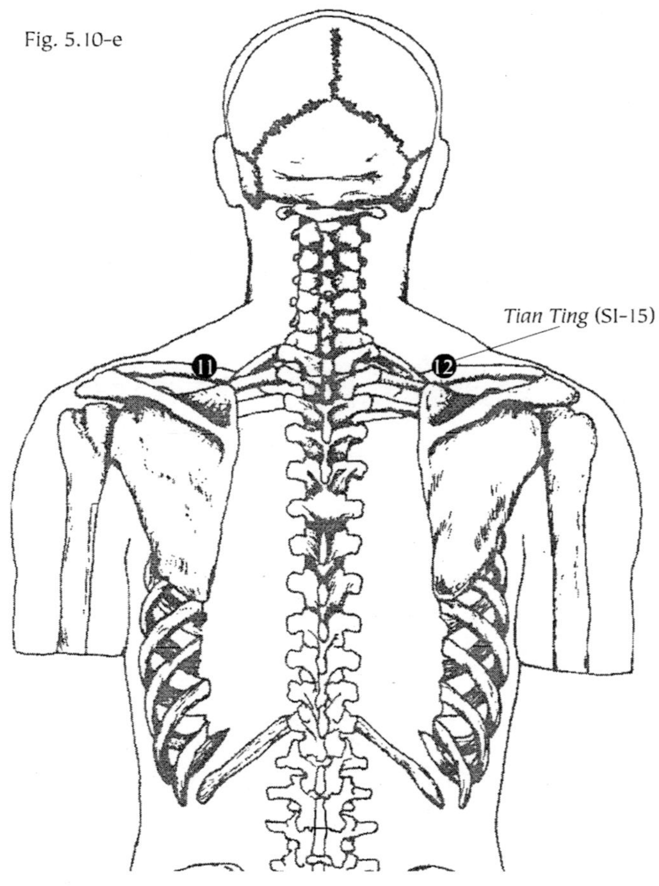

The first visualization in Section Two starts by visually connecting the qi at the left *Tian Ting* (SJ-15) point and moving upward to connect with the qi at the right *Tian Chong* (GB-9) point. (See figure 5.10-f below.)

**Esoteric *Shaoyin* Heart Window Pattern**

Fig. 5.10-f

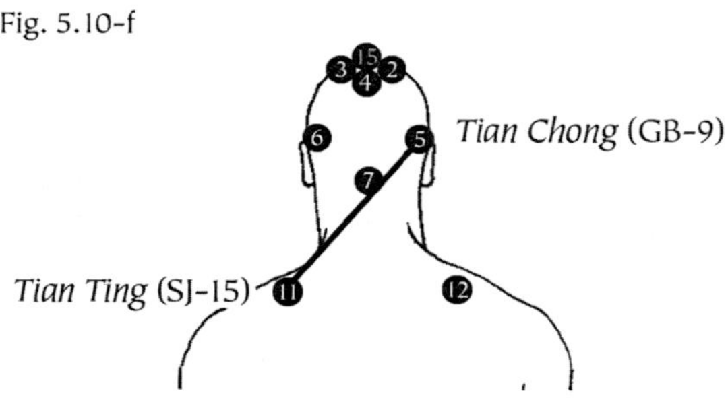


The second visualization in this section is to connect the qi at *Tian Chong* (GB-9) on the right side with the qi at *Tian Chong* (GB-9) on the left side. (See figure 5.10-g below.)

**Esoteric *Shaoyin* Heart Window Pattern**

Fig. 5.10-g

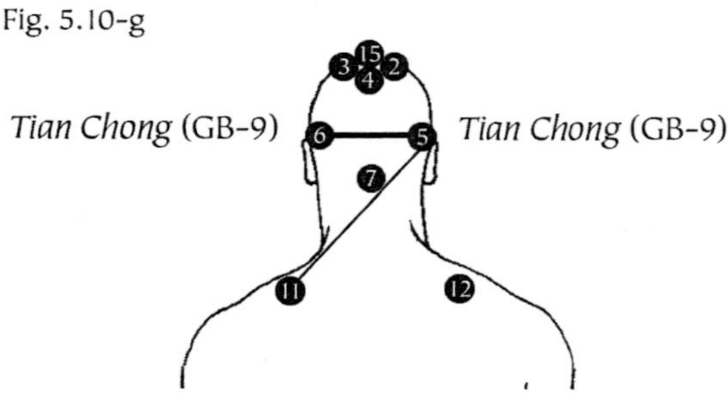

The third visualization connection in Section Two is to move the qi downward from the left *Tian Chong* (GB-9) point in a crisscross manner to connect with the qi at *Tian Ting* (SJ-15) on the right shoulder. (See figure 5.10-h below.)

## Esoteric *Shaoyin* Heart Window Pattern

Fig. 5.10-h

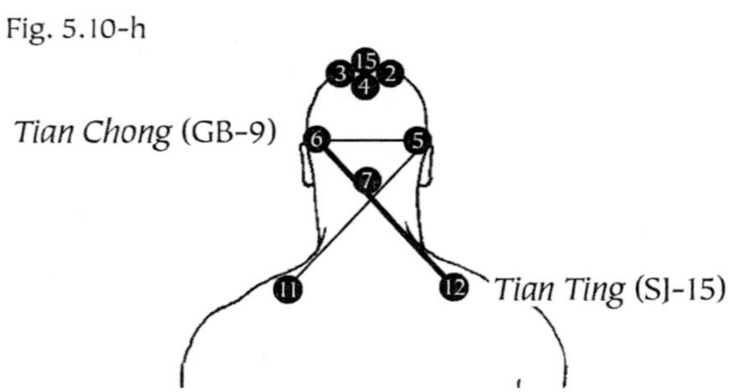


The last visualization in this section is to the bring the qi from the *Tian Ting* (SJ-15) point on the right shoulder back to connect with the *Tian Ting* (SJ-15) point on the left shoulder. (See figure 5.10-i below.)

## Esoteric *Shaoyin* Heart Window Pattern

Fig. 5.10-i

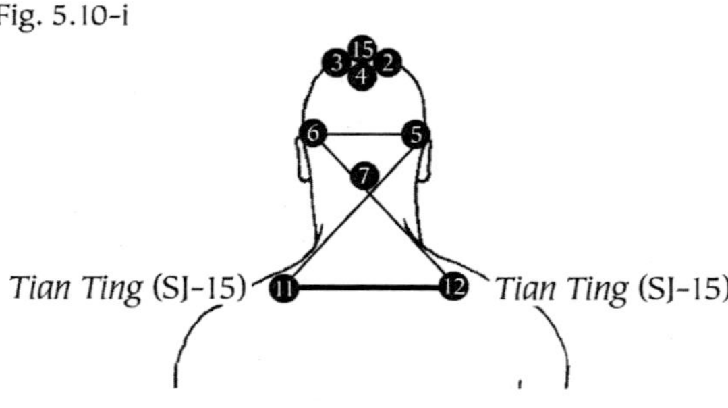

You will notice with the visual connections of the bilateral *Tian Ting* (SJ-15) points to the bilateral *Tian Chong* (GB-9) points an hourglass-shaped geometric figure has been formed. Notice the upward pointing Fire Triangle of the heart system. There is also a downward pointing Water Triangle of the kidney system. We have a condensed Esoteric *Shaoyin* field overlaid within the greater Esoteric *Shaoyin* patterning of this New Encoding Pattern. (See figure 5.10-i on the preceding page.)

The first acupuncture site needled in the Third Section is *Mingmen* (Du-4) found directly on the spine below the spinous process of the second lumbar vertebra. (See figure 5.10-j below.)

**Esoteric *Shaoyin* Heart Window Pattern**

Fig. 5.10-j

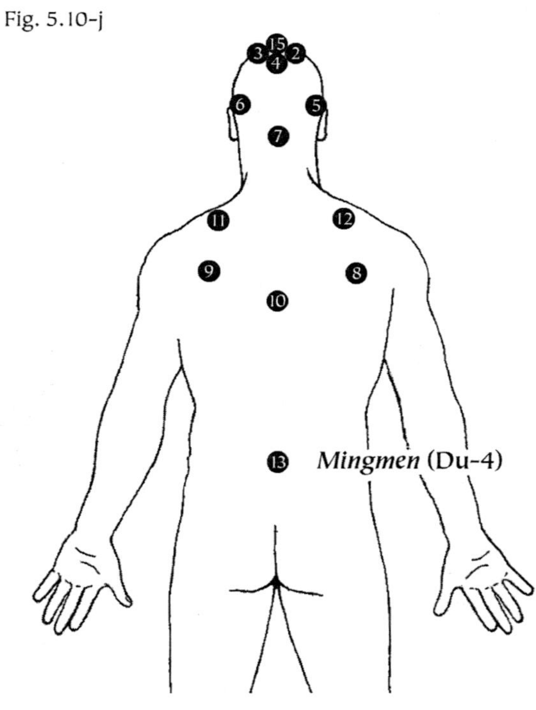

After an acupuncture needle has been inserted at the acupuncture site of *Mingmen* (Du-4), have your client visually bring qi from the acupuncture site of *Shendao* (Du-11) downward along the spine to connect with the qi at the acupuncture site of *Mingmen* (Du-4). (See figure 5.10-k below.)

## Esoteric *Shaoyin* Heart Window Pattern

Fig. 5.10-k

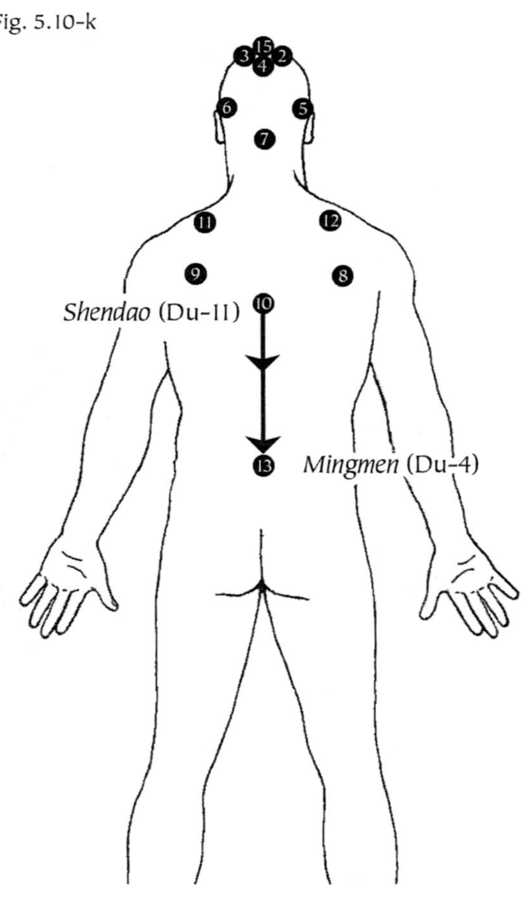

Have your client move the qi from the acupuncture site of *Mingmen* (Du-4) downward along the spine to activate the Muladhara (Root Chakra) at the coccyx (tailbone). Since there will be no needle insertion at this site, make sure that your client makes a solid visual activation with the mind and bring qi into this site. (See figure 5.10-l below.)

**Esoteric *Shaoyin* Heart Window Pattern**

Fig. 5.10-l

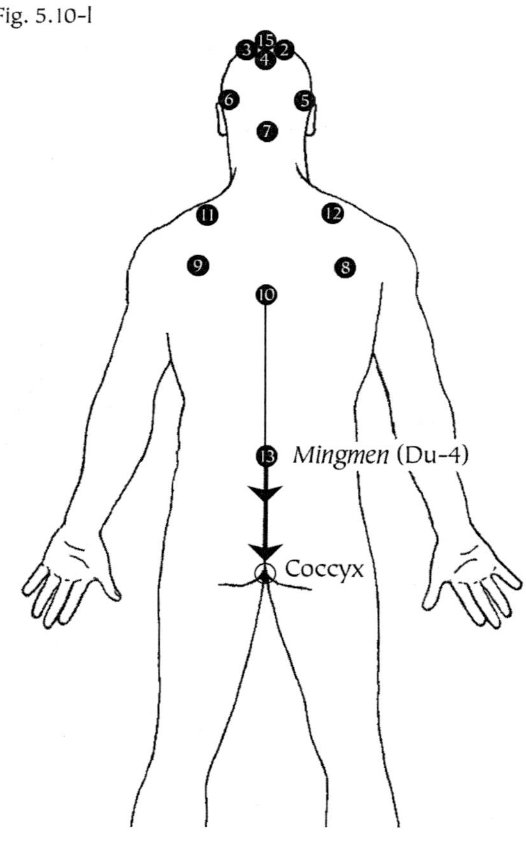

Next have your client move the qi upward from the coccyx (tailbone) back up to the acupuncture site at *Mingmen* (Du-4). (See figure 5.10-m below.)

## Esoteric *Shaoyin* Heart Window Pattern

Fig. 5.10-m

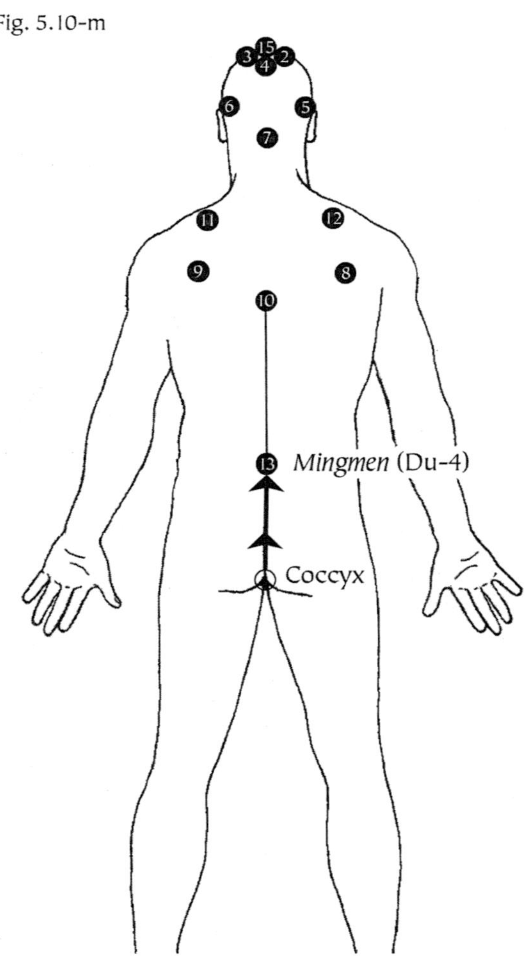

Ask your client to bring the qi up the spine from the site of *Mingmen* (Du-4) to the acupuncture site of *Shendao* (Du-11). *Shendao* (Du-11) was the tenth acupuncture point needled in this pattern. (See figure 5.10-n below.)

## Esoteric *Shaoyin* Heart Window Pattern

Fig. 5.10-n

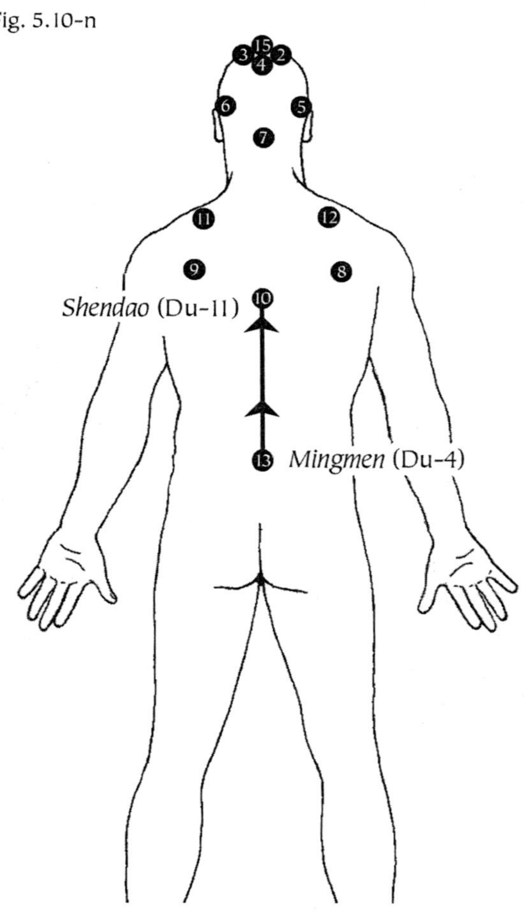

Have your client move the qi upward from the site of *Shendao* (Du-11) to connect to the qi at the acupuncture site of *Dazhui* (Du-14). (See figure 5.10-o below.)

## Esoteric *Shaoyin* Heart Window Pattern

Fig. 5.10-o

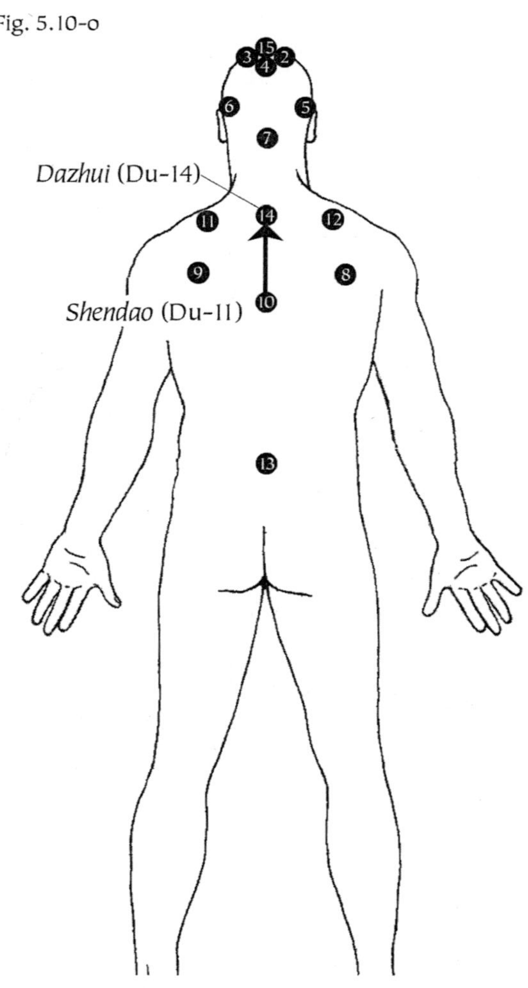

Next, have your client visually activate *Yintang* (Ajna Center), but in a non-linear fashion. Ask your client to connect the qi at *Dazhu*i (Du-14) with the qi *at Yintang* (Ajna Center). *Yintang* is located directed on the vertical midline of the forehead between the eyebrows and directly superior to the bridge of the nose. Remember your client will be facedown when this mental/visual activation takes place. You, the practitioner, will not insert an acupuncture needle or otherwise activate the qi at the site of *Yintang* (Ajna Center). Your client will do the activating at Yintang (Ajna Center). Once again, remember that the connection from *Dazhu*i (Du-14) to *Yintang* is not a linear connection but an instantaneous morphic resonant connection. (See figure 5.10-p below.)

**Esoteric *Shaoyin* Heart Window Pattern**
**Morphic Resonant Connection**

Fig. 5.10-p

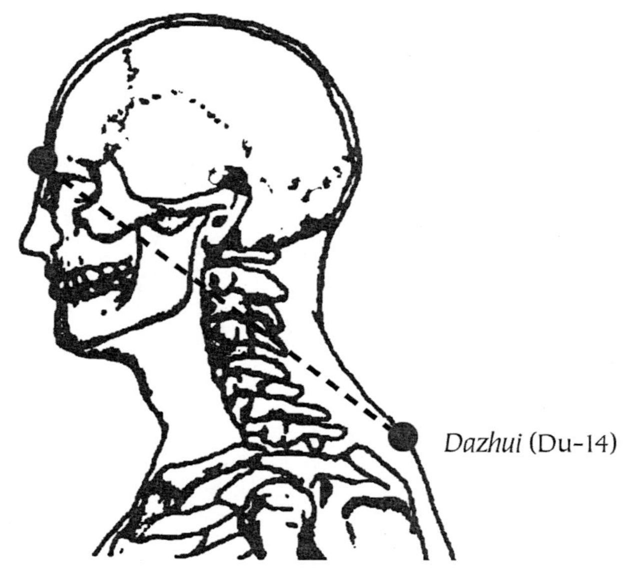

Remember that the qi opening at the acupuncture site of *Dazhui* (Du-14) will act like a wormhole from that acupuncture site to instantaneously activate one's Third Eye. This sequence of first activating *Dazhui* (Du-14) and opening up *Yintang* (Ajna Center/Third Eye) before moving the qi up to Feng Fu (Du-16) is one of the "secret" processes of being able to activate the higher head centers.

Now have your client move the qi upward from the acupuncture site of *Dazhui* (Du-14) to the acupuncture site of *Feng Fu* (Du-11) along the Du channel. (See figure 5.10-q below.)

## Esoteric *Shaoyin* Heart Window Pattern

Fig. 5.10-q

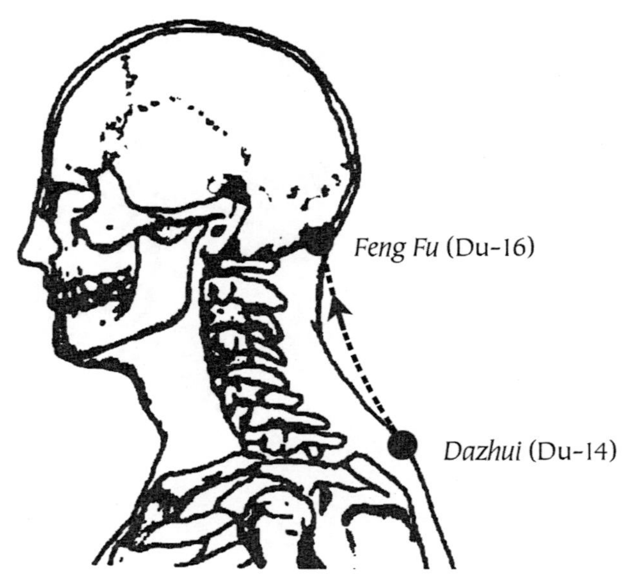

Have your client connect the qi at the acupuncture site of *Feng Fu* (Du-16) to the qi at the acupuncture site of *Yintang* (Ajna Center). This connection is a linear connection. *Feng Fu* (Du-16) is the access site of the Taluka Chakra, also known as the Alta Major Center and the "Secret Chakra." *Yintang* is the acupuncture site that can activate the Ajna Center Chakra also known as the Third Eye. (See figure 5.10-r below.)

**Esoteric *Shaoyin* Heart Window Pattern**

Fig. 5.10-r

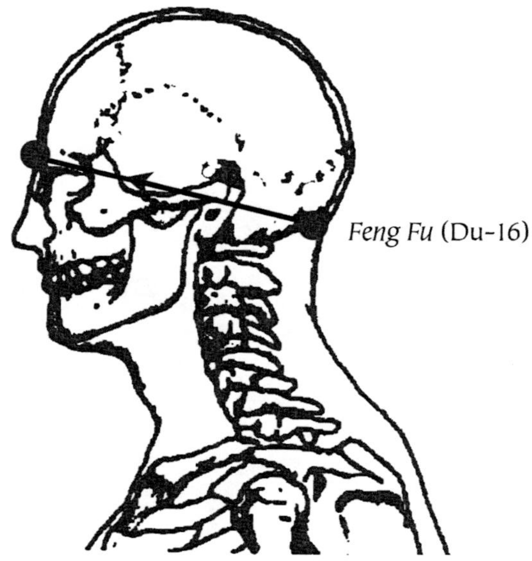

This is the very last visualization connection in the Esoteric *Shaoyin* Heart Window Pattern. Have your client simultaneously bring the qi upward from the acupuncture sites of both *Feng Fu* (Du-16) and *Yintang* (Ajna Center) in a triangular formation and connect to the qi at the acupuncture site of *Tian Man* (Du-20). We have now connected the three Major Head Centers: 1) the Taluka Chakra (Alta Major Center), 2) the Ajna Center (at *Yintang*) and 3) the Sahasrara (Crown Chakra through *Tian Man* (Du-20). (See figure 5.10-s below.)

**Esoteric *Shaoyin* Heart Window Pattern**
**The Three Major Head Centers**

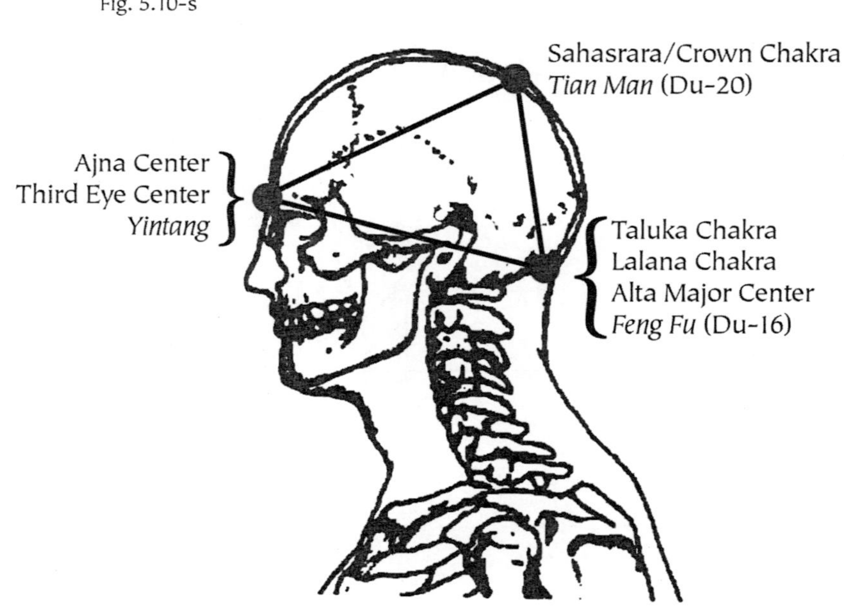

Fig. 5.10-s

## Esoteric *Shaoyin* Heart Window Pattern
### Complete Grid

Fig. 5.10-t

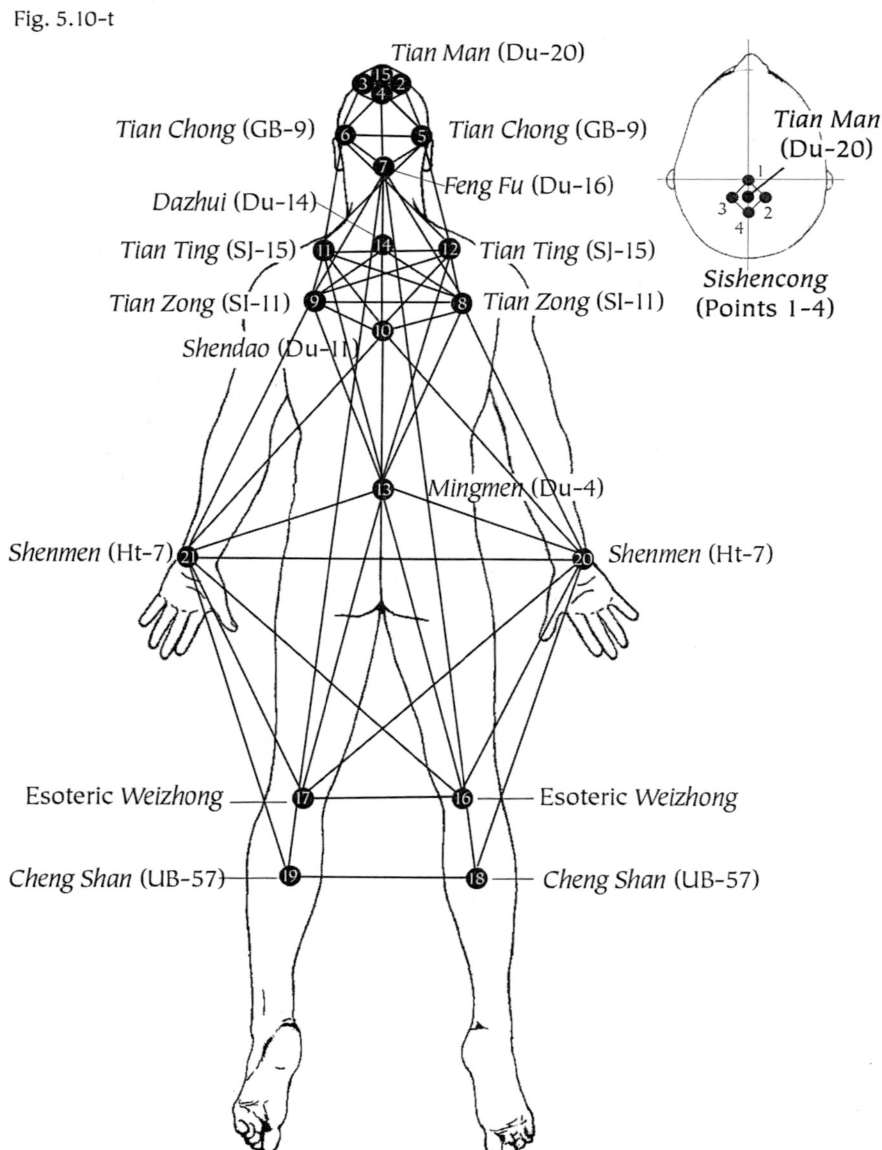

## Level IV Anterior: Option #1
## Crystalline Grid Pattern

Fig. 5.11-a

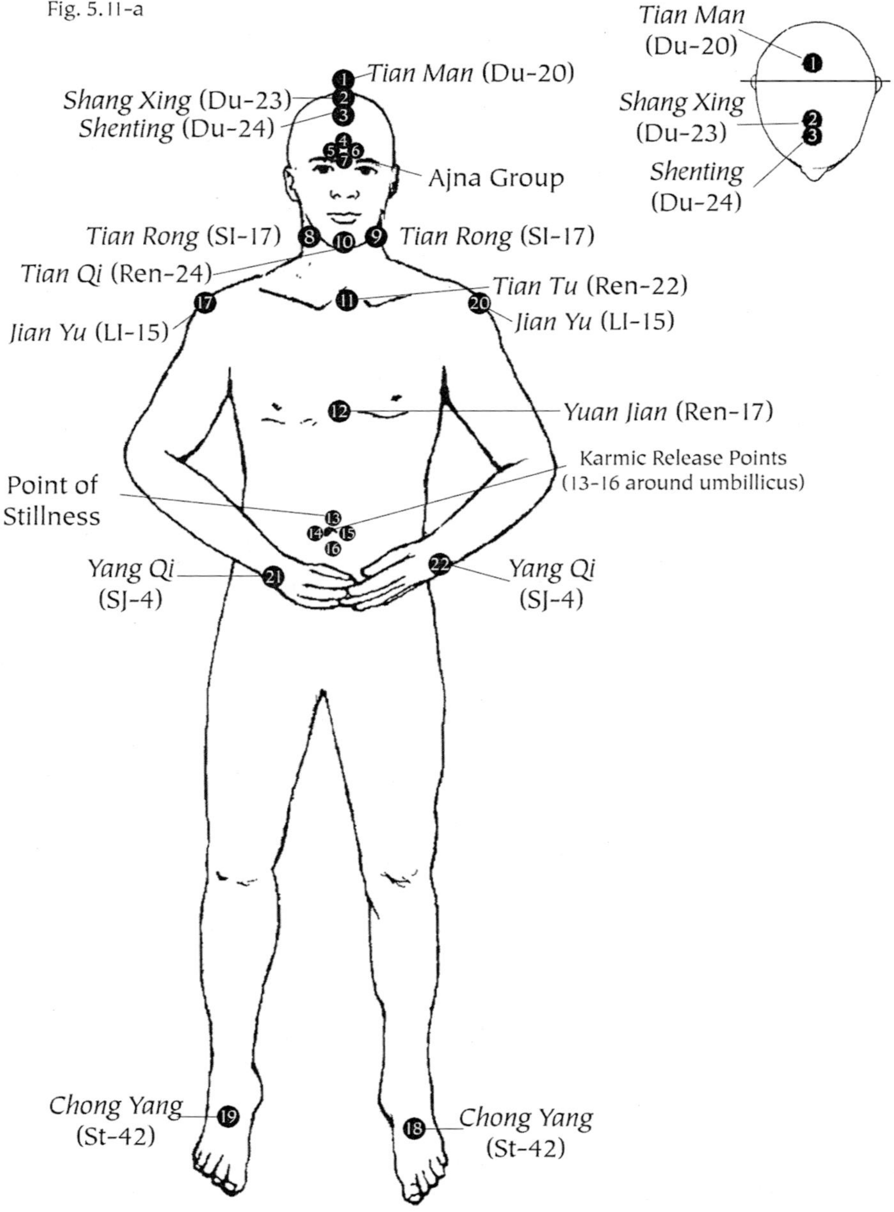

## The Crystalline Grid Pattern

The Cube on Cube Window Pattern discussed in Tier Density Level III, Awakening of the Inner *Shen* has sixteen acupuncture points. The Crystalline Grid Pattern is a continuation of the Cube on Cube Window Pattern, but with six additional acupuncture points. If you review some of the other New Encoding Patterns, you will notice that we added additional acupuncture sites to several of the less complex patterns to come up with a different pattern that covers a more complex field. With the Crystalline Grid Pattern, you will first needle the same sixteen points with the same needling sequence as the Cube on Cube Window Pattern. After the first sixteen acupuncture sites have been needled, you will add six additional acupuncture points in a very specific sequence. You will notice that the Crystalline Grid Pattern has twenty-two acupuncture points. The number twenty-two is a very powerful number and refers back to Esoteric Acupuncture's connection to the Hebrew Qabbalistic Tree of Life that has twenty-two pathways connecting the ten Sephiroth.

The Crystalline Grid Pattern has its name because many of the points, especially the last six acupuncture points, have a crystalline glow. If a person has a heightened level of very clear clairvoyance, that person will see many of the acupuncture points in this pattern glow. Although no instructions are given for making visual connections for the acupuncture points on the anterior of the body except for the two anterior patterns in Tier Density Level I, nonetheless the crystalline points will connect in a manner similar to the last diagram of the Crystalline Grid Pattern.

**Needling Sequence:**

The First Section consists of the same sixteen acupuncture points with the same needling sequence as the Cube on Cube Window Pattern. A cube has eight stars or eight angles. The first sixteen points in the Crystalline Grid Pattern represent the number of stars of one cube sitting on top of another cube. This represents spirituality resting on top of physicality. To simplify remembering the needling sequence, subdivide the first section into three smaller sections. The first subsection of the first section only contains the first ten acupuncture points. (For a detailed description of the point locations for the first sixteen acupuncture points, please refer back to the Cube on Cube Window Pattern. The point locations for those acupuncture points will not be repeated here.)

The first three acupuncture sites needled in the Crystalline Grid Pattern are those located on the top of the head and belong to the Du channel. The first point is *Tian Man* (Du-20) "Celestial Fullness" followed by *Shang Xing* (Du-23) "Upper Star, "then *Shenting* (Du-24) "Celestial Court" or "Heavenly Court." Remember to locate *Tian Man* (Du-20) at a location approximately one *cun* posterior to the traditional location of the Du-20 known as *Bai Hui*. The esoteric location of the Du-20 known as *Tian Man* will give your client an opportunity for qi and Kundalini to move from the cranium to the Sahasrara (Crown Chakra) located above the cranium. (See figure 5.11-b below.)

## Crystalline Grid Pattern

Fig. 5.11-b

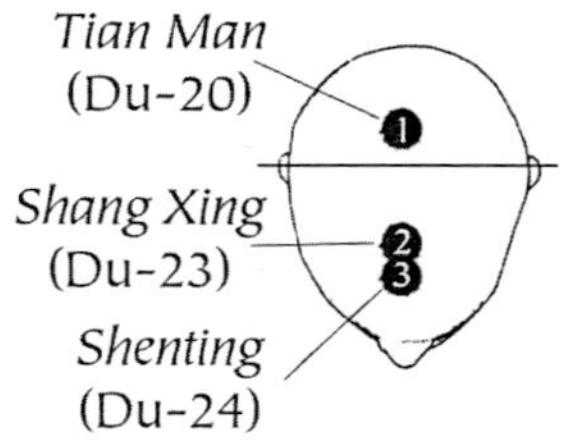


Starting with point #4, the next seven acupuncture points are same the points of the Extended Indigo Triangle Pattern.

Start by needling the four Ajna Group points (Ajna #1 through Ajna #4/*Yintang*) followed by the bilateral *Tian Rong* (SI-17) points on the neck posterior to the angle of the mandible. Insert an acupuncture needle at the site of *Tian Rong* (SI-17) on the client's right side, followed by needling *Tian Rong* (SI-17) on the client's left side. The tenth acupuncture point in this first subsection is *Tian Qi* (Ren-24) located below the lower lip and directly on the vertical midline of the face. (See figure 5.11-c.)

## Crystalline Grid Pattern

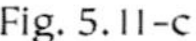
Fig. 5.11-c

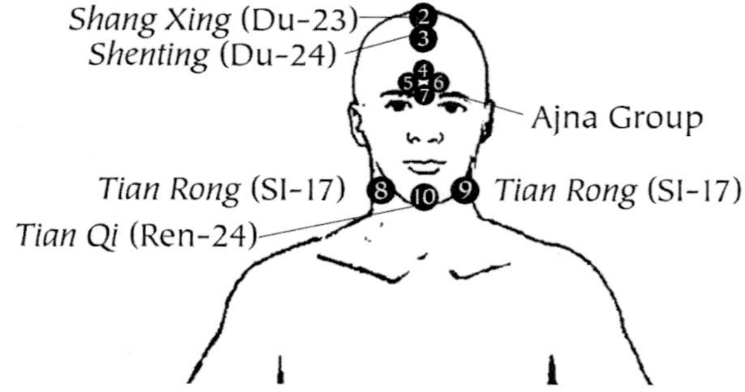


The second subsection of this first section consists of the next six points of the Crystalline Grid Pattern. The first acupuncture point needled is *Tian Tu* (Ren-22). Remember that although in Traditional Chinese Medicine *Tian Tu* (Ren-22) is usually thought of as an acupuncture site to address throat and lung issues, in Esoteric Acupuncture this point is used to activate the higher heart. The translation of *Tian Tu* to mean "Celestial Chimney" refers to the fact that *Tian Tu* (Ren-22) allows celestial or heavenly qi to connect with the frontal heart point located at the site of the twelfth acupuncture point *Yuan Jian* (Ren-17). After *Yuan Jian* (Ren-22) has been needled, insert acupuncture needles at the four acupuncture sites surrounding the umbilicus and known as the four Karmic Release Points. (See figure 5.11-d below.)

## Crystalline Grid Pattern

Fig. 5.11-d

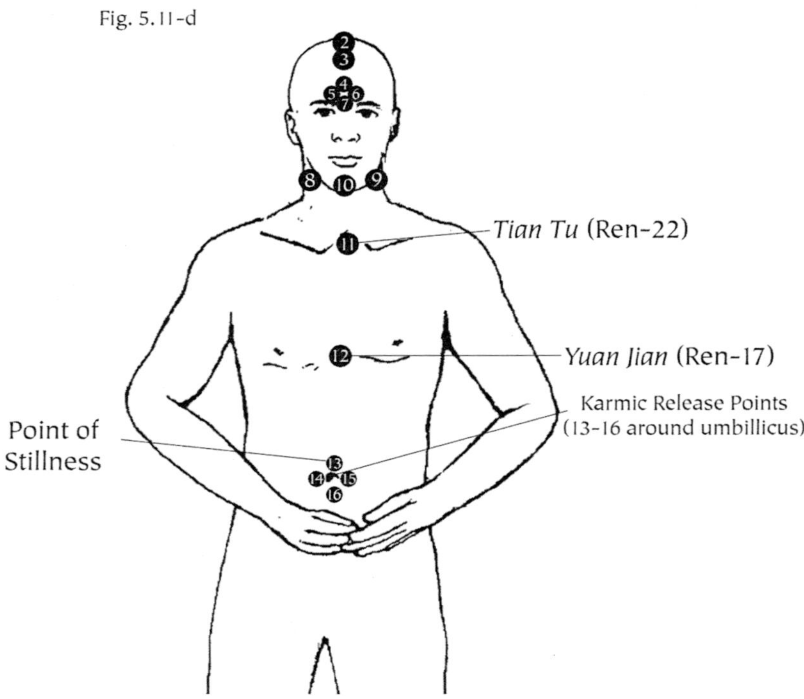


The Second Section consists of an additional six acupuncture points that are not part of the Cube on Cube Window Pattern bringing the number of acupuncture points in the Crystalline Grid Pattern to twenty-two points.

The first acupuncture point needled in the second section of the Crystalline Grid Pattern is *Jian Yu* (LI-15) located on the right outer shoulder. *Jianyu* (LI-15) is found on the upper border of the deltoideus muscle and both anterior and slightly inferior to the acromion. If you ask your client to raise his or her arm, *Jianyu* (LI-15) can be found in a distinct depression at the anterior border of the acromioclavicular joint. Most people have this depression at the acupuncture site of *Jianyu* (LI-15), but not everyone. (See figure 5.11-e below.)

**Crystalline Grid Pattern**

Fig. 5.11-e

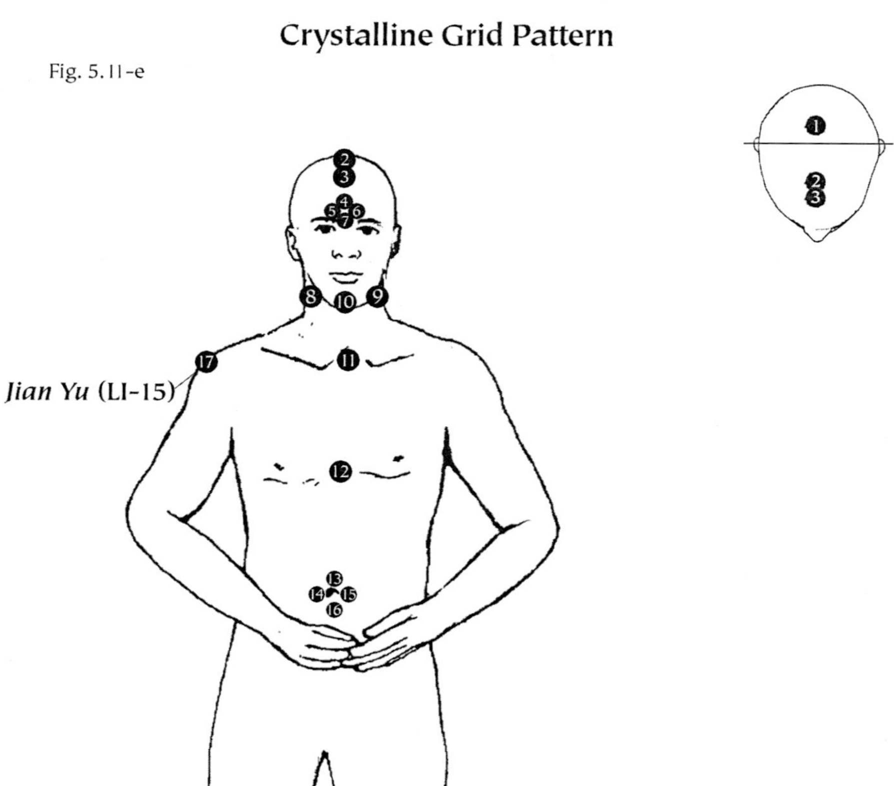


To find the second acupuncture site in this second section of six points, you will crisscross to the left foot and needle *Chong Yang* (St-42) on this left side. *Chong Yang* (St-42) is found on the highest point of the dorsum of the right foot in a slight depression found between the second and third metatarsal bones and the cuneiform bone. (See figure 5.11-f below.)

## Crystalline Grid Pattern

Fig. 5.11-f

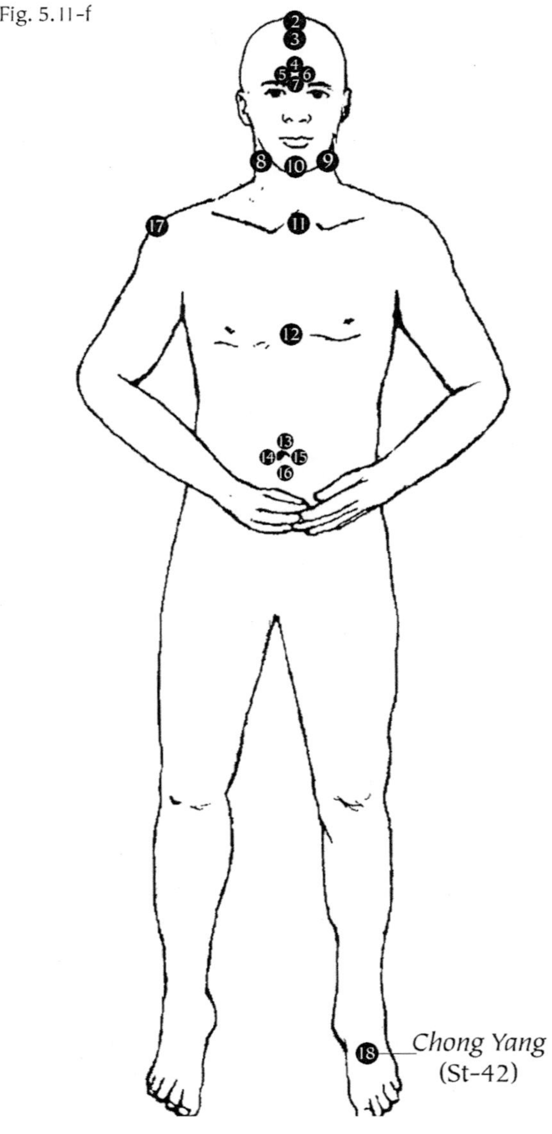

Next insert an acupuncture needle at the site of *Chong Yang* (St-42) on the right foot. (See figure 5.11-g below.)

**Crystalline Grid Pattern**

Fig. 5.11-g

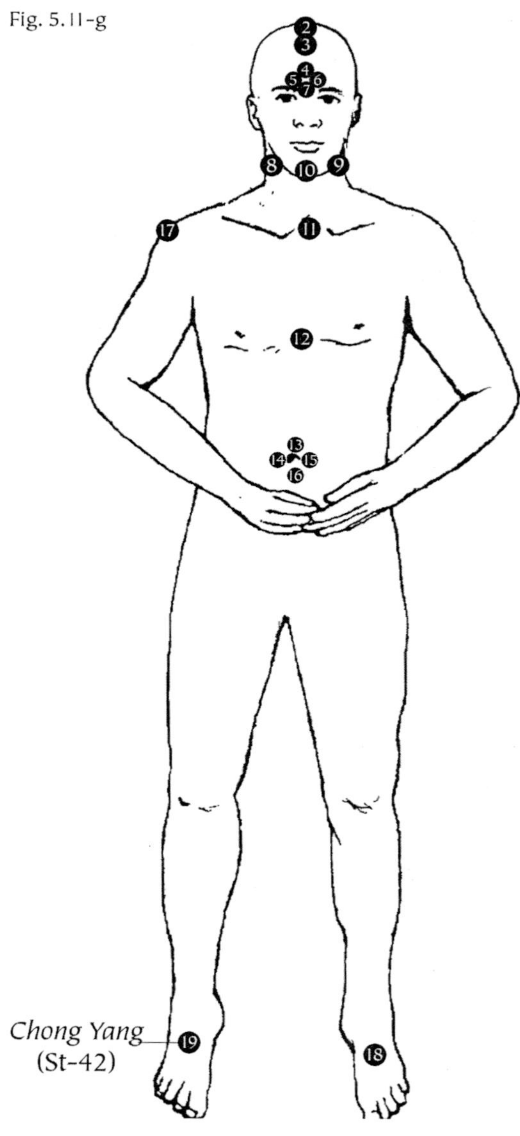

The fourth acupuncture point in this section of the Crystalline Grid Pattern is *Jianyu* (LI-15) on your client's left shoulder. You will notice with these first four acupuncture points in this section of the Crystalline Grid Pattern, we have needled two acupuncture sites of the large intestine channel and two acupuncture sites of the stomach channel. In the Chinese Six Channel Theory, the combination of the stomach channel with the large intestine channel is known as *Yangming*. Inserting acupuncture needles at the acupuncture sites of bilateral large intestines points and bilateral stomach points is known in Esoteric Acupuncture as a *Yangming* Treatment. A more common *Yangming* pairing is to insert acupuncture needles at the sites of the bilateral *Shousanli* (LI-10) points, known as "Arm Three Mile," plus the bilateral *Zhousanli* (St-36) points, known as "Leg Three Mile.,

A more traditional Chinese way for utilizing the resources available through a *Yangming* connection is to remember the phrase "more qi, more blood." The Chinese also refer to *Yangming* as the "four bigs." We are not so interested in the traditional Chinese diagnosis of *Yangming* and the "four bigs" referring to: 1) big pulse; 2) big heat; 3) big pain; and 4) big fever. These are referring to the physical plane. Just remember that with any *Yangming* treatment, the practitioner is also strengthening the immune system on the physical plane.

In Esoteric Acupuncture theory, the areas around the sites of the bilateral *Jianyu* (LI-15) points are areas that symbolize carrying a burden on one's shoulder. Have you ever felt that no matter how hard you try to climb upward on your own personal spiritual ladder, you never seem to be able to move upward? Maybe you are carrying an emotional or mental burden. The bilateral stomach points symbolize the need to "kick" something or someone out of your life. If either of the *Chong Yang* (St-42 points are tender, your higher self is reminding you how urgent it is to act immediately to remove the burden or burdens that you have be carrying with you for years. Now is the time to release this excess baggage. Kick it out of your life!

## Crystalline Grid Pattern

Fig. 5.11-h

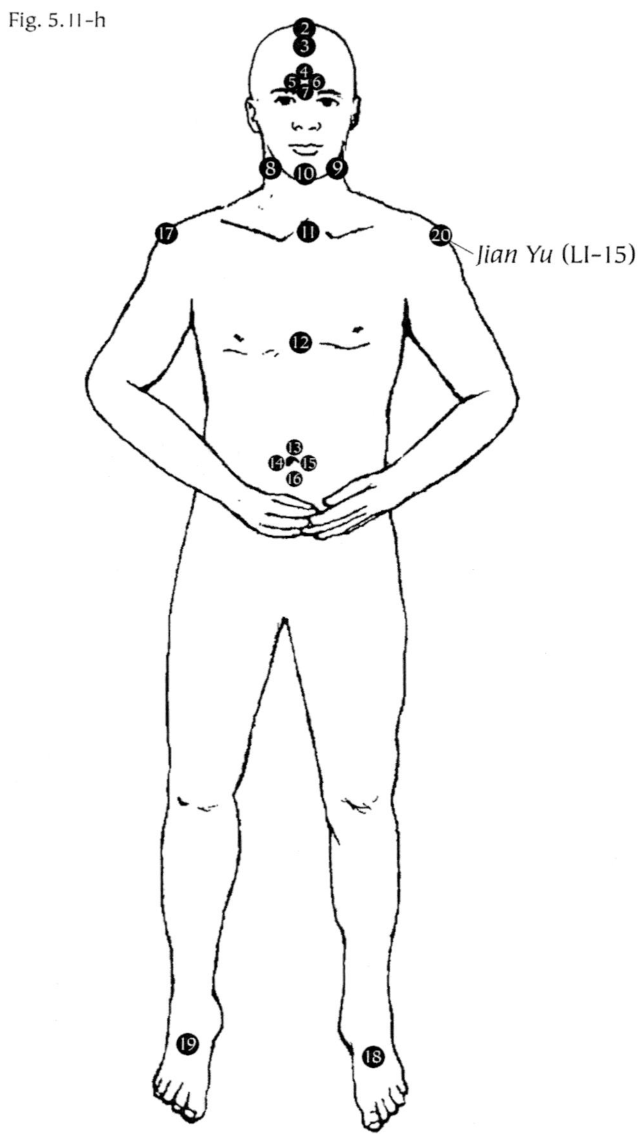

### *Shaoyin* Overlaid on *Yangming*

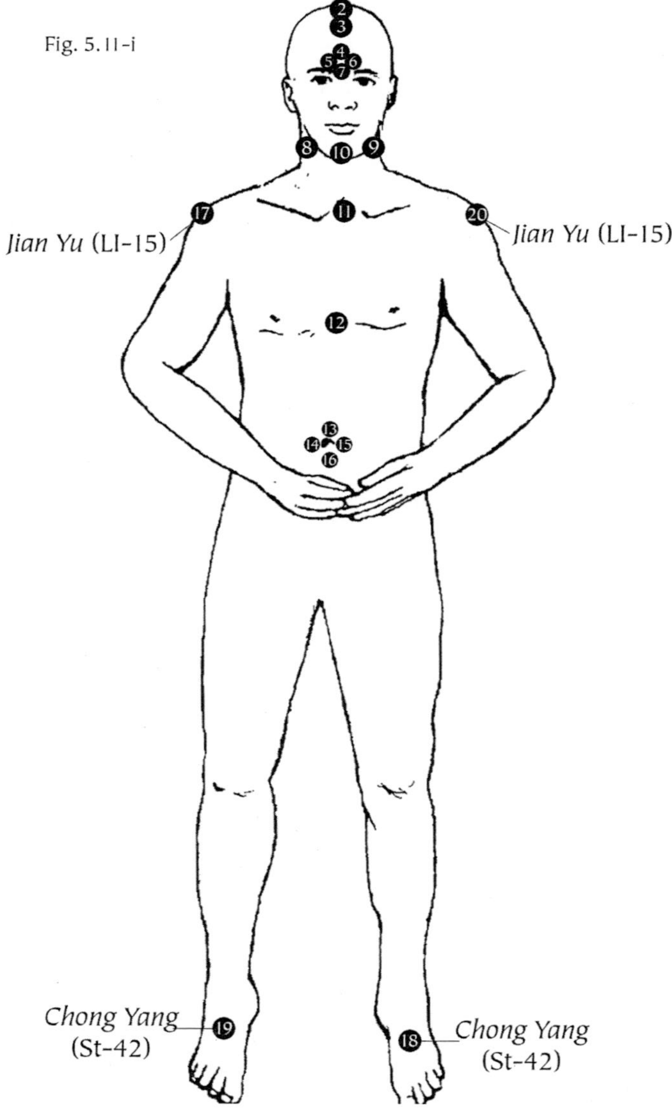


The twenty-first and twenty-second acupuncture points in the Crystalline Grid Pattern are the bilateral *Yang Qi* (SJ-4)

points. You will needle the *Yang Qi* (SJ-4) point on the right side first followed by the *Yang Qi* (SJ-4) point on the left side. According to the acupuncture text book ***Chinese Acupuncture and Moxibustion***, *Yang Qi (SJ-4) is: "the Yuan-Primary Point of the Sanjiao Meridian which maintains the qi in general."*[13] In Esoteric Acupuncture, needling the bilateral *Yang Qi* (SJ-4) points will also help the client to release something in his or her life that the person is clinging onto that needs to be released. *Yang Qi* (SJ-4) is found on the transverse crease of the dorsum of the wrist in a distinct depression lateral to the tendon of the extensor digitorum muscle. Pull the hand backward slightly to find this depression. Make sure you find the *sanjiao* channel. (See figure 5.11-j below.)

**Crystalline Grid Pattern**

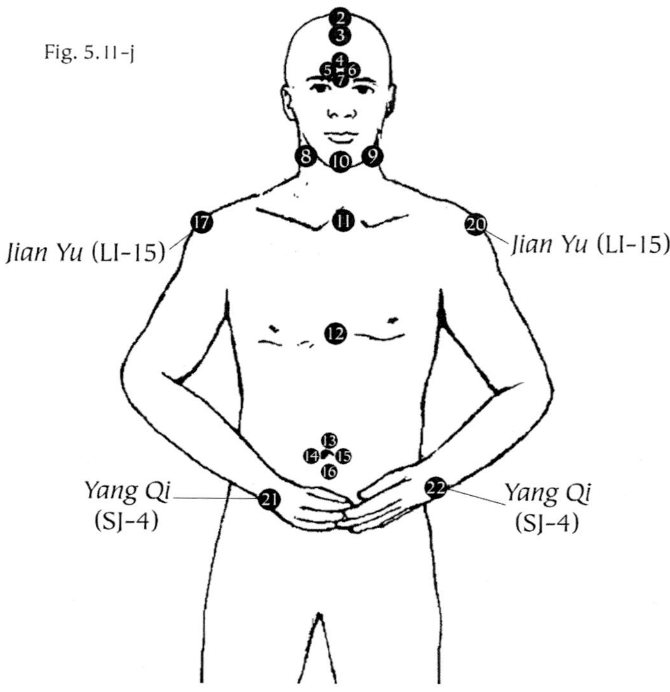

## Crystalline Grid Pattern
### Complete Grid

Fig. 5.11-k

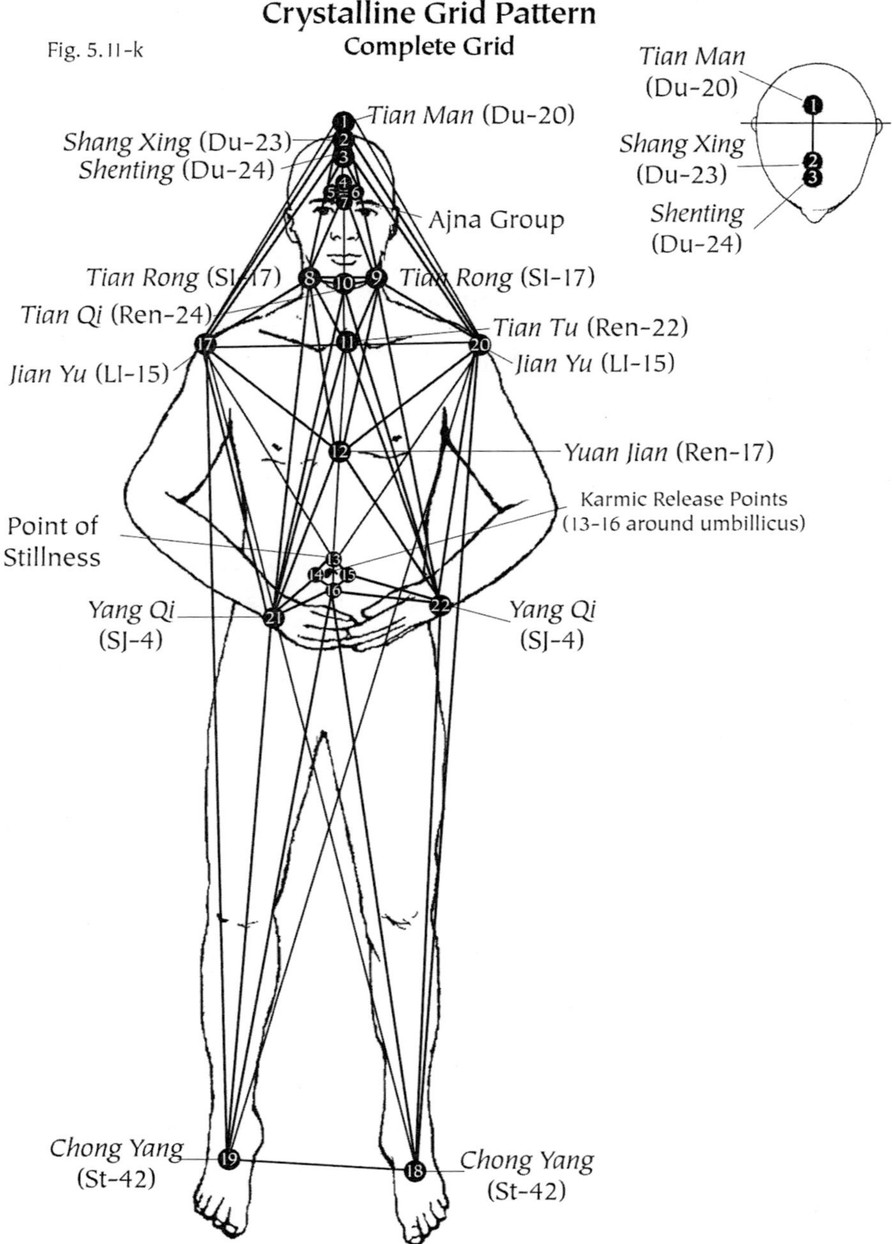

## Level IV Anterior: Option #2
## Crystalline Heart Grid Pattern

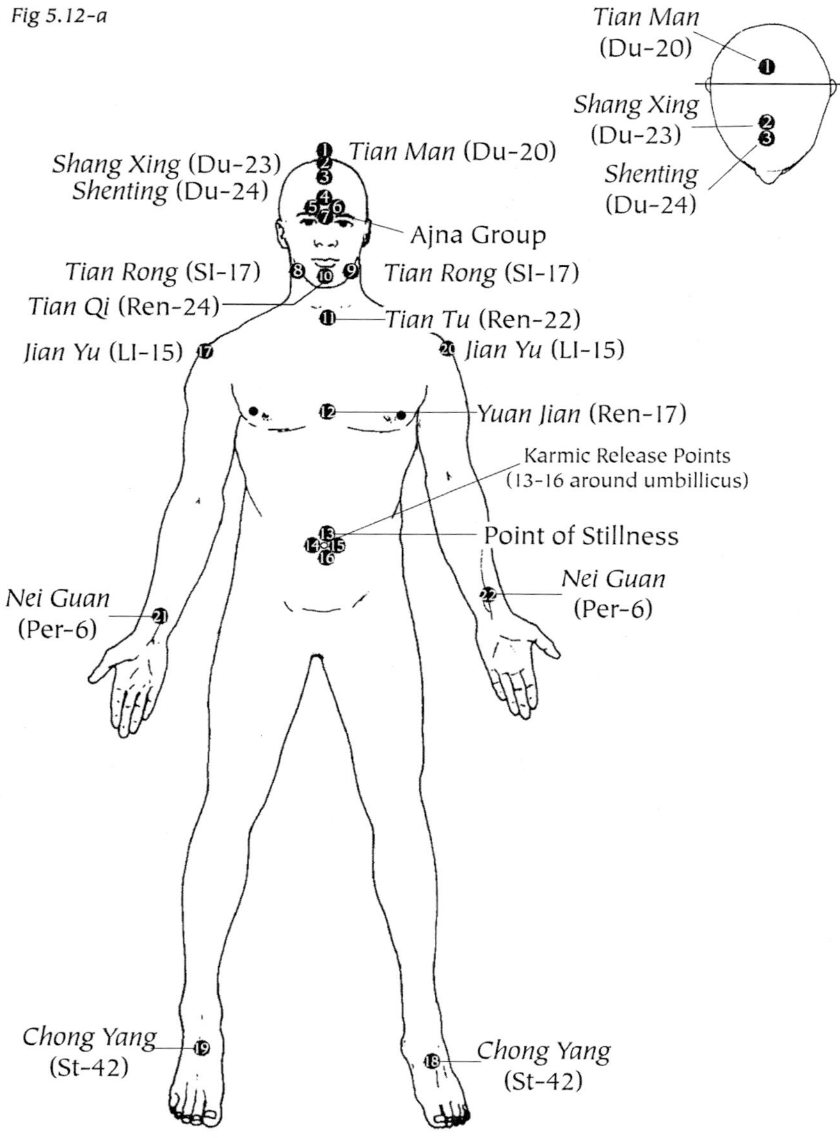

## Level IV Anterior: Option #2
## The Crystalline Heart Grid Pattern

The criteria for choosing to use the Crystalline Heart Grid Pattern rather than the original Crystalline Grid Pattern is dependent on your client you are presently treating. After you have removed the acupuncture needles from the posterior of your client, have your client turn over and lie in a supine position. If your client places his or her palms face upward, then you will use The Crystalline Heart Grid Pattern. If your client has his or her palms face downward when he or she is in a supine position, then you will use the regular Crystalline Grid Pattern. The palms upward usually indicates that your client is slightly less inhibited and has a more trusting and content heart field. Having the palms facing downward often means not wanting to reveal as much. If your client places both palms facing downward on either his or her heart or lower abdominal regions, it usually directs that the client wants to protect something associated with either of those regions.

The only difference in needling between the two patterns is that in The Crystalline Grid Pattern the last two acupuncture points are the bilateral *Yang Qi* (SJ-4) points. The bilateral *Yang Qi* (SJ-4) points are used to balance and strengthen the *Wei Qi*, also known as the protective qi. In The Crystalline Heart Grid Pattern, the last two acupuncture points are the bilateral *Nei Guan* (Per-6) points. *Nei Guan* is translated as "Inner Pass."

The pericardium system and the *san jiao* system are both components of the fire element of the heart system in the Chinese Five Element Theory. In Esoteric Acupuncture, the Inner Pass of the pericardium channel refers to the inner entrance and pathway to the Anahata (Heart Chakra). If you are working with balancing and strengthening chakras, the bilateral *Nei Guan* (Per-6) points are direct pathways to activate the Anahata (Heart Chakra).

Certain other pericardium channel points have a more direct influence on the Anahata (Heart Chakra) than even some of the acupuncture points on the heart channel. *Yuan Jian* (Ren-17) is connected to the pericardium system, yet the point is used to access the Anahata (Heart Chakra) from the anterior of the body. *Yuan Jian* (Ren-17) on the anterior of the body has similar energies and functions as *Shendao* (Du-11) on the posterior of the body.

*Nei Guan* (Per-6) is located on the inner forearm approximately two *cun* from the inner wrist crease and between the tendon of the palmaris longus muscle and the tendon of the flexor radialis muscle. Since this acupuncture point is often very tender or sensitive, I will usually rub the area where *Nei Guan* (Per-6) is located to de-sensitize the acupuncture site before inserting the acupuncture needle. Use a very thin, short needle at this site with a gentle quick insertion technique. I recommend the Seirin red handled .16 X 15 mm needle or the Seirin lime handled .14 X 15 mm needle. You do not need to insert the needle very deeply. Do not rotate or thrust the needle up and down.

Sometimes a blood vessel will be located directly between the two tendons at the location of *Nei Guan* (Per-6). In those instances, do not needle directly into the blood vessel. If your client has a blood vessel directly between the tendons on the inner wrist, use a finger or your thumb on your non-needling hand to pull the blood vessel to one side. Then you can insert the acupuncture needle between the two tendons without puncturing the blood vessel. After the acupuncture needle has been inserted, let go of the blood vessel to allow the blood vessel to return to its natural location. The blood vessel may touch the acupuncture needle, but that is perfectly fine.

There are at least two ways to find the correct location of *Nei Guan* (Per-6). One method is to know that the distance from the inner elbow crease to the inner wrist crease is approximately twelve *cun*. Divide the twelve-*cun* length in half making two lengths of six *cun* each. Take the half that is closer to the wrist crease and divide that section into three equal parts of two *cun* each. *Nei Guan* (Per-6) is located between the tendon of the palmaris longus muscle and the tendon of the flexor radialis muscle and approximately two *cun* from the inner wrist crease. (See figure 5.12-b below.)

Another way to locate *Nei Guan* (Per-6) is to find the end of your client's styloid process near the thumb. The distal end of the styloid process is approximately one and a half *cun* from the inner wrist crease. Move slightly away from the styloid process toward the elbow and insert the acupuncture needle between the two tendons. Whichever method you decide for locating *Nei Guan* (Per-6), rely on your higher intuition to locate the correct acupuncture site. The measurements are merely to point you to the vicinity of the acupuncture site and should not be the sole factor in determining the correct location. (See figure 5.12-c.)

Fig. 5.12-b

6 cun

12 cun

2 cun

*Nei Guan* (Per-6)

*Nei Guan* (Per-6) is located 2 *cun* from the wrist crease.

Fig. 5.12-c

The distal end of the Styloid Process is approximately one and a half *cun* from the wrist crease. *Nei Guan* (Per-6) is one-half *cun* distal to this measurement.

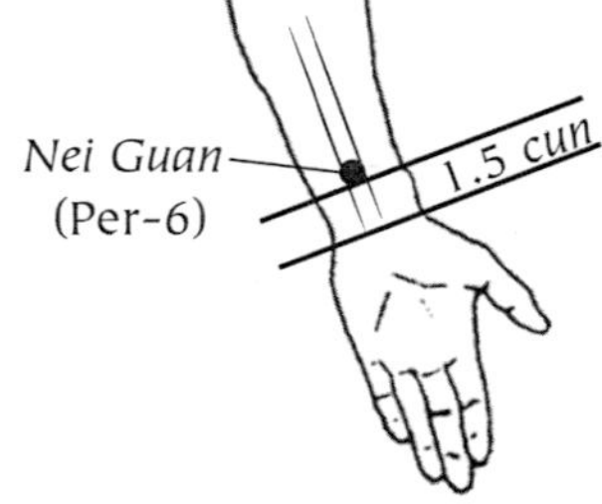

## Crystalline Heart Grid Pattern
## Complete Grid

*Fig 5.12-a*

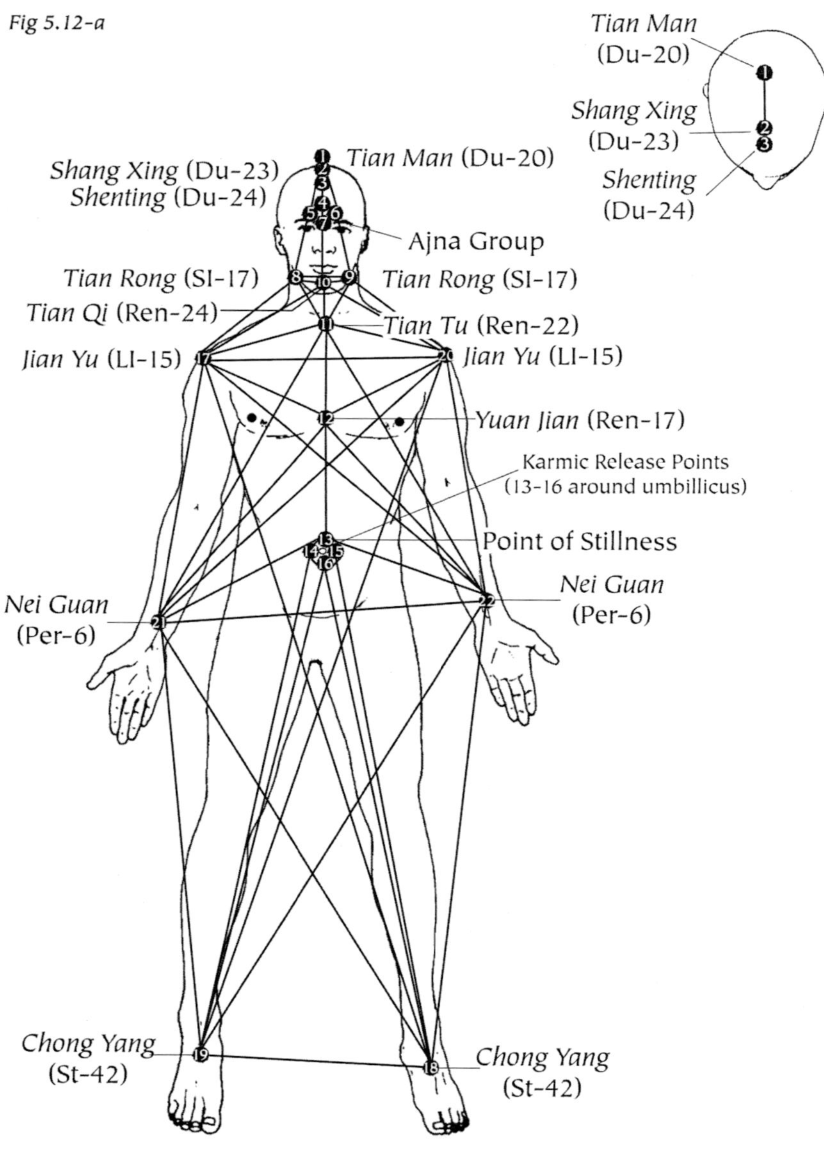

## Tier Density Level V: Supreme Balanced Inner *Shen*

At Tier Density Level V, you recognize, understand and fully embrace your calling in this lifetime. You are sure of your puzzle piece and will be following the path of your puzzle piece for the rest of your incarnation on planet Earth. Truly knowing your puzzle piece will evolve your personal piece into your peace within. You are now on your own Inner Spiritual Higher Heart path. You have already developed the skills, motivation and dedication necessary to keep you on this path you have chosen. At the Tier Density Level V, you do not deviate from your personal path. More often than not, instead of you choosing a particular path, the path choses you. This means that all of your work and lessons learned from previous lifetimes have created a certain energy field around you that almost forces you to follow a particular path. At this tier density level you have more discipline than most others on a lower density level. Once you are on the path of your puzzle piece in life, you will know in your heart that this path was preordained. It took awhile for you to figure it out.

At Tier Density Level V, you are constantly refining your qi. All of your undertakings are chosen based on knowing that these endeavors will assist you on your personal journey and will not distract you from your path.

Those who want to constantly meditate to escape or choose other methods to escape from the rigors and chores of the daily three-dimensional world are not at the Full Spiritual 3-D Density Level V. No matter what confronts you or no matter how difficult a challenge may seem, those at Tier Density Level V are up for the task. You do not find ways to escape or find idle things to do to occupy your time.

Unless your puzzle piece is to be a politician, you do not have political affiliations or attachments at this tier density. There is too much lying, deceit and lack of both honesty and integrity in the political arena. You accept others for whom they are and acknowledge their beliefs, even if those beliefs are not in alignment with your beliefs. You have compassion and understanding for those who seem to oppose you.

You stand at-one with all souls on the Soul Plane and are not interested in the realms of the Personality Plane. You connect with the Soul, not the Personality.

At Tier Density Level V, you are no longer interested in what others are doing. Sports and mindless entertainment are of no interest to you. You do not delve into mindless internet information, games and gossip. You are focused on your own inner plane work. The outside world does not pull your attention anyway from your personal Inner, Divine Heart Path. This does not mean you are unaware of external events.

Although you still exist in the three dimensional world and work to take care of any financial obligations, your second chakra work (finances) supports and reinforces your personal puzzle piece in life. You do not have to focus so much on making money, because your work (kidney system) and play (heart system) are very close now, and your own inner, higher spiritual guides are assisting you in shaping your very focused reality.

You are slowly shifting from any of the various Hatha Yoga disciplines, *tai qi*, *qi gong* and other exercises emphasizing physical movement to a place of more Stillness. You have a slight "urgency" to Be Still. You are now able to access your abstract mind as easily as your concrete mind. Your level of knowingness is fully activated and you are utilizing this aspect of clairsentience as a natural part of who you are.

If you have a family with children or young adults who are dependent on you as the principle income provider for the household, then you must take care of those obligations first. It is very difficult to place your emphasis on your own personal inner growth when you have family obligations. When your dependents are no longer dependent on you, you will be able to devote your energies to your own inner plane development and inner spiritual expansion.

Many people may not like this statement, but those on the path of Tier Density Level V do not have pets. Pets "steal" your qi. If you feel that pets give you love and energy, make you feel better and help you with your emotional growth, you are not at Tier Density Level V. It is difficult enough to travel your own personal inner spiritual journey without having to devote time to taking care of pets or children. You have eliminated things that take your qi and keep you from your inner plane work. There is no need for saviorship. You do not feel the need to save anything. Many people may not want to move into the consciousness field of Tier Density Level V.

Synchronistic events are now very common and are occurring more frequently. Your psychic awareness is now fully opened, at least to a certain level. You fully trust your higher heart. You are doing service work to uplift the planet. -Your puzzle piece is moving away from a local mindset to a more global network. At this level nobody controls you, not even your work. First and second chakra events are not issues. You do not have money or relationship issues. This does not mean you do not make money or use money. The second chakra field of money does not control you—you control that field.

Some of you are realizing if you take care of all your inner plane and outer three-dimensional karma in this lifetime, this may create an opportunity that allows you to decide if this will be your final incarnation on Earth. Some of you who make it to this level may wish to return to Earth to perform additional service work to uplift humanity as a whole. In Buddhism, this choice is known as the path of the Bodhisattva. When you have completed your wheel of karma for planet Earth and you choose not to reincarnate on Earth, it does not mean you will remain somewhere in the ethers as a tiny dot of consciousness. You will be given an opportunity to incarnate on a higher consciousness plane of existence. There are many stars and planets of a much higher vibration with much higher consciousness levels than Earth. Others may wish to delve into the realms of the solar petris and the angels, archangels and other very high spiritual beings. At Tier Density Level V, you are not focused on the astral realms of the curanderos/curanderas, shamans, sangomas, or others who work and delve in the Astral Planes.

## Tiers of Density Level V

### *Hun* Follow the *Shen* Pattern

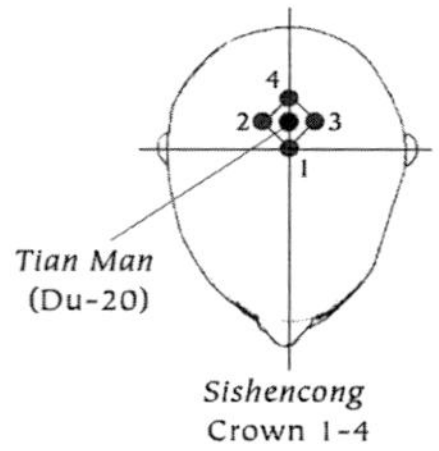
4
2
3
1
Tian Man
(Du-20)
Sishencong
Crown 1-4

Fig. 5.13-a

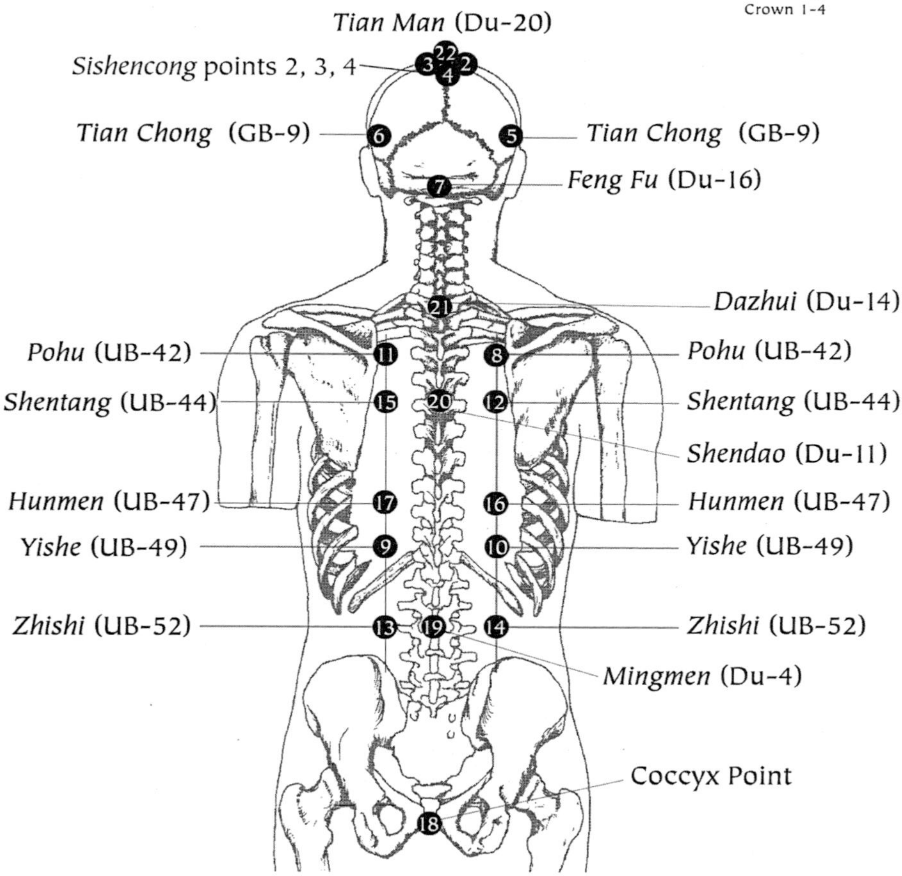
Tian Man (Du-20)
Sishencong points 2, 3, 4
Tian Chong (GB-9)
Tian Chong (GB-9)
Feng Fu (Du-16)
Dazhui (Du-14)
Pohu (UB-42)
Pohu (UB-42)
Shentang (UB-44)
Shentang (UB-44)
Shendao (Du-11)
Hunmen (UB-47)
Hunmen (UB-47)
Yishe (UB-49)
Yishe (UB-49)
Zhishi (UB-52)
Zhishi (UB-52)
Mingmen (Du-4)
Coccyx Point
22
3
2
4
6
5
7
21
11
8
15
20
12
17
16
9
10
13
19
14
18

## Needling Sequence and Point Locations

Think of this pattern having three needling sections and five visualization sections.

First Section: Crown Infinity
- 1) to 4) *Sishencong* -- "4 Spirits"
- 5) *Tian Chong* (GB-9) Right side
- 6) *Tian Chong* (GB-9) Left side
- 7) *Feng Fu* (Du-16)

The next ten acupuncture sites are located 3 *cun* lateral to the spine and level with the lower border of the spinous process of a thoracic (T) or lumbar (L) vertebra. The number of the vertebra is listed after the T or the L.

Second Section: *Taiyin* Hourglass Connection
- 8) *Pohu* (UB-42) Right side (T-3)
- 9) *Yishe* (UB-49) Left side (T-11)
- 10) *Yishe* (UB-49) Right side (T-11)
- 11) *Pohu* (UB-42) Left side (T-3)

Third Section: Double *Shaoyin* Hourglass Connection
- 12) *Shentang* (UB-44) Right side (T-5)
- 13) *Zhishi* (UB-52) Left side (L-2)
- 14) *Zhishi* (UB-52) Right side (L-2)
- 15) *Shentang* (UB-44) Left side (T-5)

Fourth Section: *Hun* connection
- 16) *Hunmen* (UB-47)--Right side (T-9)
- 17) *Hunmen* (UB-47)--Left side (T-9)

Fifth Section: Du Ascending
- 18) Coccyx Point
- 19) *Mingmen* (Du-4)
- 20) *Shendao* (Du-11)
- 21) *Dazhui* (Du-14)
- 22) *Tian Man* (Du-20)

Those of you familiar with the Chinese Five Element Theory know that the liver system is considered the mother of the fire element of the heart system. This would, in theory, make the heart the child of wood. Following the concepts and thinking of the Chinese Five Element Theory, the mother feeds the child giving the mother some level of control over the child. This means that the liver system has some control over the heart system, and that a harmonious, balanced wood system would influence and nurture the fire element in a positive, healthy manner. But, the child also influences the mother. If the liver system is out of balance, then the heart system would likewise be imbalanced to some degree.

The wood element of the liver system allows qi throughout the body to flow smoothly through the acupuncture channels, as well as allowing a smooth qi flow through the finer frequency connecting vessels and the very minute vessels. The natural characteristic of a healthy liver system is movement. An over abundance of imbalanced liver energy will often manifest as an aggressive outward or upward movement. The outward movement is seen when an angry person wants to punch someone or kick the wall. The aggressive upward movement is seen when an angry person gets a red face or aggressively shouts or uses profanity at someone. In these instances, the liver is definitely not being influenced by the characteristics and strength of the heart and the fire system.

The opposite of movement for the liver system is lack of movement often expressing itself as depression and not wanting to do anything. There is no interest to motivate the individual to doing anything of a creative or constructive nature. The normal, healthy liver qi is depleted and drained and the person has no energy or willpower to do anything except sleep or take drugs.

In Traditional Chinese Acupuncture Theory, the liver is sometimes called the "General." The liver is responsible for organizing various activities and functions of the physical, emotional and mental bodies of an individual. But, sometimes the General may covet excessive power and becomes a bully.

This is seen in the concept of wood attacks earth that can manifest as: indigestion, bloating, flatulence, abdominal pains, acid regurgitation, hiccups, belching and other symptoms of rebellious earth qi.

Those who are doing some sort of inner plane work and are also very aware of their diet will eventually reach a point where the balanced liver system will "bow" to the energetics of the heart system. This is one concept of the *Hun* follow the *Shen*. The general (wood system) recognizes the power of the emperor (heart system) and follows the emperor rather than trying to control the emperor. But on a higher level, you must understand the Monadic Ray. The Monadic Ray is a stream of consciousness that descends from the Monadic Plane down through the Soul Plane to eventually reach the Personality Plane. The Original *Hun* is an extension of the Original *Shen*. When the physical vehicle is no longer needed and the spirit ascends back to the Monadic Plane, the Original *Hun* returns to the Original *Shen*. This is the esoteric meaning of the *Hun* follow the *Shen*.

## Visualization of The *Hun* Follow the *Shen* Pattern

The visualization of The *Hun* Follow the *Shen* Pattern is divided into five sections to make it easier for the practitioner to memorize the triangular and other mental visualizations.

**Section One:** Crown Infinity Pattern

The triangular visualizations with the first seven acupuncture points in The *Hun* Follow the *Shen* Pattern are the same visual connections as the seven acupuncture points of the Crown Infinity connection in the Crown Infinity *Shaoyin* Pattern. These visual connections will not be repeated here. Please go to pages 333 to 337 for the step-by-step visualization instructions.

**Section Two:** *Taiyin* Hourglass Connection

Section two consists of the bilateral outer bladder points

of the heart and kidney systems on the trunk of the posterior of the body. Have your client visually connect *Pohu* (UB-42) on his or her right side with the acupuncture point *Yishe* (UB-49) on the left side. (See figure 5.13-b below.)

## *Hun* Follow the *Shen* Pattern

Fig. 5.13-b

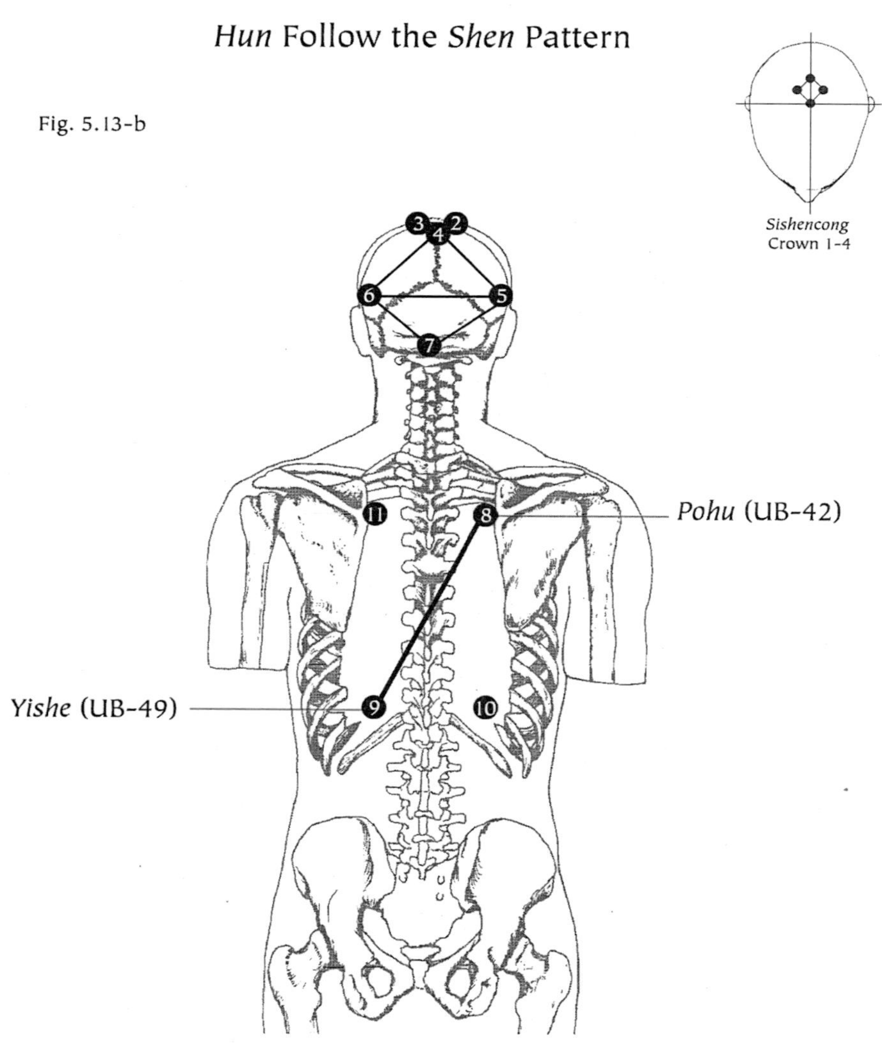

Next have your client visually connect *Yishe* (UB-49) on the left side with *Yishe* (UB- 49) on the right side. (See figure 5.13-c below.)

## *Hun* Follow the *Shen* Pattern

Fig. 5.13-c

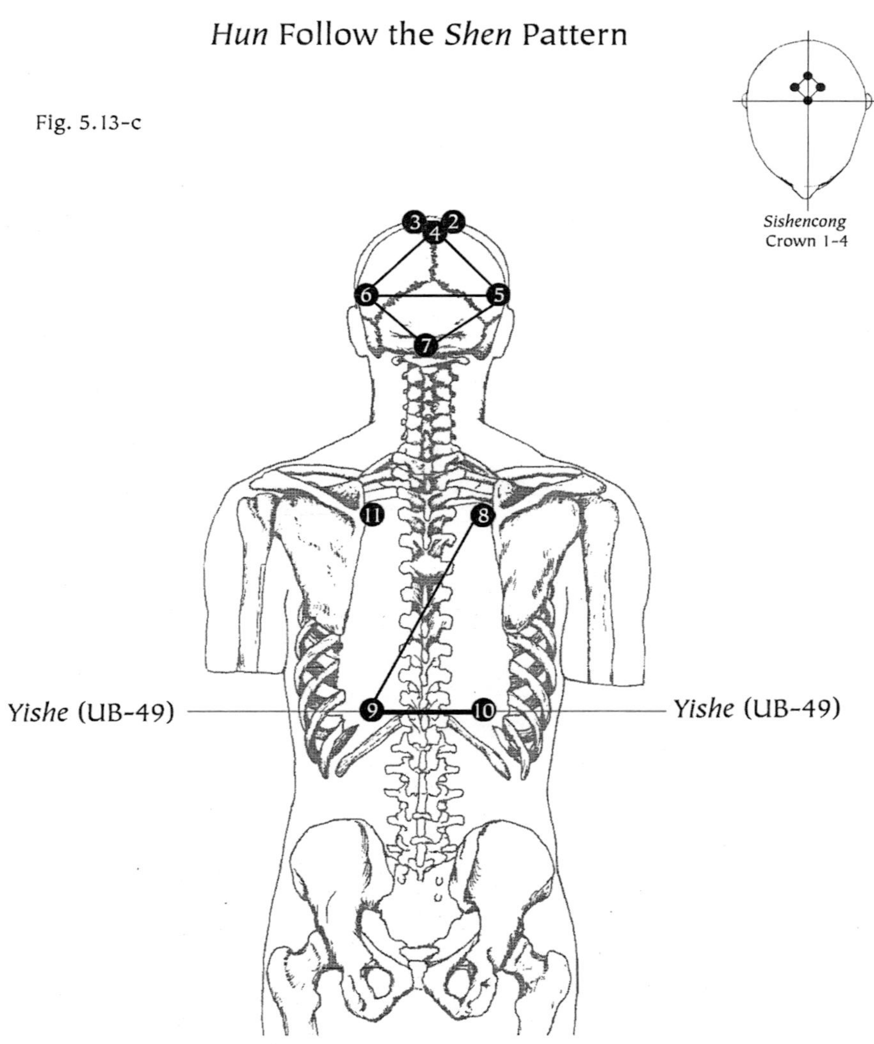

From *Yishe* (UB-49) on the right side, have your client crisscross the energy upward to connect with the acupuncture point *Pohu* (UB-42) on the left side. (See figure 5.13-d below.)

### *Hun* Follow the *Shen* Pattern

Fig. 5.13-d

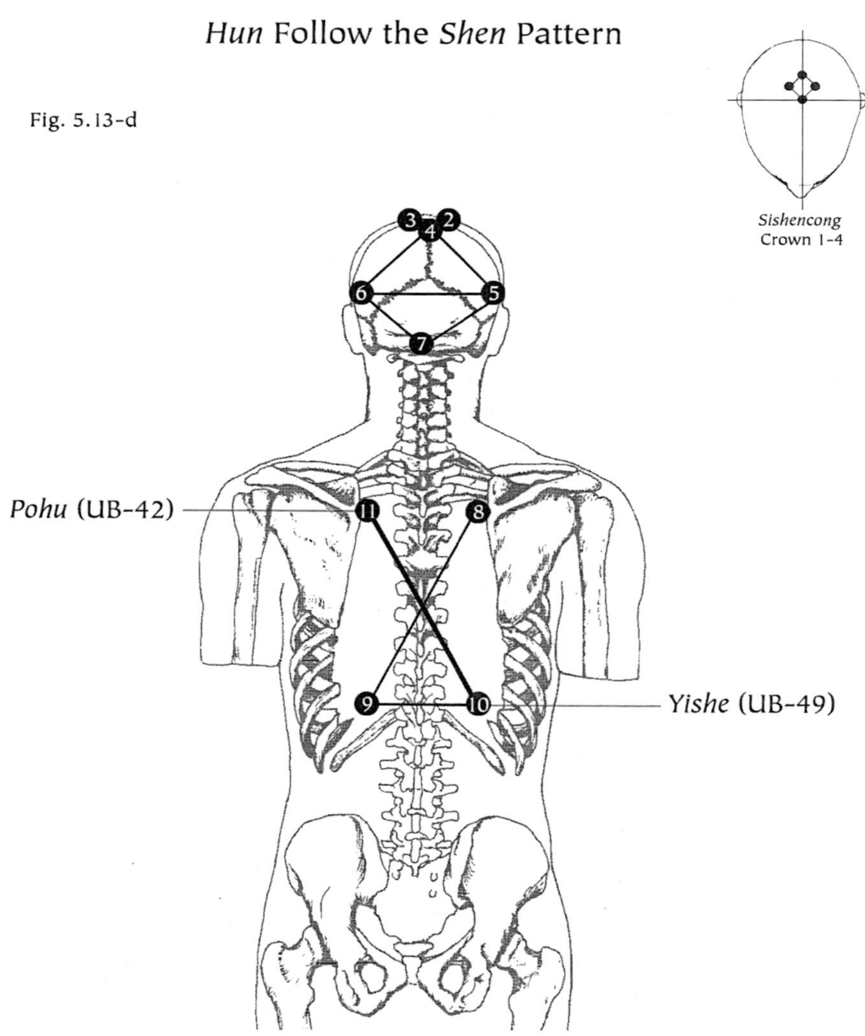

With the last connection in section two, have your client visually connect *Pohu* (UB-42) on the left side with *Pohu* (UB-42 on the right side. The lungs and spleen systems in Traditional Chinese Medicine are both connected within a pathway known as *Taiyin*. This visualization will have formed an hourglass shaped polygon. The triangle pointing upward is a Fire Triangle of the heart system. The triangle pointing downward is a Water Triangle of the kidney system. We have again created an Esoteric *Shaoyin* energy field. We have activated the lungs and spleen *Taiyin* system and have overlaid a *Shaoyin* field over the *Taiyin* connection. (See figure 5.13-e below.)

*Hun* Follow the *Shen* Pattern

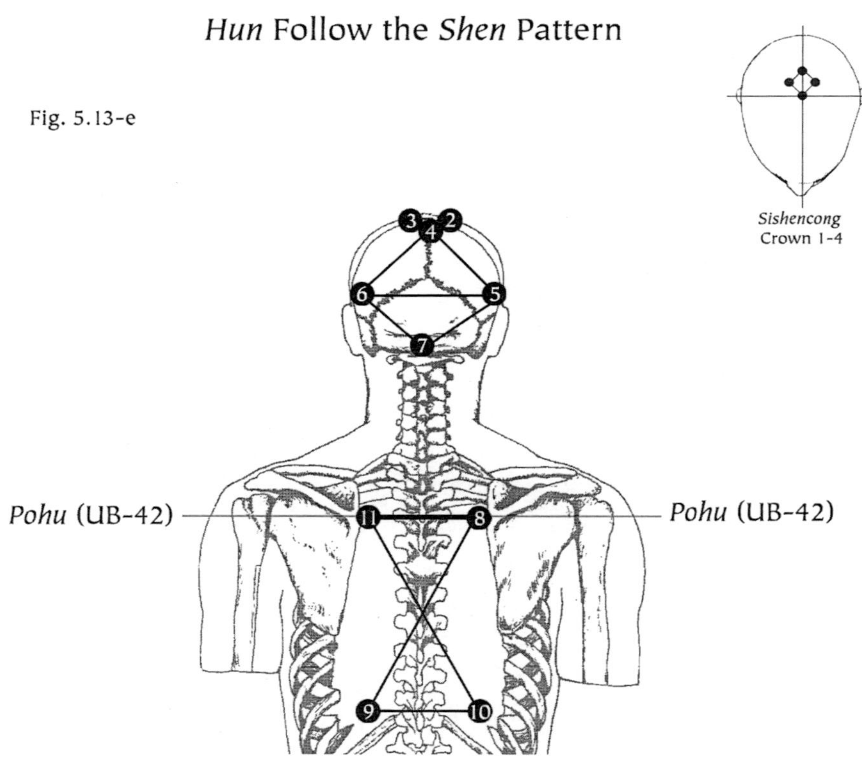


Fig. 5.13-e

**Section Three:** Double *Shaoyin* Hourglass Connection

In section three, you will have your client connect the bilateral outer heart points and the bilateral outer kidneys points of the urinary bladder meridian. First have your client visually connect the *Shentang* (UB-44) point on the right by crisscrossing down to *Zhishi* (UB-52) on the left side. (See figure 5.13-f below.)

*Hun* Follow the *Shen* Pattern

Fig. 5.13-f

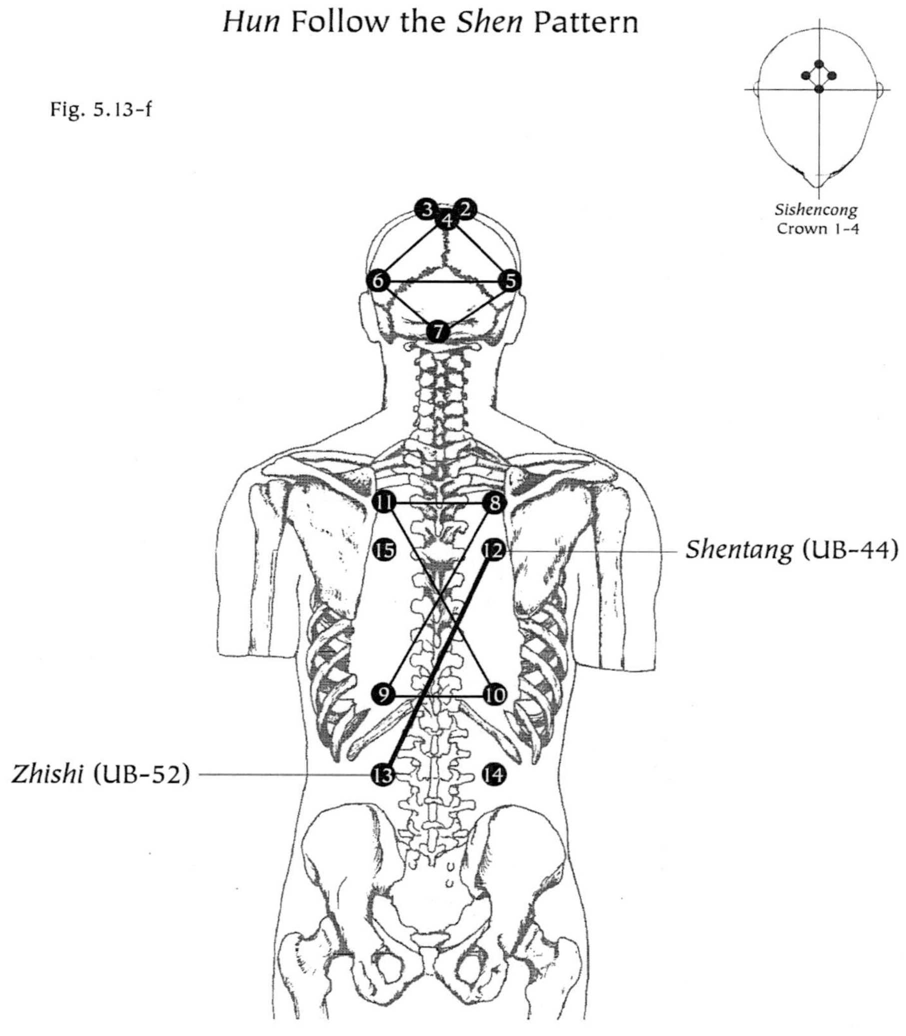

Next have your client visually move the qi from the *Zhishi* (UB-52) point on the left side and visually connect this point to *Zhishi* (UB-52) on the right side. (See figure 5.13-g below.)

### *Hun* Follow the *Shen* Pattern

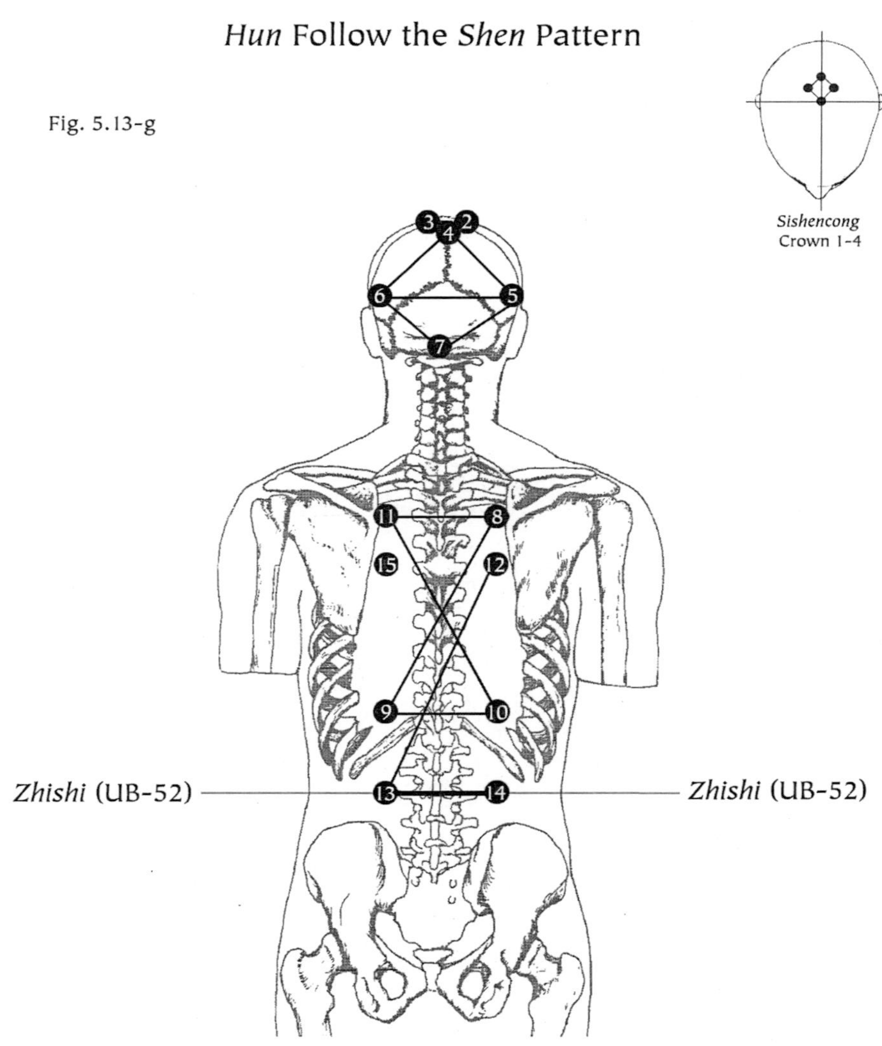


Fig. 5.13-g

Now have your client visually bring the qi from the *Zhishi* (UB-52) point on the right side and crisscross upward to connect with the *Shentang* (UB-44) point on the left. (See figure 5.13-h.)

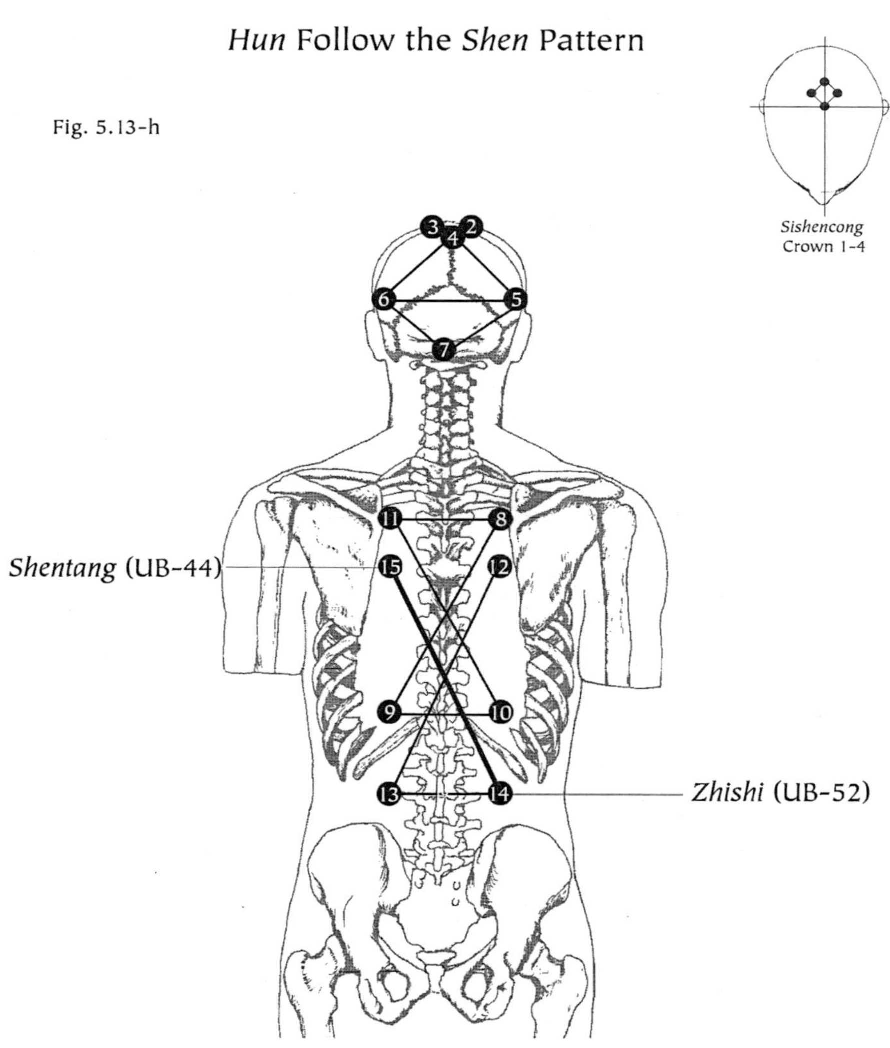


*Hun* Follow the *Shen* Pattern

Fig. 5.13-h

The last visual connection in section three is to have your client mentally connect the left *Shentang* (UB-44) with the *Shentang* (UB-44) point on the right side. We have again formed an hourglass shaped geometric pattern that is a *Shaoyin* connection. The bilateral *Shentang* (UB-44) points are connected to the heart system. The bilateral *Zhishi* (UB-52) points are connected to the kidneys. The triangle pointing downward is connected to water and the kidney system. The triangle pointing upward is connected to the fire system and heart system. We have created a double *Shaoyin* connection by visually connecting these last four acupuncture points. (See figure 5.13-i below.)

*Hun* Follow the *Shen* Pattern

Fig. 5.13-i

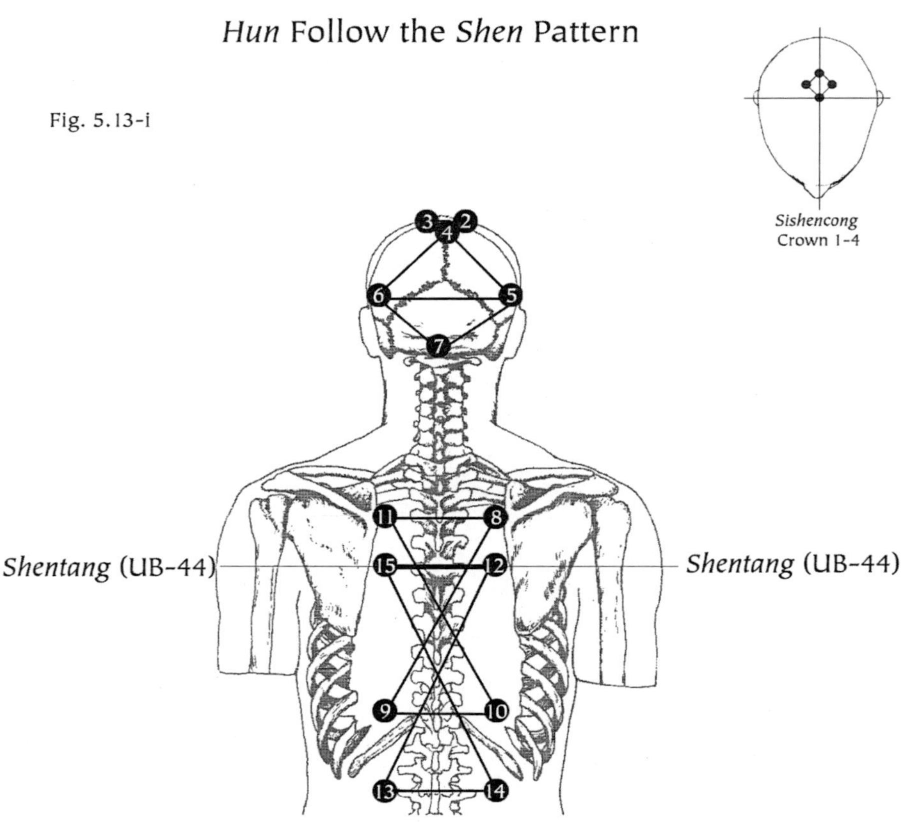

**Section Four:** *Hun* Connection

Section four consists of only two acupuncture points. Insert an acupuncture needle into the site of the right *Hunmen* (UB-47) point. Next insert an acupuncture needle into the site of the left *Hunmen* (UB-47) point. Connect the qi at these bilateral sites to one another. We will continue the upward pointing Fire Triangle connections after we start to ascend the energies upward from the Coccyx Point. (See figure 5.13-j below.)

*Hun* Follow the *Shen* Pattern

Fig. 5.13-j

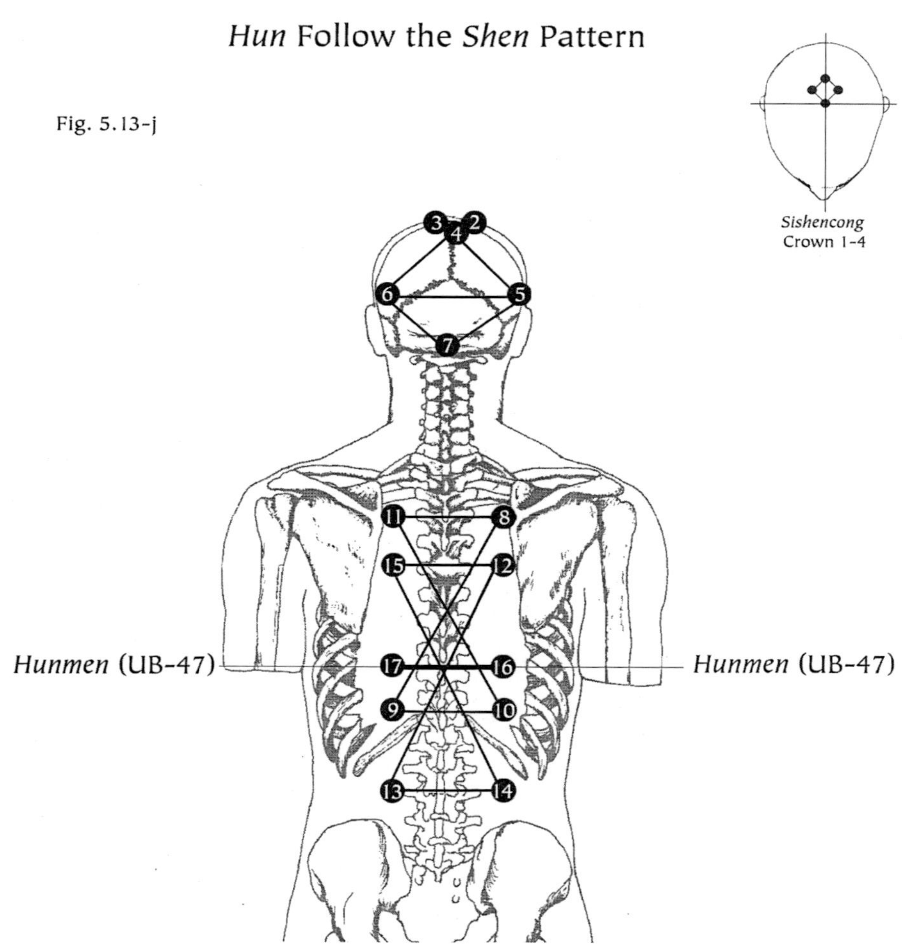

**Section Five:** Du Ascending

Section five consists of five acupuncture sites ascending along Du channel on the posterior spine and ending at *Tian Man* (Du-20). After the ten outer bladder points have been needled and visually connected in the manner described above, needle the Coccyx Point on your client. (See figure 5.13-k below.)

### *Hun* Follow the *Shen* Pattern

Fig. 5.13-k

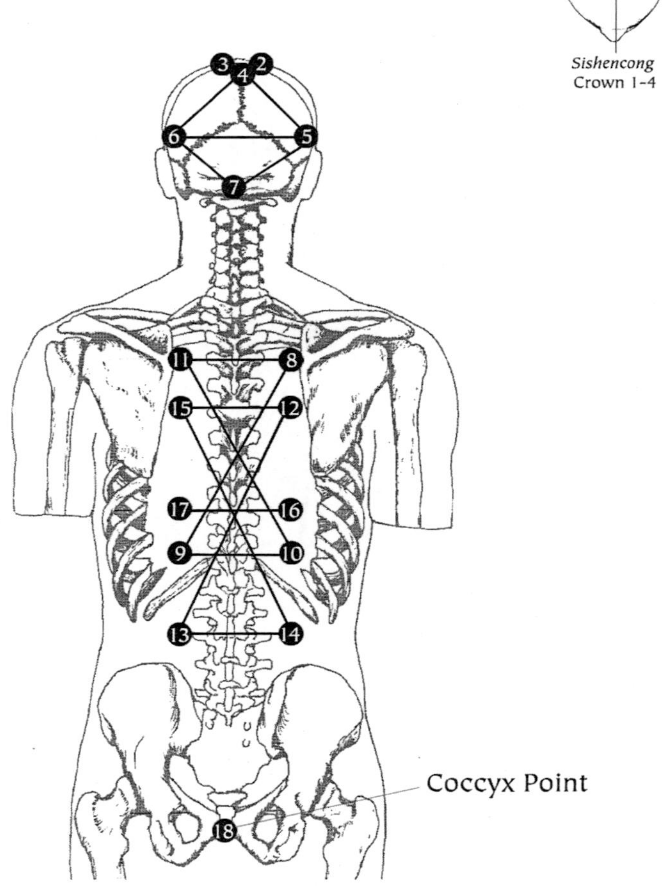

Next have your client visually bring the qi downward from the bilateral *Hunmen* (UB-47) points to connect with Coccyx Point forming a downward pointing Water Triangle. (See figure 5.13-l below.)

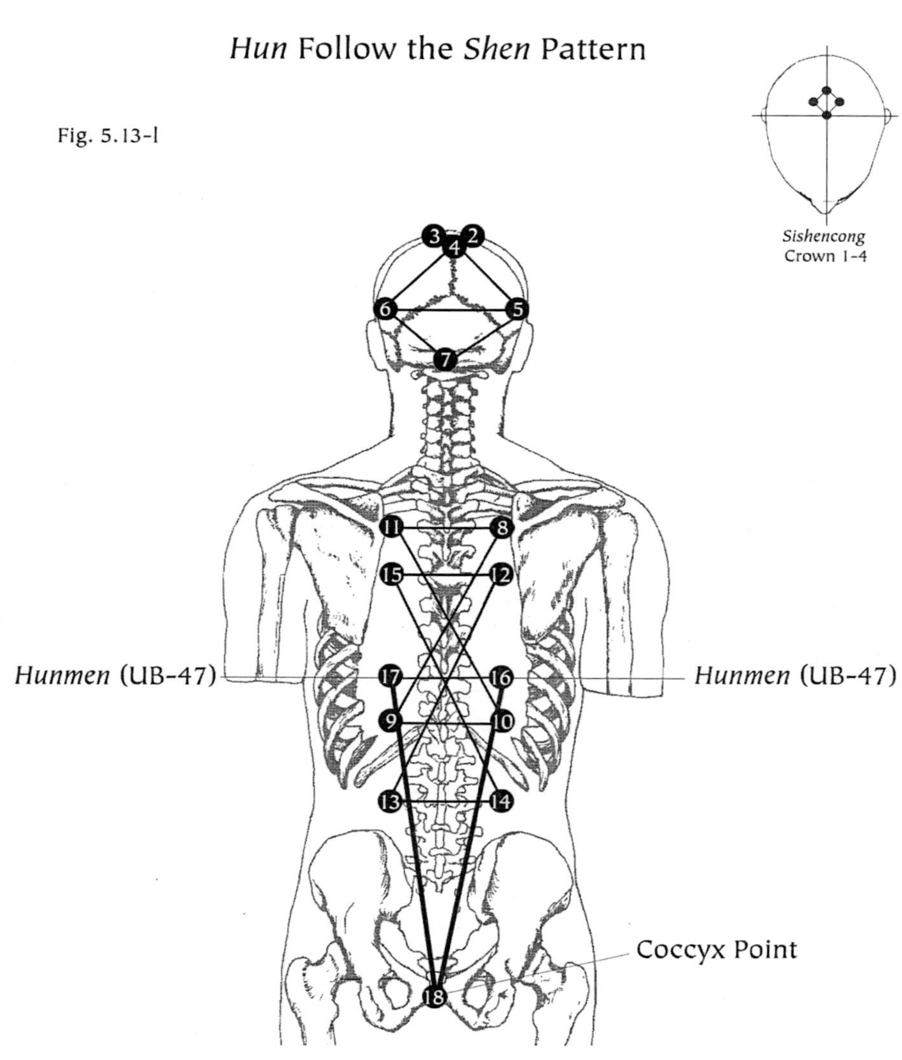

Bring the qi from the bilateral *Zhishi* (UB-52) points downward in a Water Triangle formation to connect with the Coccyx Point. (See figure 5.13-m below.)

### *Hun* Follow the *Shen* Pattern

Fig. 5.13-m

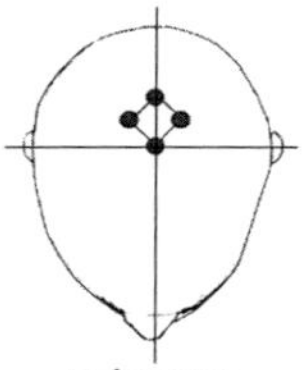

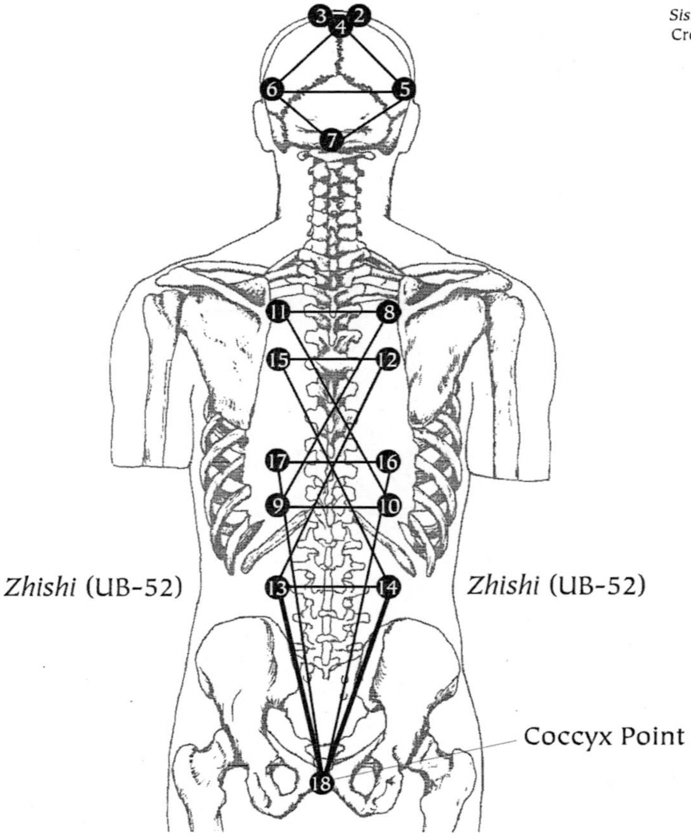

Next insert an acupuncture needle at the acupuncture site of *Mingmen* (Du-4) located directly on the spine below the lower border of the spinous process of the second lumbar vertebra. (See figure 5.13-n below.)

### *Hun* Follow the *Shen* Pattern

Fig. 5.13-n

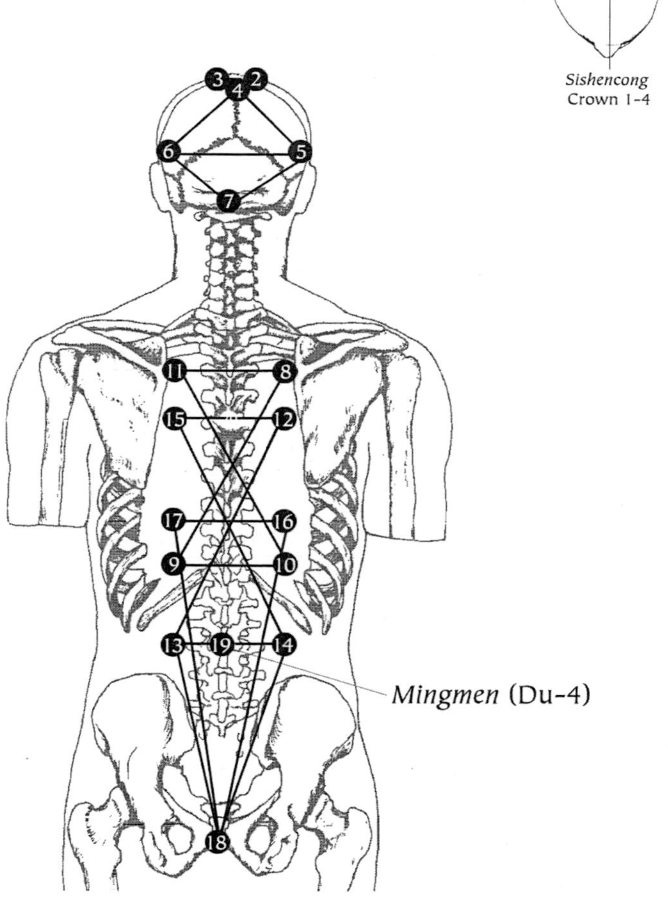

Now have your client bring qi downward from *Mingmen* to the Coccyx Point. After the Coccyx Point has been energized sufficiently, bring the energy upward from the Coccyx Point back to the site of *Mingmen* (Du-4).(See figure 5.13-o below.)

## *Hun* Follow the *Shen* Pattern

Fig. 5.13-o

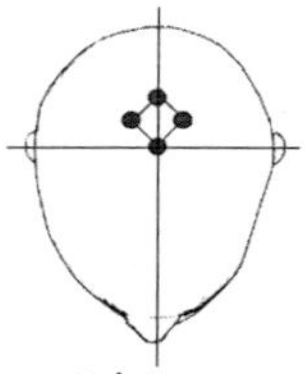

*Sishencong*
Crown 1-4

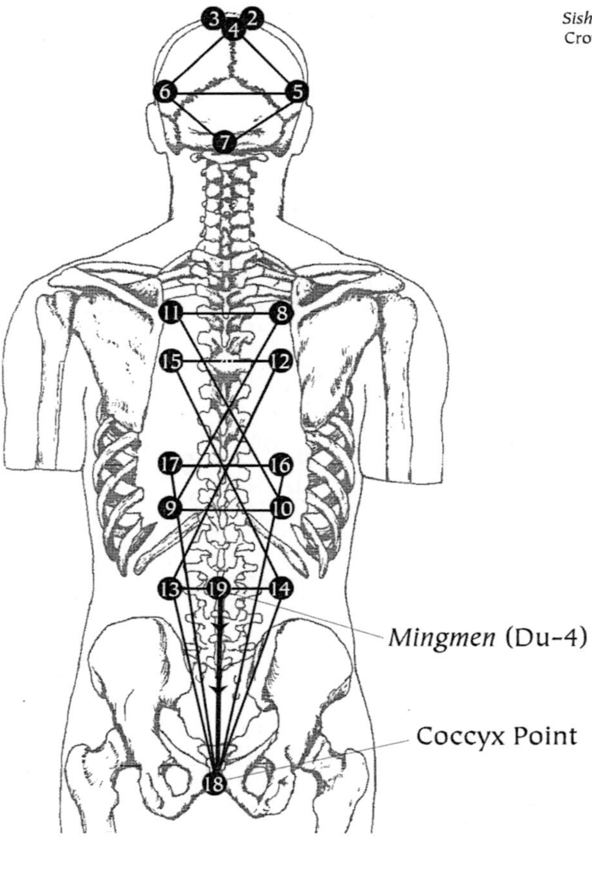

*Mingmen* (Du-4)

Coccyx Point

Next bring the qi downward from the bilateral *Yishe* (UB-49) points to connect in a Water Triangle formation with *Mingmen* (Du-4). (See figure 5.13-p below.)

*Hun* Follow the *Shen* Pattern

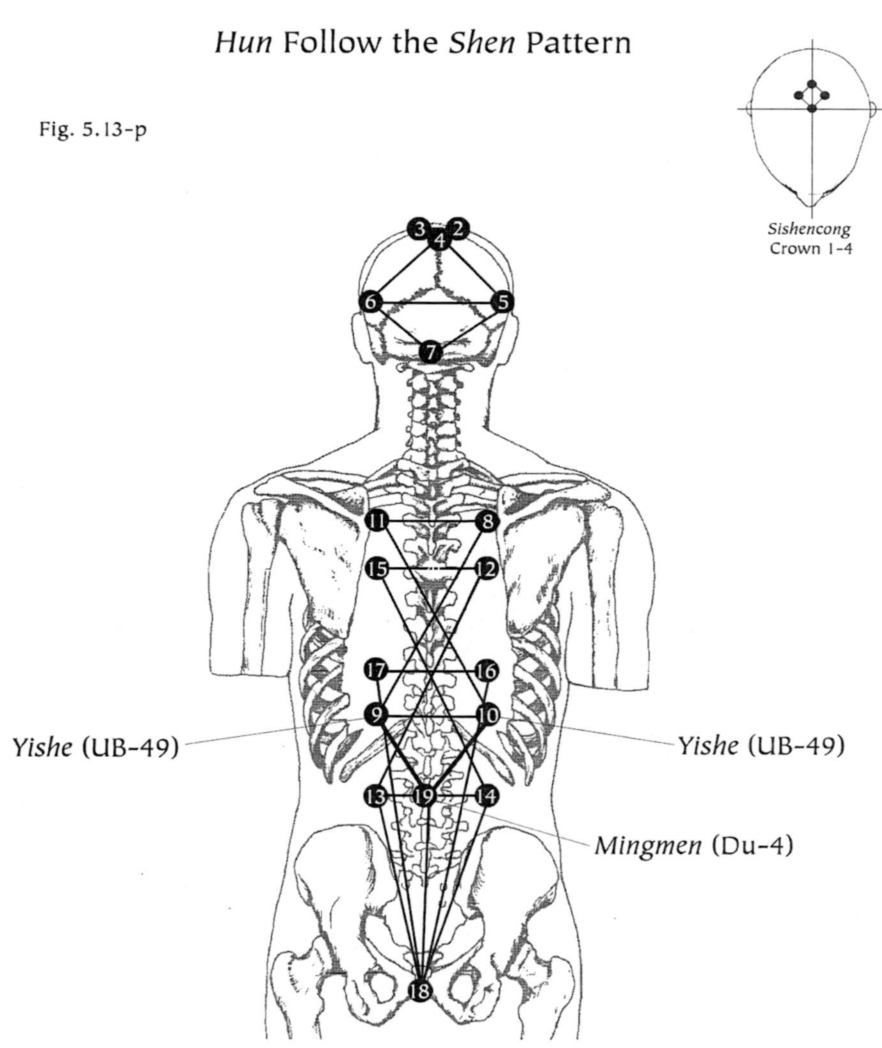


Fig. 5.13-p

Now insert an acupuncture needle at the site of *Shendao* (Du-11) located directly on the spine below the lower border of the spinous process of the fifth thoracic vertebra. (See figure 5.13-q below.)

*Hun* Follow the *Shen* Pattern

Fig. 5.13-q

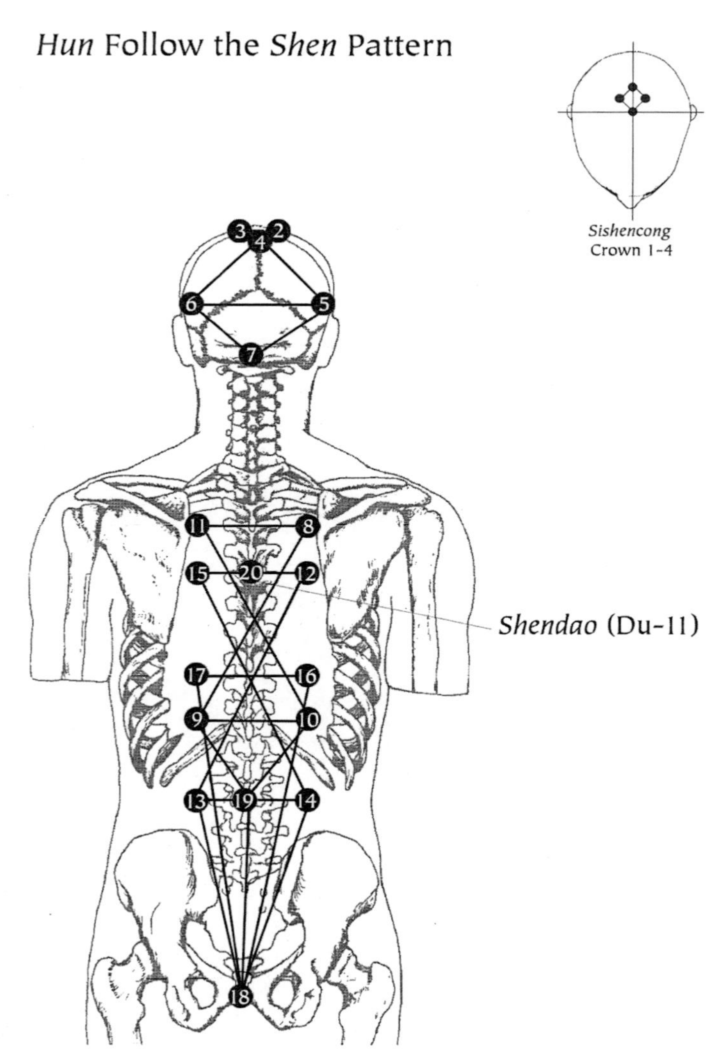

Bring the qi upward directly along the spine from *Mingmen* (Du-4) the kidney point to the site of *Shendao* (Du-11) the heart point. This is a *Shaoyin* connection of the Lower Twin Flames Within. The flame of *Mingmen* communicates with the flame of *Shendao*. (See figure 5.13-r below.)

## *Hun* Follow the *Shen* Pattern

Fig. 5.13-r

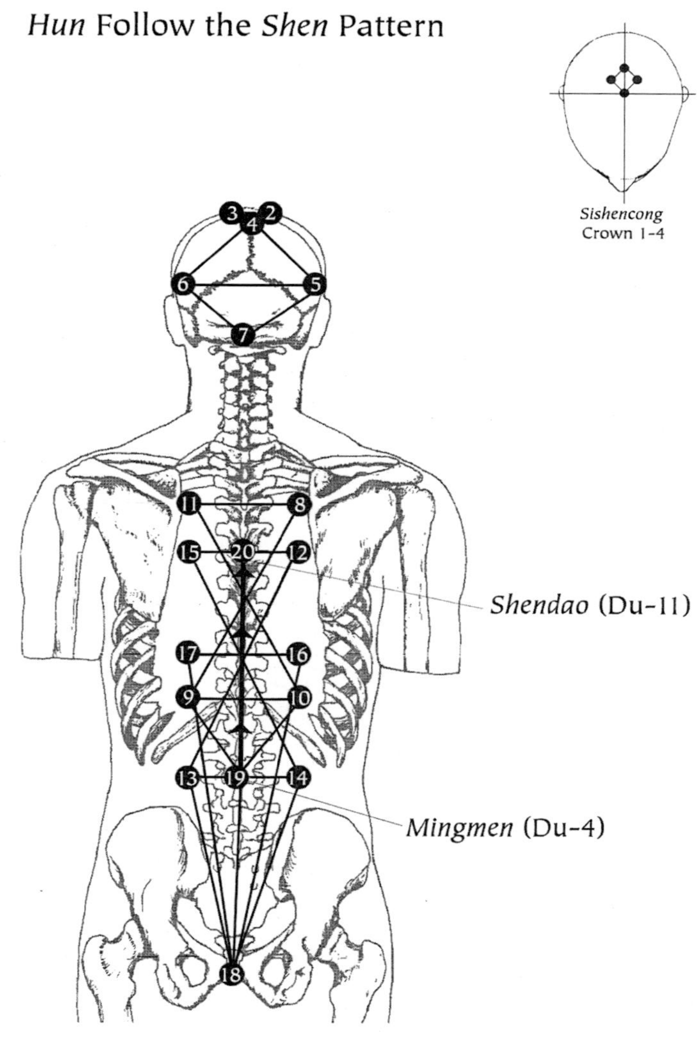

Next move the qi from the bilateral *Zhishi* (UB-52) points upward to form a Fire Triangle at the site of *Shendao* (Du-11). (See figure 5.13-s below.)

### *Hun* Follow the *Shen* Pattern

Fig. 5.13-s

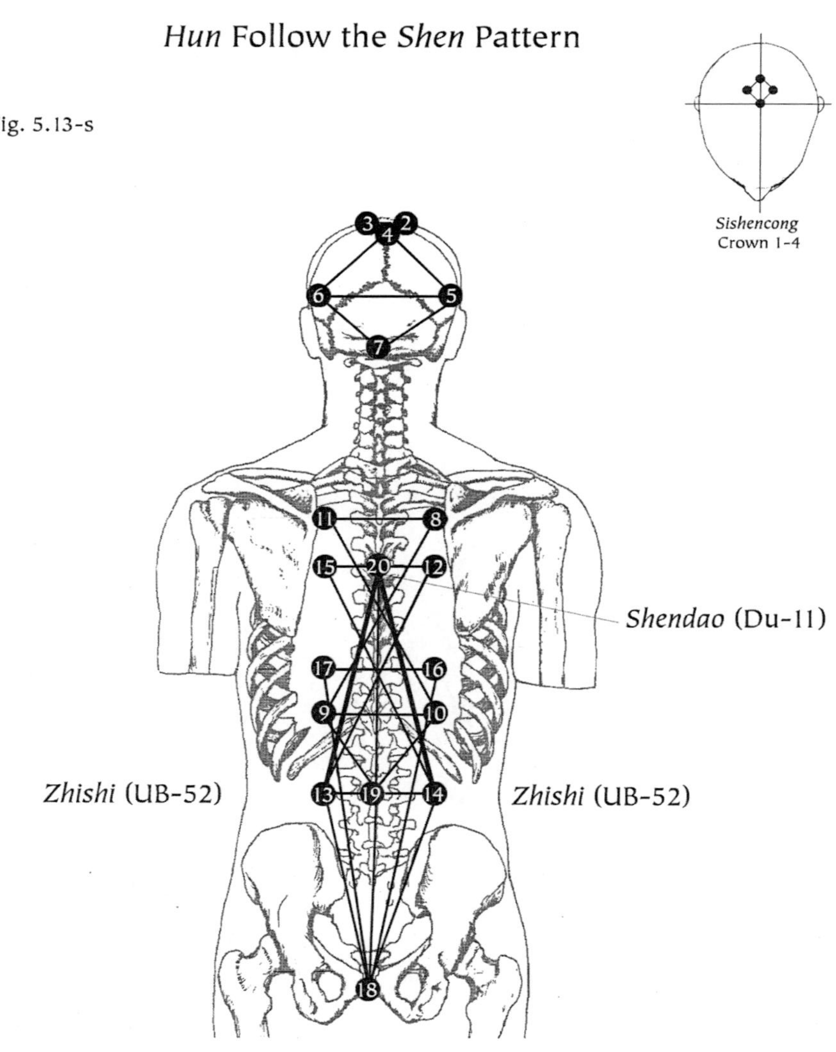

Now move the qi from the bilateral *Hunmen* (UB-47) points upward to form another Fire Triangle connecting at the site of *Shendao* (Du-11) (See figure 5.13-t)

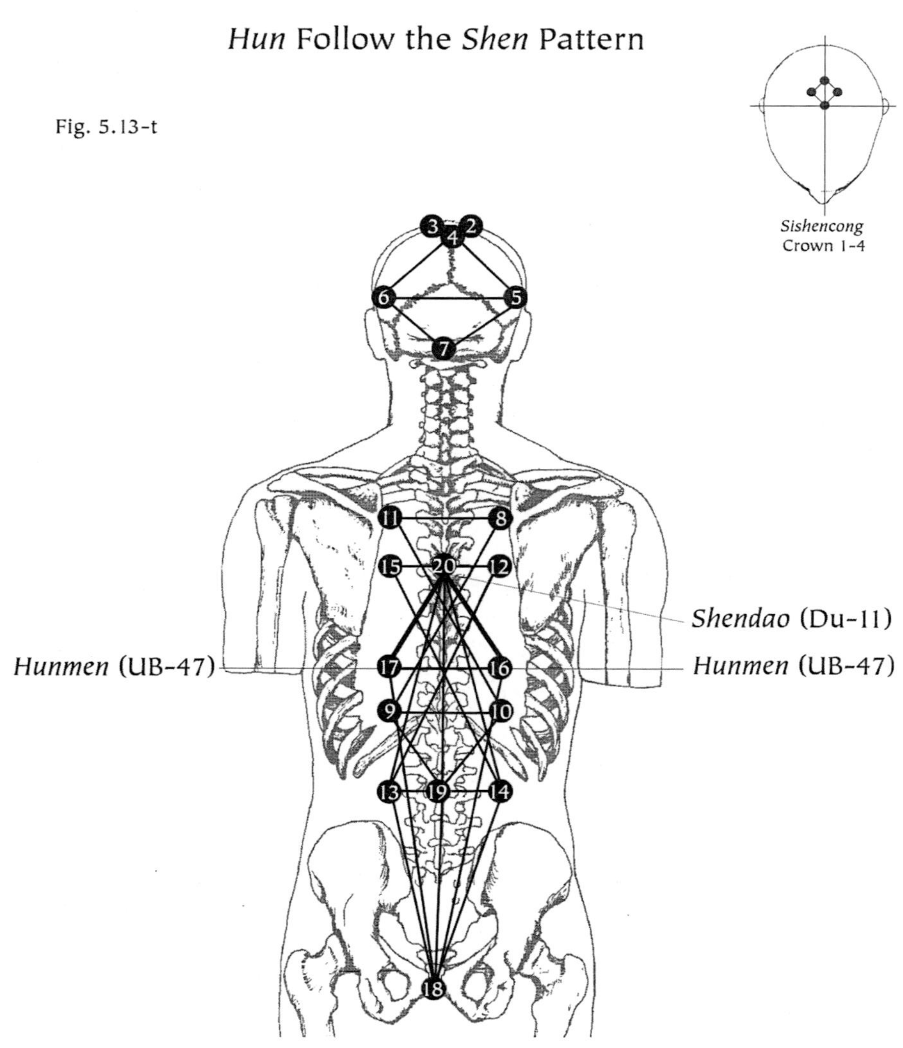

Next insert an acupuncture needle at the acupuncture site of *Dazhui* (Du-14) located directly on the spine below the lower border of the spinous process of the seventh cervical vertebra. (See figure 5.13-u below.)

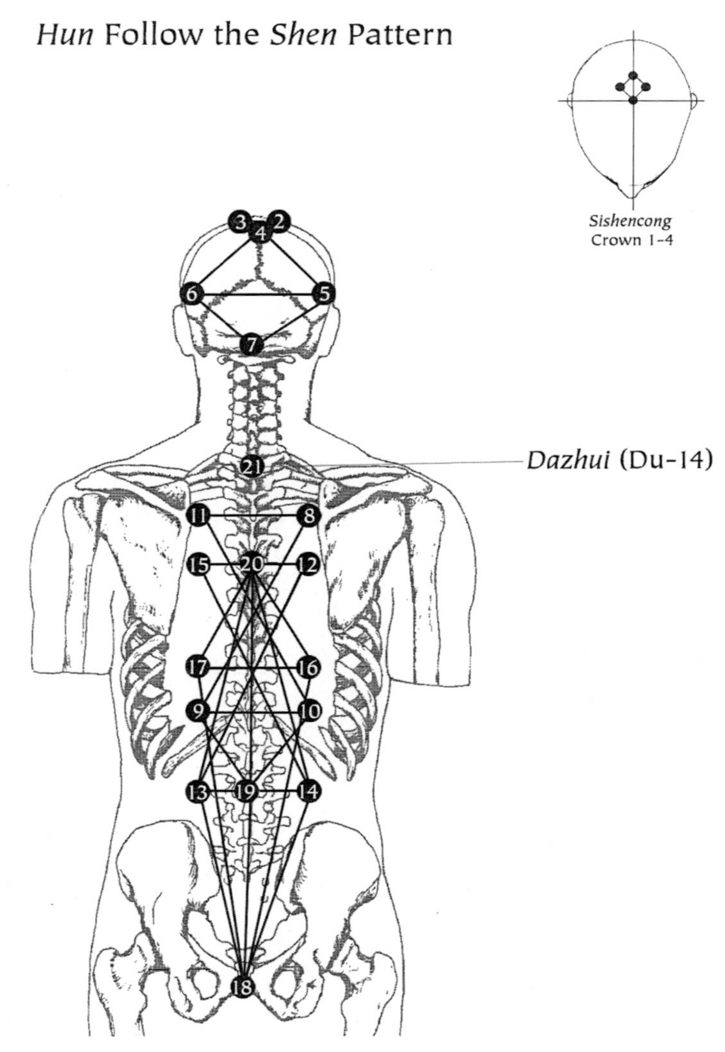


Fig. 5.13-u

Now have your client visualize an upward movement of qi from *Shendao* (Du-11) to *Dazhui* (Du-14). (See figure 5.13-v below.)

## *Hun* Follow the *Shen* Pattern

Fig. 5.13-v

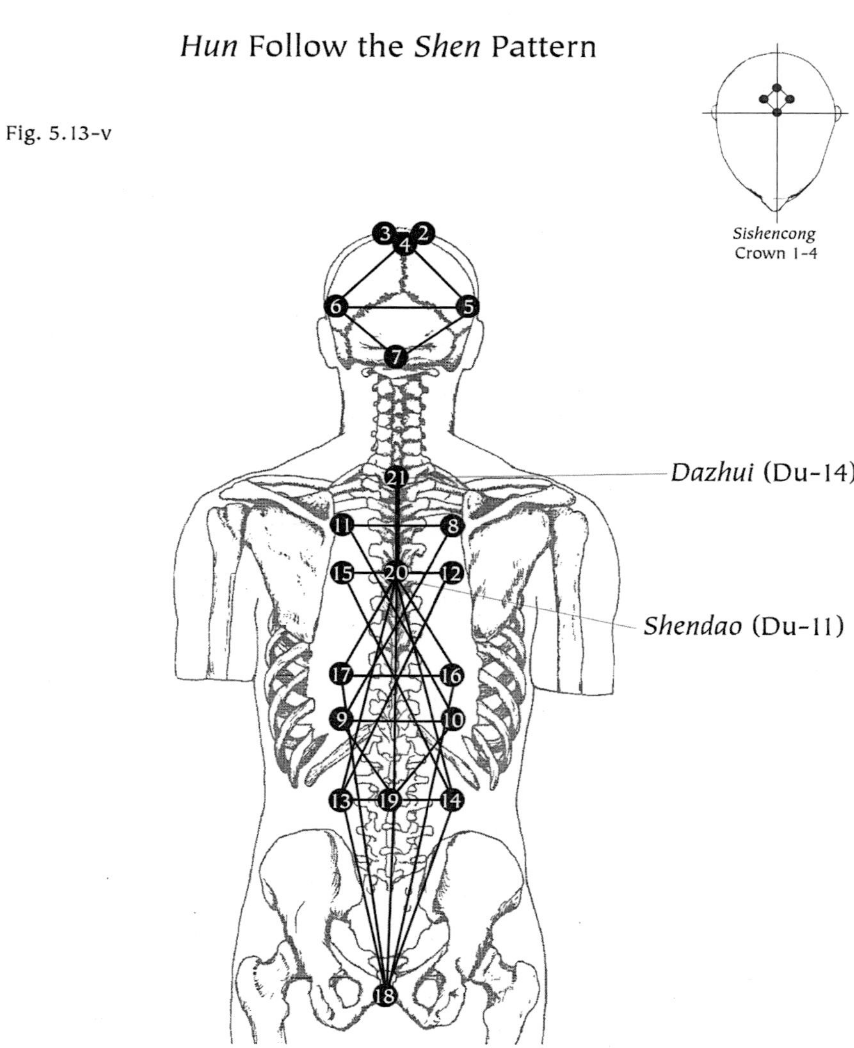

Next have your client mentally move the qi from the bilateral *Hunmen* (UB-42) points upward to connect with *Dazhui* (Du-14) to form another Fire Triangle. (See figure 5.13-w below.)

*Hun* Follow the *Shen* Pattern

Fig. 5.13-w

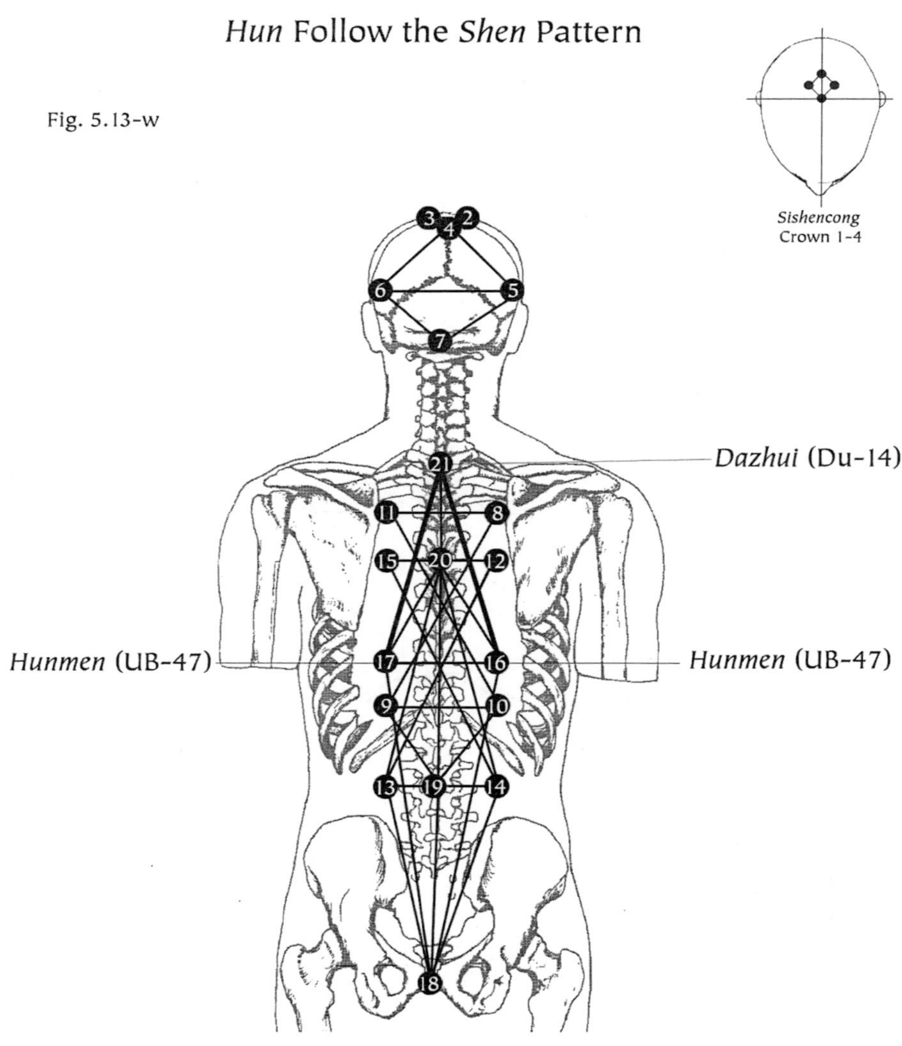

Now have your client mentally connect the qi at the site of *Dazhui* (Du-14) to the qi at the site of *Yintang* (Ajna Center) located on the anterior vertical midline of the forehead between the eyebrows and superior to the bridge of the nose. The reason this connection is so important is because since *Yintang* (Ajna Center) is not being needled, *Dazhui* (Du-14) must first activate the qi at *Yintang* (Ajna Center) before the next step of moving the qi from *Dazhui* (Du-14) upward to *Feng Fu* (Du-16). The goal is to connect the three Major Head Centers to be able to move into the Sahasrara (Crown Chakra) and beyond.

Although the connection shown in figure 5.13-x may seem like a linear connection, it is not. There is a dotted line, rather than a solid line connecting those two acupuncture sites. The dotted line from *Dazhui* (Du-14) to the Third Eye Point at *Yintang* (Ajna Center) represents a morphic resonant connection, not a linear connection. (See figure 5.13-x below.)

## Morphic Resonance Connection

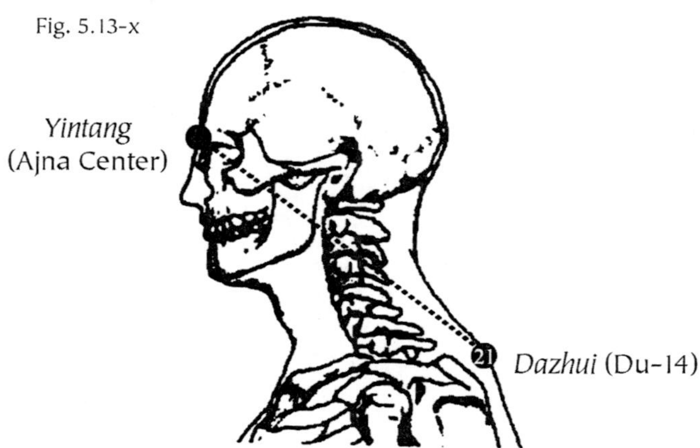

After *Yintang* (Ajna Center) has been activated from *Dazhui* (Du-14), have your client mentally see the qi move upward from *Dazhui* (Du-14) to connect with *Feng Fu* (Du-16). This connection is a linear connection. (See figure 5.13-y below.)

Fig. 5.13-y

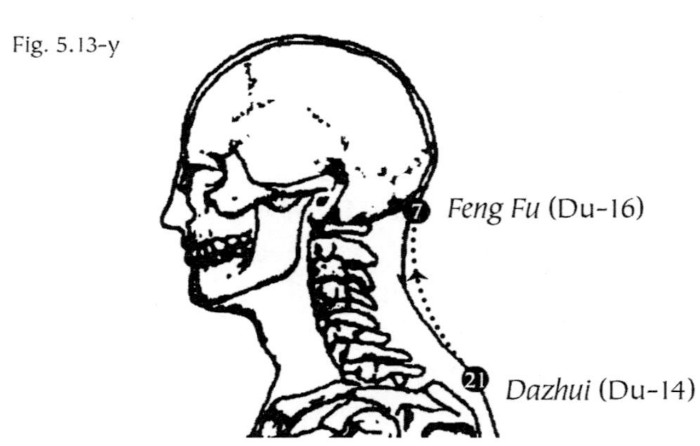


Next have your client mentally connect *Feng Fu* (Du-16) to *Yintang* (Ajna Center) by way of a linear connection. (See figure 5.13-z.)

Fig. 5.13-z

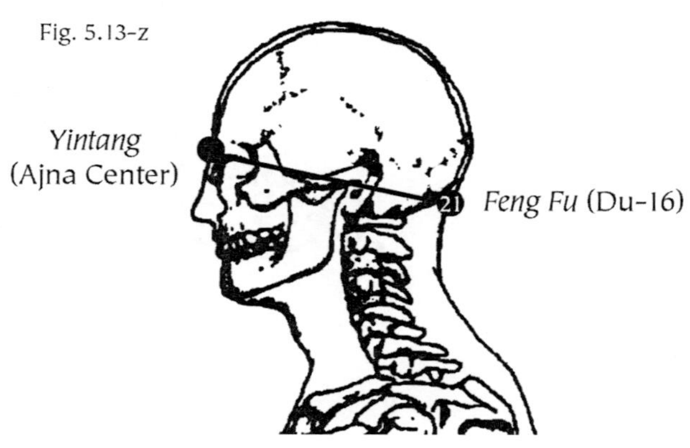

Now have your client bring the qi from the acupuncture sites of both *Feng Fu* (Du-16) and *Yintang* (Ajna Center) simultaneously upward to make a Fire Triangular connection with *Tian Man* (Du-20). As you are having your client make this Fire Triangle connection, you will now insert the twenty-second and last needle in the *Hun* Follow the *Shen* Pattern at the acupuncture site of *Tian Man* (Du-20).

The three chakra centers at those three acupuncture sites comprise what is known as the Three Major Head Centers. By inserting an acupuncture needle at the site of *Tian Man* (Du-20) in this pattern, the Sahasara (Crown Chakra) is activated. The Taluka Chakra (Alta Major Center) was activated by the insertion of the acupuncture needle at the site of *Feng Fu* (Du-16). *Yintang,* the Ajna Center (Third Eye) was activated by the morphic resonant connection with *Dazhui* (Du-14).(See figure 5.13-aa below.)

Fig. 5.13-aa

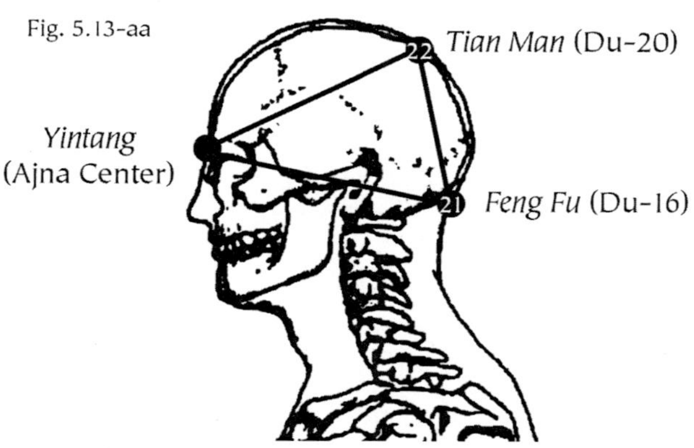

The next visual connection is to bring the bilateral *Hunmen* (UB-47) points upward in a Fire Triangle formation to join with *Feng Fu* (Du-16). (See figure 5.13-bb below.)

## *Hun* Follow the *Shen* Pattern

Fig. 5.13-bb

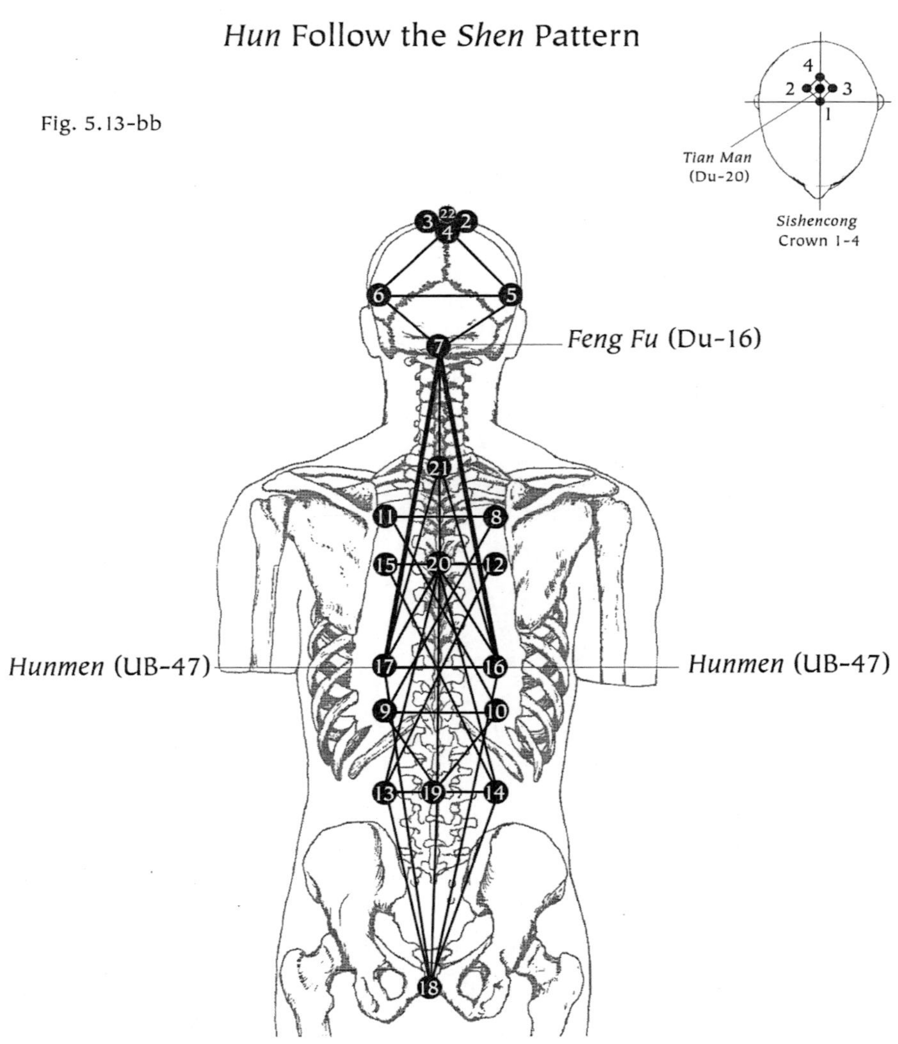

The last visual connection in The *Hun* Follow the *Shen* Pattern is to have your client mentally bring the qi upward from the bilateral *Hunmen* (UB-47) points to make a triangular connection with *Tian Man* (Du-20) located at the top of the head. (See figure 5.13-cc below)

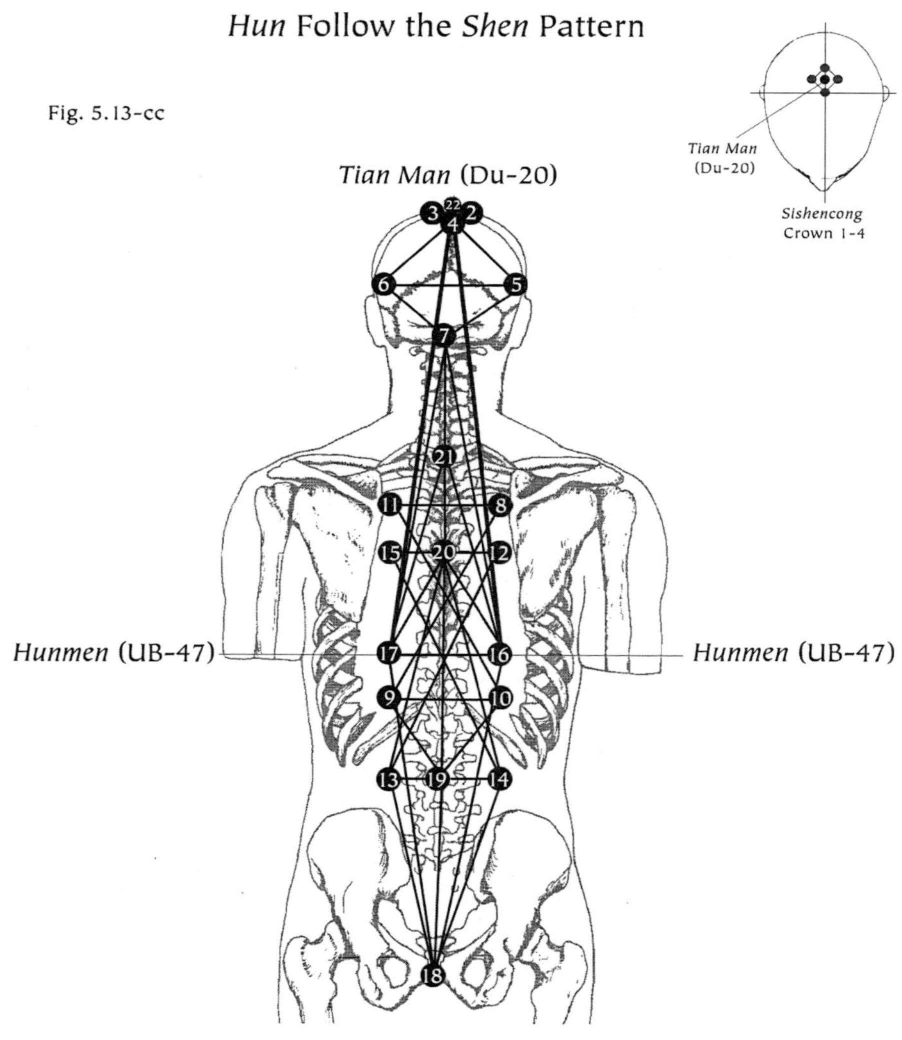


Fig. 5.13-cc

The practitioner must become very familiar with all the visualizations in the *Hun* Follow the *Shen* Pattern. Remember that as the acupuncture needles are inserted into the various acupuncture sites, the endorphins that are released throughout the body will make your client feel very relaxed. Since this New Encoding Pattern has quite a few visualization connections, your client may enter into a very calm state of mind during the needling process making it difficult for the client to continue with the mental visualization connections. It is important to have your client relax and move into a very calm field of consciousness. In those instances when your client becomes so relaxed that he or she is not able to continue with the visual connections, it is advised that the practitioner mentally completes the rest of the triangular connections and let the client relax.

We must remember that *Hunmen* is translated as the "Gate of *Hun*" or "*Hun* Gate." This implies that by needling the acupuncture site of *Hunmen* (UB-47), you will be entering the access site that communicates with the *Hun*. There are four Fire Triangle connections involving the bilateral *Hunmen* (UB-47) points in this pattern. The energy flow of the *Hun* Follow the *Shen* Pattern is designed to open the *Hun* Gates to allow the various levels of consciousness of the *Hun* to flow upward into four of the levels of the *Shen* of the heart. The energetics of the *Hun* are following the energetics of the more dominant and powerful *Shen*, the natural and rightful ruler and leader of the domain of all the fields of a person.

In many parts of the world, people have forgotten how to nurture, enrich and listen to their own heart on all the multiple levels. Do you think it is merely by coincidence that heart disease is the number one cause of death in the United States today? Here in the United States, there are so many distractions that we do not take the time to nurture and listen to our hearts. The liver fields (*Hun*) of anger, depression and not being able to see things clearly have overridden the power of calmness, sharing, joyfulness and love of the heart (*Shen*). In those instances, the

*Hun* is "leading" the *Shen* and not adhering to the natural order of the Higher *Hun* following the Inner *Shen*.

Although the visual connections in the *Hun* Follow the *Shen* Pattern may seem very complex, if you break up the connection into the sections that have been suggested in this book, it will make the mental visualizations less of a burden to memorize. Section one of the visualizations consists of the seven Crown Infinity Pattern points. Section two consists of the four outer bladder points of the *Taiyin* Channel (Lungs and spleen). Section three consists if the outer kidney and heart bladder points of the *Shaoyin* Channel. Section four is the bilateral *Hunmen* points. Section five consists of four acupuncture sites directly on the spine and the capstone site of *Tian Man* (Du-20). Section four has the most complex order of visualizations.

The last four connections are Fire Triangle connections of the *Hun* following the *Shen*. The first of these four Fire Triangle connections has the bilateral *Hunmen* connecting to *Shendao*.

Next, we connected the *Hun* frequencies, or consciousness of the *Hun*, through *Hunmen* (UB-47) directly to the acupuncture site of *Dazhui* (Du-14). The *Hun* connection to *Dazhui* (Du-14) was necessary so we could again connect to another higher heart center at the site of *Yintang* (Ajna Center).

Then the *Hun* frequencies were brought upward from the bilateral *Hunmen* (UB-47) points to communicate with *Feng Fu* (Du-16), another higher heart point. Lastly, we brought the qi from the bilateral *Hunmen* (UB-47) points directly to the Inner Spiritual Higher Heart Center activated by inserting an acupuncture needle at the site of *Tian Man* (Du-20). It is important to remember that in Esoteric Acupuncture theory *Tian Man* (Du-20) is a higher spiritual heart point. These visual connections were necessary to reinforce the concept that the *Hun* should follow the *Shen*. The *Hun* must acknowledge its place among the hierarchy of consciousness and "bow down" to the *Shen*. When this event occurs, then the general (liver system) follows the Emperor (heart system) and the *Hun* follow the *Shen*.

I want to show again the four Fire Triangles of the *Hun* following the *Shen* within the overall pattern. The first Fire Triangle connection is created by having your client bring the bilateral *Hunmen* (UB-47) points upward to connect with *Shendao* (Du-11) known as either the "Heart Path" or the "Spirit Path." (See figure 5.13-dd below.)

## *Hun* Follow the *Shen* Pattern

### *Shendao* Fire Triangle

Fig. 5.13-dd

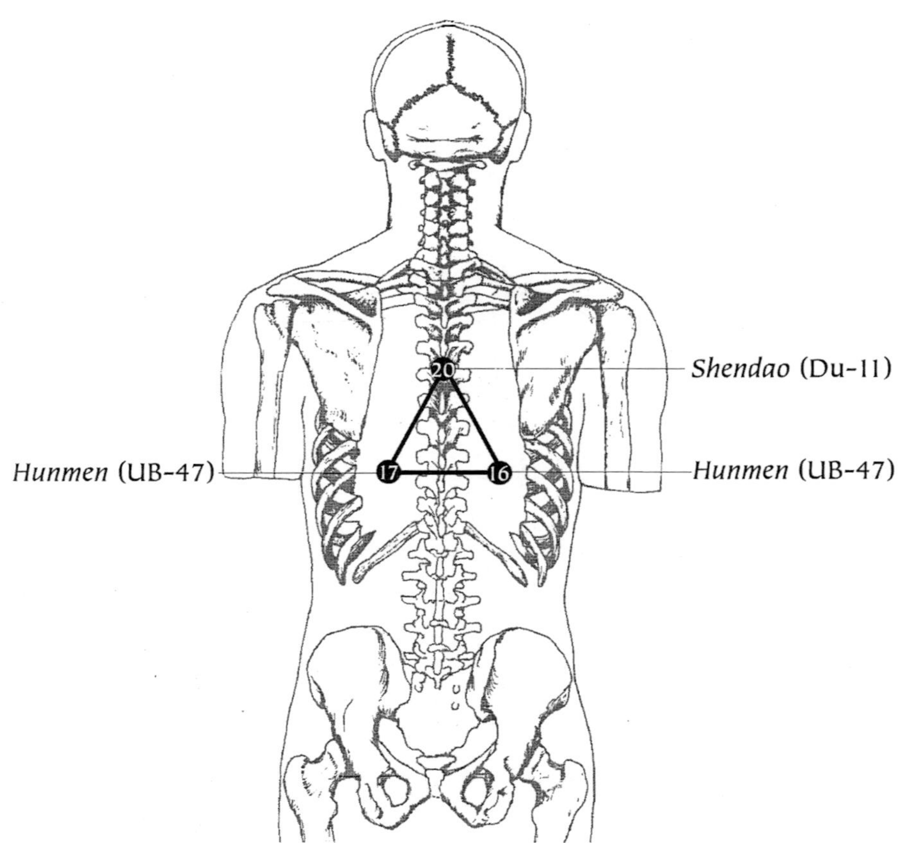

The second Fire Triangle with the bilateral *Hunmen* (UB-47) points has the consciousness of the two liver points connecting and communicating with the consciousness of *Dazhui* (Du-14). Remember *Dazhui* (Du-14) activates *Yintang* (Ajna Center), another higher heart activation point. This was discussed in the Eight Heart Gates *Shaoyang* Pattern. (See figure 5.13-ee below.)

## *Hun* Follow the *Shen* Pattern

### *Dazhui* Fire Triangle

Fig. 5.13-ee

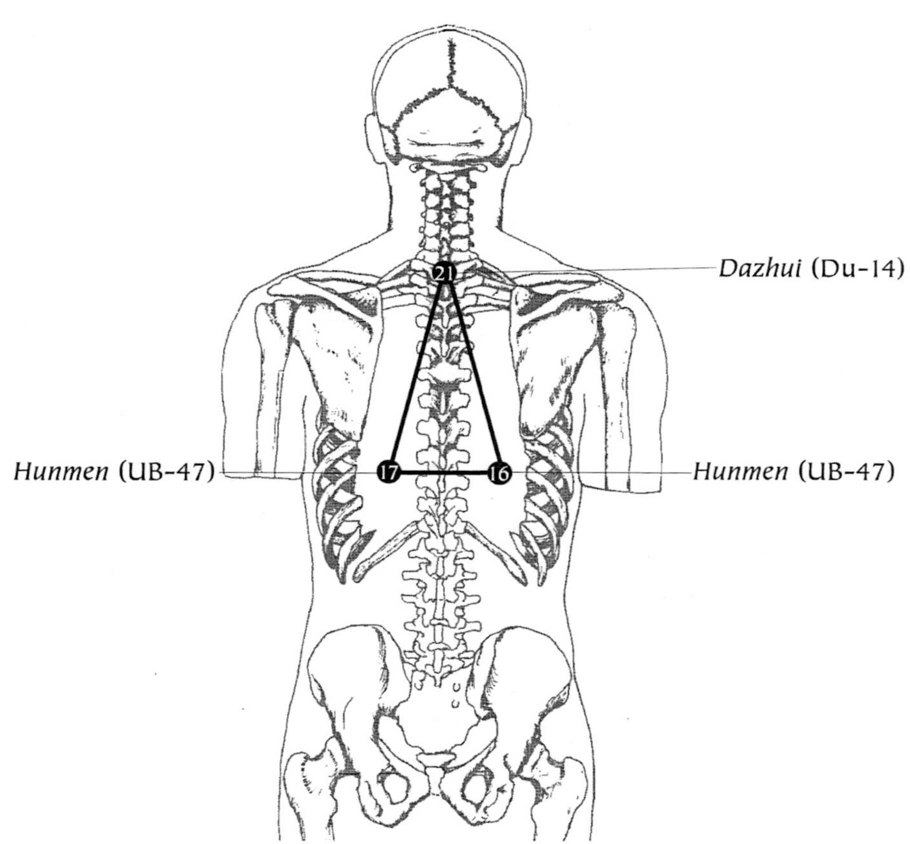

The third Fire Triangle with the bilateral *Hunmen* (UB-47) in the *Hun* Follow the *Shen* Pattern has the two liver points connecting upward with *Feng Fu* (Du-16). *Feng Fu* (Du-16) is known as the "Wind Mansion." The idea of wind can be expanded to encompass the idea of something nebulous and moving such as spirit. Remember that *Shen* includes both mind and spirit. In Esoteric Acupuncture, *Feng Fu* (Du-16) is another Inner Spiritual Higher Heart point. (See figure 5.13-ff below.)

## *Hun* Follow the *Shen* Pattern

### *Feng Fu* Fire Triangle

Fig. 5.13-ff

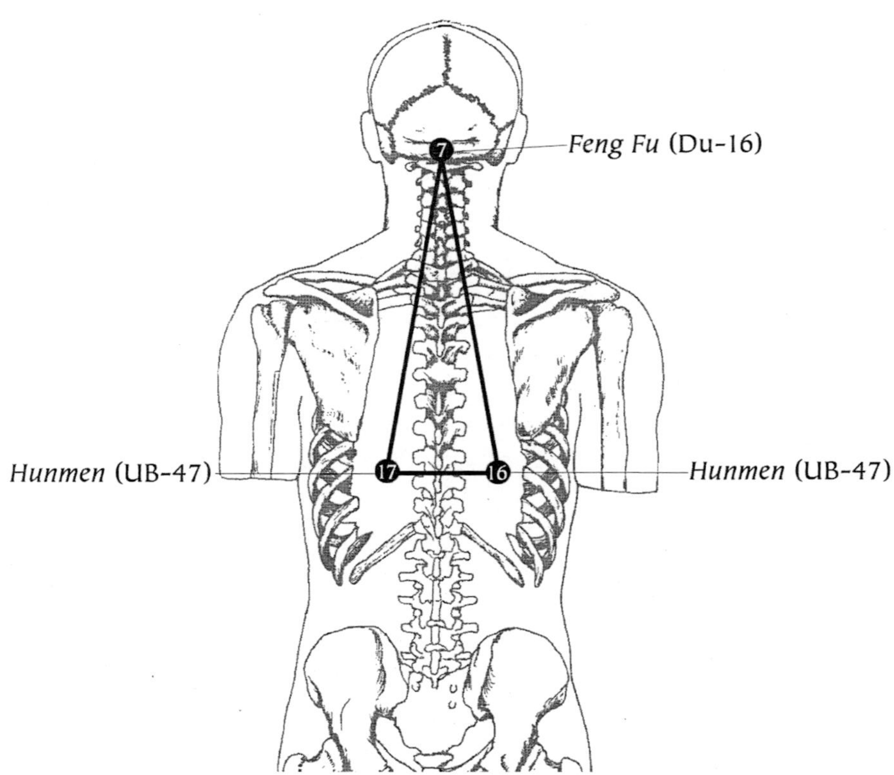

The fourth Fire Triangle formed with the bilateral *Hunmen* (UB-47) points has the two liver points connecting upward with *Tian Man* (Du-20) another celestial, higher heart point. (See figure 5.13-gg below.)

### *Hun* Follow the *Shen* Pattern

*Tian Man* Fire Triangle

Fig. 5.13-gg

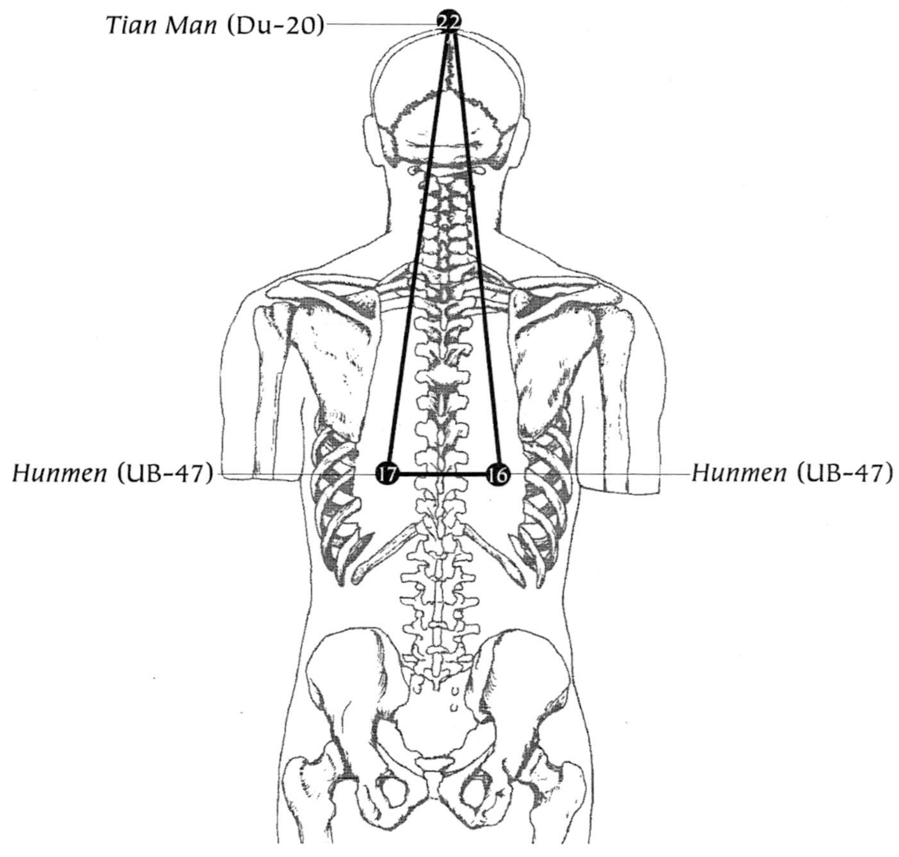

The fact that we have the client connecting the bilateral *Hunmen* (UB-47) points upward to form four Fire Triangles with those four heart centers is part of the concept of the *Hun* follow the *Shen*. (See figure 5.13-hh below.) If you go back to the Monadic Ray Connections in Chapter 3, you will notice that the Original *Hun* comes from the Original *Shen*. The Original *Hun* follows the Original *Shen*. (*Hun* is both singular and plural.)

## *Hun* Follow the *Shen* Pattern

Four Fire Triangles

Fig. 5.13-hh

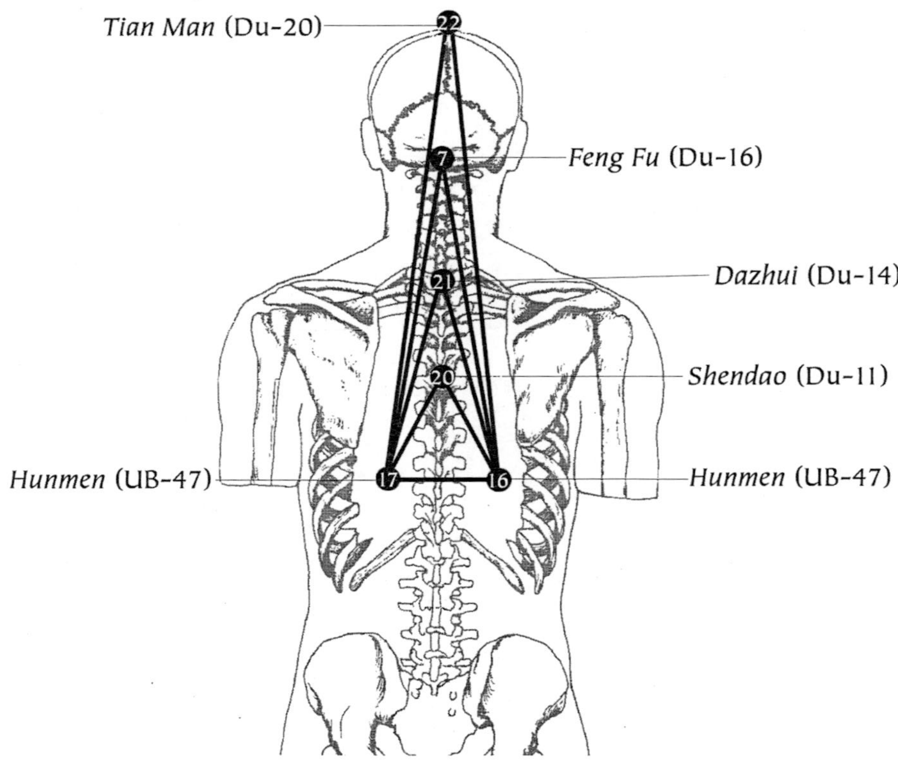

## *Hun* Follow the *Shen* Pattern
Complete Grid

Fig. 5.13-ii

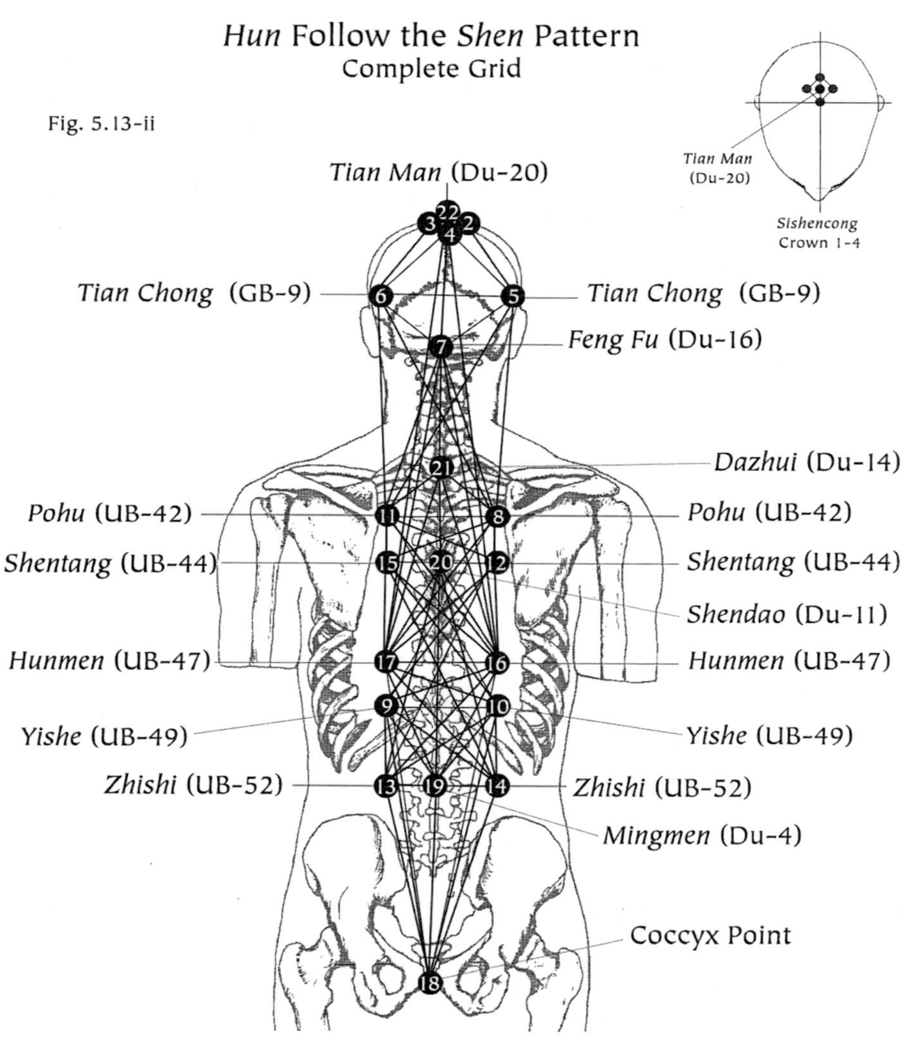

## Extended Crystalline Heart Grid Pattern

Fig 5.14-a

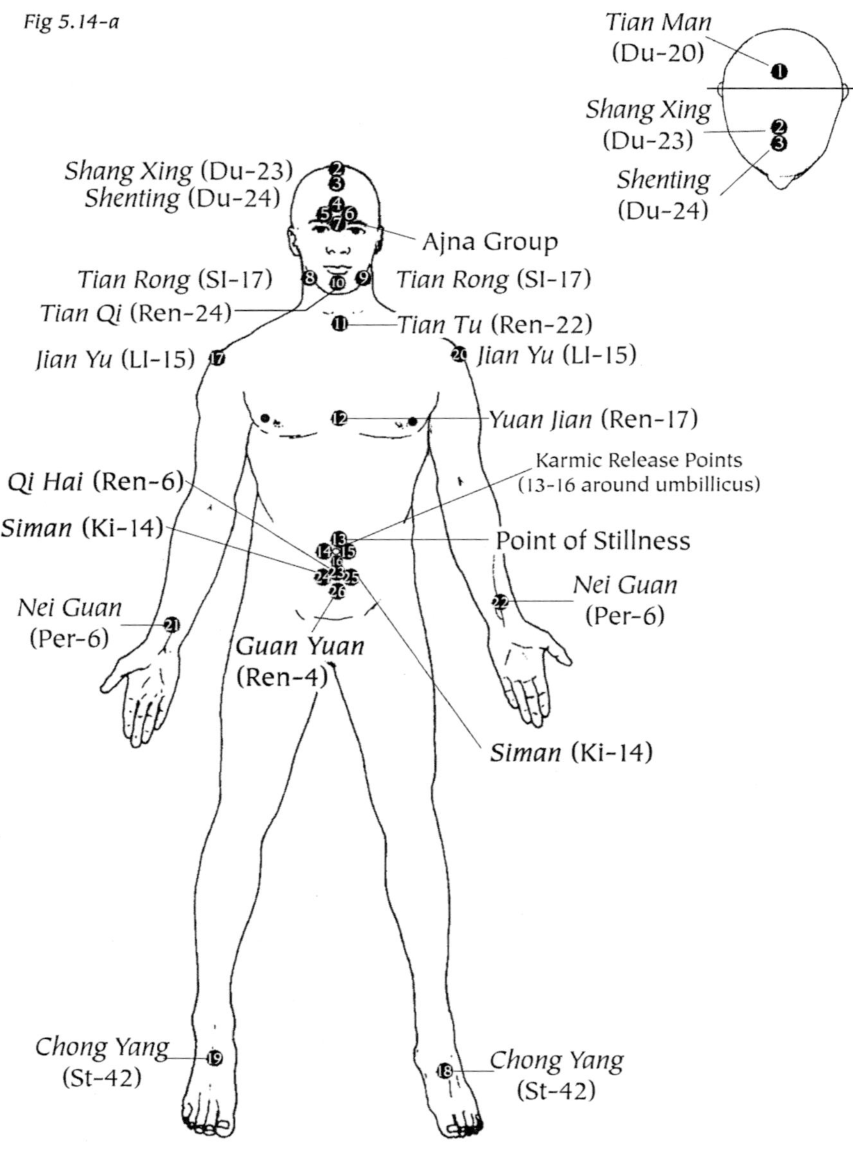

The Crystalline Heart Grid Pattern is contained within The Extended Crystalline Heart Grid Pattern. But, the Extended Crystalline Heart Grid Pattern has four additional acupuncture points. The needling sequence and the point locations for the original Crystalline Heart Patten will not be repeated here. Review the Crystalline Heart Pattern for the first twenty-two acupuncture points used and the correct needling sequence for those twenty-two acupuncture points. (See pattern starting on page 545.)

These next four acupuncture points are the "extended" part of The Extended Crystalline Heart Grid Pattern and are to be needled after the twenty-two acupuncture points of the original Crystalline Grid Pattern have been needled or otherwise activated. The four additional acupuncture points of The Extended Crystalline Heart Grid Pattern are located inferiorly to the umbilicus and superiorly to the pubic bone.

To locate these next four acupuncture points, we will first find the center of the umbilicus and the superior border of the symphysis pubis (pubic bone) on the imaginary vertical midline of the body in this area. The vertical distance from the center of the umbilicus to the superior border of the symphysis pubis is five *cun*. We will now divide this linear distance from the center of the umbilicus to the top of the pubic bone into five equal distances. (See figure 5.14-b below.)

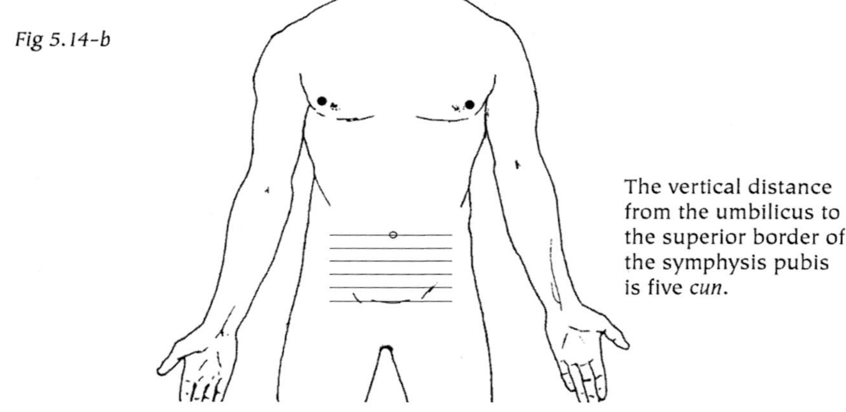


*Fig 5.14-b*

The needling sequence for these next four acupuncture points is as follows:

23) *Qi Hai* (Ren-6)
24) *Siman* (Ki-14) Right
25) *Siman* (Ki-14) Left
26) *Guan Yuan* (Ren-4)

The first acupuncture point needled in this "extended" part of the Extended Crystalline Heart Grid Pattern is *Qi Hai* (Ren-6). *Qi Hai* (Ren-6) is located directly on the vertical midline one and one half *cun* below the umbilicus. The acupuncture site of *Qi Hai* (Ren-6) is very close to the acupuncture site of the lowest Karmic Release points. (See figure 5.14-c below.)

**Extended Crystalline Heart Grid Pattern**

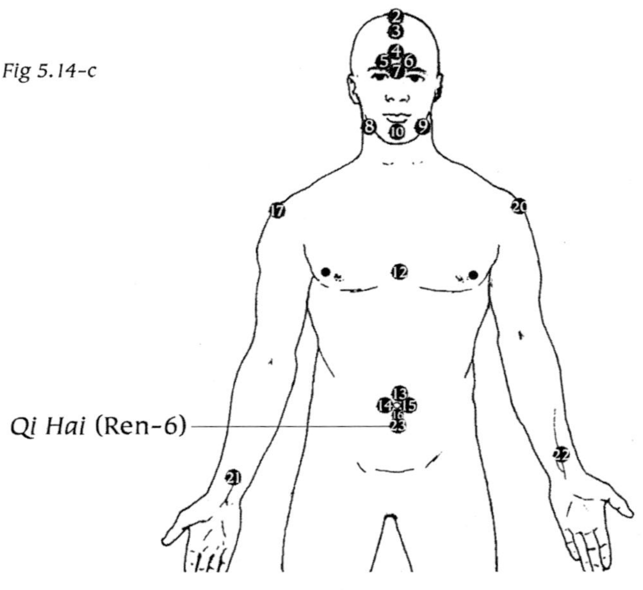

The second acupuncture point needled in this last section of the Extended Crystalline Heart Grid Pattern is *Siman* (Ki-14) located on the client's right side. *Siman* (Ki-14) is found approximately half a *cun* bilaterally to the center vertical midline two *cun* inferior to the umbilicus and three *cun* superior to the border of the symphysis pubis. (See figure 5.14-d below.)

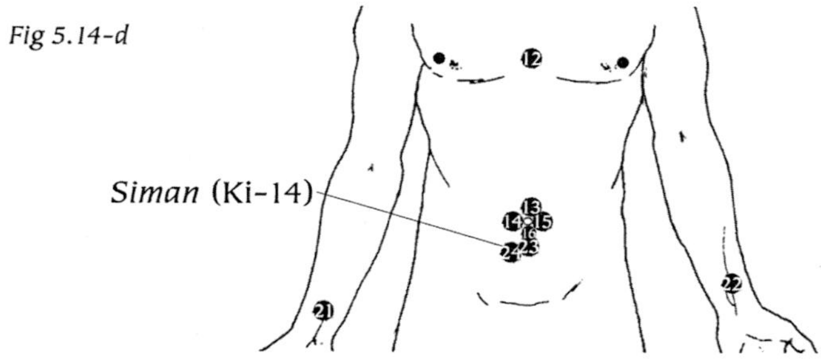

*Fig 5.14-d*

The third acupuncture point needled in the extended part of the Extended Crystalline Heart Grid Pattern is *Siman* (Ki-14 ) located on the client's left side. (See figure 5.14-e below.)

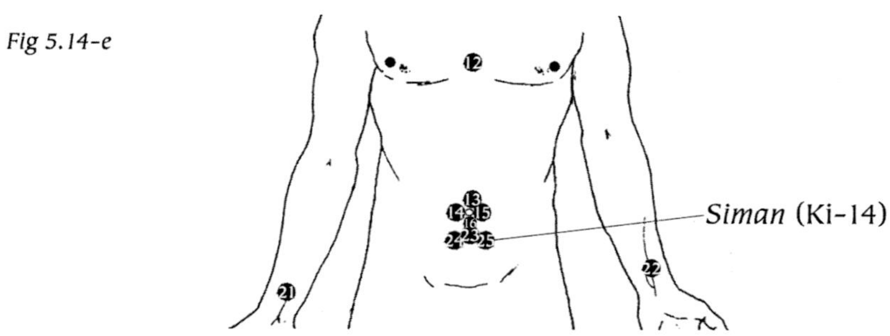

*Fig 5.14-e*

The fourth and last acupuncture point needled in the extended section of the Extended Crystalline Heart Grid Pattern is *Guan Yuan* (Ren-4). When these last four acupuncture sites are needled, they will strengthen and activate the qi at the lower *Dan Tian* area, also known as the Lower Cinnabar Field. This is the area of one's power base and the region that strengthens one's willpower to accomplish things in life. (See figure 5.14-f below.)

**Extended Crystalline Heart Grid Pattern**

*Fig 5.14-f*

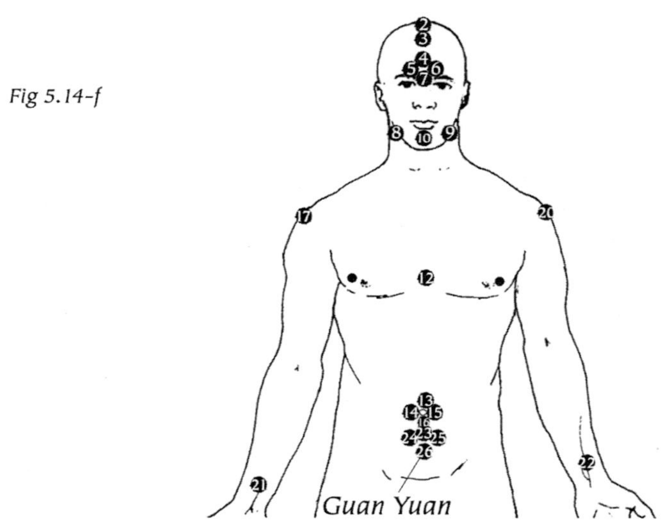


*Siman* (Ki-14) can be translated as "Fourfold Fullness." In Traditional Chinese Acupuncture, the Fourfold in the translation usually refers to: 1) Blood, 2) Qi; 3) Food; and 4) Dampness. In Esoteric Acupuncture, the Fourfold Fullness refers to the "fullness" of consciousness by the awakening of aspects of consciousness divided into two parts each with four distinct divisions. The denser part consists of: 1) The Lower Quaternary of the Physical Plane, the Etheric Plane, the Astral Plane and the Mental Plane. When the Fourfold Fullness has been activated, the lower level connects with the Upper Quaternary consisting of: 1) the Buddhic Plane; 2) the Atmic Plane; 3) the Monadic Plane; and 4) the Logoic Plane. The two levels are connected through the Causal Plane. The esoteric meaning of Fourfold Fullness requires that *Siman* (Ki-14) be an integral part of a specific field, such as created within this New Encoding Pattern.

**Esoteric Fourfold Fullness**
**Lower Quaternary Connects with The Upper Quaternary**

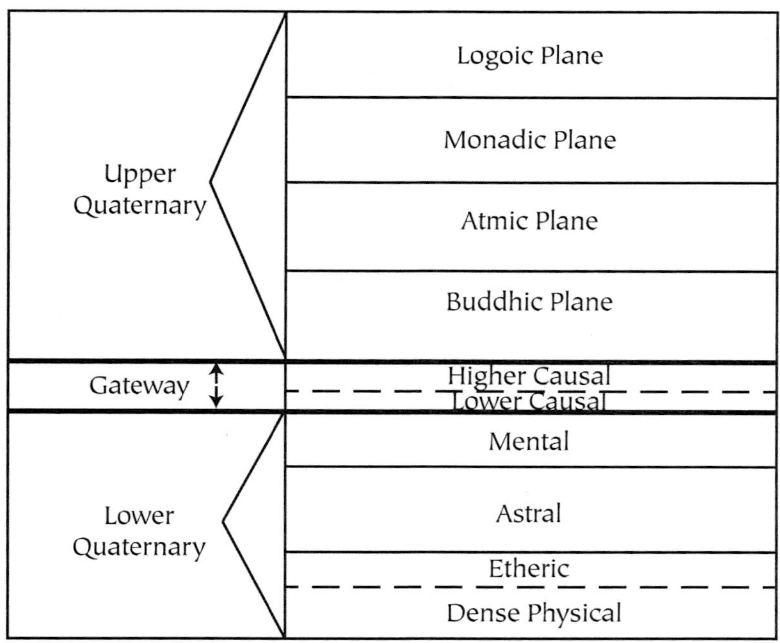

## Extended Crystalline Heart Grid Pattern
### Last Section Extended Grid

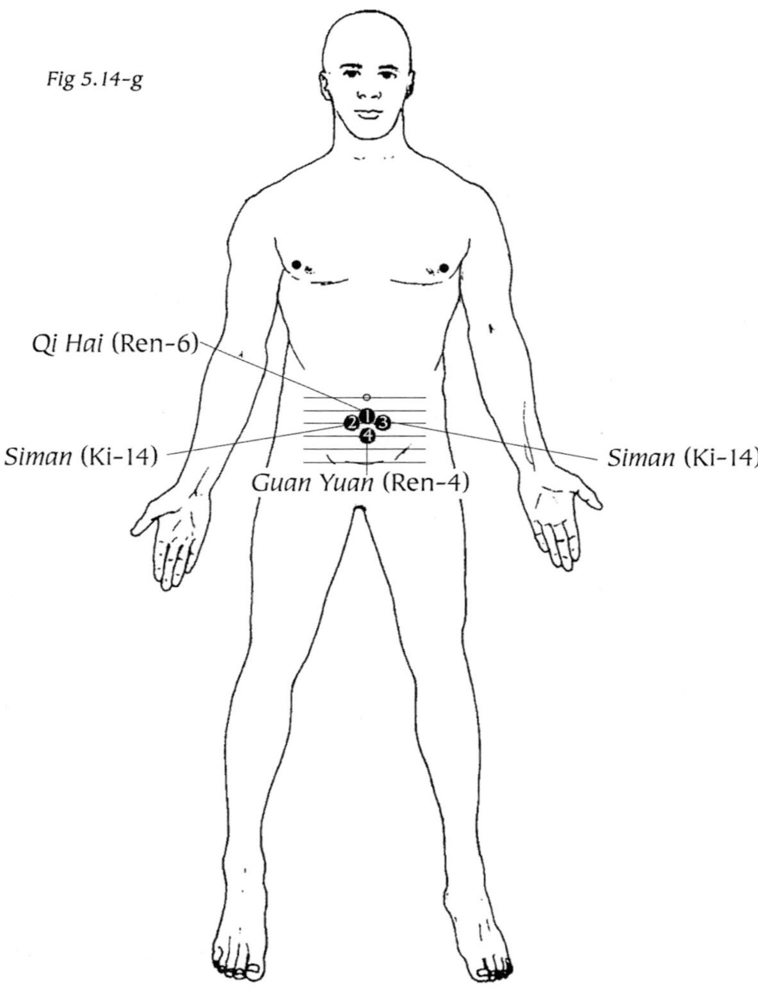

## Extended Crystalline Heart Grid Pattern
### Complete Grid

Fig 5.14-h

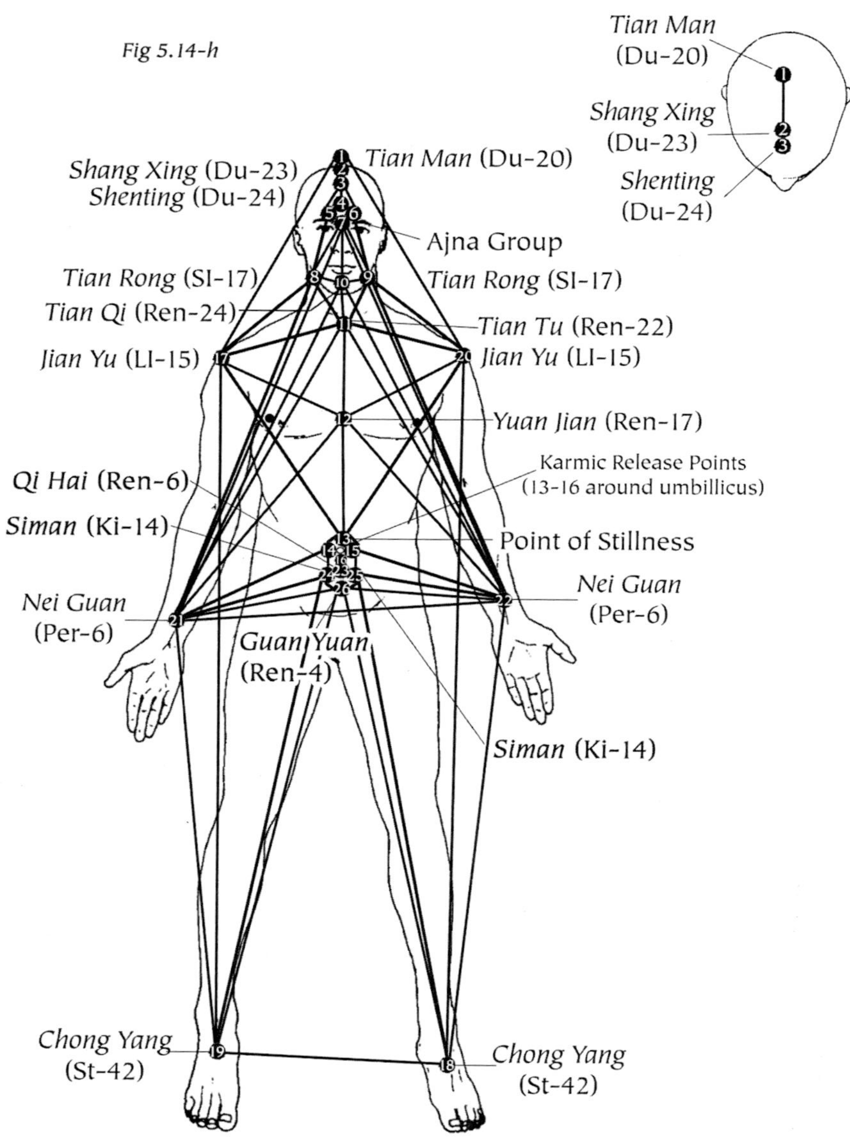

## Tree of Life Astral Pattern

Fig 5.15-a

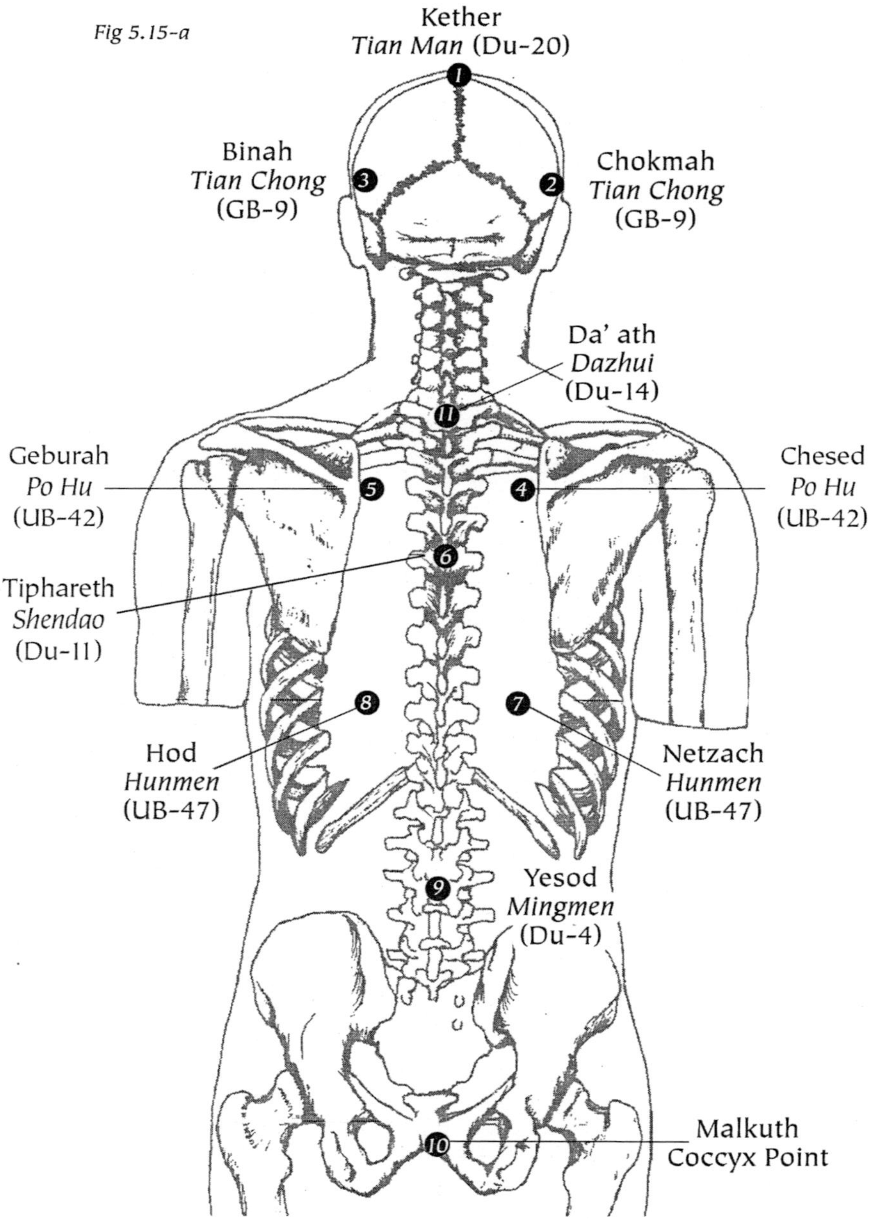

## Needling Sequence for The Tree of Life Astral Pattern

1. *Tian Man* (Du-20) = Kether
2. *Tian Chong* (GB-9) Right side = Chokmah
3. *Tian Chong* (GB-9) Left side = Binah
4. *Po Hu* (UB-42) Right side = Chesed
5. *Po Hu* (UB-42) Left side = Geburah
6. *Shendao* (Du-11) = Tiphareth
7. *Hunmen* (UB-47) Right side = Netzach
8. *Hunmen* (UB-47) Left side = Hod
9. *Mingmen* (Du-4) = Yesod
10. Coccyx Point = Malkuth
11. *Dazhui* (Du-14) = Da'ath

There are various Qabbalistic Tree of Life Patterns included within Esoteric Acupuncture. It is important to remember that although the diagram of this pattern is shown on a flat two dimensional plane, the consciousness levels available to the those utilizing any of he various Trees of Life Patterns encompass multi-dimensional planes. Although this particular Tree Life Pattern is called The Tree of Life Astral Pattern, this pattern is included in the Tiers of Density level V. The mental visualizations that are done by the client expand the scope of this pattern from merely the Etheric and Astral Planes to other planes of consciousness above the astral level. I am not going to discuss the various Sephiroth within the Tree of Life here. (Read ***Gateway to Expanded Healing: Esoteric Acupuncture, Volume I.***) Just remember that the Tree of Life does not merely have linear pathways. The two dimensional diagram of the Tree of Life with the ten or eleven Sephiroth is a representation of multiple Trees of Life stacked so as to represent the idea of multiple levels of awareness and consciousness.

It is Important to understand that merely memorizing the functions and characteristics of the various Sephiroth from a more traditional Hebrew viewpoint is not what is being presented in this work. For information of the functions and characteristics of the various Sephiroth, please consult any number of traditional books on the Hebrew Tree of Life.

Manly P. Hall in his very detailed treatise entitled ***The Secret Teachings of All Ages*** states:

> *"It must continually be emphasized that the Sephiroth and the properties assigned to them are merely symbols of the cosmic system with its multitude of parts. In the Sepher ha Zohar, it is written that there is a garment—the written doctrine—which every man may see. Those with understanding do not look upon the garment but at the body beneath it—the intellectual and philosophical code. The wisest of all look at nothing save the soul—the Spiritual doctrine—which is the eternal and ever springing Root of the law."* [14]

Another opinion on how to view the ten Sephiroth is taken from the ***Secret Doctrine, Volume 2*** by Helena P. Blavatsky:

> *"For the first Adam—the Kadmon—is the synthesis of the ten Sephiroth. Of these, the upper triad remains in the Archetypal World as the future "Trinity," while the other lower seven Sephiroth create the manifested material world."* [15]

**Point Locations for The Tree of Life Astral Pattern**

To needle the points in the Tree of Life Astral Pattern, I use Seirin "L" gauge, laser, steel handled needles. I use a very shallow oblique insertion of the needles on the head. Be sensitive to the person you are needling. Some client's may have very thin scalps and may be more sensitive to needles than some of your clients with thicker scalps. The acupuncture needles are only inserted to the depth of approximately one half inch or less on the trunk of the body.

The first acupuncture point needled in the Tree of Life Astral Pattern is *Tian Man* (Du-20). The site of this acupuncture point corresponds to Kether in the Tree of Life. The location of this acupuncture point has been discussed in previous patterns, so will not be discussed here. Just remember to insert the acupuncture needle in the location of the esoteric Du-20 that is *Tian Man* and not *Bai Hui*.

The second acupuncture point needled in the Tree of Life Astral Pattern is *Tian Chong* (GB-9) on the right side of the head and corresponds to the Sephira known in the Qabbalah as Chokmah. The third acupuncture point needled in this pattern is the *Tian Chong* (GB-9) point on the left side of the head. This third point corresponds to the Sephira known as Binah. Once again, the location of the bilateral *Tian Chong* (GB-9) points was discussed in the Crown Infinity Pattern and will not be discussed here.

The fourth and fifth acupuncture points in The Tree of Life Astral Pattern are the bilateral *Po Hu* (UB-42) points. The right side is needled first and corresponds to the Sephira known as Chesed. Next insert an acupuncture needle in the site of the left *Po Hu* (UB-42) point that corresponds to the Sephira Geburah. Both of these acupuncture sites are located bilaterally to the lower border of the spinous process of the third thoracic vertebra and are found approximately three *cun* bilaterally from the center of the spine. The most medial border of each scapula is considered to be three *cun* from a vertical midline that goes down the center of the spine. To locate the other set of bilateral urinary bladder points, draw an imaginary vertical line down from the bilateral points that are located just medial to the innermost border of each scapula. (See figure 5.15-b on the following page.)

Insert the acupuncture needles at each of these bilateral *Po Hu* (UB-42) sites angling slightly downward (oblique insertion) to a depth of approximately one-half inch or slightly less. Do not use any deep insertion of an acupuncture needle in the upper chest area where the lungs are located.

### Tree of Life Astral Pattern

Fig 5.15-b

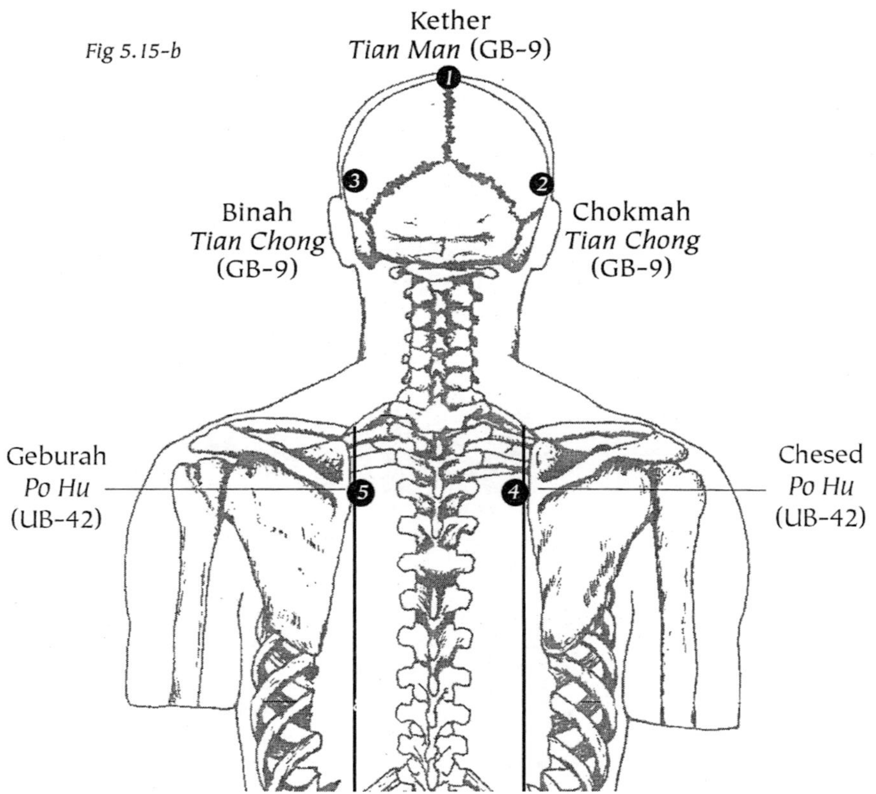


The sixth acupuncture point in The Tree of Life Astral Pattern is *Shendao* (Du-11) located directly on the spine below the lower border of the spinous process of the fifth thoracic vertebra. This is the heart point and corresponds to the Sephira called Tiphareth in the Hebrew Tree of Life. Insert the needle at a slight downward angle going into the site less than one-half inch. (See figure 5.15-c below.)

## Tree of Life Astral Pattern

Fig 5.15-c

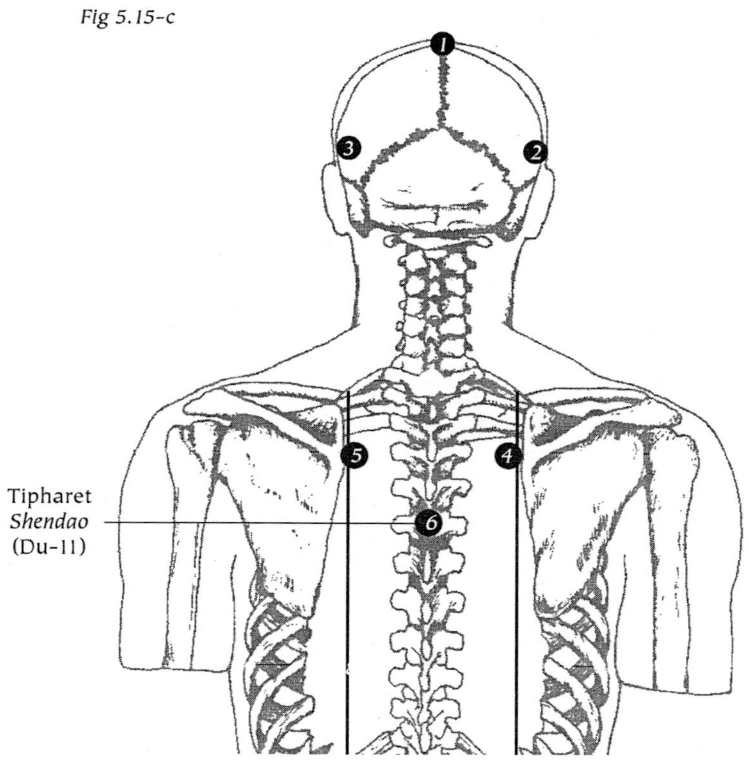


The seventh and eighth acupuncture points in The Tree of Life Astral Pattern are the bilateral *Hunmen* (UB-47) points. Both of these acupuncture points are located on the imaginary vertical lines that start at the site of the bilateral *Po Hu* (UB-42) and extend downward. You must first locate the lower border of the spinous process of the ninth thoracic vertebra. Make an imaginary horizontal line from this point (lower border of the spinous process of the ninth thoracic vertebra) that intersects both of the imaginary vertical lines. Remember that the bilateral vertical lines are approximately three *cun* outward from a vertical midline that runs down through the spine. You will needle the *Hunmen* (UB-47) point on the right side first, followed by the needling the *Hunmen* (UB-47) point on the left side. The *Hunmen* (UB-47) point on the right side first corresponds to the Sephira Netzach. The *Hunmen* (UB-47) point on the left side corresponds to the Sephira Hod. (See figure 5.15-d below.)

**Tree of Life Astral Pattern**

*Fig 5.15-d*

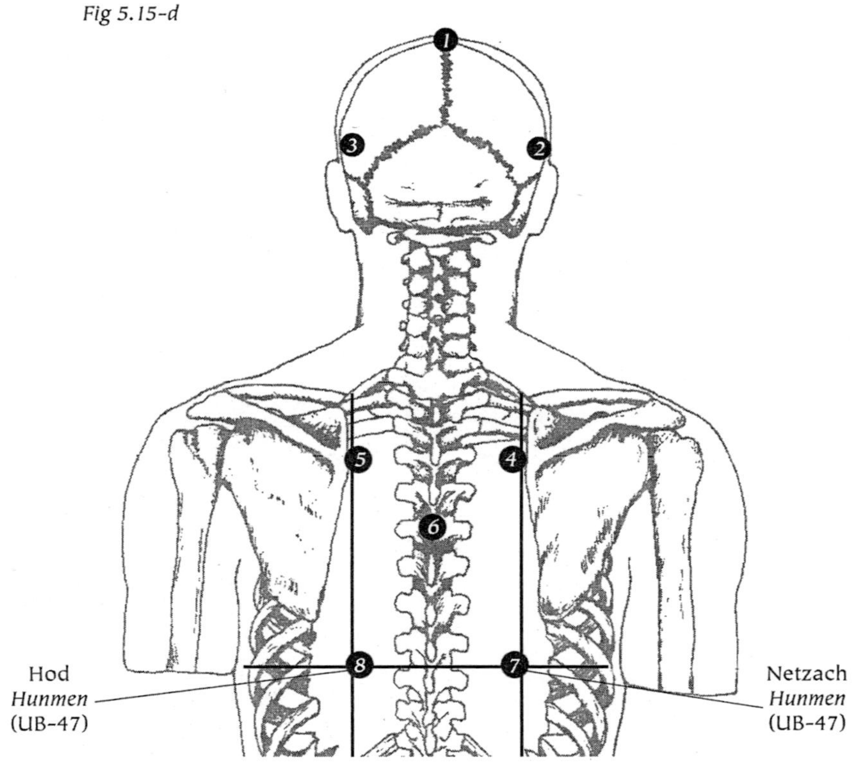

The ninth acupuncture point needled is *Mingmen* (Du-4) located directly below the lower border of the spinous process of the second lumbar vertebrae. Locate the highest points on the iliac crests (hip bones) on the lower back region. Draw an imaginary horizontal line connecting these two points. Where the imaginary horizontal line intersects the spine is usually where the fourth lumbar vertebra (L-4) is located. Count upward along the spine two vertebra from L-4 to find the location of the acupuncture site of *Mingmen* (Du-4). *Mingmen* (Du-4) is often tender, so I usually rub the point with a little force and tell the client that he or she may feel a slight sensation with the insertion of the needle. (See figure 5.15-e below.)

**Tree of Life Astral Pattern**

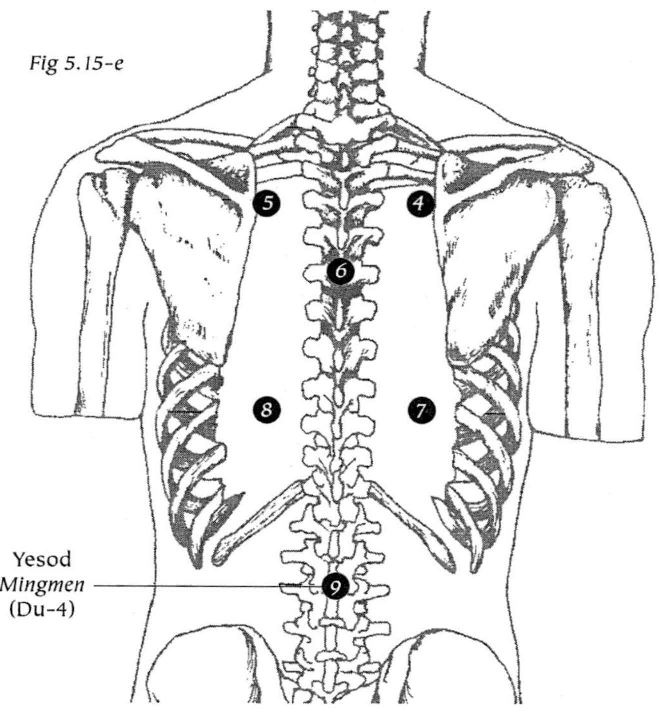

The tenth acupuncture site needled corresponds to Malkuth of the Tree of Life. This acupuncture site is located directly on the tailbone. Insert the needle very quickly with an oblique angle and to a depth of approximately one-quarter inch (.635 cm). (See figure 5.15-f below.)

**Tree of Life Astral Pattern**

*Fig 5.15-f*

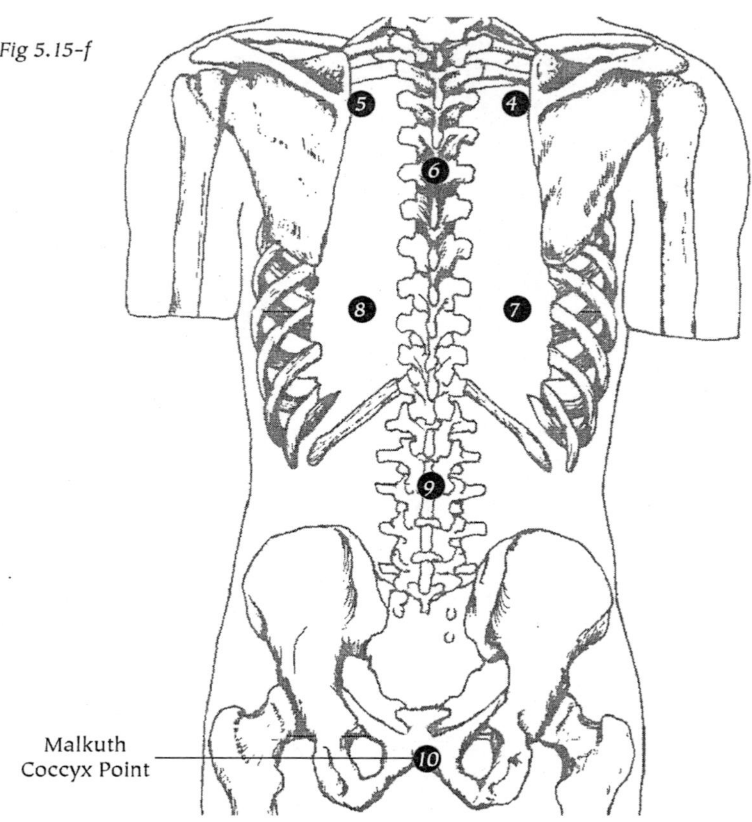

The eleventh and last acupuncture site needled in The Tree of Life Astral Pattern is called Da'ath. This point is located directly on the spine below the lower border of the spinous process of the seventh cervical vertebra. (See figure 5.15-g.)

## Tree of Life Astral Pattern

*Fig 5.15-g*

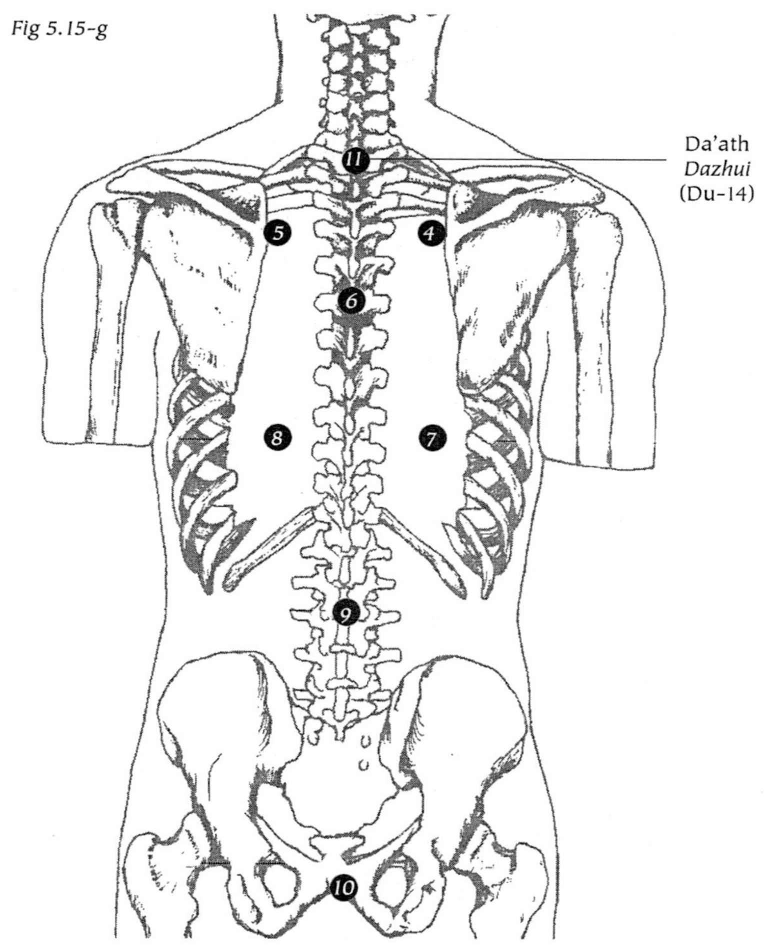

Sometimes when examining the Tree of Life in various Qabbalah (Kabbalah) texts, Da'ath is not shown. Sometimes only ten Sephiroth are shown.

There is one thing that is different with the Tree of Life Astral Pattern than with the visualization connections of the other New Encoding Patterns of Esoteric Acupuncture. With The Astral Tree of Life Pattern, do not insert the eleventh and last acupuncture needle at the acupuncture site of *Dazhui* (Du-14) until all the visualizations connections are completed. This last acupuncture site is the location of Da'ath in the Tree of Life Astral Pattern.

## The Traditional Hebrew Groupings of Paths in the Qabbalistic Tree of Life

Those of you who are knowledgeable about the Hebrew Tree of Life will quickly notice that the suggested visualizations given for the Astral Tree of Life Pattern do not follow the sequence of connections given in the traditional Hebrew Tree of Life. In Esoteric Acupuncture, we are interested in making triangular formations by visually connecting certain acupuncture points that correspond to various Sephiroth in the Hebrew Tree of Life.

It is the triangulation from the visualizations used in Esoteric Acupuncture that creates the enhanced energy for a tetrahedral geometric field. The visual triangular formations create spin point activity at the acupuncture sites. This in turn creates a Spin Field that contains more energy and has a different frequency than the energy field created by a more traditional acupuncture treatment. We are interested in accessing the planes above the Lower Quaternary field that is accessed by any traditional type acupuncture treatment. We are interested in reaching the realms of the Buddhic, Atmic, Monadic and Logoic Planes.

The traditional Hebrew groups of pathways are included in this section. There are nine groupings of pathways presented by Michael Jacob in his book ***Ten and Twenty-Two, A Journey Through the Path of Wisdom***. He integrated principles of the Tarot Cards with the pathway. As you will see from figures 5.15-h through 5.15-p, the Qabbalistic Tree of Life pathways are different from the visual triangular connections given in Esoteric Acupuncture. Nonetheless, the energetics from the visual connections of the twenty-two pathways in the Astral Tree of Life Pattern of Esoteric Acupuncture will be vibrating very closely to the energetics from the Qabbalistic Tree of Life Pathways. The diagrams of the nine groupings of pathways in the traditional Hebrew teachings are given here. The first group of paths of the Tree of Life is shown in figure 5.15-h.)

**First Group of Paths Within the Qabbalistic Tree of Life and Tarot**

*Fig 5.15-h*

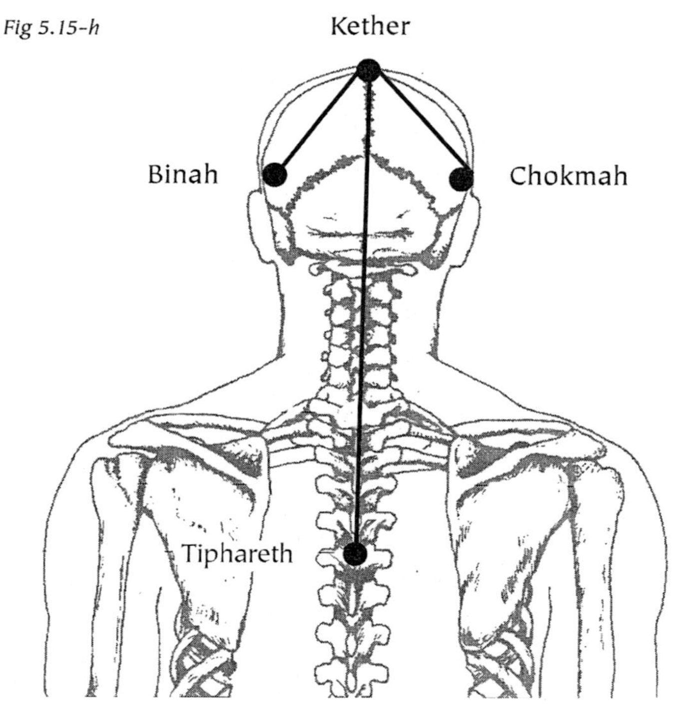

## Second Group of Paths Within the Qabbalistic Tree of Life and Tarot

*Fig 5.15-i*

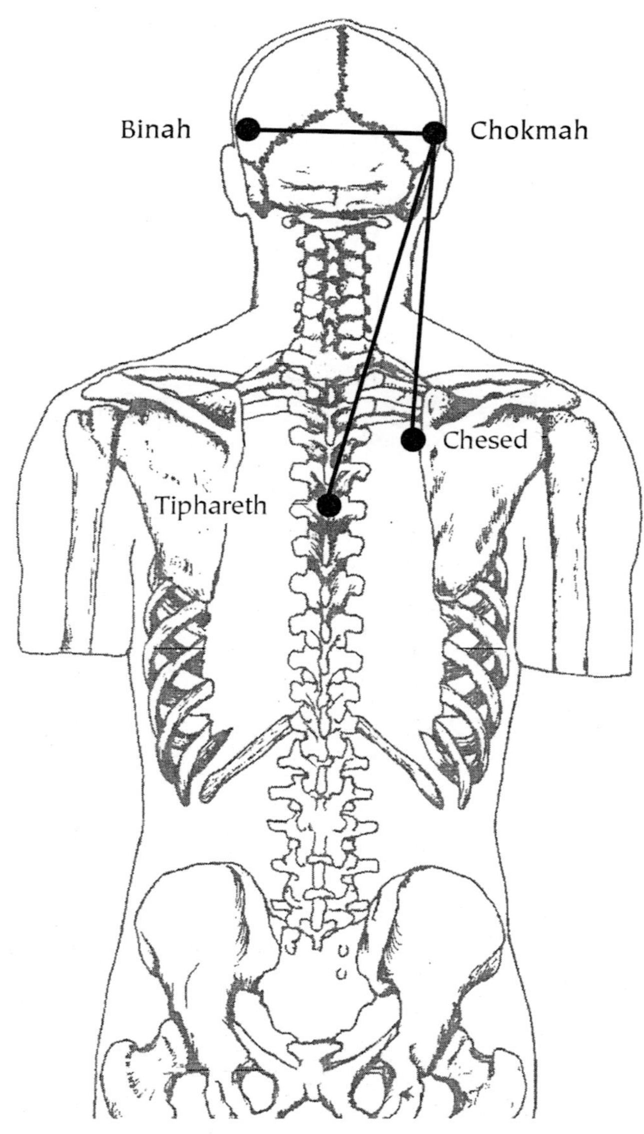

## Third Group of Paths Within the Qabbalistic Tree of Life and Tarot

Fig 5.15-j

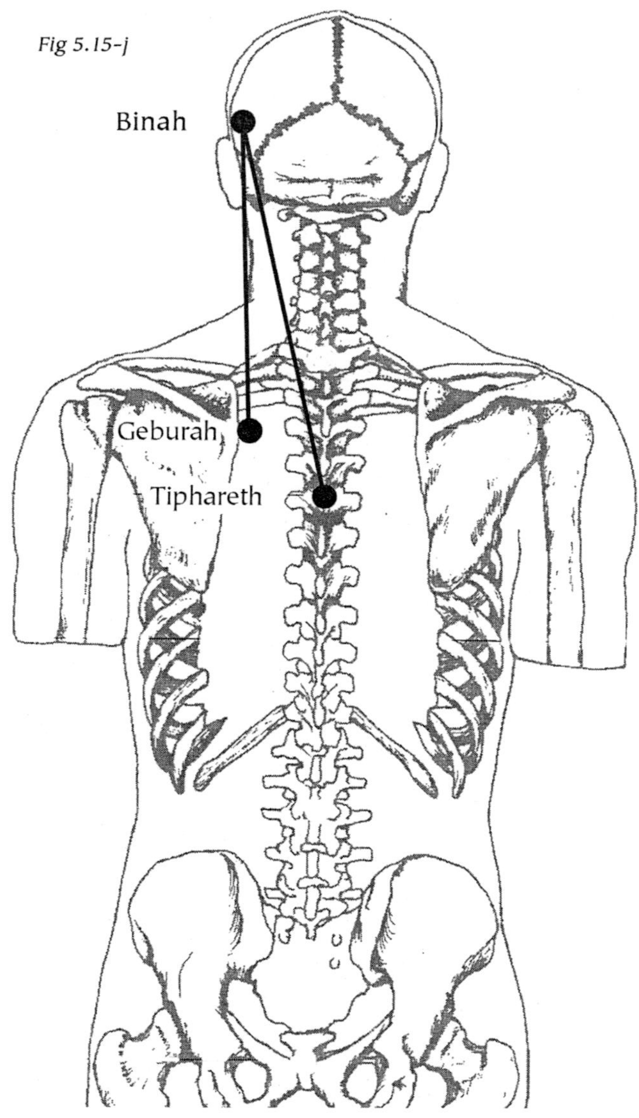

## Fourth Group of Paths Within the Qabbalistic Tree of Life and Tarot

*Fig 5.15-k*

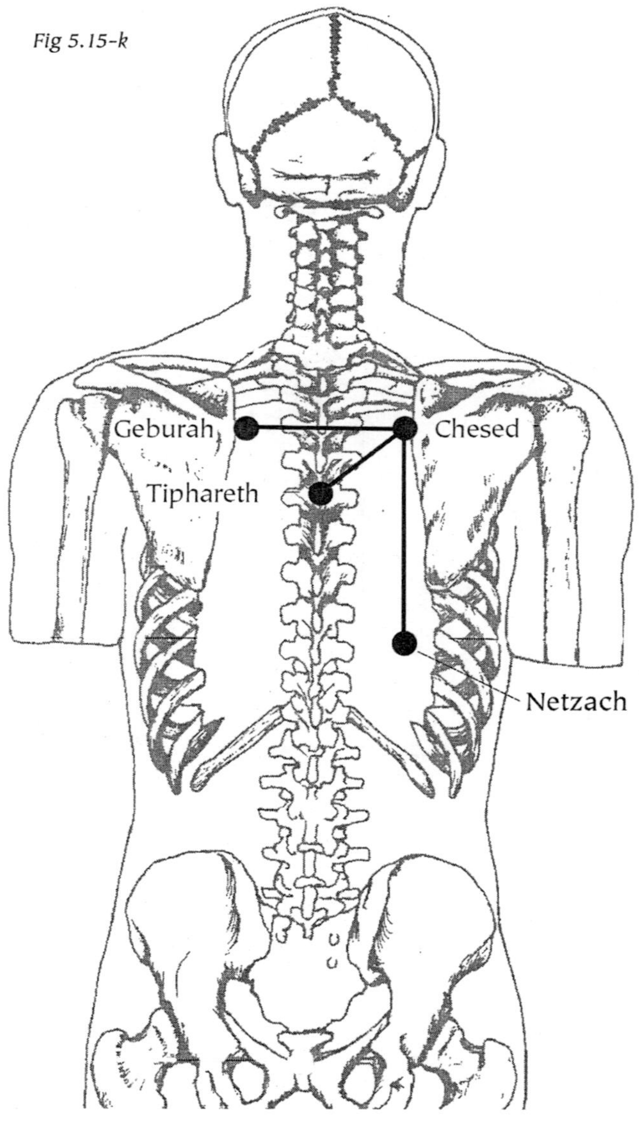

## Fifth Group of Paths Within the Qabbalistic Tree of Life and Tarot

*Fig 5.15-l*

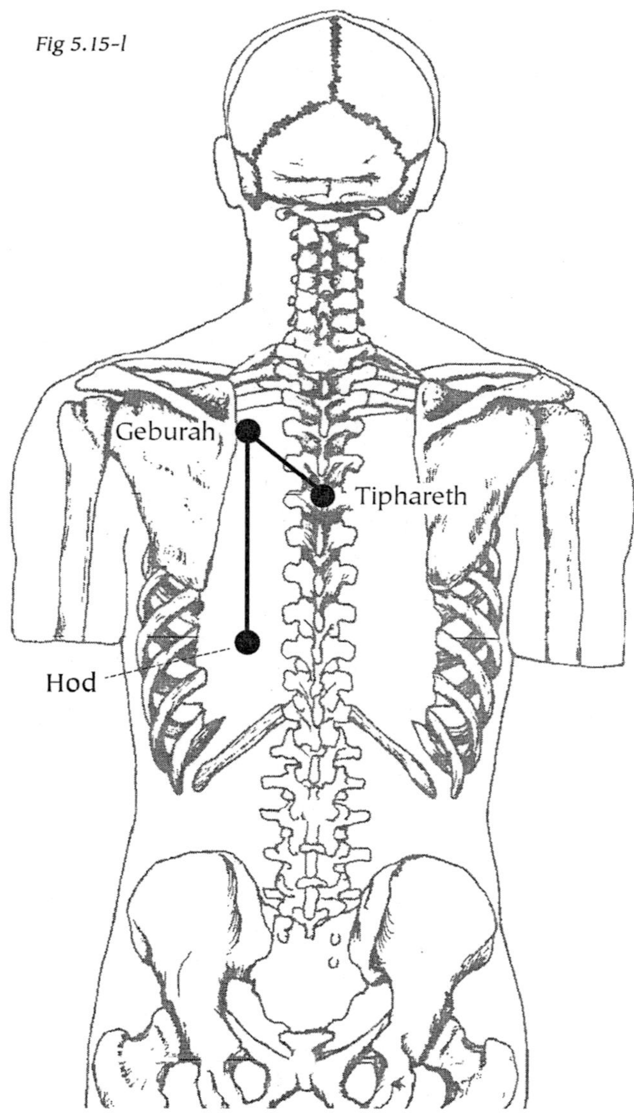

## Sixth Group of Paths Within the Qabbalistic Tree of Life and Tarot

*Fig 5.15-m*

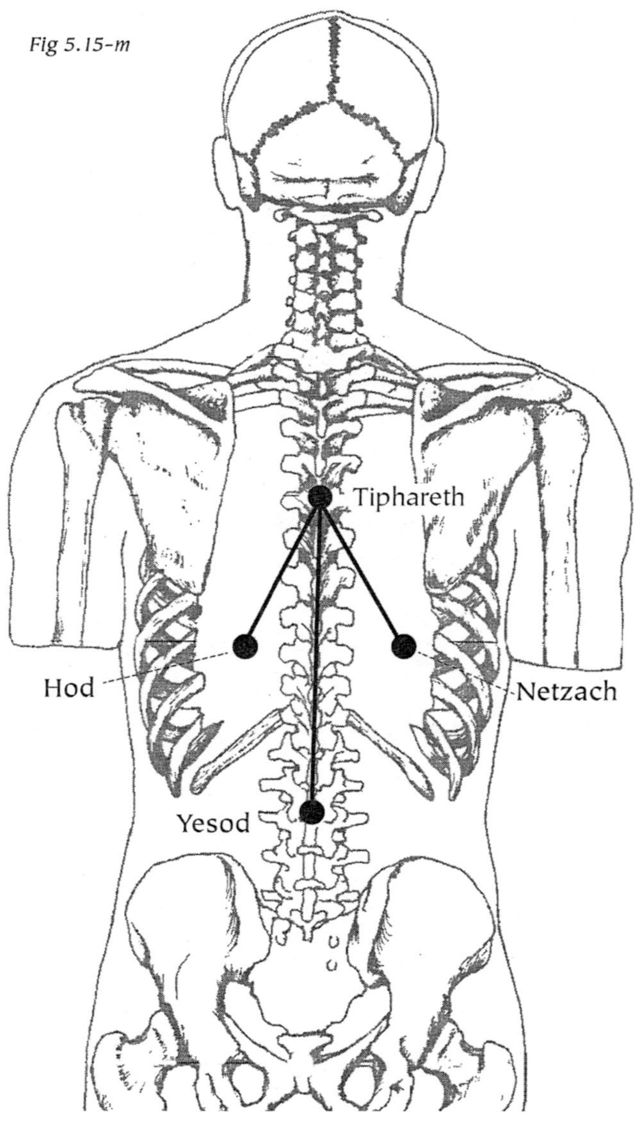

## Seventh Group of Paths Within the Qabbalistic Tree of Life and Tarot

*Fig 5.15-n*

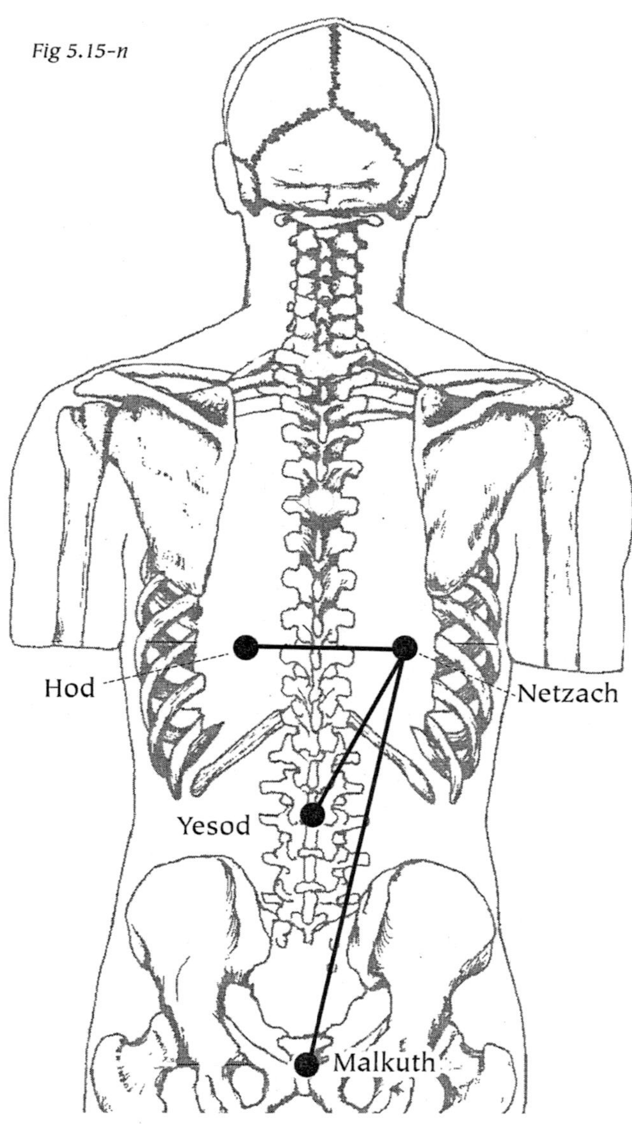

## Eight Group of Paths Within the Qabbalistic Tree of Life and Tarot

*Fig 5.15-o*

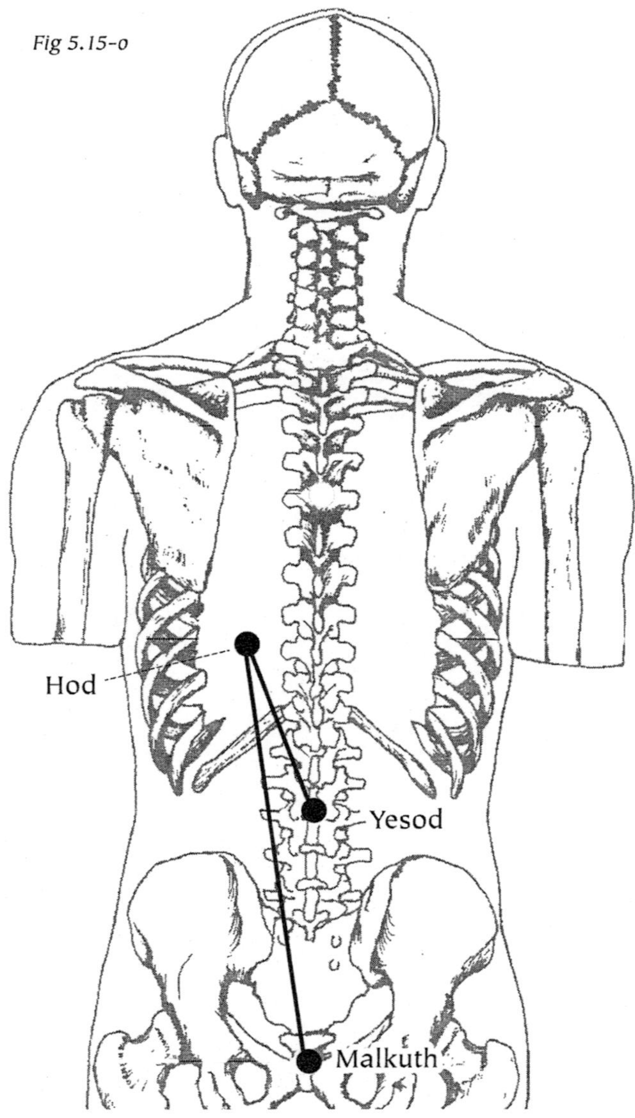

## Ninth Group of Paths Within the Qabbalistic Tree of Life and Tarot

*Fig 5.15-p*

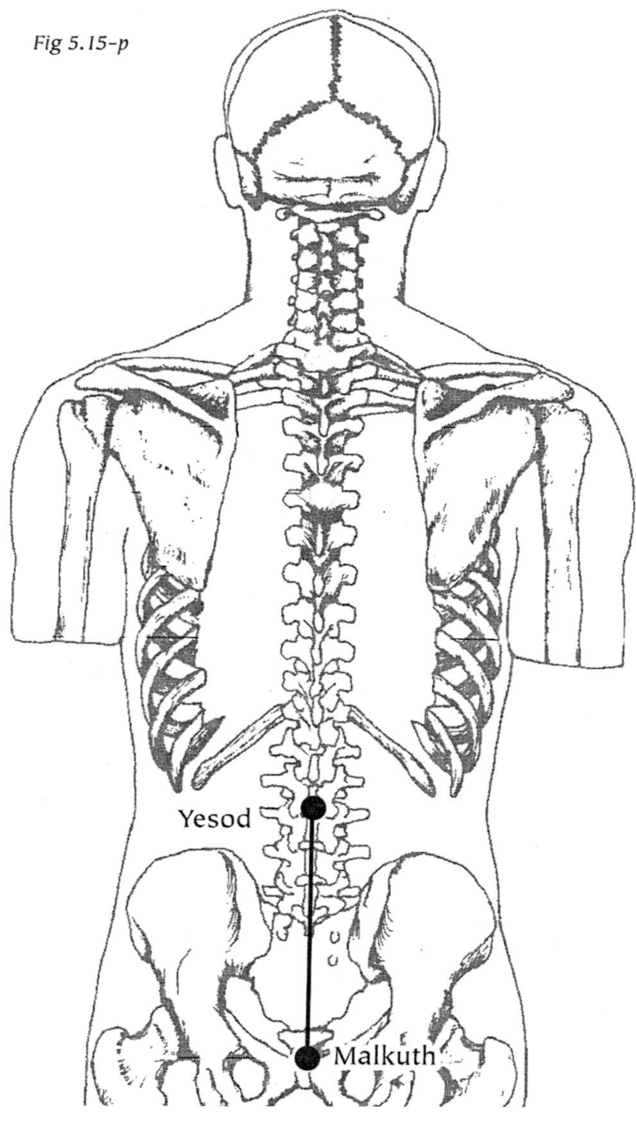

Esoteric Acupuncture includes the energetics of the Qabbalistic Tree of Life, but has been expanded to include more systems. We have merely added layers to the original pathways because of the inclusion of the Chinese theories, sacred geometry, tetrahedral geometry and various other systems. When the Tree of Life is presented in the manner given in this book and utilized by acupuncturists or other modalities of energy healers, there is greater chance that those who are not versed in the Hebrew ***Qabbalah*** (***Kabbalah***) will become curious and may even explore in depth the more traditional teachings of the ***Qabbalah***. Most acupuncturists have never even heard of the ***Qabbalah*** and would not have a clue to its interconnectedness with Chinese acupuncture without having been exposed to the basic Hebrew teachings through reading any of the books within the ***Esoteric Acupuncture*** series.

Some people say the ten Sephiroth are also pathways bringing the number of pathways in the Tree of Life to thirty-two instead of merely twenty-two. In that concept, Da'ath (the eleventh Sephira) is not included. For the visualization in Esoteric Acupuncture, we will focus on the twenty-two pathways. We are interested in the triangulation of the acupuncture sites because of the creation of a more concentrated and finer frequency energy field. We are interested in creating a Spin Field utilizing the energetics with tetrahedral geometry.

Remember, all forms of energy both store and transport information. After making the Esoteric Acupuncture visualizations, the twenty-two pathways of the *Qabbalistic* Tree of Life will be connected. Also since the traditional Hebrew groups of paths are contained within the Esoteric Acupuncture visualizations, the knowledge and esoteric wisdom contained within the traditional Hebrew groupings of pathway connections will also be activated. The physical pattern of the Tree of Life retains its memory and the twenty-two pathways will form and connect regardless of the order in which the Sephiroth (acupuncture points) are connected.

## Visualization Connections for The Tree of Life Astral Pattern

All the New Encoding Patterns of Esoteric Acupuncture contain elements of sacred geometry, sacred numbers, ***Qabbalah*** (***Kabbalah***), Platonic Solids, Pythagorean mathematics, field physics, superstring theory, Djwhal Khul's Tibetan philosophies, Dinshah's Spectro-Chrome Color Theory, Theosophy, Chinese acupuncture and Chinese Five Element Theory, the Hindu Laya Yoga (chakra system), the Hindu Nadi System and philosophies from various other people and modalities. In The Tree of Life Astral Pattern, we are working on fields beyond those activated by the more traditional Hebrew teachings. In The Tree of Life Astral Pattern, we will be activating those various fields within all the levels of the Astral Plane, plus levels from the Causal Plane and above.

We are interested in making triangular visual connections. The visualizations will begin as suggested here. This means that the visualization begins before all eleven sites have been needled or otherwise activated. You will have your client complete the visualizations before inserting the eleventh and last needle at the site of *Dazhui* (Du-14) corresponding to the eleventh "hidden" Sephira Da'ath. This means that the twenty-two pathways between the Sephiroth will be connected before you insert the eleventh and last acupuncture needle in The Tree of Life Astral Pattern at the acupuncture site of *Dazhui* (Du-14) located directly on the spine below the lower border of the spinous process of the seventh cervical vertebra.

The first visual connections begin after the first three acupuncture sites have been needled. The first acupuncture point in this pattern is *Tian Man* (Du-20), followed by *Tian Chong* (GB-9) on the right side and then *Tian Chong* (GB-9) on the left side. You will notice that we have formed a Fire Triangle with the apex pointing upward. The first visual connection in The Tree of Life Pattern is to have your client connect the sites of the bilateral acupuncture points *Tian Chong* (GB-9) to each other. We are connecting the Sephira Chokhmah (right *Tian Chong*/GB-9) with the Sephira Binah (left *Tian Chong*/GB-9). (See figure 5.16-q below.)

## Tree of Life Astral Pattern

*Fig 5.15-q*

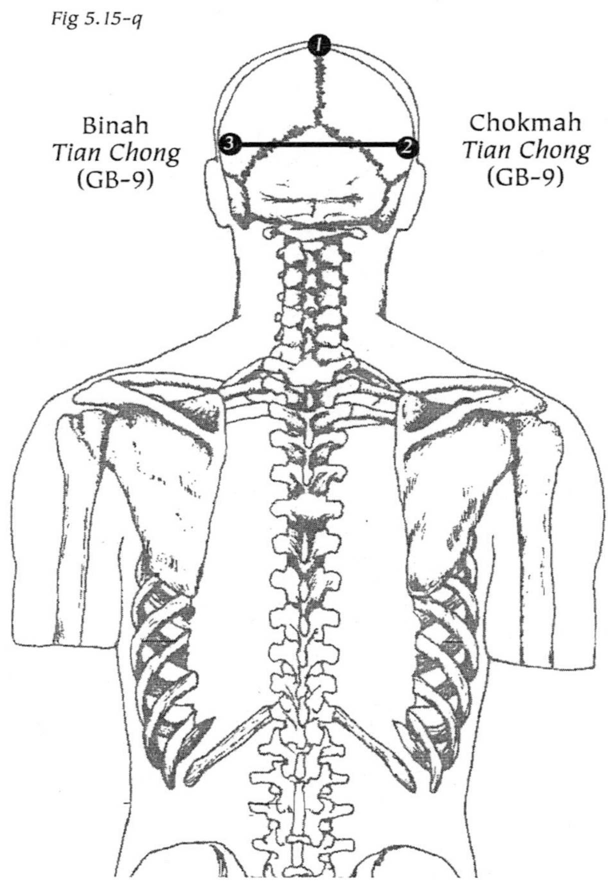

Now have your client move the energy from both of these bilateral *Tian Chong* (GB-9) acupuncture sites to form an upward pointing Fire Triangle connecting with the Sephira Kether located at the esoteric site of *Tian Man* (Du-20). This first visual fire triangle connection is very important and sets in motion the heart qi to flow to the entrance point for the Sahasrara (Crown Chakra). We are connecting Binah and Chokhmah to Kether. (see figure 5.15-r below.)

**Tree of Life Astral Pattern**

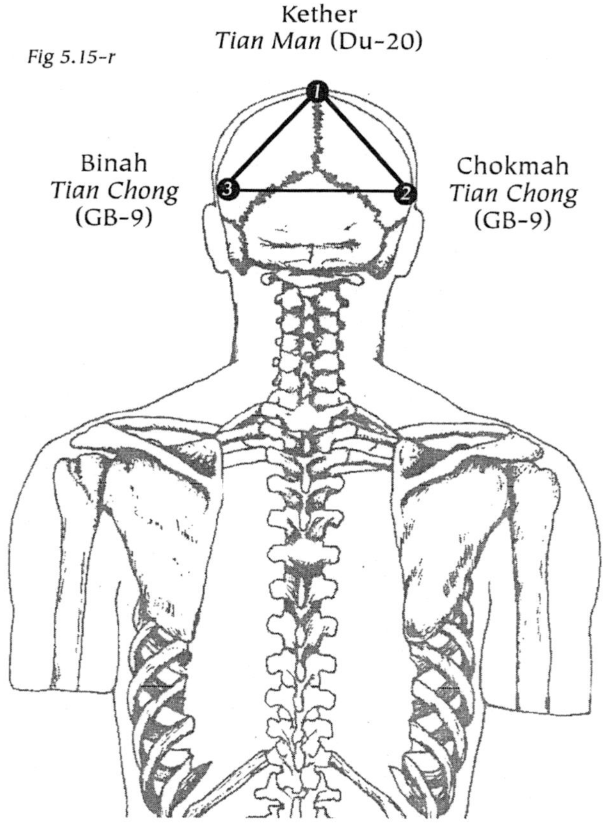

The next connection in The Tree of Life Astral Pattern is to visually connect the bilateral *Po Hu* (UB-42) points to each other. The Sephira Chesed is located at the acupuncture site of *Po Hu* (UB-42) on the right side of the client. The Sephira Geburah is located at the acupuncture site of *Po Hu* (UB-42) on the client's left side. (See figure 5.15-s below.)

**Tree of Life Astral Pattern**

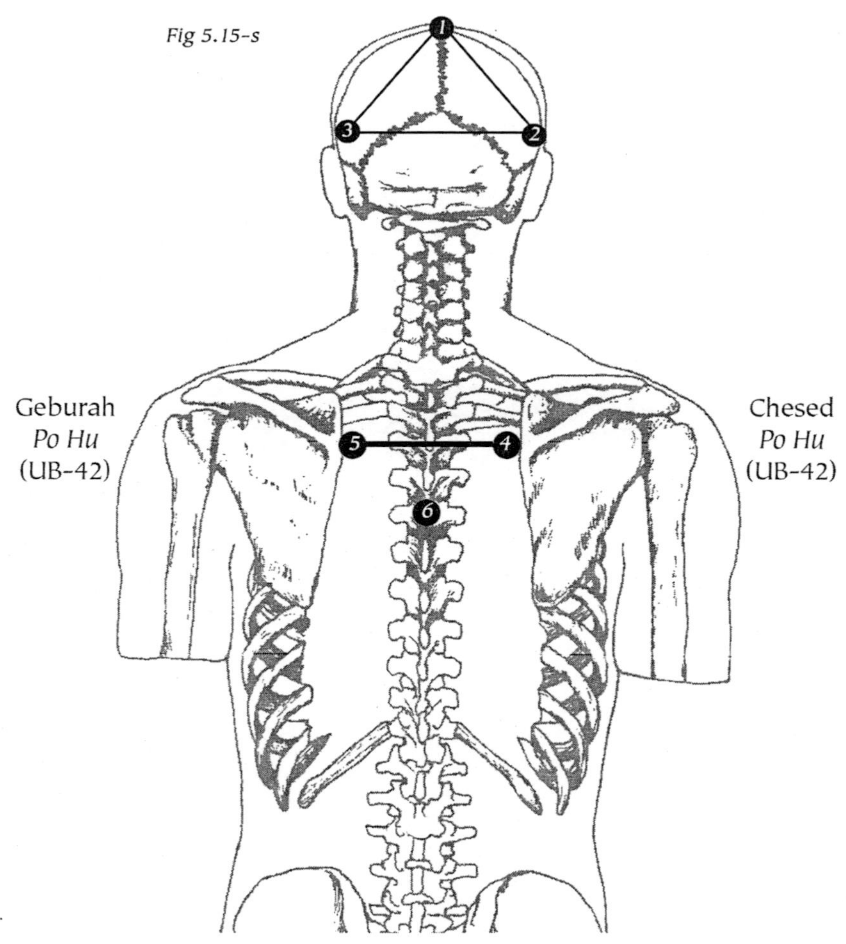


*Fig 5.15-s*

Next insert an acupuncture needle at the acupuncture site of *Shendao* (Du-11) located directly below the lower border of the spinous process of the fifth thoracic vertebra. This point corresponds to the Sephira Tiphareth. Ask your client to visually bring the energy from the bilateral *Po Hu* (UB-42) points simultaneously downward to form a Water Triangle with *Shendao* (Du-11). (See figure 5.15-t below.)

**Tree of Life Astral Pattern**

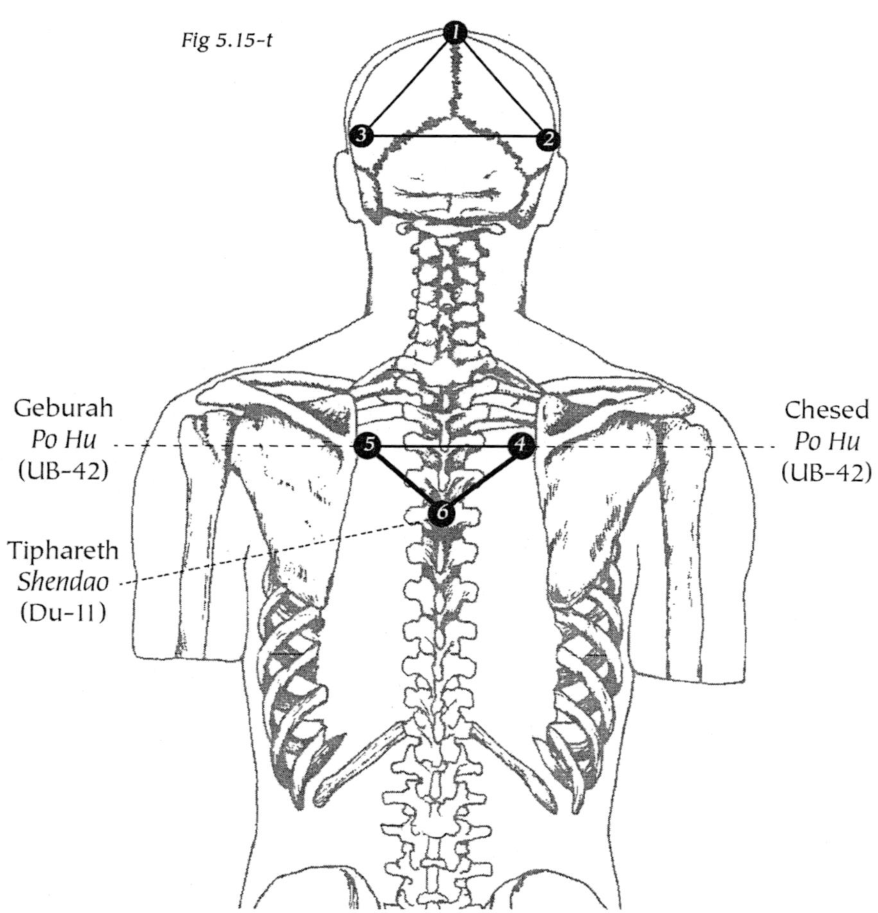


*Fig 5.15-t*

The next visual connection will be to bring the qi downward simultaneously from the bilateral *Tian Chong* (GB-9) points (Chokmah on the right side and Binah on the left side) to connect to Tiphareth at the site of the acupuncture point *Shendao* (Du-11). This connection forms another Water Triangle. (See figure 5.15-u below.)

## Tree of Life Astral Pattern

Fig 5.15-u

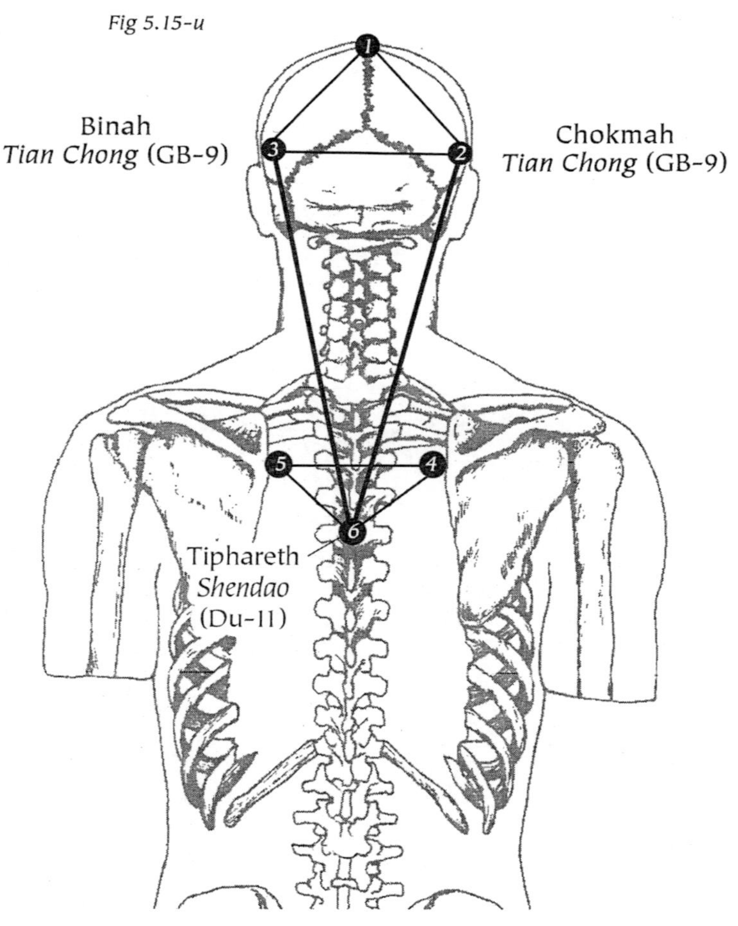

The next visual connection in The Tree of Life Astral Pattern is to bring the energy from *Po Hu* (UB-42) points on the client's right side corresponding to (Chesed) upward to connect with the *Tian Chong* ((GB-9) point on the right side corresponding to Chokmah. (See figure 5.15-v.)

## Tree of Life Astral Pattern

*Fig 5.15-v*

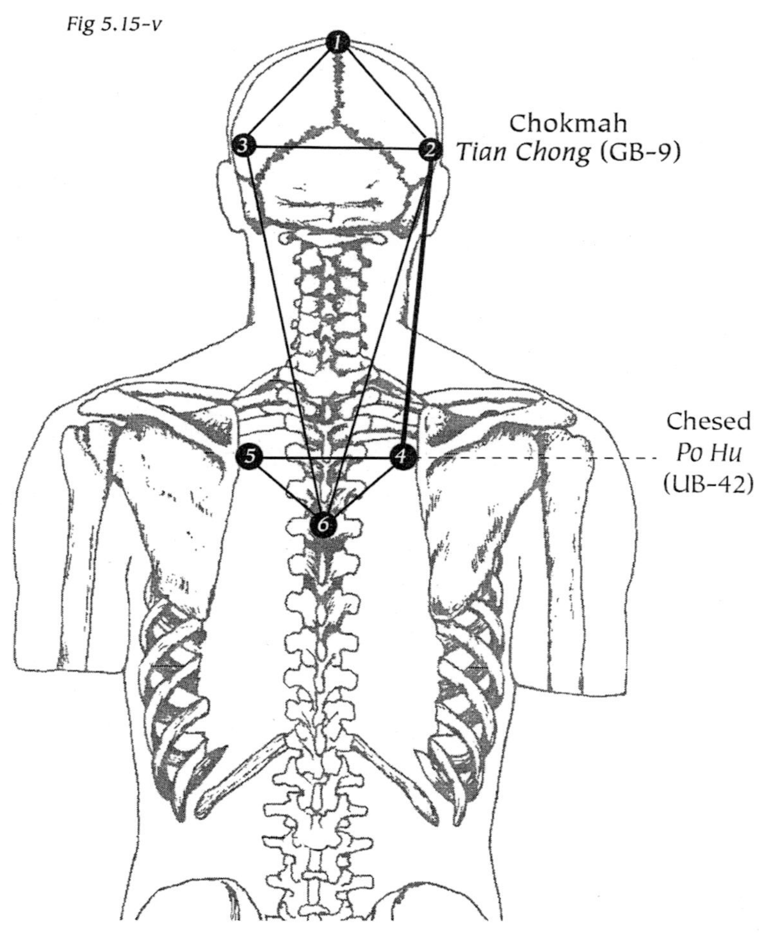

Now have your client make a visual upward connection from the left *Po Hu* (UB-42) point (Geburah) to the *Tian Chong* (GB-9) point on the left side of your client's head corresponding to Binah. (See figure 5.15-w below.)

**Tree of Life Astral Pattern**

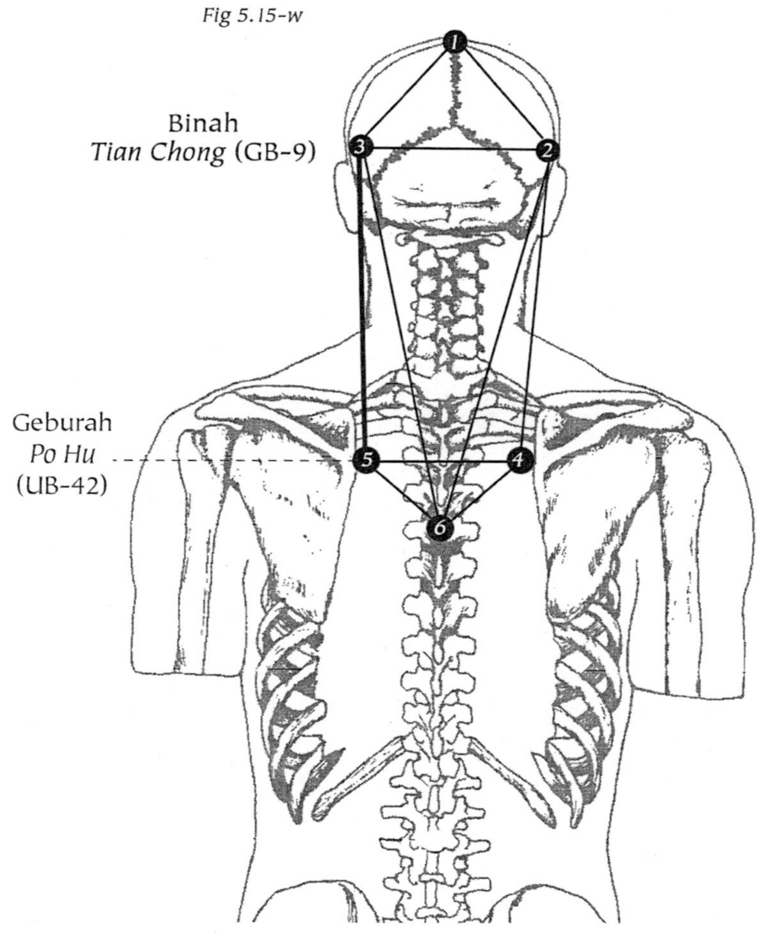

Insert acupuncture needles at the bilateral *Hunmen* (UB-47) sites. Needle the right side first, followed by the left side. *Hunmen* (UB-47) on the right side corresponds to Netzach. *Hunmen* (UB-47) on the left side corresponds to Hod. Have your client visually connect the bilateral *Hunmen* (UB-47) points. (See figure 5.15-x below.)

**Tree of Life Astral Pattern**

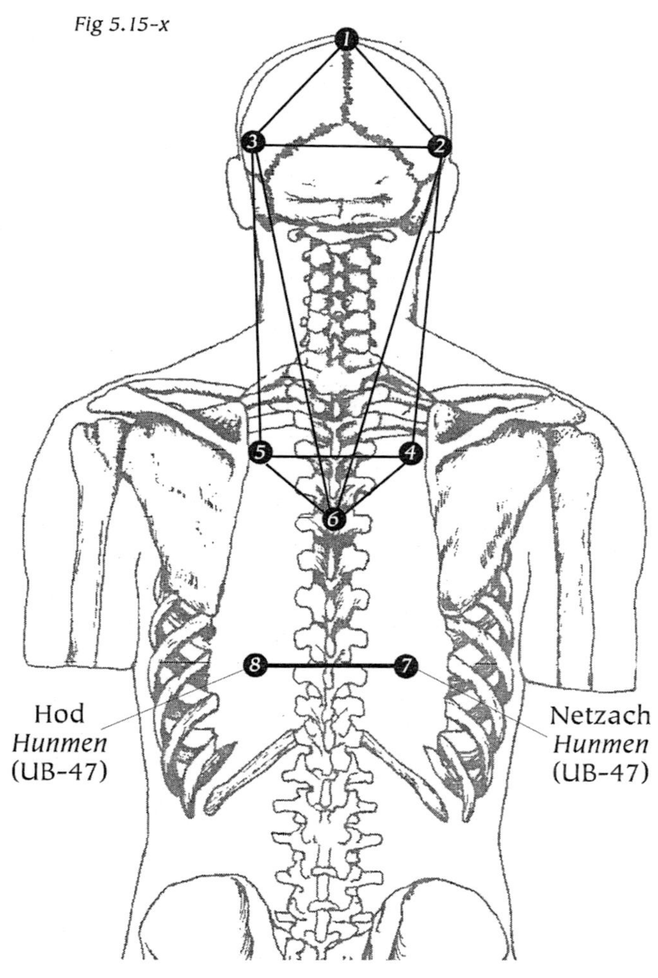

Insert an acupuncture needle at the acupuncture site of *Mingmen* (Du-4). Next have your client bring the energies downward simultaneously from the bilateral *Hunmen* (UB-47) points and connect the energies from both of those sites with *Mingmen* (Du-4) corresponding to the Sephira Yesod. (See figure 5.15-y below.)

## Tree of Life Astral Pattern

*Fig 5.15-y*

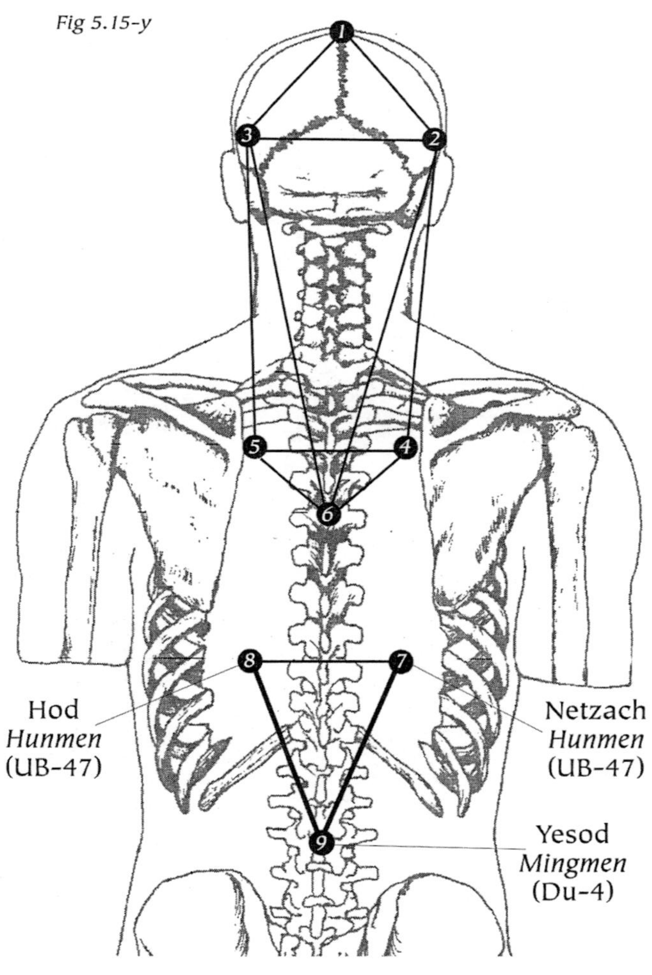

Now bring the energies simultaneously upward from the bilateral *Hunmen* (UB-47) points to connect in the center with the *Shendao* (Du-11) located directly on the spine. The acupuncture site of *Shendao* (Du-11) corresponds to the Sephira Tiphareth. (See figure 5.15-z below.)

**Tree of Life Astral Pattern**

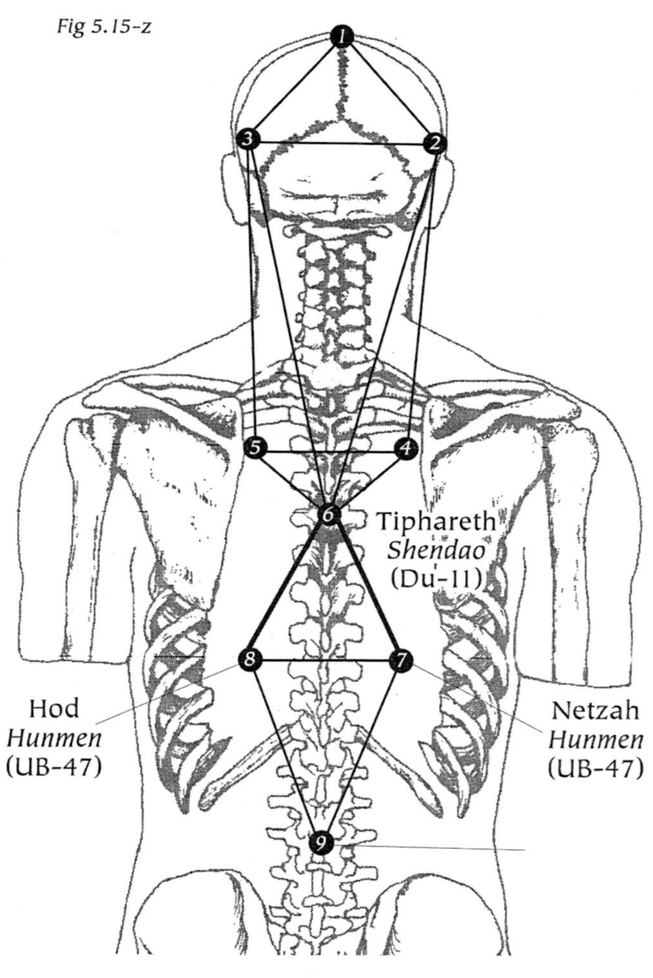


*Fig 5.15-z*

Next connect the qi at *Hunmen* (UB-47) on the client's right side that corresponds to the Sephira Netzach and bring the energy upward to connect with *Po Hu* (UB-42) also located on right side of the client. This acupuncture site corresponds to Chesed. (See figure 5.15-aa below.)

## Tree of Life Astral Pattern

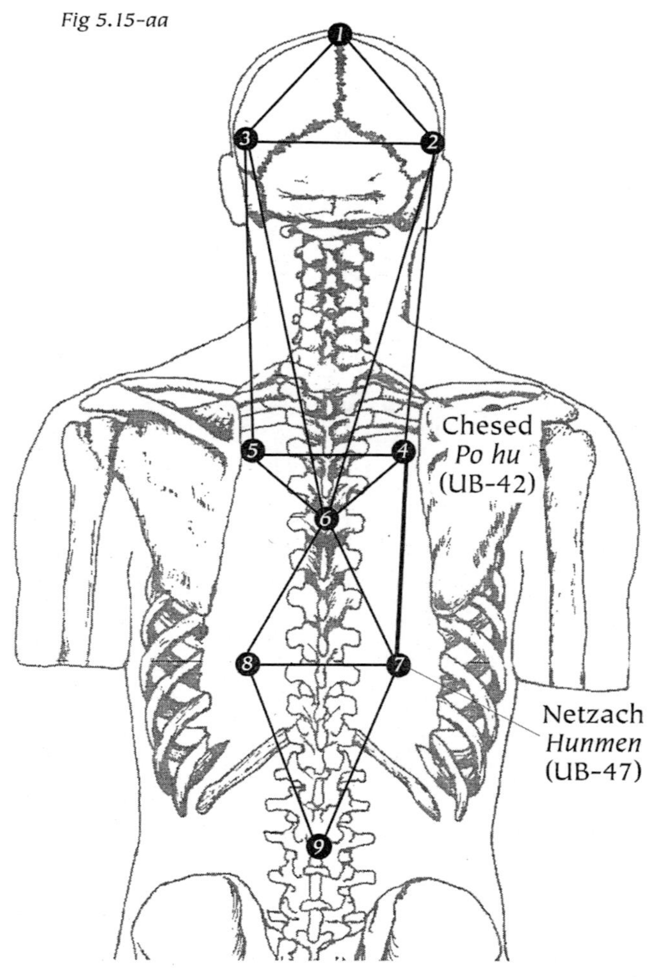

Now connect the qi from the left *Po Hu* (UB-42) point that corresponds to the Sephira Geburah with the qi at the site of the left side *Hunmen* (UB-47) that corresponds to Hod. (See figure 5.15-bb below.)

## Tree of Life Astral Pattern

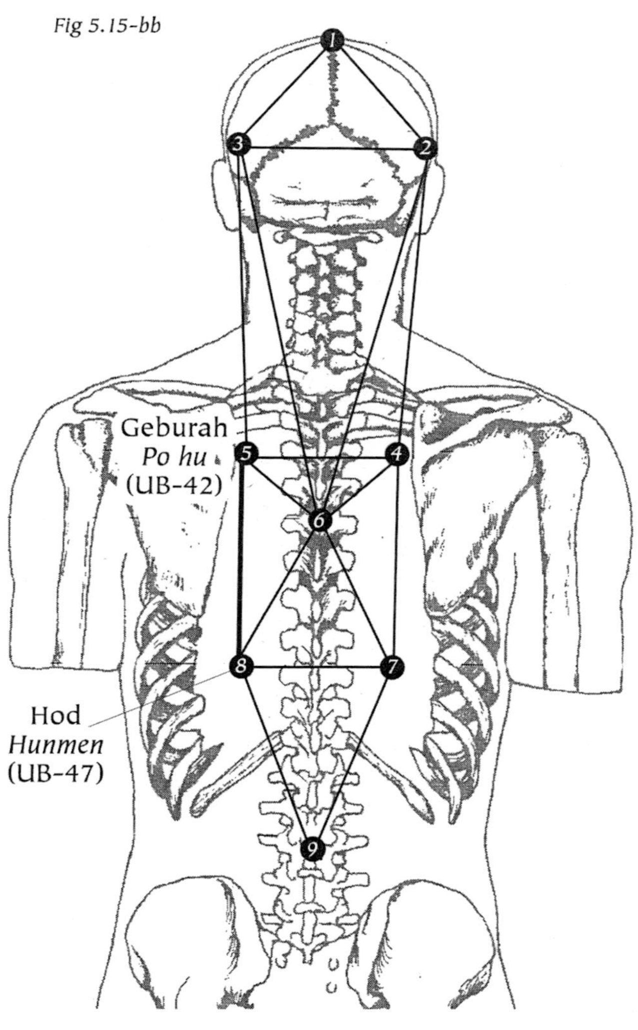

Insert an acupuncture needle at the site of the Coccyx Point. Next bring the energy straight down the spine from Yesod at *Mingmen* (Du-4) to the Coccyx Point that corresponds to Malkuth. (See figure 5.15-cc.)

**Tree of Life Astral Pattern**

*Fig 5.15-cc*

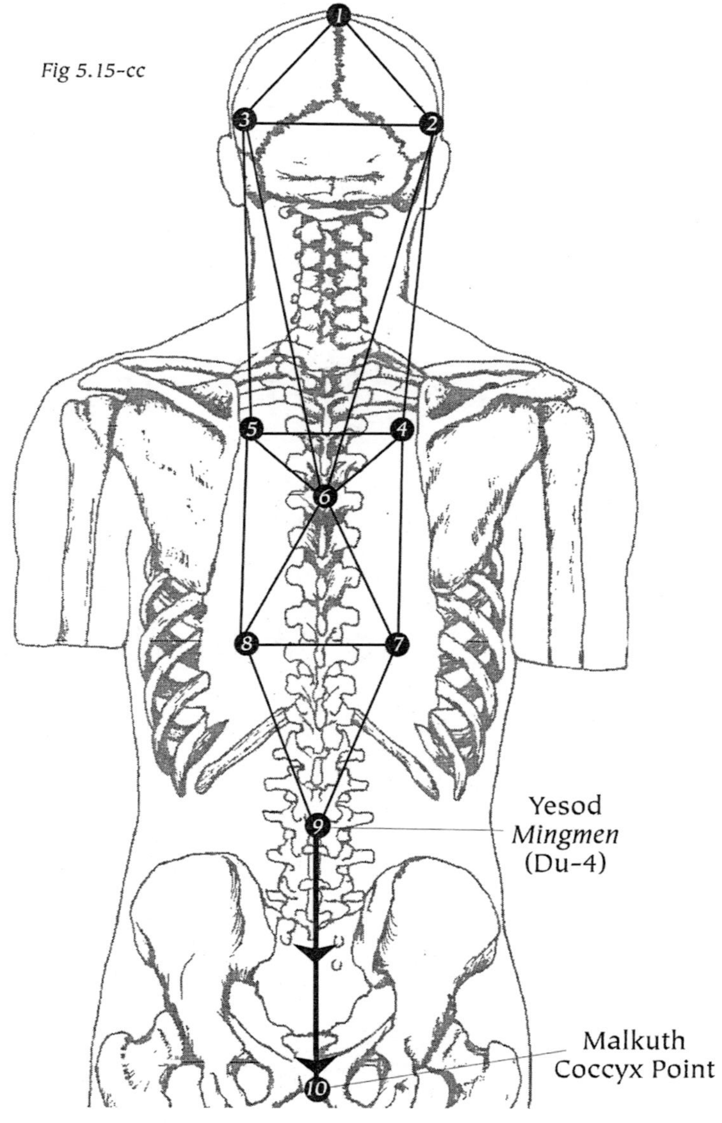

Split the energy from Malkuth and move the two rays upward to connect with the bilateral *Hunmen* (UB-47) points. (See the figure 5.15-dd below.)

**Tree of Life Astral Pattern**

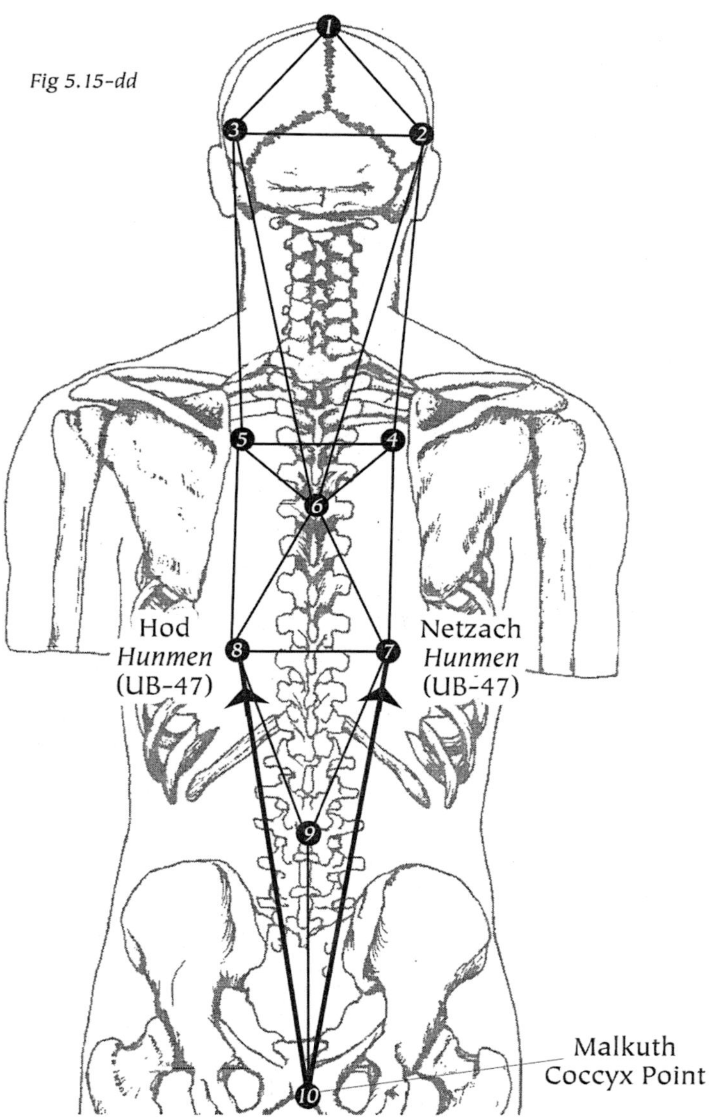


*Fig 5.15-dd*

Ask your client to visualize the energy ascending from the Coccyx Point (Malkuth to connect with *Mingmen* (Du-4). (See figure 5.15-ee below.)

### Tree of Life Astral Pattern

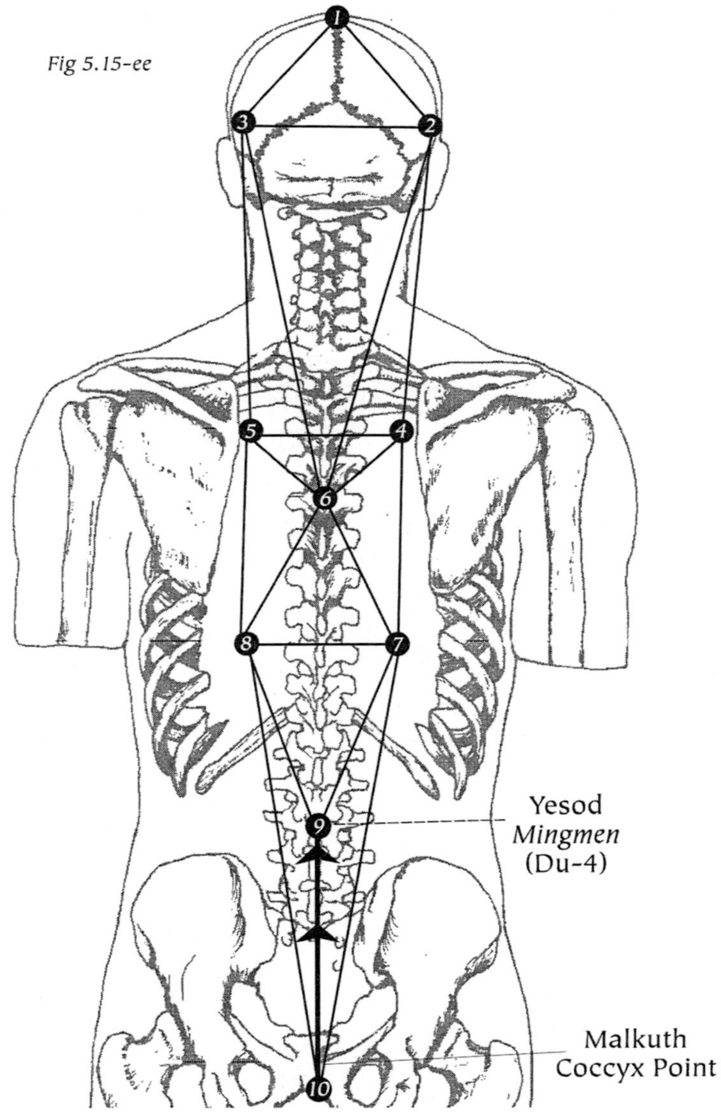


*Fig 5.15-ee*

Ask your client to bring the qi upward from Yesod at *Mingmen* (Du-4) to connect with Tiphareth at *Shendao* (Du-11). (See the above figure 5.15-ff below.)

**Tree of Life Astral Pattern**

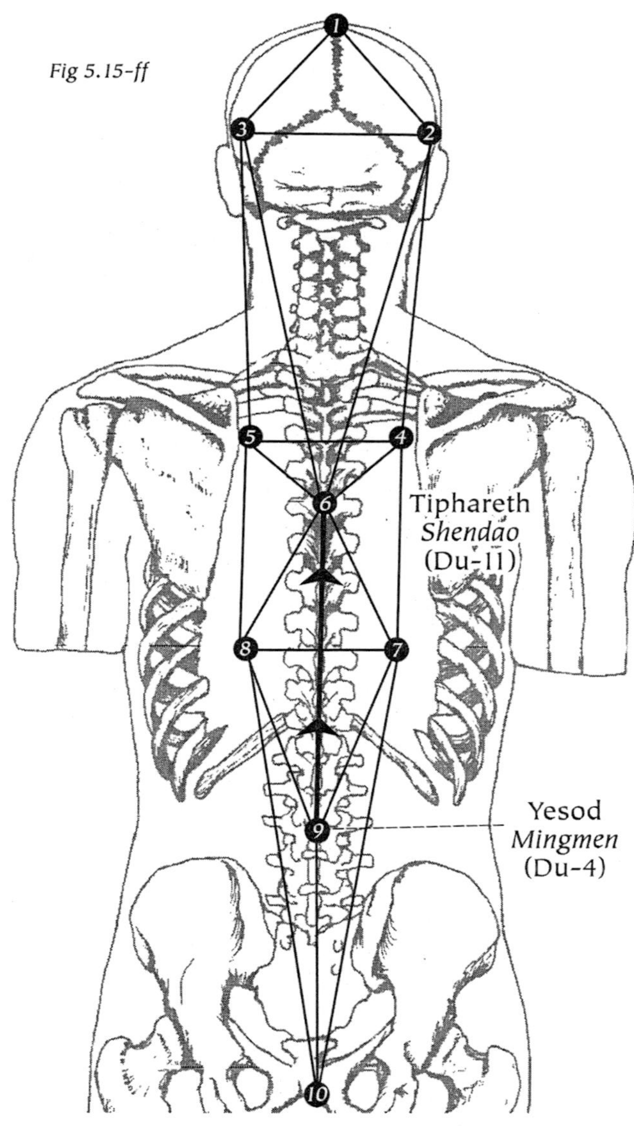


*Fig 5.15-ff*

From *Shendao* (Du-11), ask your client to move the energies upward to connect to the site of *Kether* located at *Tian Man* (Du-20). (See figure 5.15-gg below.)

**Tree of Life Astral Pattern**

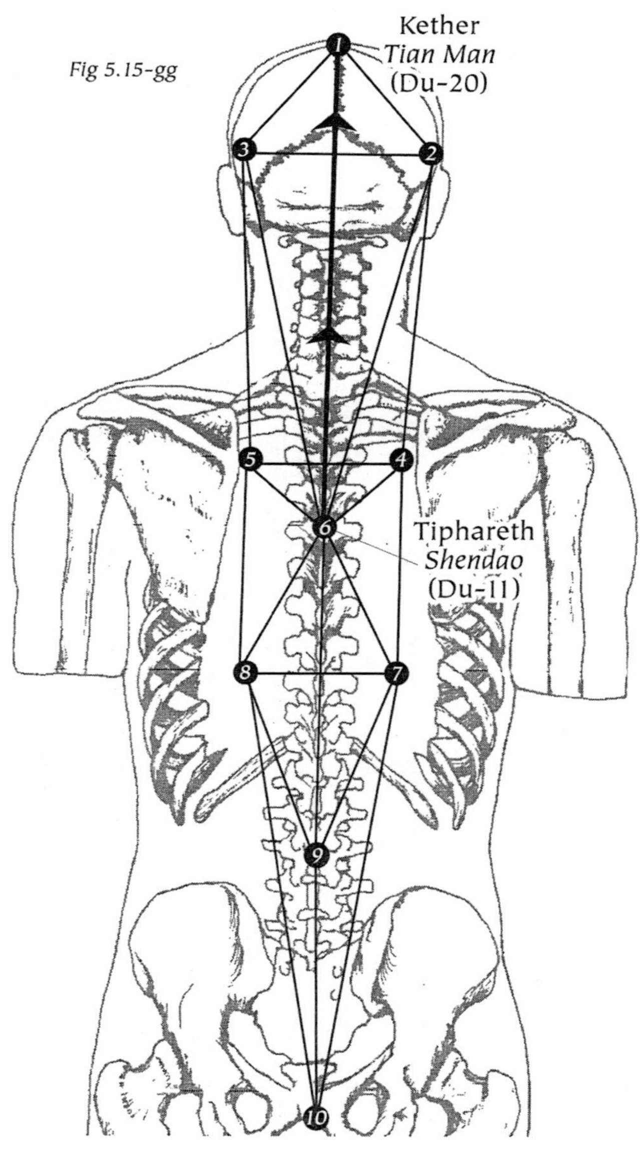


Fig 5.15-gg

After all the visual connections have been completed, needle Da'ath at the site of the last acupuncture point *Dazhui* (Du-14). (See figure 5.15-hh below.)

**Tree of Life Astral Pattern**

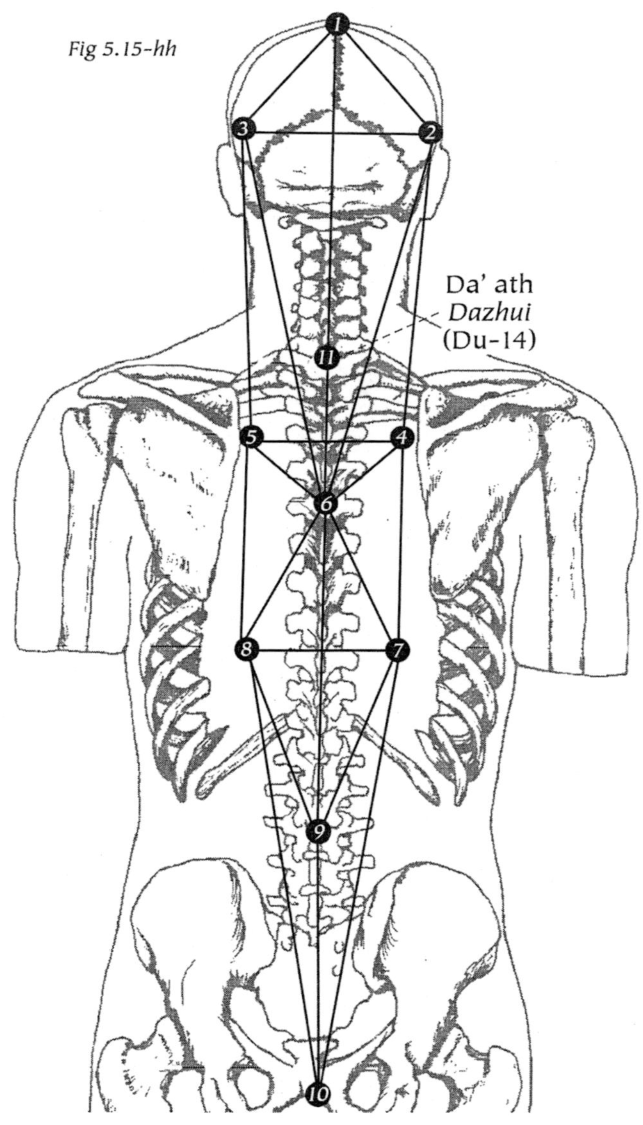


*Fig 5.15-hh*

## Complete Tree of Life Astral Pattern
### with 22 Pathways Connected

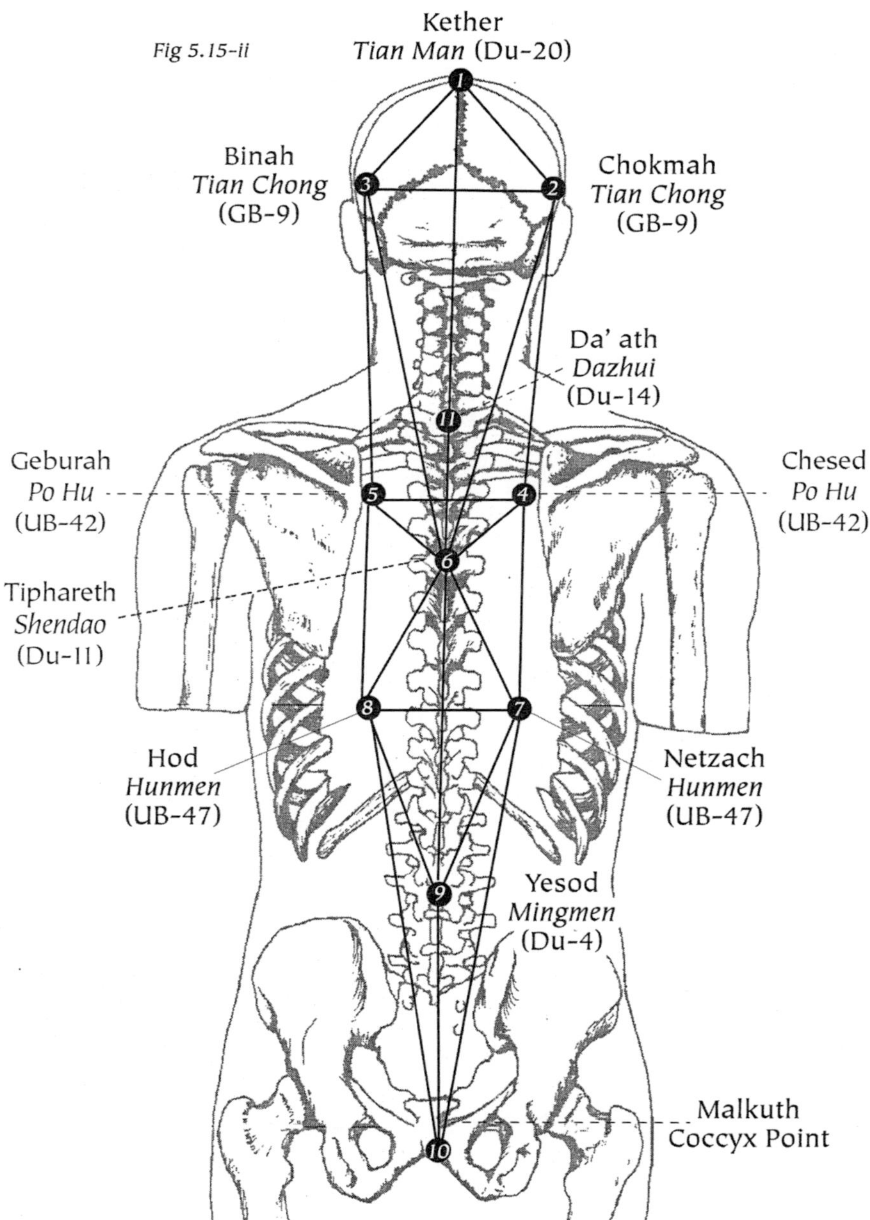


*Fig 5.15-ii*

## Treatment Protocol According to Tiers of Density

| Tiers of Density | Number of chakras imbalanced |
|---|---|
| Level 1 | Five, six or seven chakras. |
| Level 2 | Four of five chakras. |
| Level 3 | Three or four chakras. |
| Level 4 | Two or three chakras. |
| Level 5 | One chakra or none. |

| Tiers of Density | Recommended Treatment Protocol |
|---|---|
| Level 1 | Crown Infinity *Shaoyin* Pattern<br>Integration Synthesis Pattern<br>Merkebah Spin Pattern |
| Level 2 | Discern the Whisper Pattern<br>Crystalline Waters Pattern<br>Eight Heart Gates *Shaoyang* Pattern |
| Level 3 | Esoteric *Shaoyin* Heart Pattern<br>Esoteric *Shaoyin* Kidney Pattern<br>Cube on Cube Window Pattern |
| Level 4 | Esoteric *Shaoyin* Heart Window Pattern<br>Crystalline Grid Pattern<br>Crystalline Heart Grid Pattern |
| Level 5 | *Hun* Follow the *Shen* Pattern<br>Tree of Life Astral Pattern<br>Extended Crystalline Heart Grid Pattern |

| Chakras | Stored Information / Functions |
|---|---|
| Muladhara<br>Root Chakra | Survival - Fight or Flight<br>Day-to-Day Issues<br>Collecting / hoarding "things"<br>Being able to release |
| Swadthisthana<br>2nd Chakra | Money / Finances / Work<br>Sexual *qi*<br>Relationships<br>Kidney Issues<br>"Poor Me" / Fear |
| Manipura<br>Solar Plexus Chakra | Digesting Life / Emotions<br>Stomaching Life<br>Directions in Life<br>Anger<br>Sweetness in Life |
| Anahata<br>Heart Chakra | Love<br>Expansion / Expansiveness<br>Forgiveness / Acceptance<br>Trust / Compassion<br>Joy / Laughter / Play<br>Time to Rest / Relax / Meditate |
| Vishuddha<br>Throat Chakra | Speaking Out<br>Artistic Expression<br>Breathing in all life has to offer<br>Exhaling the toxins in your life |
| Ajna Center<br>Third Eye | Seeing clearly: both inwardly & outwardly<br>Higher Artistic Expressions<br>Higher Intuition |
| Sahasrara<br>Crown Chakra | Higher Spiritual Awakenings<br>Expansion of Realities: inwardly & outwardly<br>Moving into the Realms of "The Truth"<br>Selflessness |

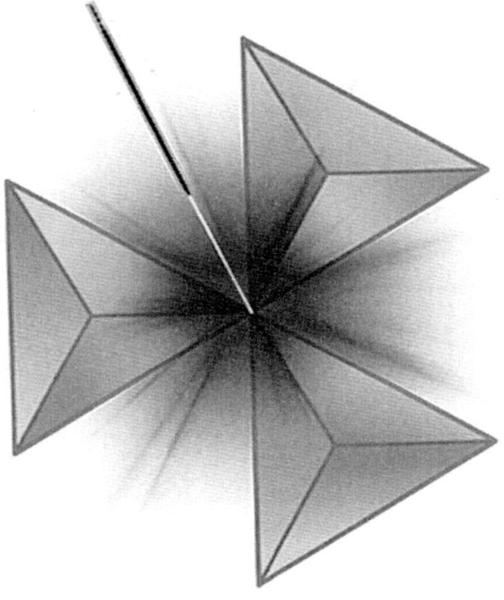

## Chapter VI: Final Thoughts

*"The answers I try to give must be from higher spiritual experiences, from a deeper source of knowledge and not lucubrations of the logical intellect trying to co-ordinate its ignorance... The inner help is quite different and there can be no confusion with it, for it reaches the substance of the consciousness, not the mind only."* [1]

Sri Aurobindo
***Life of Sri Aurobindo***

***Antahkarana, Celestial Fullness*** is a guide to assist in the journey of our own initial Inner Spiritual Awakening and the development and focusing of this journey by strengthening, balancing and awakening our Inner *Shen* of the Spiritual Heart. Everything is connected through energy. Even when things seem far apart or there is much space between particles, everything is still connected through energy. Esoteric Acupuncture is one attempt to show how various philosophies such as: Chinese Acupuncture Theory, the Hindu Nadi systems and the chakras, the ***Qabbalah***, Sacred Geometry, Pythagoras's theories on triangles and music, Platonic Solids and mathematics, superstring physics, Darius Dinshah's Chromo-Spectrum Metry Color Theory, Djwhal Khul's Tibetan philosophies and various Buddhist, Hindu, Muslim and Christian theories are all related and are branches of a puzzle that connects everything to everything. One way to make sense of these seemingly separate concepts is to develop and refine one's Inner *Shen* of Knowing of the Heart. The New Encoding Patterns of Esoteric acupuncture are designed to assist in the awakening of one's Inner, Spiritual *Shen* of the Higher Heart.

Some of you may have noticed that most of the New Encoding Patterns seem to be symmetrical in design. Symmetry is very pleasing to the physical eyes. Most people seem to like symmetry and symmetrical things and designs. Under the apparent symmetry created by the insertion of acupuncture needles in the acupuncture sites of the New Encoding Patterns is a less apparent underlying field of asymmetry. The brain and the inner vision respond well to the stimulus of asymmetry. Although the acupuncture patterns may all seem symmetric, the human body is not symmetrical. The physical heart and physical spleen systems are located on the left side of the human body. The physical liver is located on the right side of the body. Even if we are using bilateral acupuncture points in an acupuncture pattern, the energetics of the meridians, and thus the energetics of the acupuncture points are not the same on each side of the body. We are overlaying symmetry on top of asymmetry.

Symmetry seems to make sense in most instances, even in the world of particle physics. Presently, some theoretic physicists in particle physics are doubting the concept of supersymmetry. What if the tiniest particles do not have a hidden superpartner? Perhaps, asymmetry requires us to view our own world of knowledge with an expanded view.

The subtitle of this book, ***Celestial Fullness***, implies some level of inner awakening. Some people may call this a moment of Nirvana, Satori, Samadhi, Kundalini Awakening or by other names. These are only states of consciousness with many levels above. Most people will not reach these levels with only one or several Esoteric Acupuncture treatments. But the desire to reach these heightened, awakened realms of consciousness and the process to reach them may be aided by needling certain acupuncture sites on the body in a specific sequencing order. In Esoteric Acupuncture, one is utilizing the energetics of Sacred Geometry, Sacred Numbers, utilizing energy grids and using the energetics behind select acupuncture points as a transporter of information to bring the client into a quiet, centered state of Stillness.

In my search for the most fundamental starting point for determining how to change or modify one's level of health, I came to understand that **it must begin with the heart**. The fundamental inner starting point that determines where everything begins is the Original Consciousness and the Original *Shen* of our Higher Heart. The focus of treatments with Esoteric Acupuncture revolves around first correcting imbalances within the *Shen* of the heart, then harmonizing, strengthening and awakening the dormant spiritual aspects of our Higher, Inner *Shen*. Although Esoteric Acupuncture (as well as all styles of acupuncture) can address and correct many levels of *Shen* disturbances, the focus of Esoteric Acupuncture is on awakening our Higher, Inner Spiritual *Shen*. The Higher, Inner Spiritual *Shen* is not discussed in any of the traditional Asian schools of acupuncture theory. Awakening the Higher, Inner Spiritual *Shen* is a journey of the 21$^{st}$ Century that some people have chosen to follow.

Those seekers who have the determination, discipline and dedication to further refine their Inner Heart frequency and have taken care of the "pull" of the lower chakras, will be shown the path to their Higher Spiritual Journey. The Spiritual Journey will strengthen, define and bring us closer to our true Inner, Spiritual Higher Heart Center. The refinement and strengthening of our Inner Spiritual *Shen* can be accomplished through any number of ways, and will in turn help to cultivate both the Inner Soul Journey and the Inner Spiritual Journey. Both the pathways of one's Soul Journey and the Spiritual Journey will lead to one's discovering his or her true puzzle piece in life.

Although it may seem unobtainable at this present time

in humanity's journey, the goal for Esoteric Acupuncture is to be an instrument that will assist Earth on a full awakening for the population of the entire planet. At some point a critical mass will be reached through a morphogenetic grid, and the "Hundredth Monkey" theory will take place. There is no One Way, or One Pathway to reach these multiple levels of consciousness. There are infinite pathways. Somewhere along this inner journey, you will discover your true puzzle piece in life. Although some portions of the more difficult Inner Plane Ageless Wisdom may not appeal to the masses, I am hopeful that those of you who are reading this material will appreciate and utilize some of the Ageless Wisdom teachings that have been interwoven into a healing modality presented as Esoteric Acupuncture.

Although the initial Inner Awakenings may be very subtle, these subtle shifts often awaken the dormant inner spiritual seed inside of you that jolts you into looking at your life from a higher vantage point. You may refocus your lifestyle so that you are feeding your body only the purest organic foods and drinks available. This process of ingesting this quality of foods will alter your mind, thoughts and qi to the point where you will naturally gravitate toward the journey to discover your own Inner Spiritual Higher Heart Center. This journey and the pathway you choose to follow become a part of everything you do from this point onward.

The Inner Awakening will enable to you expand your consciousness to accept truths about your everyday three-dimensional reality. This does not mean that you will like all the truths you are exposed to, but you will not use the phrases: "I don't want to hear or talk about that. It is too scary." That is a program to shield your mind from being exposed to things your consciousness cannot comprehend or does not want to accept. If your consciousness is not expanded, you cannot accept certain facts that are outside of your comfort zone.

There are many levels of an inner awakening. Often

awakening without the heart energy of the spiritual side will bring the individual into a fear-based reality. A person can be well versed in certain types of information unknown by the masses that may bring up anger, resentment or fear in that person. In Esoteric Acupuncture, we are more interested in an Inner Spiritual Awakening of the heart. Of course, when you have an Inner Spiritual Awakening you will also be exposed to a multitude of truths and information not all of which are pleasant. If you are working on your Higher Heart, you will not fall into the dark pit of fear.

Esoteric Acupuncture is merely one modality to assist in the planetary awakening that is currently happening. Although the goal of this work has been mentioned in other Esoteric Acupuncture books and throughout this one, I would like to repeat it again. Esoteric Acupuncture is designed to help you find your own, individual puzzle piece in life. This requires that you first go inward to your Inner Spiritual Higher Heart and take an inventory of your life and what you are doing with your life. This requires you to be truthful to yourself. Then find or develop a technique that fits your personality to help you quiet your chattering mind. If you find any teacher or school of thought that tells you their style is the only way, I would suggest that you go to your heart and re-evaluate that teacher and style of teaching. Again, I will repeat: there is no One Way or One Pathway. There are infinite choices.

An Esoteric Acupuncture treatment will align your lower levels of consciousness with your Inner Spiritual Higher Heart Center. The beauty of this work is that it "forcefully" nudges you to take an active part in your spiritual journey. You have to do the real work, which is inner plane development, and not merely rely on a quick-fix solution by an outside source. Although an outside source may be able to point you in the right direction and even place you on your correct pathway, you have to be wise enough to know that you must still do the inner plane work. The New Encoding Patterns of Esoteric Acupuncture are only able to unlock some of your inner locks.

You have to decide what steps you want to take (if any) after the treatment. Of course, the Esoteric Acupuncture treatments are able to simultaneously address physical challenges. But, working merely on the physical level is not the primary goal of Esoteric Acupuncture. The goal is to create a new paradigm of thinking in healthcare management for the masses and to help you uncover what is your "true" purpose here on planet Earth in this particular incarnation.

One of the keys for your own Spiritual Quest is to do some sort of service work. The service work must be done with joy and love in your heart and not with resentment or merely a sense of obligation. Service work is not synonymous with a saviorship mentality where a person must "save the world' or save someone or something. Saviorship is a very noble cause, but is not the same as the service work that is being discussed here. The service work can either be inner plane service work, such as true quiet mind meditation, or external service work where you are physically in contact with other individuals. Once you tap into the field of your Inner Spiritual Higher Heart Center, you will know that everyone and everything is connected. There is a fabric of consciousness that connects us all. Once you truly tap into this force field, you cannot forget it or ignore its importance. This interconnecting fabric of consciousness becomes a part of who you are and guides your individual Soul Journey.

Although Chapter Five gives the practitioner a guideline for selecting certain New Encoding Patterns based on the number of imbalanced chakras and the Tiers of Density of consciousness, Esoteric Acupuncture is not focused on merely the chakra levels. The chakras are on the Astral Plane. Esoteric Acupuncture is designed to move consciousness into the planes of the causal body and higher. It is important to understand this point. Think of the Astral Plane as the bridge between the Mental Plane and the Physical Planes (dense physical and Etheric Plane).

With the visualizations and the specific sequencing of the acupuncture points within the New Encoding Patterns, one is able to bridge the gap from the dense Mental Plane (concrete mind) through the higher Mental Sub Planes (the Causal Planes of the abstract mind) to connect with levels of consciousness above the Causal Plane and move into the Buddhic Plane, the Atmic Plane, the Monadic Plane, the Logoic Plane and even into the cosmic levels of consciousness.

When balancing each of the individual chakras, a person's physical challenges may not completely disappear after one treatment. The Astral Plane is the realm of the emotional body that has a finer frequency vibration than the denser Physical Plane. If the person receiving a chakra balancing and alignment treatment has a deeply ingrained emotional attachment to his or her past experiences, the denser reality of the physical vehicle often requires more time to resolve issues than the astral realms. It was mentioned in another volume of Esoteric Acupuncture that every level of density has its own laws. Generally speaking, the denser levels usually require more linear time to obtain noticeable positive, permanent changes.

Even though it has been mentioned in this book that some of the theories of Traditional Acupuncture and Chinese Medicine from Asia that were developed in the Ages of Pisces and Aries are outdated, does not mean that Traditional Acupuncture and herbs are not useful today. I am one of the most enthusiastic and avid followers of the ancient Chinese doctrines of acupuncture as the building blocks for the new acupuncture of the 21st Century. In the herbal world, many, if not most of the pharmaceutical drugs were developed after first researching and studying the efficacy of herbs, then synthesizing the active ingredient of these herbs to come up with a synthetic pharmaceutical copy now called Western Allopathic Medicine. The statement about Piscean thinking being outdated is intended to bring to the attention of the reader the fact that the old paradigm of waiting for an imbalance to develop before taking action is an ineffective and very costly way to address health and wellness in this very complex, diverse society of the 21st Century.

Also, I want to make it perfectly clear that I am not suggesting that a practitioner has to choose between Traditional Asian Acupuncture protocols or Esoteric Acupuncture. My intention is not to create division, but to be able to accept and utilize all protocols and modalities that best fit each individual practitioner's needs. We are a much more complex society than even a few decades ago. I am envisioning the professional scope and practice of acupuncture by licensed acupuncturists to encompass those parts of traditional acupuncture and herbs that are still useful for the needs of the 21st Century, and embrace a type of thinking and attitude similar to Esoteric Acupuncture that emphasizes wellness, inner spiritual growth and expansion of consciousness on the many levels of the heart field. I feel that this type of thinking and approach will benefit not only the acupuncture community and our profession as a whole, but will greatly benefit the general population seeking answers outside of the old paradigm of addressing diseases or other physical and emotional challenges after the imbalances have already manifested.

A concern to me is that after intensive schooling and study to gain a certain depth in understanding Chinese and Western Medicine and after passing the California Acupuncture State Board Examination to receive licensure to practice, a great number of licensed acupuncturists in California do not renew their acupuncture license after five years in business. Part of this dilemma may be due to lacking the business acumen to acquire enough income to stay in business. Maybe the acupuncture schools should address that issue. But the more concerning part of this dilemma may be that much of what is taught in the accredited acupuncture schools is not in alignment with what is needed by a sophisticated clientele/patient base that utilizes acupuncture treatments today. Much of the scope within the curriculum in acupuncture schools in the United States today is more in direct alignment with the Western models from the Allopathic, Chiropractic and Osteopathic schools of thought, overriding much of the wisdom and philosophies that drew students to study acupuncture in the first place.

We should not forget that outside of sports injuries and those people addressing pain with acupuncture treatments, most of the clientele in the United States who utilize acupuncture on a consistent basis throughout the year (not merely for immediate physical issues) are very diverse, well-read and progressive thinking individuals. Unless you are a well-read, open-minded person with knowledge of what true acupuncture is, you might think that acupuncture is only used to alleviate pain due to injuries or aging, to relieve stress and for relaxation.

Therefore, I feel that the key focus is to gradually attract the type of clientele who recognize and understand the "real" strength and beauty of acupuncture enough to seek treatments on a regular basis throughout the year. Most of this clientele are aware of organic foods and wholesome diets. Many of these same clients practice Hatha Yoga, *Qi Gong* and *Tai Qi,* meditate and are generally into the more natural ways of acquiring and maintaining health and wellness. That is our client base here in a progressive thinking city such as Los Angeles, California. This is how acupuncture in the West will grow and expand.

There is a very large group of people who want "something else" besides the western model of taking drugs to temporarily relieve stress or physical ailments. Treating those who seek prevention from disease, a better quality of health and expanded levels of consciousness should become the goal for expanding the influence of acupuncture in the United States. Our real power as an acupuncture profession is prevention, wellness and expanding consciousness. Allopathic Medicine is trying to corner the market of the paradigm of treating people after a concern or problem has already occurred. That is not the real power of acupuncture. This is not to say that acupuncturists should abandon our present paradigm of treating disease. I am suggesting that as healthcare professionals we need to expand our clientele base not only to survive as a profession, but to thrive and grow in the decades to come in the fast paced societies of the modern 21st Century world.

The healthcare industry today is in reality a "disease treatment" industry. The political agenda of the acupuncture community in the United States in our time is focused on disease, thus becoming integrated into the western medical model. Even so, we will never be equals to western doctors by following their rules and criteria of how to treat health issues. If we follow the western pharmaceutical model, using their rules and protocols as we are presently doing, we will be swallowed up under their system as second-class doctors. We should not to bow down to the dictates of the western role model. The opposite is true. Our profession needs to preserve our identity and strengthen our own unique power. In the hospital settings today in California, we are merely looked upon as technicians instead of the primary healthcare practitioner status given to us by California law. The power of acupuncture is working with qi/prana for wellness, health and the prevention of diseases before they manifest. This is our mastery and is what we should always practice and enforce. Esoteric Acupuncture is designed to help move our profession into accepting our inherent strengths and be the role model of health, prevention and wellness.

Although there have been some movement and changes happening in the health profession and in all events throughout the world, the acupuncture community as a whole has not adopted the thinking to embrace this new paradigm shift. As a group, we still do not believe in the inherent powers of moving energy for health and disease prevention before the disease or imbalance manifests. And we have not embraced the idea of ingesting organic, high vibrational foods for raising consciousness.

### Bringing It All together

Is building the Antahkarana, as a spiritual antenna, an accomplishment we should strive for in the fast-paced world of the 21st Century? Is building the Antahkarana necessary today? Some people may feel that the dedication and mental work necessary to build one's Antahkarana is a slow, tedious system that is outdated by our current shift into a fourth and fifth dimensional reality of consciousness and beyond. I have also heard people express their opinion that working with Kundalini is an outdated way to access a higher state of total awakened consciousness. With the consciousness shift of planet Earth today, we are definitely able to activate portions of the pineal gland and move into higher, altered states of reality (different from 3-D reality) by other methods besides working with Kundalini and building our Antahkarana. It has been mentioned throughout the Esoteric Acupuncture series of books the importance of connecting with your Inner Spiritual Higher Heart. It is through the Inner Spiritual Higher Heart that one is able to begin the process of spiritual awakening to the unlimited mind of Universe. Working with Kundalini and the process of building, maintaining and expanding the Antahkarana are merely methods of awakening. If awakening is the goal, or if further expansion of your already awakened state is the goal, then you might consider what is offered by way of utilizing the New Encoding Patterns of Esoteric Acupuncture for expanding consciousness in an organic manner. Esoteric Acupuncture will not give you instant cosmic consciousness, but this system will help to awaken your Inner Spiritual *Shen* for a centered, harmonious Spiritual Awakening.

Esoteric Acupuncture emphasizes an organic, natural spiritual awakening, not merely a consciousness awakening. There are ways to awaken and expand consciousness that are not necessarily what Esoteric Acupuncture refers to as a spiritual awakening. One can have a consciousness expanding experience with the proper computer generated mind control frequencies, or by using sound frequencies to open certain aspects of the brain. But in my opinion, we must become aware on all levels and not just be a happy, content spiritual being in our own small bubble of reality. We must become aware of all sides, both dark and light, but live with an expanded mindset of love, expansion and abundance.

Trust is the key. Trust yourself and know that the road to your Inner Spiritual *Shen* of the Higher Heart is through trust. Remove the tentacles of self-doubt and pity. The level of trust referred to here does include the lower, child-like naivety that lacks inner awareness. The true higher vibrations of trust lead to the heart, not to the fear tentacles of the kidney system. If you are expanding levels of consciousness and you allow fear to take hold of your consciousness, then the dark will win. Trust is an extension of love and the purity of goodness, sharing and compassion. The true, higher realms of trust (not the naïve trust of an unawakened soul) will always lead to the inner heart field.

The whole process of what each person feels is his or her individual spiritual awakening is a journey with countless paths, countless challenges, countless obstacles, countless joys and infinite possibilities. Some people may have inner spiritual journeys that are not consciously initiated. Those of you who have spiritually awakened, at least to a certain degree, may have gathered the desire, or already have an urgency and passion for a more encompassing, more revealing inner spiritual journey that does not merely rely on what is told to you by organized religion. Next, it may be beneficial for you to be spiritually awakened enough to understand Kundalini and the existence of the methods of building one's own Antahkarana (spiritual antenna). You will then be able to ask yourself the question: "are those concepts necessary to learn and expand upon for my Inner Spiritual Journey in this day and age?"

I do not say that working with Kundalini and building the Antahkarana (spiritual antenna) are absolutely necessary procedures for awakening and that they are the only way. In this accelerated time frame for this planet, our solar system and our galaxy as a whole, many individuals will, or may have already, experienced a sudden consciousness awakening of some degree. These same individuals may feel that their sudden awakening is all that is necessary. Other people may have emotional and mental challenges from those premature consciousness awakenings because the process may have expanded an awareness the individual was not prepared to handle or comprehend. Some people who have experienced Kundalini rising may have had a smooth journey and not experienced any excessively abrupt spiritual awakening.

The building of one's own Antahkarana (spiritual antenna) is merely one method I feel is a positive step to assist you in your personal journey of spiritual unfoldment and to help bring about a gentler awakening of Kundalini. My opinion is that consciousness has no boundaries or no outer limits and resides in an infinite field that is not a linear field. Since we only have this one lifetime in this particular physical vehicle, why not try to access as much of the field as you are able to handle? The only lifetime that really matters is the one you are experiencing now. As Ram Dass once said: "Be Here Now." Memories are fine, but do not dwell in the past. Although hope and aspirations are positive objectives, do not dwell on the future. Be in the moment. Fear and its many tentacles are the only obstructions blocking you from freeing your concrete mind and expanding to the multidimensional realities that are awaiting you.

Expanding beyond one's concrete mind does not mean we do not need our concrete mind. No matter how much you think you know or how much information you can store and regurgitate, that is still considered lower knowledge. Swami Rama states in his book entitled ***Wisdom of the Ancient Sages, Mundaka Upanishad*** that:

> *"Lower knowledge actually means that the aspirant earns the means to facilitate his or her search and to create favorable circumstances for prayer, meditation, and contemplation, which are the real means to attain final liberation or realize*

> *Absolute Truth... If lower knowledge is not gained, it creates obstacles for the aspirant. The goal is to attain the higher knowledge, which directly helps one to liberate himself from all bondage."* [2]

Working with the spiraling frequencies inherent within the New Encoding Patterns is a safe way to align and strengthen your central pathway that is your path to Higher Wisdom. The New Encoding Patterns will also assist with the harmonious upward flow of Kundalini through the astral spine via the Chitrini nadi for most people, or through the Brahma nadi for the advanced practitioners of Kundalini. Having the patience and dedication to devotedly pursue your goal on various levels of spiritual awakenings require a mature, quiet heart. Being impatient and wanting to find the short cut is the consciousness of an unawakened or an immature heart. If you are very Still, you will discover your natural path which may seem like a "short cut." It will feel that way because when you are on your own true individual, inner heart path, everything will seem smooth with very few obstacles. Those who are on their own true inner heart journey but still encounter challenges or obstacles need those particular challenges to assist them with their biggest steps of growth on their own journey.

There will be no abrupt, premature Kundalini rising by receiving an Esoteric Acupuncture treatment, unless you are taking certain pharmaceuticals or are on mind-altering plants such as: ayahusca, peyote, psilocibin mushrooms or other types of mind-altering chemicals or plants.

I have repeated in the Esoteric Acupuncture series of books that Esoteric Acupuncture is not merely a different acupuncture system, but rather a way of life. It is important to know that everything you eat and drink, as well as your emotions and thoughts are transferred through your mind, your hands and acupuncture needle into your client. But, the real purpose of Esoteric Acupuncture and the New Encoding Patterns is to assist you in discovering your puzzle piece in life. I mentioned in Chapter One that I have shifted the focus on Esoteric Acupuncture to emphasize awakening, rather than the idea of healing. Each of us has a purpose for why we chose to incarnate on planet Earth at this particular time. We are not here merely to find a job so we can take care of our daily Muladhara (root chakra) and Swadthisthana (second chakra) issues, or to find a better job so we can have more money to make our daily existence more pleasant. Since we are in this three -dimensional world, we must take care of our three-dimensional needs. Of course there is absolutely nothing wrong with striving for a better and more comfortable lifestyle for yourself, your loved ones and your family. But, I feel there has to be a real purpose of why each of us decided to reincarnate again, in this particular time frame, with this particular physical vehicle.

Receiving an Esoteric Acupuncture treatment or even a series of Esoteric Acupuncture treatments will not automatically lift you into an elevated level of awakening. Unless you are mentally, emotionally and spiritually ready to accept newer, finer frequency vibrations of reality, you may not feel that much different after an Esoteric Acupuncture treatment than you would from any generic, traditional acupuncture treatment. Most of my clientele are awakened to some degree and most have been coming for Esoteric Acupuncture treatments for a number of years. Each treatment will strengthen and refine the frequencies of the Spiritual Heart Center. Sometimes because of past karmic inner plane discipline work, you may be elevated to an accelerated pace of awakening by an Esoteric Acupuncture treatment with one or more New Encoding Patterns. Your "awakening," or perhaps a better word may be your acceptance of this new awareness may occur very suddenly.

Many of the clientele who have received Esoteric Acupuncture treatments from me have told me they experienced an elevated altered state of consciousness and felt very light. Some people felt as if they were floating above the treatment table during the session. Others have said they went into a very deep consciousness state where they were not quite asleep, yet were not in their normal 3-D level of consciousness. Sometimes the client will go into a very deep sleep and enter a realm unlike their normal sleep. This is also beneficial for your clients. In large cities such as Los Angeles where I reside, many people "run" on false energy. They may drink caffeine, alcohol, ingest products with white sugar for quick energy or feed off the concentrated, dense energy of being in a congested urban environment. The sessions when your client goes into a short yet very deep sleep after receiving a New Encoding Patterns of Esoteric Acupuncture allows the client to align with his or her central pathway and will balance the seven major chakras. When he or she awakens from the deep sleep, he or she will usually feel very refreshed and may later experience an "ah ha" moment.

Very often teachers of the esoteric Ageless Wisdom schools will give their students or followers of the Ageless Wisdom teachings some knowledge about a certain subject or topic without fully explaining in an easier-to-understand format what the teaching really meant esoterically. The true esoteric teachers often leave "hints" for the students or readers of the Ageless Wisdom teaching to allow the students or followers an opportunity to individually unravel the puzzle of that teaching. I have likewise in the Esoteric Acupuncture series given the reader certain esoteric teachings without revealing more insights into what I was conveying. This was also done on purpose.

Those of you who have read ***Climbing Jacob's Ladder: Esoteric Acupuncture, Volume III*** will remember that it originally came out as a workbook and not much detail was given with the New Encoding Patterns. During one of my meditations while I was writing that book, it was revealed to me that true teachers of the esoteric Ageless Wisdom do not reveal all the information at one time and basically "force" the students to go to his or her abstract mind to pull out the esoteric meanings.

With ***Antahkarana: Celestial Fullness, Esoteric Acupuncture, Volume VI***, I did the opposite and tried to make the section on the

New Encoding Patterns as simple as possible by including more diagrams. I hope this makes it easier to understand and less of a burden for the practitioner to retain both the visualizations and sequencing order of the New Encoding Patterns.

I would like to clarify the importance of having your clientele make certain visual connections and why it is equally important for the practitioner to intimately know all the posterior visual connections. It was mentioned in an earlier volume in the Esoteric Acupuncture series that the acupuncture meridians were located on the etheric levels of the physical plane. The etheric sub planes are less dense than the gross physical levels. The fact that the etheric sub planes are located above the skin helps to explain how a very gentle system such as Toyo Hari Style Acupuncture from Japan is so effective. Very often the practitioner of Toyo Hari will not even pierce the skin with the acupuncture needle. The fact that the acupuncture meridians are located on the outside of the skin and the meridians have branches that go inward to the various organs and other parts of the body explains how inserting a needle into an acupuncture site without piercing the skin has the capability to strengthen, disperse or otherwise move *qi* in the dense physical plane.

Auras are projected on the astral plane and are visible to those who have the sensitivity and clarity of refinement of eyesight to see on that plane. Think of the Etheric Plane as the intermediary between the dense physical body and the Astral Plane. Where the outer edge of the Etheric Plane and the denseness of the etheric frequencies touch the more refined frequencies of the Astral Plane is where the Atomic Shield is located. The Atomic Shield touches the very outer border of one's *Wei Qi,* our protective barrier. In order to insert acupuncture needles into specific sites on the dense physical body, the practitioner must pierce the Atomic Shield and penetrate the Etheric Plane. This action opens gateways for qi from the dense physical vehicle to communicate with the Astral Planes.

When we make visual connections, such as the triangular visualizations used in Esoteric Acupuncture, we are working on the Mental Plane by accessing and activating our visual powers of the right brain. The Mental Plane is made up of finer frequencies than the frequencies of the Astral Plane.

There are seven sub planes within each of the seven planes of consciousness. Above the four lower Mental Sub Planes are the three Causal Sub Planes. The four lower Mental Sub Planes plus the three higher Causal Sub Planes make up the seven levels of our mental body or Mental Plane. The four lower sub planes of the Mental Plane make up the concrete mind of academia, rational thinking and constriction.. The three upper sub levels of the Mental Plane make up the abstract mind of intuition, artistic creativity, imagination and freedom.

I just want to make clear the distinction between the left-brain activities of the lower Mental Sub Planes versus the right-brain activities of the three higher Causal Sub Planes. The visualization process of the right brain adds a layer on top of the energized etheric layer that activates the qi within the acupuncture meridians. The insertion of needles in specific acupuncture sites following a very specific sequencing order in Esoteric Acupuncture creates a more active and more expansive energetic grid pattern. The act of making mental visual connections between certain acupuncture points now allows the acupuncture sites to act as gateways to the levels above the lower Mental Sub Planes to connect with the consciousness on the Buddhic Plane and higher. We are creating a communication platform grid called our Axiatonal Grid System that links into the greater astral and the other Axiatonal Grid Systems of our universe. The complete process of correctly inserting acupuncture needles in a specified sequence in a New Encoding Pattern, plus the visualization connections between the acupuncture sites now expands the frequencies to allow the recipient of the Esoteric Acupuncture treatment to move into the hyperspatial realms of consciousness. The only barrier to reaching and understanding what is happening on the higher planes is one's cluttered, lower mental mind.

If reaching the higher planes of consciousness above the

mental levels is a goal, then it is recommended that you involve yourself with serious dedication and discipline in some form of meditation, *Qi Gong*, pranayama (breathing exercises) or other methods to center and quiet your triad of the body, mind and spirit, to allow the lower consciousness fields to connect to the higher consciousness realms. But if your goal is becoming "smart" and being able to show off your intellectual prowess by repeating interesting tidbits of information, no matter how difficult and esoteric the information may be, shows that you have not acknowledged and paid homage to the greater spiritual aspect of the totality of who you are. Knowledge is not synonymous with Wisdom. Knowledge is connected to the kidneys system. Wisdom is part of one's heart system. Knowledge and Wisdom are the opposing, yet complimentary aspects, of Esoteric *Shaoyin*. All the New Encoding Patterns within Esoteric Acupuncture contain and strengthen the frequencies of Esoteric *Shaoyin*, the heart and love versus the kidneys and fear. To access and remain in our True Spiritual Nature requires that we understand the importance of remaining in our higher heart space at all times, as much as possible.

Being able to quickly and easily make the visual triangular connections will tell you much about your client. Those who are able to quickly make the visual triangular connections have a more developed right brain and a freer, expansive nature. Those that have a difficult time making the triangular visual connections are not as opened in their artistic, imaginative aspects of their brain and may sometimes show certain tendencies of being more constricted. The visualizations used in Esoteric Acupuncture are exercises to assist in the development and unfolding of one's bicameral mind.

You will notice how many times I have gone over the visual morphic resonant connection between *Dazhui* (Du-14) located directly below the lower border of the spinous process of the seventh cervical vertebra to *Yintang* (Ajna Center) located on the vertical midline of the anterior of the body at the site between the eyebrows and directly superior to the bridge of the nose.

This is the key connection for allowing qi to flow smoothly through the three Major Head Centers. (See figure 6.1-a.) The next connection is to move the energy upward from *Dazhui* (Du-14) to *Feng Fu* (Du-16) "The Wind Mansion". (See figure 6.1-b.) Next the energies from *Feng Fu* (Du-16) are connected to *Yintang* (Ajna Center). (See figure 6.1-c.) And lastly, connect the energies at both *Feng Fu* (Du-16) and *Yintang* (Ajna Center) to *Tian Man* (Du-20) in a triangular manner. (See figure 6.1-d.)

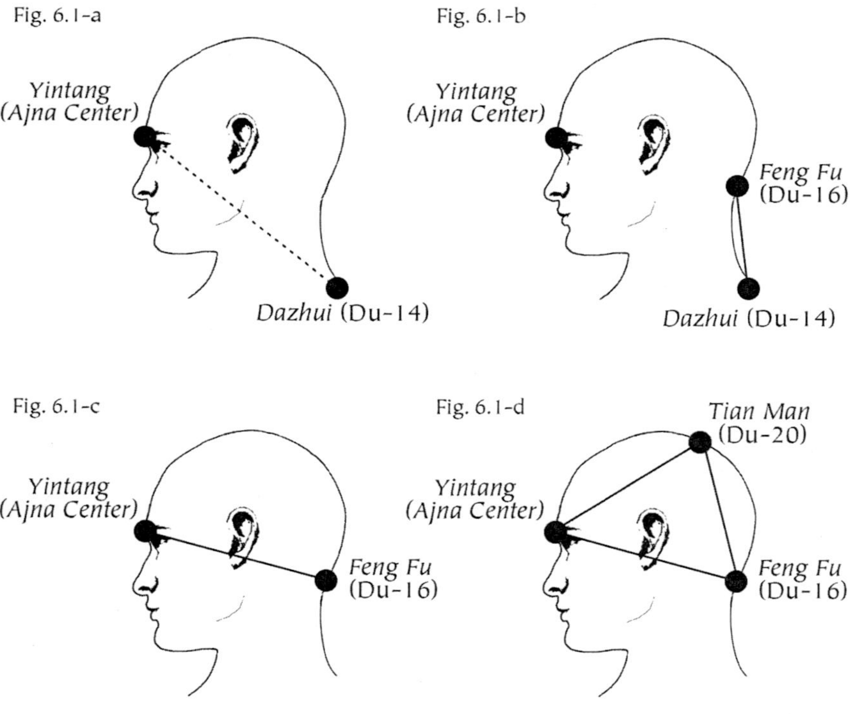


Although a straight line is drawn from *Dazhui* (Du-14) to *Yintang* (Ajna Center) in figure 6.1-a, this particular connection of these two acupuncture sites is not a straight mental linear connection. The connection from *Dazhui* (Du-14) to *Yintang*

(Ajna Center) is a nonlinear communication known as a morphic resonant connection. This is an instantaneous consciousness connection. Since the client is lying in a prone position in this sequence of connections and *Yintang* is not needled. *Yintang* is only activated by this connection. This is a key element in working with the 3-6-1/Six Surrounding the One Grid used in Esoteric Acupuncture.

There is a phrase in Stanza III in ***Sea of Fire-Cosmic Fire: Esoteric Acupuncture, Volume IV*** that stated: "To reveal the Hidden Gateways, you must go through the Mother to fully embrace the Father (Guru) Within." It was stated earlier in this book that the Inner Light without Light of the Ajna Center was the feminine or Mother Frequency. This frequency blended with and complimented the masculine or Father Frequency of the Inner Sound Without Sound hidden within the medulla oblongata. If you are interested in connecting to the male polarity of your inner teacher within (the Guru Chakra), you have to open the higher aspects of the feminine heart. The female principle of Love-Wisdom controls the higher consciousness.

Certain Hindu traditions place the symbolism of the inner light principle of the feminine mother frequencies in a high place of reverence. According to the book ***Babaji and the 18 Siddha Kriya Yoga Tradition,*** the fully self-realized and fully cosmically conscious Saint of Vadalur, Tamil Nadu in southern India, Ramalinga Swamigal, is said to have: "*entreated his listeners to meditate upon the Lord of Light seated in one's heart and pray to the Supreme Grace Light.*" [3] Later Ramalinga Swamigal noticed that his disciples and followers were not listening to his advice to meditate upon the inner light and stated: "*We disclosed the treasure, but no one was willing to have it. We close down.*" [4]

Placing an acupuncture needle in the acupuncture site of *Yintang* may activate the feminine inner light. Placing an acupuncture needle in the "correct" site at *Feng Fu* (Du-16) may activate the hidden Inner Sound without Sound within the medulla oblongata. Notice how we connect the opposite polarities of the Father with the Mother when we make the visual connection from *Feng Fu* (Du-16) at the area of the medulla oblongata to the acupuncture point *Yintang* at the Ajna Center. But, this is not exactly what is meant by "you must go through the Mother to fully embrace the Father." It is not quite enough to merely receive Esoteric Acupuncture treatments. First of all, the recipient of the Esoteric Acupuncture treatment must already be doing sort of inner plane work, whether it is meditating, practicing *qi gong*, doing pranayama (breath work) or any of the higher forms of yoga concentrating on the planes above the dense physical. These practices will assist you to be able to calm the *Shen* of your heart to be able to Still the Mind. This requires strengthening and harmonizing the heart qi of the lower planes. The Inner, Spiritual Higher Heart is the Mother referred to in Stanza III ***of Sea of Fire-Cosmic Fire: Esoteric Acupuncture, Volume IV***. The Mother may include the physical heart and the Anahata (Heart Chakra), but it specifically refers to the Inner Spiritual Higher Heart that holds the vibrations of Light without Light.

When the *Shen* of the heart is vibrating at a certain very high frequency where you are able to Still the Mind, then the hidden Inner Light without Light of the Mother at the Ajna Center and the hidden Inner Sound without Sound of the Father hidden within the medulla oblongata have a opportunity to communicate and interlink as One.

If the above action takes place, then this means that the hidden Jewel within the twelve Lotus Petals of the Heart (also known as the Jewel within the Lotus) has an opportunity to connect and merge with the Jewel immersed within the twelve petals of the Guru Chakra. The Guru Chakra is wrapped underneath the Sahasrara and is not known to most people. The Sahasrara (Crown Chakra) is a higher heart center to the Anahata (Heart Chakra). When the two heart centers are resonating and communicating with similar frequencies, then the twelve petals of the Anahata (Heart Chakra) start to communicate with the twelve petals of the Guru Chakra. At this time, the Guru Chakra may slowly begin to separate from the Sahasrara (Crown Chakra) and start to reveal itself. Eventually the Guru Chakra will completely separate from the Sahasrara (Crown Chakra). This separation is accelerated by the construction of our Antahkarana, our inner antennae.

The phrase in Stanza III in the ***Sea of Fire-Cosmic Fire: Esoteric Acupuncture, Volume IV*** means that we must work on the higher levels of our heart, which is the greater Mother, to allow us the opportunity and ability to connect and merge the Mother aspect of the Ajna Center with the Father aspect at the Taluka Chakra (Lalana Chakra or the Alta Major Center) through *Feng Fu* (Du-16). When the Jewel within the Guru Chakra opens and the Guru Chakra splits from the Sahasrara (Crown Chakra), this signals that we have gone through the greater Mother to embrace the greater Father within the Guru Chakra. We now do not need an outside guru, because we have activated and are utilizing our own guru within.

Whenever there was mention of our Inner Spiritual Higher Heart, this was a reference to the place that houses our Divine Love-Wisdom. Just like "The Truth," Divine Love-Wisdom is singular. The field of Divine Love-Wisdom is available to all.

When we have awakened and are embracing our Inner Spiritual Higher Heart, true goodness, kindness and love unfolds and emanates outward from us. True goodness, kindness and love do not envelope the idea of advantage. You are not being kind or showing goodness with the expectation of receiving something in return, or building up merits or "points" to be redeemed at a later date. The field of Divine Love-Wisdom does not expect anything in return.

Djwhal Khul, through his teachings in the Alice Bailey books, speaks of the Halls of Ignorance. This is the field of consciousness where much of humanity resides. This merely means that most people today are still on the beginning phases of their journey in three-dimensional reality and have not yet realized their individual inner Soul Journey and the Inner Joy, Love-Wisdom that is within each of us but is not yet awakened in most. The masses in this field are ruled by their lower desires and are searching for the objects of their lower chakras' pull. The Halls of Ignorance contains the murky consciousness of the densest Maya that is also known as illusion and glamour. Illusion does not mean non-existent, but rather that what most people strive to obtain in the material world of money or fame and self-recognition are only fleeting objects and fleeting moments. Maya is not the same as working on one's inner planes for inner spiritual growth and wisdom. At the present time, most of humanity is only concerned with either their own individual or group scheme or to a more planetary scheme that only involves physical, emotional or mental pleasures.

Always try to keep your word. The tongue is controlled by the spleen system and the heart system. The heart controls how we vocalize and express our thoughts. The heart also influences the choices of words that we use and what we say. The frequency of how we say something is almost as important as what we say and is controlled by the tongue.

If you are constantly late to an agreed upon meeting with others, you definitely have a blockage in your heart system. I am not talking about occasionally being late because of unforeseen traffic or other unforeseen obstacles that contributed to you being late. I am talking about those who are constantly late. If you cannot keep a commitment after agreeing upon a certain time, this is an indication that you are either deceitful, have little respect for the person you agreed to meet, you have an inflated ego that tells you "everything will start when I arrive" or you cannot tell the truth. It may seem harsh, but if you are constantly late to agreed upon appointments or meetings, you are indeed deceitful and cannot keep your word. In your Soul Journey and your Spirit Journey, it is important to try and keep your word.

As we move inward and begin to awaken our dormant Inner Spiritual Higher Heart, the murkiness and denseness of the old reality begins to lift. This process makes our reality "lighter." We may then begin to change our consciousness to that of a higher plane of reality of sharing and caring for others and understanding our interconnectedness with planet Earth.

It has been mentioned in this book the concept of Energy Consciousness. Energy Consciousness is that consciousness that extends to the most fundamental "things" we are presently aware of, which means particles or waves. Both particles and waves carry information and consciousness. Energy Consciousness includes what is known as Atomic consciousness.

> *"An atom revolves around its axis. In its revolution it comes within the field of activity of other atoms. These it either attracts and swings into its own field of operation, or it repulses and drives them outside its range of activity causing separation. One thing to be borne in mind in the concept of mutual attraction is the preservation of identity in cohesion."* [5]
>
> Djwhal Khul

In ***Sea of Fire-Cosmic Fire: Esoteric Acupuncture, Volume IV*** a phrase was presented:

> *When I don't know who I am, I follow You.*
> *When I know who I am, You and I are One*

It is important for acupuncturists, as a group, as well as all healthcare practitioners to find their puzzle piece in life. Know who you are. When you know who you are and listening to and following your heart, this consciousness, as information, will be passed on to your clientele. When you do not know who you are and are merely working because healthcare is a "nice way to make a living," this information is also being passed onto your clientele. It has been stressed that the practitioners of Esoteric Acupuncture must also become intimately familiar with the visualization of the New Encoding Patterns that are activated on your clientele. This process of visually making the triangular connections activates the energetics of your Inner Spiritual Higher

Heart, as well as that of your client whom you are treating. The visualization process is one method to bring you into alignment with your own Unified Field. You will be in your own Unified Field after the needles have been inserted in any of the New Encoding Patterns of Esoteric Acupuncture. It is the responsibility of your client to retain and maintain his or her individual Unified Field by correct eating, correct mental thoughts and some method to quiet the mental chatter of his or her "monkey mind" to reach that level of inner peace. There are many levels.

When you have gone through your "Mother" (higher heart) to embrace your "Father" (Guru) you are now One with the Universe and on the same level as all your teachers, masters and gurus that you have followed and admired. Going through your Mother means awakening to your Inner Spiritual Higher Heart. Embracing your Father means that the petals of your Anahata have fully opened and the Jewel Within the Lotus of your heart has embraced the Jewel Within the twelve opened petals of your Guru Chakra. You have connected your Higher Twin Flames Within. You now know your puzzle piece in life and are unfolding the various levels within your puzzle piece as you continue on your individual Inner Spiritual Journey. You have risen from your individual Soul Journey to your true Inner Spiritual Journey.

Unless you find your puzzle piece in life (your heart journey) and are on that journey, you will always give out more qi (scatter more qi) than you will receive or gain. Think about this. No matter what job you have or how much money you make, or no matter what partner you are with unless you have found your puzzle piece in life, all those situations will take more qi out of you. The opposing and complementing energies are fear from the kidney system and love from the heart system. Money is only energy connected to the Swadthisthana Chakra that also controls fear. At some point toward the end of your life, you may question yourself about the meaning of life and how you lived your life. Finding your true puzzle piece means that you opened your heart and listened to that inner voice within. Your heart and inner love will give you all the qi you require. When you are living your puzzle piece of life, then work and play become very close. The energies of the kidneys that control working and fear become very close to the energies of the heart that controls playing and love. At that moment your whole life changes.

I am hoping that the Ageless Wisdom Teachings in this book and the other books in the Esoteric Acupuncture series will inspire and trigger your innate spiritual quest to discover your puzzle piece in this lifetime. Find your inner health, your inner strength and your field of inner Love-Wisdom. My intention is not to merely present interesting ideas and concepts to be intellectually analyzed, discussed, dissected and debated for purely academic jousting among scholars or students of the Esoteric Ageless Wisdom Schools. I have tried to integrate the Ageless Wisdom Teachings in a way that has a practical application, as well as being an intellectual stimulus. The Ageless Wisdom Teachings presented in the Esoteric Acupuncture series are preserved and presented in a slightly different light to better align with, and be of use in the 21$^{st}$ Century. These works are presented to hopefully assist you in your own individual journey in life to uplift humanity and the Earth in our present evolution as a group body.

Your choices in life and everything you do should revolve around your heart and higher heart fields. It was mentioned earlier that the tongue has two main energy fields, the spleen of Earth and the heart of the fire element. When your heart is in control of what you choose to consume and not the Earth energies of the stomach and spleen, then you can no longer put things into your system that may be detrimental to you or to others. When your heart controls your tongue, you will not speak badly about others and will be very aware of the tone of your voice and how you choose to language your expressions and thoughts to others. You do not gossip and do not listen to gossip.

Also, the liver system must not be in control of your life. In Traditional Chinese Medicine, the liver and liver system allow qi to flow smoothly throughout the acupuncture channels and the very minute meridians and connecting channels. The key word is "allow" the qi to flow. The heart and heart system must take the lead role as being in charge. We have presented the concept of the *Hun* follow the *Shen* and how the Original *Hun* is an offshoot from the Original *Shen*. This means that the proper order of a heart-based individual is that the heart is the most prevailing energy field of that person.

> *Hun must follow the inspiration of the spirit (shen)....But, in order to conform to the original true and authentic life, the hun has to conform to the initiative of the shen.*[6]

> *You are the hope you have been waiting for.*
> *You are the solution for a better planet and a better life.*
> *Let your Higher Shen shine brightly.*

I suggest regular Esoteric Acupuncture treatments of one session every three weeks (exactly twenty one days apart) or one treatment per month. Most of my clientele come once a month. For practitioners choosing to treat others with Esoteric Acupuncture, be very aware of the emotional and mental state of your client. Do not treat heavily fear-based people with an Esoteric Acupuncture treatment. These treatments move energy very quickly and may exacerbate your client's fear. Also use caution with those on high blood pressure medications and psychotropic drugs.

Repeated Esoteric Acupuncture treatments are designed to strengthen the memory of your individualized Unified Field to make it easier to return to your center, the field of your Inner Spiritual Higher Heart and your Higher *Shen*.

Do not be envious of others and merely strive to be like someone else. There is a saying: "The grass is always greener on the other side of the fence." I have added: "until you get there and find the grass is astro turf." Things that other people possess are not always what they appear to be to an outsider. Find your own path. Discern the quiet whisper in your heart. Follow the inner yearning of your own heart. You will then know your true puzzle piece in life. This is the purpose of Esoteric Acupuncture—to assist you in awakening to the journey of your Inner Spiritual Path. Know yourself. Be true to yourself.

*"You were born an original. Don't die a copy."*

author unknown

*"Zen is the stream of life. We enter Zen when we let go of everything. Like the mind of a newborn infant who comes in with a clean slate without the taint of education and socialization, we can flow with whatever is. Zen is a practice of non-grasping, non-rejecting."*

Jikun Kathleen Sankey, O.M.D., L.Ac.

A portion of my own inner journey has been to unravel the deeper esoteric Truths and Wisdom to share with those who gravitate toward this field. My search for The Truth has always led me to seek the most fundamental source, or the beginning source for anything I was trying to understand. It has been stated that in our known universe, the only constants are particles and waves. Waves came first. Waves are consciousness. It may be a goal for some to discover their own Original *Shen* and Original Consciousness, our fundamental starting points. This book may serve as a guideline on that quest.

Be in the moment. No regrets. No looking backwards.

Namaste,
Still I Seek
With Much Love,
Mikio

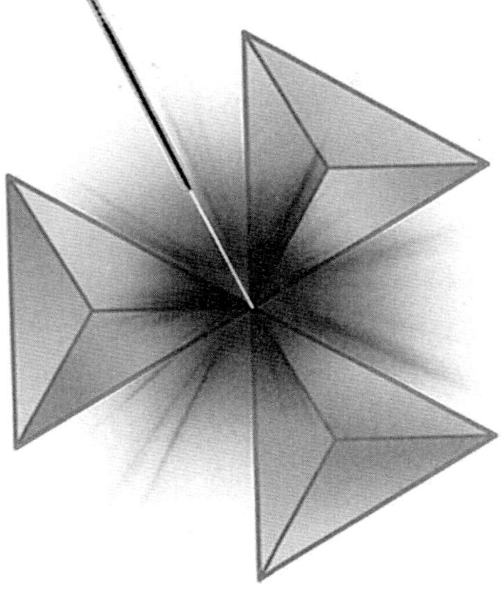

**Addendum:** The *Wei Qi* Grid Strengthening Pattern

Up until this point, I have been very reluctant to introduce to the acupuncture community of the United States the concept of how to protect oneself from psychic attacks. Students attending acupuncture schools today in the United States are not really taught much energy healing, especially in the world of the shamans, curanderos, sangomas, santerias and the other Nature-Earthly realms.

Most acupuncture schools in the United States teach the very simplest, most basic concepts of acupuncture and are much more concerned with Chinese herbs and internal medicine utilizing the diagnostic protocols from a traditional Asian herbal perspective. Also, the acupuncture schools today, at least the schools in California, are being heavily influenced and shaped by the western, allopathic role model.

In Traditional Chinese Medical thought in the United States today, the idea of an exogenous pathogenic attack by a non-physical force is either dismissed by the majority of practitioners as old fashioned and superstitious, a figment of one's imagination or that the practitioner should recommend that the client seek an immediate psychiatric evaluation. The more expansive minded healthcare professionals who have a background in Traditional Chinese Medicine may explain these unseen exogenous energetic attacks as an attack by Evil Qi.

Although I have taught the Advanced Energy Healers in Australia for the past several years one variation of the Psychic Grid Protection Pattern, I have only taught a couple of very small advanced groups here in the United States about protection from psychic attacks. The Advanced Energy Healers in Australia, as a group, seem to be more open to "true" energy healing and understand events outside of the ordinary physical or emotional realms that may challenge one's well being. Although the majority of licensed acupuncturists may seem to be very conservative in their scope of understanding of energy and exogenous energy attacks, the acupuncturists who attend my advanced Esoteric Acupuncture workshops are much more open to ideas outside the limiting box of traditional academia.

The *Wei Qi* Grid Strengthening Pattern is designed to activate and strengthen the "crystalline" sites on the posterior of the body. In my experience with clientele who have had psychic attacks, most of the tears, cords and hooks are seen on the posterior side of the body on the astral level. Astral debris, energy blockages or other astral objects attached to the body are seen on both the anterior and posterior of the body. Tears in the fabric of space, on the astral plane, are different than the tears in the fabric of the higher, compacted dimensional planes, such as the tears in the Calabi-Yau compacted multi-dimensions that are quite normal in those realms. The astral tears on people are also different from qi leakages. Astral tears are the results from an outside force. Qi leakage is due to one's own weakened systems, usually the lung system and the kidney system. The most common areas of attack that I have seen are the posterior areas of the body on the regions of heart/pericardium region, the head, the neck and the lower kidney regions. Once in awhile I may see an attack on the anterior of the body, but mostly I see the attacks from the posterior of the body. Dark energy attacks may occur when a person has a weak or weakened kidney qi that pulls energy from one's spiritual heart. The kidney system controls our sexual qi. Negative entities and Evil Qi have an opportunity to attack those who have a weakened second chakra field (sexual field) and may attack those who are holding onto to one of the many tentacles of fear such as: anger, hatred, jealousy, envy, sadness, regrets, unworthiness, lack of self esteem, excessive worrying and other similar vibrations. The last four acupuncture sites in the *Wei Qi* Grid Strengthening Pattern are the designed to strengthen the kidney qi and to tie in the kidney system with the crystalline grid sites on the posterior of the body. The upper *jiao* (upper chest region) houses the physical heart and the physical lungs. The lungs (also the large intestines) are responsible for building and maintaining our protective qi known as the *Wei Qi*. The

*Wei Qi* system is contained within the etheric planes. When a weakened kidney system pulls qi from both the heart and lung systems, this will create a weakened *Wei Qi* barrier. Exogenous attacks, whether the source is pathogenic, from cold, wind, heat or other more physical sources, or from an unseen source on the lower fourth dimensional planes, cannot usually invade a person's physical, emotional (astral) or mental planes, if the etheric planes of the *Wei Qi* barrier are strong. The grid of the *Wei Qi* Grid Strengthening Pattern is designed to strengthen the etheric levels in a specific gridding and protective network system.

The *Wei Qi* Grid Strengthening Pattern is divided into three sections for ease in remembering the needling sequence. The first section contains the same twenty-one acupuncture points and the same needling sequence as the Esoteric *Shaoyin* Heart Window Pattern. The second section of the *Wei Qi* Strengthening Grid Pattern has six acupuncture sites that, when needled, will activate and strengthen one's crystalline sites and link the connections of these sites together with the sites of the Esoteric *Shaoyin* Heart Window Pattern that have already been activated. Again, these six acupuncture points of the second section must be needled in a very specific sequence. The third and last section of the *Wei Qi* Grid Strengthening Pattern consists of four acupuncture points that reinforce the kidney qi and must also be needled in a very specific sequence.

For the *Wei Qi* Grid Strengthening Pattern, have your client make the triangular visual connections with the first twenty-one acupuncture sites of the Esoteric *Shaoyin* Heart Window Pattern. Refer back to that pattern for the visualization instructions. After the twenty-one acupuncture sites of the Esoteric *Shaoyin* Heart Window Pattern have been visually connection (gridded), let your client relax. The last ten acupuncture sites will automatically connect and grid up your client's field and strengthen his or her protective barrier. The practitioner must insert the needles in the specific order given in this book.

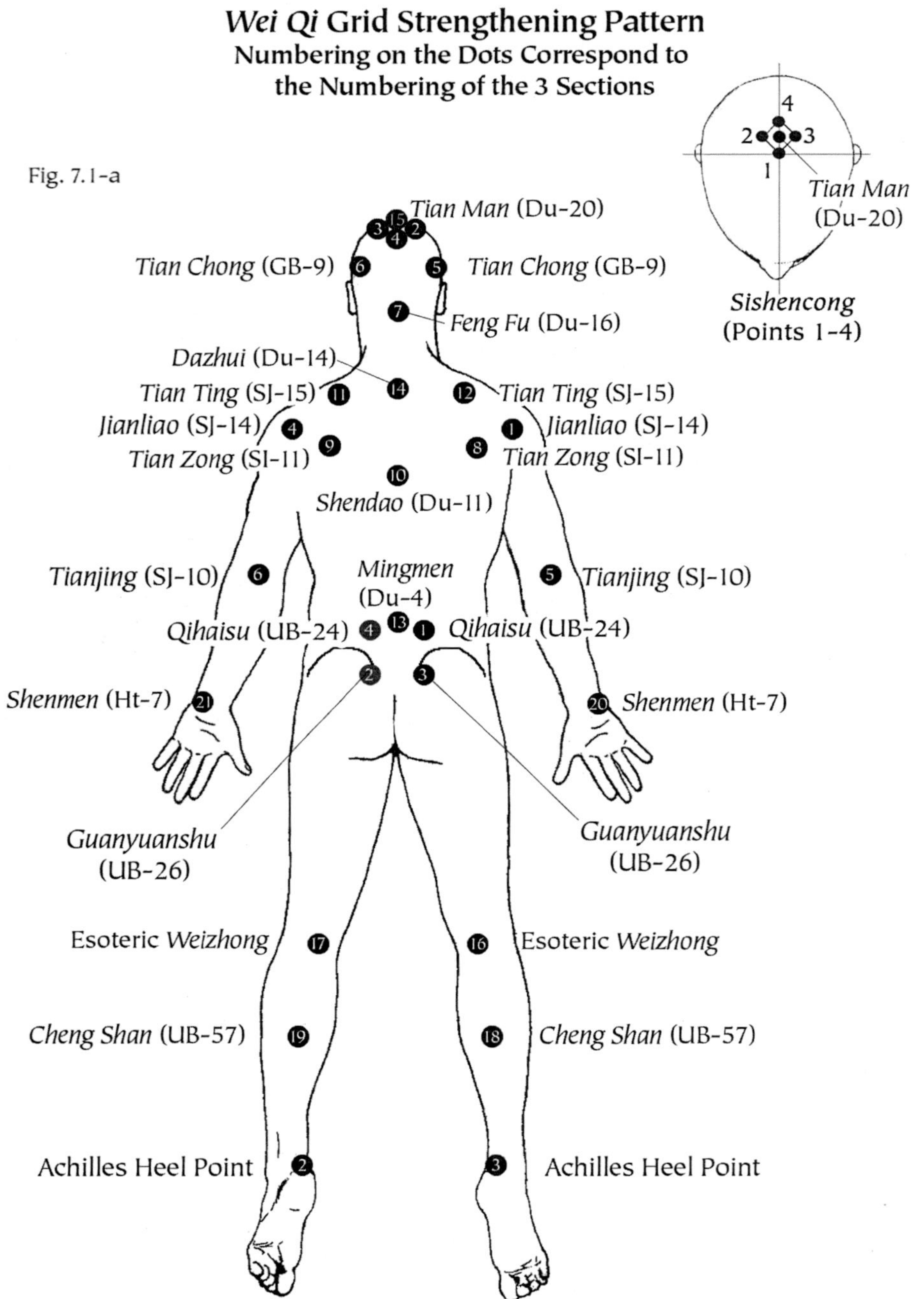
*Wei Qi* Grid Strengthening Pattern
Numbering on the Dots Correspond to
the Numbering of the 3 Sections
Fig. 7.1-a
*Tian Man* (Du-20)
*Tian Chong* (GB-9)
*Tian Chong* (GB-9)
*Feng Fu* (Du-16)
*Dazhui* (Du-14)
*Tian Ting* (SJ-15)
*Tian Ting* (SJ-15)
*Jianliao* (SJ-14)
*Jianliao* (SJ-14)
*Tian Zong* (SI-11)
*Tian Zong* (SI-11)
*Shendao* (Du-11)
*Tianjing* (SJ-10)
*Mingmen* (Du-4)
*Tianjing* (SJ-10)
*Qihaisu* (UB-24)
*Qihaisu* (UB-24)
*Shenmen* (Ht-7)
*Shenmen* (Ht-7)
*Guanyuanshu* (UB-26)
*Guanyuanshu* (UB-26)
Esoteric *Weizhong*
Esoteric *Weizhong*
*Cheng Shan* (UB-57)
*Cheng Shan* (UB-57)
Achilles Heel Point
Achilles Heel Point
*Tian Man* (Du-20)
*Sishencong* (Points 1-4)

## *Wei Qi* Grid Strengthening Pattern
### First Section with Points

Fig. 7.1-b

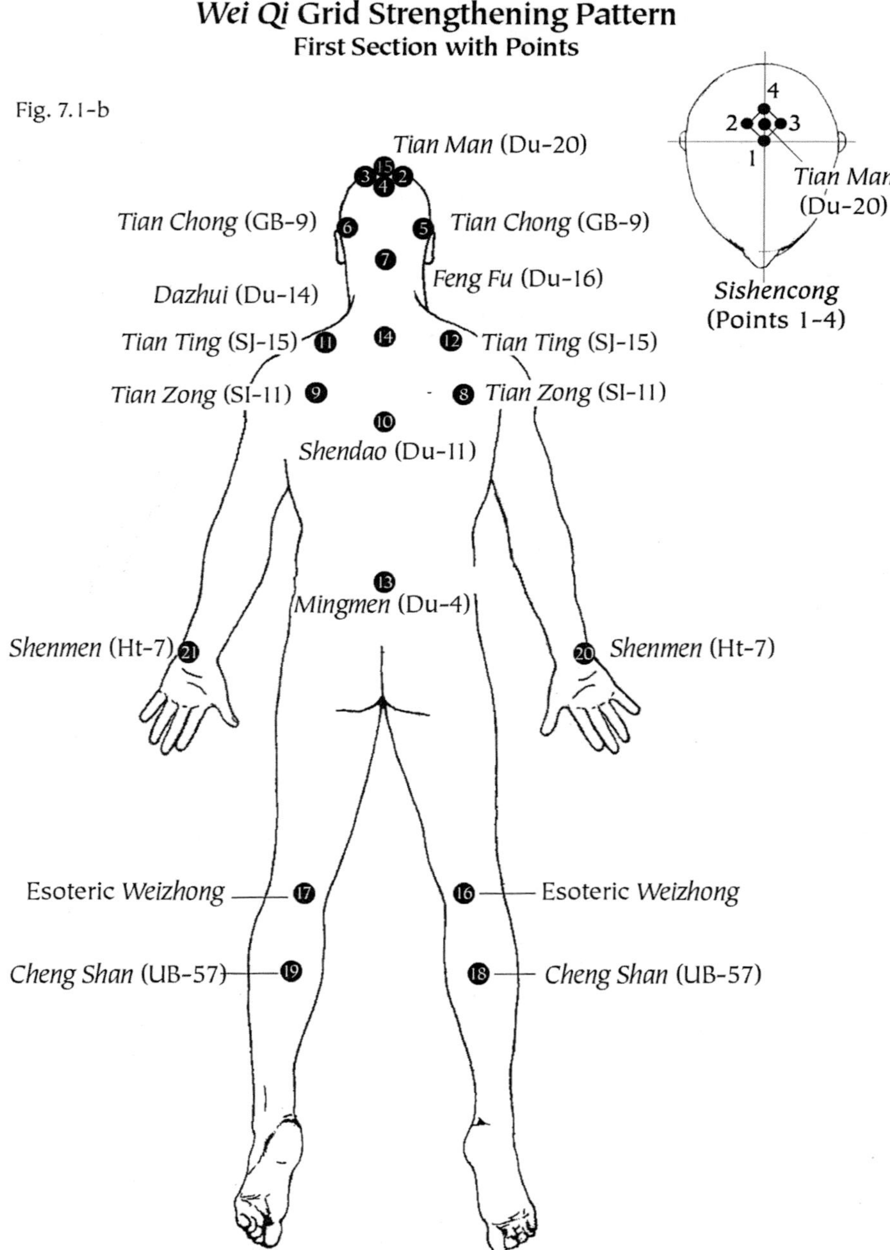

## *Wei Qi* Grid Strengthening Pattern
### First Section with Grid

Fig. 7.1-c

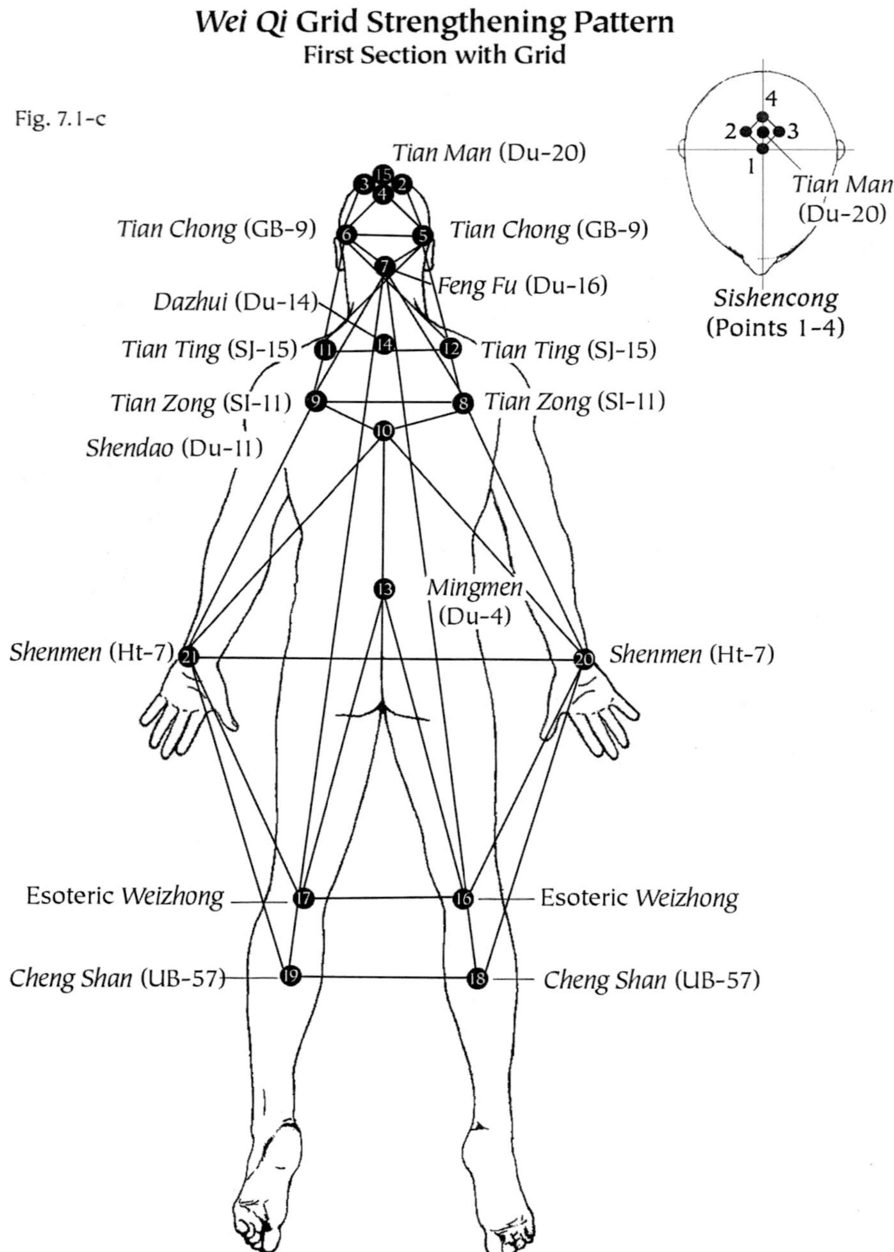

## *Wei Qi* Grid Strengthening Pattern
### Second Section with Points
### No Visualizations

Fig. 7.1-d

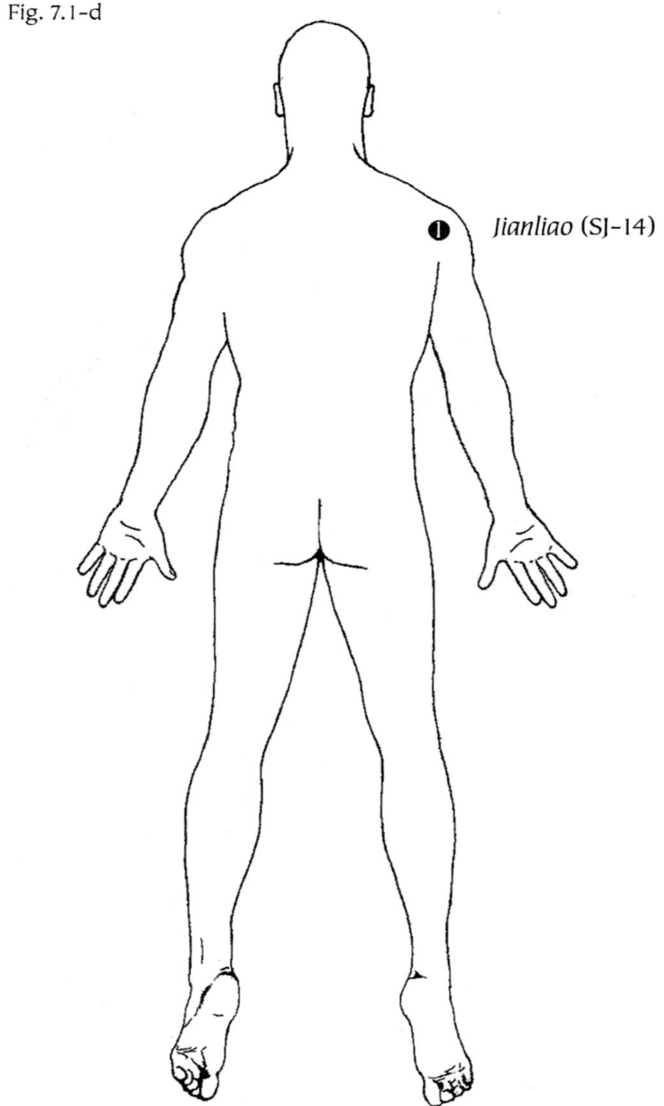

## *Wei Qi* Grid Strengthening Pattern
### Second Section with Points
### No Visualizations

Fig. 7.1-e

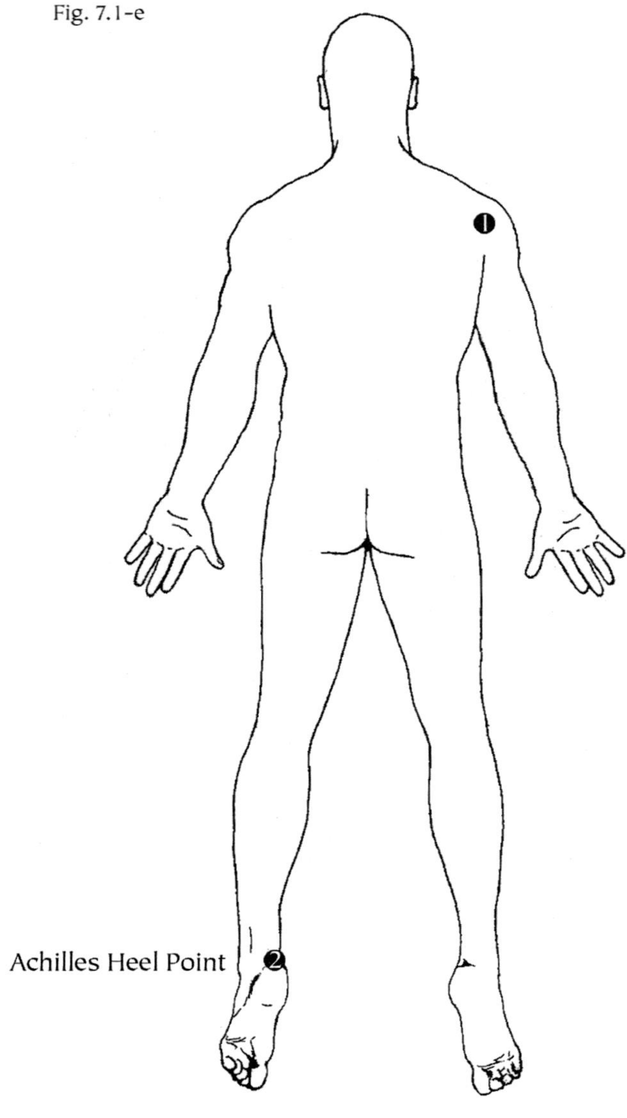

## *Wei Qi* Grid Strengthening Pattern
### Second Section with Points
### No Visualizations

Fig. 7.1-f

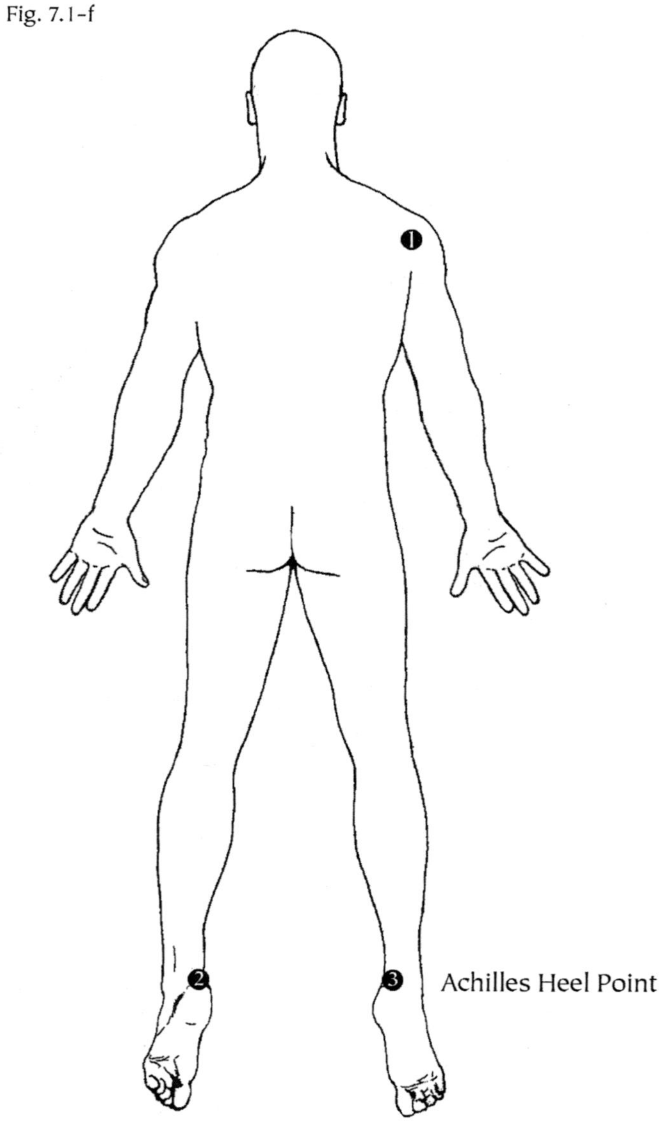

## *Wei Qi* Grid Strengthening Pattern
### Second Section with Points
### No Visualizations

Fig. 7.1-g

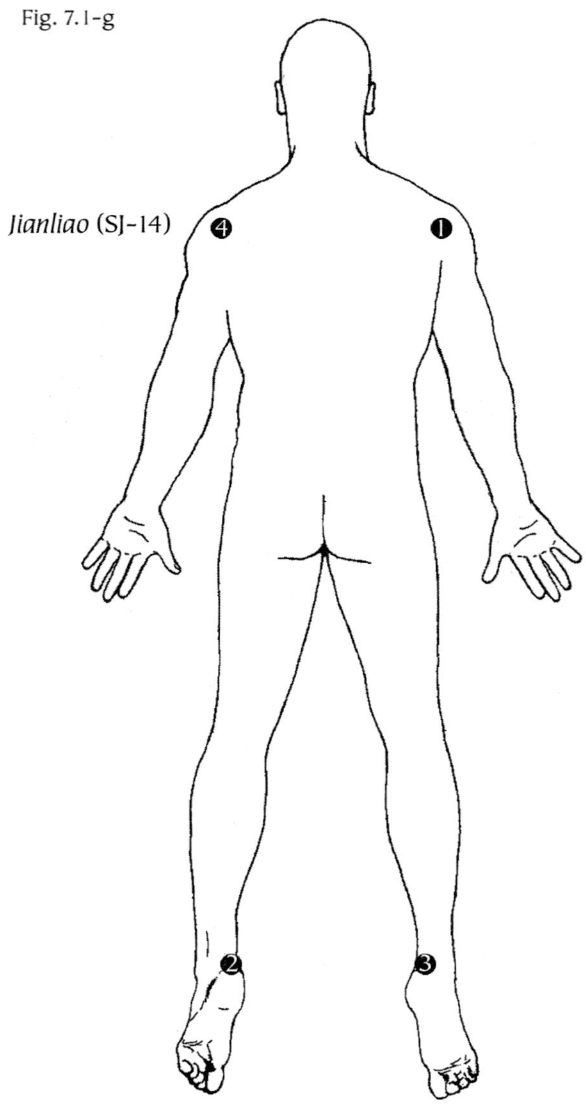

## *Wei Qi* Grid Strengthening Pattern
### Second Section with Points
### No Visualizations

Fig. 7.1-h

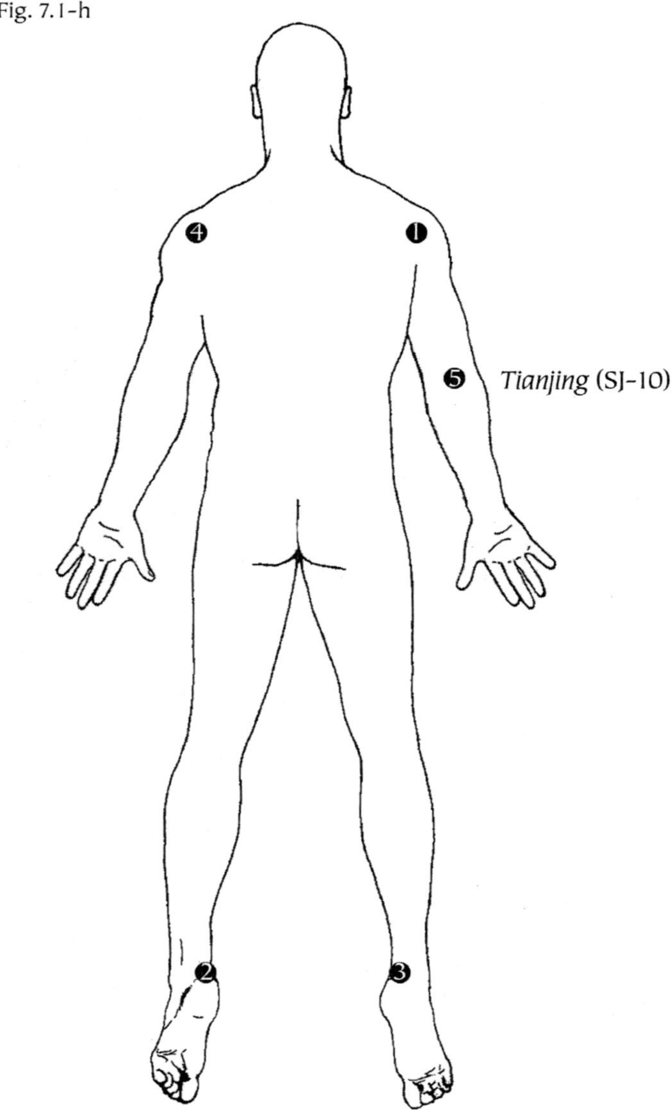

## *Wei Qi* Grid Strengthening Pattern
### Second Section with Points
### No Visualizations

Fig. 7.1-i

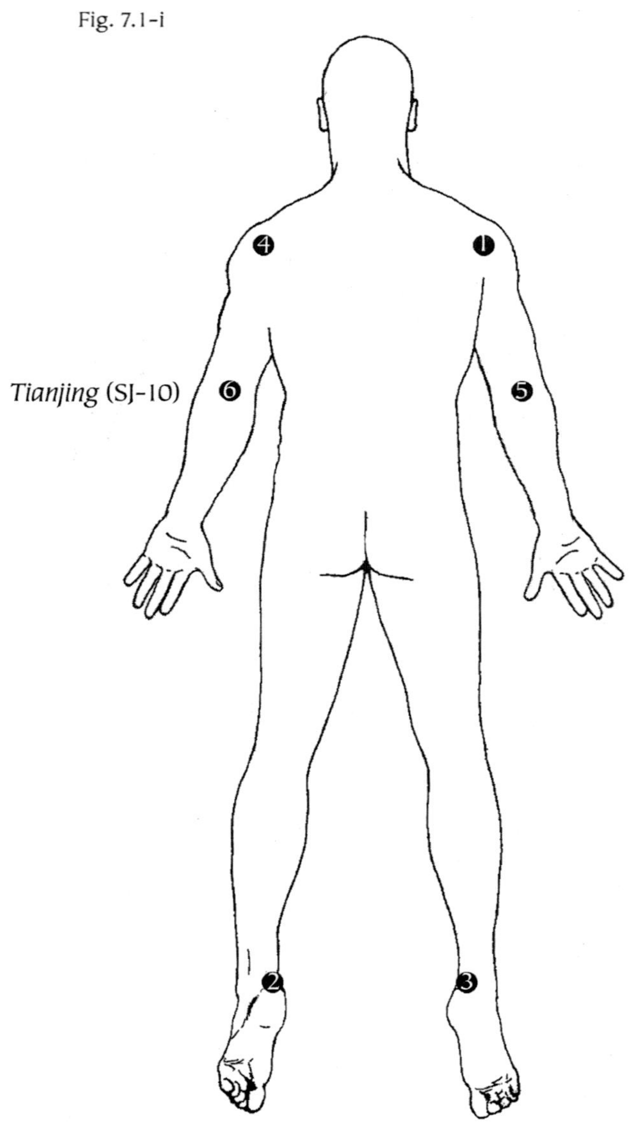

## *Wei Qi* Grid Strengthening Pattern
### Second Section with Grid
### No Visualizations

Fig. 7.1-j

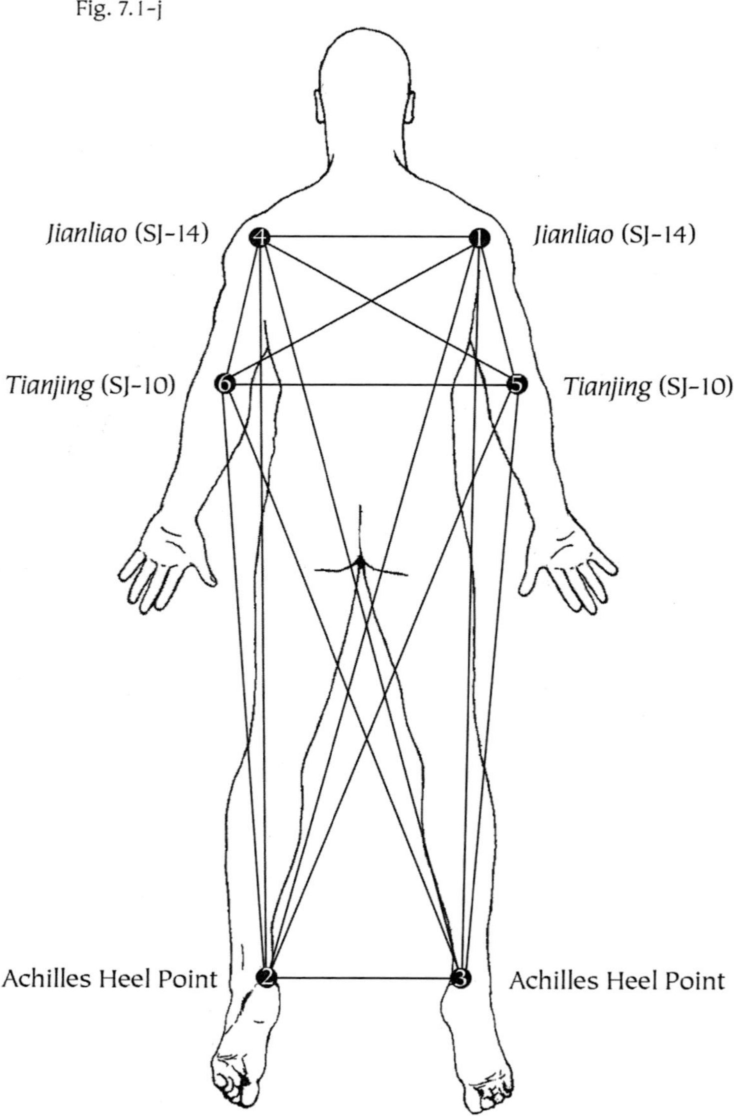

## *Wei Qi* Grid Strengthening Pattern
### Third Section with Points
### No Visualizations

Fig. 7.1-k

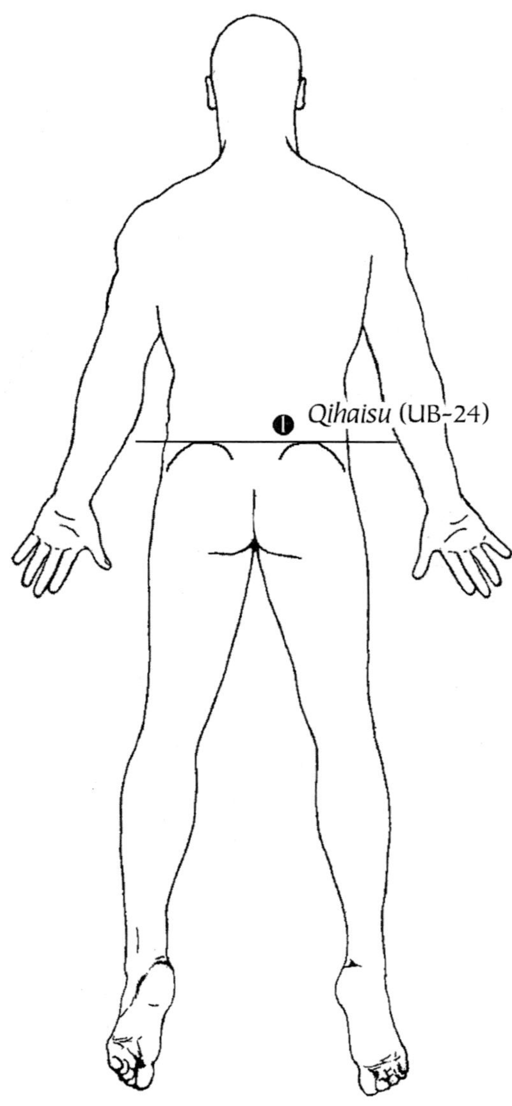

## *Wei Qi* Grid Strengthening Pattern
### Third Section with Points
### No Visualizations

Fig. 7.1-l

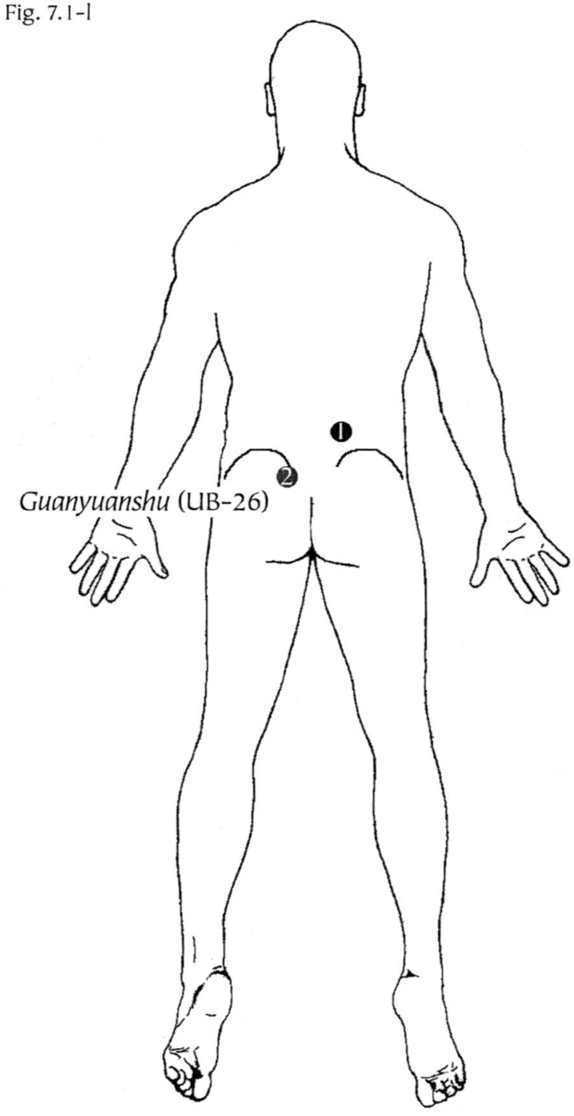

## *Wei Qi* Grid Strengthening Pattern
## Third Section with Points
### No Visualizations

Fig. 7.1-m

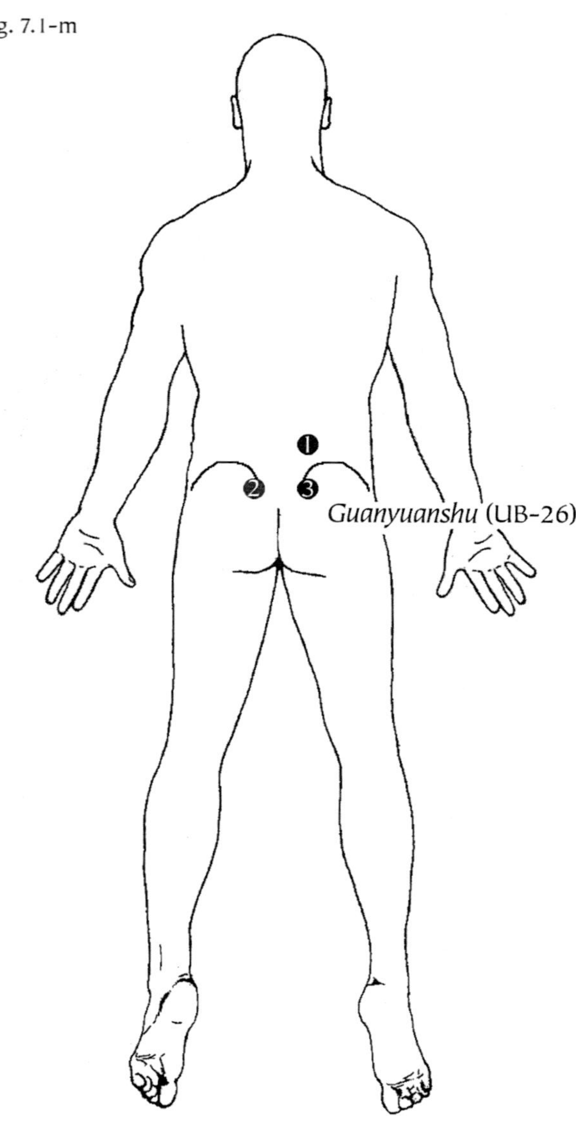

## *Wei Qi* Grid Strengthening Pattern
### Third Section with Points

Fig. 7.1-n

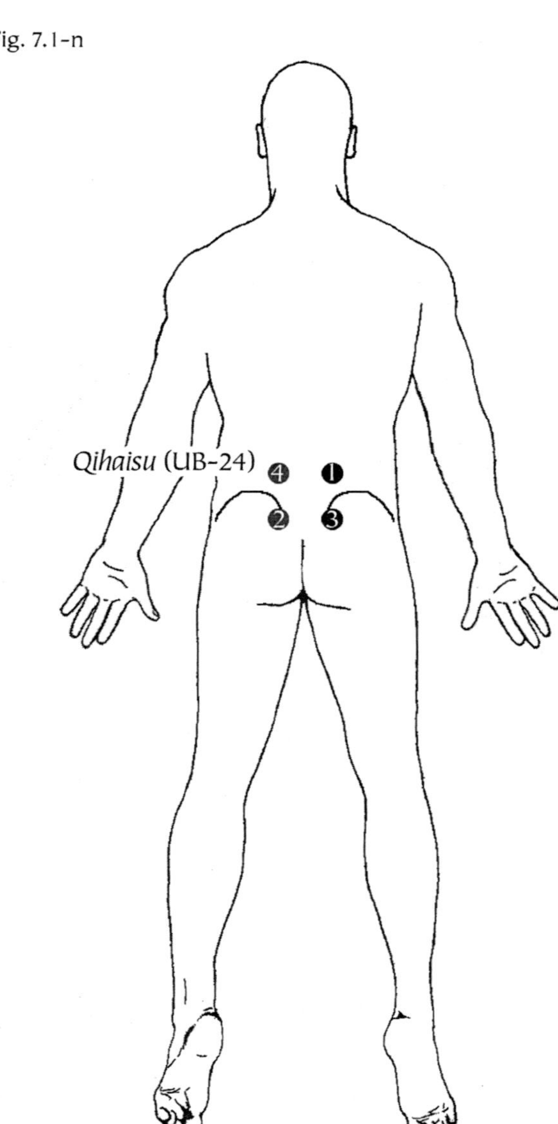

## *Wei Qi* Grid Strengthening Pattern
### Third Section with Grid
### No Visualizations

Fig. 7.1-o

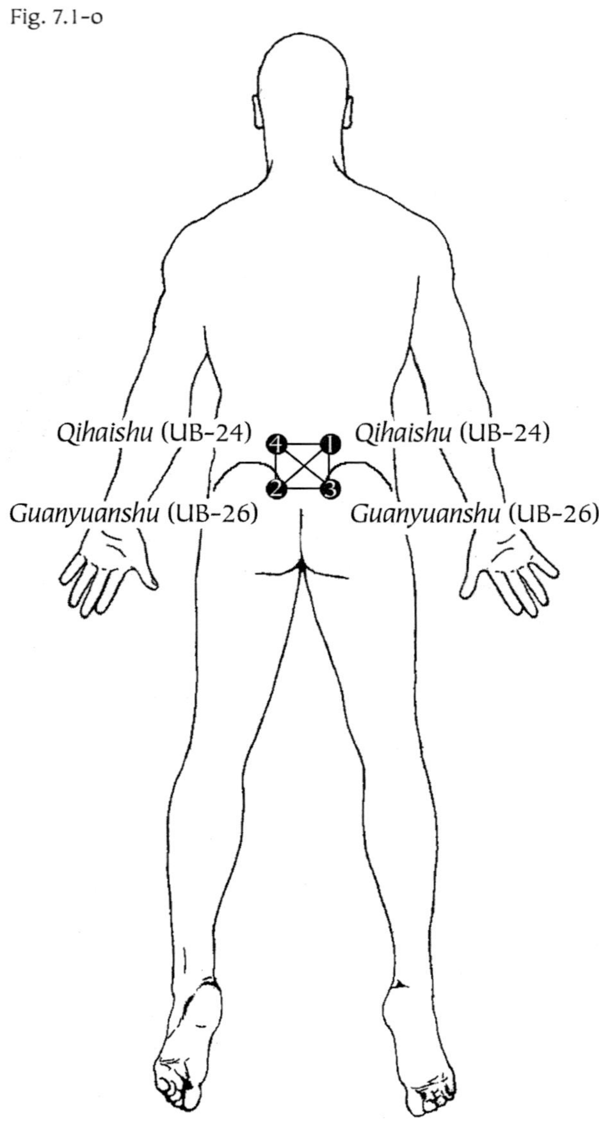

## *Wei Qi* Grid Strengthening Pattern
### Complete Grid

Fig. 7.1-p

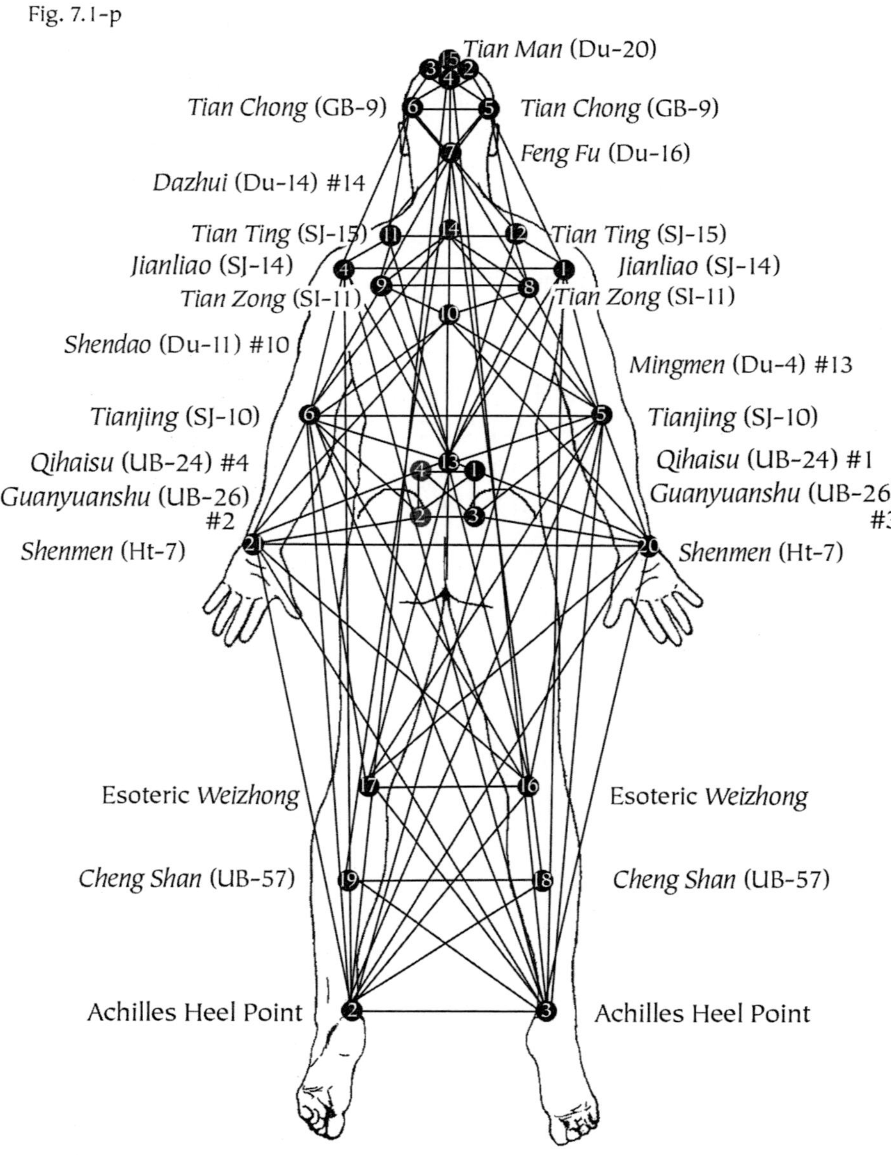

You will notice that the complete grid diagrams at the very end of all the posterior New Encoding Patterns in Chapter V and in the Addendum had a more complete grid than the visualization connections given as the guideline for the practitioner. There were some grid connections that were not mentioned in the visualization sections, but were connected in the complete grid diagrams. Those connections that were not visually connected will automatically form and complete the grid for each of those New Encoding Patterns.

The first acupuncture site needled in the second section of the *Wei Qi* Protection Grid Pattern is *Jianliao* (SJ-14) on the client's right posterior shoulder. *Jianliao* (SJ-14) is found at the lateral extremity of the acromion in a slight depression that is more pronounced when the client abducts his or her right arm. The depression is posterior and inferior to the lateral end of the acromion. The practitioner will make the visual triangular connections, instead of the client. After receiving the twenty-one needles in section one, the client will be so relaxed that he or she will most likely not be able to consciously make the intricate visualization connections. You will also notice that the last figure with the complete grid has more connections than the practitioner was asked to visualize. Those extra grid connections will automatically form after the acupuncture needles have been inserted in the proper sequencing.

The second acupuncture needle inserted is placed in the site located directly on the client's left heel and in alignment with the Achilles tendon. The acupuncture site is on the heel where the smoother skin of the foot touches the rougher skin of the heel. This acupuncture point and the next point are both called the Achilles Heel Points. On the earlier Psychic Protection Grid Patterns, I used to insert an acupuncture needle in the esoteric site of the Ki-1 point called *Dichong* ("Earth's Thoroughfare") in Esoteric Acupuncture. The location where the acupuncture needle is inserted in the esoteric *Dichong* (Ki-1) point is closer to the toes than the location of the traditional Ki-1 point known as *Yongquan*. (For diagrams of the locations of the acupuncture site of *Dichong* versus the site of *Yonguan*, see Chapter V page 497.) After working with Evil Qi (psychic) attacks for several years, the bilateral *Dichong* (Ki-1) points were changed to the bilateral Achilles Heel Points. According to ***Webster's Third New International Unabridged Dictionary***, the definition of an Achilles heel means "a point of vulnerability or weakness." [1] Be aware that for those who have experienced or are presently experiencing psychic energy attacks that drain the body of qi and prana, the Evil Qi will penetrate the person's weakest area(s) first. So we are closing up any vulnerable areas by including the bilateral Achilles Heel Points in the *Wei Qi* Grid Strengthening Pattern.

The bilateral Achilles Heel Points are often very sensitive on most clientele. I will rub the heel at the site of this point prior to inserting an acupuncture needle and tell the client that there may be some sensation when the needles are inserted at these two sites. Although I usually do not use guide tubes when inserting acupuncture needles, if the client has tough skin on the heel, I may use a guide tube on the heel points. I use Seirin Laser needles .20 mm X 30 mm in length with a straight, firm horizontal insertion with no twisting or thrusting in and out.

The third acupuncture needle inserted in this second section of the *Wei Qi* Protection Grid Pattern is the Achilles Heel Point on the client's right heel. The acupuncture site is on the heel in alignment with the client's Achilles' tendon

The fourth acupuncture site needled in this section of the *Wei Qi* Protection Grid is *Jianliao* (SJ-14). (See figure 7.1g.) As you are inserting the needles, make sure you are mentally connecting these four points in an hourglass shaped configuration. Start with the first point on the right shoulder and crisscross the energy downward to the Achilles Heel Point on the client's left heel. Connect the qi on the left heel to the qi at the site of the right Achilles Heel Point. Next bring the qi upward in a crisscross fashion from the right Achilles Heel Point to the left *Jianliao* (SJ-14) point. Now connect the left *Jianliao* (SJ-14) point to the *Jianliao* (SJ-14) point on the right shoulder to complete the hourglass configuration for these first four acupuncture sites in the second section of the *Wei Qi* Grid Strengthening Pattern.

The fifth and sixth acupuncture sites needled in this second section of the *Wei Qi* Protection Pattern are the bilateral *Tianjing* (SJ-10) points known as "Celestial Well" or "Heavenly well" points. In Esoteric Acupuncture, these bilateral points are considered to be acupuncture sites that reinforce the qi of one's higher heart. They are thought of as supplemental heart points. The bilateral *Tianjing* (SJ-10) points are found proximal to the olecranon in a slight depression when the elbow is flexed. This means that the point is found above the elbow in the posterior of the arm in the depression that is closer to the armpit and farther from the fingers. The right acupuncture site is needled first, followed by needling the acupuncture site on the posterior of the left elbow. As you insert an acupuncture needle in the site of the right *Tianjing* (SJ-10) point, visually crisscross the qi upward to connect with the acupuncture site of *Jianliao* (SJ-14) on your client's left shoulder. Next move the qi at the site of the left *Jianliao* (SJ-14) point horizontally across to connect with the qi at the acupuncture site of *Jianliao* (SJ-14) on your client's right shoulder. From this acupuncture site on the right shoulder, crisscross the qi downward to connect to the qi of the left *Tianjing* (SJ-10) point. The last visual connection in the second section is to move the qi horizontally from the acupuncture site of the left *Tianjing* (SJ-10) site to connect with the qi at acupuncture site of *Tianjing* (SJ-10) on the client's right elbow.

The last four acupuncture points in the *Wei Qi* Protection Grid Pattern are the bilateral *Qihaishu* (UB-24) and the bilateral *Guanyuanshu* (UB-26) points. These four acupuncture sites are needled in a crisscross, hourglass shaped configuration starting with the *Qihaishu* (UB-24) point on the client's right side.

The first acupuncture site activated in the third section of the *Wei Qi* Protection Grid Pattern is *Qihaishu* (UB-24) on the client's right side. *Qihaishu* (UB-24) is found at the acupuncture site that is horizontally level with the lower border of the spinous process of the third lumbar vertebra and located directly on the inner bladder line that is approximately one and a half *cun* lateral from the center of the spine. You can insert the needle at the site of *Qihaishu* (UB-24) horizontally to a depth of approximately 20 mm or slightly more. (See figure 7.1-k.)

The second acupuncture site activated in this section is the *Guanyuanshu* (UB-26) point located on the client's left side and level with the lower border of the spinous process of the fifth lumbar vertebra. Again, you can insert the acupuncture needle horizontally into that acupuncture site to a depth of approximately 20 mm or slightly more. (See figure 7.1-l.) As you are inserting the acupuncture needle or using another method to activate the energy at that site, make sure you visually make the connection from the *Qihaishu* (UB-24) point on the right side and connect this energy with the qi at the acupuncture site of *Guanyuanshu* (UB-26) on the left side.

The third acupuncture site needled in the third section is the *Guanyuanshu* (UB-26) point located on the client's right side. As you are inserting an acupuncture needle into this site, move the qi from the *Guanyuanshu* (UB-26) point on the client's left side horizontally to connect with the energies at the site of *Guanyuanshu* (UB-26) point located on the client's right side.

The last acupuncture site in the *Wei Qi* Grid Strengthening Pattern is *Qihaishu* (UB-24) on the client's left side. As you are inserting a needle into this site, bring the qi upward in a crisscross fashion from the *Guanyuanshu* (UB-26) point located on the client's right side to connect with *Qihaishu* on the left side. The last connection in this third section of the *Wei Qi* Grid Strengthening Pattern is to move the qi horizontally across from the acupuncture site of *Qihaishu* (UB-24) on the client's left side to the acupuncture site of *Qihaishu* (UB-24) on the right side.

## Extended Crystalline Heart Grid Pattern
### Anterior Pattern for *Wei* Qi Attack

Fig 7.2

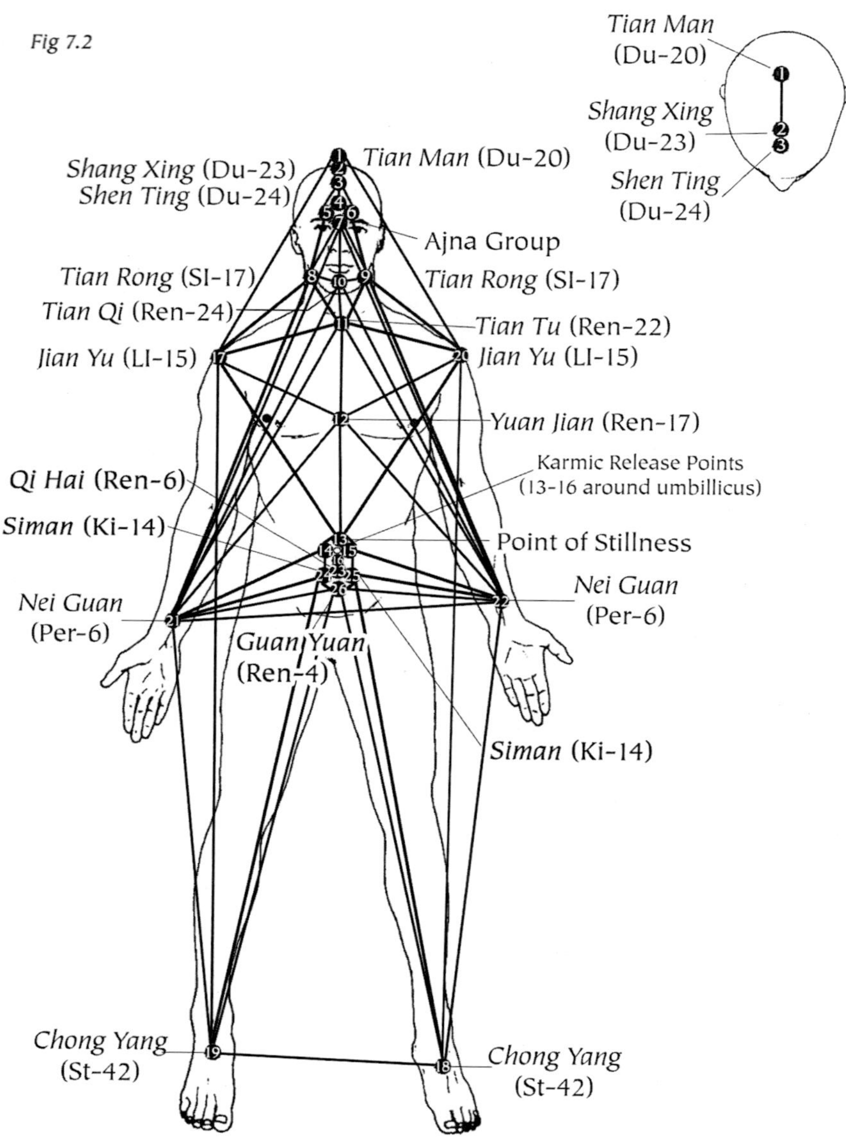

### Extended Crystalline Heart Grid Pattern

For an individual who may need protection from an exogenous non-physical attack, known as an attack by Evil Qi, the Extended Crystalline Heart Grid Pattern is the recommended anterior pattern to use after a posterior treatment with the *Wei Qi* Grid Strengthening Pattern. You are reinforcing the qi at the anterior crystalline points. Since the grid connections from all the acupuncture sites that were needled will form automatically as shown in figure 7.2, no visual connections are needed.

For the point location of the acupuncture sites in the Extended Crystalline Heart Grid Pattern, first go to that same pattern in Chapter V. Then use the last four acupuncture points of the *Siman* Fourfold Window Group that is discussed in Chapter II. The last four *Siman* Fourfold Fullness Window points protect the Lower Cinnabar Field that activates the Swadthisthana, the second chakra.

It is important to note that Most Evil Qi attacks will occur because the client has very low energy in the Anahata, the heart field of love compared to a heavy imbalance in the sexual kidney field of fear. In the field of Esoteric *Shaoyin*, the client must work on the heart field and strengthen all the branches extending from love. Those who have been constantly attacked by external Evil QI must learn to transmute the fear energy of the victim mentality to a place of strength from the heart. Although the two New Encoding Patterns given here will help those who are experiencing Evil Qi attacks or want to prevent being drained and controlled by outside forces, the person must still do much inner plane work.

## The Wind Mansion Pattern
### That Which Has No Form

Fig. 7.3-a

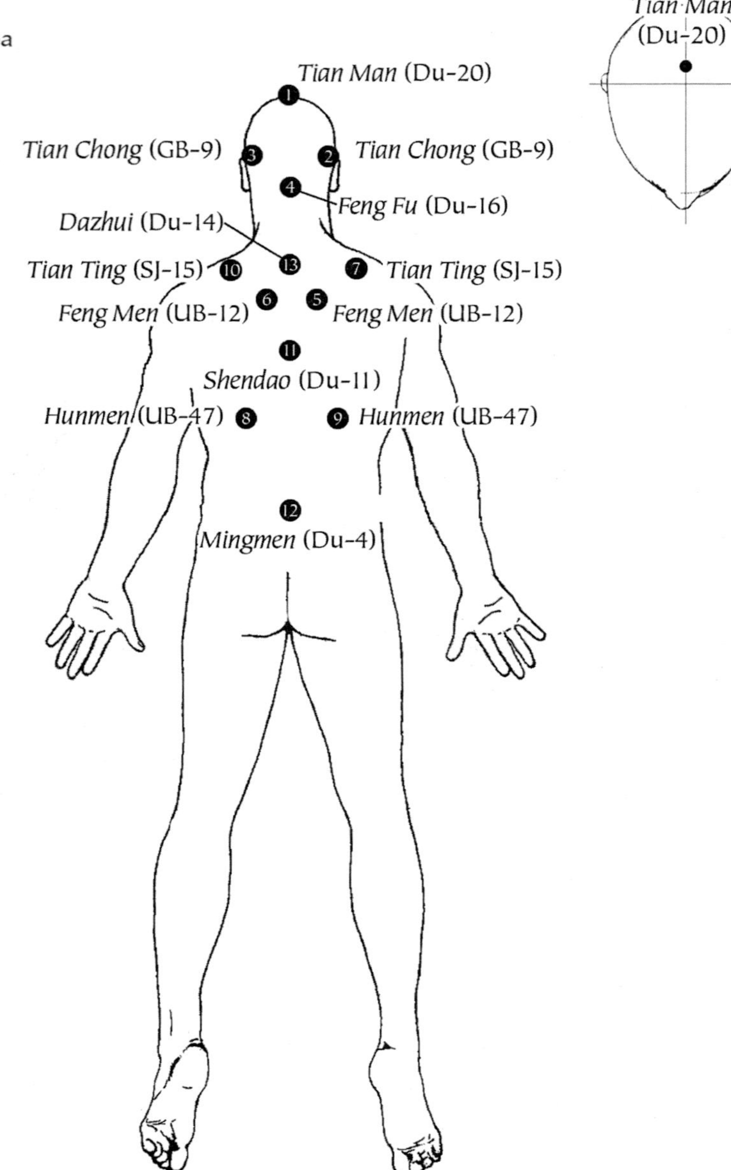

## The Wind Mansion Pattern

The Wind Mansion Pattern is another of the "Window" patterns and consists of thirteen acupuncture sites. The number 13 refers to The Twelve with the "hidden" Thirteenth Gateway. The first four acupuncture sites reveal another *Shaoyin* connection with the upward pointing Fire Triangle of the heart system opposing, while simultaneously complimenting, the downward pointing Water Triangle of the kidney system.

All the acupuncture points of the traditional acupuncture meridians are located within the etheric plane. The connection of the lower level of the Inner Twin Gates Within occurs on both the etheric plane and the mental plane. The kidney point in this pattern is *Mingmen* (Du-4) located directly on the spine and on the Du pathway. The heart point in the Wind Mansion *Shaoyin* Pattern is *Shendao* (Du-11) also located directly on the spine and in the Du pathway. *Mingmen* (Du-4) and *Shendao* (Du-11) communicate on the Etheric Plane because of the fact that both of those acupuncture points are on the same meridian pathway that is within the etheric field of the client. Those same two acupuncture points communicate on the mental plane because of the visual connect of those two points done by the client.

On a higher level, the Twin Gates Within refer to the higher aspects of the Anahata (Heart Chakra) communicating with the Sahasrara (Crown Chakra). Remember that the central heart point in this pattern is *Shendao* (Du-11). *Shendao* is often translated as either "Heart Path" or "Spirit Path." The inner Heart Path/Spirit Path is the connection to the Sahasrara (Crown Chakra) through *Tian Man* (Du-20). This connection may, in turn, lead to connections with the higher chakras above the Sahasrara (Crown Chakra). Just because *Shendao* (Du-11) *and Tian Man* (Du-20) are both on the Du meridian pathway and are naturally linked together by the relationship of being on the same meridian is not what is referred to as the inner Heart Path. Although there will be an etheric connection, we are not interested in the etheric levels in this New Encoding

Pattern. The inner connection from the higher Anahata (Heart Chakra) to *Tian Man* (Du-20) occurs through a morphic resonant connection, an instantaneous consciousness connection.

The Wind Mansion Pattern is designed to move consciousness through the Anahata (Heart Chakra) into the higher head chakras. The acupuncture site of *Mingmen* (Du-4) is the anchoring second chakra kidney energy activation point in this pattern. But, we are more interested in the Wind Mansion Pattern to ascend the energetics of *Mingmen* (Du-4) to the Anahata (Heart Chakra) and the upper head centers, rather than emphasizing the grounding aspects of the kidney qi at that point. *Mingmen* (Du-4) is known as both the Gate of Vitality and the Life Gate. Both of these names for the translation of *Mingmen* (Du-4) indicate how much power is contained within this point and also how important this acupuncture point is for a person's wellbeing and quality of life. We are using the qi and consciousness from this kidney gate to reinforce the heart qi at *Shendao* (Du-11) before moving the qi to *Dazhui* (Du-14) and subsequently to the Ajna Center, Brahmarandra Chakra and the Sahasrara (Crown Chakra).

Wind Mansion is a very interesting name. Remember that names carry specific vibrations. Wind can be thought of as a type of energy created by nature or created by non-natural means such as a fan or other mechanical or electromagnetic devices that create frequency patterns. People that talk a lot and ramble on are often said to be: "big winded." In Esoteric Acupuncture, wind is used to describe a field or higher state of consciousness that does not include mindless ramblings of an individual. Wind is a nebulous field and can be thought of as being connected to spirit and to the spiritual realms.

The window within this pattern is the connection of *Feng Fu* (Du-16) with the bilateral *Feng Men* (UB-12) points known as "Wind Gates." An interesting note is that an alternative name for the bilateral (UB-12) points is also *Feng Fu* which is Wind Mansion. The upward pointing Fire Triangle that is formed by bringing the qi of the bilateral (UB-12) (*Feng Men*/Wind Gate) points upward to connect with Du-16 (*Feng Fu*/Wind Mansion) creates the "window" in the Wind Mansion Pattern. We are activating and moving the qi from the bilateral Wind Gate sites and directing the bilateral energies to the Wind Mansion site that may trigger a consciousness shift into the Field of "Sound without Sound." We mentioned that Celestial Hearing is connected to the higher heart system. Physical hearing with your ears is connected to the kidney system. The Field of Sound without Sound is definitely an Inner Higher Heart Field.

The reason that the Wind Mansion Pattern is placed in the addendum rather than in the Tiers of Density Levels in Chapter V is because this pattern was originally designed to use without a follow-up anterior New Encoding Pattern. After you have needled this posterior pattern and you feel that your client would benefit from a frontal treatment, it is perfectly fine to turn your client over and use an anterior New Encoding Pattern of your choice. But, the Wind Mansion Pattern was originally intended to be a "stand alone" pattern.

Needling Sequence for the Wind Mansion Pattern

1) *Tian Man* (Du-20) : "Celestial Fullness"
2) *Tian Chong* (GB-9) Right side: "Celestial Hub"
3) *Tian Chong* (GB-9) Left side: "Celestial Hub"
4) *Feng Fu* (Du-16) "Wind Mansion"
5) *Feng Men* (UB-12) Right side: "Wind Gate"
6) *Feng Men* (UB-12) Left side: "Wind Gate" (An alternative name for these bilateral UB-12 points is also *Feng Fu* "Wind Mansion," the same as Du-16.)
7) *Tian Ting* (SJ-15) Right side: "Celestial Hearing"
8) *Hunmen* (UB-47): Left Side: "*Hun* Gate" or "Soul Gate"
9) *Hunmen* (UB-47): Right Side: "*Hun* Gate" or "Soul Gate"
10) *Tian Ting* (SJ-15) Left side: "Celestial Hearing"
11) *Shendao* (Du-11): "Spirit Path" or "Heart Path"
12) *Mingmen* (Du-4): "Life Gate" or "Gate of Vitality
13) *Dazhui* (Du-14): "The Big Hammer"

The first figure shows three acupuncture sites: *Tian Man* (Du-20) and the bilateral *Tian Chong* (GB-9) points. The point location for these three acupuncture sites have been discussed in other New Encoding Patterns and will not be repeated here. (See figure 7.3-b below.)

## The Wind Mansion Pattern

Fig. 7.3-b

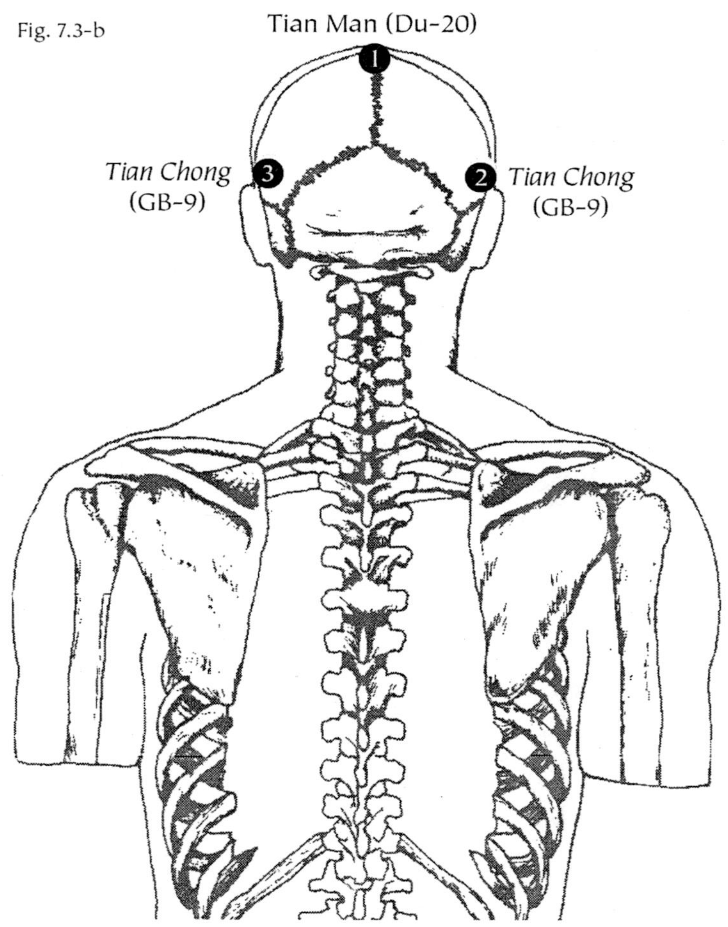

After acupuncture needles have been inserted in the first three acupuncture sites of the Wind Mansion Pattern, have your client visually connected the bilateral *Tian Chong* (GB-9) points to each other. (See figure 7.3-c below.)

**The Wind Mansion Pattern Visualization**

Fig. 7.3-c

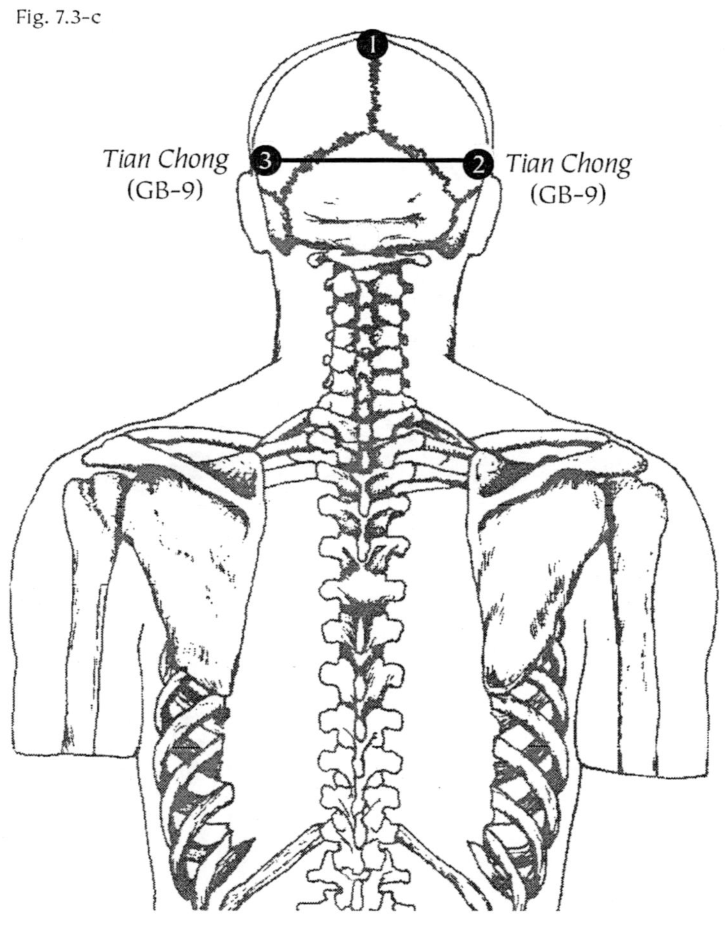

Next have your client bring the qi simultaneously upward from the bilateral *Tian Chong* (GB-9) points in a triangular formation to connect with *Tian Man* (Du-20) at the top of the head. (See figure 7.3-d below.)

## The Wind Mansion Pattern Visualization

Fig. 7.3-d

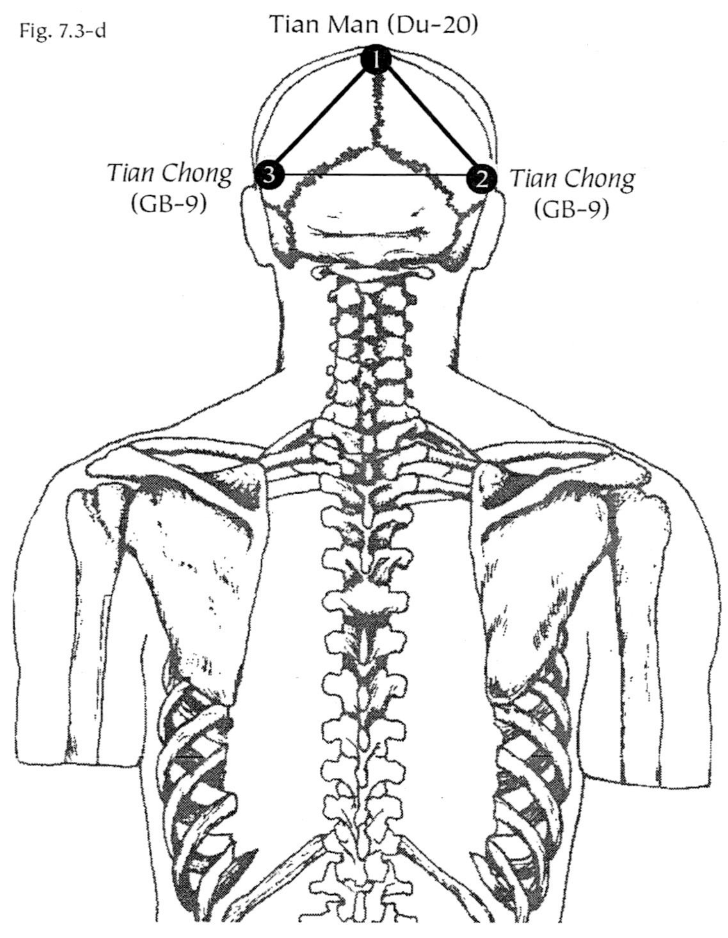

Now insert an acupuncture needle at the acupuncture site of *Feng Fu* (Du-16), the entrance gateway to the Taluka Chakra (also known as the (Lalana Chakra or the Alta Major Center). (See figure 7.3-e below.)

**The Wind Mansion Pattern Visualization**

Fig. 7.3-e

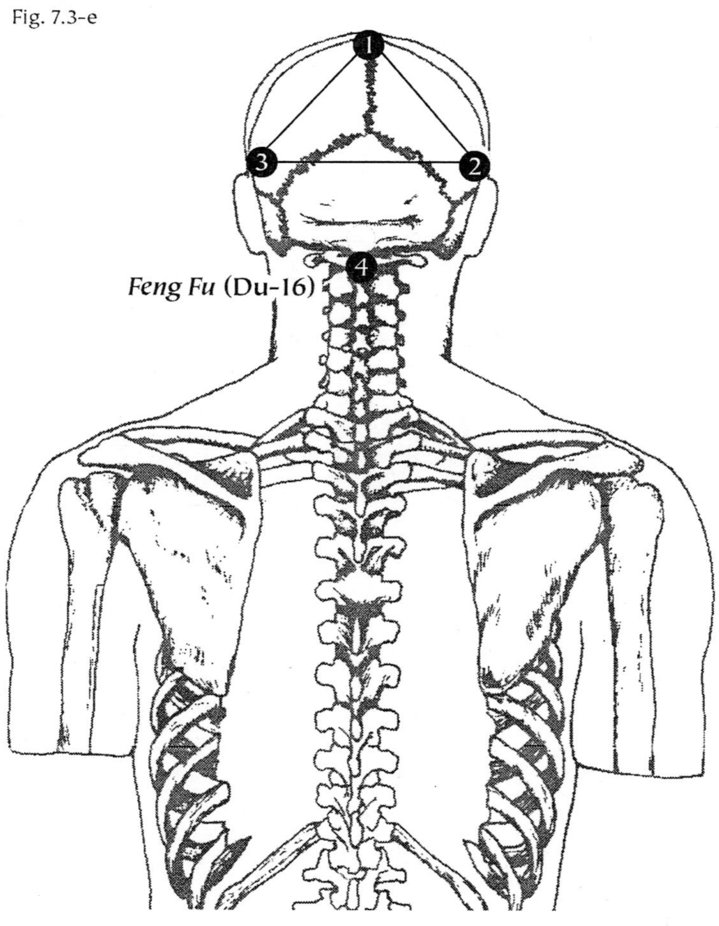

Next have you client visually bring the qi downward simultaneously from the bilateral *Tian Chong* (GB-9) points in a triangular formation to connect with *Feng Fu* (Du-16). Notice the upward pointing Fire Triangle opposing the downward pointing Water Triangle creating another Esoteric *Shaoyin* configuration. (See figure 7.3-f below.)

### The Wind Mansion Pattern Visualization

Fig. 7.3-f

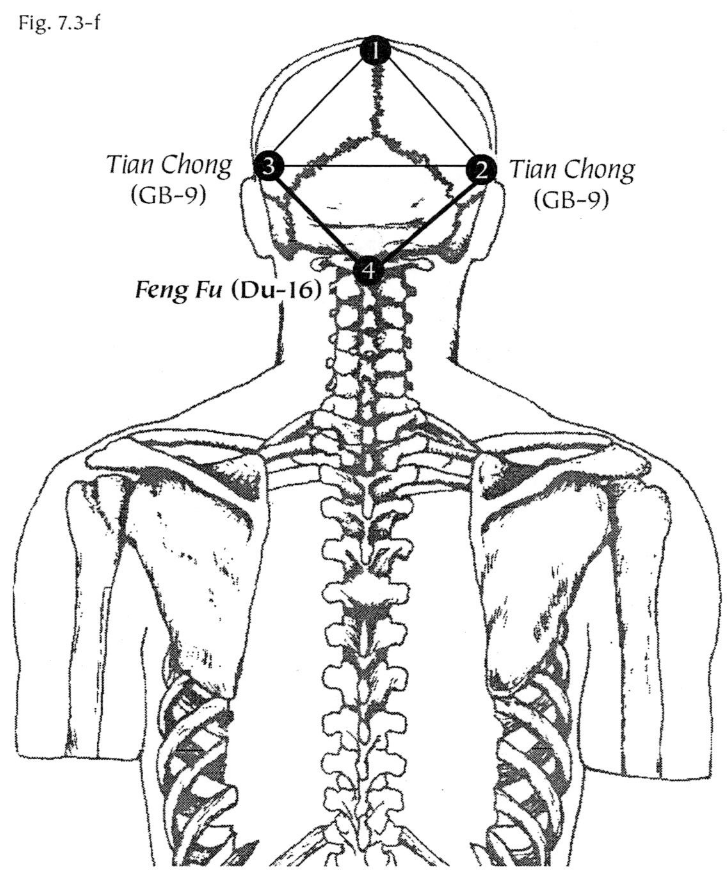

Now insert an acupuncture needle at the fifth acupuncture site in this pattern at *Feng Men* (UB-12) located approximately one and a half *cun* lateral to the center of the spine on the client's right side and level with the lower border of the spinous process of the second thoracic vertebra. *Feng Men* (UB-12) can be translated as "Wind Gate." (See figure 7.3-g below.)

## The Wind Mansion Pattern Visualization

Fig. 7.3-g

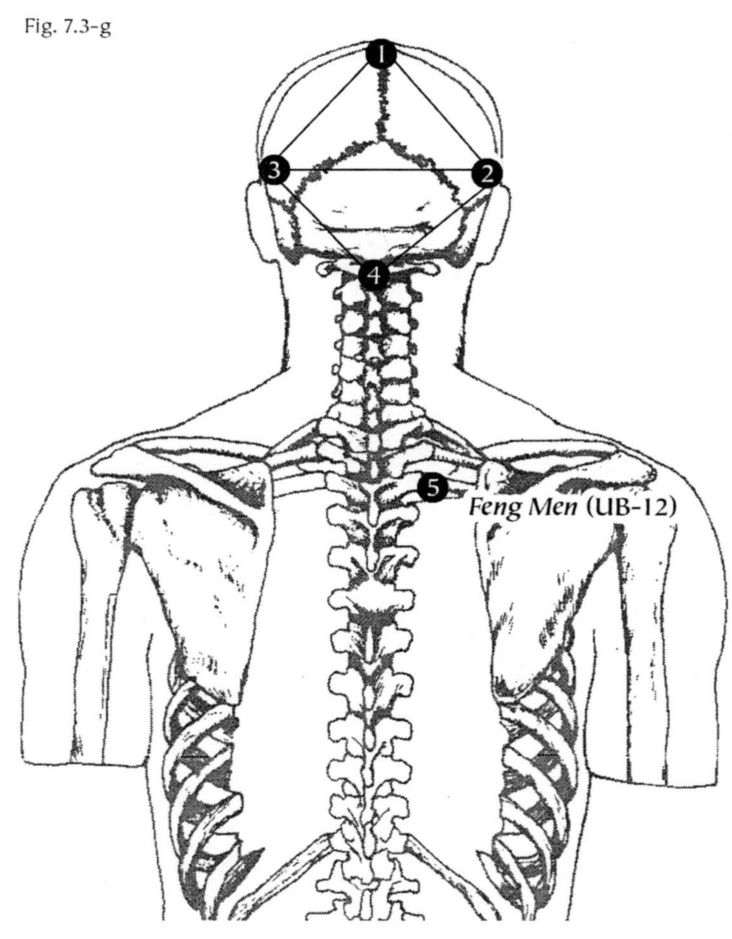

The sixth acupuncture needle is on the client's left side at the acupuncture site of *Feng Men* (UB-12). The point location is similar to the preceding location, except that this point is on the client's left side. (See figure 7.3-h below.)

## The Wind Mansion Pattern Visualization

Fig. 7.3-h

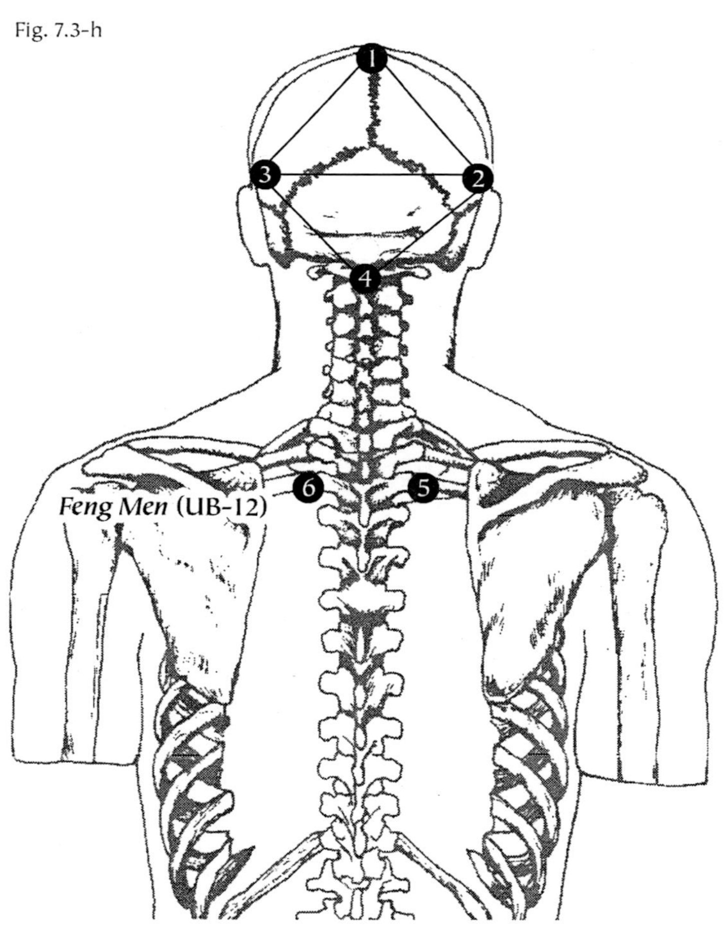

Have your client visually connect the bilateral *Feng Men* (UB-12) "Wind Gate" points as shown in figure 7.3-I below.

## The Wind Mansion Pattern Visualization

Fig. 7.3-i

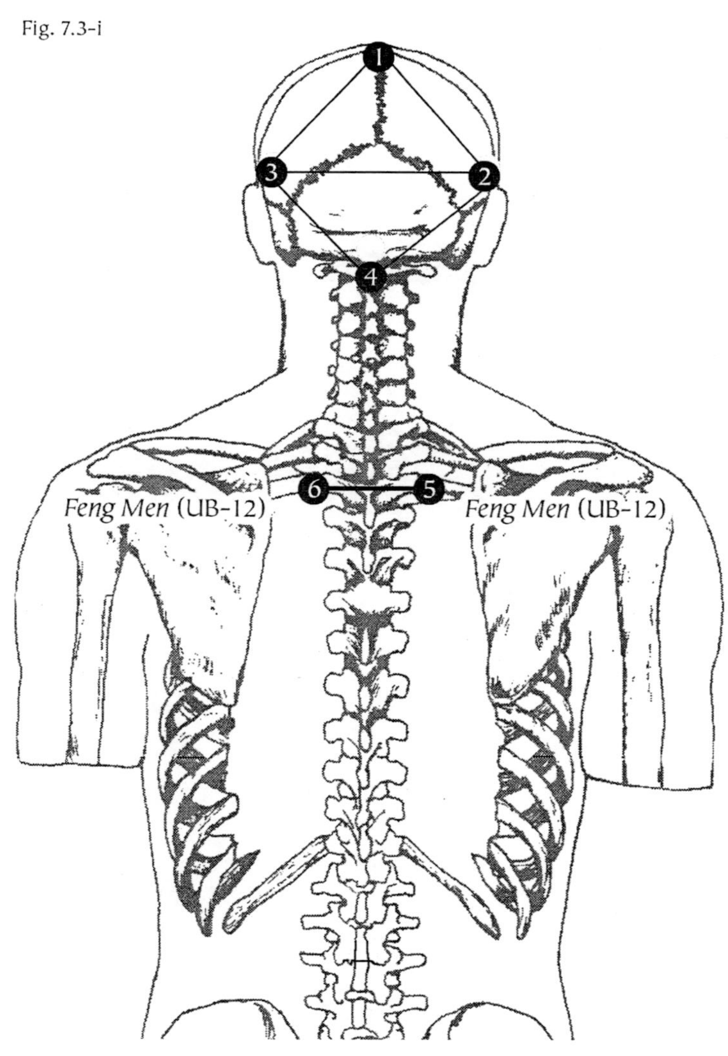

Now ask your client to bring the qi upward simultaneously from the bilateral *Feng Men* (UB-12) "Wind Gate" points in a triangular fashion to connect to the Wind Mansion at *Feng Fu* (Du-16) located in the depression below the external occipital protuberance. (See figure 7.3-j below.)

### The Wind Mansion Pattern Visualization

Fig. 7.3-j

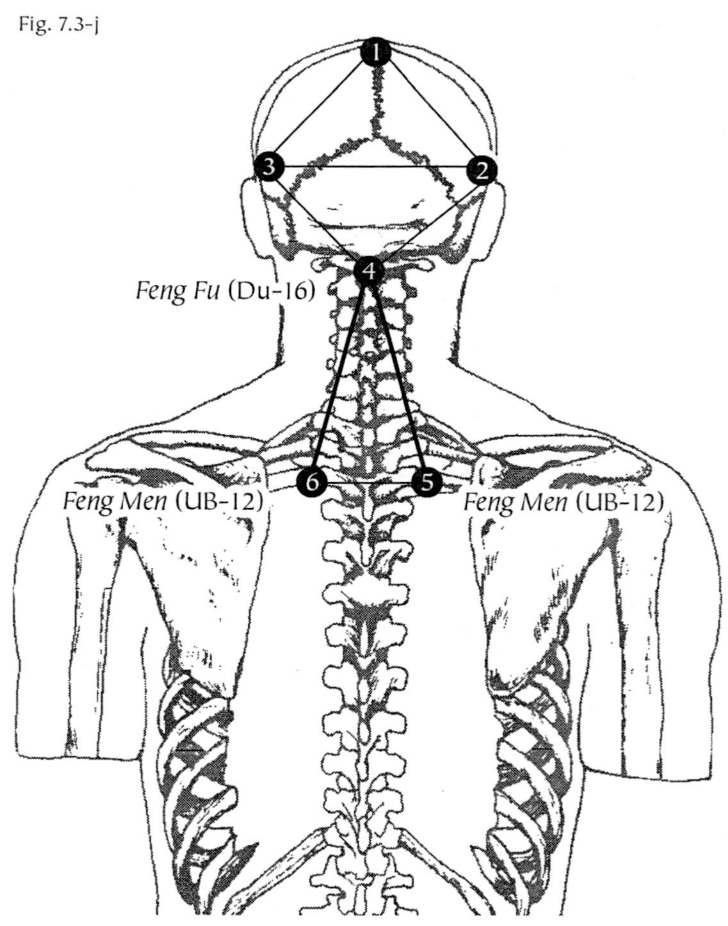

The seventh acupuncture site needled is at the acupuncture site of *Tian Ting* (SJ-15) on the client's right side. The needle sequence in the Wind Mansion Pattern is different from the needling sequence in the Esoteric *Shao*yin Heart Window Pattern where the *Tian Ting* (SJ-15) point on the client's left side was activated before the *Ting* (SJ-15) point on the client's right side. Here we are activating the *Tian Ting* (SJ-15) point on the client's right side first. (See figure 7.3-k below.)

**The Wind Mansion Pattern Visualization**

Fig. 7.3-k

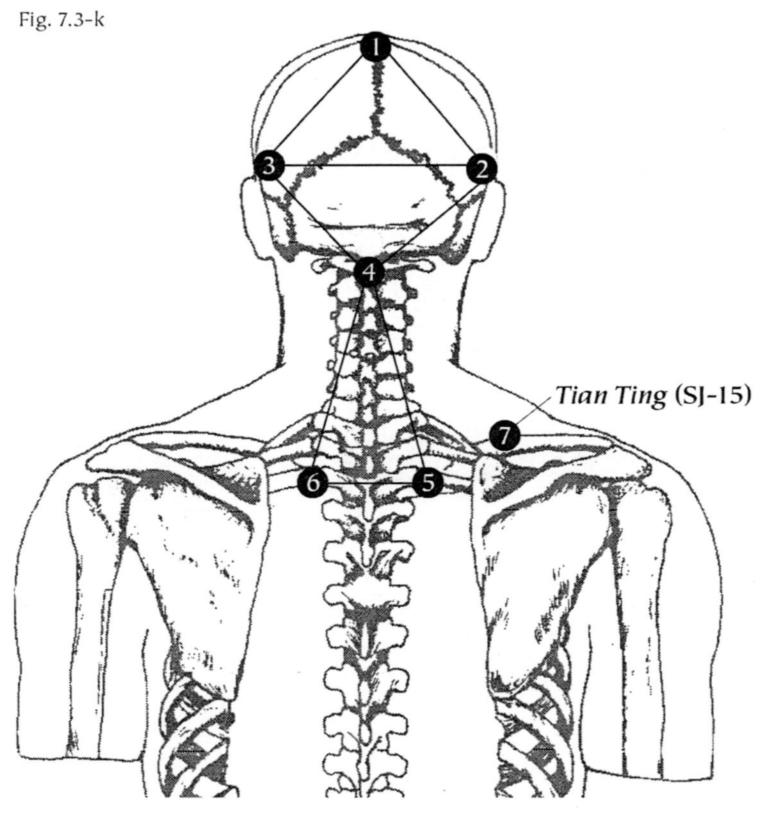

The eighth acupuncture site needled in the Wind Mansion Pattern is *Hunmen* (UB-47) on the client's left side. *Hunmen* is located approximately three *cun* lateral to the center of the spine and horizontal to the lower border of the spinous process of the ninth thoracic vertebra. (See figure 7.3-l below.)

## The Wind Mansion Pattern Visualization

Fig. 7.3-l

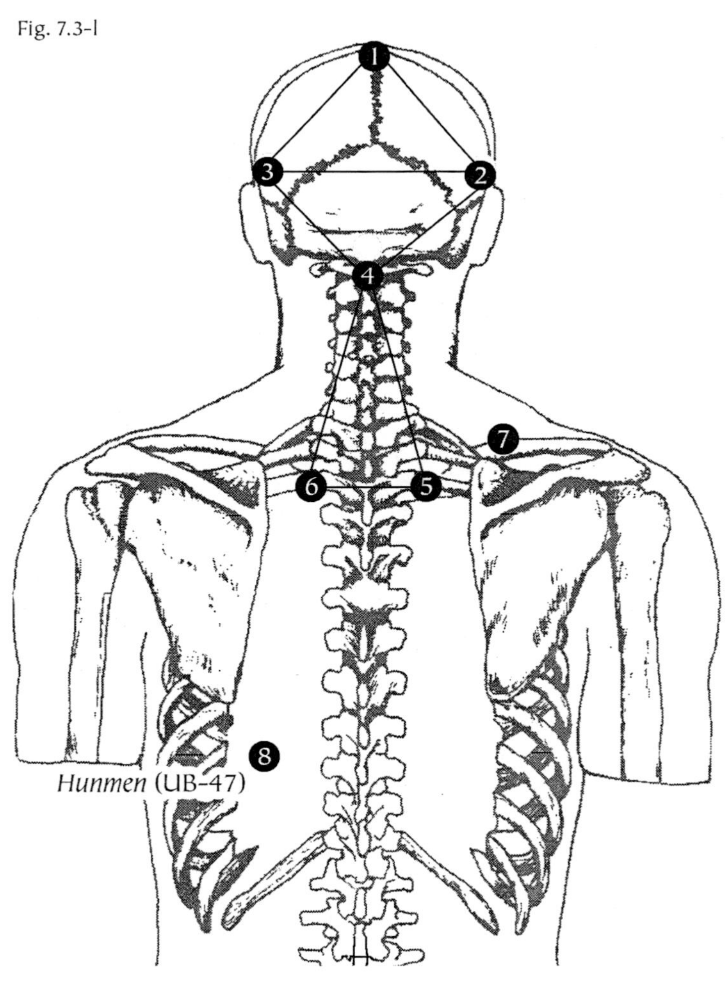

Have your client visually connect the *Tian Ting* (SJ-15) point on the posterior of the right shoulder with the *Hunmen* (UB-47) point on the left side. (See figure 7.3-m below.)

## The Wind Mansion Pattern Visualization

Fig. 7.3-m

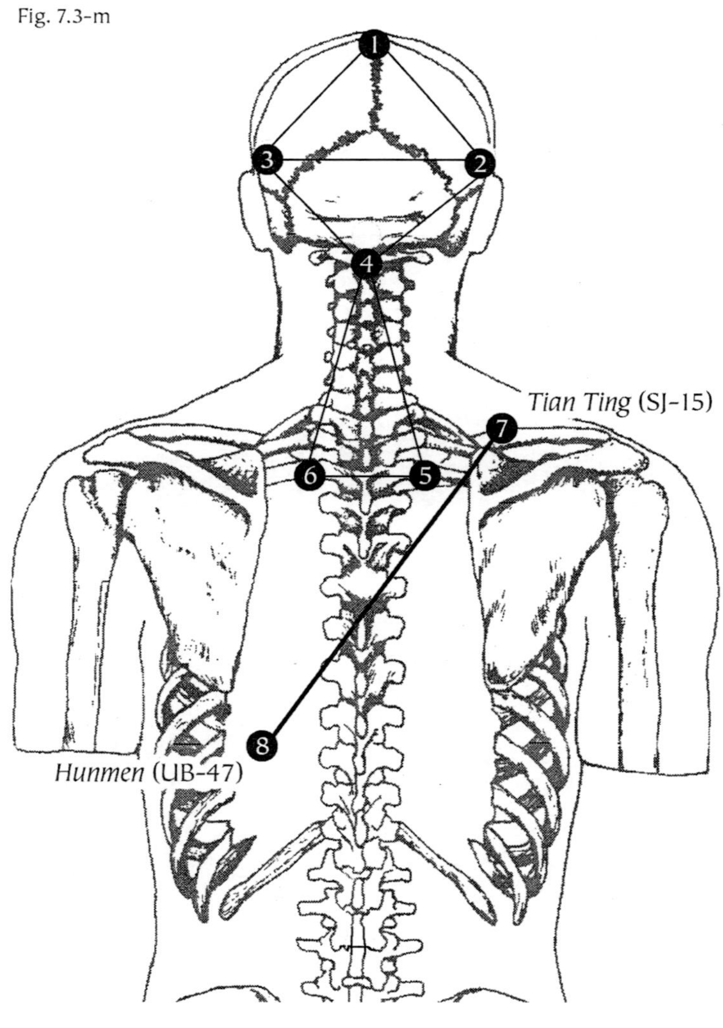

Next insert your ninth acupuncture needle in the acupuncture site of *Hunmen* (UB-47) on the client's right side. (See figure 7.3-n below.)

## The Wind Mansion Pattern Visualization

Fig. 7.3-n

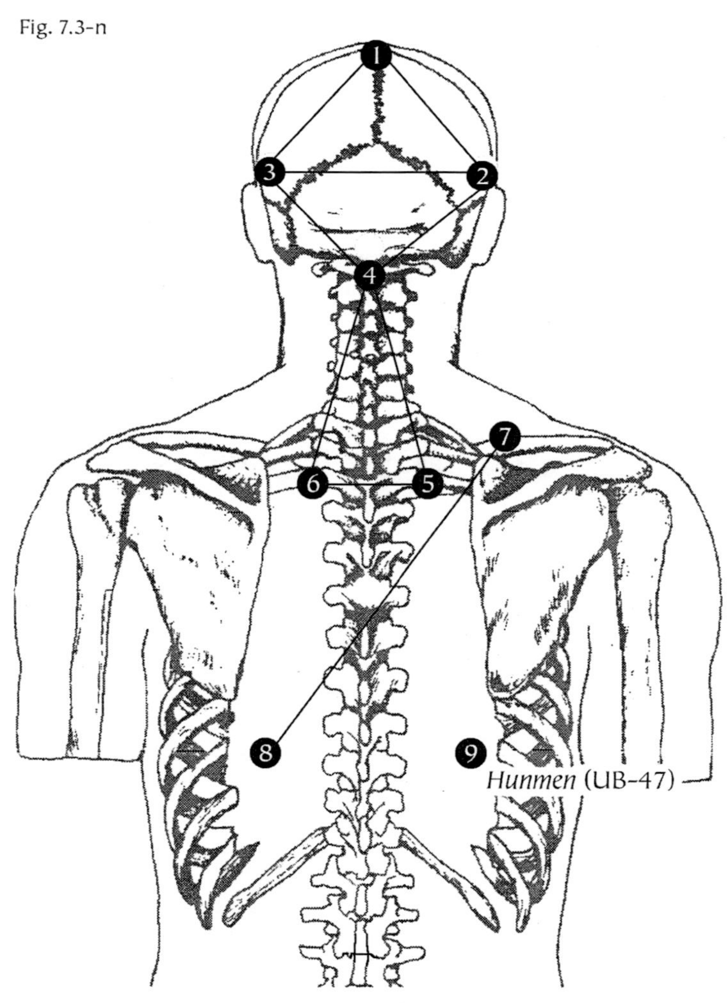

Now have your client visually connect the qi at the site of *Hunmen* (UB-47) on the left side with the qi of *Hunmen* (UB-47) on the right side. (See figure 7.3-o below.)

## The Wind Mansion Pattern Visualization

Fig. 7.3-o

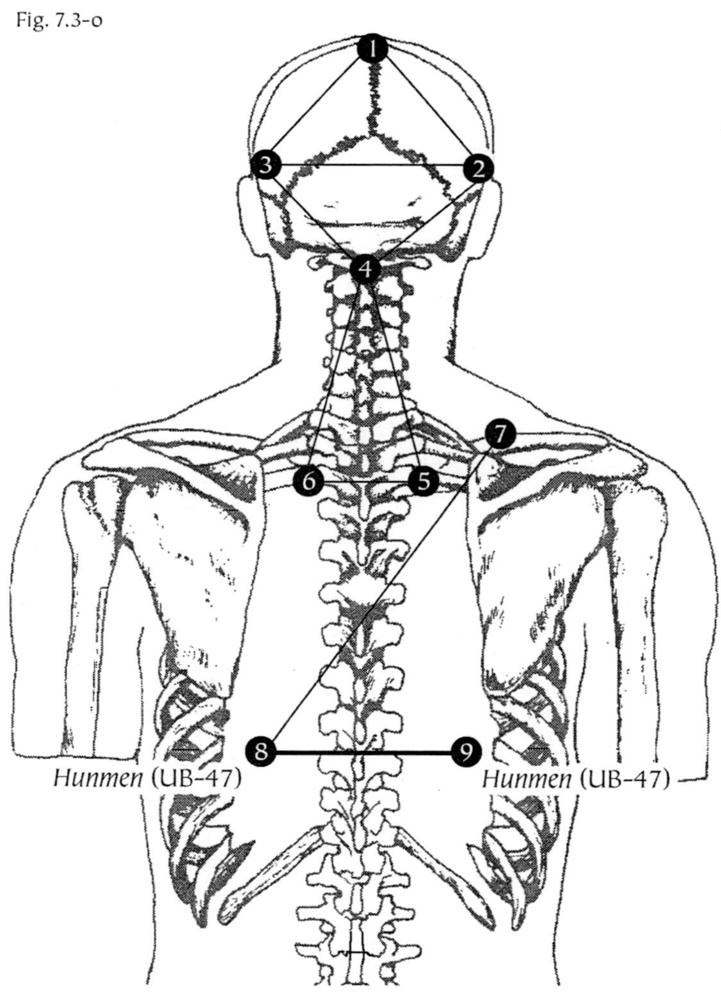

Insert your tenth acupuncture needle at the acupuncture site of *Tian Ting* (SJ-15) on the client's left posterior shoulder. (See figure 7.3-p below.)

## The Wind Mansion Pattern Visualization

Fig. 7.3-p

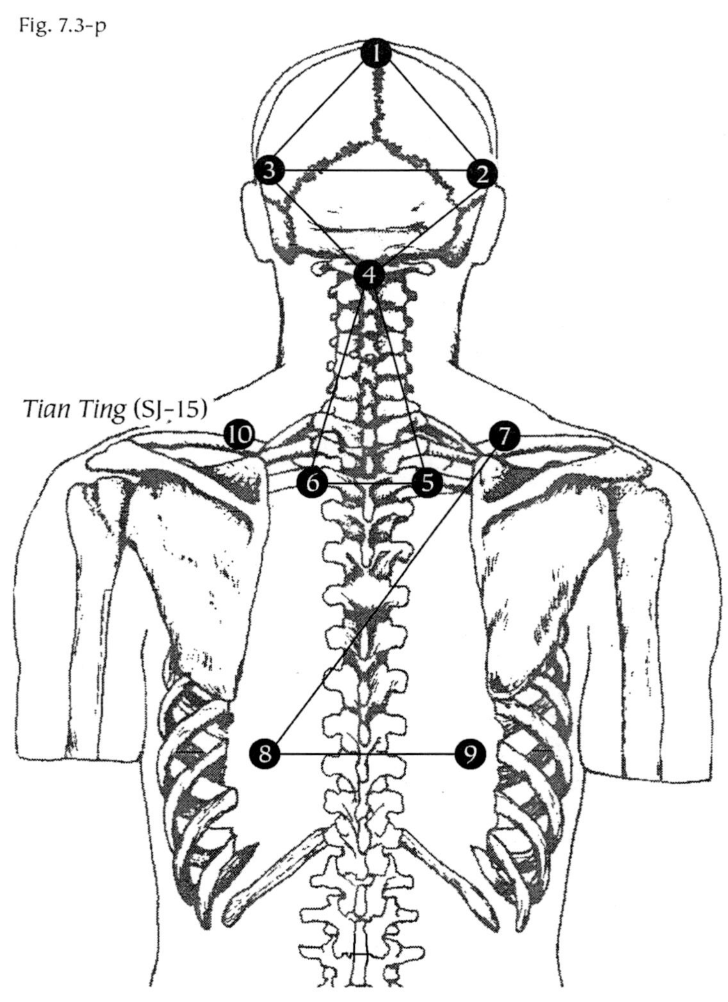

Next bring the qi upward in a crisscross manner from the acupuncture site of *Hunmen* (UB-47) on the right side to connect with the qi at the acupuncture site of *Tian Ting* (SJ-15) on the left side. (See figure 7.3-q below.)

### The Wind Mansion Pattern Visualization

Fig. 7.3-q

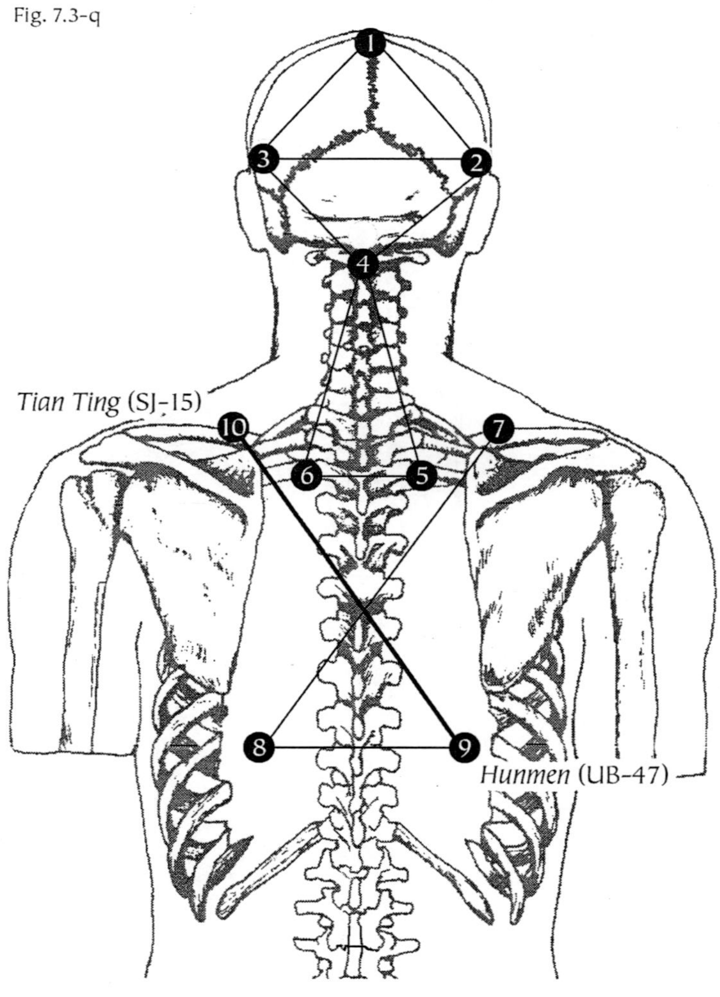

Have your client connect the qi at the sites of the bilateral *Tian Ting* (SJ-15) points. The bilateral *Tian Ting* (SJ-15) points are Celestial Hearing points. The field of Celestial Hearing is under the domain and control of the higher heart. The bilateral *Hunmen* (UB-47) points are liver points moving upward toward the Celestial Hearing points. The hourglass-shaped geometric shape is both a *Hun* Follow the *Shen* Hourglass layered above the overall Wind Mansion Pattern. (See figure 7.3-r below.)

## The Wind Mansion Pattern Visualization

Fig. 7.3-r

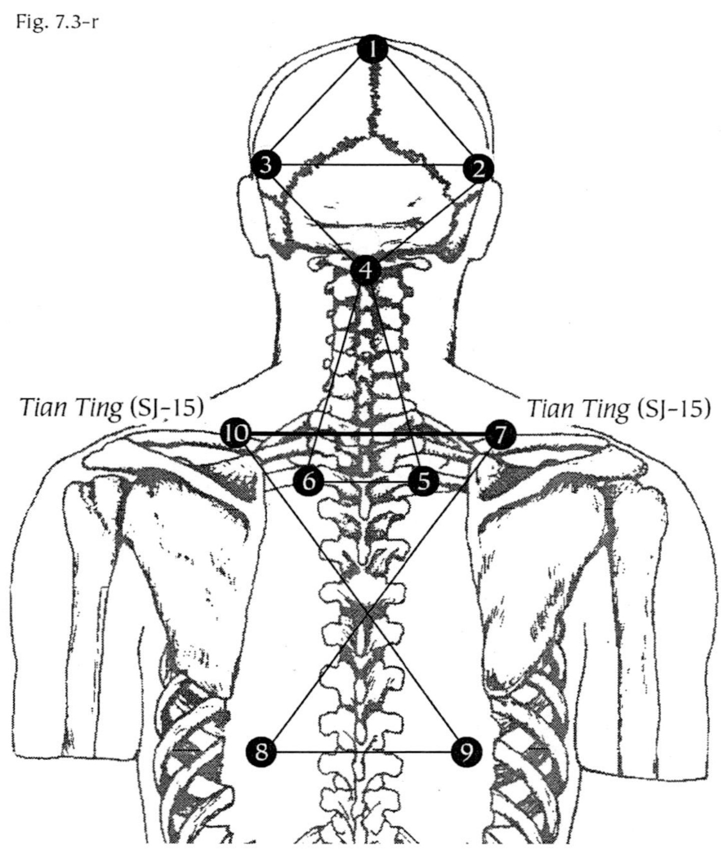

Next have your client create the Upper *Shaoyang* Field of "That Which Has No Form." The formation of this hourglass geometric figure is different than in the Esoteric *Shaoyin* Heart Window Pattern where we started this hourglass connection from the *Tian Ting* (SJ-15) point on the client's left side. In the Wind Mansion Pattern, we will start this hourglass connection from the *Tian Ting* (SJ-15) point on the client's right side connecting to the *Tian Chong* (GB-9) point on the client's left side of the head. (See figure 7.3-s below.)

### The Wind Mansion Pattern Visualization

Fig. 7.3-s

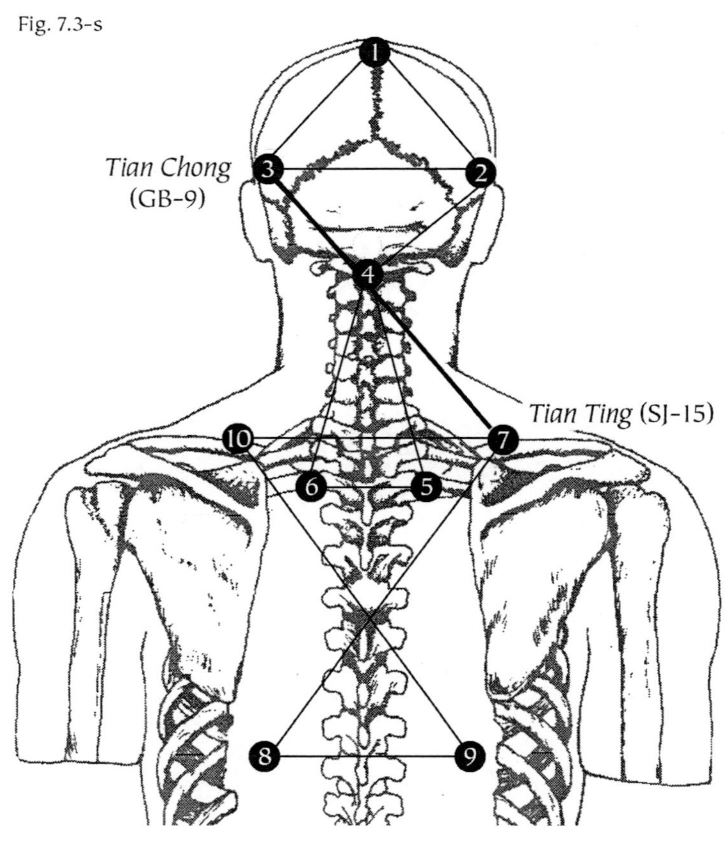

The bilateral *Tian Chong* (GB-9) and the bilateral *Tian Ting* (SJ-15) points are "Celestial Hearing" points. Although the bilateral *Tian Chong* (GB-9) points are part of the gallbladder meridian system, in Esoteric Acupuncture this set of gallbladder points are used to activate one's "Celestial Hearing" connected to one's higher heart system. Again, connect the bilateral *Tian Chong* (GB-9) together as shown in figure 7.3-t below.

## The Wind Mansion Pattern Visualization

Fig. 7.3-t

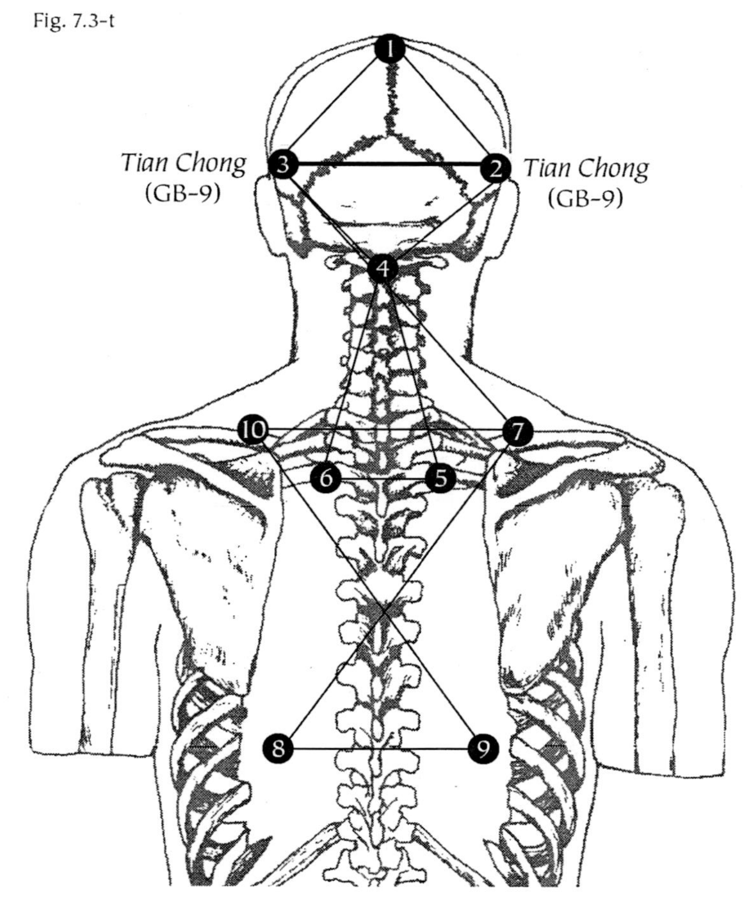

Next ask your client to visualize the qi moving downward in a crisscross fashion from the acupuncture site of *Tian Chong* (GB-9) on the right side to connect with the qi at the acupuncture site of *Tian Ting* (SJ-15) on the left side. (See figure 7.3-u below.)

## The Wind Mansion Pattern Visualization

Fig. 7.3-u

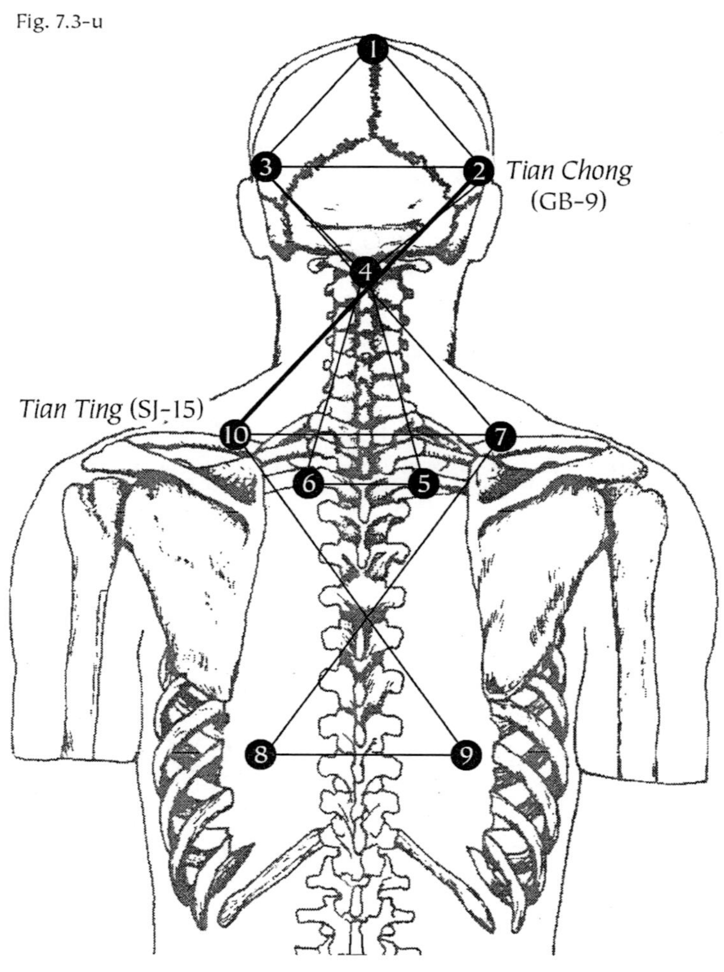

Once again ask your client to visualize the qi at the acupuncture sites of the bilateral *Tian Ting* (SJ-15) points connecting to each other. (See figure 7.3-v below.)

### The Wind Mansion Pattern Visualization

Fig. 7.3-v

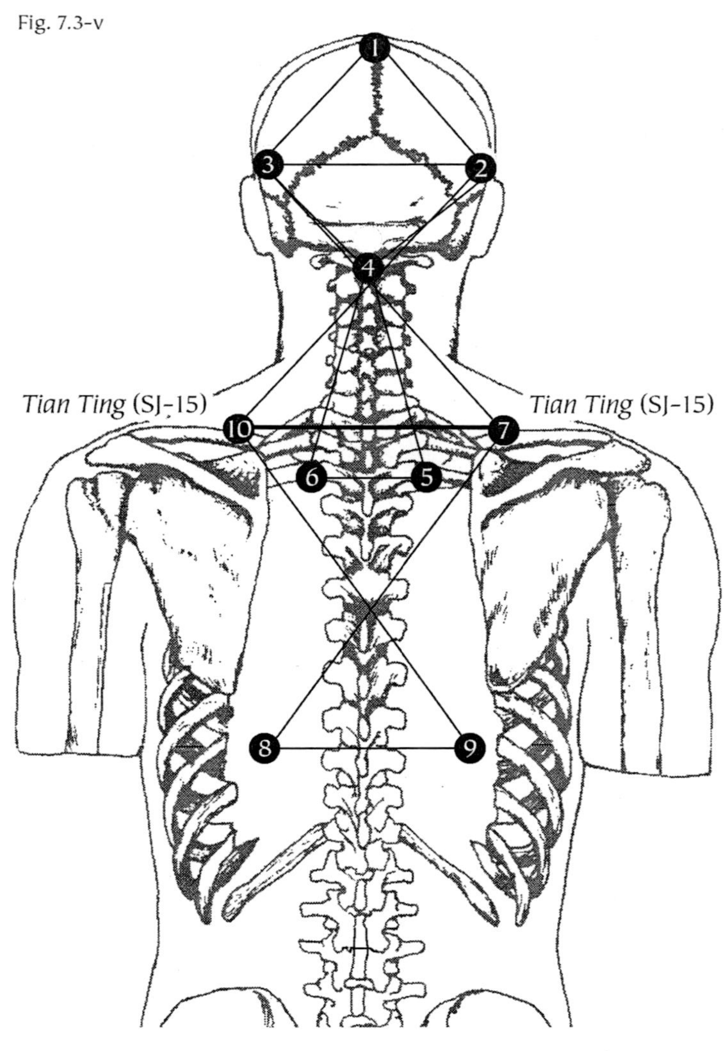

We have created two very powerful overlapping fields with the hourglass formation. The *san jiao* to gallbladder connection is the Upper *Shaoyang* Field of "That Which Has No Form." This field includes the "Sound Without Sound" activation point of *Feng Fu* (Du-16) the "Wind Mansion." These five acupuncture sites create the celestial hearing "Heart Field of One Hand Clapping." The crisscross hourglass pattern is also an Esoteric *Shaoyin* Field with the Water and Fire Triangles. (See figure 7.3-w below.)

**The Wind Mansion Pattern Visualization**

**Hourglass Field**
**"That Which Has No Form"**
**"The Heart Field of One Hand Clapping"**

Fig. 7.3-w

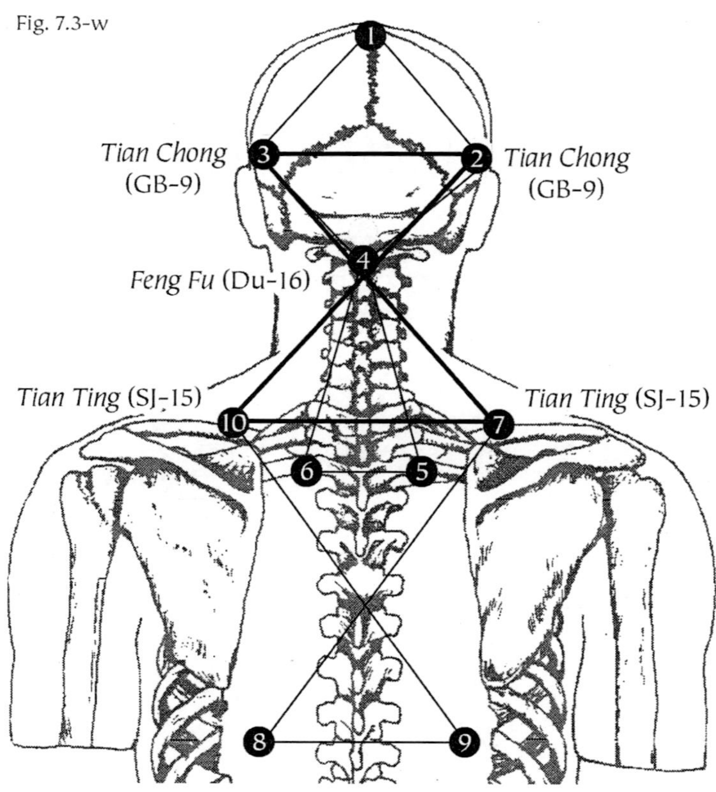

To reinforce the Celestial Hearing Field and expand the outer grid, visually connect *Tian Ting* (SJ-15) on the right side with the *Tian Chong* (GB-9) point on the right side. (See figure 7.3-x below.)

## The Wind Mansion Pattern Visualization

**Hourglass Field**
**"That Which Has No Form"**
**"The Heart Field of One Hand Clapping"**

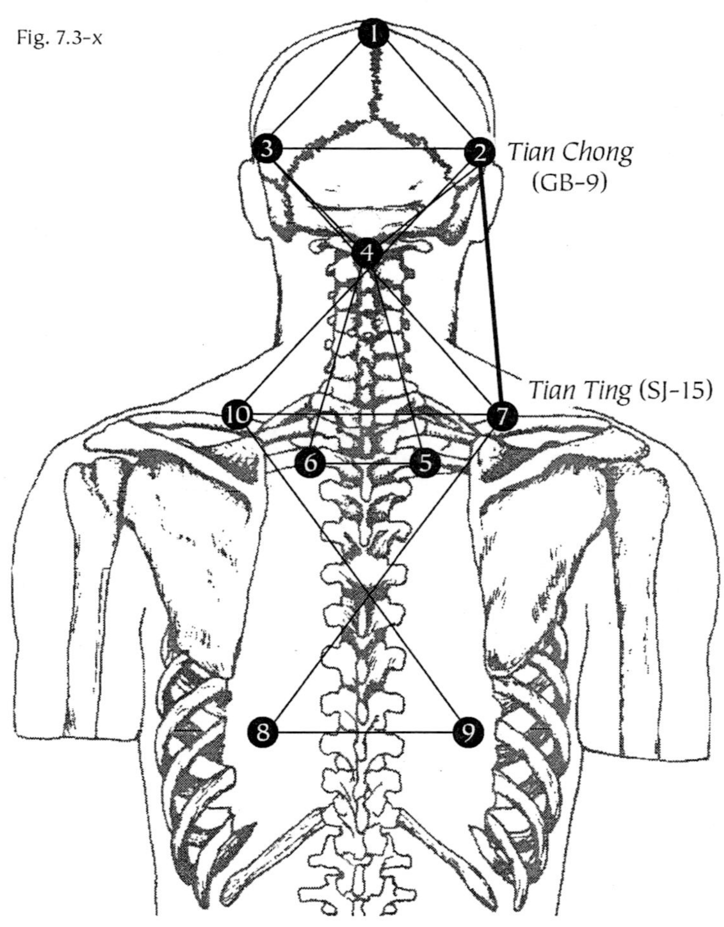

Again, we are reinforcing the outer Celestial Hearing Grid by visually connecting *Tian Ting* (SJ-15) on the left with the *Tian Chong* (GB-9) point on the left. (See figure 7.3-y below.)

### The Wind Mansion Pattern Visualization

**Hourglass Field**
**"That Which Has No Form"**
**"The Heart Field of One Hand Clapping"**

Fig. 7.3-y

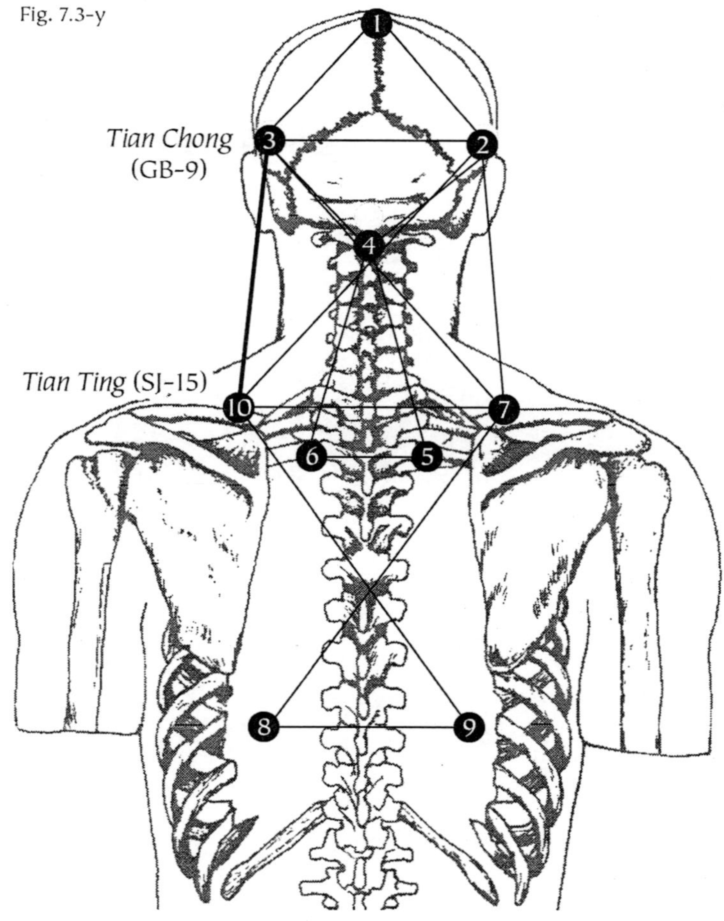

Insert your eleventh acupuncture needle directly in the spine below the spinous process of the fifth thoracic vertebra at the acupuncture site of *Shendao* (Du-11). (See figure 7.3-z below.)

## The Wind Mansion Pattern Visualization

Fig. 7.3-z

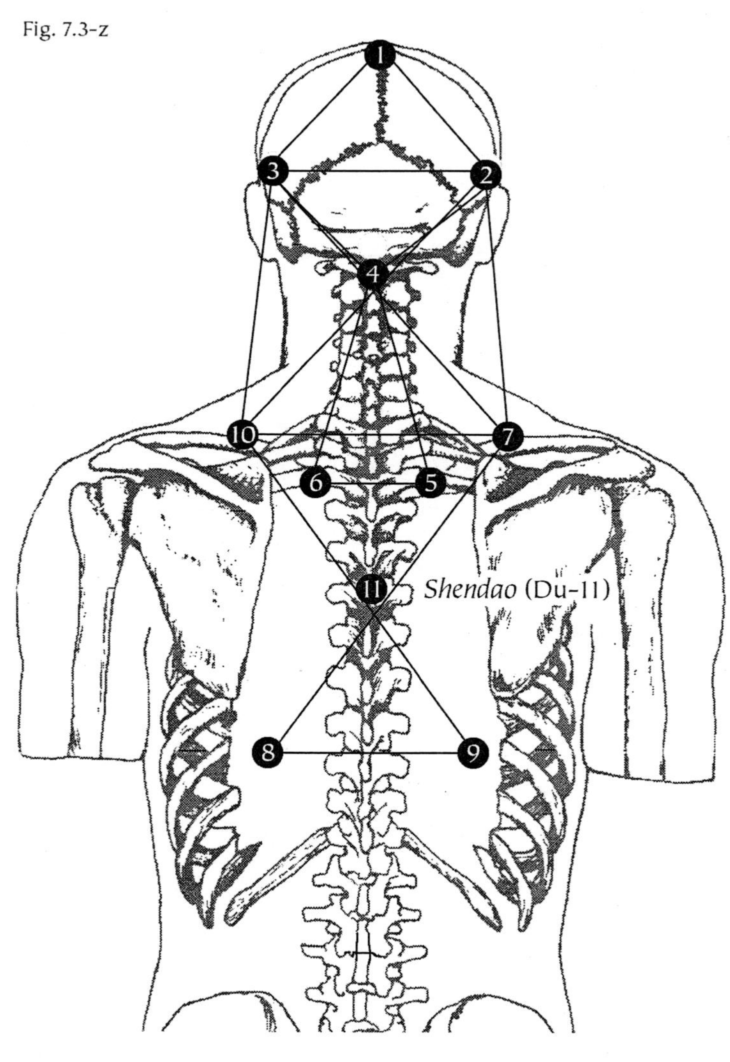

Next have your client visually bring the qi from the bilateral *Tian Ting* (SJ-15) points downward in a triangular formation to the center of the spine at the acupuncture site of *Shendao* (Du-11). This visual connection is a downward pointing Water Triangle. But, since the bilateral *Tian Ting* (Sj-15) are heart points and are connecting with *Shendao* (Du-11), we have again created an Esoteric *Shaoyin* Field. (See figure 7.3-aa below.)

## The Wind Mansion Pattern Visualization

Fig. 7.3-aa

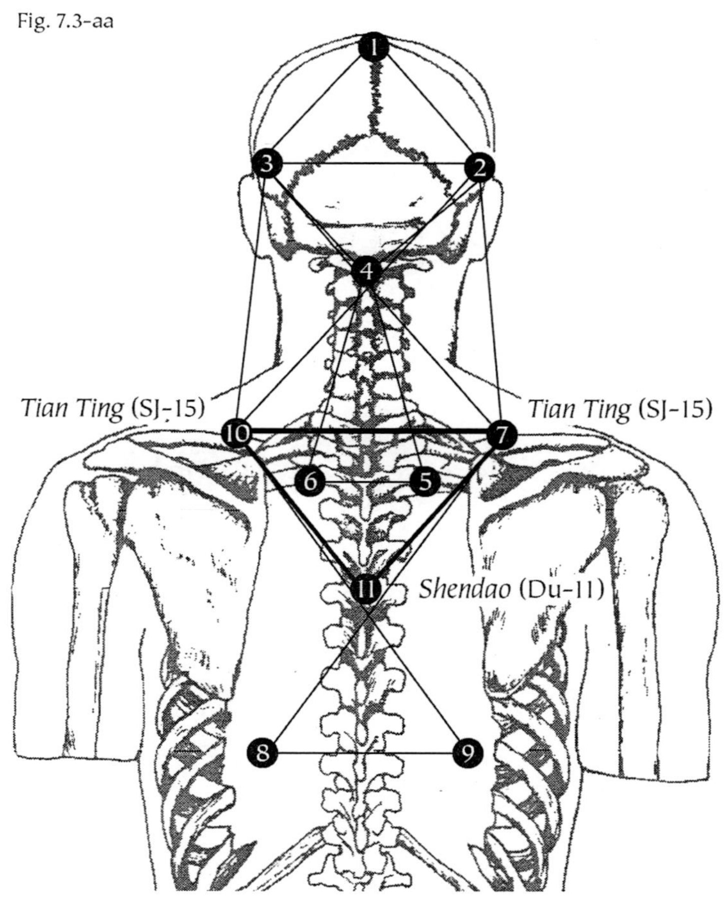

Now ask your client to visually bring the qi from the bilateral *Feng Men* (UB-12) "Wind Gate" points downward in a triangular manner to connect with the center "Heart Path" at *Shendao* (Du-11). (See figure 7.3-bb below.)

## The Wind Mansion Pattern Visualization

Fig. 7.3-bb

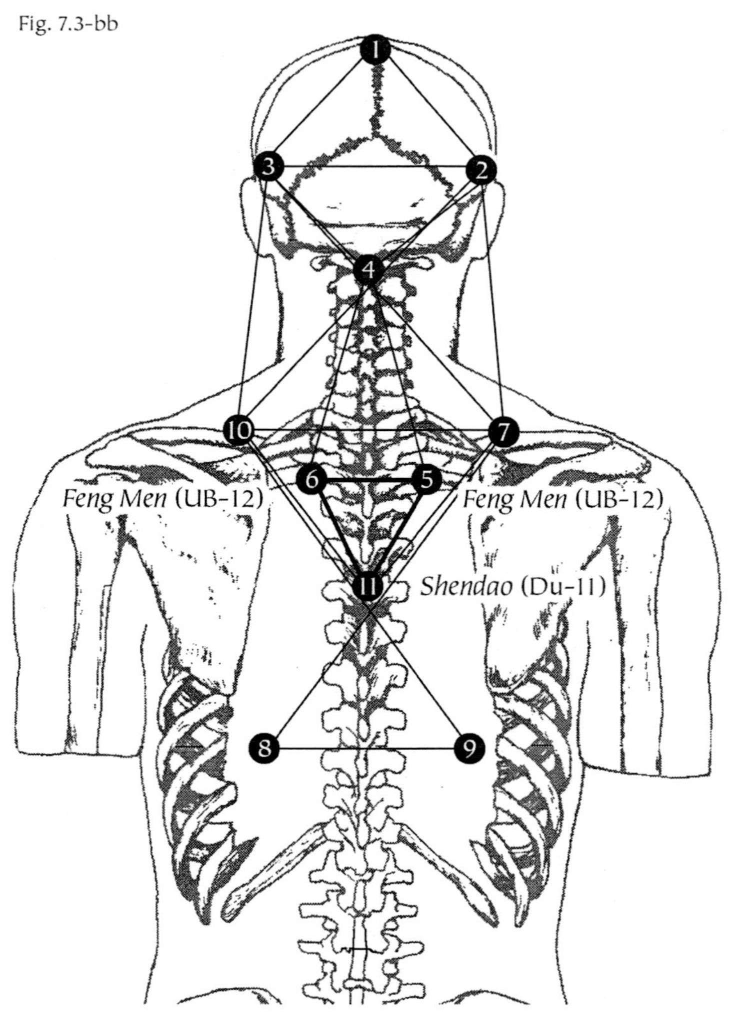

Have your client visualize an outer connection from *Hunmen* (UB-47) on the right side to *Tian Ting* on the right side. (See figure 7.3-cc below.)

## The Wind Mansion Pattern Visualization

Fig. 7.3-cc

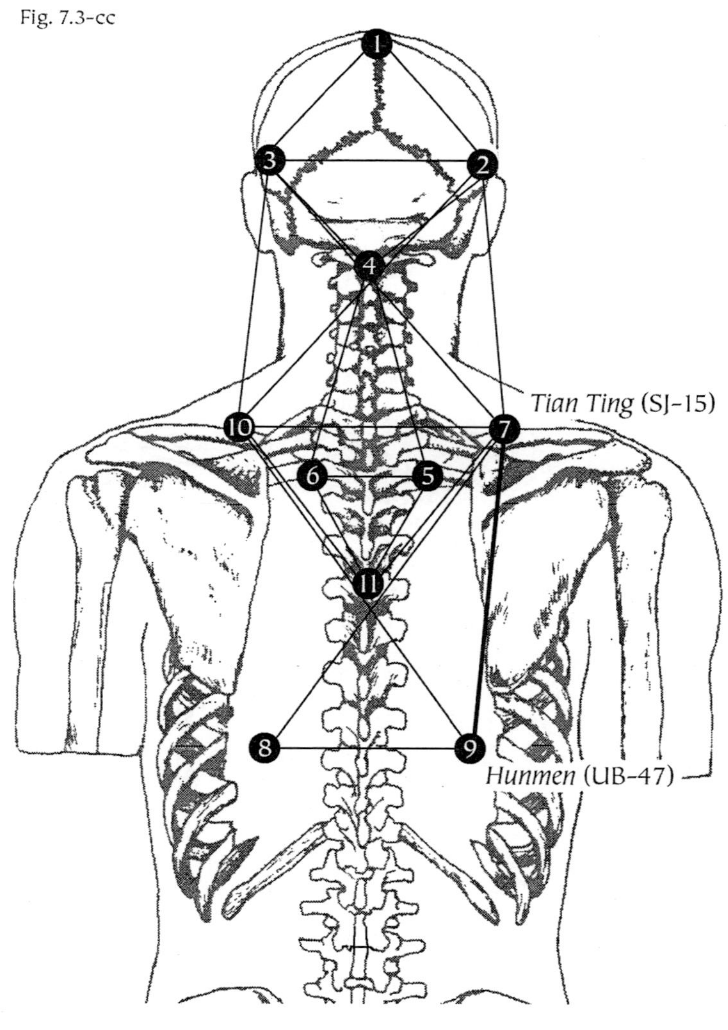

Next have your client visualize an outer connection, but this time from the acupuncture site of *Hunmen* (UB-47) on the left side to the acupuncture site of *Tian Ting* (SJ-15) on the left side. (See figure 7.3-dd below.)

### The Wind Mansion Pattern Visualization

Fig. 7.3-dd

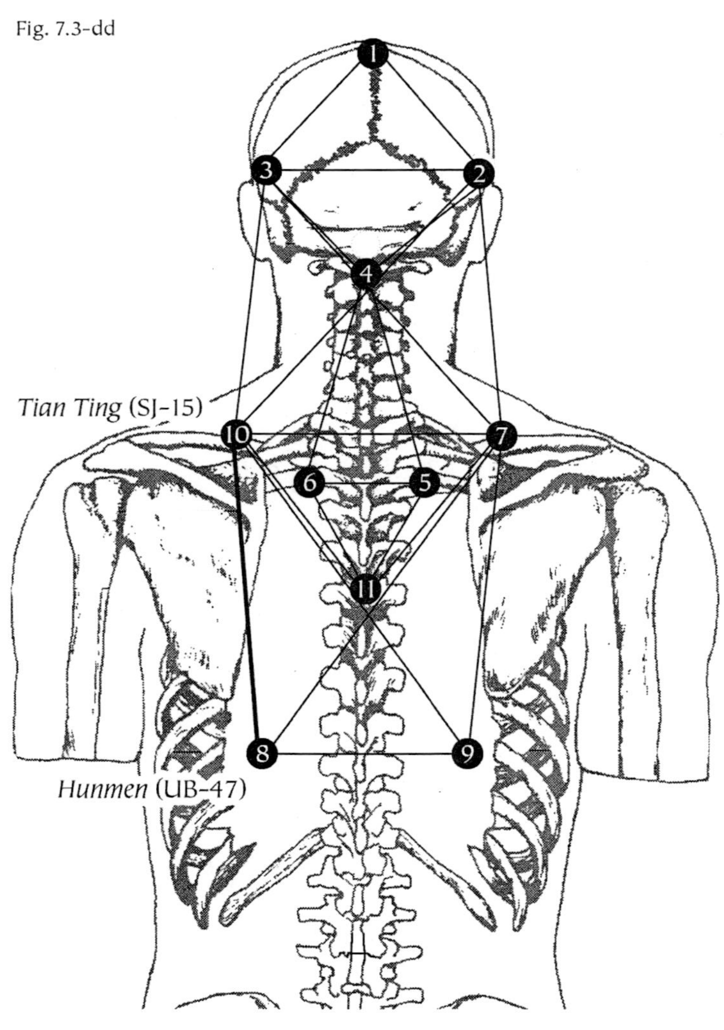

Next insert your twelfth acupuncture needle at the acupuncture site of *Mingmen* (Du-4) located directly on the spine below the spinous process of the second lumbar vertebra. (See figure 7.3-ee below.)

## The Wind Mansion Pattern Visualization

Fig. 7.3-ee

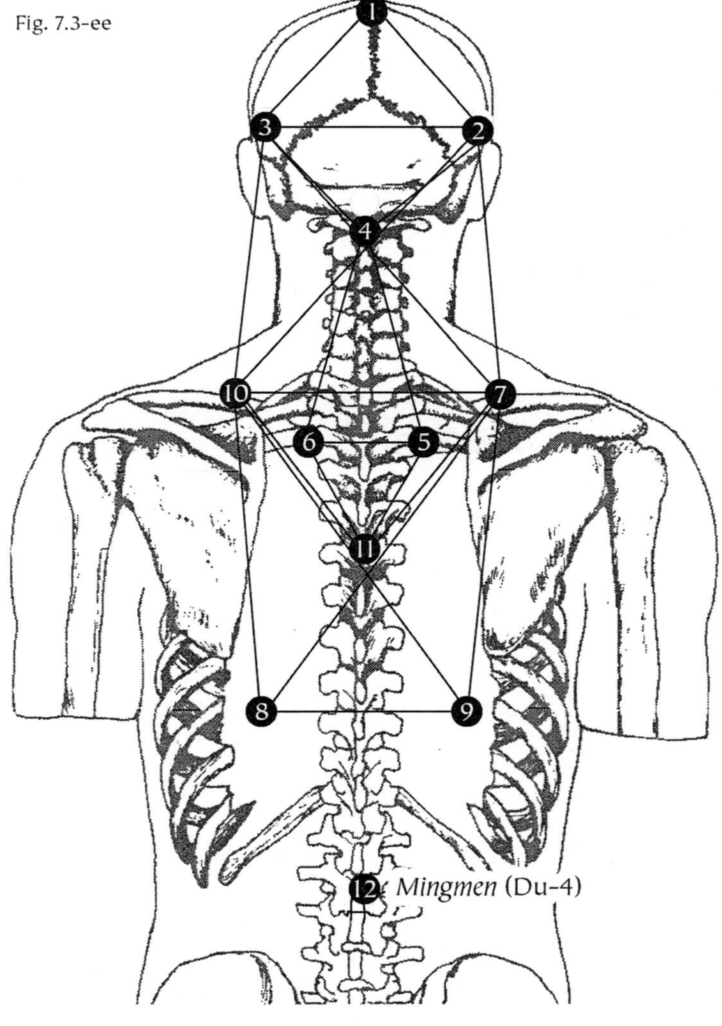

Have your client visually bring the qi downward along the spine from the acupuncture site of *Shendao* (Du-11) to the acupuncture site of *Mingmen* (Du-4). Your client is connecting his or her the Lower Twin Flames Within of the heart and kidney systems. (See figure 7.3-ff below.)

## The Wind Mansion Pattern Visualization

Fig. 7.3-ff

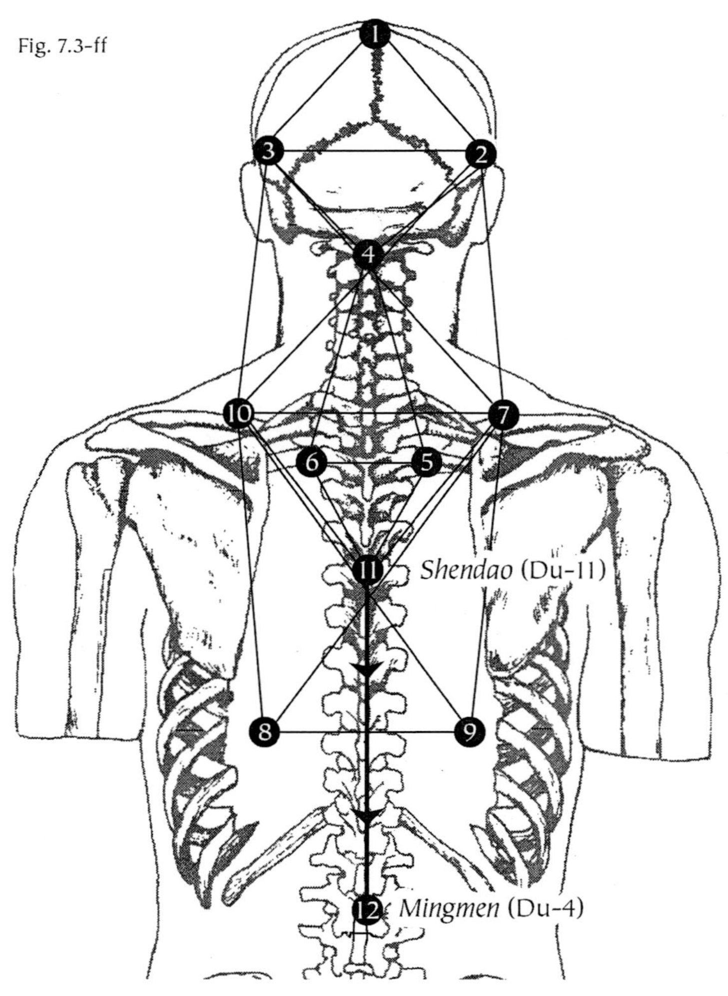

Now have your client bring the qi simultaneously downward from the acupuncture sites of the bilateral *Hunmen* (UB-47) points to connect with *Mingmen* (Du-4) on the spine. (See figure 7.3-gg below.)

**The Wind Mansion Pattern Visualization**

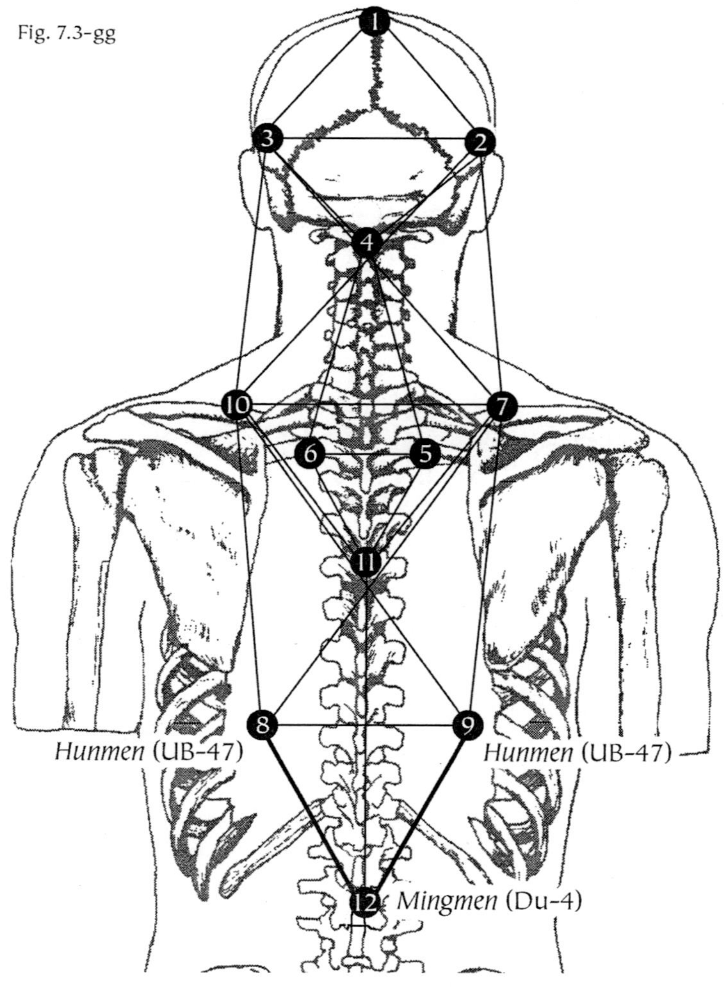


Fig. 7.3-gg

After anchoring the qi at the acupuncture site of *Mingmen* (Du-4) for a few moments, ask your client to bring the qi upward from *Mingmen* (Du-4) to connect again with *Shendao* (Du-11), thus reinforcing the Lower Twin Flame Within connection. (See figure 7.3-hh below.)

## The Wind Mansion Pattern Visualization

Fig. 7.3-hh

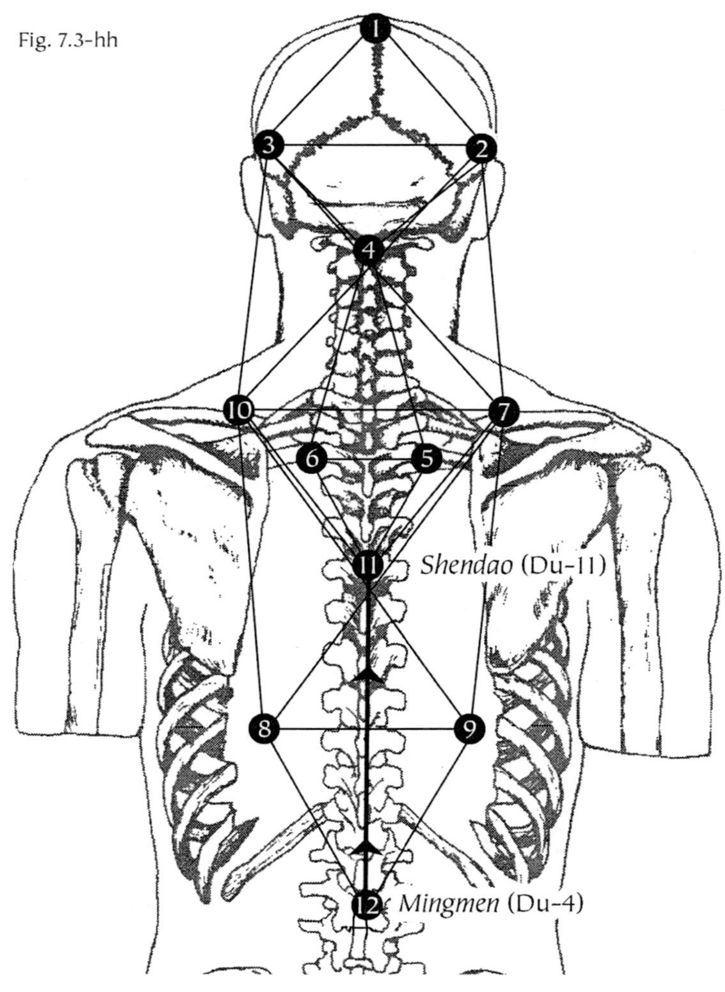

Insert your thirteenth and last acupuncture needle at the acupuncture site of *Dazhui* (Du-14) "The big Hammer" located directly on the spine below the lower border of the spinous process of the seventh cervical vertebra. (See figure 7.3-ii below.)

## The Wind Mansion Pattern Visualization

Fig. 7.3-ii

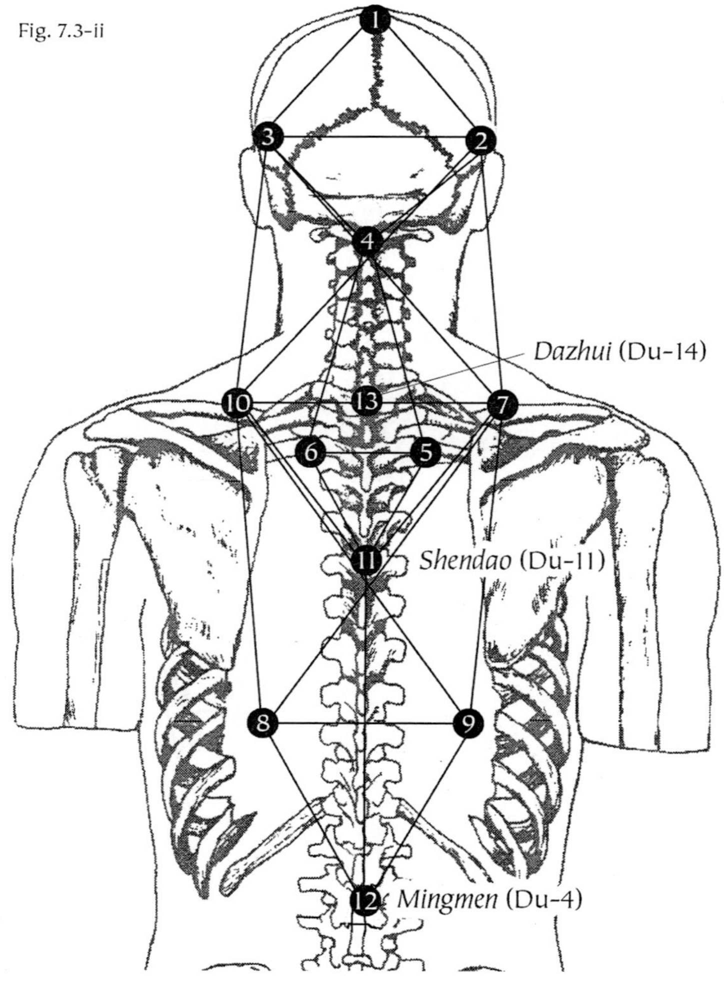

Next have your client move the qi directly up the spine from the acupuncture site of *Shendao* (Du-11) to connect to *Dazhui* (Du-14). (See figure 7.3-jj below.)

## The Wind Mansion Pattern Visualization

Fig. 7.3-jj

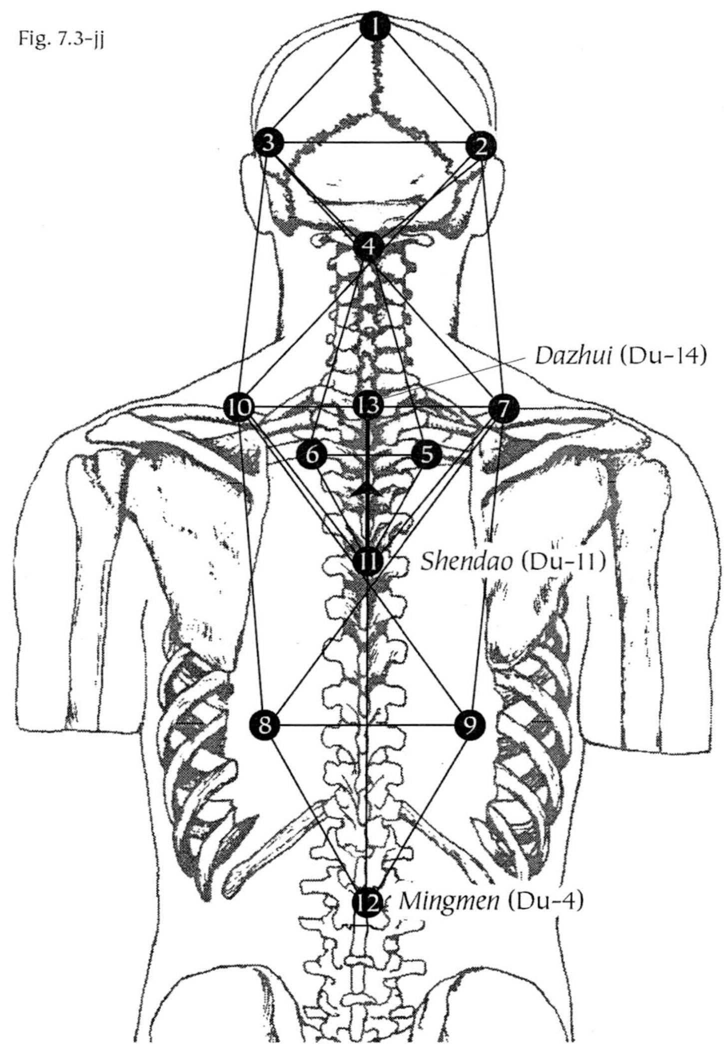

Remember what was said earlier about the "Big Hammer" *Dazhui* (Du-14) point being the key acupuncture point that introduced the concept of morphic resonance to the vocabulary for acupuncturists. Have your client connect *Dazhui* (Du-14) to *Yintang* (Ajna Center) in a non-linear fashion. *Dazhui* (Du-14) is located on the spine below the lower border of the spinous process of the seventh lumbar vertebra. *Yintang* is located on the vertical midline of the forehead between the eyebrows and directly superior to the bridge of the nose. Although the figure below shows a broken line connecting *Dazhui* (Du-14) to *Yintang*, the communication between the two acupuncture points is a non-linear, instantaneous consciousness connection. (See figure 7.3-kk below.)

**The Wind Mansion Pattern Visualization**
**Morphic Resonant Connection**

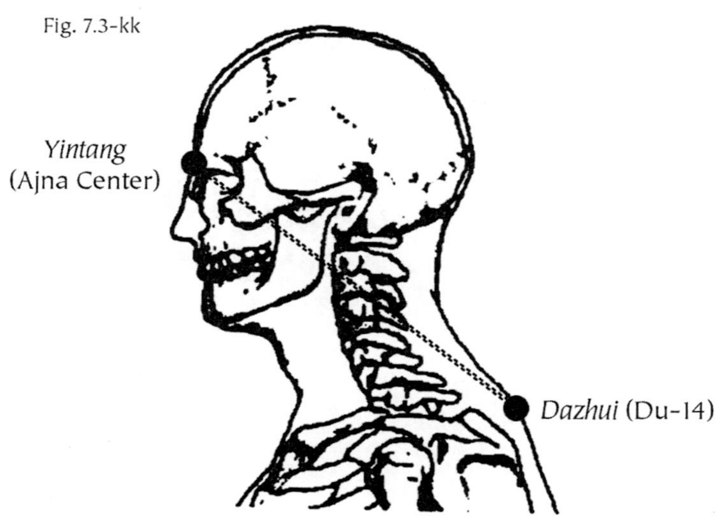


Fig. 7.3-kk

Next ask your client to move the qi upward from the acupuncture location of *Dazhui* (Du-14) to *Feng Fu* (Du-16) located on the vertical midline of the posterior of the head in the slight depression inferior to the external occipital protuberance. The upward movement of qi from *Dazhui* (Du-14) to *Feng Fu* (Du-16) follows the Du meridian pathway of the Etheric Plane. (See figure 7.3-ll below.)

**The Wind Mansion Pattern Visualization**

Fig. 7.3-ll

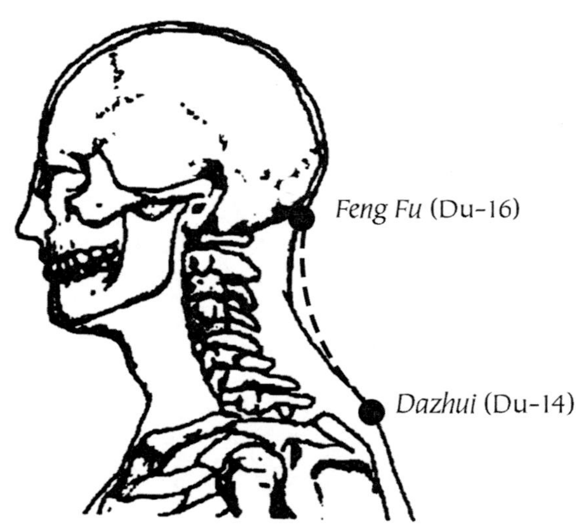


From the acupuncture site of *Feng Fu* (Du-16), you will ask your client to make a linear connection to the acupuncture site of *Yintang* located on the vertical midline of the forehead superior to the bridge of the nose. *Yintang* (Ajna Center) is not needled in the Wind Mansion Pattern. *Dazhui* (Du-14) had to be needled first to activate *Yintang* (Ajna Center). Once *Yintang* (Ajna Center) had been activated, the correct energy field was set up so we could make the linear connection from the acupuncture site of *Feng Fu* (Du-16) to the acupuncture site of *Yintang* (Ajna Center). (See figure 7.3-mm below.)

### The Wind Mansion Pattern Visualization

Fig. 7.3-mm

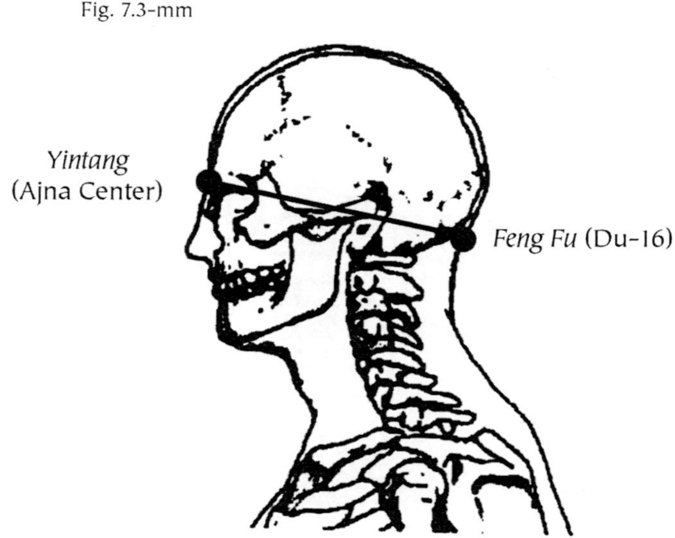


Now ask your client to simultaneously move the qi at the acupuncture sites of both *Yintang* (Ajna Center) and *Feng Fu* (Du-16) upward in a triangular formation to connect with the qi at the acupuncture site of *Tian Man* (Du-20). Just remember that the triangular connection of *Feng Fu* (Du-16) *Yintang* (Ajna Center) and *Tian Man* (Du-20) is the connection of the Three Major Head Centers. The formation of this particular triangular connection will benefit your meditations. (See figure 7.3-nn below.)

**The Wind Mansion Pattern Visualization**
**Three Major Head Centers**

Fig. 7.3-nn

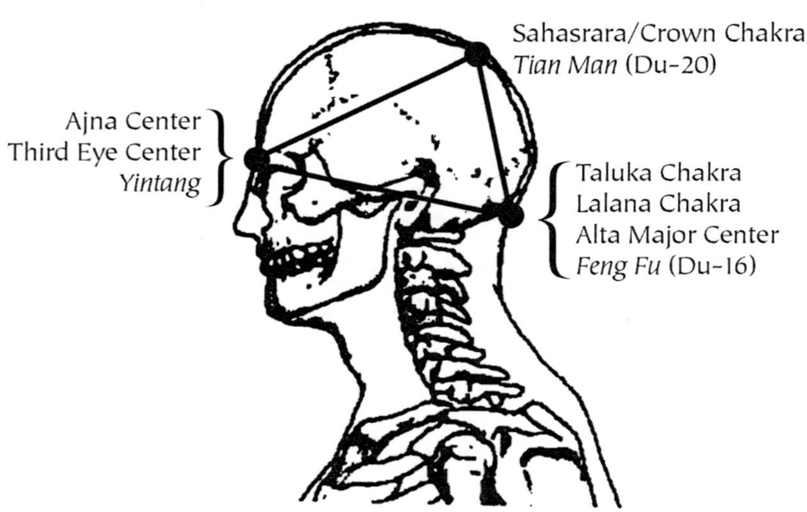


The Wind Mansion Pattern is similar in one way to the *Hun* Follow the *Shen* Pattern represented in Chapter V. Both of these patterns are designed to harmonize the liver system to flow with the natural order of energy within a balanced moving system. The *Hun* of the liver system must give way to the *Shen* of the heart system to allow the greatest inner plane awakenings for an individual. In both of these New Encoding Patterns, we are focusing on strengthening the *Hun* of the liver in a balanced harmonious manner to be able to move into the higher spiritual aspects of our hearts.

The liver likes activity and movement. Stillness comes from the heart system. Sometimes an overactive *Hun* will cause too much chaos in the mind, not allowing the *Shen* to calm the mental chatter.

With the Wind Mansion Pattern, there are two sets of hourglass-shaped geometric formations. One is called the *Hun* Follow the *Shen* Hourglass. The other is called the Heart Field of One Hand Clapping. With every hourglass formation, we have created a Water Triangle with its apex pointing downward and a Fire Triangle with its apex pointing upward. We now have a duel field of complimentary and opposing energies known as the field of Esoteric *Shaoyin*. The two fields are the heart field and the kidney field. Having the Esoteric *Shaoyin* field means that each of the two hourglass fields of the *Hun* Follow the *Shen* and the Heat Field of One Hand Clapping have an overlaying Esoteric *Shaoyin* Field above them.

The Wind Mansion Pattern also has an underlying field of "Wind" points. The bilateral *Feng Men* (UB-12) points and *Feng Fu* (Du-16) strengthen the one's access to the Thirteenth Gate and help move the recipient of the treatment closer to his or her Inner, Spiritual Higher Heart. Our spiritual field has no set form or set location.

The Celestial Hearing Field within the Wind Mansion Pattern also has no form. Celestial Hearing is not located in the physical heart, but rather in a higher vibration of the heart field.

## The Wind Mansion Pattern
### Complete Grid

Fig. 7.3-oo

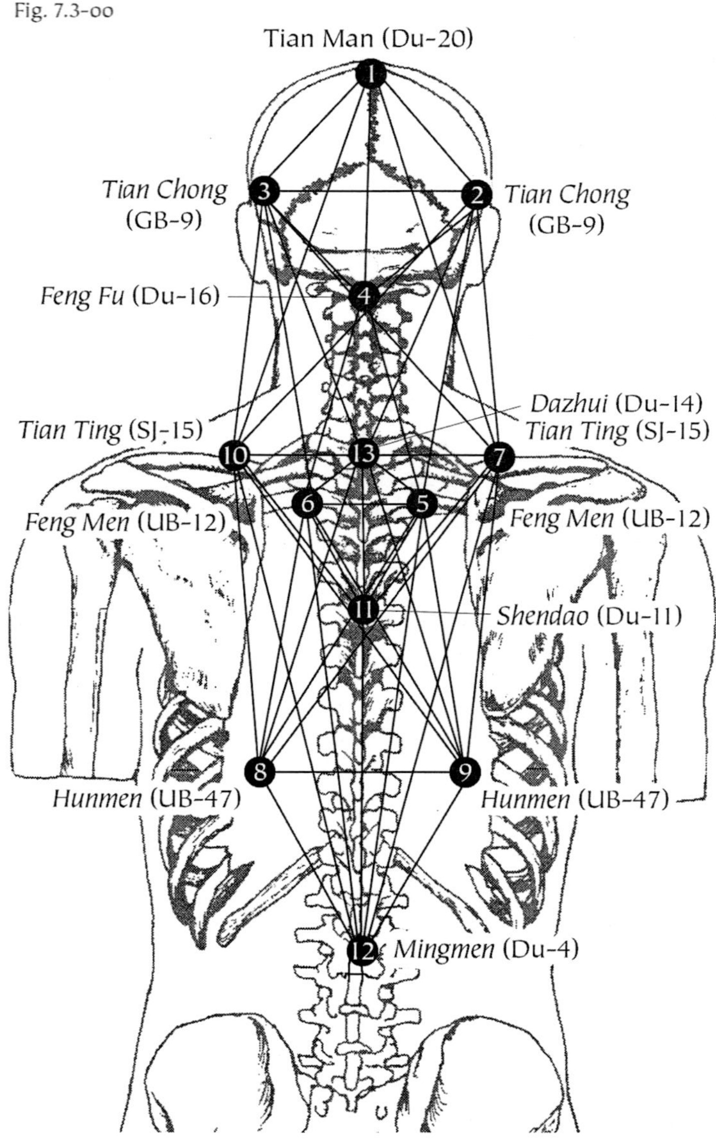

# Glossary:
## Antahkarana, Celestial Fullness: Esoteric Acupuncture, Volume VI

**Alta Major Center**: See Taluka Chakra

**Akashic Records:** This is a field of very fine frequencies that is believed to house everything throughout time for all of humanity. This includes storing all thoughts, deeds and actions of every person who has ever existed in our three-dimensional reality here on Earth. One who is able to acquire a very Still vibratory frequency is allowed an opportunity to reach into and access information stored in this timeless "library" of knowledge and wisdom.

**All Field**: This is a term created in Esoteric Acupuncture to mean an all-encompassing field that includes: all dimensions and no dimensions, all space and spacelessness, all time and timelessness, all of the multiple universes, galaxies, solar systems, old black holes and new black holes, realms much smaller than those containing superstrings and all realities known and those as yet unimaginable to even the greatest human minds of today.

**Antahkarana**: This is the term used in Theosophy to mean a frequency of light or a frequency of consciousness that is built by mental manner, usually during meditation, to assist that individual in accessing, refining and furthering his or her inner, spiritual journey and inner, spiritual awakening. There are many, many levels of spiritual awakenings. The Antahkarana can also be thought of as a personal spiritual antenna for accessing and retrieving a more refined type of stream of consciousness that's different than from our 3-D concrete mind. This stream of consciousness is above the level of the fourth sub-plane of the mental plane. It was discussed earlier in this book that each plane of consciousness has seven sub-planes within. The highest sub-plane is numbered as the first sub-plane. The level above the fourth sub-plane of the mental plane is the third sub-plane that is the lowest level of the causal body. When built and utilized, the Antahkarana accesses and connects the lower concrete mind (sub-planes seven to four) to the higher Causal Sub Planes (sub-levels three to one) of the abstract mind. The Causal Plane acts as the bridge between the concrete mind to connect to the spiritual levels of the Buddhic Plane, Atmic Plane and the higher planes of consciousness.

The stream of consciousness that can be seen emanating upward from the top of a person's head is also known as "The Rainbow Bridge." The various colors will reveal a general level of consciousness for that person. Gold, violet, silver, white, lavender, purple or indigo colored emanations of light are usually indications of being in the consciousness field of the higher head centers or beyond. In my opinion, charcoal, shades of grey, red or orange colored lights emanating from the head are not the most desirable energy fields to be maintained. Building the Antahkarana and utilizing this bridge is one method to move from the dense concrete mind to the higher spiritual heart frequencies.

In the past, some of those who were aware of the Antahkarana may have attempted to build the bridge through meditation. Today the Antahkarana can also be built by another method through certain New Encoding Patterns brought forth in the Esoteric Acupuncture series of works. After the initial Antahkarana is built, you can strengthen and further refine the Antahkarana through meditation and/or by regular Esoteric Acupuncture treatments.

**Atomic Shield**: The Atomic Shield is different from the protective qi known as *Wei Qi* in Chinese medicine. The *Wei Qi* forms the outermost portion of the etheric plane. The etheric plane connects with the astral plane. There is a certain quality of density that is attached to the very outer level of the *Wei Qi* separating the etheric plane from the astral plane. This barrier separating the etheric planes from the astral planes is called the Atomic Shield. Dreams occur on the astral levels that are above the etheric levels. The atomic shield acts as a precautionary barrier to keep certain types of information retrieved on the astral planes from downloading into one's day-to-day consciousness, unless that individual is at a certain level of conscious awareness. Often during dream states, we are shown various levels of information that are of an extremely fine frequency. When a person is not at a certain level of spiritual awareness, that individual may misuse the information. The misuse of certain information does not always mean that the individual is using or sharing the information for negative reasons. That individual may not have developed his or her inner plane discretionary abilities to share or use the information wisely. The Atomic Shield also acts as a barrier to protect oneself from exogenous astral entities or astral debris that may attach directly onto the physical body.

**Axiatonal Grid**: This is a phrase that describes a non-physical system made up of both linear and non-linear, non-physical pathways that collectively have the capability to be able to connect to systems outside of the actual defined pathways within the system. The Axiatonal Grid systems will allow one an opportunity to connect to people, things and places that are of tremendous distances and even to be able to transcend multi-dimensional realities and timelines. There are many Axiatonal Grids. The New Encoding Patterns of Esoteric Acupuncture anchor various grids within your field and create an Axiatonal Grid system. In order to experience a reality by "traversing" an Axiatonal Grid System, the person must be able to Still the Mind and to resonate smoothly with the frequency created by the New Encoding Pattern.

**Bara Shith or Bara Shesh**: Bara is a word used in the ***Old Testament*** to mean Creator and is sometimes used to mean created. The words Shith, Sheth or Shesh can be translated to mean six. When Bara and Shith are combined, the term can be translated to mean: "In Begining, Created Six."

**Bereshith**: This is a Hebrew term that can be translated as: "In Beginning" and comes from Bara Shith which is sometimes translated as Created Six.

**Big Hammer**: This is the name of an acupuncture point medically known as *Dazhui* in Chinese or Du-14 for English speaking acupuncturists, professors or students. *Dazhui*/Du-14 is located directly on the posterior spine below the spinous process of the seventh cervical vertebrae. (For those not familiar with anatomy, picture an imaginary horizontal line drawn on a person's back from the top of one shoulder to the other shoulder. The Big Hammer is located directly on the back on the spine somewhat level with where this imaginary horizontal line intersects the spine. This is only a rough location of the point. (See ***Dazhui*** below.)

**Brahmarandra Chakra**: This is one of the higher head centers and is located within the cranium below the esoteric *Sishencong* location of four acupuncture points. When Kundalini ascends through the Sushumna (central pathway), the Pingala (right side pathway) and the Ida (left side pathway), the energy will usually only ascend as far as the Brahmarandra Chakra located within the cranium. The Brahmarandra Chakra is referred to as the inner "Mountain within the Mountain." This is also the region where the higher light ("light without light") from an fully awakened Ajna Center (at the acupuncture site of *Yintang*) merges and integrates with the higher sound ("sound without sound") of the Taluka Chakra (Alta Major Center) at the acupuncture site of *Feng Fu* (Du-16).

**Celestial Fullness** (*Tian Man*/Du-20): Celestial Fullness is a phrase that implies that some level of spiritual awakening has already occurred. Celestial Fullness is the translation of the acupuncture point known as *Tian Man* in Chinese. *Tian Man* (Du-20) is also the site of the "hidden" thirteenth gateway. This hidden gateway is found approximately one *cun* (one inch) posteriorly to the traditional location of *Bai Hui* (Du-20). You will not activate the hidden gateway to Celestial Fullness by inserting an acupuncture needle at the site of the traditional location of *Du-20*/Bai Hui. The site of Celestial Fullness is also esoterically known as the "Center of the Center."

**Chohan**: This is a term usually applied to great souls who have left the physical body and are working in the higher, non-physical realms to assist humanity and the planet Earth in our ascension process to a finer frequency realm. In Esoteric Acupuncture, Chohan is used to designate an ascended master.

**Cinnabar Fields**: These are three energetic regions on the anterior of the body that hold much qi and special encodings. The Lower Cinnabar Field is located inferiorly to the umbilicus approximately two to three *cun* below the umbilicus. The acupuncture point known as *Guan Yuan* (Ren-4) is located directly on the anterior vertical midline of the body and three *cun* below the umbilicus. An alternative name for this point is *Dan Tian* that is translated as Cinnabar Field. The Lower Cinnabar Field houses the Mingmen Fire and is a region that holds and generates much power.

The Central Cinnabar Field is located in the region of the acupuncture site of *Yuan Jian* (Ren-17). This is the heart region that encompasses and controls more than the heart system of Traditional Chinese Medicine. The Anahata (Heart Chakra) is located here, as well as the *Hun* influencing the energetics of the Central Cinnabar Field.

The Upper Cinnabar Field is located in the upper forehead and anterior hairline region of the body. The energetics of the upper Cinnabar Field includes some aspects of the Inner, Spiritual Higher Heart field, as well as holding keys to the gateway to access the Sahasrara (Crown Chakra) and the higher chakras above. The Upper Cinnabar Field is in the region of the Brahmarandra Chakra within the cranium directly below the Sahasrara (Crown Chakra),

**Clairaudience**: The ability to hear beyond the realms of what is termed our three-dimensional hearing. There are multiple levels of clairaudience.

**Clairsentience**: This is a state of heightened awareness and a very expanded level of consciousness where a person just "knows things" by being able to access the higher realms of his or her higher heart. This knowingness comes without prior studies or prior exposure to that information or knowledge in the more traditional three-dimensional methods. You just "know things by heart." There are also multiple levels of clairsentience.

**Clairvoyance**: This is a state of being able to see in the realms beyond the normal three-dimensional reality. There is an outer level of clairvoyance where people are able to use their physical eyes to see beyond the three-dimensional realms. There is also a higher, inner vision or internal insight where a person can close his or her eyes and "see" within the inner realms to view with clarity events, people and places without the use of the physical eyes.

***Cun***: This is a distance of measurement in the Chinese medical system for acupuncture that does not have an exact measurement like in the West. Sometimes one *cun* may be equal to approximately one inch or 2.54 cm. Other times one *cun* may be smaller or larger than one inch. The measurement of one *cun* depends on each person and the anatomical location that the acupuncturist is trying to measure.

The distance from the center of the spine to the medial

border of each scapula is considered three *cun* in Chinese medicine. On some people this distance seems quite large. On other people this distance seems very small. No matter what the actual length is in terms of centimeters or inches, the distance from the center of the spine to the medial border of each scapula is three *cun*. This means that the distance from the medial border of the left scapular to the medical border of the right scapula is six *cun*.

The vertical distance from the umbilicus to the superior border of the pubic bone is considered five *cun*. The actual distance varies tremendously depending on the body type of the individual. On those with a relatively short upper torso, that distance may be very short. I have treated some Asian men who have long upper torsos and the distance from the umbilicus to the superior border of the pubic bone is very long versus those with short upper torsos. No matter what the distance is in centimeters or inches, the Chinese say that the measurement is one *cun*. If this explanation is still confusing, please consult any of the acupuncture textbooks used in the acupuncture and Oriental Medical schools

***Dazhui* (Du-14)** is a very important key acupuncture point in Esoteric Acupuncture. The Chinese say that the name "Big Hammer" refers to the fact that the seventh cervical vertebrae is often (but not always) the most prominent protrusion in this area of the spine. Some Chinese also translate *Dazhui* as meaning "Big Vertebrae."

Using a hammer usually means there is some level of physical force, or striking, applied to insert a nail somewhere or to insert some level of force to break or pry open something. Esoterically, the Big Hammer refer to the fact that the gentle insertion of an acupuncture needle at this posterior site has a gentle, "esoteric hammering" action that creates the "correct" frequency, when used within a New Encoding Pattern in Esoteric Acupuncture, to activate the Third Eye point through a consciousness connection known as morphic resonance. This "hammering" on the posterior of the body directly on the spine has the ability to signal and activate a specific acupuncture site located on the anterior midline of the forehead and directly superior to the bridge of the nose. This acupuncture site is known as *Yintang* in Chinese. In the Chakra system, this acupuncture site is called "The Third Eye." We are "striking" an acupuncture site on the back (gentle insertion of an acupuncture needle) to communicate with an acupuncture site on the front. This communication process does not involve a linear connection between these two acupuncture sites. The traditional accepted explanation of connections between acupuncture sites is that there is a linear connection through the acupuncture meridian pathways or connections through an inner connecting pathway. This type of connection is a linear connection. In Esoteric Acupuncture, inserting a needle at the site of *Dazhui*/Du-14 instantaneously allows *Dazhui*/Du-14 to communicate with *Yintang*/the Third Eye. No manner how quickly one acupuncture site communicates with an another acupuncture via a linear connection, it is not an instantaneous consciousness connection that occurs instantly with morphic resonance.

Esoterically, "The Big Hammer" point refers to the fact that with very little force, but force with the correct, gentle frequency at the correct location will give us "big" results as if we had used a Big Hammer.

The connection of *Dazhui* (Du-14) to *Yintang* was the first acupuncture connection that was shown to me to be able to incorporate Rupert Sheldrake's concept of morphic resonance into an expanded language of acupuncture for the 21st century.

**Djwhal Khul**: Djwhal Khul was a Tibetan teacher and lama often referred to as an Ascended Master in the Theosophical teachings. He is the person responsible for the information given in most of the Alice Bailey works and also assisted Helena P. Blavatsky with information in her massive works called ***The Secret Doctrine***. Djwhal Khul has overlighted some of the works in the Esoteric Acupuncture series, especially ***Sea of Fire, Cosmic Fire: Esoteric Acupuncture, Volume IV***.

**Essence (*Jing*)**: This is the substance written about in Traditional Chinese Medicine that is a fundamental energy of the body and of a person's existence. The *jing* is controlled by the lung system and is essential for life. One's *jing* is formed at the very beginning of the conception of a newly created fetus. At the moment of death, the jing no longer exists on the Personality Plane and returns to the Soul Plane.

**Essence, Monadic**: This is an extremely fine frequency of matter that exists in the atomic sub plane of each of the seven levels of consciousness. The monadic essence is contained within the finest frequency of our Higher, Inner *Shen*. Unlike one's regular essence/*jing*, discussed in the Traditional Chinese Medical texts, our Monadic Essence returns to the Monadic Plane at the time of the death of the physical vehicle by way of our Monadic Ray.

**Granthi(s)**: This is the term for astral knots or areas of astral blockages along the Kundalini pathways. The granthis will stop Kundalini from ascending further. You must work with refined mental matter to shatter these astral blockages.

**Hartmann Grid:** This is a network of geopathic lines or pathways discovered by Dr. Ernest Hartmann, a German medical doctor in the early 20th Century. These geopathic lines cover the entire planet. One set of lines run approximately North and South and is intersected by another set of lines that run approximately East and West. One set of lines are approximately six feet to seven feet apart and are intersected by lines that are approximately eight feet to eight and a half feet apart creating rectangular grids.

Dr. Hartmann noticed that when some patients were placed in certain beds at the hospital, those patients seemed to become more stressed and their conditions seemed to worsen compared to patients sleeping on other beds in different parts of the same room. Was there another explanation that was not taught in the medical school? Dr. Hartmann discovered that there were certain underground forces along certain pathways that emitted electromagnetic waves detrimental to humans. When two of those pathways intersected, it created a greater stress field for humans. That is the Hartmann Grid.

For those of you with household pets, dogs will not sleep in an area that is emanating upward rays that are detrimental to humans. On the other hand, cats seem to gravitate to the spots that are emanating those types of rays that are detrimental to humans. If you have a pet cat and that cat sleeps in a specific spot in your house or apartment, it may be best to not sit or sleep in that same spot. If you have a household dog that likes a spot in your house or apartment, you might considered placing your favorite chair or couch on top of that specific area that your dog rests. (Do not worry. Your dog will find another stress free spot in your house or apartment where the dog will rest.)

**Heart Gate**: This is one translation of the Chinese name *Shenmen* for the acupuncture point located on the medial lateral portion of the wrist and known as Heart-7 (Ht-7) to English-speaking practitioners. *Shenmen* is also translated to mean Spirit Gate.

**Heart Path**: This is one translation of the acupuncture point located directly on the spine below the lower border of the spinous process of the fifth thoracic vertebra. The English-speaking practitioners call this acupuncture point Du-11, while the Chinese speaking practitioner calls this acupuncture point *Shendao*. *Shendao* is also translated as Spirit Path.

**I Am That I Am**: This is the stage of consciousness where one knows who he or she is and spiritually and intuitively knows that the True-Self and the God-Self are one. In Hebrew this is known as Ahiye Asher Ahiye. In Esoteric Acupuncture, the consciousness of "I Am That I Am" corresponds to the Monadic Plane. "I Am That" is the level of consciousness that corresponds to the Soul Plane. "I Am" is the level of consciousness that corresponds to the Personality Plane.

**Indu Chakra**: This is a minor chakra that is situated superiorly to the Manas Chakra and reflects our god-mind, also called the Spiritual Mind. The Indu Chakra contributes to certain attributes that are also connected to the higher aspects of the Anahata (Heart Chakra). These attributes may include: acquiring patience, cultivating gentleness and mercy in dealing with others and for obtaining the state of mind of non-attachment. This chakra gives us the ability to make intelligent decisions and maintain discrimination, similar to attributes of the small intestines system in the Chinese Medical Model. The Indu Chakra also controls our ability to always have presence of mind (Mindfulness), to maintain supreme Wisdom in all of one's thoughts and actions, assists one to always be in the moment (at-one-ment) and is attracted to The Truth, especially one's own Truth. When this chakra is activated, you will not be one of the mindless sheep with a herd mentality obeying the sheepdog and blindly following the sheep herder (shepherd).

**Key Codes**: This is a term used in Esoteric Acupuncture to describe a gathering of consciousness that holds the most fundamental essence of the particles and waves that have made up who we are in every incarnation. The Key Codes are more refined than our DNA or other physical, emotional or mental traits or characteristics that define an individual. Our individual Key Codes hold the "secrets" to who we are and are stored in our Original Encodings.

We are able to begin the unraveling process for gaining a clearer picture of our own Key Codes when permanent atoms of the lower planes bridge the gap to communicate the permanent atoms on the higher levels. Bridging the gap between the two levels is what we are doing with the building of one's Antahkarana.

**Lalana Chakra** (See Taluka Chakra)

**Light Quotient**: This is a term used in Esoteric Acupuncture to describe the level of awakening by an individual. The brighter the light emanating from a person indicates a greater spiritual awareness and an expanded awakening for that individual. Less light emanating from an individual indicates a denser vibratory rate and a lower vibrational reality with a lesser degree of spiritual awakening. It is desirable, in my opinion, to strive to obtain the highest light quotient possible.

The amount of one's Light Quotient can be seen in one's aura, in the soul of one's eyes or in the depth and beauty of a smile. Do not be fooled by a sexual smile or a staged smiled by a politician or celebrity. You can also sense and know one's Light Quotient by trusting your own higher heart and tapping into your own clairsentient powers.

**Light without Light**: See Original *Hun*.

**Lower Quaternary:** This is the phrase that describes the four lowest levels, or planes of reality in human consciousness. These four planes consist of: the dense physical planes, the etheric planes, the astral planes and the four lower sub planes of the mental plane.

**Manas Chakra:** This is a minor chakra that is situated above the Ajna Center (The Third Eye) and is sometime known as the Forehead Chakra, compared to the Ajna Center that is sometimes called the Brow Chakra. The Manas Chakra is connected to the higher mind and also the subconscious mind. Some attributes of the lower aspect of this chakra have given birth to the phrase "In the prison of thought of the thinking mind." The higher aspect of the mind is called the $6^{th}$ sense in the East and is not the $6^{th}$ sense of the West that is associated with the power of clairvoyance.

**Maya**: This is a term that means illusion or not real in relationship to the inner plane realities. Illusion does not mean non-existent in the same manner as when someone is imagining something or making something up. Illusion in the context of Maya means being swayed by materialistic things and endeavors and allowing the lower ego of fame, fortune and accumulating things to take precedence over the inner spiritual work. Maya refers to the emotional levels of the Astral Plane and to the outer world of glamour and recognitions that are not as lasting as one's inner plane work and inner plane accomplishments.

**Monadic Plane:** In the three-plane model of consciousness, this plane is considered the top plane above the Soul Plane and the Personality Plane. In the seven-plane model of consciousness, the Monadic Plane is the sixth plane directly below the top plane of consciousness called the Logoic Plane.

**Monadic Ray:** This is a fabric of consciousness that exists in everyone and descends from the Monadic Plane through the Soul Plane down into the physical vehicle on the Personality Plane. This fabric of consciousness transports information contained in the finest frequencies of our Original Consciousness and Original Encoding to the dense lower planes of existence. Because most people have not bothered to awaken the consciousness of their inner world, most people not aware of this level of consciousness.

**Morphic Resonance:** This is the term used in Esoteric Acupuncture to explain an instantaneous consciousness connection between any numbers of sites or locations that are distant from one another, but are not connected in a linear fashion. This term is credited to Rupert Sheldrake and his concept of the morphogenetic grid.

**Nadi system**: This is an extremely complex HIndu system of the inner pathways of prana/qi flow within the various planes of consciousness of the human body. According to Swami Muktananda, the nadi system contains seventy-two thousand inner pathways. These are pathways and not acupuncture points. The Hindu nadi system preceded the Chinese acupuncture meridian system and is much more complex than the acupuncture meridian system.

To contrast the Hindu nadi system with the Chinese system of pathways, the Chinese acupuncture meridian system has twelve major bilateral pathways, a central vertical anterior pathway, a central vertical posterior pathway, one major horizontal pathway, pathways known as extraordinary meridians and inner pathways known as *luo* connecting pathways or *luo* channels. The acupuncture meridian system is a more manageable system for the human mind of today. It would literally be impossible for the human mind of today to memorize, locate and discuss seventy-two thousand pathways, let alone memorize the crossing pathways or the energy sites that would correspond to a very expansive and massive new acupuncture system.

**Original Consciousness**: Original Consciousness is an extremely fine frequency contained within each monad. As the monad divides into the twelve different Soul Extensions, each of those twelve Soul Extensions will carry the Original Consciousness from the same monad. As consciousness densifies in the Soul Plane, the twelve Soul Extensions begin to gather different frequencies. The process of gathering consciousness of a denser vibrations develop slightly different references back to the Original Consciousness that each share from the monad on the Monadic Plane.

One portion of Original Consciousness is also the term used in Esoteric Acupuncture to describe the state of extreme Stillness that is "The Gateway" to the Universal Mind and to Universal Mind/The All Field. (The Universal Mind is contained within Universal Mind, but not vice versa.) At this state of consciousness, everything in Universe is connected. Original

Consciousness is not confined to a reality that only includes our planetary, galactic, solar or cosmic conscious mind.

On a lower level, our Original Consciousness is the very beginning, or starting point, of our consciousness as we prepare to descend into a denser level of three-dimensional realities in a human physical body. Our Original Consciousness is contained within our personal monad at the level of the Monadic Plane. This is the plane of All-Knowing and the state of complete Knowingness. This is the vibrational state of Fundamental Clairsentience and is one of the Three Vapors state of reality.

**Original Encodings:** This consciousness separates slightly from the Original Consciousness of the monad as each monadic extension prepares for the journey through the Soul Plane into the densest level of the Personality Plane. The Original Encoding is contained within the Original Consciousness. Since there are twelve possible monadic extensions from each monad, there are twelve different, but similar, Original Encodings from each monad. The consciousness from both our Original *Hun* and our Original *Shen* contribute to our Original Encoding.

**Original *Hun*:** This is an extremely fine frequency of consciousness that originates at the Monadic Plane level. Our Original *Hun* contributes to the consciousness of our Original Encoding. Although the Original *Hun* is very closely tied in with the Original *Shen,* they are different and distinct fabrics of consciousness. As one's consciousness becomes more densified, the Original *Hun* returns to the liver system within the individual.

Our Original *Hun* is the seat of a refined reality known as "Light without Light." It requires an extremely fine frequency of the *Hun* of the liver system to move into clairvoyance to be able to see beyond the three-dimensional realms. "Light without Light" is a much higher realm of insight and does not include anything associated with outer sight or seeing. "Light without Light" is a plane of reality known as one of the Three Vapors.

The gateway to initially open up this field is through activating the Ajna Center at the acupuncture point of *Yintang*.

**Original *Shen***: The Original *Shen* is an extremely fine frequency of consciousness, even more refined than the consciousness of our Original *Hun*. Both the Original *Hun* and the Original *Shen* are contained within our Original Consciousness. The Original *Shen* is that portion of our Original Consciousness, along with our Original *Hun*, that flow from the Monad Plane down into the denseness of our concrete minds at the Personality Plane. Since most people are not aware of the concept of our Original Consciousness, they will not know, or may not have the desire to unravel the mysteries of our Original Consciousness. Contained within the fabrics of consciousness of our Original *Shen* is the answer to the "mystery" of our puzzle piece in life.

Original *Shen* contains the field of "Sound without Sound." In Traditional Chinese Medicine, one's physical hearing is controlled by the kidney system. For celestial hearing, the heart system controls this realm of reality. "Sound without Sound" is a state of consciousness and is not dependent upon any degree of physical hearing. Remember it is controlled by the Higher, Inner Spiritual Heart.

The gateway for the initial activation of the reality of the field of "Sound without Sound" is through the Taluka/Lalana Chakra. The initial activation can be set in motion by inserting an acupuncture needle at the site of *Feng Fu* (Du-16) "The Wind Mansion." Remember, in Traditional Chinese Medicine, the liver system controls wind. The Taluka/Lalana Chakra is the seat of reality of the field of '"Sound without Sound." But, the field of "Sound without Sound" is contained within the Original *Shen* of the higher heart system. This is another example of the heart leading and controlling the liver, or "The *Hun* follow the *Shen*".

**Permanent Atoms**: These are very minute frequencies, or centers of force, which form the central focal point and the attractive force that act as the building blocks for the incoming Monad to manifest as an individual on the Personality Plane. Each monad comes down from the Monadic Plane to the Soul Plane and eventually to the Personality Plane where an individual resides as a new incarnate in the three-dimensional realms.

***Po***: Think of this term as various levels of consciousness that are connected with the lung system within the Chinese Medical role model. One aspect of the Po is our Corporeal Soul that usually doe not survive after the death of the physical vehicle.

***Shaoyin*, Esoteric**: In the Six Channel Theory of Traditional Chinese Medicine (TCM), *Shaoyin* is a connection and communication system involving the heart system and the kidney system. When *Shaoyin* is used in TCM, the practitioners are interested in what is known as yang deficiency referring to cold symptoms such as: copious and frequent urination, lower back pain, low energy or lethargy, low sex drive, cold limbs, loose stools, no thirst and a dull, pale complexion.

In Esoteric Acupuncture, we are interested in fields, rather than the signs and symptoms of imbalances taught to TCM practitioners. The field within and without of an upward pointing triangle is called a Fire Triangle of the heart system. The field within and without of a downward pointing triangle is a Water Triangle of the kidney system. These opposing, yet complimentary upward and downward pointing triangles represent the fields of Esoteric *Shaoyin*. The kidneys control fear and all its tentacles. The heart contains love and all of its many branches.

***Shen***: This is a consciousness realm controlled by the heart. In Traditional Chinese Medicine, *Shen* is said to mean both mind and spirit.

***Shendao*** (Du-11) see Heart Path.

**Spirit Gate**: See Heart Gate.

**Spirit Path**: See Heart Path.

**Taluka Chakra**: This chakra or frequency (information) storage site is also known as the Alta Major Center in the Djwhal Khul system or the Lalana Chakra or Talu Chakra by other Hindu systems. These are merely different names for the same chakra site. This chakra can be activated by inserting an acupuncture needle into the acupuncture site of *Feng Fu* (Du-16) located on the vertical midline of the posterior of the body in the depression below the occipital protuberance on the back of the head. Needling the Taluka Chakra will activate the stored memory that is connected to our Inner Sound, or "Sound without Sound," of our higher male (father) aspect.

*Feng Fu* (Du-16) is often translated as "Wind Mansion." In Chinese Medical theory, wind usually refers to the liver system and may cause physical symptoms such as: twitching, tics, stiffness of the body or joints or symptoms of Bell's Palsy.

But, "wind" can also refer to the nebulous realms of spirit and spiritual ideas. This particular region of the body on the posterior of the head, in the depression inferior to the occipital protuberance, is one key activation site for all of the "head" centers including: the Ajna Center, Manus Chakra, Indu Chakra, Brahmarandra Chakra (Lalana Chakra), Guru Chakra and the Sahasrara (Crown Chakra). The Taluka Chakra (Alta Major Center) is anatomically located at the lowest level of the seven head centers.

Inserting an acupuncture needle at the acupuncture site of *Feng Fu* (Du-16) will also connect the head centers with a higher aspect of the Muladhara (Root Chakra). Needling and activating the qi at *Feng Fu* (Du-16) stimulates the medulla oblongata that is the part of the brain connected and controls the Muladhara (Root Chakra).

**Tetrahedral Consciousness**: In the Esoteric Acupuncture works, this is the "new" type of consciousness that was needed by the larger brains of the early Homo Sapiens known as Cro-Magnon. Tetrahedral consciousness was not needed by the species of human-like entities with the smaller brains that existed before the Cro-Magnons made their appearance on planet Earth. A tetrahedron has six vectors. Tetrahedral Consciousness is the phrase that explains the saying: "In beginning, created six.

**Three Planes of Consciousness**: According to this particular model, one's consciousness and existence are broken down into three distinct levels.

The Monadic Plane is the top level of consciousness in this three tiered model. This is the level that the spirit eventually returns to after the death of the physical vehicle. This is the level from where our Monadic Ray originates. Our Monadic Essence is stored here within our Inner Spiritual Higher *Shen*.

The Soul Plane is the level of consciousness above our everyday three-dimensional reality. This is the level where one's "Spirit Guides" reside. This is one level that is obtainable for those who are able to quiet the mind during meditation.

The Personality Plane is the consciousness of our everyday three-dimensional reality. This is the plane where our physical, astral (emotional) and mental consciousnesses reside.

**Upper Quaternary**: This is a phrase used in Esoteric Acupuncture to describe the four upper levels of consciousness. Going from the lowest of the four levels to the highest level, these planes of consciousness consist of: the Buddhic, Atmic, Monadic and Logoic Planes of consciousness. In Esoteric Acupuncture, the Causal Plane is considered the gateway from the Lower Quaternary to the Upper Quaternary and from the Upper Quaternary down to the Lower Quaternary.

**Wayu**: This is a Hindu term to describe a very refined, subtle stage of Kundalini. The subtle frequency of Wayu requires that it ascends through the Brahma Nadi, the most refined Nadi pathway within the Sushumna. The less refined stages of Kundalini will ascend though the Sushumna and other pathways within the Sushumna that are less refined than the Brahma Nadi.

Wayu contains no electrical charge, contains no particles and has no mass. Wayu is able to travel faster than the speed of light. This frequency is not included within the theoretical physicist's model of Superstring Theory or with TOE, the Theory of Everything. Wayu is not an electromagnetic wave, it is not gravity or either of the nuclear waves of Superstring Theory. Also, Wayu is not part of the electro-weak field. Yet, according to Hindu scholars and serious meditators, if Wayu is not contained within the Theory of Everything, how can the Theory of Everything be complete?

***Wei Qi***: This is a term used in Traditional Chinese Medicine to describe the outermost protective barrier on the etheric layer that acts as a protective barrier for the dense physical body. The *Wei Qi* is built by the lung qi and the large intestine qi. The *Wei Qi* is also known as our protective qi due to the fact that this outer layer protects the body from exogenous pathogenic factors that may adversely challenge a person such as: dampness, wind, heat and other outside factors that may attack the body causing disease or problems. This outer etheric layer borders the astral plane. (See Atomic Shield.)

**Wisarga:** This is a term meaning "power bridge" and is used in Esoteric Acupuncture to denote an energetic connection that connects two energetic areas. The main wisarga (power bridge) we are concerned with is the connection from the intracranial Brahmarandra Chakra through the esoteric *Tian Man* (Du-20) gateway to the Sahasrara (Crown Chakra) that is located above the cranium. This power bridge can be built through extreme concentration using refined mental matter, or by an Esoteric

Acupuncture treatment by a practitioner who is well versed in the Ageless Wisdom Teachings and is also doing inner plane work. There is another wisarga above the head that connects the Sahasrara (Crown Chakra) to the more advanced Cosmic Chakras that are located above the Sahasrara (Crown Chakra). This particular wisarga connects the Sahasrara (Crown Chakra) to the Mahan Chakra located directly above the Sahasrara.

***Wuji:*** In the context of Esoteric Acupuncture, *Wuji* is thought of as the Chinese term to describe the state of reality somewhat equivalent to the Qabbalistic realm of reality known as Ain. Ain is called Negative Existence or The No-Thing. Using the translation of *Wuji* by Jan Diepersloot in his book ***Warriors of Stillness***, he states: *"Ji means beginning and wu is negation, so Wuji means before the beginning, i.e., the big void or nothingness."* *Wuji* is the state of being before the split into yin and yang.

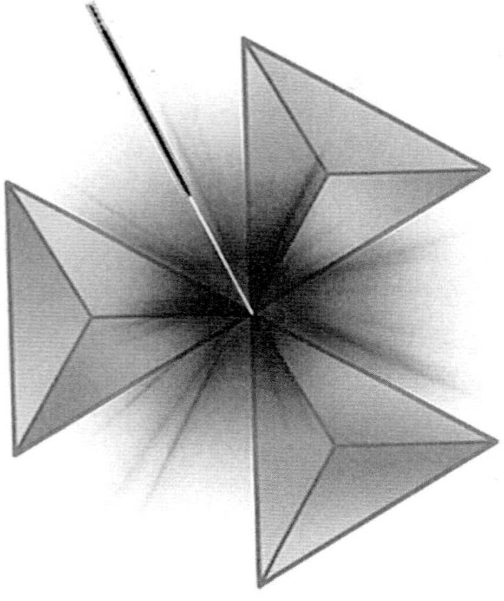

# Vol. VI - Footnotes by Chapter

## Chapter 1: The Spiritual Side Of Esoteric Acupuncture

1. Louis Sahagun. ***Master of the Mysteries: The Life of Manly Palmer Hall***. Port Townsend, WA: Process Media, 2008, p. 189.

2. Alice Bailey. ***A Treatise on Cosmic Fire***. New York, NY: Lucis Publishing Co., 1925, p. 848.

3. Elisabeth De La Vallee. . ***A Study of Qi***. Monkey Press: Norfolk, UK, 2006, p.36.

4. Izla Veith (a translation). ***The Yellow Emperor's Classic of Internal Medicine***. Berkeley, CA: University of California Press, 1949, p. 152.

5. Philip Babcock Gove, Ph.D., (editor-in-chief). ***Webster's Third New International Unabridged Dictionary***. Springfield: MA: Merriam-Webster, Inc., 1986, p. 776.

6. ***Webster's Third New International Unabridged Dictionary***. p. 1043.

7. Swami Muktananda. ***Play of Consciousness***. South Fallsburg, NY: SYDA Foundation, 1978, .31.

8. J.J. Hurtak. ***The Book of Knowledge: The Keys of Enoch***. Los Gatos, CA.: The Academy for Future Science, 1977, p. 523.

9. Jose Arguelles, Ph.D. ***Time & The Technosphere***. Rochester, VT: Bear & Company, 2002, p. 72.

10. R. Buckminster Fuller. ***Synergetics***. New York, NY: Macmillan Publishing Company, 1975, p. 239.

11. Ibid., p. 314.

12. Ibid., pp. 238-239.

13. ***Webster's***. p. 1802.

14. Henrietta Bernstein. ***Cabalah Primer***. Marina Del Rey, CA: DeVorss & Company, Publisher, 1984, p. 100.

15. Isaac Myer. ***Qabbalah, The Philosophy of Ibn Geberol***. San Diego, CA: Wizards Bookshelf, reprinted 1988. (First published in 1888.), p. 127.

16. Manly P. Hall. ***The Secret Teachings of All Age,*** Los Angeles, CA: The Philosophical Research Society, Inc., 1977, p. CXVII.

17. George Musser. ***Scientific American, Which Came First—Galaxies or Black Holes?*** (Internet article), January 7, 2009, p. 2.

18. Thompson, Andrea. ***Black Holes Preceded Galaxies, Discovery Suggests***. (Internet article), p. 1.

19. Ibid., p. 1.

20. Pam Frost Gorder. ***Black Holes Form First, Galaxies Follow: New Quasar Study***. (Internet article), February 15, 2014, p. 1.

21. Jan Diepersloot. ***Warriors of Stillness, Meditative Traditions in the Chinese Martial Arts Volume I***. Walnut Creek, CA: Center for Healing and the Arts, 1995, p. 6.

22. ***Secret Teachings***. p. CXVII.

23. ***Secret Teachings***. p. CXVII.

## Chapter II: Master Window Groups of Esoteric Acupuncture

1. Wallace Wattles. ***The Wisdom of Wallace Wattles***.(Compilation of ***The Science of Getting Rich, The Science of Being Great*** and ***The Science of Being Well***), Printed in U.S.A.: BN Publishing, 2007, p. 115.

2. Miyamoto, Musashi. ***A Book of Five Rings***. The Overlook Press: New York, NY, 1974, p. 39.

3. Deadman, Peter, and Mazin Al-Kafaji with Kevin Baker. ***A Manual of Acupuncture***. Vista, CA: Journal of Chinese Medicine Publications, 1998, p. 48.

4. Andrew Ellis, Nigel Wiseman and Ken Boss. ***Grasping the Wind***. Brookline, MA: Paradigm Publications, 1989, p. 209.

5. ***A Manuel of Acupuncture***, p. 354.

6. *Xinnong Cheng*, (Chief editor). ***Chinese Acupuncture and Moxibustion***. Beijing, China: Foreign Language Press, 1987, p. 185.

7. Giovanni Maciocia. ***The Foundations of Chinese Medicine***. Edinburgh, Scotland: Churchill-Livingston, 1989, p. 99.

8. Ibid., p. 99.

9. Ibid., p. 98.

## Chapter III: Fabrics of Consciousness in Chinese Medicine

1. Claude Larre and Elisabeth Rochat de la Vallee. ***The Heart in Ling Shu Chapter 8***. Norfolk, UK: Monkey Press, 1989, p.61.

2. Wallace Wattles. ***The Wisdom of Wallace Wattles***. (Compilation of ***The Science of Getting Rich, The Science of Being Great*** and ***The Science of Being Well***), Printed in U.S.A.: BN Publishing, 2007, p. 37.

3. Giovanni Maciocia. ***The Practice of Chinese Medicine***. Edinburgh, Scotland: Churchill Livingstone, 1989, pp. 197.

4. Ibid., p.198.

5. Ted J. Kaptchuk, O.M.D. ***The Web That Has No Weaver***. New York, NY: Congdon & Weed, 1983, pp. 45 & 46.

6. Joseph *Changqing Yang*, Ph.D., L.Ac. ***Shen Disturbance, A Guideline for Psychiatry In Traditional Chinese Medicine***. Los Angeles, CA: Self Published, 2002, pp. 24 & 25.

7. ***The Heart in Ling Shu Chapter 8***. p. 10.

8. Claude Larre and Elisabeth Rochat De La Vallee. ***The Liver.*** Norfolk, UK: Monkey Press, 1994, pp. 71 & 72.

9. Ibid., pp. 68 & 68.

10. Philip Babcock Gove, Ph.D. (editor-in-chief). ***Webster's Third New International Unabridged Dictionary***. Springfield,, MA: Merriam-Webster, Inc., 1986, p. 780.

11. Giovanni Maciocia. ***The Practice of Chinese Medicine***. Edinburgh, Scotland: Churchill Livingston, Inc., 1994, p. 201.

12. ***The Liver***. p. 69.

13. ***Webster's***, p. 510.

14. Ibid., p.2176.

15. ***The Web That Has No Weaver.*** P. 55.

16. ***The Liver.*** p. 73.

17. Ibid., p. 73.

18. Dr. Elihu Pleasant-Bey. ***The Biography of Noble Drew Ali.*** Seven Seals Publications, (no city or date of publication is given), p. 389.

## Chapter IV: What is the Antahkarana

1. Divine Grace Acharya Keshav Dev. ***A Mystery.*** Delhi, India: Acharya Shri Enterprises, 2001, p. 114.

2. Swami Satyeswarananda Giri Babaji Maharaj. ***Babaji***, San Diego, CA: The Sanskrit Classics, Publishers, 1983, p. 180.

3. Charles W. Leadbetter. ***The Monad***. Adyar, Madras, India: The Theosophical Publishing House, 1920, p. 11.

4. Yogi Ramacharaka. ***The Life Beyond Death***. Chicago, IL: Yogi Publication Society, 1937, p. 40.

## Chapter V: Tiers of Density and New Encoding Patterns

1 Open Your Eyes You Can Fly sung by Flora Purim Milestone Records. Composed by Chick Corea and Neville Potter, 1976.

2. Alice Bailey. ***A Treatise on Cosmic Fire***. New York, NY: Lucis Publishing Co., 1925, p. 609.

3. R. Buckminster Fuller. ***Synergetics***. New York, NY: Macmillan Publishing Company, 1975. p.326.

4 Ibid., p.96.

5 Elisabeth Rochat De La Vallee. ***A Study of Qi***. Monkey Press: Norfolk, UK, 2006, p. 26.

6. Peter Deadman and Mazin Al-Kafaji with Kevin Baker. ***A Manuel of Acupuncture***. Vista, CA: Journal of Chinese Medicine Publications, 1998, p. 27.

7. Ibid., p. 29.

8. Xinnong Cheng, (Chief editor). ***Chinese Acupuncture and Moxibustion***. Beijing, China: Foreign Language Press, 1987, p. 37.

9. George Soulie de Morant. ***Chinese Acupuncture***. Brookline, MA: Paradigm Publications, 1994, p. 133.

10. David Icke. ***The David Icke Guide to Global Conspiracy (and how to end it)***. Isle of Wight, UK: David Icke Books Ltd., 2007, p. 584.

11. Alice Bailey. ***Discipleship In The New Age, Volume I***. New York, NY: Lucis Publishing Co., 1944, p. 663.

12. Andrew Ellis, et. ai.. ***Grasping the Wind***. Brookline, MA: Paradigm Publications, 1989, p. 259.

13. ***Chinese Acupuncture and Moxibustion,*** p. 456.

14. Manly P. Hall. ***The Secret Teachings of All Ages***. Los Angeles, CA: The Philosophical Research Society, Inc., 1977, p. CXXI.

15. Helena P. Blavatsky. T***he Secret Doctrine Volume 2***. Pasadena, CA: Theosophical University Press, 1977, (A facsimile of the Original Edition of 1888.), p. 2.

## Chapter VI: Final Thoughts

1. A.B. Purani. ***The Life of Sri Aurobindo***. Pondicherry, India: Sri Aurobindo Ashram Publication Department, p. 285.

2. Swami Rama. ***Wisdom of the Ancient Sages, Mundaka Upanishad***. Honesdale, PA: The Himalaya International Institute of Yoga Science & Philosophy of the U.S.A., 1990, p. 37.

3. Marshall Govindan, M.A.. ***Babaji and the 18 Siddha Kriya Yoga Tradition***. St. Etienne de Bolton, Quebec, Canada: Kriya Yoga Publications, 1991, p. 128.

4. Ibid., p. 128.

5. Alice Bailey. ***A Treatise on Cosmic Fire***. New York, NY: Lucis Publishing Co., 1925, p. 279.

6. Claude Larre and Elisabeth Rochat De La Vallee. ***The Heart***. Norfolk, UK: Monkey Press, 2004, pp. 62 & 63.

## Addendum:

1. Achilles Heel: Philip Babcock Gove, Ph.D.,(editor-in-chief) ***Webster's Third New International Unabridged Dictionary***. Springfield,, MA: Merriam-Webster, Inc., 1986, p. 16.

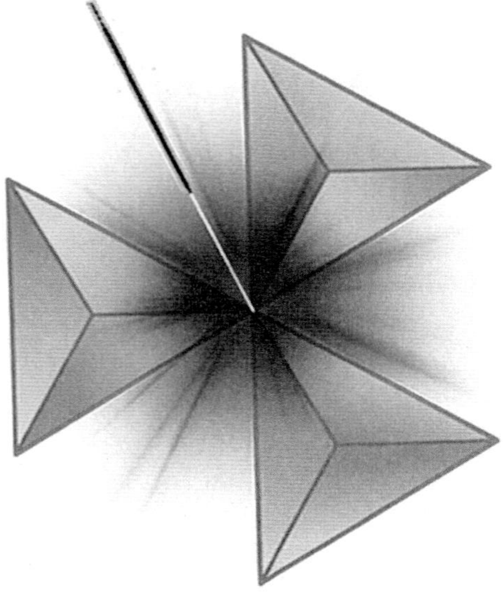

# Bibliography: *Antahkarana, Celestial Fullness*


Acharya Keshav Dev, His Divine Grace. ***A Mystery***. Delhi, India: Acharaya Shri Enterprises, 2001.

Acharaya Shri Dev Ji Maharaj, His Divine Grace Shri Shri 1008, ***Kundalini, A Cosmic Energy***. Delhi, India: Acharaya Shri Enterprises, 1998.

Bailey, Alice. ***Discipleship In The New Age, Volume I***. New York, NY: Lucis Publishing Co., 1944.

Bailey, Alice. ***Discipleship In The New Age, Volume II***. New York, NY: Lucis Publishing Co., 1955.

Bailey, Alice. ***A Treatise on Cosmic Fire***. New York, NY: Lucis Publishing Co., 1925.

Blavatsy, Helena P. T***he Secret Doctrine Volume 2***. Pasadena, CA: Theosophical University Press, 1977, (A facsimile of the Original Edition of 1888.)

Bernstein, Henrietta. ***Cabalah Primer***. Marina Del Rey, CA: DeVorss & Company, Publisher, 1984.

Capra, Fritjof. ***The Web of Life***. New York, NY: Anchor Books, 1996.

Cheng, Xinnong (Chief editor). ***Chinese Acupuncture and Moxibustion***. Beijing, China: Foreign Language Press, 1987.

Deadman, Peter, and Mazin Al-Kafaji with Kevin Baker. ***A Manual of Acupuncture***. Vista, CA: Journal of Chinese Medicine Publications, 1998.

Diepersloot, Jan. ***Warriors of Stillness, Meditative Traditions in the Chinese Martial Arts Volume I***. Walnut Creek, CA: Center for Healing and the Arts, 1995.

Dixon, Jane. ***Biology of Kundalini***. No publication city listed: Lulu Publishing, 2008.

Eisen, William. ***The Essence of The Cabalah***. Marina Del Rey, CA: Devorss & Company, Publisher, 1984.

Ellis, Andrew, Nigel Wiseman and Ken Boss. ***Grasping the Wind***. Brookline, MA: Paradigm Publications, 1989.

Ferguson, Marilyn. ***The Aquarian Conspiracy***. Los Angeles, CA: J.P. Tarcher, Inc.,1980.

Friedman, Norman. ***The Hidden Domain***. Eugene, OR: The Woodbridge Group, 1997.

Fuller, R. Buckminster. ***Synergetics***. New York, NY: Macmillan Publishing Company, 1975.

Gaunt, Bonnie. ***Beginnings, the Sacred Design***. Kempton, IL: J.P. Tarcher, Inc., `1976.

Gorder, Pam Frost. ***Black Holes Form First, Galaxies Follow: New Quasar Study***. (Internet article), February 15, 2014.

Goswami, Shyam Sundar. ***Layayoga***. Rochester, VT: Inner Traditions International, 1999.

Gove, Ph.D., Philip Babcock (editor-in-chief) ***Webster's Third New International Unabridged Dictionary***. Springfield,, MA: Merriam-Webster, Inc., 1986.

Govindan, M.A., Marshall. ***Babaji and the 18 Siddha Kriya Yoga Tradition***. St. Etienne de Bolton, Quebec, Canada: Kriya Yoga Publications, 1991.

Griffith, Samuel B. ***Sun Tzu, The Art of War***. London, U.K.: Oxford University Press, 1963.

Hall, Manly P. ***The Secret Teachings of All Ages***. Los Angeles, CA: The Philosophical Research Society, Inc., 1977.

Hawkins, M.D., Ph.D., David R. ***Transcending The Level of Consciousness***. W. Sedona, AZ: Veritas Publishing, 2006.

Helms, M.D., Joseph M. ***Acupuncture Energetics***. Berkeley, CA: Medical Acupuncture Publishers, 1995.

Hurtak, J.J. ***The Book of Knowledge: The Keys of Enoch***. Los Gatos, CA.: The Academy for Future Science, 1977.

Icke, David. ***The David Icke Guide to Global Conspiracy (and how to end it)***. Isle of Wight, UK: David Icke Books Ltd., 2007.

Jacobs, Michael. ***Ten and Twenty-Two, A Journey Through the Paths of Wisdom***. Northvale, NJ: Jason Aronson, Inc., 1977.

Kaptchuk, O.M.D., Ted J. ***The Web That Has No Weaver***. New York, NY: Congdon & Weed, 1983.

Kenyon, Tom. ***Brain States***. Lithia Springs, GA: New Leaf, 1994.

Krishna, Gopi. ***Kundalini, The Evolutionary Energy in Man***. Boston, MA: Shambhala Publications, Inc., 1997.

Krishna, Gopi. ***Kundalini, The Secret of Yoga***. Ontario, Canada: Institute for Consciousness Research, 1972.

Larre, Claude and Elisabeth Rochat De La Vallee. ***The Extraordinary Fu***. Norfolk, UK: Monkey Press, 2003.
Larre, Claude and Elisabeth Rochat De La Vallee. ***The Heart***. Norfolk, UK: Monkey Press, 2004.

Larre, Claude and Elisabeth Rochat De La Vallee. ***Heart Master, Triple Heater***. Norfolk, UK: Monkey Press, 1992.

Larre, Claude and Elisabeth Rochat De La Vallee. ***The Kidneys***. Norfolk, UK: Monkey Press, 1989.

Larre, Claude and Elisabeth Rochat De La Vallee. ***The Liver.*** Norfolk, UK: Monkey Press, 1994.

Larre, Claude and Elisabeth Rochat De La Vallee. ***The Lung***. Norfolk, UK: Monkey Press, 1989.

Larre, Claude and Elisabeth Rochat De La Vallee. ***Spleen and Stomach.*** Norfolk, UK: Monkey Press, 1990.

Leadbetter, C.W. ***The Monad***. Adyar, Madras, India: The Theosophical Publishing House, 1920.

Maciocia, Giovanni. ***The Foundations of Chinese Medicine***. Edinburgh, Scotland: Churchill-Livingston, 1989.

Maciocia, Giovanni. ***The Practice of Chinese Medicine***. Edinburgh, UK: Churchill- Livingston, 1994.

Maciocia, Giovanni. ***The Psyche in Chinese Medicine***. Edinburgh, Scotland: Churchill-Livingston, 2009.

Miyamoto, Musashi. ***A Book of Five Rings***. The Overlook Press: New York, NY, published in U.S. in 1974.

Montgomery, Ruth. ***Born To Heal***. New York, NY: Popular Library, 1973.

Muktananda, Swami. ***Play of Consciousness***. South Fallsburg, NY: SYDA Foundation, 1978.

Musser, George. ***Scientific American, Which Came First—Galaxies or Black Holes?*** (from Internet), January 7, 2009.

Myer, Issac. ***Qabbalah, The Philosophy of Ibn Geberol***. San Diego, CA: Wizards Bookshelf, 1988. (First published in 1888.)

Pleasant-Bey, Dr. Elihu. ***The Biography of Noble Drew Ali***. Seven Seals Publications, (no city or date of publication is given).

Purani, A.B. ***The Life of Sri Aurobindo***. Pondicherry, India: Sri Aurobindo Ashram Publication Department, 1958.

Rama, Swami. ***Wisdom of the Ancient Sages, Mundaka Upanishad***. Honesdale, PA: The HimalayaInternational Institute of Yoga Science and Philosophy of the U.S.A., 1990.

Ramacharaka, Yogi. ***The Life Beyond Death***. Chicago, IL: Yogi Publication Society, 1937.

Ramacharaka, Yogi. ***Mystic Christianity***. Chicago, IL: Yogi Publication Society, 1907.

Ramacharaka, Yogi. ***Raja Yoga or Mental Development***. Chicago, IL: Yogi Publication Society, 1934.

Ramacharaka, Yogi. ***The Hindu-Yogi Science of Breath***. Chicago, IL: Yogi Publication Society, 1904.

Rochat De La Vallee, Elisabeth. ***A Study of Qi***. Monkey Press: Norfolk, UK, 2006.

Saraswati, Swami Satyananda. ***Hatha Yoga Pradipika***. Munger, India: Bihar School of Yoga, 1985.

Musser, George. ***Scientific American, Which Came First—Galaxies or Black Holes?*** (Internet article), January 7, 2009.

Sahagun, Louis. ***Master of the Mysteries: The Life of Manly Palmer Hall***. Port Townsend, WA: Process Media, 2008.

Satyeswarananda Giri Babaji Maharaj, Swami. ***Babaji. The Divine Himalayan Yogi and His Legacy.*** San Diego, CA: The Sanskrit Classics, Publishers, 1984.

Shinoda Bolen, M.D., Jean. ***The Tao of Psychology***. San Francisco, CA: Harper Collins Publishers, 1979.

Silverstone, Matthew. ***Blinded by Science***. No city, country listed: Lloyd's World Publishing, 2011.

Sivananda, Sri Swami. ***The Science of Pranayama***. Himalayas, India: Swami Krishnananda for The Divine Life Society, 1984.

Soulie de Morant. ***Chinese Acupuncture***. Brookline, MA: Paradigm Publications, 1994.

Svoda, Robert E. ***Aghora II: Kundalini***. Las Vegas, NV: Brotherhood of Life, 1993 Vivekananda, Swami

Thompson, Andrea. ***Black Holes Precede Galaxies, Discovery Suggests***, (Internet article), January 6, 2009.

Veith, Izla. ***The Yellow Emperor's Classic of Internal Medicine***. Berkeley, CA: University of California Press, 1949.

Vivekananda. ***The Yogas and Other Works***. New York, NY: Ramakrushna-Vivekananda Center, 1953.

Wattles, Wallace. ***The Wisdom of Wallace Wattles***. (Compilation of ***The Science of Getting Rich, The Science of Being Great*** and ***The Science of Being Well***), Printed in U.S.A.: BN Publishing, 2007.

*Yang,* Joseph *Changqing,* Ph.D., L.Ac. ***Shen Disturbance, A Guideline for Psychiatry In Traditional Chinese Medicine***. Los Angeles, CA: Self Published, 2002.

*Yau, Shing-Tung* and Steve Nadis. ***The Shape of Inner Space***. New York, NY: Basic Books, 2010.

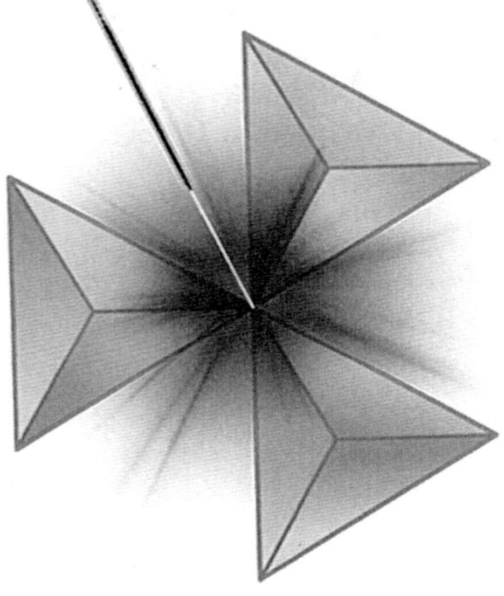

# Index

## A

## B



## C

## D



## E



## F

## G



## H



## I

## M



## N

## O



## P

## Q



## R



## S

## T



## U

## V



## W

## Y



## Z

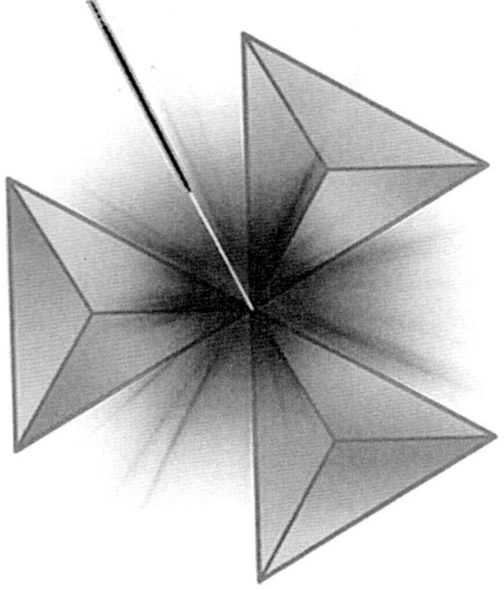

# About the Author

Mikio Sankey, Ph.D., L.Ac.

Dr. Mikio Sankey, Truth Seeker, lecturer, professor, energy healer, naturopathic physician and acupuncturist has been studying the teachings of the Ageless Wisdom for over 45 years. He has integrated the Ageless Wisdom Teachings with Traditional Acupuncture Theory to present Esoteric Acupuncture.

Mikio Sankey received his initial formal acupuncture and Chinese medical education at Samra University of Oriental Medicine in Los Angeles, California. He received a Ph.D. degree in Oriental Medicine from American Liberty University in Fullerton, California. He has a Doctorate in Health Sciences from Honolulu University, specializing in nutrition.

Dr. Sankey was recognized as the 2006 Acupuncture Author of the Year by the National Acupuncture and Oriental Medical Organization known as AAOM (now AAAOM) for the book ***Sea of Fire—Cosmic Fire: Esoteric Acupuncture, Volume IV***. He currently has five other books in the Esoteric Acupuncture Series.

Dr. Sankey is listed in ***AOM Pioneers and Leaders, 1982 to 2007, A Commemorative Book of Challenge and Courage, Volume I.*** This is a collaborative work of the various acupuncture organizations in the United States including: the AAAOM, NCCAOM, CCAOM and the ACAOM honoring the leaders who were responsible for shaping the direction of acupuncture and Oriental Medicine in the first twenty-five years of practice in the United States.

Dr. Mikio Sankey is a licensed acupuncturist in the state of California and is currently in private practice in the Los Angeles area with his wife Jikun Kathy Sankey, O.M.D., L.Ac.